Seventh Edition

Career Information, Career Counseling, and Career Development

Lee E. Isaacson
Professor Emeritus, Purdue University

Duane Brown
University of North Carolina at Chapel Hill

Allyn and Bacon
Boston • London • Toronto • Sydney • Tokyo • Singapore

To
Ardis and Sandra

Vice President, Editor in Chief: Paul A. Smith
Senior Editor: Virginia C. Lanigan
Editorial Assistant: Karin Huang
Marketing Manager: Brad Parkins
Editorial-Production Administrator: Annette Joseph
Editorial-Production Coordinator: Susan Freese
Editorial-Production Service and Electronic Composition: Omegatype Typography, Inc.
Composition Buyer: Linda Cox
Manufacturing Buyer: Suzanne Lareau
Cover Administrator: Linda Knowles

Copyright © 2000, 1997, 1993, 1986, 1977, 1971, 1966 by Allyn & Bacon
A Pearson Education Company
160 Gould Street
Needham Heights, MA 02494
Internet: www.abacon.com

Between the time website information is gathered and then published, it is not unusual for some sites to have closed. Also, the transcription of URLs can result in unintended typographical errors. The publisher would appreciate being notified of any problems with URLs so that they may be corrected in subsequent editions. Thank you.

Library of Congress Cataloging-in-Publication Data
Isaacson, Lee E.
    Career information, career counseling, and career development /
Lee E. Isaacson, Duane Brown. — 7th ed.
        p.   cm.
    Includes bibliographical references and indexes.
    ISBN 0-205-30650-0
    1. Vocational guidance.   2. Vocational guidance bibliography.
3. Vocational guidance—Information services.   4. Information
storage and retrieval systems—Vocational guidance.   I. Brown,
Duane.   II. Title.
    HF5381.I675   2000
    371.4'25'07—dc21   99-28938
                                                              CIP

Printed in the United States of America
10 9 8 7 6 5 4 3 2   04 03 02 01 00

OVERVIEW

CONTENTS

8   Computer-Assisted Career Guidance Systems (CACGS)   209

PART 4   *The Career Development Process*

PART 5   *Career Development Procedures*

PART 6   *Special Settings and Future Possibilities*

17   Career Development in Business and Industry   **465**

18   Career Counselors in Private Practice   **486**

PREFACE

Since the publication of the sixth edition 3 years ago, numerous changes have occurred in the workplace, and some changes have occurred in the manner in which career development services are provided. However, the problems confronting career counselors have not changed greatly in this time span. American business has, for the moment at least, fought off the challenges from businesses in other countries and emerged as the most profitable in the world. The result is that new jobs are being produced at a steady rate and unemployment is at a relatively low rate.

Recently, there has been a reaffirmation of the need for high school–age students to make early career decisions. Although career development specialists have long debated the wisdom of having students in the middle of their adolescence make career decisions, this debate seems moot at this time. The emergence of articulated programs of study between high schools and community colleges called *tech–prep programs* has made it incumbent on counselors in public schools to encourage career exploration during the elementary and middle school years and for high school counselors to engage students in career decision making so that they can choose their educational and career paths wisely. Young workers, particularly those without well-developed job skills, are finding the workplace unfriendly and unforgiving, just as they did when the sixth edition was published.

Some career development problems that have existed in this country for decades still confront career development specialists. One long-standing problem, the need to help people who are poor find ways to climb onto a career ladder and pull themselves out of the doldrums of poverty, has actually intensified since 1997. The conservative agenda that grips the country at this time includes limiting welfare benefits and replacing them with workfare programs. This shift makes finding careers that will provide the necessities of life essential for all.

Although it is probably safe to say that the problem of equality in the workplace for minorities and women has not intensified in the last 3 years, it has not improved either. Preparing women and minorities for the workplace presents a major challenge to career development specialists. Discrimination against women and minorities exists, but they are by no means the only groups that face this hurdle. As the work force ages, an already existing problem, age discrimination, will challenge career counselors and others to prepare older workers to face it. Mentally and physically challenged individuals will also require increasing attention if they are to achieve their potential as workers because of long-standing misperceptions about them.

This book was prepared to help aspiring career counselors, counseling psychologists, and others engaged in providing career development services cope with the problems identified above as well as other more routine concerns. Specifically, the purposes of this book are to help students:

- Become aware of some of the key historical events that have shaped career development theory and practice
- Understand the career development of all people across the life span
- Become aware of the sources of career information, the advantages and disadvantages of each source, and the methods of storing and disseminating information
- Understand how career development programs can be organized and delivered to groups ranging from elementary children to workers who are disengaging from the labor force
- Understand the intricacies of career development assessment and career counseling
- Understand the trends that will shape the workplace over the next decade
- Understand the process of finding and securing jobs in an electronic era

New Features of This Edition

The major goal in this revision was to update all material contained in the sixth edition. However, some new aspects of this edition are noteworthy:

- Many references are made to new developments involving the Internet. For example, on-line placement services are discussed in Chapter 16, along with the use of the Internet in the job search. Where appropriate, website addresses are provided to help students become acquainted with this exciting new resource.
- O*NET is featured in Chapter 5. Many years of developmental work have resulted in this on-line database that will be the primary source of occupational information for decades to come. However, information regarding the *Dictionary of Occupational Titles,* currently the primary source of occupational information, has been retained because it will take some time to make the transition to O*NET.
- One new and one revised system of classifying occupational information, the Standard Occupational Classification (SOC) System and the North American Industry Classification System (NAICS), are introduced in this volume. The

SOC is a revision of the existing system, whereas the NAICS replaces the Standard Industry Classification System.
- The discussion of providing career development services to cultural minorities has been extended. In Chapter 2 a theory of career choice based on cultural values is presented, and throughout the book additional references to providing career development services to cultural and ethnic minorities are provided.

Audience

This book is intended to help those who are now engaged, or who expect to be engaged, in facilitating the career development process. It is written expressly with school counselors, rehabilitation counselors, counseling psychologists, employment counselors, placement officers, and career counselors in mind. However, teachers, media specialists, social workers, and others who are influential in the career development process can benefit from the contents of the book.

Approach

This edition, like the previous ones, includes both theory and practical applications. The theoretical background is included as one means of helping the reader understand why certain practical approaches may be useful and why work is an important aspect of people's lives. The practical tools allow the reader to gain specific knowledge and skills needed to assist with career development problems. The practical applications also help the reader understand how to design and deliver career development programs in various settings.

Organization

This book is divided into six sections. Part 1, Foundations of Career Development, examines career development theory and the factors that influence workers in their careers. Part 2, The World of Work, contains discussions of the occupational structure in existence today and the trends that will influence it tomorrow, along with presentations about classifying and describing the world of work. Information about the World of Work is the title of Part 3. In this section various approaches to gathering, organizing, and disseminating occupational information are presented, including an in-depth discussion of computerized systems. Part 4, The Career Development Process, contains four chapters that deal with career development programming across the life span. Chapter 12 deals with the needs of special groups and populations. Part 5, Career Development Procedures, deals with the vital processes of preparation for the workplace, appraisal and assessment, career counseling, and job placement. Part 6 is titled Special Settings and Future Possibilities. The special settings discussed are business and industry and private practice. Chapter 19, focusing on future possibilities, includes predictions about the changes in career development theorizing, career counseling, the development and utilization of occupational information, and career development programming.

As has been the case with past editions, every effort has been made to be sensitive to the many issues involved in career development theory, research, and practice, particularly those related to the career development of women, minorities, older adults, and physically and mentally challenged individuals. Extended discussions of these issues can be found throughout the book.

Acknowledgments

Many groups and individuals deserve special thanks for making this volume possible. These include our graduate students, whose questions often started the search for better ways to relay information, our professional colleagues who have provided invaluable feedback about the contents of the book, reviewers of earlier editions who provide the impetus for refinements and improvements in the content, and the host of authors whose contributions to the career development literature have stimulated our thinking and helped us understand career development.

We also wish to acknowledge the work of Robin Wooley and Kim Reykdal. Not only did they help update the research in this volume, they checked the Instructor's Manual for accuracy.

Finally, we wish to thank our wives, Ardis and Sandra, who have encouraged and supported us throughout our careers, been patient when writing took precedence over what were more important matters, and willingly gave of their time and talent to make this volume and other accomplishments possible.

L. E. I.
D. B.

1

Introduction to Career Information, Career Counseling, and Career Development

The purpose of this book is to provide a foundation for practitioners who are interested in helping others explore career options that are available to them and make informed career choices as a result. All available evidence suggests that the need for this type of service is great. For example, a series of nationwide surveys developed and commissioned by the National Career Development Association (NCDA) and carried out by the Gallup Organization (Brown & Minor, 1989, 1992; Hoyt & Lester, 1995) revealed that only one-third of adults in this country were in their current jobs as a result of conscious planning. The remaining two-thirds entered their jobs because of chance circumstances, the influence of others, or because they took the only job available. Not surprisingly, only about half of the workers surveyed reported that they were very satisfied with their jobs.

The NCDA surveys also identified other dimensions of the problem confronting career development practitioners. Two-thirds of the adults responding to the surveys had never consulted a counselor about possible career choices, although the percentage of younger respondents who had seen a counselor to discuss career options approached 50 percent. Moreover, although two-thirds of the adults responding to the surveys reported accessing some type of career information during their lives, their chief source of information about careers was newspapers and/or television. Because information about careers is typically reported in a piecemeal—and at times haphazard—manner in the media, the fact that the media was the chief source of information about careers raises a question about the validity of the information. Only about 7 percent of the people surveyed had used the career resource centers in their high schools. Seventeen percent of the people responding to the survey had sought information about careers in college or community college career information centers. Perhaps more startling is the fact that nearly one-third of the respondents reported that they had never used career information from any source. When the respondents to each of the three surveys were asked if they would get more information if they were starting over, 65 percent of the white, 71 percent of the Asian American, 75 percent of the Hispanic, and 79 percent of the African American respondents said they would get more information (Brown & Minor, 1992). Other findings from the most recent NCDA survey (Hoyt & Lester, 1995) are reported below. These percentages have been converted into numbers to give the reader a feel for the magnitude of the problem facing career development professionals. The numbers are reported in ranges that take into account sampling error:

1. Twenty-eight percent of the workers surveyed anticipated changing their jobs within three years. Over 6 percent of those surveyed expected to change jobs because their businesses would close or they would be terminated. In terms of numbers, if the figures are generalized to the labor force in this country, between 26 and 40 million people anticipated changing jobs in the 3 years after the survey was conducted.

2. Sixteen percent of the respondents indicated that the information they needed about jobs was not available when they needed it. This suggests that between 12 and 24 million people did not have the information they needed about jobs when they were making critical career decisions or trying to obtain a job.

3. Nine percent of the respondents had needed assistance selecting, changing, or getting a job in the year prior to the survey. This suggests that between 3 and 18 million people needed assistance in these areas.

The NCDA surveys are not the only sources that identify the need for increased emphasis on career development services. Two reports, one developed by the United States Department of Labor (DOL, 1991b) and the other by United States General Accounting Offices (GAO, 1992) addressed the needs of high school students who are attempting to make the transition from school to work. The GAO study indicated that one-third of young workers (16–24) do not have the skills they need to perform entry-level, semiskilled jobs. This is a total of 9.1 million young workers. The GAO also concluded that the United States does not have a coherent strategy for preparing youth for work. The GAO recommended that Congress act to help non–college bound students and dropouts make the transition from school to work.

The GAO (1992) echoes the findings of the Secretary of the Department of Labor's Commission on Achieving Necessary Skills (SCANS) findings (DOL, 1991b). This commission was asked to "examine the demands of the workplace and whether our young people are capable of meeting those demands" (p. xv). The commission reported the following: "What we found was disturbing: more than half our young people leave schools without the knowledge foundation required to find and hold a good job" (p. xv). They went on to identify both academic and career development competencies that would help students bridge the gap between school and work.

Both the DOL (1991b) and GAO (1992) reports focus on young workers. A 1994 report developed by the American Association of Retired Persons (AARP) indicates that "less than one-quarter of Americans between the ages of 65–74 describe themselves as retired and less than one-third of Americans age 75 and older do" (p. 2). Perhaps more importantly for career development professionals is that large numbers of older workers, many of whom had left the labor force, are returning to the work force because of boredom or financial reasons (TERM, 1993). These workers often require assistance because of employer discrimination against older workers (AARP, 1994). Other older workers will require assistance because the nature of the job hunt has changed since they last were engaged in the process or because they have never been involved in a search for a job (AARP, 1992).

The problems facing career counselors, counseling psychologists, and others concerned with career development are great. Their tasks are to find effective ways to deliver career information and to improve career choice making in ways that will significantly increase the number of people who enter careers as a result of making a conscious, informed choice.

The perception that the citizens of this country need more assistance with career planning is not new. Picchioni and Bonk (1983) traced the history of guidance and counseling in the United States and documented that concerns about career planning began to surface formally in the post–Civil War era. In 1881 Lysander Salmon Richard published a book, *Vacophy,* that called for the establishment of a new profession made up of individuals who would (1) understand the technical and moral requirements of each occupation, (2) be located in every town, and (3) have the same professional standing as lawyers and doctors. In 1895 George Arthur Merrill began providing systematic career guidance to students enrolled in Cogswell High School in San Francisco, a service that was also initiated in 1897 by another pioneer, Jessee B. Davis, in Central High School in Detroit. In 1905 Frank Parsons founded the Breadwinner's Institute as a portion of the Boston Civic House. The Breadwinner's Institute offered life skills training to immigrants and others, but Parsons was not satisfied with the amount of guidance offered in the classes at the Institute. In 1908 Parsons established the Vocation Bureau as a separate agency within Civic House to help people who came to the settlement house make vocational choices. From these disparate efforts by educators, social workers, and concerned citizens, the guidance and counseling movement was born. In 1913 the National Vocational Guidance Association, the first professional organization for practitioners interested in career development, was formed. Today thousands of school counselors, rehabilitation counselors, career counselors, counseling psychologists, teachers, social workers, and others are involved in facilitating some aspect of the career development of children, adolescents, and adults. Their efforts include such diverse activities as helping elementary school children explore careers in their neighborhoods, assisting adolescents make initial career choices, helping college students acquire job interviewing skills, providing career counseling to adults who have lost their jobs due to plant closings, and facilitating the retirement process by helping retirees find part-time jobs.

Unlike late-nineteenth- and early-twentieth-century practitioners who had few guidelines for their work and fewer tools to aid them in their efforts, modern practitioners have ethical, legal, and practical guidelines to draw from to guide their work. The number of tools such as tests and inventories, like the number of guidelines for practice, exploded in the twentieth century and will likely increase as we move into the twenty-first century. The impetus for the proliferation has many sources, but none more important than the need to assist people with their career development and choice making. Today the problem for the prospective practitioner is to understand the guidelines that govern professional practice and to develop a command of a reasonable number of the tools and strategies that can be employed to help various client groups with their career development.

The Language of Career Development

Like all educational and psychological practitioners, career development practitioners, whether they be counselors, psychologists, or placement specialists, have a specialized vocabulary that must be mastered by the neophyte. Some words in this specialized vocabulary have already been introduced including *career, career development,* and *work.* Although most of the jargon relating to career choice and development will be interspersed throughout the book, some of the specialized vocabulary related to career development will be defined and discussed in this section.

It should be noted that universal agreement regarding some of the words used to describe various aspects of career choice and development has not been reached. For example, some counselors and psychologists (e.g., Holland, 1997) have retained the word *vocation* and use it synonymously with words like *job* and *occupation.* On the other hand, many career counselors and psychologists have rejected the term vocation because it is associated with the idea that people are "called," sometimes by God, to their occupations instead of being active participants in choosing them. This latter group has adopted the term *career choice* to denote the process of selecting a career while some practitioners have retained the term *vocational choice.* One of the leading publications of research dealing with career/vocational development is the *Journal of Vocational Behavior.* Another leading journal in this area is the the *Career Development Quarterly.* Both journals publish material related to career choice and development, but their titles reflect the preferences of the groups that publish them. As will be seen, the semantic argument about which terms are most meaningful and descriptive is not restricted to the terms *career* and *vocation.* Disagreements abound about which terms are most useful to describe various aspects of career development.

Value Judgment

The Meaning of Work

Two words that are often used interchangeably in day to day language are *work* and *job*. "Don't call me at work." is a frequently used admonition. "My line of work is ———." is an often heard phrase. From a technical point of view, these terms do not mean the same thing. The early Puritans defined work as laboring in a skilled trade or vocation. They believed that one of the best ways to serve God was through honest labor, and in fact, it was the Christian's duty to serve God in this manner (Picchioni & Bonk, 1983). Puritans and poets, scientists and despots, all have advanced ideas about work, some of which follow:

> *It is work which gives flavor to life.*
> —Amiel

> *To youth I have but three words of counsel—work, work, work.*
> —Bismarck

> *All work, even cotton-spinning, is noble; work is alone noble. . . . A life of ease is not for any man, nor for any god.*
> —Carlyle

> *There is no substitute for hard work.*
> —Edison

> *I look on that man as happy, who, when there is question of success, looks into his work for a reply.*
> —Emerson

> *Work is love made visible. And if you cannot work with love but only with distaste, it is better that you should leave your work and sit at the gate of the temple and take alms of those who work with joy.*
> —Gibran

> *Every child should be taught that useful work is worship and that intelligent labor is the highest form of prayer.*
> —Ingersoll

> *Never is there either work without reward, nor reward without work being expended.*
> —Livy

> *Though a little one, the master-word (work) looms large in meaning. It is the open sesame to every portal, the great equalizer in the world, the true philosopher's stone which transmutes all the base metal of humanity into gold.*
> —Osler

> *Hard work is the best investment a man can make.*
> —Schwab

Because of our concern for the importance of work in people's lives, more technical definitions of work have evolved. *Webster's New Universal Unabridged Dictionary* defines work as, "exertion or effort directed to produce or accomplish something" among some forty definitions offered. This definition, which is similar to most modern definitions advanced by sociologists and psychologists recognizes that work can occur outside of jobs. Housewives and househusbands work, as do volunteers of all kinds. However, simply viewing work as the exertion of energy in not sufficiently clear, because one can exert energy or effort in the pursuit of leisure goals such as hitting a tennis ball or backpacking through a national forest. Work then is exertion aimed at the attainment of various objectives other than those pursued solely for pleasure or sport.

Why People Work.   The foregoing definition, while useful because it helps differentiate work from leisure, does not fully explain why people work.

Work is seldom, if ever, only a means by which an individual sustains life. Work has many other functions of equal or sometimes greater importance to both society and the individual. It is one way in which the individual relates to society. Work provides the person, and often the family as well, with status, recognition, affiliation, and similar psychological and sociological products essential for participation in a complex society.

Work has religious and theological meanings. In early Hebrew writings, work was viewed as punishment. Early Christians were offended by work for profit, but this view was reversed by the Middle Ages. During the Reformation, work was considered the only way to serve God. Luther and Calvin viewed work positively, and their attitude combined with Social Darwinism and laissez-faire liberalism to form the foundation of what is now called the Protestant work ethic.

Another psychological product of work is the development of self-esteem. People feel a sense of mastery in dealing with objects of work, and their self-esteem is enhanced because they are engaging in activities that produce something that other people value. Unemployed people often suffer low self-esteem because they believe that they cannot produce something that other people value.

If we assume that work is one of the central components of life activities for most adults, it is easy to assume that the satisfaction derived from work is an important determinant in an individual's total satisfaction. This is obviously a nebulous concept. One research approach to determining job satisfaction has been to ask workers, "What type of work would you try to get into if you could start all over again?" One might logically infer that workers who choose the same occupation see greater likelihood of satisfaction in their present occupation than in any other field. Occupations named most frequently in response are those in which incumbents appear to have the greatest degree of control and the feeling that what they do is recognized as important by others. Such studies usually reveal that professions such as university professor, mathematician, biologist, and chemist show high percentages (80 or 90 percent) stating that they would choose the same occupation again. Unskilled and blue-collar workers show the lowest percentages (in the teens or low 20 percent level), and white-collar and skilled workers fall in the middle range. As noted earlier, nearly two-thirds of all workers would get more information about jobs if they were starting over. Apparently many workers feel that they might find more satisfactory jobs than the ones they held at the time of the surveys.

Work and Education.   Many business and industry leaders are expressing concern about the difficulty of finding workers who either have the skills required in new jobs or are trainable to meet the demands of those positions. As advancing technology takes over assembling, painting, welding, and other activities, workers are expected to operate or monitor the robot or computer that does the task. Increasing industrial competitiveness demands higher efficiency and productivity in these more technical occupations.

Since the mid-1980s, numerous organizations have released studies focusing on the interrelated problems of work and education. Johnston and Parker (1987) discuss the problems to be faced in the work force after the turn of the century. Both of the reports from the National Alliance of Business (1986) and the W. T. Grant Commission (1988) urge the formation of cooperative efforts among community organizations, business, labor, and government to resolve developing problems. The report by the Commission on the Skills of the American Workforce (1990), based on extensive interviews with management and workers in several European and Asian industrial nations, recommends vast changes in our educational system to prepare workers for the increasingly competitive future.

A survey by the National Alliance of Business (1990) states that 64 percent of the 1200 largest U.S. corporations reported dissatisfaction with the reading, writing, and reasoning skills of high school graduates entering the work force. Defining reading competency as beyond the seventh-grade level and math competency at a fifth-grade level, the companies report having to interview seven to eight applicants to find one that meets this level of skill.

Keller and Piotrowski (1987) indicated that only about one-tenth of the *Fortune* 500 companies had career development programs for their employees. Modernizing the work force, upgrading skills, increasing worker satisfaction, and remaining competitive in a changing world require the attention of all institutions and organizations in our society, both public and private. In addition, government agencies and schools must make these goals a priority.

The Future of Work.   It is extremely important that career development practitioners assume the mind-set of futurists because they often assume the formidable task of helping the people they serve predict what is ahead in the work world. Later we will look at projected changes in the occupational structure of this country in some detail. However, at this point it may be useful to consider the forces that may influence work in the future and potential changes that may occur in general terms.

The earliest prehistoric people maintained themselves by hunting and fishing. Anthropologists have shown how this simple, essentially nomadic life was replaced, as cultures became less primitive, by a system of division of labor, in which men were primarily occupied as hunters, fishermen, herdsmen, and traders. As social structures became more sophisticated, the occupations of farmers and craftsmen evolved. During this social change, individual family involvement in task specialization was a limited, part-time, almost incidental activity, perhaps growing out of individual interest or group recognition of an unusual skill. Nevertheless, the trend toward focusing effort on a specific group of tasks had started, and at that point the concept of *career* was born.

From prehistoric times, work has been a crucial factor in social organization. Greek and Roman civilizations each had a complex occupational structure. Many of the turning points in history were a result of changing relationships between humans and work. The early medieval craft guilds were created for occupational purposes, but the guilds exerted a social force that further weakened the semislavery of the feudal period. The Hanseatic League and similar groups of free cities organized, at least in part, to promote trade. The medieval university developed essentially to provide educational preparation for certain professional fields. The Protestant Reformation laid the foundation for a new view of humanity, and the historic period of discovery and exploration provided a vision of new opportunities. The Industrial Revolution accelerated occupational specialization and provided the means of transforming resources into new forms of wealth. The opening of vast geographic areas in the Western Hemisphere for settlement and development suggested that almost any man could, if he wished, acquire some of the ingredients of independence and self-actualization—a homestead, a business, a mine, a factory, a profession, or a job.

Recent decades have produced tremendous expansion in the number and nature of jobs. New relationships between human and machine, employer and employee, society and citizen have evolved and, in the dynamic structure of today's world, will continue through endless mutations and modifications. The continuous interaction between work and society modifies both. Often, transitions can be seen well in advance, and the principal uncertainty focuses on the timing of the event. The transformations, usually gradual and anticipated, are occasionally sudden and unexpected.

Although authors such as Toffler (1980), Johnston and Parker (1987), and Naisbett and Aburdene (1990) correctly predicted many of the changes that have occurred, they failed in many instances to gauge the magnitude of many of the recent shifts. The current and continuing importance of the computer in the workplace has been accurately predicted by many, as have some of the other changes that have occurred. For example, the idea that workplaces will become increasingly decentralized was expected. Now many workers (e.g., airline reservation agents for one major carrier) who use computers work offsite, and their work is monitored by computers as well. Similarly the idea that computers would replace certain workers has long been predicted. Automatic teller machines (ATMs) are replacing bank tellers, and secretaries are being replaced by "smart" software that "learns" to interpret the voice of a user and type the message relayed.

In this same vein, most futurists who studied the workplace expected that, while technology would decrease employment opportunities in some areas, it would increase the opportunities in others. Not surprisingly, given the use of computers in all phases of education, health care, business, and elsewhere, the demand for people who can create software that educates, monitors, and entertains is at an all-time high. Systems analysts who can design computer systems that increase efficiency and productivity are also in demand. Construction companies need specialists who can install fiber-optic cable that can connect computers and telephones, technological equipment repairers are in demand, and knowledgeable sales people who can explain the potential of various types of technological innovations are needed.

One area, the rapid impact of the Internet on the dissemination of information, communication, and as a sales tool, has surprised all but the most savvy prognosticator. Webmasters are in demand. A webmaster is a person who designs and maintains websites on the Internet. Sales people with specialized skills needed to market products on the Internet are also in demand, along with the people who can create software and hardware that can take advantage of the Internet's potential. Finally, all experts agree that technology will continue to change the face of the workplace throughout the twenty-first century by eliminating and creating jobs, by changing the physical nature of the workplace, and by creating new tools for use by workers.

Decentralization of the work force, variable time schedules, and technological innovations will influence work force participation for all workers, particularly parents who are raising children. The shifts in the population makeup of this country will also have a significant impact on the workplace. Currently, approximately three in ten workers in the United States are nonwhite. Some time during the first half of the twenty-first century nonwhites will make up a majority of workers. This may be why the USDOL Commission on Achieving Necessary Skills (1991b) noted that one of the skills needed by future workers was the ability to function in a multicultural workplace. Although the trend in the past has been toward earlier retirement, changes in Social Security that increase the age at which payments may be received and improved health care may reverse this trend, with the result that more older workers will work longer. Regardless of the impact of Social Security and longevity, it is likely that the average age of workers will increase in the short term because of the sheer number of workers in the cohort known as "baby boomers" who are now in their fifties.

Because one's occupation generally determines where and how one lives, the community activities and organizations in which one participates, and many other aspects of life, social status has long been associated with one's job. It is difficult to predict whether this relationship will become more or less intense. If, as some writers predict, technological change results in a small group of highly trained technical experts and a great mass of low-skilled workers who work infrequently at uninteresting and unrewarding positions, then it is likely that social status will become detached from occupation and will shift to some other basis. On the other hand, if technological change produces a general upgrading of most workers and provides most people with an opportunity to participate in activities that not only appear to be worthwhile but *are* challenging and satisfying, then social status may become even more closely related to one's job.

In addition to technological change, population factors, and changing social status, many other pressures in present-day society influence both work and society. Some of these factors include the number of scientists whose research has an impact on everyday life; the availability and application of energy sources; increased innovation and the shortened time between discovery and general application; the uneven distribution of population, food, and natural resources on a worldwide basis; and the accelerated rate of industrialization in underdeveloped countries.

Fifty years ago the economy of this country operated in isolation. Today the United States participates in a global economy in which the economic well-being of other countries influences the economy of this country and vice versa. Our businesses, industries, and workers compete head to head with those of other countries. Because of tariffs and trade barriers, such as Japan's restrictions on the importing of rice and automobiles, the competition among countries is not entirely open and is unlikely to become so. But when the United States, Mexico, and Canada ratified the North American Free Trade Agreement (NAFTA), which guaranteed these countries virtually unrestricted access to the markets of the other countries involved, many of the restrictions fell. Earlier, establishment of the European Common Market had eliminated many of the barriers to open trade among many European countries. Currently, negotiations are under way to further reduce the barriers to free trade throughout the world. One impact of lowering restriction will be fewer opportunities for unskilled workers, because the jobs they do can be performed for less money in underdeveloped countries. Other implications of the global economy will be increased emphasis on efficiency and productivity, less job security because of the options for placing "jobs offshore" to get work performed for less, and the need for a better educated work force because the jobs likely to be created are in the information and technology areas.

Some generalizations regarding changes in the workplace that are likely in the twenty-first century follow:

- Work will continue to change and will be dramatically different in the future.
- Many new jobs will be created and old jobs eliminated. The new jobs will require higher levels of technological sophistication than the jobs that are eliminated.
- The academic skills required for new workers to be successful will escalate.
- Workers will not only change jobs more often in the future, they will change the types of jobs they will do more often.
- Because of the need for rapid, up-to-date information about jobs, the Internet will become a primary job search tool for workers and a primary worker recruitment device by employers.
- Training and retraining will become a life requirement. Much of this training will take place in virtual reality workplaces.
- Many of the new skills needed by workers will be acquired through the use of distance learning via the Internet or through intranets established by businesses.
- Although overall geographic mobility will be required for many workers, numerous jobs will be located in decentralized locations including other countries.

Defining Position, Job, Occupation, Career, and Career Development

Just as *work* and *job* are often used interchangeably, so are the terms *position, job, occupation,* and *career.* Four decades ago, occupational sociologists such as Shartle (1959) advanced useful definitions of these terms that have since been endorsed by the National Career Development Association. He defined a *position* as a group of tasks performed by one individual and thus there are as many positions as there are individuals working. A *job,* according to Shartle, is a group of similar positions in a single business, and an *occupation* is a group of similar jobs in several businesses. The *Dictionary of Occupational Titles* (DOL, 1991a) contains definitions of 12,741 occupations that exist in this country. Because different businesses and industries have not adopted a uniform set of titles, it is difficult to assess how many jobs there are, but the number probably exceeds 20,000.

The definitions of *position, job,* and *occupation* are relatively straightforward and are widely accepted, but there is some controversy about the meaning of *career.* Five relatively recent definitions of *career* follow:

The totality of work one does in a lifetime (Sears, 1982).

Career = work + leisure (McDaniels, 1989).

...a sequence of positions that one holds during a lifetime of which occupation is only one (Hansen, 1997) (based on Super, 1951).

...the course of events which constitutes a life; the sequence of occupations and other life roles which combine to express one's commitment to work in his or her total pattern of self-development (Super, 1976, p. 4).

Careers are unique to each person and created by what one chooses or does not choose. They are dynamic and unfold throughout life. They include not only occupations but prevocational and postvocational concerns as well as integration of work with other roles: family, community, leisure (Herr & Cramer, 1996).

By examining the five definitions listed above, one can immediately get a sense of the problem involved in defining *career.* Super's (1976) and Herr and Cramer's (1996) definitions are based on a holistic, lifestyle concept of career and reflect their beliefs that all life roles are interrelated. While few people would dispute the idea that life roles are interrelated, it is obvious that the definition of *career* advanced by these authors is not universally accepted. McDaniels's (1989) definition is more circumscribed in that it limits *career* to two roles which he sees as inseparable. Sears's (1982) definition, which is the one adopted for this book, is based on the concept that one's career is a series of paid or unpaid occupations or jobs that one holds throughout his or her life. We have also adopted Sears's (1982) definition of *career development.* He suggests that *career development* is a lifelong process involving psychological, sociological, educational, economic, physical factors, as well as chance factors that interact to influence the career of the individual.

However, we would add culture to Sears's list of factors that influence career development. Leong (1991), Luzzo (1992), and Fitzgerald and Betz (1994) correctly note that the influence of cultural background has not been adequately considered in theories of career development, in research on the process of career development, or in career development practice. Research suggests that there are important factors among cultural groups in areas such as career decision-making attitudes and work values (Leong, 1991; Luzzo, 1992). Given the increasingly multicultural nature of our society, our conceptualizations of career development and our approaches to intervening in the process must take into consideration cultural background.

Career Interventions Defined

A *career intervention* is a deliberate act aimed at enhancing some aspect of a person's career development including influencing the career decision-making process (Spokane, 1991). There are many types of career interventions including career guidance, career counseling, career information, career education, career development programs, and career coaching.

Career guidance is a broad construct that, like career intervention, encompasses most of the other strategies listed above and has been used traditionally as the rubric under which all career development interventions were placed. Often, authors speak of career guidance programs (e.g., Herr & Cramer, 1996), which are organized, systematic efforts designed to influence various aspects of career development of a client group such as high school or college students (Herr & Cramer, 1996; Spokane, 1991). Career guidance programs may contain some or all of the following: systematic attempts to dispense career information, activities to enhance self-awareness, career planning classes or individual career counseling, job placement, and so forth. The term *career guidance programs* is increasingly being replaced by the term *career development programs*, but it is still widely used, particularly in referring to the career development efforts of counselors working in public schools.

Career education, which is a term that was coined in the 1970s (e.g., Hoyt, 1977), is a systematic attempt to influence the career development of students and adults through various types of educational strategies including providing occupational information, infusing career-related concepts into the academic curriculum, taking field trips to businesses and industries, having guest speakers representing various occupations talk about their jobs, offering classes devoted to the study of careers, establishing career internships and apprenticeships, and setting up laboratories that simulate career experiences. *Career education programs*, like career development programs, is sometimes used synonymously with career guidance programs, although the scope of career education programs has typically exceeded the scope of career guidance programs. The term *career education*, like *career guidance*, is being rapidly replaced by the term *career development programs* because of the efforts of the National Occupational Information Coordinating Agency. This agency is actively involved in promoting career development programs that contain both the elements of career education and career guidance programs. These ideas will be discussed more fully in Chapter 9.

Career counseling is a service provided to a single client or group of clients who come seeking assistance with career choice or career adjustment problems. The process of career counseling involves establishing rapport, assessing the nature of the problem, goal setting, intervention, and termination. The outcomes of career counseling are expected to be some or all of the following: the selection of a career, increased certainty about a career choice that was made prior to the beginning of counseling, enhanced self-understanding, increased understanding of one or more occupations, strategies for making adjustments within the work role, strategies for coordinating work role with other life roles, and enhanced mental health (Brown & Brooks, 1991).

One question about the foregoing definition of career counseling that is receiving increasing attention is the relationship between career and mental health issues. Many (e.g., Betz & Corning, 1993; Krumboltz, 1993) have argued that the two are inseparable while admitting that, at times, they may occur as independent processes. Others, such as Super (1993), have argued that, while career counseling and personal counseling are related, they fall on a continuum with career counseling focusing on the specific and personal counseling on the more general concerns of the individual. Still others (Brown, 1995; Brown and Brooks, 1991) argue that, while counselors may address both personal and career problems simultaneously, in some instances it will be impossible to proceed with career counseling because the psychological state (e.g., depression) of the individual precludes some clients from engaging in goal setting and rational approaches to career decision making.

Career information is sometimes referred to as labor market information (LMI), particularly when it involves providing comprehensive information about job trends, the industries in this country, or comprehensive information systems. Career information comes in a variety of formats including print, film, audiotape, and videotape. However, in the future, career resources centers will increasingly rely on information available on the Internet. For example, the United States Department of Labor now places all of its major publications online, including the most used pieces of occupational information, the *Occupational Outlook Handbook*, all occupational projections, and the newly developed O*NET. The Occupational Information Network (O*NET) is the most up-to-date source of information available today and is destined to become the basis for all types of occupational information. Thousands of other sources of information are also available on the Internet.

Career coaching is the term used in business and industry to signify the efforts engaged in by managers to facilitate the career development of employees (Hall & Associates, 1986). Career coaching efforts are directed at helping employees identify the opportunities that exist within their work settings and to prepare and enter these careers. The motivation for these efforts grows out of the joint concern for employees and helping the business identify the talent it needs to be successful.

Organizations and Publications

A few of the organizations that are instrumental in promoting career development in this country have already been named. The National Career Development Association, a division of the American Counseling Association, was founded in 1913 as the National Vocational Guidance Association. It publishes the *Career Development Quarterly*. Career counselors, school counselors, counseling psychologists, and other professionals who are interested in the career development process often affiliate with this division. Counseling psychologists, along with career counselors, have historically provided leadership for the career development movement. They typically belong to Division 17, Counseling Psychology, a division of the American Psychological Association. That division's journal, the *Journal of Counseling Psychology*, publishes a wide array of articles, but typically has a section devoted to career development. The editorial board of the *Journal of Vocational Behavior*, which is a journal not affiliated with a professional organization, has traditionally been dominated by counseling psychologists. Another journal that focuses on career development and is not affiliated with a professional organization is the *Journal of Career Development*. Finally, the Association of Training and Development (ASTD) has a special interest group that focuses primarily on career development within business and industry.

Another organization that is instrumental in the promotion of career development is the National Occupational Information Coordinating Committee (NOICC). NOICC, unlike NCDA and Division 17, is not a professional organization. It is a federal interagency organization that works with the Department of Defense, the Department of Labor, and the Department of Education to improve the quality of occupational information as well as to enhance the delivery of information. Each state has a State Occupational Information Coordinating Committee (SOICC) that works with NOICC and within the states to accomplish the goals of NOICC. One of the overarching concerns of NOICC and the SOICC is to improve career information delivery systems (CIDS). For this reason NOICC in particular has taken the lead in improving career development programs and systems at all levels.

Summary

Career development has been, and continues to be, a major concern of lay people and professionals alike. Because of the impact of a variety of forces including technology, a changing population, and the emergence of a truly global economy, the need for people to make well-considered career choices has never been greater. Professionals concerned about career development come from a variety of disciplines, but they have two common concerns: finding ways to deliver career information more effectively and facilitating the career choice making process. In order to address these concerns they must understand the guidelines that govern professional practice and be able to use the tools and techniques that have been developed since the inception of the career development movement.

References

AARP. (1992). *Returning to the job market: A woman's guide to employment planning.* Washington, DC: Author.

AARP. (1994). *America's changing work force.* Washington, DC: Author.

Betz, N. E., & Corning, A. F. (1993). The inseparability of "career" and "personal" counseling. *Career Development Quarterly, 42,* 137–142.

Brown, D. (1995). A value-based approach to facilitating career transitions. *Career Development Quarterly, 44,* 4–11.

Brown, D., & Brooks, L. (1991). *Career counseling techniques.* Boston: Allyn & Bacon.

Brown, D., & Minor, C. W. (Eds.). (1989). *Working in America: A status report.* Alexandria, VA: NCDA.

Brown, D., & Minor, C. W. (Eds.). (1992). *Career needs in a diverse workplace: A status report on planning and problems.* Alexandria, VA: NCDA.

Commission on the Skills of the American Workforce. (1990). *America's choice: High skills or low wages.* New York: National Center on Education and the Economy.

DOL. (1991a). *Dictionary of occupational titles* (4th ed.). Washington, DC: U.S. Government Printing Office.

DOL. (1991b). *What work requires of schools: A SCANS report for America 2000.* Washington, DC: USDOL.

Fitzgerald, L. F., & Betz, N. E. (1994). Career development in a cultural context: Race, social class, and sexual orientation. In M. L. Savickas & R. W. Lent (Eds.), *Convergence in career development theories* (pp. 103–119). Palo Alto, CA: CPP Books.

General Accounting Office (1992). *Educational issues.* Washington, DC: Author.

Hall, D. T., & Associates. (1986). *Career development in organizations.* San Francisco: Jossey-Bass.

Hansen, L. S. (1997). *Integrative life planning: Critical tasks for career development and changing life patterns.* San Francisco: Jossey-Bass.

Herr, E. L., & Cramer, S. H. (1996). *Career guidance and counseling through the lifespan: Systemic approaches.* New York: HarperCollins.

Holland, J. L. (1997). *Making vocational choices* (3rd ed.). Englewood Cliffs, NJ: Prentice-Hall.

Hoyt, K. B. (1977). *A primer for career education.* Washington, DC: Department of Education.

Hoyt, K. B., & Lester, J. L. (1995). *Learning to work: The NCDA Gallup survey.* Alexandria, VA: NCDA.

Johnston, W., & Parker, A. (1987). *Workforce 2000: Work and workers for the twenty-first century.* Indianapolis, IN: The Hudson Institute.

Keller, J., & Piotrowski, C. (1987). Career development programs in *Fortune* 500 corporations. *Psychological Reports, 61,* 920–922.

Krumboltz, J. D. (1993). Integrating career and personal counseling. *Career Development Quarterly, 42,* 143–148.

Leong, F. T. L. (1991). Career development attributes and occupational values of Asian American and white American students. *Career Development Quarterly, 39,* 221–230.

Luzzo, D. A. (1992). Ethnic group and social class differences in college students' career development. *Career Development Quarterly, 41,* 161–173.

McDaniels, C. (1989). *The changing workplace.* San Francisco: Jossey-Bass.

Naisbitt, J., & Aburdene, P. (1990). *Megatrends 2000.* New York: Morrow.

National Alliance of Business. (1986). *Employment policies: Looking to the year 2000.* Washington, DC: Author.

National Alliance of Business. (1990). *Survey of competency level of new job applicants.* Washington, DC: Author.

Picchioni, A. P., & Bonk, E. C. (1983). *A comprehensive history of guidance in the United States.* Austin, TX: Texas Personnel and Guidance Association.

Richards, L. S. (1881). *Vacophy.* Marboro, MA: Pratt Brothers.

Sears, S. (1982). A definition of career guidance terms. A National Vocational Guidance Association perspective. *Vocational Guidance Quarterly, 31,* 137–143.

Shartle, C. L. (1959). *Occupational information—Its development and application* (3rd ed.). Englewood Cliffs, NJ: Prentice-Hall.

Spokane, A. R. (1991). *Career interventions.* Englewood Cliffs, NJ: Prentice-Hall.

Super, D. E. (1951). Vocational adjustment: Implementing self-concept. *Occupations, 30,* 88–92.

Super, D. E. (1976). *Career education and the meaning of work.* Washington, DC: Office of Education.

Super, D. E. (1993). The two faces of counseling: Or is it three? *Career Development Quarterly, 42,* 132–136.

TERM. (1993). *TERM school-to-work news, research & opinion.* Atlanta, GA: Technical Education Resource Monitor.

Toffler, A. (1980). *The third wave.* New York: Morrow.

W. T. Grant Commission on Work, Family, and Citizenship. (1988). *The forgotten half: Pathways to America's youth and young families.* Washington, DC: W. T. Grant Foundation.

2

Theories of Career Choice and Development

One purpose of this chapter is to provide an overview of the history of theorizing about career choice and development. It is generally recognized that the fore-runner of modern theories of career development appeared in 1909 in *Choosing Your Vocation* by Frank Parsons. Parsons's tripartite model—understand one's self, understand the requirements of the jobs available, and choose based on true logic—underpinned career counseling and career development practice into the middle of the twentieth century. However, in the 1950s and 1960s a period of intense theorizing about career development occurred. The result was eight new theories of career choice and development, many of which are still viable today. From 1970 to 1984 five new theories of career choice and development were advanced, three of which focused largely on women's career development. Another intense period of theorizing began in 1991, and four new theories of career choice and development were presented in this period since 1991. A chronological account of these events can be found in Table 2.1.

The second objective of the chapter is to discuss the most influential of the theories that have been presented to date, that is, the theories that have stood the test of time. The third objective of the chapter is to briefly present some of the new attempts at theorizing about career choice and development. However, prior to embarking on discussions of the established, influential theories or the new, emerging theories, a more general discussion of the purpose and evaluation of theories of career choice and development will be provided.

The Purposes and Evaluation of Theory

In Chapter 1, career development was defined as a lifelong process involving psychological, sociological, economic, and cultural factors that influence individuals' selection of, adjustment to, and advancement in the occupations that collectively make up their careers. Career development is, to say the least, a complex process. Theories provide us with simplified pictures, or as Krumboltz (1994) prefers, road maps to the career development process.

There are "good" theories and "bad" theories. As Krumboltz (1994) states, "Our psychological theories are as good as we know how to make them so far, but in all probability they are far short of being accurate" (p. 11). However, good theories have distinct characteristics such as well-defined terms and constructs that can easily be interpreted by practitioners and researchers. Just as importantly, the relationships among the constructs in the theory are clearly articulated. If the terms are clearly defined and logically interrelated, practitioners can use them as guides to practice, and researchers can generate research to test the assumptions of the theory. Moreover, good theories are comprehensive in that they explain the career development process for all groups, including men and women, people from various cultures, and individuals from various socioeconomic strata.

Well-constructed theories serve other purposes. For example, they help us to understand why people choose careers and become dissatisfied with them. They also allow us to interpret data about career development that have been generated in the past, are being generated in the present, and will be generated in the future. Researchers and practitioners have long been aware that women and men choose sex-typed careers. Gottfredson's theory (1981) helped us to understand why this occurs. Well-developed theories also help us account for all internal and external influences that influence career development, including cognitions about careers and affective responses to various career-related events (Brown & Brooks, 1996; Krumboltz, 1994). Finally, well-constructed theories are parsimonious, which means they are set forth in the simplest, most succinct fashion necessary to describe the phenomena involved.

To summarize, theories of career choice and development are needed to:

1. Facilitate the understanding of the forces that influence career choice and development
2. Stimulate research that will help us better clarify the career choice and development process
3. Provide a guide to practice in the absence of empirical guidelines

A History of Career Development Theorizing

The 18 initial theoretical statements listed in Table 2.1 are by no means the only attempts at developing theories of career choice and development, and as will be shown later, most of these theories listed have been revised numerous times. Today the theories of Holland (1997), Super (1990), Lofquist and Dawis (Dawis, 1996; Lofquist & Dawis, 1991), Krumboltz (Mitchell & Krumboltz, 1990, 1996), and Gottfredson (1981, 1996) are making a major impact on research and/or practice. These theories will be discussed in some detail in the section, The Developmental Theories, along with Status Attainment Theory (Blau & Duncan, 1967; Hotchkiss & Borow,

TABLE 2.1   A History of Career Development Theorizing

Year	Event
1909	Parson's book, *Choosing Your Vocation*, is published posthumously.
1951	Eli Ginzberg and associates publish *Occupational Choice: An Approach to a General Theory* which outlines a developmental theory of career development.
1953	Donald Super publishes "A Theory of Vocational Development" in the *American Psychologist* which outlines a second developmental theory of career development.
1956	Ann Roe publishes *The Psychology of Occupations* which contains her personality-based theory of career development.
1959	John Holland publishes "A Theory of Vocational Choice" in the *Journal of Counseling Psychology* which sets forth some of the propositions of his theory of vocational choice.
1963	David Tiedeman and Robert O'Hara publish *Career Development: Choice and Adjustment* which contains a theory rooted in the idea that careers satisfy needs.
1963	Edward Bordin and associates publish "An Articulated Framework for Vocational Development" in the *Journal of Counseling Psychology* which sets forth a psychodynamic framework for career development.
1967	Blau and Duncan publish *The American Occupational Structure* which sets forth the premises of status attainment theory, a sociological theory of career development.
1969	Lloyd Lofquist and Renè Dawis publish *Adjustment to Work* which outlines the premises of a trait-factor model of occupational selection and adjustment.
1976	John Krumboltz and associates publish "A Social Learning Theory of Career Selection" in *The Counseling Psychologist*.
1981	Linda Gottfredson publishes "Circumscription and Compromise: A Developmental Theory of Occupational Aspirations" in the *Journal of Counseling Psychology* which focuses on how sex role identification limits occupational aspirations.
1981	Gail Hackett and Nancy Betz publish "A Self-Efficacy Approach to the Career-Development of Women" in the *Journal of Vocational Behavior* which uses Bandura's self-efficacy construct to explain important aspects of the career decision-making process.
1984	Helen Astin publishes "The Meaning of Work in Women's Lives: A Sociopsychological Model of Career Choice and Work Behavior" in *The Counseling Psychologist* which outlines a general theory of the career development of women.
1984	Tiedeman and Miller-Tiedeman publish "Career Decision Making: An Individualistic Perspective" which is one of the early attempts at framing a theory based on constructivist philosophy.
1991	Gary Peterson and associates publish *Career Development and Services: A Cognitive Approach* which contains their Cognitive Information Processing model of career choice and development.
1995	Robert Lent and associates publish "Toward a Unifying Social Cognitive Theory of Career and Academic Interest, Choice and Performance" in the *Journal of Vocational Psychology*, which is based on Albert Bandura's (1986) sociocognitive theory.
1996	Duane Brown's "Values-Based Model of Career and Life-Role Choices and Satisfaction" is published in the *Career Development Quarterly* and *Career Choice and Development*.
1996	Richard Young and associates publish "A Contextual Explanation of Career" which is based on constructivist philosophy.

1996). These theories have become influential because they possess the characteristics of a "good" theory described above, although each of them has shortcomings.

It is difficult to say why some theories become influential while others do not. One theory, Bordin's Psychodynamic Theory (1984) was well constructed, but it may not have become popular because it was built on psychodynamic theory which has never been widely accepted by counselors or counseling psychologists. Roe's theory (Roe, 1956, 1984; Roe & Lunneborg, 1990) gradually lost favor because researchers were unable to verify her basic propositions that early childhood environments gave rise to personality types that in turn resulted in career selection. No perfect theory of career choice has yet to emerge and it is unlikely that this will occur. However, to return to Krumboltz's (1994) map metaphor, some theory builders do a better job of providing maps to the vast array of phenomena that influence career development than others.

Some of the relatively new theories of career choice and development may become influential in the future. For example, the constructivists theories (e.g., Tiedeman & Miller-Tiedeman, 1984; Young, Valach, & Collin, 1996) are receiving a great deal of attention from scientists and practitioners alike. Some theories are so new that they have not had an opportunity to attract large numbers of adherents. The learning-based models generated by Lent and his associates (Lent, Brown, & Hackett, 1995, 1996) is one of these because it is based in the widely accepted sociocognitive theory of Albert Bandura (1986). The Career Information Processing model (Peterson, Sampson, & Reardon, 1991; Peterson, Sampson, Reardon, & Lenz, 1996), and the values-based theory of Brown (Brown, 1996; Brown & Crace, 1995) are also in the group that will be discussed in the emerging theories section. As will be shown in that section, each of these theories has generated research studies and has been the basis of articles in scholarly journals.

Theories for Special Groups
Some writers (e.g., Astin, 1984; Hackett & Betz, 1981) have proposed that, since many of the early theories (e.g., Super, 1953) were oriented primarily to white males, they are inappropriate explanations of the career development of women and males and females from other than European backgrounds. Theorists such as Holland (1982) and Super (1990) contend that these criticisms are unwarranted, although Super has made some changes in his theory over time to accommodate the changing career patterns of women. Efforts to develop alternative theories that focus on specific subgroups have not been met with much enthusiasm. For example, Astin's (1984) psychosociological model of career choice and work behavior has attracted few supporters. Moreover, Gail Hackett, who in collaboration with Nancy Betz addressed the role of self-efficacy in women's career choice making, is now a coauthor of a more comprehensive theory that focuses on the social cognitive factors that influence the career development of both men and women (Lent, Brown, & Hackett, 1995, 1996). Interestingly, Betz, along with Fitzgerald (Fitzgerald & Betz, 1994) have argued forcefully that current theories have limited applicability to minority groups, persons with gay or lesbian sexual orientation, and women.

Is Career Development Theory Unintentionally Racist?

Sue and Sue (1990) and Pedersen (1991) have proposed that most of the theories included in training programs for professional counselors, psychologists, and others are culturally oppressive because they are rooted in Eurocentric beliefs. The Western European worldview is that people should act independently when they make career decisions, a belief that arises from the cultural belief that the individual is the most important social unit (Carter, 1991). However, many American Indians, Asian Americans, and Hispanics believe that the welfare of the group should be placed ahead of the concerns of individuals. They hold a collateral social value and thus may reject the ideas that independence and competition are acceptable. Leong (1991) found that the Asian American students in his sample had a dependent decision-making style, not the independent style that would flow from Eurocentric values. One implication of this finding is that some Asian American students may find it perfectly appropriate to allow their parents to play a major role in the selection of their occupations. Unfortunately, most of the theories included in this chapter (e.g., Dawis, 1996; Gottfredson, 1996; Holland, 1997; Super, 1990) make this assumption, along with the assumption that job satisfaction is the result of the individual's interaction with his or her work environment. It seems entirely likely that job satisfaction and factors such as achievement in one's career are related to a much more complex set of variables including family or group approval of the career choice and their performance in it. When studying the theories that are presented in the next section, it is important to recall the nature of their bias and to consider the real possibility that they have at least one major shortcoming. Theories that lack cultural sensitivity are not comprehensive, and thus they fail one of the major tests of a theoretical statement. Moreover, if the theories lack cultural sensitivity, career counselors who interpret and apply them as set forth by their authors are likely to be engaging in culturally oppressive activities (Pedersen, 1991).

Introduction to the Theories

The theories that follow fall into several categories—trait and factor theories, developmental theories, learning theories, socioeconomic theories, and recent theoretical statements. Trait and factor theories stress that individuals need to develop their traits, which include their interests, values, personalities, and aptitudes, as well as select environments that are congruent with them. Developmental theories are based to some degree on the assumption that the factors that influence career choice and development are related to stages of personal and psychological development. The tenets of various learning theories have been used to describe both the process by which the individual develops and the choice making process itself. Socioeconomic theories pay less attention to psychological traits, although they typically address the matter of intellect as a factor in career choice. However, these theories focus on the socioeconomic status of the decision maker and/or the influence of sociological and economic factors on the occupational choice making process. In the recent theoretical statements section, two theories based in learning theory, one trait and factor model, and a contexualist theory will be presented.

Trait and Factor Theories

Holland's Theory of Vocational Choice

Holland developed a theoretical position gradually revealed in a series of published theoretical and research studies (Holland, 1959, 1962, 1963a, 1963b, 1963c, 1963d, 1966a, 1966b, 1968, 1972, 1973, 1985, 1987, 1997; Holland & Gottfredson, 1976; Holland & Lutz, 1968; Holland & Nichols, 1964). Holland's theory of vocational choice is based on several assumptions. These are:

1. An individual's personality is the primary factor in vocational choice.
2. Interest inventories are in fact personality inventories.
3. Individuals develop stereotypical views of occupations that have psychological relevance. These stereotypes play a major role in occupational choice.
4. Daydreams about occupations are often precursors to occupational choices.
5. Identity, the clarity of an individual's perceptions of his or her goals and personal characteristics, is related to having a small number of rather focused vocational goals.
6. In order to be successful and satisfied in one's career it is necessary to choose an occupation that is congruent with one's personality. A congruent occupation is one in which the other people in the work environment have the same or similar characteristics as one's own.

Personality develops as a result of the interaction of inherited characteristics, the activities to which the individual is exposed, and the interests and competencies that grow out of the activities (Holland, 1997). Holland believes that to some degree "types beget types," but recognizes that children shape their own environments to an extent, and they are exposed to a number of people in addition to their parents who provide experiences and reinforce certain types of performance. The combination of these influences produces 'a person who is predisposed to exhibit a characteristic self-concept and outlook and to acquire a characteristic disposition" (Holland, 1997, p. 19). Ultimately, the personality emerges. Holland posits that there are six pure personality types that occur rarely if at all in their pure form. These "pure" types are realistic, investigative, artistic, social, enterprising, and conventional. Descriptions of these types follow.

Realistic people deal with environment in an objective, concrete, and physically manipulative manner. They avoid goals and tasks that demand subjectivity, intellectual or artistic expressions, or social abilities. They are described as masculine, unsociable, emotionally stable, and materialistic. They prefer agricultural, technical, skilled-trade, and engineering vocations. They like activities that involve motor skills, equipment, machines, tools, and structure, such as athletics, scouting, crafts, and shop work.

Investigative people deal with environment by the use of intelligence, manipulating ideas, words, and symbols. They prefer scientific vocations, theoretical tasks, reading, collecting, algebra, foreign languages, and such creative activities as art, music, and sculpture. They avoid social situations and see themselves as unsociable, masculine, persistent, scholarly, and introverted. They achieve primarily in academic and scientific areas and usually do poorly as leaders.

Artistic individuals deal with environment by creating art forms and products. They rely on subjective impressions and fantasies in seeking solutions to problems. They prefer musical, artistic, literary, and dramatic vocations and activities that are creative in nature. They dislike masculine activities and roles such as auto repair and athletics. They see themselves as unsociable, feminine, submissive, introspective, sensitive, impulsive, and flexible.

Social people handle environment by using skills in handling and dealing with others. They are typified by social skills and the need for social interaction. They prefer educational, therapeutic, and religious vocations and such activities as church, government, community services, music, reading, and dramatics. They see themselves as sociable, nurturant, cheerful, conservative, responsible, achieving, and self-accepting.

Enterprising people cope with environment by choices expressing adventurous, dominant, enthusiastic, and impulsive qualities. Characterized as persuasive, verbal, extroverted, self-accepting, self-confident, aggressive, and exhibitionistic, they prefer sales, supervisory, and leadership vocations and activities that satisfy needs for dominance, verbal expression, recognition, and power.

Conventional people deal with the environment by choosing goals and activities that carry social approval. Their approach to problems is stereotyped, correct, and unoriginal. They create a good impression by being neat, sociable, conservative. They prefer clerical and computational tasks, identify with business, and put a high value on economic matters. They see themselves as masculine, shrewd, dominant, controlled, rigid, and stable and have more mathematical than verbal aptitude.

According to Holland, a person can be typed into one of these categories by expressed or demonstrated vocational or educational interests, by employment, or by scores obtained on such instruments as the Vocational Preference Inventory, the Strong Interest Inventory, or the Self-Directed Search. The last, an instrument developed by Holland, consists of occupational titles and activities that can be divided equally among the six type areas. Each method of determining personality type yields a score. Although Holland (1997) believes that all six types play a role in the personality, he suggests that the top three scores are the most influential factors. Thus the result of the assessment of type is a three-letter code (e.g., SAE), known as a *Holland code*. If the three-letter code is consistent and differentiated, the primary (first type) is expected to be the most influential, the second type the second most influential, and the tertiary or third type the third most influential in factors such as vocational decisions and aspirations and academic achievement. The consistency of a personality profile can be determined by use of the hexagon shown in Figure 2.1. If the personality types are adjacent (e.g. realistic and investigative), they are said to be consistent. Inconsistent types are those that are located opposite each other on the hexagon (e.g., investigative and enterprising). A personality profile is well differentiated if the scores on the primary type of the profile are significantly higher than the lowest score. Holland (1997) believes that consistency and differentiation are indirect estimates of identity, which he defines as the clarity of an individual's goals and self-perceptions. Identity can be measured directly by the instrument My Vocational Situation (Holland, Daiger, & Powers, 1980).

Holland (1985, 1997) also proposes that there are six work environments (realistic, investigative, artistic, social, enterprising, and conventional) that are analogous to the pure personality types just described. As already noted, individuals must select vocation environments that are congruent with their personalities to maximize their job satisfaction and achievements. These environments are described in the following sections.

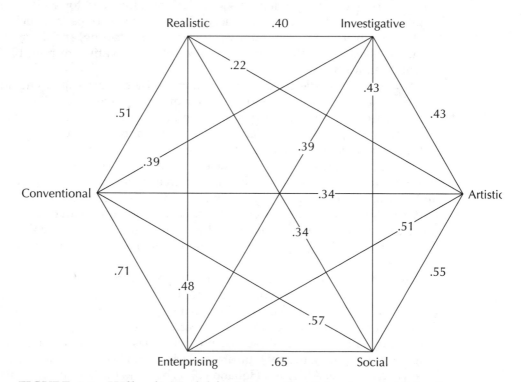

FIGURE 2.1 Holland's Model for Interpreting Interclass and Intraclass Relationships

Source: Reproduced by special permission of the publisher, Psychological Assessment Resources, Inc., Odessa, FL, 33556. From the *Self-Directed Search Technical Manual* by J. L. Holland, Ph.D. Copyright 1985, 1987, 1994, by PAR, Inc. Further reproduction is prohibited without permission from PAR, Inc.

The *realistic* environment involves concrete, physical tasks requiring mechanical skill, persistence, and physical movement. Only minimal interpersonal skills are needed. Typical realistic settings include a filling station, a machine shop, a farm, a construction site, and a barber shop.

The *investigative* environment requires the use of abstract and creative abilities rather than personal perceptiveness. Satisfactory performance demands imagination and intelligence; achievement usually requires a considerable time span. Problems encountered may vary in level of difficulty, but they will usually be solved by the application of intellectual skills and tools. The work is with ideas and things rather than with people. Typical settings include a research laboratory; a diagnostic case conference; a library; and a work group of scientists, mathematicians, or research engineers.

The *artistic* environment demands the creative and interpretive use of artistic forms. One must be able to draw on knowledge, intuition, and emotional life in solving typical problems. Information is judged against personal, subjective criteria. The work usually requires intense involvement for prolonged periods. Typical settings include a play rehearsal, a concert hall, a dance studio, a study, a library, and an art or music studio.

The *social* environment demands the ability to interpret and modify human behavior and an interest in caring for and dealing with others. The work requires frequent and prolonged personal relationships. The work hazards are primarily emotional. Typical work situations include school and college classrooms, counseling offices, mental hospitals, churches, educational offices, and recreational centers.

The *enterprising* environment requires verbal skill in directing or persuading other people. The work requires directing, controlling, or planning activities of others, and an interest in others at a more superficial level than in the social environment. Typical settings include a car lot, a real estate office, a political rally, and an advertising agency.

The *conventional* environment involves systematic, concrete, routine processing of verbal and mathematical information. The tasks frequently call for repetitive, short-cycle operations according to an established procedure. Minimal skill in interpersonal relations is required, since the work is mostly with office equipment and materials. Typical settings include a bank, an accounting firm, a post office, a file room, and a business office.

Holland suggests that each model environment is sought by individuals whose personality type is similar to those controlling the environment. It is assumed that they will be comfortable and happy in a compatible environment and uneasy in an environment suited to a different personality type. A congruent person–environment match presumably results in a more stable vocational choice, greater vocational achievement, higher academic achievement, better maintenance of personal stability, and greater satisfaction.

Finally, Holland developed an occupational classification system based on the model environment construct. Occupations are categorized according to the extent to which they involve activities representing the different points on the hexagon. An occupation that is mainly realistic in nature, but involves some investigative activities and a lesser amount of conventional characteristics, would be labeled as RIC. This code would be considered consistent because the types are adjacent on the hexagon. A code of RSC, however, would be inconsistent because it involves opposites.

Status of Holland's Theory.   Holland's theory of vocational choice and adjustment stands as the most influential of the extant theories. In 1990 Holland and Gottfredson compiled a list of nearly 500 publications that had been stimulated by the theory, and the number has grown steadily in the years since that publication was compiled. Practitioners are also attracted to the theory, probably because instruments, such as the Self-Directed Search (Forms R & E) (Holland, 1990a), are relatively easy to administer and interpret to a wide range of adolescents and adults. Holland (1990b) has also provided an Occupations Finder that allows practitioners and their clients to identify job options rather easily once their Holland code is identified.

Theory of Work Adjustment (TWA)

TWA has been set forth in a series of publications (Dawis, 1996; Dawis, England, & Lofquist, 1964; Dawis & Lofquist, 1984; Dawis, Lofquist, & Weiss, 1968; Lofquist & Dawis, 1991). In each of these publications the theory has been changed somewhat, but with few exceptions the assumptions underpinning the theory have not changed. The basic assumption of TWA is that people have two types of needs: biological (or survival) needs such as the need for food and psychological needs such as social acceptance. These needs give rise to drive states which in turn lead to volitional behavior. Whenever the behavior results in the needs being satisfied, reinforcement occurs and the behavior is strengthened. A second assumption is that work environments have "requirements" that are analogous to the needs of individuals. Both individuals and environments develop mechanisms for satisfying their needs. When the needs of individuals in an environment (work) and those of the environment are satisfied, correspondence exists. Workers select jobs because of their perception that the job will satisfy their needs, and workers are selected because of the perceptions that their skills will meet the needs of the workplace. If the reinforcer pattern of the workplace matches the need pattern of the worker, satisfaction and satisfactoriness occur. Satisfaction results when the worker is reinforced. Workers are judged to be satisfactory when they reinforce the need pattern of the work environment. The tenure, or time spent in a job by workers, is the result of their satisfaction with the job and satisfactoriness in performance.

Three variables—skills, aptitudes, and personality structure—can be used to predict the success of the worker if the reinforcement pattern of the work environment is known. The skills referred to in this predictive equation are the job-related skills the individual can offer to a work environment. Aptitude is the potential an individual has to develop the skills needed by the work environment, and the structure of the personality of the individual is determined by a combination of aptitudes and values. Values are determined by the importance attached to classes of reinforcement (e.g., pay, independence of functioning, etc.). Gender and minority group status are assumed to be critical variables in the development of personality structure within TWA.

Figure 2.2 is a graphic description of the occupational choice making process in TWA terms. As can be seen, decision making begins with an analysis of values and abilities, followed by an analysis of the ability patterns and value patterns of the several occupations. Ultimately individuals compare all occupations being considered in terms of the extent to which they can perform the job satisfactorily and the degree to which the occupation will satisfy their needs.

In order to understand work adjustment, the structure of the work environment and the characteristics of the worker must be known. Predictions of success depend on the celerity, pace, rhythm, and endurance of both the worker and the work environment. Celerity is the quickness with which workers engage their work environment to get their needs met. Successful workers quickly and vigorously try to get their needs met prior to leaving a job. Moreover, work environments respond with varying degrees of speed when a worker is unsatisfactory. The vigor with which individuals and work environments try to get their needs met denotes pace. Endurance is used in TWA to indicate the tolerance of the individual or the work environment for dealing with unsatisfactory work conditions or workers in the case of the work environment. Rhythm denotes the pattern of attempts (e.g., steady, erratic) by individuals and work environments to get their needs met.

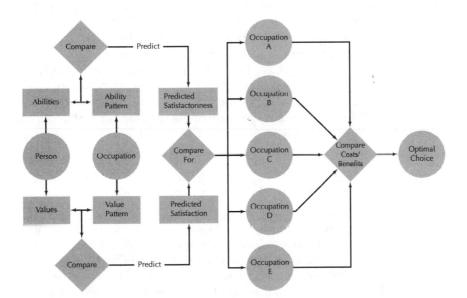

FIGURE 2.2   TWA's Graphic Explanation of Career Choice

Source: Dawis, R. V. (1996). The theory of work adjustment and person-environment-counseling. In D. Brown, L. Brooks, & Associates, *Career choice and development* (3rd ed.). San Francisco: Jossey-Bass. Used by permission of the publisher.

Another factor that must be considered in the adjustment to work process is whether individuals take an active or reactive approach. Active attempts are those direct attempts to make the work environment more responsive to the needs of the worker. When workers respond reactively they change themselves to respond to the perceived demands of the workplace. For example, reactive workers might reconsider the needs they deem important and substitute security for high pay. Some people have more tolerance (endurance) for unsatisfying situations than others and may make a series of reactive and active attempts to make the environment respond to their needs before ending their tenure in the job. Similarly work environments may have greater or lesser tolerance for unsatisfactory efforts by workers. The development of work adjustment styles, including reactive and active approaches, celerity, endurance, pace, and rhythm is influenced by a variety of factors including inherited characteristics, gender, and cultural background.

Counselors who wish to apply TWA in their work will find that inventories and tests are available to measure the theoretical constructs of the theory (Dawis, 1996). Two scales, the Minnesota Satisfaction Questionnaire and the Minnesota Satisfactoriness Scales, can be used to measure satisfaction and satisfactoriness respectively. The Minnesota Importance Questionnaire can be used to measure need preferences, and the Minnesota Ability Test Battery can be used to measure aptitudes. Occupational Reinforcer Patterns is an inventory that can be used to measure preferences for patterns of reinforcers.

Status of TWA.   TWA has been in existence for over 30 years and is one of the most carefully crafted theories of career choice and development available. Researchers have been attracted to the theory because its constructs are carefully defined and have been operationalized in the instruments mentioned above. Also, the authors of the theory have been careful to specify the interaction of the constructs, which makes the job of the researcher who wishes to generate testable hypotheses easier. Conversely, the theory has stimulated relatively little interest among practitioners, probably because of the presence of Holland's theory which parallels TWA in many respects.

The Developmental Theories

Developmental theories focus on the biological, psychological, sociological, and cultural factors that influence career choice, adjustments to and changes in careers, and withdrawal from careers. These theories focus on stages of development (e.g., childhood and adolescence). The first developmental theory was presented in 1951 by Ginzberg, Ginsburg, Axelrad, and Herma, but their theory has been overshadowed by Super's life-space, life-span theory which will be presented here. A second developmental theory will also be presented here, Gottfredson's (1981, 1996) Theory of Circumscription and Compromise. Her theory, while not as comprehensive as Super's theory, focuses on an extremely important aspect of the career development process, the impact of sex-typing of occupations on career choice.

Super's Life-Span, Life-Space Theory

Probably no one has written as extensively about career development or influenced the study of the topic as much as Donald Super. His earliest theoretical statements were influenced by researchers in differential psychology, developmental psychology, sociology, and personality theory.

Super's writing on career development is so extensive that even the highly motivated student faces a major challenge in reviewing all of it. The references listed here provide considerable depth but are not intended to be all-inclusive (1951, 1953, 1954, 1955, 1957, 1960, 1961a, 1961b, 1964a, 1964b, 1969, 1972, 1974, 1977, 1980, 1981, 1983, 1984, 1990; Super & Bachrach, 1957; Super et al., 1957; Super & Hall, 1978; Super & Kidd, 1979; Super, Starishevsky, Matlin, & Jordaan, 1963).

Super has often stated that his view is a "segmented" theory consisting of several related propositions, out of which he hopes an integrated theory will ultimately emerge. He has, from time to time, restated these segments, broadening slightly earlier statements and on two occasions adding more segments. His 1953 article presented the initial 10 postulates. He added two more in the 1957 book written with Bachrach. The 1990 article expands the list to 14 propositions. We use this latest listing as the basis for our consideration of Super's life-span theory. In this sequence, the original 10 propositions are listed as 1–6 and 9–12, with 7, 8, 13, and 14 being later additions. Super's 1990 statements are listed in italics, followed, where appropriate, with a brief discussion of the proposition.

1. *People differ in their abilities and personalities, needs, values, interests, traits, and self-concepts.* The concept of individual differences is so widely recognized and accepted that no one seriously challenges it. The range of personal characteristics varies widely both within each individual and between individuals. Within each person are traits or abilities so pronounced that often these are used to caricature the individual. At the same time there are areas in which the person is relatively weak or inept. Although most of us are more or less like other people in many traits, the uniqueness of the person is apparent in the individualized combination of strengths and weaknesses.

2. *People are qualified, by virtue of these characteristics, each for a number of occupations.* The range of abilities, personality characteristics, and other traits is so wide that every person has within his or her makeup the requisites for success in many occupations. Research in the field of rehabilitation has demonstrated that even severely disabled individuals have a choice of many occupations in which they can perform satisfactorily. For people without serious physical or emotional impairment, the gamut of possibilities is wide indeed.

Few occupations require special abilities, skills, or traits in excessive quantity. Just as most athletic activities involve only certain muscles or muscle groups, so too most jobs require only a few specific characteristics. A person, then, can perform successfully in any occupation for which he has the qualifying characteristics. The lack of a certain skill, or its presence in minute quantities, excludes the person from an occupation only if that skill is important in meeting the demands of that occupation.

3. *Each occupation requires a characteristic pattern of abilities and personality traits—with tolerances wide enough to allow both some variety of occupations for each individual and some variety of individuals in each occupation.* For each ability or trait required in the performance of a particular occupation, one might expect to find a modal quantity that best fits the nature of the work. On either side of this amount, however, is a band or range of this characteristic that will meet satisfactorily the demands of the work. For example, picture an extremely simple task that requires, hypothetically, only a single characteristic. In studying this task, we might ascertain the quantity of this trait that would best meet the requirements of the job. We would also expect that a person could perform satisfactorily even though he or she possessed less than the ideal amount of the trait, as long as the person surpassed the minimum demanded by the job. On the other hand, we could also expect satisfactory performance even if the worker possessed more of the trait than was required for optimum performance.

Since the patterns of abilities required in various occupations will rarely be unique, one can expect to find considerable overlap. Thus there will be a number of occupations in which a particular distribution of assets can result in satisfactory performance, just as there will be a number of patterns of ability that can result in satisfactory performance in a given occupation.

4. *Vocational preferences and competencies, the situations in which people live and work, and, hence, their self-concepts change with time and experience, although self-concepts, as products of social learning, are increasingly stable from late adolescence until late maturity, providing some continuity in choice and adjustment.* As individuals exercise certain skills or proficiencies, they may increase or expand them to a higher level. As these higher-level skills develop, workers may be drawn to occupational outlets that provide opportunities to use them. Similarly, as workers perform successfully in given work situations, they may realize that there are more rewarding or more responsible positions in which participation would offer even more satisfaction. On the other hand, there may be work situations that are so demanding on workers that they may look for positions that do not tax the pattern of abilities so heavily.

Since the pattern of skills and preferences, as well as the work situation, undergoes constant change, it is likely that the job that the worker once found entirely satisfactory is no longer viewed in that way. The individual whose self-concept changes may also find that the once satisfactory job is no longer so. Either of these changes may result in the worker seeking a new work situation or attempting to adjust the position held in some way so it will again be comfortable and satisfying. Since neither the worker nor the job is static, either change or adjustment is necessary to keep the two in balance.

Super (1984, 1990) emphasizes that self-concept should be defined broadly to include not only an internalized personal view of self, but also the individual's view of the situation or condition in which he or she exists. This is a significant factor because the situation surrounding the individual always bears on the person's behavior and self-understanding. Super suggests that *personal-construct* might be a more useful term than *self-concept* because it permits this broader definition.

5. *This process of change may be summed up in a series of life stages (a "maxicycle") characterized as a sequence of growth, exploration, establishment, maintenance, and decline, and these stages may in turn be subdivided into (a) the fantasy, tentative, and realistic phases of the exploratory stage and (b) the trial and stable phases of the establishment stage. A small (mini) cycle takes place in transitions from one stage to the next or each time an individual is destabilized by a reduction in force, changes in type of personnel needs, illness or injury, or other socioeconomic or personal events. Such unstable or multiple-trial careers involve new growth, reexploration, and reestablishment (recycling).*

The *growth* stage refers to physical and psychological growth. During this time the individual forms attitudes and behavior mechanisms that will be important components of the self-concept for much of life. Simultaneously, experiences are providing a background of knowledge of the world of work that ultimately will be used in tentative choices and in final selections.

The *exploratory* stage begins with the individual's awareness that an occupation will be an aspect of life. During the early or fantasy phase of this stage, the expressed choices are frequently unrealistic and often closely related to the play life of the individual. Examples can be seen in young children's choices of such careers as cowboy, movie star, pilot, and astronaut. These choices are nebulous and temporary and usually have little, if any, long-term significance for the individual. Some adolescents and even some adults, of course, have not advanced beyond the fantasy phase. Often, the understanding of themselves or of the world of work needed to make more effective choices is either missing or is disregarded.

In the tentative phase of the exploratory stage, the individual has narrowed choice to a few possibilities. Because of uncertainty about ability, availability of training, or employment opportunity, the list may contain choices that will later disappear. The final phase of the exploratory stage, still prior to actual entrance into the world of work, narrows the list to those occupations that the individual feels are within reach and provide the opportunities she feels are most important.

The *establishment* stage, as the name implies, relates to early encounters within actual work experiences. During this period the individual, at first perhaps by trial and error, attempts to ascertain whether choices and decisions made during the exploratory period have validity. Some of this period is simply tryout. The individual may accept a job with the definite feeling that he or she will change jobs if this one does not fit. As he or she gains experience and proficiency, the individual becomes stabilized; that is, aspects of this occupation are brought into the self-concept and the occupation is accepted as one that offers the best chance to obtain those satisfactions that are important.

During the *maintenance* stage, the individual attempts to continue or improve the occupational situation. Since both the occupation and the individual's self-concept have some fluidity, this involves a continual process of change or adjustment. Essentially the person is concerned with continuing the satisfying parts of the work situation and revising or changing those unpleasant aspects that are annoying but not so repulsive that they drive the individual from the field.

The *decline* stage includes the preretirement period, during which the individual's emphasis in work is focused on keeping the job and meeting the minimum standards of output. The worker is now more concerned with retaining the position than with enhancing it. This period terminates with the individual's withdrawal from the world of work.

Research by Levinson, Darrow, Klein, Levinson, and McKee (1978) and by Gould (1978) on postadolescent male development appears to support Super's life stages approach. Both report patterns of adult male development consisting of relatively stable, structure-building periods separated by transitional, structure-changing periods. The Levinson group found that their subjects made occupational choices between ages 17 and 29 and often made different choices later. This age period is somewhat later than Super theorized. They also report that the preparatory phase of occupational development is completed in the 28–33 age period, also later than previously assumed. The discrepancy in ages may be because data for the Levinson subjects were obtained by interviewing adult men who were recalling earlier events in their lives.

Murphy and Burck (1976), using Super's life stages concept, suggest that the increasing frequency of midlife career changes may indicate that an additional stage, the renewal stage, be inserted between the establishment stage and the maintenance stage. During this period, approximately between ages 35 and 45, the individual reconsiders earlier goals and plans, and then either rededicates self to pursuing those goals or decides to move in other directions with a midlife career change.

6. *The nature of the career pattern—that is, the occupational level attained and the sequence, frequency, and duration of trial and stable jobs—is determined by the individual's parental socioeconomic level, mental ability, education, skills, personality characteristics (needs, values, interests, traits, and self-concepts), and career maturity and by the opportunities to which he or she is exposed.*

All factors in the individual's experiential background contribute to attitudes and behavior. Some factors obviously contribute more significantly than others. The socioeconomic level of the individual's parents may be one of these, since the individual's early contact with the world of work is largely brought about through parents, family, and friends. Hearing parents and their friends discuss experiences at work; observing the impact of occupational success, failure, or frustration within the family; and obtaining or losing chances at education, travel, or other experiences because of family circumstances all greatly influence the individual's later work history. The individual's mental ability is an important factor in academic success that will open or close doors to many occupations. Ability to deal with others is important in most work situations. "Being in the right place at the right time" or "getting the breaks" is also important, since the individual must first have an opportunity to demonstrate competency before becoming established in a job.

We often think that, in the Horatio Alger tradition, anyone can attain any goal if he or she only tries hard enough. In reality, however, factors over which we often have no control set limits that can be surpassed or extended only by Herculean effort, if at all.

7. *Success in coping with the demands of the environment and of the organism in that context at any given life-career stage depends on the readiness of the individual to cope with these demands (that is, on his or her career maturity).* Super identifies career maturity as a group of physical, psychological, and social characteristics that represent the individual's readiness and ability to deal with the developmental problems and challenges that are faced. These personal aspects have both emotional and intellectual components that produce the individual's response to the situation. The person whose maturity is equal to the problem probably resolves it with minimal difficulty or concern; when the maturity is not sufficient for the task, inadequate responses of procrastination, ineptness, or failure are likely to occur.

8. *Career maturity is a hypothetical construct. Its operational definition is perhaps as difficult to formulate as is that of intelligence, but its history is much briefer and its achievements even less definite.* Super's early research (e.g., the 25-year longitudinal study called the Career Pattern Study) included attention to the concept of maturity as related to career or vocational development problems. He and coworkers searched for ways to define and assess this concept. Out of these efforts have emerged Super's Career Development Inventory.

9. *Development through the life stages can be guided partly by facilitating the maturing of abilities and interests and partly by aiding in reality testing and in the development of self-concepts.* Individuals can be helped to move toward a satisfying vocational choice in two ways: (1) by helping them to develop abilities and interests and (2) by helping them to acquire an understanding of their strengths and weaknesses so they can make satisfying choices.

Both aspects of this postulate emphasize the role of the school and its guidance program in assisting the individual to maximize development as a person. The teacher, with frequent contacts with a young person, has the best opportunity to observe latent or underdeveloped abilities in the classroom. The teacher has numerous chances to challenge the individual to push toward higher, but nevertheless reachable, goals. The counselor, similarly, through data obtained from tests or other guidance techniques may encounter undeveloped potential. Out-of-school adults may need similar types of help.

One of the authors of this book has occasionally found three questions useful in the counseling relationship in providing some indication of the extent to which the counselee has already engaged in some reality testing of vocational aspirations. The first question—What would you like to be if you could do anything you wanted?—frequently evokes a fantasy response which the individual usually soon labels as such. The second question—What do you expect to be 10 years from now?—often elicits a reply that still includes considerable fantasy, but may also include a sizable display of self-evaluation and insight. The third question—What is the least you would settle for, 10 years from now?—requires the client to discard fantasy entirely and to cope with strengths, weaknesses, and potential as she sees them.

10. *The process of career development is essentially that of developing and implementing occupational self-concepts. It is a synthesizing and compromising process in which the self-concept is a product of the interaction of inherited aptitudes, physical makeup, opportunity to observe and play various roles, and evaluations of the extent to which the results of role playing meet the approval of superiors and fellows (interactive learning).*

As the individual develops and matures, he or she acquires a mental picture of self—a self-concept. Since in U.S. culture one's position in the world of work is important, this becomes a major influence on the individual's self-concept. During the educational period, before actual entrance into work, one's anticipated occupational role plays a part in the development of self-concept. Each person attempts to maintain or enhance a favorable self-concept and thus is led toward those activities that will permit him or her to keep or improve the desired self-image. As the inner drive toward this ideal self-concept pushes the individual strongly, he or she encounters restricting factors, which may come from personal limitations or from the external environment. These factors interfere with attainment of the ideal self-concept and result in the individual's compromising or accepting somewhat less than the ideal.

Also influential is the extent to which individuals can gain insight into a variety of occupations and see to what extent each occupation permits them to be the kind of persons they want to be in their own eyes and in the eyes of family, teachers, peer group, and others whose opinions they value.

Super's (1980) description of a Life-Career Rainbow (see Figure 2.3) emphasizes the different roles played by each individual during his or her lifetime and the influence these roles have on lifestyle and career. Typical roles for most people include child, student, citizen, worker, spouse, homemaker, parent, and pensioner. These roles emphasize the lifelong aspect of career development.

11. *The process of synthesis of or compromise between individual and social factors, between self-concepts and reality, is one of role playing and of learning from feedback, whether the role is played in fantasy, in the counseling interview, or in such real-life activities as classes, clubs, part-time work, and entry jobs.*

Modifications of the vocational aspects of the self-concept may occur in many ways. Since the world of work is so complex and entrance requirements in many areas so difficult, it is not feasible to experiment with actual participation in more than a few actual work situations. This leaves the necessity of matching the self-concept and its demands against what occupations have to offer in a situation that is essentially abstract. This may be a daydream or reverie, it may involve seeking professional assistance through counseling, or it may mean seeking related experiences that will help the individual evaluate the suitability of the occupation in terms of self-concept.

12. *Work satisfactions and life satisfactions depend on the extent to which the individual finds adequate outlets for abilities, needs, values, interests, personality traits, and self-concepts. They depend on establishment in a type of work, a work situation, and a way of life in which one can play the kind of role that growth and exploratory experiences have led one to consider congenial and appropriate.*

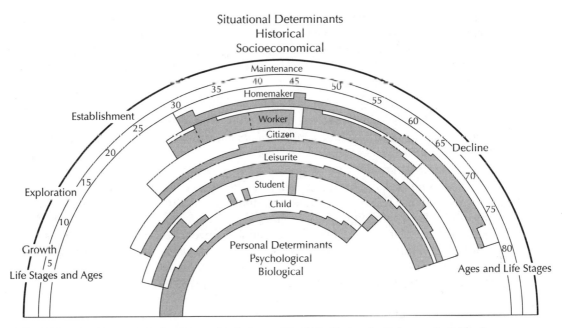

FIGURE 2.3   Super's Life-Career Rainbow: Six Life Roles in Schematic Life Space

Source: Super, D. E. (1980). A life-space, life-span approach to career development. *Journal of Vocational Behavior, 16,* 282–298. Used by permission of the publisher.

The individual who finds pleasure and satisfaction in work does so because the position held permits the use of characteristics and values in a way that is seen as important. In other words, the experiences encountered in work are comparable with the mental image held of self—they give sufficient opportunity to be the kind of person one pictures oneself to be.

If the work performed does not provide the possibility to be the type of person one pictures oneself to be, one becomes discontented. This dissatisfaction will usually cause a person to look for a work situation where the possibility to play the desired role seems likelier.

13. *The degree of satisfaction people attain from work is proportional to the degree to which they have been able to implement self-concepts.* The relationship of the work situation to the individual's role must be thought of in the broad sense. The professions and higher managerial positions probably provide the greatest opportunities, as viewed by most people, for the intrinsic satisfactions that come from work itself. But many individuals gain great satisfaction from work that to some appears boring and monotonous. Other workers find satisfaction in jobs that they too may consider routine and unchallenging but that provide them the chance to be the kind of people they want to be, to do the things they want to do, and to think of themselves as they wish to think. Super proposes that the amount of satisfaction is directly related to the extent the job fits the self-concept. Super and Kidd (1979) explore career change and modification in adults, recognizing the increase in midlife career change. They suggest that *career adaptability* may be an appropriate term to identify the individual's ability to face, pursue, or accept changing career roles.

   14. *Work and occupation provide a focus for personality organization for most men and women, although for some persons this focus is peripheral, incidental, or even nonexistent. Then other foci, such as leisure activities and homemaking, may be central. (Social traditions, such as gender-role stereotyping and modeling, racial and ethnic biases, and the opportunity structure, as well as individual differences, are important determinants of preferences for such roles as worker, student, leisurite, homemaker, and citizen.)*

   Essentially, this proposition says that most adults are what they do—the individual is a reflection of that person's job or major role. To a large degree this proposition relates to the Life-Career Rainbow proposed by Super (1980) as representative of life-span, life-space career development. As indicated in this proposition, Super believes that the various segments of his theory apply to both men and women, if modified slightly to provide for women's childbearing role.

Status of Super's Theory.   At the time of his death in 1994, Super had authored or coauthored nearly 200 articles, books, book chapters, monographs, and other publications, many of them dealing with his theory. His students and others have also contributed dozens, if not hundreds, of publications to the professional literature, all stimulated by his theory. His theory is, by his own admission (Super, 1990) not well constructed because there is no cement to hold the various segments together. This is probably the reason that many of the research studies stimulated by the theory focused on some of the constructs (e.g., career maturity) contained in the theory as opposed to testing its assumptions directly (Super, Savickas, & Super, 1996). Unquestionably the theory will remain an influential one, but it remains to be seen if it will maintain its position of preeminence with its leading advocate gone from the scene.

Gottfredson's Theory of Circumscription and Compromise

Gottfredson's (1996) theory is concerned with how career aspirations develop and is predicated on four basic assumptions: (1) the career development process begins in childhood; (2) career aspirations are attempts to implement one's self-concept; (3) career satisfaction is dependent on the degree to which the career is congruent with self-perceptions; and (4) people develop occupational stereotypes that guide them in the selection process. Obviously, these assumptions about self-concept have much in common with Super (1990), and Gottfredson's views on occupational stereotypes are identical to Holland's (1997).

   Gottfredson departs from other theorists in that she believes the self-concept consists of a social self and a psychological self, with the former being the more important determinant of occupational aspirations. The social self is made up of those aspects of self-perceptions regarding intelligence, social status, and gender, while the psychological self is made up of variables such as values and personality variables. Gottfredson believes that the major thrust of choosing a career is to establish a social identity based on the choice. According to Gottfredson (1996) people develop cognitive maps of occupations that are organized along the following dimensions:

1. Masculinity/femininity of the occupation
2. The prestige of the occupation
3. Fields of work

For Gottfredson, prestige goes beyond the social status of the occupation and includes an intellectual complexity or ability dimension. Of these dimensions, the sex-type assigned to the occupation and the prestige associated with it are the most important in the career choice making process. In the choice making process individuals estimate the degree to which they are compatible with a given occupation. In making these estimates, preserving one's self-percepts regarding one's masculinity/femininity will be the most powerful concern, followed in descending order by protecting one's social standing, and representing one's interests and personality. Obviously, in the consideration of potential occupational choices, the accessibility of the occupation must also be considered. Career aspirations are the result of the interaction between estimates of accessibility and compatibility estimates.

As children grow and develop perceptions of themselves and occupational fields, they begin to narrow or circumscribe their range of occupations based on their estimates of compatibility (sex-type, prestige, and interests) and accessibility. Gottfredson believes that once self-percepts are developed and occupations discounted as incompatible with them, it is unlikely that the process will be reversed unless there is some type of intervention such as an influential person telling them that they have the intellectual capacity to perform the tasks associated with entering the occupation.

Often the final occupational choice is a compromise as adolescents and adults give up their most preferred choices in favor of those that are more accessible. Compromise, that is, the process of selecting occupations that are viewed as a less than optimal fit with the self-view, occurs as a result of many factors including the availability of work in some fields (e.g., artistic jobs), availability and quality of educational and employment opportunities, and discrimination. When people are forced to compromise they give first consideration to sex-type, second consideration to prestige, and third consideration to interests. Using these three variables and their knowledge about the accessibility of careers, individuals develop a zone of acceptable occupations within their cognitive map of the occupational structure.

Status of Gottfredson's Theory
Gottfredson's theory has had a substantial impact on research and has stimulated approximately 40 published and unpublished studies at this juncture (Gottfredson, 1996). It has also served as the basis for programs aimed at eliminating or reducing

the impact of sex-typing and other factors that result in the circumscription of occupation choice (Hesketh, Pryor, & Gleitzman, 1989; Lapan, Loehr-Lapan, & Tupper, 1993). It seems likely that it will continue to be an influential theory in the future.

Theories Based in Learning Theory

In 1976 Krumboltz's theory based in the social learning theory of Albert Bandura (1977) was presented. Although Bandura's ideas about the acquisition of behavior have changed to some degree (e.g., Bandura, 1986) Krumboltz has not altered his theory in any significant way. As will be seen in the Recent Theoretical Statements section of this chapter, two other learning theories of career choice and development have been presented recently. What differentiates theories rooted in learning theory from trait and factor theories is that they are not as concerned about the role of traits such as interests and values in the career decision-making process. Rather, their focus is on the learning processes that lead to beliefs such as self-efficacy beliefs and interests and how these impact the career decision-making process. They differ from the developmentalists in some key aspects as well, namely in that they are not concerned with developmental stages. Learning theorists believe that since many of the factors surrounding career choice and adjustment are learned, their theories need to account for the learning processes that lead to the acquisition of the beliefs and behaviors that are critical to the career development process.

Krumboltz's Social Learning Theory

Krumboltz (1979), Krumboltz, Mitchell, and Jones (1976), and Mitchell and Krumboltz (1984, 1990, 1996) describe a social learning theory of career selection based on the behavioral theory of Bandura (1977) and others, emphasizing reinforcement theory.

Krumboltz identifies four kinds of factors that influence career decision making:

1. *Genetic endowment and special abilities.* Krumboltz recognizes that certain inherited characteristics can be restrictive influences on the individual, as Tiedeman similarly identifies biological constitution. Some examples are race, gender, and physical appearance. There are other factors for which inheritance, at least in part, may set limits, including various special abilities such as intelligence, musical and artistic ability, and physical coordination.

2. *Environmental conditions and events.* This factor includes those influences that may lie outside the control of anyone but that bear on the individual through the environment in which the individual exists. Some influences may be synthetic in the broadest sense; others may be due to natural forces. These human or natural elements may cause events to occur that also bear on the individual in the educational and career decision process. Examples of influences of this type include the existence of job and training opportunities, social policies and procedures for selecting trainees or workers, rate of return for various occupations, labor and union laws and regulations, physical events such as earthquakes and floods, the existence of natural resources, technological developments, changes in social organization, family training experiences and resources, educational systems, and neighborhood and community influences.

3. *Learning experiences.* All previous learning experiences influence the individual's educational and career decision making. Recognizing the extreme complexity of the learning process, Krumboltz identifies only two types of learning as examples: instrumental learning experiences and associative learning experiences. He describes *instrumental learning experiences* as those situations in which the individual acts on the environment to produce certain consequences. *Associative learning experiences* are described as situations in which the individual learns by reacting to external stimuli, by observing real or fictitious models, or by pairing two events in time or location.

4. *Task approach skills.* The skills that the individual applies to each new task or problem are called *task approach skills.* Examples of these include performance standards and values; work habits; and such perceptual and cognitive processes as attending, selecting, symbolic rehearsing, coding, and so on. The application of these skills affects the outcome of each task or problem and in turn is modified by the results.

Krumboltz sees the individual as constantly encountering learning experiences, each of which is followed by rewards or punishments that in turn produce the uniqueness of the individual. This continuous interaction with learning experiences produces three types of consequences, which Krumboltz labels as self-observation generalizations, task approach skills, and actions. A *self-observation generalization* is an overt or covert self-statement that evaluates one's own actual or vicarious performance in relation to learned standards. The generalization may or may not be accurate, just as one's self-concept may or may not coincide with the concept others have of an individual. *Task approach skills* are thought to be efforts by the person to project into the future self-observation generalizations to make predictions about future events. They include work habits, mental sets, perceptual and thought processes, performance standards and values, and the like. *Actions* are implementations of behavior such as applying for a job or changing a major field of study. The behavior produces certain consequences that affect future behavior.

In summary, an individual is born into the world with certain genetic characteristics: race, gender, physique, and special abilities or disabilities. As time passes, the individual encounters environmental, economic, social, and cultural events and conditions. The individual learns from these encounters, building self-observations and task approach skills that are applied to new events and encounters. The successes and failures that accrue in these encounters influence the individual in choosing courses of action in subsequent learning experiences, increasing the likelihood of making choices similar to previous ones that led to success and of avoiding choices similar to those that led to failure. The process is complicated by aspects of instability, since the individual changes as a result of the continuous series of learning experiences, and the situation also changes because environmental, cultural, and social conditions are dynamic.

Status of Krumboltz's Theory

Krumboltz's theory, while widely discussed and always presented in books of this type, has not been a significant influence on either research or practice to this time. While it is unclear what, if anything, will occur with regard to research, it seems certain that the theory will have increasing impact on practice because of two publications highlighting the application of the theory in career counseling (Krumboltz, 1996; Mitchell & Krumboltz, 1996). The publication of the Career Beliefs Inventory (CBI) (Krumboltz, 1991) has already provided counselors with a measure of the beliefs that may guide the career decision making of their clients. A recently published workbook (Levin, Krumboltz, & Krumboltz, 1995) should also be instrumental in helping counselors apply some of the constructs in Krumboltz's theory.

Socioeconomic Theories

The theories considered thus far are basically psychological in that they assume that individuals exert control over their lives. While most theorists would agree that the degree of control varies from individual to individual and situation to situation, most would also agree with the proposition that individuals do have control and it is the job of the career counselor to increase the degree of self-direction.

Unlike psychologists, sociologists and economists are inclined to concern themselves with small and large group behavior. Sociologists often focus on small groups such as the family, but they may be concerned with large groups such as women or minority groups. Some economists may focus on the economic forces that influence the career development of the entire labor force such as the global economy, the so-called dual labor market, or the impact of supply and demand of workers on wages and tenure. Hotchkiss and Borow (1990, 1996) report an increasing emphasis by sociologists and economists on structural variables such as socioeconomic status, barriers to career development such as discrimination and occupational segregation, and labor market considerations that influence careers. These broad-brush approaches place greater emphasis on factors outside the control of the individual than do the psychological approaches presented to this point.

Status Attainment Theory

According to Hotchkiss and Borow (1984, 1990, 1996) the publication *The American Occupational Structure* (Blau & Duncan, 1967) marks the advent of Status Attainment Theory (SAT). Initially SAT posited that the socioeconomic status of one's family influences education, which in turn affects the occupation entered. Later variables such as mental ability, and what were termed social–psychological processes, were added to this model. Hotchkiss and Borow (1996) suggest that, as the model now stands, its basic assumption is that family status and cognitive variables combine through social psychological processes to influence educational attainment, which in turn impacts occupational attainment and earnings. Some sociologists and economists have criticized SAT as being too simplistic and have sought alternatives to it. For example, some have tried to explain occupational attainment by focusing on the type of firm in which they are employed.

Dual Labor Market Theory

Dual Labor Market Theory posits that there are two types of businesses in our labor market, core and peripheral. Core firms have internal labor markets that have rather well-developed career paths that offer opportunities for upward mobility. These firms have dominant roles in the markets in which they compete and make use of technology and other tools to enhance their positions in their markets. Peripheral firms make no long-term commitment to their employees. Instead employees are paid by the job and furloughed when no longer needed. Workers in these firms have little chance of upward mobility according to the theory and research provides some support for this assertion (Borow & Hotchkiss, 1996).

Race, Gender, and Career

Sociologists have been at the forefront in the research of the impact of race and gender on occupational attainment and earnings. This research has consistently shown that African Americans earn less than whites (e.g., Saunders, 1995). Wage data regarding males and females show a similar pattern, with women earning consistently less than men (e.g., Reskin, 1993; Roos & Jones, 1993). Reskin's research also suggests that males and females are largely segregated in the workplace, with women often relegated to occupations with lower earnings and status.

Status of Socioeconomic Theory.   Status Attainment Theory and Dual Labor Market Theory have stimulated a surprising amount of research (Hotchkiss & Borow, 1996) and will undoubtedly continue to do so in the future. On the other hand it is unlikely that these theories will become influential to practitioners who are oriented to psychological perspectives.

Recent Theoretical Statements

As was noted in the beginning of this chapter, four emerging theories of career choice and development will be presented in this section. Two of these theories are based in learning theory, one is a trait and factor theory. The fourth theory falls outside the classifications presented thus far because it is based in constructivist philosophy while the other theories presented are based in positivism. There are many differences between these two philosophical positions, but none more important than the positions they advance regarding cause and effect relationships.

Positivists believe in cause and effect relationships and constructivists do not. For example, the congruence models that are at the heart of trait and factor models hold that if individuals select careers that match to a large degree their interests, values, or personality, the result will be job satisfaction. Constructivists make no parallel assumption. Other differences between these positions will be discussed later in this section.

A Social-Cognitive Perspective

This theory, which is based in the sociocognitive theory of Albert Bandura (1986), parallels Krumboltz's theory to some degree. It also departs from his theory in some significant ways. The most significant of the departures is that Lent, Brown, and Hackett (1995, 1996) place more emphasis on self-regulatory cognitions, particularly those associated with self-efficacy expectations, which is in keeping with Bandura's current position. Self-efficacy beliefs are dynamic, ever-changing self-percepts that individuals hold about their ability to perform particular tasks. They state, "In formulating SCCT we tried to adapt, elaborate, and extend, those aspects of Bandura's theory that seemed to be most relevant to the process of interest formation, career selection, and performance" (Lent, Brown, & Hackett, 1996). The central propositions of social cognitive theory are as follows:

1. The interaction of people with their environments is highly dynamic; the result is that individuals are at once influenced by, and influence, their environments.

2. Career-related behavior is influenced by four aspects of the person: behavior, self-efficacy beliefs, outcome expectations, and goals, in addition to genetically determined characteristics.

3. Self-efficacy beliefs and expectations of outcomes interact directly to influence interest development. People become interested in things that they believe they can perform well which will produce valued outcomes.

4. Gender, race, physical health, disabilities, as well as environmental variables, influence self-efficacy development as well as expectations of outcomes and, ultimately, goals and performance.

5. Actual career choice and implementation will be influenced by a number of direct and indirect variables other than self-efficacy, expectations of outcomes, and goals. Direct influences on career choice and development include discrimination, economic variables that influence supply and demand, and the culture of the decision maker. Indirect influences include chance happenings.

6. Performance in educational activities and occupations is the result of the interactions among ability, self-efficacy beliefs, outcome expectations, and the goals that have been established. All things being equal, people with the highest level of ability and the strongest self-efficacy beliefs will perform at the highest level. However, self-efficacy beliefs and outcome expectations are altered continuously as individuals interact with their environment.

Lent and his associates (Lent, Brown, & Hackett, 1995, 1996) believe that their theory is in keeping with the increasing emphasis on cognitive functioning in psychology. They believe that earlier learning theories, such as Krumboltz's social learning theory (Krumboltz, 1979; Mitchell & Krumboltz, 1996), rely too much on learning histories and not enough on cognitive processes to explain career-related behavior. For example, there is no mention of role of operant and classical conditioning in their theory, which is not the case with Krumboltz. It remains to be seen whether others will subscribe to their ideas.

A Career Information Processing Model of Career Choice

The CIP was first presented in 1991 (Peterson, Sampson, & Reardon, 1991) and was recently revised (Peterson, Sampson, Reardon, & Lenz, 1996). It, like the social-cognitive model described above, is based in learning theory. However, unlike Lent, Brown, and Hackett who relied on Bandura's (1986) work as the basis for their theory, Peterson and associates drew upon the branch of learning theory that has focused on information processing. Additionally, they drew upon the work of Meichenbaum (1977), a cognitive therapist, as the basis for some of their recommendations for interventions into career problems.

Figure 2.4 is a graphic representation of CIP theory. It shows that, with regard to career decisions, people develop two types of knowledge: self-knowledge and

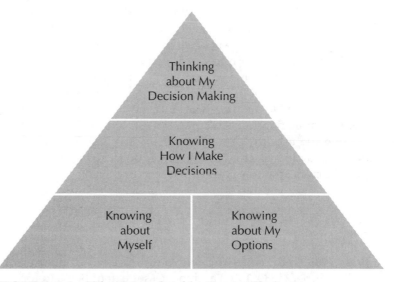

**FIGURE 2.4   What's Involved in Career Choice:
The CIP Model**

Source: From *Career Development and Services: A Cognitive Approach, 1st edition,* by G. W. Peterson, J. P. Sampson, Jr., and R. C. Reardon. © 1991. Reprinted with permission of Wadsworth Publishing, a division of International Thomson Publishing. Fax 800-730-2215.

knowledge about careers. When the time to make a career decision arrives, individuals draw on the generic information processing skills they have developed which are subsumed under the acronym CASVE: communication, analysis, synthesis, valuing, and execution. The communication (C) phase begins with a signal from inside or outside the organism that a problem exists. In response to this signal individuals try to determine the aspects (A) of the problem that exists. In the synthesis (S) stage, individuals generate potential solutions and then identify realistic options. In the valuing (V) stage a costs/benefits analysis is conducted based on the values systems of the individual. Finally, plans are developed and executed (E) to act on the alternatives that have been chosen.

The metacognitions referred to at the top of the pyramid (Figure 2.4) are the cognitive functions that are essential in the monitoring and regulation of the decision-making process. These include the acquisition, storage, retrieval, and processing of information relevant to the career problem at hand. The primary metacognitions involve self-talk, self-awareness, and monitoring and control. Self-talk is the internal dialogue carried on by decision makers with themselves. For the decision-making process to be optimal the overall nature of this self-talk must be positive (e.g., I am a good decision maker; There are many things I can do). Self-awareness is the metacognition that keeps the decision makers on task by producing the realizations that they are the ones most directly involved and by keeping out superfluous factors. The monitoring and control function has a temporal dimension (Where am I in the decision-making process? and Where do I need to be at this time?). This metacognition also allows people to understand when they have collected enough information, when they need to backtrack, and when it is time to move from stage to stage in the process.

Of greatest concern to career counselors and counseling psychologists is the client who, for whatever reasons, is not a good decision maker. The Career Thoughts Inventory (CTI) (Sampson, Peterson, Lenz, Reardon, & Saunders, 1996) was developed to diagnose various aspects of decision-making problems. The CTI has items relating to each compartment shown in the pyramid in Figure 2.4 including the executive processes, the CASVE cycle, self-knowledge, and occupational knowledge. This instrument should make the CIP theory more useful to practitioners and may stimulate research as well.

A Values-Based Model of Career and Life-Role Choices and Satisfaction

Brown (1996; Brown, 1997; Brown & Crace, 1995) built on the work of Rokeach (1973), Super (1980, 1990) and to a lesser extent Beck, to formulate his holistic theory of career and life-role choice and satisfaction. However, as Brown (1996) noted, the first draft of his theory was aimed only at people who hold traditional Eurocentric values: individualism, future time orientation, activity orientation, moderate emphasis on self-control of one's feelings and thoughts, and domination of nature.

Cultural values have been identified as important variables in career development and vocational behaviors (e.g., Fouad, 1995; Super & Sverko, 1995), but because these values vary across cultures, a comprehensive theory of career choice and development must take into account this variation. What is presented in this section is a major revision of Brown's (1996) theory that focuses for the most part on the role of values in a single life role: career.

However, cultural values are not the only variables that influence the career choice making process or the resulting satisfaction and/or success. Contextual variables such as socioeconomic status (SES) (e.g., Hotchkiss & Borow, 1996), family or group influence (e.g., Leong & Serafica, 1995), and discrimination (e.g., Melamed, 1996) are also considered in this revision, along with factors such as gender (e.g., Gottfredson, 1996; Melamed, 1995), and aptitudes (e.g., Jencks, Crouse, and Mueser, 1983; Phillips & Imhoff, 1997) because they have been linked empirically to career decision making and occupational attainment.

Variables That Influence Career Choice and Satisfaction

Values

Values are beliefs that are experienced by the individual as standards regarding how he or she should function. They are cognitive structures, but they have behavioral and affective dimensions. Values develop so that individuals can meet their needs in socially acceptable ways (Rokeach, 1973), and thus the behavioral aspect of values is shaped by the cultural context in which they develop. An individual's values are the basis for his or her self-evaluation and the evaluation of others, and they play a major role in the establishment of personal goals (Rokeach, 1973).

Research (e.g., Carter, 1991; Kluckhorn & Strodtbeck, 1961) has indicated that some values seem to be more prevalent in certain cultural groups than others, although it is not uncommon for various cultural groups to hold some of the same values (Carter, 1991). Numerous efforts have been aimed at developing a taxonomy of cultural values that illustrates the similarities and differences among the values held by various cultural groups in this country (e.g., M. Ho, 1987; Ibrahim, 1985; Sue & Sue, 1990). These taxonomies draw upon the pioneering research of Kluckhorn and Strodtbeck 1961), and typically they include categories for values regarding human nature (human beings are good, bad, or neither), person-nature relationship (nature dominates people, people dominate nature, living in harmony with nature is important), time orientation (past, past-future, present, or circular— oriented to changes that recur in nature as opposed to time as measured by watches and calendars), activity (being, i.e., spontaneous self-expression is important; being-in-becoming, i.e., controlled self-expression is important; doing, i.e., action-oriented self-expression is important), self-control (it is either highly or moderately important to control one's thoughts and emotions), social relationships (individualism, the individual is the most important social unit), collateral (also referred to as filial piety [Lee, 1991]), and allocentrism (it is important to put the group's concerns ahead of the concerns of the individual [Marin & Marin, 1991]).

How Values Develop

Enculturation is the process by which individuals incorporate the beliefs/values of their cultural group and form a values system (D. Ho, 1995; Rokeach, 1973). Although the process of enculturation is not fully understood, it seems likely that it occurs initially as a result of a complex process of modeling, reinforcement, and experience (Bandura, 1986; Rokeach, 1973). Cultural values and the work values that develop later may be vaguely perceived or crystallized. When values are crystallized, individuals can label them (I value competition) and apply them to their own behavior (and that is why I try to work harder than other people). Values are relatively stable, but they may change throughout the life span as a result of conflict or contemplation (Rokeach, 1973).

The result of enculturation for most individuals is monoculturalism, that is, they incorporate the values and beliefs of one culture. Bienculturation or multienculturation occurs when the beliefs of two or more cultures are internalized. Biculturalism or multiculturism may be the result of involvement in a bicultural or multicultural family (D. Ho, 1995) or acculturation resulting from sustained contact with other cultural groups.

Although the concept of biculturalism is often discussed in the context of multicultural literature (e.g., Leong & Gim-Chung, 1995), it is unlikely that an individual can adopt the values of two or more cultures because some of these values conflict. However, this should not be interpreted to mean that individuals cannot understand and appreciate the cultural values of more than one cultural group and adapt some of their behavior to match various cultural contexts. The enculturation process is influenced by the cultural group membership (M. Ho, 1987), gender (e.g., Brenner, Blazini, & Greenhaus, 1988; M. Brown, 1995), SES (Arbona, 1995; Blau & Duncan, 1967), and family membership (D. Ho, 1995; M. Ho, 1987).

Acculturation may or may not influence the cultural values that individuals incorporate into their values system. Acculturation involves the enculturation of beliefs from a culture different from one's own (Berry, 1990). It may also involve adopting the language, customs, and traditions of the other culture. Individuals who are in contact with another culture often receive "messages" that conflict with their own beliefs. For example, an Asian American student who believes that it is important to make a career choice that is in keeping with his family's wishes may be "told" by members of his peer group and his counselor that the "appropriate" way to make a career choice is to act independently. The result of these conflicting messages is acculturative stress (Chan & Ostheimer, 1983; Smart & Smart, 1995). Acculturative stress can be resolved in several ways, including adopting the values of the dominant culture. However, as Rokeach (1973) noted, although values may change as a reaction to conflict, they may also change as a result of contemplation. Therefore, acculturation probably does not occur solely as a reaction to conflicts.

Members of minority groups are continuously exposed to the values of the dominant culture, values that are often at odds with those they have acquired from their own culture (e. g., McWhirter & Ryan, 1991; Smart & Smart, 1995). Acceptance and inclusion of Eurocentric values in the values system and the behavioral norms and traditions accompanying them result in acculturation. One of the outcomes of acculturation may be the rejection of one's cultural beliefs. If the conflicting images and messages that are transmitted from the different culture are rejected, no acculturation occurs (LaFromboise, Trimble, & Mohatt, 1990). Two additional points should be made at this time. First, acculturation is not necessarily a one-way process: it is reversible (LaFromboise, Trimble, & Mohatt, 1990). Secondly, acculturation is a process that may affect individuals from all cultural groups, including members of the dominant culture who interact with cultural groups with different values (Berry, 1990). Because of the dynamic nature of the enculturation process in a multicultural society, it is a mistake to make assumptions based solely on cultural group membership.

Cultural Group Membership versus Internalized Culture

Cultural group membership, which is a demographic designation, has typically been used in lieu of internalized culture (D. Ho, 1995). Ho recommends that the psychological characteristic, internalized culture, be substituted for demographic designations. Internalized culture consists of the beliefs and values of the individual. Research has consistently supported the idea that there are differences in values systems among the major cultural groups as well as *within* group variation (e.g., Carter, 1991), and thus assuming that an individual has a particular set of cultural values is likely to lead to erroneous conclusions.

Factors That Retard Motivation to Act on Values

As noted above, values are the major force in the goal-setting process (Rokeach, 1973; Feather, 1988). However, five factors may lead individuals to lower their expectations of success if they act on their values: mental health problems (Casserly, 1982; Pietromonaco & Rock, 1987), history of personal/cultural group discrimination (M. Brown, 1995; Leong & Serafica, 1995; Melamed, 1996), lack of information (D. Brown, 1996), poverty (Hotchkiss & Borow, 1996), and self-efficacy (e.g., Lent, Brown, & Hackett, 1996). These variables will all be incorporated into the statements that follow.

Propositions of Brown's Values-Based Theory

1. Highly prioritized work values are the most important determinants of career choice if (A) individuals perceive that they are unconstrained to act on their values; (B) at least one option available will satisfy the values held by the individual; (C) the individual has values-based information about his/her options and accurate information about values (see Judge & Bretz, 1992); (D) the difficulty level of implementing the options is approximately the same (see Feather, 1988); and (E) the financial resources available to the individual are sufficient to support

the implementation of values-based options. Consequently, without intervention, people who feel that they are constrained, by either their cultural values or contextual forces, will enter occupations that are less related to their values than those who feel unconstrained.

1.A. Perception that one is relatively free to act on her/his values in choosing a career will be related to the gender of the decision maker (see Melamed, 1995), the presence (or absence) of mental health problems (see Pietromonaco & Rock, 1987), perceptions regarding the likelihood of experiencing discrimination, the availability of resources to implement the decision, and the presence or absence of certain cultural values.

1.A.1. Individuals who value individualism will feel less constrained to act on their values in the choice of a career than will individuals who value collateral relationships (see Leong, 1991) if they are relatively free from mental health problems, have values-based information about their options, hold similar perceptions regarding the likelihood of experiencing discrimination, and perceive that the resources are either available or attainable to implement their career decisions.

1.A.2. Although none of the values regarding activity (doing; being; being-in-becoming) will be experienced as constraints to the career decision-making process, when doing is paired with a future or past-future time orientation, the likelihood of engaging in career decision making will be enhanced when compared to being and/or being-in-becoming activity values paired with either circular or present-time orientations.

1.A.3. All other things being equal, among people who have the same values, women will feel more restricted than men in the career decision-making process (see Melamed, 1995).

1.A.4. Poor individuals, regardless of their ethnicity, will have lower career expectations than nonpoor individuals (see Jacobs, Karen & McClelland, 1991).

1.A.5. Poor individuals and unacculturated members of minority groups will have less access to occupational information than will nonpoor individuals and acculturated members of minority groups (see Brown & Minor, 1992).

1.A.6. Individuals who have conflicts in their values systems (having two highly prioritized values that are relatively incompatible) will feel constrained in the decision-making process because of the ambivalence (concern for others and independence) resulting from the conflict.

1.A.7 Individuals who have highly prioritized values that must be satisfied (for example, concerning work and other competing life roles such as family) will feel constrained in the decision-making process. Ultimately the result of this process will be to compromise and attend less to one of the roles than the individuals would if they were less constrained.

2. Because their values systems differ, as do their decision-making strategies, members of ethnic and cultural minority groups and European Americans will enter occupations at variable rates. The impact of their decision-making processes will be accentuated by historic patterns of discrimination (see Phillips & Imhoff, 1997).

3. For individuals who make their own career decisions and for others involved in the career decision-making process, the process of choosing a career

involves a series of "estimations." These include (A) estimates regarding ability, (B) estimates regarding values (see D. Brown, Fulkerson, Vedder, & Ware, 1983), and (C) estimates regarding the nature of the occupational choices available. For individuals who place group concerns ahead of their concerns and defer to other decision makers, these estimations will be made primarily by the decision maker, not the individual who will implement the choice. Regardless of who makes these estimates, there will be no significant difference in their accuracy.

3.A. Individuals who hold collateral values and come from backgrounds where little emphasis is placed on providing feedback to individuals will (1) underestimate their ability if humility is one of their cultural values, or (2) simply be less able to make these estimates because there is less emphasis in their groups on providing feedback about individual strengths and weaknesses. One result of conditions 1 and 2 is that instruments that are highly dependent on self-estimates of abilities to identify career options will be less reliable and valid for groups that value humility or receive little feedback about their capabilities, and these individuals will make more "errors" defined as mismatched values between the person and the workplace.

4. Individuals who highly prioritize collateral relationships and cooperative achievement values will experience greater stress in roles characterized by conflict, and will be less satisfied in those roles, than people who value individualism and competitive achievement. They will also have shorter tenure in roles with high levels of conflict than people who value individualism and competitive achievement. Moreover, individuals with collateral values will experience greater stress than those who value individualism when their work roles interfere with their family roles.

4.A. Job tenure will be partially the result of matching cultural values regarding achievement and social relationships to those of role incumbents, particularly supervisors (see Meglino, Ravlin, & Adkins, 1989).

4.B. The primary sources of job satisfaction will vary for individuals with collateral and individualism social values. The primary source of job satisfaction for individuals with collateral social values will be based mainly on feedback from significant others and secondarily from self-evaluations. The importance of these two sources will be reversed for people who hold an individualism social value.

5. Success in the work role depends upon a combination of factors including scholastic aptitude, special aptitudes, the quality and number of educational opportunities available, family socioeconomic status, participation in the work role, having a past-future or future time orientation, and the barriers in the workplace resulting from discrimination. Motivation, which results from individuals' interpretation of the appropriateness of their functioning in the job based on the match between their values in the workplace and perceptions regarding the fairness of their treatment, will interact with job-related skills and aptitudes and other background variables to determine performance when the influence of economic variables that result in chaotic occupational restructuring is removed.

5.A. Success, as measured by tenure and performance in the career role, requires an awareness of future events in both the initial choice and subsequent choices that must be made to accommodate the dynamic nature of the workplace.

Accordingly, success in the career role will be directly related to time orientation (see Savickas, 1991), with individuals who have a past-future or future orientation being most successful, followed in descending order by individuals with present and circular time orientations, respectively.

5.B. Success, as measured by tenure and performance, will not be influenced by values regarding the nature of people or person-environment relationships.

A Contexualist Theory of Career

As was mentioned in the introduction of this section one of the theories to be presented is grounded in constructivism as opposed to positivism. The Contextualist Theory (Young, Valach, & Collin, 1996) to be presented here is that theory. Young and his associates suggest that the dichotomous approaches used by trait and factor theorists to describe the person and the work environment are inappropriate. They believe that the only way to understand individuals is in the context of their environment as they experience it and make sense or meaning of the experience.

Contextualists do not see the actions of the individual as being caused by past or present events. Career-related behaviors are goal-directed results of the individuals' construction of the context in which they function. In order to understand an event one must start with the event, determine the individual's view of it, and work from that point.

Young, Valach, and Collin (1996) maintain that action taken with regard to career is a goal-oriented series of behaviors that occur in a stream of behavior that is guided simultaneously by individuals and the social contexts of which they are a part. They break action into three parts: unobservable behavior, the internal processes that cannot be observed, and the meaning or results as interpreted by the individuals and others who observe the action. Joint actions occur between people, such as those that occur in career counseling. In this process, joint goals are formed and the players engage in joint action that also has personal and social meaning. Projects are longer-term joint or individual actions such as preparing for a career. When people construct meaning among actions and projects they can engage in endeavors such as careers.

Actions take place in a series of sequential steps that occur in a social context from which the actor cannot be separated. The meaning associated by career-related actions and projects is interpreted not only in terms of its immediate context, but in terms of the goals of the individual (Young et al., 1996). Interpretations are also influenced by the gender and culture of the actor because of the variations in perceptions that have developed as a result of those variables. Interpretation occurs at two levels, in the present context, which is built on a stream of actions, and in the anticipated context of the future. In order to describe these events, individuals construct narratives, which are temporal interpretations of life events that pertain to a career. If individuals are asked, Why did you enter your present career? they construct narratives based on their interpretations of the events that led to their careers as well as their interpretations of what the person who asked the question needs or wants to know. One role of career counselors is to assist clients to project their narratives into future contexts.

A number of publications are available that illustrate how Contextual Theory can be applied in career counseling (e.g., Savickas, 1995; Young et al., 1996). Savickas (1995) suggests a five-step approach beginning with evoking stories that allow the identification of themes. Themes are frequently mentioned ideas about the nature of the career problem. Once the theme or themes are described the counselor "narrates" or describes the theme to the client. The client and counselor then interpret the problem in the light of the theme, edit or change the theme, and extend it into the future. The final step in the process involves helping the client develop the behavioral skills needed to implement the future narrative theme that has been developed.

Status of Recent Theoretical Statements
Contexualism and other descriptions of contructivists theories and their applications in practice have probably commanded the most attention since they began to emerge in the eighties. Most of these publications (e.g., Savickas, 1995) have focused on practice, and the theory has generated little research (Young et al., 1996). The social-cognitive theory (constructed by Lent et al., 1995, 1996) comes out of tradition of empiricism, a tradition that is likely to continue. However, because of the pervasive influence of trait and factor theories such as Holland's (1997), the theory may not be widely accepted by practitioners. The CIP Theory (Peterson et al., 1996) has not stimulated a great deal of research to this point, but that may change as the theory becomes better known. The theory has much to offer practitioners interested in the career decision-making process and may receive greater attention from that group. Finally, Brown's (1996) Values-Based Theory may have trouble finding supporters because of the presence of two very well-developed trait and factor theories. It has stimulated half a dozen research studies to this point, and practitioners who have been exposed to the theory have been enthusiastic. In the long run the acceptance of this theory, and the other theories mentioned here, will be dependent on the extent to which they are supported empirically and their utility to practitioners.

Theories of Decision Making

Each theory discussed in this chapter incorporates decision making as an impor tant aspect of career choice and career development. However, with the exception of Krumboltz's social learning theory, most give little attention to how individuals make those decisions. The purpose of this section is to alert the reader to the importance of this process, to review briefly a few of the major approaches to understanding the decision-making process, and to direct the reader to more extended discussions of the topic.

Jepsen and Dilley (1974) and Wright (1984) provide discussions of several relevant models useful to the reader. Jepsen and Dilley separate the models they discuss into two groups: *prescriptive models* that describe how decisions ought to be made, and *descriptive models* that describe how decisions are actually made. They also state that the process involves a decision maker and a situation in which two or more alternatives exist that carry potential outcomes of variable significance to the decision maker. The essence of the process is for the decision maker to identify and assign relative values to the alternatives and their consequences so he or she can maximize the outcome. We examine briefly two models of each type.

Mitchell (1975) modifies a model proposed earlier by Restle (1961) so it can be applied to the career decision-making process. Restle states that the decision maker matches the confronting situation to his view of an ideal one and then chooses the alternative that most closely resembles that ideal situation. Mitchell identifies four elements of preferences held by the decision maker:

1. *Absolute constraints* are the factors that must be present or absent for the alternative to be viable.
2. *Negative characteristics* are undesirable aspects.
3. *Positive characteristics* are desirable aspects.
4. *Neutral characteristics* are aspects present but irrelevant to the choice to be made.

The decision maker can use these elements in a variety of ways, such as comparing only positive characteristics; considering alternatives singly, matching positive versus negative characteristics; rejecting an alternative because of negative characteristics; and other combinations.

Tversky (1972) proposes a model that he names *elimination by aspects*. This approach focuses on all choices simultaneously, with each choice having a variety of characteristics. In this model, the characteristic (e.g., job security) for each alternative is matched, and those that fail to meet the decision maker's minimum standard are eliminated.

Examples of descriptive models include Vroom's expectancy model and Janis and Mann's conflict model. Vroom (1964) uses two key terms in developing his model: *valence,* which can be equated with preference, and *expectancies,* which are comparable to the belief that choices can be realized. Both aspects are crucial to each decision and interact in the process. The force or pressure to make a particular choice is directly related to the sum of the valences of all outcomes and the strength of the expectancies that the choice will result in the attainment of desired outcomes.

Janis and Mann (1977) assume that conflict is caused whenever a person is faced with making a decision, thus producing stress and uncertainty. The process starts when the decision maker becomes aware of a threat that he or she feels compelled to consider (e.g., the sounding of a fire alarm). The process continues through several steps that can be illustrated by a series of questions that, when answered positively, require action leading to the next question and when answered negatively interrupt the decision-making process. The questions are as follows:

1. Are there risks involved if I do not change?
2. Are the risks serious if I do not change?
3. Can I hope to find a viable solution to the problem?
4. Is there sufficient time to search for viable alternatives?

The individual who answers the final question affirmatively is considered to be in a state of vigilance, where attention can be given to acquiring information about alternatives and to weighing the advantages and disadvantages of each. This is considered to be the most favorable situation for reaching an appropriate decision.

The career counselor faces a serious dilemma in helping clients in the decision-making process. At present, none of the models described has been incorporated into the prevalent theories. It appears likely that one model may fit some clients and some situations better and another may be more satisfactory in different circumstances. The irony is that the counselor must apply a model in deciding which model is likely to be most useful to this client at this time.

Some of the major difficulties for the counselor focus on the inability to be certain of judgments of client characteristics (e.g., one cannot be certain of the client's motivation, clarity of self-understanding, and precision of values ascribed to various factors). It is often impossible to be sure that the client has incorporated his most important values and has weighted them properly. Nevertheless, the client must be helped and the counselor must choose a model or combination of models that appears most viable.

Summary

Theories of career choice and development offer researchers and practitioners guides to the complex phenomena involved in these processes. Theorizing began at the turn of the twentieth century (Parsons, 1909) and continues today. Today trait and factor theories, particularly Holland's (1997) model, are of greatest influence, probably because of their parsimony and ease of application. However, there is increasing interest in the theories based on learning theory, and the constructivists' theories are receiving increasing attention.

References

Arbona, C. (1995). Theory and research on racial and ethnic minorities: Hispanic Americans. In F. T. L. Leong (Ed.), *Career development and vocational behavior of ethnic and racial minorities* (pp. 37–66). Mawah, NJ: Lawrence Erlbaum.

Astin, H. S. (1984). The meaning of work in women's lives: A sociopsychological perspective. *The Counseling Psychologist, 12,* 117–126.

Bandura, A. (1977). *Social learning theory.* Englewood Cliffs, NJ: Prentice-Hall.

Bandura, A. (1986). *Social foundations of thought and action: A social-cognitive theory*. Englewood Cliffs, NJ: Prentice-Hall.

Beck, A. (1976). *Cognitive therapy and the emotional disorders*. New York: International Universities Press.

Berry, J. W. (1990). Psychology of acculturation: Understanding people moving between cultures. In R. W. Brislin (Ed.), *Applied cross-cultural psychology* (pp. 232–253). Newbury Park, CA: Sage.

Blau, P. M., & Duncan, O. D. (1967). *The American occupational structure*. New York: Wiley.

Bordin, E. S. (1984). Psychodynamic model of career choice and satisfaction. In D. Brown, L. Brooks, & Associates, *Career choice and development* (pp. 94–136). San Francisco: Jossey-Bass.

Bordin, E. S., Nachmann, B., & Segal, J. S. (1963). An articulated framework for vocational development. *Journal of Counseling Psychology, 10*, 107–116.

Brenner, O. C., Blazini, A. P., & Greenhaus, J. H. (1988). An examination of race and sex differences in manager work values. *Journal of Vocational Behavior, 32*, 336–344.

Brown, D. (1995). A values-based approach to facilitating career transitions. *Career Development Quarterly, 44*, 3–11.

Brown, D. (1996). A holistic, values-based model of career and life role choice and satisfaction. In D. Brown, L. Brooks, & Associates, *Career choice and development* (3rd ed.). San Francisco: Jossey-Bass.

Brown, D., & Brooks, L. (1996). Introduction to theories of career choice and development. In D. Brown, L. Brooks, & Associates. *Career choice and development* (3rd ed., pp. 1–32). San Francisco: Jossey-Bass.

Brown, D. (1997). Brown's values-based theory of career and life-role choice and satisfaction: A revision focused on the work role. Unpublished manuscript, University of North Carolina, Chapel Hill.

Brown, D., & Crace, R. K. (1995). Values and life role decision making: A conceptual model.

Brown, D., Fulkerson, K. F., Vedder, M., & Ware, W. B. (1983). Self-estimate ability in Black and White 8th, 10th, and 12th grade males and females. *Career Development Quarterly, 32*, 21–28.

Brown, D., & Minor, C. W. (1992). *Career needs in a diverse workforce: Implications of the NCDA Gallup Survey*. Alexandria, VA: NCDA.

Brown, M. T. (1995). The career development of African Americans: Theoretical and empirical issues. In F. T. L. Leong (Ed.), *Career development and vocational behavior of racial and ethnic minorities* (pp. 7–30). Mahwah, NJ: Lawrence Erlbaum.

Carter, R. T. (1991). Cultural values: A review of empirical research and implications for counseling. *Journal of Counseling and Development, 70*, 164–173.

Casserly, M. (1982). Effects of differentially structured career counseling on the decision quality of subjects with varying cognitive styles. Unpublished doctoral dissertation, University of Maryland, College Park.

Chan, K. S., & Ostheimer, B. (1983). *Navajo youth and early school withdrawal*. Los Alamitis, CA: National Center for Bilingual Research.

Dawis, R. V. (1996). The theory of work adjustment and person-environment–correspondence counseling. In D. Brown, L. Brooks & Associates, *Career choice and development* (3rd ed.). San Francisco: Jossey-Bass.

Dawis, R. V., England, G. W., & Lofquist, L. H. (1964). A theory of work adjustment. *Minnesota Studies in Vocational Rehabilitation No. XV*. Minneapolis: University of Minnesota.

Dawis, R. V., & Lofquist, L. H. (1984). *A psychological theory of work adjustment*. Minneapolis: University of Minnesota Press.

Dawis, R. V., Lofquist, L. H., & Weiss, D. J. (1968). A theory of work adjustment (A revision). *Minnesota Studies in Vocational Rehabilitation No. XXIII.* Minneapolis: University of Minnesota.

Feather, N. T. (1988). Values systems across cultures: Australia and China. *International Journal of Psychology, 21,* 697–715.

Fitzgerald, L. F., & Betz, N. E. (1994). Career development in a cultural context. In M. L. Savickas & R. W. Lent (Eds.), *Convergence in career development theories* (pp. 103–118). Palo Alto, CA: CPP Books.

Fouad, N. A. (1995). Career behavior of Hispanics: Assessment and intervention. In F. T. L. Leong (Ed.), *Career development and vocational behavior of racial and ethnic minorities* (pp. 165–192). Mawah, NJ: Lawrence Erlbaum.

Ginzberg, E., Ginsburg, S. W., Axelrad, S., & Herma, J. L. (1951). *Occupational choice: An approach to a general theory.* New York: Columbia University Press.

Gottfredson, L. S. (1981). Circumscription and compromise: A developmental theory of occupational aspirations (Monograph). *Journal of Counseling Psychology, 28,* 545–579.

Gottfredson, L. S. (1996). A theory of circumscription and compromise. In D. Brown, L. Brooks, & Associates, *Career choice and development* (3rd ed., pp. 179–281). San Francisco: Jossey-Bass.

Gould, R. (1972). The phases of adult life: A study in developmental psychology. *American Journal of Psychiatry, 129,* 521–531.

Hackett, G., & Betz, N. E. (1981). A self-efficacy approach to the career development of women. *Journal of Vocational Behavior, 24,* 326–339.

Hesketh, B., Pryor, R., & Gleitzman, M. (1989). Fuzzy logic: Toward measuring Gottfredson's concept of occupational social space. *Journal of Counseling Psychology, 36,* 103–109.

Ho, D. Y. F. (1995). Internal culture, culturocentrism, and transcendence. *The Counseling Psychologist, 23,* 4–24.

Ho, M. K. (1987). *Family therapy with ethnic minorities.* Newbury Park, CA: Sage.

Holland, J. L. (1959). A theory of vocational choice. *Journal of Counseling Psychology, 6,* 35–45.

Holland, J. L. (1962). Some explorations of a theory of vocational choice: I. One- and two-year longitudinal studies. *Psychological Monographs, 76* (26, Whole No. 545).

Holland, J. L. (1963a). Explorations of a theory of vocational choice and achievement: II. A four-year prediction study. *Psychological Reports, 12,* 547–594.

Holland, J. L. (1963b). A theory of vocational choice: Part I. Vocational images and choice. *Vocational Guidance Quarterly, 11,* 232–239.

Holland, J. L. (1963c). A theory of vocational choice: Part II. Self descriptions and vocational preferences. *Vocational Guidance Quarterly, 12,* 17–24.

Holland, J. L. (1963d). A theory of vocational choice: Part IV. Vocational daydreams. *Vocational Guidance Quarterly, 12,* 93–97.

Holland, J. L. (1966a). A psychological classification scheme for vocations and major fields. *Journal of Counseling Psychology, 13,* 278–288.

Holland, J. L. (1966b). *The psychology of vocational choice.* Waltham, MA: Blaisdell.

Holland, J. L. (1968). Explorations of a theory of vocational choice: Part VI. A longitudinal study using a sample of typical college students. *Journal of Applied Psychology, 52* (Monograph Suppl.).

Holland, J. L. (1972). The present status of a theory of vocational choice. In J. M. Whiteley & A. Resnikoff (Eds.), *Perspectives on vocational development.* Washington, DC: American Personnel and Guidance Association.

Holland, J. L. (1973). *Making vocational choices: A theory of careers.* Englewood Cliffs, NJ: Prentice-Hall.

Holland, J. L. (1982). The SDS helps both males and females: A comment. *Vocational Guidance Quarterly, 30*, 195–197.

Holland, J. L. (1985). *Making vocational choices: A theory of vocational personalities and work environments* (2nd ed.). Englewood, Cliffs, NJ: Prentice-Hall.

Holland, J. L. (1987). Current status of Holland's theory of careers: Another perspective. *Career Development Quarterly, 36*, 31–44.

Holland, J. L. (1990a). The self-directed search. Odessa, FL: PAR.

Holland, J. L. (1990b). The occupations locator. Odessa, FL: PAR.

Holland, J. L. (1997). *Making vocational choices* (3rd ed.). Englewood Cliffs, NJ: Prentice-Hall.

Holland, J. L., & Gottfredson, G. D. (1976). Using a typology of persons and environments to explain careers: Some extensions and clarifications. *Counseling Psychologist, 6*, 20–29.

Holland, J. L., & Gottfredson, G. D. (1990). *An annotated bibliography for Holland's theory of vocational personality and work environment.* Baltimore: Johns Hopkins University.

Holland, J. L., & Lutz, S. W. (1968). The predictive value of a student's choice of vocation. *Personnel and Guidance Journal, 46*, 428–436.

Holland, J. L., & Nichols, R. C. (1964). Explorations of a theory of vocational choice: III. A longitudinal study of change in major fields of study. *Personnel and Guidance Journal, 43*, 235–242.

Hotchkiss, L., & Borow, H. (1984). Sociological perspectives on career choice and attainment. In D. Brown, L. Brooks, & Associates, *Career choice and development* (pp. 137–168). San Francisco: Jossey-Bass.

Hotchkiss, L., & Borow, H. (1990). Sociological perspectives on work and career development. In D. Brown, L. Brooks, & Associates, *Career choice and development* (2nd ed., pp. 262–307). San Francisco: Jossey-Bass.

Hotchkiss, L., & Borow, H. (1996). Sociological perspectives on work and career development. In D. Brown, L. Brooks, & Associates, *Career choice and development* (3rd ed., pp. 281–336). San Francisco: Jossey-Bass.

Ibrahim, F. A. (1985). Effective cross-cultural counseling and psychotherapy: A framework. *The Counseling Psychologist, 13*, 625–638.

Jacobs, J. A., Karen, D., & McClelland, K. (1991). The dynamics of young men's occupational aspirations. *Sociological Forum, 6*, 609–639.

Janis, I. L., & Mann, L. (1977). *Decision making: A psychological analysis of conflict, choice, and commitment.* New York: Free Press.

Jencks, C., Crouse, J., & Mueser, P. (1983). The Wisconsin model of status attainment: A national replication with improved measures of ability and aspiration. *Sociology of Education, 56*, 3–19.

Jepsen, D. A., & Dilley, J. S. (1974). Vocational decision making models: A review and comparative analysis. *Review of Educational Research, 44*, 331–349.

Judge, T. A., & Bretz, R. D., Jr. (1992). Effects of work values on job choice decisions. *Journal of Applied Psychology, 77*, 261–271.

Kluckhorn, F. R., & Strodtbeck, F. L. (1961). *Values in values orientations.* Evanston, IL: Row Peterson.

Krumboltz, J. D. (1979). A social learning theory of career choice. In A. M. Mitchell, G. B. Jones, & J. D. Krumboltz (Eds.), *Social learning theory and career decision making.* Cranston, RI: Carroll Press.

Krumboltz, J. D. (1991). *Manual for the career beliefs inventory.* Palo Alto, CA: CPP.

Krumboltz, J. D. (1994). Improving career development theory from a social learning theory perspective. In M. L. Savickas & R. W. Lent (Eds.), *Convergence in career development theory* (pp. 9–32). Palo Alto, CA: CPP Books.

Krumboltz, J. D. (1996). A learning theory of career counseling. In M. Savickas & Bruce Walsh (Eds.), *Integrating career theory and practice*. Palo Alto, CA: CPP Books.

Krumboltz, J. D., Mitchell, A. M., & Jones, G. B. (1976). A social learning theory of career selection. *The Counseling Psychologist, 6*, 71–81.

LaFromboise, T. D., Trimble, J. E., & Mohatt, G. V. (1990). Counseling intervention and Native American tradition: An integrative approach. *The Counseling Psychologist, 18*, 624–628.

Lapan, R. T., Loehr-Lapan, S. J., & Tupper, T. W. (1993). *Tech-prep career workbooks: Counselor's manual*. Columbia, MO: University of Missouri, Department of Educational and Counseling Psychology.

Lee, K. C. (1991). The problem of the appropriateness of the Rokeach Values Survey in Korea, *International Journal of Psychology, 26*, 299–310.

Lent, R. W., Brown, S. D., & Hackett, G. (1995). Toward a unifying social cognitive theory of career and academic interest, choice, and performance. *Journal of Vocational Behavior, 45*, 79–122.

Lent, R. W., Brown, S. D., & Hackett, G. (1996). Career development from a social cognitive perspective. In D. Brown, L. Brooks, & Associates, *Career choice and development* (3rd ed.). San Francisco: Jossey-Bass.

Leong, F. T. L. (1991). Career development attributes and occupational values of Asian American and White high school students. *Career Development Quarterly, 39*, 221–230.

Leong, F. T. L. (Ed.). (1995). *Career development and vocational behavior of ethnic minorities*. Mahwah, NJ: Lawrence Erlbaum.

Leong, F. T. L., & Gim-Chung, R. H. (1995). Career assessment and intervention with Asian Americans. In F. T. L. Leong (Ed.), *Career development and vocational behavior of racial and ethnic minorities* (pp. 193–226). Mahwah, NJ: Lawrence Erlbaum.

Leong, F. T. L., & Serifica, F. C. (1995). Career development of Asian Americans: A research area in need of a good theory. In F. T. L. Leong (Ed.), *Career development and vocational behavior of ethnic and racial minorities* (pp. 67–102). Mahwah, NJ: Lawrence Erlbaum.

Levin, A. S., Krumboltz, J. D., & Krumboltz, B. L. (1995). *Exploring your career beliefs: A workbook for the Career Beliefs Inventory with techniques for integrating your Strong and MBTI results*. Palo Alto, CA: CPP.

Levinson, D. J., Darrow, C. N., Klein, E. B., Levinson, M. H., & Mckee, B. (1959). *The seasons of a man's life*. New York: Knopf.

Lofquist, L. H., & Dawis, R. V. (1969). *Adjustment to work*. New York: Appleton-Century-Crofts.

Lofquist, L. H., & Dawis, R. V. (1991). *Essentials of person-environment-correspondence counseling*. Minneapolis: University of Minnesota Press.

Marin, G., & Marin, V. M. (1991). *Research with Hispanic populations*. Newbury Park, CA: Sage.

McWhirter, J. J., & Ryan, C. A. (1991). Counseling the Navajo: Cultural understanding. *Journal of Multicultural Counseling and Development, 19*, 74–82.

Meglino, B. M., Ravlin, E. C., & Adkins, C. L. (1989). A work values approach to corporate culture. A field test of the value congruence process and its relationship to individual outcomes. *Journal of Applied Psychology, 74*, 424–432.

Meichenbaum, M. (1977). *Cognitive behavior-modification*. New York: Plenum.

Melamed, T. (1995). Career success: The moderating effects of gender. *Journal of Vocational Behavior, 47*, 295–314.

Melamed, T. (1996). Career success: An assessment of a gender-specific model. *Journal of Occupational and Organizational Psychology, 69*, 217–226.

Mitchell, L. K., & Krumboltz, J. D. (1984). Social learning approach to career decisions: Krumboltz's theory. In D. Brown, L. Brooks, & Associates, *Career choice and development* (pp. 235–280). San Francisco: Jossey-Bass.

Mitchell, L. K., & Krumboltz, J. D. (1990). Social learning approach to career decisions: Krumboltz's theory. In D. Brown, L. Brooks, & Associates, *Career choice and development* (2nd ed., pp. 308–337). San Francisco: Jossey-Bass.

Mitchell, L. K., & Krumboltz, J. D. (1996). Krumboltz's theory of career choice and counseling. In D. Brown, L. Brooks, & Associates, *Career choice and development* (3rd ed.). San Francisco: Jossey-Bass.

Mitchell, W. D. (1975). Restle's choice model: A reconceptualization. *Journal of Vocational Behavior, 9,* 315–330.

Murphy, P., Burck, H. (1976). Career development of men in middle life. *Journal of Vocational Behavior, 9,* 337–343.

Parsons, F. (1909). *Choosing your vocation.* Boston: Houghton-Mifflin.

Pedersen, P. B. (1991). Multiculturalism as a generic approach to counseling. *Journal of Counseling and Development, 70,* 6–12.

Peterson, G. W., Sampson, J. P., Jr., & Reardon, R. C. (1991). *Career development and services: A cognitive approach.* Pacific Grove, CA: Brooks/Cole.

Peterson, G. W., Sampson, J. P., Jr., Reardon, R. C., & Lenz, J. G. (1996). A cognitive information processing approach. In D. Brown, L. Brooks, & Associates, *Career choice and development* (3rd ed.) (pp. 423–476). San Francisco: Jossey-Bass.

Phillips, S. D., & Imhoff, A. R. (1997). Women and career development: A decade of research. *Annual Review of Psychology, 48,* 31–60.

Reskin, B. F. (1993). Sex segregation in the workplace. *Annual Review of Sociology, 19,* 241–271.

Restle, F. (1961). *Psychology of judgment and choice.* New York: Wiley.

Roe, A. (1956). *The psychology of occupations.* New York: Wiley.

Roe, A. (1984). Personality development and career choice. In D. Brown, L. Brooks, & Associates, *Career choice and development* (pp. 31–53). San Francisco: Jossey-Bass.

Roe, A., & Lunneborg, P. W. (1990). Personality development and career choice. In D. Brown, L. Brooks, & Associates, *Career choice and development* (2nd ed.) (pp. 68–101). San Francisco: Jossey-Bass.

Rokeach, M. (1973). *The nature of human values.* New York: Free Press.

Roos, P. A., & Jones, K. W. (1993). *Work and Occupations, 20,* 395–428.

Saunders, L. (1995). Relative earnings of black and white men by region. *Monthly Labor Review, 118,* 68–73.

Sampson, J. P., Jr., Peterson, G. W., Lenz, J. G., Reardon, R. C., & Saunders, D. (1996). *Career beliefs inventory.* Odessa, FL: Personality Assessment Resources.

Savickas, M. L. (1991). Improving career time perspective. In D. Brown & L. Brooks, *Career Counseling Techniques* (pp. 236–249). Boston: Allyn & Bacon.

Savickas, M. L. (1995). Constructivist counseling for career indecision. *Career Development Quarterly, 43,* 363–373.

Savickas, M. L., & Lent, R. W. (1994). A convergent project for career psychology. In M. L. Savickas, & R. W. Lent (Eds.), *Convergence in career development theory* (pp. 9–32). Palo Alto, CA: CPP Books.

Smart, J. F., & Smart, D. W. (1995). Acculturative stress: The experience of the Hispanic immigrant. *The Counseling Psychologist, 23,* 25–42.

Sue, D. W., & Sue, D. (1990). *Counseling the culturally different* (2nd ed.). New York: Wiley.

Super, D. E. (1951). Vocational adjustment: Implementing a self-concept. *Occupations, 30,* 1–5.

Super, D. E. (1953). A theory of vocational development. *American Psychologist, 8,* 185–190.

Super, D. E. (1954). Career patterns as a basis for vocational counseling. *Journal of Counseling Psychology, 1,* 12–20.

Super, D. E. (1955). Personality integration through vocational counseling. *Journal of Counseling Psychology, 2,* 217–226.

Super, D. E. (1957). *The psychology of careers.* New York: Harper & Row.

Super, D. E. (1960). The critical ninth grade: Vocational choice or vocational exploration. *Personnel and Guidance Journal, 39,* 106–109.

Super, D. E. (1961a). Consistency and wisdom of vocational preference as indices of vocational maturity in the ninth grade. *Journal of Educational Psychology, 52,* 35–43.

Super, D. E. (1961b). Some unresolved issues in vocational development research. *Personnel and Guidance Journal, 40,* 11–14.

Super, D. E. (1964a). A developmental approach to vocational guidance. *Vocational Guidance Quarterly, 13,* 1–10.

Super, D. E. (1964b). Goal specificity in the vocational counseling of future college students. *Personnel and Guidance Journal, 43,* 127–134.

Super, D. E. (1969). Vocational development theory. *The Counseling Psychologist, 1,* 2–30.

Super, D. E. (1972). Vocational development theory: Persons, positions, processes. In J. M. Whiteley & A. Resnikoff (Eds.), *Perspectives on vocational guidance.* Washington, DC: American Personnel and Guidance Association.

Super, D. E. (Ed.). (1974). *Measuring vocational maturity for counseling and evaluation.* Washington, DC: American Personnel and Guidance Association.

Super, D. E. (1977). Vocational maturity in mid-career. *Vocational Guidance Quarterly, 25,* 294–302.

Super, D. E. (1980). A life-span, life-space approach to career development. *Journal of Vocational Behavior, 16,* 282–298.

Super, D. E. (1981). A developmental theory: Implementing a self-concept. In D. H. Montros & C. J. Shinkman (Eds.), *Career development in the 1980s: Theory and practice.* Springfield, IL: Thomas.

Super, D. E. (1983). Assessment in career guidance: Toward truly developmental counseling. *Personnel and Guidance Journal, 61,* 555–562.

Super, D. E. (1984). Career and life development. In D. Brown, L. Brooks, & Associates (Eds.), *Career choice and development.* San Francisco: Jossey-Bass.

Super, D. E. (1990). A life-span, life-space approach to career development. In D. Brown, L. Brooks, & Associates (Eds.), *Career choice and development* (2nd ed.). San Francisco: Jossey-Bass.

Super, D. E., & Bachrach, P. B. (1957). *Scientific careers and vocational development theory.* New York: Teachers College, Columbia University.

Super, D. E., Crites, J. O., Hummel, R. C., Moser, H. P., Overstreet, P. L., & Warnath, C. F. (1957). *Vocational development: A framework for research.* New York: Teachers College, Columbia University.

Super, D. E., & Hall, D. T. (1978). Career development: Exploration and planning. *Annual Review of Psychology, 29,* 333–372.

Super, D. E., & Kidd, J. M. (1979). Vocational maturity in adulthood: Toward turning a model into a measure. *Journal of Vocational Behavior, 14,* 255–270.

Super, D. E., Savickas, M. L., & Super, C. (1996). A life-span, life-space approach to career development. In D. Brown, L. Brooks, & Associates, *Career choice and development* (3rd ed.). San Francisco: Jossey-Bass.

Super, D. E., Starishevsky, R., Matlin, R., & Jordaan, J. P. (1963). *Career development: Self-concept theory.* New York: College Entrance Examination Board.

Super, D. E., & Sverko, B. (Eds.). (1995). *Life roles, values, and careers: International findings of the work importance study.* San Francisco: Jossey-Bass.

Tiedeman, D. V., & Miller-Tiedeman, A. (1984). Career decision making: An individualistic perspective. In D. Brown, L. Brooks & Associates, *Career choice and development* (pp. 281–310). San Francisco: Jossey-Bass.

Tiedeman, D. V., & O'Hara, R. P. (1963). *Career development: Choice and adjustment.* New York: College Entrance Examination Board.

Tversky, A. (1972). Elimination by aspects: A theory of choice. *Psychological Review, 79,* 281–291.

Vroom, V. H. (1964). *Work and motivation.* New York: Wiley.

Wright, G. (1984). *Behavioral decision theory.* Newbury Park, CA: Sage.

Young, R. A., Valach, L., & Collin, A. (1996). A contextual explanation of career. In D. Brown, L. Brooks, & Associates (Eds.), *Career choice and development* (3rd ed., pp. 477–512). San Francisco: Jossey-Bass.

3

Factors Influencing Workers and Their Careers

The concept of individual differences confirms the uniqueness of each individual. These differences result from the interaction of each individual's biological inheritance and specific characteristics of the particular environment that surrounds the person. The theories of career development considered in Chapter 2 address the principle of individual differences. Holland (1997), Super (1990), and the Theory of Work Adjustment (Dawis, 1996) place particular emphasis on the idea that traits such as interests, values, and aptitudes are important determinants of occupational satisfaction and choice and that these individual differences are easily identifiable.

The spectrum of personal characteristics of each individual is broad enough for the typical person to meet the patterns required in a wide variety of jobs. Conversely, the pattern demanded by the specific job has sufficient flexibility and tolerance to accommodate a wide variety of prospective job holders. This set of premises may be misinterpreted in two ways. If it is taken erroneously in the broadest possible context, one might say that each individual has the personal characteristics that make success possible in *any* job and that the pattern required by *every* job is a universal one found in all people. The indefensibility of such a position is obvious when one contemplates the possibility of a color-blind paint mixer or an accountant without numerical aptitude. At the other extreme, one might postulate that each individual is entirely unique so there is only one job or, more precisely, one position, that one can fill successfully, and that each position is so demanding that only one individual can perform it successfully. If such specificity were widespread, our complex society would be totally immobilized by the impossible task of matching individuals and positions.

A more realistic viewpoint assumes that most human characteristics, like most job requirements, are spread out over a normal distribution. A few individuals, and some jobs, do have such unique characteristics that only a few possible matches exist at any give time (e.g., the position of a soloist at the Metropolitan Opera). A few characteristics are so universal and a few tasks so elemental that practically every person meets at least the minimum requirements for some jobs. Most people and most occupations fall somewhere between these two extremes; we conclude, therefore, that some consideration must be given to balancing human characteristics against occupational demands, if success and satisfaction are to be maximized for the individual and productivity and effectiveness assured for the occupation.

The objective of this chapter is to identify and to discuss briefly some of these human and occupational differences that influence the likelihood of a given individual selecting an occupation, preparing for it, entering it, succeeding at the work, and gaining satisfaction from that participation. Those factors that relate directly to the individual are labeled *internal factors* and are subdivided into three categories—generic, personal-psychological, and personal-sociological. Those factors that relate to the job, work setting, or societal items are labeled *external factors* and also are divided into three categories—work situation, sociological, and economic.

Internal Factors

Generic Characteristics

Grouped under this heading are those characteristics that are broadly shared with many other individuals but that contribute significantly to the uniqueness of the individual. Among the many that can be subsumed here, we discuss briefly three examples—gender, ethnic and cultural background, and physique.

Gender
In 1996 the Bureau of the Census reported that the average male's income was $32,144, whereas women earned $23,710. This report is simply a confirmation of a long-standing wage gap between males and females. Melamed (1995; 1996) concluded on the basis of her own research and a review of the empirical literature regarding the occupational choices of women that three factors contribute to the wage discrepancy that exists among men and women: initial occupational choice, time spent in the work role, and discrimination. However, one of these factors— initial occupational choice—seems to be changing to some degree. The U.S. Department of Labor (1997) contrasted the percentages of women in certain occupations in 1975 and 1995. In 1995, 52 percent of accountants and auditors were women versus 44 percent in 1975. Moreover, when contrasting 1975 and 1995, women made up 52 percent of the total employment of accountants and auditors (vs. 44%), 32 percent of the chemists (vs. 21%), 8 percent of the engineers (vs. 1%), and 16 percent of the law enforcement officers (vs. 8%). Just as importantly there

was a decline in the relative percentage of women employed in some traditional female careers such as cashier. Earlier, Castro (1990) had reported that the percentage of physicians who were women was approaching 20 percent and that 32 percent of computer analysts were women. Both of these figures have undoubtedly increased.

Nearly 20 years ago Huston (1983) and Astin (1984) pointed out that the early socialization of women leads to differences in career choices between the sexes. Gottfredson's (1996) theory, as presented in Chapter 2, has as one of its basic premises that some occupational choices are eliminated because they are perceived to be incompatible with the individuals' sex-role identity. Although women make up only about 1 percent of the employment of carpenters and mechanics, it appears that women are ruling out fewer occupations on the basis of sex-role appropriateness. Although there is less evidence that men are acting in a similar fashion, many males will be forced to enter female-dominated fields because of competition from women in traditional fields. Others will choose to do so because of the attractiveness of these careers. For example, in 1995, 7 percent of nurses were men, up from 3 percent in 1975.

It also seems likely that the role of discrimination, sometimes referred to as the "glass ceiling," will be less a factor in limiting women's careers in the future because of the results of some successful high-profile lawsuits and because of the changing views of women in the workplace. In 1995, 50 and 57 percent (up from 24% and 45% in 1975) of all financial and personnel managers were women. However, it would be naïve to think that unfair labor practices will not continue to be a problem. Similarly, it seems likely that the relative participation of men in the work role will equalize to some degree in the future, thus eliminating another barrier to upward occupational mobility and increased earnings.

Ethnic and Cultural Background

In the year 2006 the labor force in this country is expected to total 149 million. Approximately 70 percent of these workers will be white. The remainder will be cultural and ethnic minorities (DOL, 1997). With the exception of Asian Americans, minority status has proved to be a barrier to upward occupational mobility and higher earnings. In 1996 the average earnings of the major cultural groups in this country were Asian Americans, $43,276; whites, $37,171; Hispanics, $24,906; and African Americans, $23,482. These differences in earnings, like those reported for women in the previous section, are due to a number of factors including discrimination (Arbona, 1995; Leong & Roote, 1992; Smith, 1983), access to education, and initial occupational choice. Brown (1997) documented that minorities are overrepresented in lower-paying occupations. Smith (1983) credits the success of Asian Americans in the workplace with their emphasis on educational achievement, which opens up educational opportunities, as well as retention of their culture, a supportive family structure, and their unwillingness to rely on governmental support programs. Her 20-year-old observation that minorities need to focus on school achievement and become more aware of the occupations available to them is still valid. Brown and Minor (1992) found that African American parents were more supportive of career development activities than parents from other groups, which suggests that this group may be in agreement with Smith's (1983) recommendation. However, discrimination against minorities at all levels in the workplace must be greatly reduced if they are to achieve their full occupational potential.

Physique

Differences between individuals in height and weight are immediately obvious. Other physical differences may be less apparent, but their existence can be demonstrated easily. Certain physical capacities must be present if the person is to meet the minimum requirements for some jobs. In a later section of this chapter, we consider in more detail the physical requirements for various jobs. Professional athletes provide an example of how this factor relates to qualifications for different occupations; picture for a moment a stereotypical jockey, basketball player, weight lifter, and a marathon runner. It is most unlikely that the jockey could compete successfully in basketball or in weight lifting, or that participants in those activities could bring a horse to the winner's circle of a derby. Most people have sufficient amounts of the various physical capacities to meet the minimum requirement in a wide range of occupations; nevertheless, the absence of a needed capacity can exclude that individual from successful participation in an occupation.

We refer to an individual as *disabled* or *impaired* when certain physical or mental capacities are nonexistent or limited. The presence of such conditions can influence career participation in many ways. Often unwarranted assumptions are made about people with disabilities (e.g., if the person cannot walk, then there is no work he can do). If one really pushed, it would be possible to identify some physical or mental capacity that approaches zero for each of us, but we work around it in some way that usually satisfies the situation and do not think of ourselves as people with disabilities. The term *disability* usually refers to a more serious impairment such as loss of a limb or its use. Of course, such disability is serious, frustrating, and inconvenient, often limiting participation in a wide range of activities. It requires the individual to focus on those fields where the absent capacity is not needed. Inability to walk is irrelevant vocationally if the work setting and the job do not require that ability.

Kraus and Stoddard (1989) describe the extent of physical disability and its impact on work. For example, about 20 percent of noninstitutionalized people over age 15 have a physical limitation. Over 18 million people in the United States are unable to lift and carry a 10-pound bag of groceries, nearly 13 million are unable to see words or letters in newsprint, and 2.5 million are unable to speak clearly because of physical restrictions. About 8.6 percent of the working-age population has some form of work disability. Among African American workers, 13.7 percent have a work disability, and among Hispanics the figure is 7.9 percent. The impact of disability is dramatic, with 19.7 percent of those with a work disability being employed full time compared to 59.4 percent of those without a work disability.

Personal-Psychological Characteristics

In this section we look at some of the psychological requirements that affect the individual's career choice and participation. Our examples include aptitude, interests, and personality (including temperament and values).

Aptitude

Aptitudes are defined as specific capacities and abilities required of an individual to learn or adequately perform a task or job duty. Much psychological research has focused on this topic for over half a century. An early classic work by Bingham (1937), *Aptitudes and Aptitude Testing*, describes the state of the art at that point. Later work includes books by Anastasi (1988), and Kapes, Mastie, and Whitfield (1994).

Recent research suggests that *aptitude* refers to specific psychological factors that contribute in varying degrees to success in various occupations. It is a capacity or potential that has stability, unity, and independence. Different authors report varying numbers of aptitudes, partly due to variable input factors such as types of psychological measurements, statistical treatment, and subjective factors (e.g., groupings or classifications). However, the developers of O*NET (1998) identified 52 *abilities.* These abilities fall into four categories: cognitive, psychomotor, physical, and sensory. Examples of abilities that fall into each domain follow.

Cognitive	Fluency of ideas—the ability to come up with a number of ideas
	Inductive reasoning—the ability to combine separate pieces of information or specific answers to problems to form general rules or conclusions
	Originality—the ability to come up with unusual or clever ideas about a specific topic or situation or to develop creative ways to solve problems
Psychomotor	Arm-hand steadiness—the ability to keep the arm and hand steady while making an arm movement or while holding the arm and hand in one position
	Rate control—the ability to time the adjustments of a movement or equipment control in anticipation of changes in speed and/or direction of a continuously moving object or scene
	Wrist-finger speed—the ability to make fast, simple, repeated movements of the fingers, hand, and wrist
Physical	Extent flexibility—the ability to bend, stretch, twist, or reach out with body, arms, or legs
	Speed of limb movement—the ability to quickly move the arms or legs

	Static strength—the ability to exert maximum force to lift, push, pull, or carry objects
Sensory	Perceptual speed—the ability to quickly and accurately compare letters, numbers, objects, or patterns
	Peripheral vision—the ability to see objects or movement of objects to one's side when the eyes are focused
	Sound localization—the ability to tell the direction from which a sound originated

Obviously, not all of the 52 abilities identified in O*NET are required for all jobs. However, the data in O*NET provide ratings regarding the level of each ability needed to perform a given occupation, the importance of the ability of performing the occupation, the frequency with which the ability must be exercised in each occupation, as well as other types of information. The level of ability required for each occupation is presented in using a 0 (not relevant) to 7 (highly relevant) scale. The importance of the ability to successful performance of each occupation is presented using a 1 (not important) to 5 (extremely important) scale, and frequency data are presented using a 1 (almost never) to 4 (always) scale.

As was stated at the outset, most people have a wide range of aptitudes and most occupations are structured so that people with differing levels of aptitudes can perform them. However, whereas these tolerances are wide, they are so wide that individuals should not rule out occupations for which they have little aptitude. The problem then becomes finding methods for estimating one's aptitudes in the career decision-making process. These methods will be discussed in Chapter 13.

Interests

Perhaps the most used type of information to determine the appropriateness of an occupation for an individual is interests. Interests are likes or preferences, or, somewhat differently, things that people enjoy.

Super (1957) describes four types of interests, varying primarily with the method of assessment:

Expressed interests: Verbal statements or claims of interest

Manifest interests: Shown through actions and participation

Inventoried interests: Estimates of interest based on responses to a set of questions concerning likes and dislikes

Tested interests: Revealed under controlled situations

As can be seen in Super's taxonomy, interest may be assessed in a number of ways. Although they are most frequently assessed using psychometric devices, stated or expressed interests are as valid a predictor of factors such as occupational choice, satisfaction, and achievement as are inventoried interests (Whitney, 1969). However, when individuals involved in career decision making have limited experiences, the likelihood that either stated or inventoried interests will be good predictors of occupational behavior is reduced. Moreover, interest measures are aimed at quantifying what individuals like or prefer, not why they like or prefer them. Personality and values measures are more likely to provide this type of information.

Personality

The theoretical positions of Holland (1997) and Super (1990) identify personality as a key factor in vocational choice and career development. However, although Holland claims that interest inventories are personality inventories, his assertion is probably not accepted outside the area of career development, and his instruments are typically classified as interest inventories because they measure likes and preferences (cf. Kapes, Mastie, & Whitfield, 1994). Personality is typically defined as the sum total of an individual's beliefs, perceptions, emotions, and attitudes and may be extended to include the behavior of the personality as well (Drummond, 1996). Historically, the role of personality in career choice has been secondary to interests, a situation that still exists. However, since the development of the Myers-Briggs Type Indicator (MBTI), there has been a resurgence in interest in personality's role in occupational selection, and it is likely that many of the millions of people who have taken the MBTI did so as a means to facilitate their career choice and development. This interest was fueled partially by the career data collected regarding this instrument, which are presented in the appendix to the technical manual of the MBTI (Myers & McCaulley, 1998).

The MBTI yields included four polar scales. These are:

Extroversion ——————Introversion

Sensing————————iNtuition

Thinking ————————Feeling

Judging————————Perceiving

The personality profile resulting from the Myers-Briggs consists of the highest scores on Introversion versus Extroversion; Sensing versus iNtuition; Thinking versus Feeling, and Judging versus Perceiving. Thus each individual is categorized as one of 16 personality types such as ENFP or ISTJ. Each personality type has certain preferences, including preferences for work environments. For example approximately half of the individuals in the helping professions surveyed by Myers and McCaulley (1998) have NF in their personality profile. This means that their preferred way of taking in data is through their intuition (versus the five senses for Ss), and their preferred manner of using information is on the basis of their feelings (as opposed to their thoughts, as would be the case for Ts).

Values

The most widely accepted definition of values stems from the seminal work of Rokeach (1973), who defined values as cognized needs that guide our behavior and serve as standards against which we judge our behavior and the behavior of others. Needs are transitory because once they are satisfied they no longer motivate behavior. Values function across situations and are not transitory. Values differ from interests in that they serve as standards while interests do not. Earlier Spranger (1928) had proposed that values could be used to classify people according to their values types which he enumerated as theoretical, economic, social, political, aesthetic, and religious. More recently Super (1957, 1990) Brown & Srebalus (1996) and others such as Leong (1991) have identified values as important determinants of various aspects of career development and career choice and satisfaction, propositions that have received wide support. The Values Scale (Nevill & Super, 1986) and the Life Values Inventory (Crace & Brown, 1996) are examples of values inventories.

Personal-Sociological Characteristics

This category includes those characteristics that are personal in the sense that they have an impact on a particular individual, but they involve others close to that person. We consider three examples: family socioeconomic status, access to education, and lifestyle.

Family Socioeconomic Status

Sociological literature from its beginning has included studies of relationships between family and work, social status and work, and the impact of family status on individuals. Oppenheimer (1982) studied census records to compare family data for eight different occupational groups. She further divided the sample into income levels to identify periods of economic stress. She found that most families face three periods of such stress, labeled life-cycle squeezes. These usually occur when the couple establishes an independent household, when children reach adolescence, and when the couple reaches the postretirement period. The strategies used by the family to resolve the financial crunch appear to be related to the occupational status of the father. For example, during the second squeeze (children at the late adolescent period), children of low-income, blue-collar families frequently discontinued schooling and went to work either to help with family finances or to provide self-support, usually at low-level jobs, while children of high-income, white-collar families continued their education, thus increasing their eligibility for higher level jobs.

Higher socioeconomic status of parents provides many opportunities for children that may influence their later career planning. In addition to longer and richer educational advantages, they are more likely to engage in travel, summer camp, or similar enrichment experiences and to have contact with a wide range of occupational role models within the family circle of friends and acquaintances.

Meantime, their peers from lower status families are restricted from such contacts not only by financial factors but by lack of access to such opportunities. Blau and Duncan (1967) and Sewell and Hauser (1975) are classic sociological studies showing the relationship between family status and later occupational attainment. Hotchkiss and Borow (1996) reviewed many of the sociological studies on this topic.

Access to Education

Americans commonly take pride in their free public education system, implying that equal opportunity for quality elementary and secondary education exists for all. There are at least two problems in this assumption: first, access to education may not be uniformly equal; and second, the quality available may not be equal.

Statewide competency testing programs have demonstrated regularly a wide discrepancy in the percentage of students from different schools and school systems who pass the test successfully. Undoubtedly, many factors produce this variation, but those schools with higher failure rates consistently have limited funding, crowded classes, lower quality staff, restricted facilities and resources, and other aspects that reflect lower quality education. Statewide, such schools are frequently found in two locations—isolated rural areas with limited financial resources, or inner-city urban areas with high ratios of low-income and welfare families. Such schools also frequently show poor attendance records, high dropout rates, and a limited number of educational programs. Recent court rulings in several states have required reorganization of state educational systems to reduce obvious discrepancies.

We oversimplify when we assume that because a school exists and tuition fees are not charged, it is accessible to all. There are numerous hidden costs in most school attendance situations, such as book fees, activity fees, transportation costs, and clothing expenses. Some potential students are absent because they must care for family members, either younger siblings or ill adults, or because they must engage in work that is often irregular, seasonal, or part time. Increasing numbers of nonattending or irregularly attending students are members of single-parent families, and sometimes that parent is dysfunctional or lacks parental skills.

Several researchers have explored the impact of school tracking, where students are assigned to programs such as college preparatory or vocational. Among these are studies by Alexander and McDill (1976), Garet and DeLany (1988), Gamoran and Mare (1989), and Vanfossen, Jones, and Spade (1987). The research shows a close relationship between family status and the track to which a student is assigned. This, in turn, has a direct impact on subsequent career participation.

There are striking exceptions to these generalizations. Every school teacher and counselor can identify individual students who face overwhelming odds in getting to school and staying in school and who nevertheless succeed academically. However, it often is the comparison between this unusual, highly motivated student and the generally typical student that makes the stark reality so apparent.

Our discussion, thus far, has focused on the elementary and secondary levels. Access to postsecondary education is restricted by a number of factors, including geographic location, costs, eligibility for admission, and limitation of enrollment.

Lifestyle

Lifestyle factors in the parental home influence the childhood and adolescent years in ways that carry over into adulthood and have an impact on career. One example, mentioned earlier, is the single-parent family. In many such families, especially where finances are adequate, child care or other resources fill the gap caused by the absent parent. In other situations, particularly in low-income settings, the result may be little or no supervision, involvement with high-risk activities, lack of encouragement and motivation, absence of role models, and lack of access to developmental and enlightening experiences. Smith (1983) describes the many problems faced by inner-city poor black children, many of whom live in single-parent families. These conditions discourage, and sometimes prevent, motivated involvement in education, thus later severely restricting successful career involvement.

An example of lifestyle influence on adult career behavior that is a well-established phenomenon is the dual-career family. The trend during the past decade has clearly been an increase in two-earner families. This appears likely to increase in the years ahead. Dual-career families find both positive and negative aspects to their status. On the plus side, these families report a greater degree of flexibility in partners being able to relinquish unsatisfactory career paths and either search for new opportunities or take up a training program that might open new paths. This is obviously the result of the security provided by the second income. On the negative side are reports that dual-career families must sometimes forgo career opportunities that require relocating because such a move would be disruptive for the partner's career. Indirectly related to career development are other problems faced by dual-career families, such as increased pressure on time allocation, the difficulty of finding time for family activities, and the sharing of household tasks.

External Factors

Work Situation

In this section we consider factors influencing career participation that are direct outgrowths of the job or the work situation. The training time required for various jobs, the physical demands required to do the work, and the environmental conditions imposed by the work are examined.

Training Time

Except in very simple occupations, the acquisition of general and specialized knowledge and skills is necessary for successful performance by the worker. The particular mix of general and specific knowledge and skill obviously varies from occupation to occupation.

General educational development includes the broad academic preparation acquired in elementary and secondary school and in college that does not have a specific occupational objective. It usually refers to aspects of education that develop reasoning and adaptability to environment, ability to understand and follow directions, and such tool knowledges as mathematics and language.

The latest projections issued by the U.S. Department of Labor (DOL, 1997) clearly show that the occupations growing the fastest are those that require the highest educational level, and the specific vocational preparation for these jobs will require a solid educational foundation. Additionally, what is clear is that the level of general educational preparation required for entry into the best jobs is increasing and diversifying. Traditionally general educational development has focused on two areas: mathematics and language proficiency. Currently problem solving, human relations, and leadership skills and a variety of other skills are seen as foundations for many careers. Jones (1996) identified 17 foundational skills that are needed by students entering the work force. These are:

Basic Skills

Reading   Writing   Mathematics   Speaking   Listening

Cognitive Skills

Creative thinking   Problem solving   Decision making   Visualization

Interpersonal Relationship Skills

| Communication | Negotiation | Leadership | Ability to work as team member | Ability to function effectively in multi-cultural setting |

Personal Qualities

Self-esteem   Self-management   Responsibility

Specific vocational preparation is training time required to learn the techniques and knowledge and to develop the skills needed for average performance in a specific job-worker situation. The training includes the acquisition of skills and knowledge needed to do the job, but it does not include the orientation training that is usually required to familiarize the worker with the special conditions or procedures existing at the specific work site. Specific vocational preparation is usually obtained in one or a combination of the following:

1. Vocational education
2. Apprentice training
3. In-plant training

4. On-the-job training
5. Essential experience in other jobs

Currently information about training time can be ascertained from a variety of sources including O*NET, the *Dictionary of Occupational Titles*, the *Occupational Outlook Handbook (OOH)*, and the *Guide for Occupational Exploration*. The data in O*NET were developed using the classification system found in the third edition of the *Dictionary of Occupational Titles (DOT)* (DOL, 1992) as the foundation. Data from other sources were combined with the *DOT* information to provide the data that are now available in O*NET. The system used to classify occupations in the *DOT* is presented below.

Nine levels are used to categorize specific vocational preparation:

Level	*Time*
1	Short demonstration
2	Anything beyond short demonstration up to and including 30 days
3	Over 30 days up to and including 3 months
4	Over 3 months up to and including 6 months
5	Over 6 months up to and including 1 year
6	Over 1 year up to and including 2 years
7	Over 2 years up to and including 4 years
8	Over 4 years up to and including 10 years
9	Over 10 years

Physical Demands

Every work situation requires some physical involvement of the worker; conversely, every worker brings to the work situation certain physical capacities that are used in the process of performing the work. Just as one might expect the physical characteristics of individuals to vary, so too might one expect the physical demands associated with different types of work to vary. Some occupations require minimum output of physical activity, some require vigorous action of one or two types, and others involve strenuous activity across a broad range. As was noted in the section on aptitude, the new O*NET (USDOL, 1998) system has identified what they term abilities including physical, sensory, and psychomotor abilities. These abilities are based on the system that can be found in the *DOT* (DOL, 1992). The *DOT* system is shown below.

1. *Strength:* This factor is expressed in terms of *Sedentary, Light, Medium, Heavy,* and *Very Heavy.* It is measured by involvement of the worker with one or more of the following activities:
   a. Worker position(s):
      (1) *Standing:* Remaining on one's feet in an upright position at a workstation without moving about.
      (2) *Walking:* Moving about on foot.

    (3) *Sitting:* Remaining in the normal seated position.

  b. Worker movement of objects (including extremities used):

    (1) *Lifting:* Raising or lowering an object from one level to another (includes upward pulling).

    (2) *Carrying:* Transporting an object, usually holding it in the hands or arms or on the shoulder.

    (3) *Pushing:* Exerting force upon an object so that the object moves away from the force (includes slapping, striking, kicking, and treadle actions).

    (4) *Pulling:* Exerting force upon an object so that the object moves toward the force (includes jerking).

  c. The five degrees of Physical Demands, Factor No. 1 (strength), are as follows:

S—Sedentary Work: Lifting 10 pounds maximum and occasionally lifting and/or carrying such articles as dockets, ledgers, and small tools. Although a sedentary job is defined as one that involves sitting, a certain amount of walking and standing is often necessary in carrying out job duties. Jobs are sedentary if walking and standing are required only occasionally and other sedentary criteria are met.

L—Light Work: Lifting 20 lbs. maximum with frequent lifting and/or carrying of objects weighing up to 10 lbs. Even though the weight lifted may be only a negligible amount, a job is in this category when it requires walking or standing to a significant degree, or when it involves sitting most of the time with a degree of pushing and pulling of arm and/or leg controls.

M—Medium Work: Lifting 50 lbs. maximum with frequent lifting and/or carrying of objects weighing up to 25 lbs.

H—Heavy Work: Lifting 100 lbs. maximum with frequent lifting and/or carrying of objects weighing up to 50 lbs.

V—Very Heavy Work: Lifting objects in excess of 100 lbs. with frequent lifting and/or carrying of objects weighing 50 lbs. or more.

2. *Climbing and/or Balancing:*

    (1) *Climbing:* Ascending or descending ladders, stairs, scaffolding, ramps, poles, ropes, and the like, using the feet and legs and/or hands and arms.

    (2) *Balancing:* Maintaining body equilibrium to prevent falling when walking, standing, crouching, or running on narrow, slippery, or erratically moving surfaces; or maintaining body equilibrium when performing gymnastic feats.

3. *Stooping, Kneeling, Crouching, and/or Crawling:*

    (1) *Stooping:* Bending the body downward and forward by bending the spine at the waist.

    (2) *Kneeling:* Bending the legs at the knees to come to rest on the knee or knees.

(3) *Crouching:* Bending the body downward and forward by bending the legs and spine.

(4) *Crawling:* Moving about on the hands and knees or hands and feet.

4. *Reaching, Handling, Fingering, and/or Feeling:*

(1) *Reaching:* Extending the hands and arms in any direction.

(2) *Handling:* Seizing, holding, grasping, turning, or otherwise working with the hand or hands (fingering not involved).

(3) *Fingering:* Picking, pinching, or otherwise working with the fingers primarily (rather than with the whole hand or arm as in handling).

(4) *Feeling:* Perceiving such attributes of objects and materials as size, shape, temperature, or texture, by means of receptors in the skin, particularly those of the fingertips.

5. *Talking and/or Hearing:*

(1) *Talking:* Expressing or exchanging ideas by means of the spoken word.

(2) *Hearing:* Perceiving the nature of sounds by the ear.

6. *Seeing:* Obtaining impressions through the eyes of the shape, size, distance, motion, color, or other characteristics of objects. The major visual functions are: (1) acuity, far and near, (2) depth perception, (3) field of vision, (4) accommodation, and (5) color vision.

The functions are defined as follows:

(1) Acuity, far—clarity of vision at 20 feet or more.
Acuity, near—clarity of vision at 20 inches or less.

(2) Depth perception—three-dimensional vision. The ability to judge distance and space relationships so as to see objects where and as they actually are.

(3) Field of vision—the area that can be seen up and down or to the right or left while the eyes are fixed on a given point.

(4) Accommodation—adjustment of the lens of the eye to bring an object into sharp focus. This item is especially important when doing near-point work at varying distances from the eye.

(5) Color vision—the ability to identify and distinguish colors.

Obviously, the worker must have sufficient physical capacity to perform the activities required in the occupation. The inability to perform certain physical tasks is important only if the ability is required to do the work. The reverse is also true: The ability to lift a heavy weight is irrelevant unless this is required to do the work. Some individuals with physical disabilities may generalize their inability to do certain tasks to all activities; other people who do one activity better than most others expect to excel in all. The crucial factor concerning physical demands is that the worker must be able to meet the minimum requirements.

Environmental Conditions

Just as an occupation requires a worker to meet certain physical demands, it frequently requires that the work be performed in a particular setting that may impose certain demands on the worker's physical capacities. Those of us who work in comfortable, climate-controlled, well-lighted offices are likely to give little thought to the minimal demands that our work situation makes of us. Many workers, however, are confronted with specific circumstances, imposed by the location and nature of the work, that place far heavier demands on them. For example, a blast furnace keeper in a steel mill encounters extreme temperatures as a normal part of the work; a coal miner is faced with noise, hazards, dust, and poor ventilation.

In the O*NET database, environmental data about jobs are referred to as Job Characteristics. The data presented are far more complete than anything that has been produced to date. Information about hazardous conditions is noted, as are listings about unpleasant working conditions such as noxious fumes, loud noises, or cramped working conditions. Further, scales that detail the nature and relative importance of the human conditions found in the workplace such as role relationships, communication methods, and responsibility for others are also present in the database. Finally, information about the need for special or protective clothing is in O*NET when it is appropriate.

Sociological Influences

The relationship between individuals and their occupations is, in many ways, similar to that between individuals and their spouses. Both partners contribute to meeting each other's needs; both impose demands on the other. If compatibility is to develop, there must be adaptability, mutual interest and concern, tolerance, and acceptance. In an earlier section of this chapter, we discussed the sociological factors in the immediate family environment of the individual. In this section we are concerned with the broad view beyond the family, as sociologists study the impact of work on individuals and their lives. Helpful sources to consult for further information include Terkel (1972); O'Toole, Scheiber, and Wood (1981); Stewart and Cantor (1982); Hall (1986); and Rothman (1987). Recent, relevant sociological research can often be found in professional journals such as *American Journal of Sociology,* the *American Sociological Review,* and *Work and Occupations.* Our examples of this sociological focus include occupational prestige, occupational mobility, regulating admission to occupations, and regulation of worker behavior.

Occupational Prestige

The importance of occupational prestige for the counselor and the teacher can be focused primarily on (1) recognizing the considerable variation in the amount of prestige generally given to various occupations, and (2) recognizing the impact that such prestige values have on individuals who are considering and evaluating occupations.

Occupational prestige has been defined in many ways. In some research studies reported in the literature, specific efforts have been made to avoid definition in order to draw from the respondents their ideas and attitudes concerning the meaning of the term. For the purpose of this chapter, occupational prestige is considered to be the esteem or social status accorded to an occupation by the general population. It is important to recognize that the concern here is the prestige of the occupation, not that of the individual.

Garbin and Bates (1966) studied 20 factors that appear to influence the prestige ranking of an occupation. Of the 20 factors reported, six showed positive correlations of .90 to .95 with occupational prestige. In descending order, these are as follows:

1. Regarded as desirable to associate with
2. Intelligence required
3. Scarcity of personnel who can do the job
4. Interesting and challenging work
5. Training required
6. Education required

Five other factors produced correlations of .80 or better:

1. Work calling for originality and initiative
2. Toil for improving others
3. Having influence over others
4. Security
5. Opportunity for advancement

Counts (1925) asked a group of 450 people to rank 25 occupations. Counts's study has been replicated at least four times: (1) Deeg and Paterson, 1946; (2) Hakel, Hollman, and Dunnette, 1967; (3) Kanzaki, 1975; and (4) Fredrickson, Lin, and Xing, 1992. One striking aspect of the results of these studies, which are summarized in Table 3.1, is that occupational status has remained relatively stable in the United States. In a related study, Parker and his associates (1995) compared the occupational rankings of 100 occupations by high school students to data collected in previous studies by Reiss (1961) and Treiman and Terrell (1975). They conclude that the results of their study also support the idea that prestige ratings and rankings are generally stable across groups and time. However, they did find that high school students generally rate social service occupations lower than other groups.

The results of the study just cited by Fredrickson and associates (1992) also suggest that occupational status transcends geographic and cultural differences. He and his colleagues compared occupational status in Taiwan, The Peoples Republic of China, and the United States and found that the rankings were remarkably similar. Bankers, engineers, army captains, physicians and lawyers were consistently ranked high by college students from The Peoples Republic of China,

TABLE 3.1   Social Status of 25 Occupations: 1925, 1946, 1967, 1975, and 1992

Occupation	1925	1946	1967	1975	1992
Banker	1	2.5	4	3	5
Physician	2	1	1	1	1
Lawyer	3	2.5	2	5	2
Superintendent of Schools	4	4	3	4	4
Civil Engineer	5	5	5	2	3
Army Captain	6	6	8	8	6
Foreign Missionary	7	7	7	9	NR
Elementary School Teacher	8	8	6	6	7
Farmer	9	12	19	7	16
Machinist	10	9	12	11	14
Traveling Salesperson	11	16	13	16	13
Grocer	12	13	17	13	18
Electrician	13	11	9	10	8
Insurance Agent	14	10	10	14	9
Mail Carrier	15	14	18	17	15
Carpenter	16	15	11	12	10
Soldier	17	19	15	19	11
Plumber	18	17	16	15	12
Motorman (Bus Driver)	19	18	20	22	19
Barber	20	20	14	18	17
Truck Driver	21	21.5	21	21	20
Coal Miner	22	21.5	23	20	21
Janitor	23	23	22	24	23
Hod Carrier	24	24	24	23	22
Ditchdigger	25	25	25	25	24

Source: Kanzaki, G. A. (1976). Fifty years of stability in the social status of occupations. *Vocational Guidance Quarterly*, 25, 101–105; and Fredrickson, R. H., Lin, J. G., & Xing, S. (1992). Social status ranking of occupations in The People's Republic of China, Taiwan, and the United States. *Career Development Quarterly, 40,* 351–360. Used by permission of NCDA.

Taiwan, and the United States. Moreover, occupations such as truck driver, janitor, and ditchdiggers were accorded low status by all three groups. The differences found among the groups seem to be related to the differing nature of the jobs in the three countries studied.

Occupational Mobility
The Horatio Alger concept of the poor but industrious and ambitious boy who starts at the bottom and rises to the top of his career field has long been a part of

U.S. heritage. In the dynamic, expanding, and classless society that has existed in the United States for the past two centuries, such opportunities have existed; and every community has within it examples of self-made successes.

Sociologists have assigned the term *vertical mobility* to movement from one occupational stratum to a higher or lower one. When the change is essentially one of function but the person remains at the same level, the term *horizontal mobility* is used.

The biographies of self-made men and women often imply that the individual's success has come about through the persistent application of hard work, faithfulness, and virtue. This view, of course, takes the position that only the individual was active and that the situation in which a person worked was passive and inert. The stories of failures, on the other hand, all too often cast the individual in the role of the helpless, storm-tossed victim of ruthless and uncontrollable circumstances. In such a picture, we must assume that the individual is passive and the situation is all-powerful. If, however, we view people and their work as an interacting relationship, to which both contribute and from which both benefit, then both parties are seen as active. A realistic consideration of mobility must proceed from this assumption of interrelatedness.

Hotchkiss and Borow (1996) summarize sociological research that explores "status attainment"—the sociological term for how individuals pursue and reach status goals such as education, occupation, and income. Most research on status attainment is an outgrowth of earlier research on occupational mobility. The general basis assumed is that parental status heavily influences, both directly and indirectly, the status achieved by their children. Early studies (pre-1967) also identified education, achievement motivation, influence of peers, and intelligence as other important determinants of occupational mobility. Blau and Duncan (1967) established the pattern for current research on status attainment by developing a model of occupational attainment and also a graded scale of occupational prestige.

Blau and Duncan's model showed that the father's occupation (heavily influenced by his education) has an important effect on the son's education and subsequent occupation. Simultaneously, Sewell and others started a longitudinal study in 1957 with Wisconsin high school seniors; they followed the group until 1975 (Sewell & Hauser, 1975). Sewell and others modified the Blau–Duncan model by proposing that family status and certain cognitive variables (such as mental ability and school performance) influence what they call "social-psychological processes" (including such items as educational and occupational aspiration, parental encouragement to attend college, teacher encouragement, and peer plans); these in turn influence educational attainment, which then influences occupational attainment. The so-called Wisconsin model has been applied to other data samples, with supporting results obtained. Factors such as geographic or cultural isolation do appear to reduce aspiration levels. Evidence suggests that economic restraints may also have a negative effect.

Early sociological research (Form & Miller, 1949; Thomas, 1956) showed the influence of first full-time employment on later-attained occupational level. Both studies suggest that workers tend to remain at about the same occupational level as the one where they begin to work. More recently, Borow (1981) reemphasizes that one's first job has an important influence on one's entire work history—it can be constrictive and limit future advancement, or it can broaden future options by providing the base from which mobility is facilitated. Borow contends that youth and others should be helped to see what chances each position offers to move on or upward to other jobs. This again emphasizes the interrelatedness of people and work and the importance of information, planning, educational opportunity, and support or encouragement from parents and significant others for effective and satisfying career development.

Regulating Admission to Occupations

Colleges and universities with strong athletic programs have used various techniques to attract outstanding high school athletes. The military services participate vigorously, even competitively, to attract new recruits. Many occupations and professions similarly exert considerable effort to attract new entrants to the field. In some cases, the procedures used are as open and spirited as those of the military. In many other situations, however, the process is performed with subtlety and diplomatic finesse.

Conversely, many occupational groups have established various methods of restricting entrance into the occupation. Most of these regulating devices serve one or the other of two basic purposes. Some of the restrictions are established to protect the public (those outside the occupation) from incompetence and inefficiency and thus are intended to uphold adequate standards. Other regulations are established primarily to protect the group within the occupation, particularly to maintain the level of income by preventing an oversupply of workers.

Some occupations, especially many of the professions, have successfully established formal control of admission procedures. This is usually accomplished by requiring the completion of specific schooling of a particular type and duration, or by demanding that the prospective applicant serve an apprenticeship or internship of a specified period. The imposition of a lengthy training program on potential candidates controls the number of applicants in two ways: first, a long period of preparation discourages some by reducing the attractiveness of the work; and second, the training establishments often serve as a selective instrument, restricting the members admitted to preparatory programs.

As an occupational group becomes strongly established and clearly recognized, it may successfully develop additional means of controlling admission by arranging for legally recognized bodies to have the power to issue licenses or certificates. As the group becomes more professionalized, it may reach the point at which the profession itself controls the preparatory program and the licensing procedure. This concentration of power and control evolves gradually, with the profession increasing its position because of technical complexities in the preparatory program or in the actual practice of the profession.

Shimberg, Esser, and Kruger (1973) emphasize that the passage of regulatory legislation is usually the result of vigorous efforts by practitioners in the field. If these efforts are successful, as they often are, a regulatory board is established, usually under the jurisdiction of the Attorney General's office. The purposes of the regulatory board are set forth in the enabling legislation, but they generally fall into two categories: regulation of the title of an occupational group or regulation of both the title and the practices of an occupation (Brown & Srebalus, 1996). For example, in some states that have regulatory laws for counselors, psychologists, and social workers, unregulated individuals may adopt the title of psychotherapist and practice because the boards that have been established cannot regulate practice. Boards that regulate title only have very limited authority and thus very little influence on practice except for those people who wish to adopt the title that is regulated. Boards that regulate title are often certification boards (e.g., Certified Public Accountant) or registry boards (e.g., Registered Nurse), but they may be called licensing boards with essentially the same function: regulating titles used. Powerful regulatory boards, almost always called licensing boards, have great influence on the behavior of the individuals of the group they regulate. They typically establish minimum training standards for entry into the occupation, continuing education requirements, and ethical standards of practice, and accept and adjudicate complaints from the public about the behavior of the people who are regulated.

Regulatory boards typically include representatives from the public at large, but powerful regulatory boards are made up primarily of practitioners from the profession or occupation being regulated. Weaker boards, such as those for dental hygienists, may be dominated by members from other occupational groups such as dentists.

Many skilled crafts use apprenticeship programs to regulate admission. Although there is usually nationwide agreement concerning the length and content of the apprenticeship, the extent to which it is actually enforced may vary considerably depending on a number of factors. In extensively organized occupational groups, enforcement is more widespread than in groups that are only partially organized. With the latter groups, apprenticeships may exist in those geographic areas (often in metropolitan or highly industrialized sections) where organization is strong, and may be nonexistent or spotty in areas that are not organized.

Preparatory programs, both formal classroom and practical or applied on-the-job plans, are often used to develop the initiate's identification with the occupational group. This is done by teaching occupational history; identifying significant contributors to the development of the occupation; promoting myths or legends related to the occupation (e.g., Florence Nightingale and the nursing profession, Casey Jones and railroad locomotive engineers); encouraging attitudes and values congruent with those held by practitioners; and teaching the rules that apply to the work.

Regulating Behavior on the Job

Regulations, both formal and informal, exist to control the behavior of workers in most occupations. How apparent these controls are varies from occupation to occupation, and sometimes even from workplace to workplace. Careful observation of settings that appear to be relatively open will often reveal subtle influences that set limits and thus control worker behavior. The existence of these rules, where they are openly recognized, is usually justified on the same grounds used for rules regulating admission to occupations—protection either of the public or of the occupational group.

Self-regulating professions maintain their self-regulatory status by developing and enforcing a code of ethics for practitioners in the profession. These codes usually include fairly explicit descriptions of prohibited behavior (abuse of clients, antisocial acts, unfair business practices); descriptions of expected or exemplary behavior; and claims to any legal exemptions that are assumed necessary to perform the occupational duties (such as privileged communication or immunity from prosecution in the event of accidents).

Another aspect of on-the-job behavior is the degree of autonomy granted to the worker to determine what he or she will do, how it will be done, and when it will be done. Assembly line workers have very little control of this type, whereas skilled craft workers and professionals have a great deal. Riemer (1982) has studied this autonomy among building-trades craft workers; he states that individual autonomy arises from three sources—apprenticeship training, tool ownership, and the portable nature of the worker's skills. Group autonomy for building craft workers comes from recruitment control, informal work group control, and formal union control.

Behavior on the job is sometimes established by attitudes and/or behaviors acquired during the formal preparatory programs, so the worker arrives on the job already conditioned in a particular way. Just as physicians are taught (primarily by role-model behavior of supervising physicians), during their internship assignments, that their decisions regarding patient care are to be accepted unhesitatingly by other health care workers, so, too, are nurses and others taught the primacy of the physician's orders. It is difficult for either professional group to accept any other relationship. Haas and Shaffir (1982) describe the process that transpires as medical students attempt to professionalize their behavior—that is, how they attempt to convince fellow students, faculty, and supervising physicians of their *appearance* of competency. Actually possessing skill and knowledge is less important than being able to appear competent.

Employers, or those who control the work site, have considerable input into worker behavior on the job. This is evident in negotiated or decreed work rules, influence in code-of-ethics statements, and involvement in preparatory programs. Fellow workers also influence worker behavior. This can come through the same channels used by employers, or it can appear in informal relationships on the job.

Beginning teachers, office workers, and sales representatives identify the range of acceptable attire either by observing other workers in the workplace or by consulting fellow workers. Although specific dress codes are rarely spelled out, the informal identification of appropriate and inappropriate clothing is well known and followed by the workers. Those who deviate beyond the set limits subject themselves to criticism by fellow workers and, often, by employers or supervisors.

Occupations are occasionally caught up in periods of change and transition during which workers are confused because the role they are expected to play (the on-the-job behavior displayed) is unclear. Such episodes may be produced by the impact of technological change, revised public expectations, or efforts by the occupation to change its activities or public perception. During these periods of turmoil, workers are uncertain as to whether they should behave in the old way or in the new way.

Not long ago, pharmacists were primarily responsible for compounding drugs to fill prescriptions written by physicians. Their place of employment was usually a small pharmacy or apothecary shop, and occasionally a hospital or similar health-care setting. Modern technology multiplied the drugs available for human use and at the same time delivered them ready for sale, already compounded and usually prepackaged as well. The pharmacist faced a transitional period in which the occupation changed roles from scientist-technician to sales-businessperson.

Similarly, the creation of Health Maintenance Organizations (HMOs) and the active participation of insurance companies in the decision-making process about health care have caused conflicts for physicians caught between the traditional concept of a personalized doctor–patient relationship and the need for cost-effective services. Some older physicians have retired as a result. Others have fought the changes while still others have joined the trend and formed their own managed-care companies.

Almost every worker can provide illustrations of control exerted on off-the-job behavior. This can result from direct, unequivocal demands made by the employer, or from very subtle, unexpressed social pressures of public expectation, or from any step between these two extremes. Public school teachers, especially in smaller communities, are often expected to maintain standards of decorum usually exceeding the established level of the community. Principals or school board members often are very explicit about what is acceptable behavior in the community. Successful lawyers and physicians may encounter public expectations that require them to maintain expensive automobiles, homes, or club memberships as symbols of their professional success. Business executives and governmental administrators are often expected to contribute both time and money to local United Fund campaigns.

Economic Aspects

In this section, we look primarily at the elements affecting the income that workers obtain from their efforts. Surprisingly little literature bears directly on the economic aspects of careers. Specific statistical information on such items as wages and hours can be obtained from the Bureau of Labor Statistics and other sections of the Department of Labor. These data are published annually in such publications as *Monthly Labor Review* and are sometimes summarized in *Occupational Outlook Quarterly*. State Employment Security offices compile and publish data for both statewide and regional areas. Detailed information for each Standard Metropolitan Statistical Area (SMSA) within the state is collected, collated, and published on a regular basis. Typical publications include occupational employment statistics, industry and occupational employment projections, and compensation and wage data. Most states also now have computerized systems of occupational information that include current economic data. Four topics that reflect economic influences—supply and demand, employment and unemployment, payment systems, and the influence of structural changes—will be considered at this time.

Supply and Demand

Economists generally contend that over the long run in a free economy, the basic determinant of occupational income is the ratio between the supply of a given type of worker and the demand for them. In other words, wages and salaries are determined by the number of workers with a particular skill who can be induced to sell their skill at a certain rate of pay and the number of employers who desire to purchase that skill and make wage offers at certain rates of pay. Any factor that tends to increase the number of workers willing to sell their skill will usually cause wage levels to go lower. Any factor that decreases the number of available workers will tend to cause wages to rise. Similarly, any factor that increases employer demand for workers will cause wages to rise, whereas any factor reducing employer demand will cause wages to fall. Hotchkiss and Borow (1996) provide a thorough discussion of these economic factors.

In actuality, the basic supply-and-demand ratio rarely operates with total freedom. A number of factors exist that control, or at least restrict, the free operation of the supply-demand ratio. Some of these factors have been developed to protect the general public; others have been designed to protect or assist the specific group of workers. Some of these restricting elements are social custom; others have been established as legal regulations. All of them impede the free operation of the supply–demand ratio.

These impediments to the free operation of supply–demand interaction usually come from one or more of three sources—the public, the employers, or the workers. Examples of interference or control emerging from the public include both legislation and social practice. Minimum-wage laws and child labor regulations are typical of such action. Minimum-wage laws provide a floor in covered industries below which workers cannot be paid. Obviously, this control has an influence beyond the particular industries specified in the legislation, since non-covered industries must usually offer a competitive wage to attract workers.

Child labor laws restrict not only the number of workers available, but also employer practices with workers who are less than 18 years of age. For example the laws stipulate that 16- and 17-year-olds may work unlimited hours, but they may not be employed in hazardous occupations. Fourteen- and 15-year-olds may work in nonmanufacturing, nonmining, nonhazardous jobs for no more than 3 hours on a school day and no more than 18 hours when school is in session. Moreover, work may not begin sooner than 7:00 AM or last longer than 7:00 PM for this group (DOL, 1992). Another law, the Americans with Disabilities Act (ADA) (EEOC, 1992) also restricts employers and protects the rights of employees. For example, this act precludes discrimination against individuals with disabilities who are qualified to work in all phases of the employment process. For example, Title I of ADA requires employers to develop procedures that will allow qualified individuals to apply for jobs (e.g., making written materials available in Braille for people who are visually impaired who would otherwise be able to perform the job). It also requires that employers make the workplace accessible (e.g., by providing ramps for wheelchairs) and imposes several other limitations of employers such as restricting their ability to dismiss employees who develop disabilities. Other legislation, such as that requiring special licenses to practice, also interferes with the supply and demand of labor, primarily by limiting the supply.

Employers can interfere with the free operation of supply and demand by engaging in certain hiring practices that limit access to jobs by certain workers. At first glance, one might assume that such restrictive practices would result in limited supplies of workers and therefore produce higher wages—a situation inimical to the interests of the employer. Such restriction, however, may limit some workers' access to jobs, thus depressing the wages to be paid in those positions. Though now illegal, these practices have not totally disappeared.

Workers, or their representatives (e.g., unions) can interfere with the supply–demand equation. Worker groups can insist on establishing wage rates by negotiation—a process that assures that all involved workers will require the same wage rate for the same job, thus eliminating the possibility for single workers to accept employment at lower wage rates. Workers may also control admission to the training programs by which workers become qualified for employment. An example of this is limiting the number of apprentices admitted to a craft to a certain percentage of employed journeymen, regardless of the number of unfilled positions existing in that craft.

The factors listed identify conditions that influence the supply–demand ratio. Additional factors that affect the supply of qualified labor include the following:

1. The qualifications demanded of a given kind and grade of labor differ. The types of special traits required in all kinds of work are too numerous to mention. Illustrative of these factors would be specific physical or mental skills required in certain work, the amount and type of effort demanded, and the amount and type of responsibility that the work carries.

2. The general appeal of a given kind of work varies. The more attractive the occupation, the greater the likelihood that a large number of potential workers will attempt to qualify for placement. The effect of some factors related to a given occupation is difficult to evaluate in terms of appeal. What is challenging and interesting to one person may be monotonous and distasteful to another. There are, however, certain characteristics that tend to be commonly evaluated. Remuneration relative to other occupations is one such factor.

3. Regularity of employment is often an attractive feature, and many workers will accept a lower wage if they can be assured that the work is steady. Another factor that adds to the general appeal of an occupation is the opportunity for advancement. Some fields are stepping-stones and training jobs for other, more advanced and attractive occupations. The possibility of moving ahead later to such an opportunity is often sufficient to attract a large supply of workers willing to work for a relatively low wage.

4. Workers are often reluctant to move to other geographic areas. This can affect the labor supply in two ways. First, it may cause a surplus in an area where employment is decreasing, thus forcing wages even lower. Second, the reluctance to move may prevent the solution of a shortage of workers in an expanding labor market, thus forcing wages still higher in an attempt to find sufficient workers.

5. The difficulty of transferring from one occupation to another without extensive retraining affects the labor supply in expanding fields. As the demand for low levels of skill continues to decrease and greater demands are made for skilled workers, this problem will intensify.

6. Unequal access to educational opportunities restricts the labor supply to some extent, since training opportunities are limited and not available to all who might like to take advantage of them. Restricting factors may be due to location, cost, entrance requirements, discrimination, or other reasons.

7. Organized labor exerts influence and control on the supply of workers available. Restriction on the number of members, apprenticeship or initiation requirements, and conditions of work impose limitations on the supply of workers.

8. The labor supply can be influenced by activities of employers and employers' groups. Positive influences would include such things as publicizing opportunities, providing training, and improving wages and working conditions.

9. Government assistance, such as welfare, may influence the supply of labor by reducing the number seeking low-paying jobs.

10. Another factor having a definite effect on the demand for labor is the general status of business. When producers are confident of a continuing or increasing public demand for goods or services, their demand for labor goes up. If producers feel that the business cycle is headed downward toward less demand for goods or services, they reduce their demand for labor.

Employment and Unemployment

One frequently hears on radio or television newscasts, or sees in daily newspapers or weekly news magazines, statements about changing rates of employment and unemployment and similar information. Although we often do not stop to think precisely who is included in these data, it is important to understand the terminology if the data are to have any meaning.

Considered from the standpoint of the worker, employment appears to be a simple concept that can be identified by asking the worker, Do you have a job? The worker who says yes would be classified as employed; if the answer is no, we would consider him or her unemployed. Complications (and there are many of them) arise when the answer is, Well, yes and no. For the purposes of state and national statistical data, employment requires pay or the sharing of benefits in a family-operated enterprise. Thus homemakers and volunteers are not considered to be employed because they are not paid.

A further complication arises in obtaining employment data. There is no way to maintain an accurate count of who is working for pay, so sampling methods must be applied. For governmental purposes, using a nationwide sample of 60,000 households, *employed* people include the following:

1. All civilians who worked for pay any time during the week that includes the twelfth day in the month for at least an hour, or who worked unpaid for at least 15 hours in a family-operated enterprise.
2. Those who were temporarily absent from their regular jobs because of illness, vacation, industrial dispute, or similar reasons during that week.
3. Members of the armed forces stationed in the United States.

Unemployed people are those who did not work during the survey week but were available for work and had looked for jobs within the preceding 4 weeks. Individuals on layoff who did not look for work or who are expecting to start new jobs within 30 days are counted as unemployed. There are generally thought to be three types of unemployment:

Frictional unemployment is the temporary joblessness of individuals who are between jobs, are engaged in seasonal work, have quit their jobs and are looking for better ones, or are looking for a first job.

Cyclical unemployment is the situation that arises from changes in the level of business activity during the course of the business cycle. The factory worker on layoff because product demand has fallen is an example.

Structural unemployment is the joblessness that occurs when technological change or similar factors eliminate the need for that worker. Workers can no longer sell their skills because there is no demand for them.

The term *underemployment* is also frequently encountered. The underemployed worker is employed but is in a job below his or her level of skill or experience, usually because there is no job available at the higher level.

A *discouraged worker* is a person without a job who is no longer looking for work because he or she believes no job is available. Because he or she is not looking, this worker is no longer counted as unemployed. Sometimes unemployment figures appear to improve because people stop looking for jobs and are dropped from the figures.

Labor force is another term that is sometimes used in different ways. The total labor force includes all employed civilians and the armed forces within the United States, plus those who are unemployed but seeking work and available to work. Unemployment figures are usually quoted as a percentage of this total figure. Individuals not in the labor force include retirees, those engaged in their own housework, students, the long-term ill, discouraged workers, and those voluntarily idle.

Payment Systems

The income provided to workers for their efforts can be categorized as follows:

Entrepreneurial withdrawal
Fees
Compensation of employees
    Salaries
    Wages

Entrepreneurial withdrawal is the income taken by the owner of a business or industry as compensation for the responsibility and risk that he or she has assumed in establishing and undertaking the business.

Fees constitute the income paid to the various free professions when the worker is engaged in the actual independent practice of the profession. An example is the income of lawyers and physicians in private practice.

Employees of organizations are paid in the form of either salaries or wages. *Salary* is usually a fixed compensation regularly paid for services over a specific period of time, such as a year, quarter, month, or week. *Wages* are similarly compensation for services (usually labor) paid at short, stated intervals. Salaries are usually paid to managerial, administrative, professional, clerical, and supervisory employees. Although the amount of salary may be on the basis of a year, it is often paid in installments each week or month.

Workers described as laborers, even though highly skilled, are usually paid wages. These may be based on either a time rate or a piece rate. *Time-rate wages* pay the worker a fixed rate per unit of time. The time unit ordinarily is 1 hour, and workers often describe their income in terms of so much an hour. The *piece-rate system* compensates the worker in terms of the number of units produced.

In many work situations, some combination of time- and piece-rate wages may be in effect. This permits the worker to gain from the advantages of both systems, but he or she may also be subject to some of the disadvantages of both systems. A combination method usually provides a minimum guarantee and a bonus if the standard output established for that job is exceeded. Many workers and worker groups are suspicious of piece-rate or so-called incentive systems, since they fear that the superior worker who develops a method of higher production may cause either the piece rate to be lowered or the number of needed workers to be reduced. Every organization can point to instances when unscrupulous employers have done exactly that.

Many workers, especially service workers such as waiters and waitresses, receive their income either partly or entirely from tips provided by the customers they serve. Such compensation is based on neither the unit of time nor the unit of work. Similarly, individuals in sales positions may be paid a commission—a percentage of their total sales.

In addition to cash payments received by workers, two other methods of payment are part of the total picture of worker reimbursement: fringe benefits and payment in kind. *Fringe benefits* include indirect payments to workers that can amount to an important part of their total income. Typical fringe benefits include paid vacations and holidays and various types of insurance coverage such as medical, accident, or life. Other examples include retirement programs, supplemental unemployment income, and military or maternity leave with pay. *Payment in kind* includes meals provided without charge by the employer, company housing free or at a reduced rental, expense accounts, free travel, use of a company automobile, uniforms or other clothing, and so forth.

In recent years, several modifications of the basic wage system have appeared. Some companies have adopted a profit-sharing system, in which a certain proportion of the company's annual profit is divided among the workers, often in the form of an end-of-the-year, Christmas, or vacation bonus. Other companies have established a guaranteed annual wage by which workers are assured of a specified income regardless of the number of weeks worked. Still other companies have linked wage rates to a cost-of-living index, so wages are increased to compensate for increases in the cost of living. Presumably, such systems would also lower wages with a declining cost of living.

Influence of Structural Change

In Chapter 4 we examine the world of work in some detail, including its present structure and the causes of changes that are likely to influence its nature in future years. We consider this topic here only to emphasize that one factor influencing workers and their careers is the continuous change that occurs in the occupational format. For example, the utilization of computers has made some jobs simpler, such as those of checkers in supermarkets, and eliminated manufacturing and bank teller jobs because of the use of computer-operated machines and automatic teller machines, respectively. Computers have also made other jobs, such as accounting, more complex because of the need to master complicated software packages.

Change is a persistent part of our lives, and as that change influences the way we live, it also modifies the occupational structure that surrounds us. One change that continued through the 1990s is the reduction of manufacturing jobs and their replacement by service industry occupations. For example, the jobs expected to experience the most growth between 1982 and 2005 include building custodians, cashiers, secretaries, general clerks, sales clerks, nurses, waiters and waitresses, elementary and kindergarten teachers, truck drivers, and nursing aids. As manufacturing jobs decline, workers are displaced from positions with relatively high rates of pay and favorable fringe benefits such as pension and health insurance programs. If they are to transfer to expanding areas, most will need extensive retraining before qualifying for positions that offer lower rates of pay, greater job insecurity, and fewer fringe benefits.

Appraisal of the individual in terms of ability, temperament, interest, and educational achievement is used routinely in career development. Of equal importance are the factors beyond the individual's psychological self that shape and influence the world of work and the individual's relationship to it. If it is appropriate to discuss ability as it bears on the possibilities of entering a particular field, it is equally sound to look at admission restrictions, social selectivity, and lifestyle. Selection of career goals should include consideration of how the individual fits the occupational mold and how the occupation fits the individual.

Summary

One might say that it is obvious that almost every characteristic of the individual as well as the situation in which that individual lives influence the relationship between the worker and his or her work. Nevertheless, it is often helpful to consider this interaction in an orderly and methodical frame of reference.

Factors that directly relate to the person have been labeled *internal factors;* these factors are subdivided into generic, personal-psychological, and personal-sociological categories. In the generic group we looked at gender, ethnic and cultural background, and physique. The psychological sector included aptitude, interests, personality, temperament, and values. The sociological unit consisted of family socioeconomic status, access to education, and lifestyle.

External factors include those influences situated beyond the individual and the immediate family. These are subdivided into the work situation, sociological, and economic aspects. Topics considered under the work situation label included training time, physical demands, and the environmental conditions in which the work is performed. Sociological topics included prestige ratings, mobility, the control of admission to specific occupations, and control of worker behavior on and off the job. Economic items included the effect of supply and demand, the meaning of employment and unemployment, and how workers are paid for their efforts.

References

Alexander, L., & McDill, E. L. (1976). Selection and allocation within schools: Some causes and consequences of curriculum placement. *American Sociological Review, 41,* 963–980.

Anastasi, A. (1988). *Psychological testing* (6th ed.). New York: Macmillan.

Arbona, C. (1995). Theory and research on racial and ethnic minorities: Hispanic Americans. In F. T. L. Leong (Ed.), *Career development and vocational behavior of ethnic and racial minorities* (pp. 37–66). Mahwah, NJ: Erlbaum.

Astin, H. S. (1984). The meaning of work in women's lives: A sociopsychological model of career choice and work behavior. *Counseling Psychologist, 12,* 117–126.

Bingham, W. V. (1937). *Aptitudes and aptitude testing* New York: Harper & Row.

Blau, P. M., & Duncan, O. D. (1967). *The American occupational structure.* New York: Wiley.

Borow, H. (1981). Career guidance uses of labor market information: Limitations and potentialities. In D. H. Montross & C. J. Shinkman (Eds.), *Career development in the 1980s: Theory and practice.* Springfield, IL: Charles C. Thomas.

Braun, J., & Bayer, F. (1973). Social desirability of occupations: Revisited. *Vocational Guidance Quarterly, 21,* 202–205.

Brown, D. (1997). Cultural and work values as determinants of career decisions: A revision of Brown's values-based theory. Unpublished manuscript. School of Education, University of North Carolina, Chapel Hill.

Brown, D., & Minor, C. W. (1992). *Career needs in a diverse workforce: Implications of the NCDA Gallup Survey*. Alexandria, VA: NCDA.

Brown, D., & Srebalus, D. J. (1996). *Introduction to the counseling profession* (2nd ed.). Boston: Allyn & Bacon.

Castro, J. (1990). Get set: Here they come. *Time*, special issue, Fall 1990, 50–51.

Crace, R. K., & Brown, D. (1996). *Life values inventory*. Chapel Hill, NC: Life Values Resources.

Counts, G. S. (1925). The social status of occupations. *School Review, 33*, 16–27.

Dawis, R. V. (1996). Theory of work adjustment and person–environment–congruence counseling. In D. Brown, L. Brooks, & Associates, *Career choice and development* (3rd ed.). San Francisco: Jossey-Bass.

Deeg, M. E., & Paterson, D. G. (1946). Changes in social status of occupations. *Occupations, 25*, 205–208.

DOL. (1992). *Dictionary of occupational titles* (3rd ed.). Washington, DC: U.S. Government Printing Office.

DOL. (1992). *Handy reference guide to the fair labor standards act*. Washington DC: U.S. Department of Labor.

DOL. (1997). *News*. Washington, DC: Bureau of Labor Statistics, USDOL.

DOL. (1998). *The Occupational Information Network*. (*http://www.doleta/gov/programs/onet*) Washington, DC: U.S. Department of Labor.

Droege, R. C., & Boese, R. (1982). Development of a new occupational aptitude pattern structure with comprehensive occupational coverage. *Vocational Guidance Quarterly, 30*, 219–229.

EEOC. (1992). *The American with Disabilities Act: Questions and answers*. Washington, DC: U.S. Equal Employment Opportunity Commission.

Ferguson Publishing. (1998). 1996 Census Bureau report in *Career Opportunities News, 15*, p. 7. Chicago: Author.

Form, W. H., & Miller, D. C. (1949). Occupational career pattern as a sociological instrument. *American Journal of Sociology, 54*, 317–329.

Fredrickson, R. H., Lin, J. G., & Xing, S. (1992). Social status ranking of occupations in The People's Republic of China, Taiwan, and the United States. *Career Development Quarterly, 40*, 351–360.

Gamoran, A., & Mare, R. D. (1989). Secondary school tracking and educational inequality: Compensation, reinforcement, or neutrality? *American Journal of Sociology, 94*, 1146–1183.

Garbin, A. P., & Bates, F. L. (1966). Occupational prestige and its correlates: A reexamination. *Social Forces, 44*, 295–302.

Garet, M. S., & DeLany, B. (1988). Students, courses, and stratification. *Sociology of Education, 61*, 61–77.

Gottfredson, L. (1996). A theory of circumscription and compromise. In D. Brown, L. Brooks, & Associates, *Career choice and development* (3rd ed.). San Francisco: Jossey-Bass.

Haas, J., & Shaffir, W. (1982). Ritual evaluation of competence. *Work and Occupations, 9*, 131–154.

Hakel, M. D., Hollman, T. D., & Dunnette, M. D. (1967). Stability and change in the social status of occupations over 21 and 42 year periods. *Personnel and Guidance Journal, 46*, 762–764.

Hall, R. H. (1986). *Dimensions of work*. Newbury Park, CA: Sage.

Hodge, R. W., Siegel, P. M., & Rossi, P. H. (1964). Occupational prestige in the United States, 1925–63. *American Journal of Sociology, 70*, 286–302.

Holland, J. L. (1997). *Making vocational choices* (3rd ed.). Englewood Cliffs, NJ: Prentice-Hall.

Hotchkiss, L., & Borow, H. (1996). Sociological perspectives on career development and attainment. In D. Brown, L. Brooks, & Associates, *Career choice and development: Applying contemporary theories to practice* (3rd ed.). San Francisco: Jossey-Bass.

Huston, A. C. (1983). Sextyping. In M. E. Hetherton (Ed.), *Socialization, personality and social development: Vol. IV. Handbook of child development*. New York: Wiley.

Jones, L. K. (1996). Job skills for the 21st century: A guide for students. Phoenix, AZ: Oryx.

Kanzaki, G. A. (1975). Fifty years (1925–1975) of stability in the social status of occupations. *Vocational Guidance Quarterly, 25*, 101–105.

Kapes, J. T., Mastie, M. M., & Whitfield, E. A. (1994). *A counselor's guide to career assessment inventories* (3rd ed.). Alexandria, VA: National Career Development Association.

Kraus, L. E., & Stoddard, S. (1989). *Chartbook on disability in the United States*. Washington, DC: National Institute on Disability and Rehabilitation Research.

Leong, F. T. L. (1991). Career development attributes and occupational values of Asian American and white American college students. *Career Development Quarterly, 39*,   221–230.

Leong, F. T. L., & Raote, R. (1992). On the hidden cost of being a Chinese American. Unpublished paper, The Ohio State University, Columbus.

Melamed, T. (1995). Career success: The moderating effects of gender. *Journal of Vocational Behavior, 47*, 295–314.

Melamed, T. (1996). Career success: An assessment of a gender-specific model. *Journal of Occupational and Organizational Psychology, 69*, 217–226.

Myers, I. B., & McCaulley, M. H. (1998). *Manual: A guide to the development and use of the Myers-Briggs Type Indicator* (3rd ed.). Palo Alto, CA: Consulting Psychologist Press.

Nevill, D., & Super, D. E. (1986). *The Values Scale manual: Theory, application, and research.* Palo Alto, CA: Consulting Psychologist Press.

Oppenheimer, V. K. (1982). *Work and the family: A study in social demography.* New York: Academic Press.

O'Toole, J., Scheiber, J. L., & Wood, L. (Eds.). (1981). *Working: Changes and choices.* New York: Human Sciences Press.

Parker, H. J., & Associates (1995). Prestige ratings of contemporary occupations: Perceptions of high school students and implications for counselors. *The School Counselor, 43*, 19–28.

Reiss, A. J. (1961). *Occupation and social status.* New York: Free Press.

Riemer, J. W. (1982). Worker autonomy in the skilled building trades. In P. L. Stewart & M. G. Cantor (Eds.), *Varieties of work.* Beverly Hills, CA: Sage.

Rothman, R. A. (1987). *Working: Sociological perspectives.* Englewood Cliffs, NJ: Prentice-Hall.

Sewell, W. H., & Hauser, R. M. (1975). *Education, occupation, and earnings: Achievement in early career.* New York: Academic Press.

Shimberg, B., Esser, B. F., & Kruger, D. H. (1973). *Occupational licensing: Practices and policies.* Washington, DC: Public Affairs Press.

Smith, E. J. (1983). Issues in racial minorities career behavior. In W. B. Walsh & S. H. Osipow (Eds.), *Handbook of vocational psychology: Vol. 1. Foundations.* Hillsdale, NJ: Lawrence Erlbaum Associates.

Spranger, E. (1928). *Types of men.* Translated from 5th German edition. Halle: Max Niemeyer.

Stewart, P. L., & Cantor, M. G. (Eds.). (1982). *Varieties of work.* Beverly Hills, CA: Sage.

Super, D. E. (1957). *The psychology of careers.* New York: HarperCollins.

Super, D. E. (1990). A life-span, life-space approach to career development. In D. Brown, L. Brooke, & Associates (Eds.), *Career choice and development* (2nd ed.). San Francisco: Jossey-Bass.

Super, D. E., & Nevill, D. (1986). *The Values Scale.* Palo Alto, CA: Consulting Psychologist Press.

Terkel, S. (1972). *Working.* New York: Pantheon.

Treiman, D. S., & Terrell, K. (1975). Sex and the process of status attainment: A comparison of men and women. *American Sociological Review, 40,* 174–200.

Vanfossen, E., Jones, D., & Spade, J. S. (1987). Curriculum tracking and status maintenance. *Sociology of Education, 60,* 104–122.

Whitney, D. R. (1969). Predicting from expressed choice: A review. *Personnel and Guidance Journal, 48,* 279–286.

4

Occupational Structure Today and Tomorrow

Both scholars and philosophers have frequently declared that the most constant factor in life is change. Each of us encounters change in some way every day. Even those of us who describe ourselves as young remark regularly that things aren't the way they used to be. In some parts of life, change occurs very slowly and gradually, whereas elsewhere it may be sudden, unexpected, and massive; and there are gradations between these two extremes. The occupational world is also constantly changing and readjusting.

Predicting the future is hazardous business, and even the best estimates often leave many factors unaccounted for. The risk of error increases with the need for precision and the distance projected into the future. For example, in the United States, we can say with some confidence that January is likely to be colder than November or March. But matching high temperature at a given location on January 15 against that of November 15 or March 15 is less reliable. Similarly, we can usually make a better prediction of tomorrow's weather than that of a year from tomorrow. Even though we cannot build a formula that will weight all factors accurately, we can usually identify those factors that are most likely to be influential. Then we can either proceed on the basis of all other things being equal or, as the Bureau of Labor Statistics does, with a best-case and worst-case approach that will identify the range within which reality will likely be found.

In this chapter we discuss four broad topics that relate to anticipated change and present structure in the world of work:

Causes of long-term trends
Causes of short-term trends
The occupational world through 2005
Sources of information on change and structure

Causes of Long-Term Trends

Some changes in the world of work occur slowly and may be anticipated or identified long before their influence becomes significant. Their eventual impact can be massive and can last for a very long time. These big changes are grouped into four categories, but it is important to recognize that these often may be interrelated, so some items could be listed under more than one heading. These causal forces are labeled population, sociological, economic, and technological factors.

Population Factors

Three factors influence the growth of our population: the birth rate, the death rate, and the net immigration (the excess of immigration over emigration). Birth rates began to decline in the mid-1960s and have continued to decline since that time, although they began to turn upward in the mid-1990s. The impact of declining birth rates has a delayed effect on the numbers in the labor force because newborns do not go to work. The delayed impact begins to appear 16 to 20 years later, so the children of the baby-boom generation are entering the work force during the 1990s. However, a declining birth rate does influence the existing labor force by reducing the need for child care workers, elementary teachers, factory workers who manufacture school equipment, and so forth.

Improved nutrition, greater access to medical care, and other life-extending factors have also changed the death rate, so people live longer than previously. More older people in the population create a different demand for goods (e.g., leisure equipment) and services (e.g., medical care). This increased longevity, added to a decreased birth rate, compounds the rate at which the average age of our population moves upward.

The 16–24 age group is expected to make up 16 percent of the work force by the year 2005, which indicates that the proportion of the work force made up of younger workers is expected to remain relatively steady in the 1992–2005 period. If projections are correct, the 25–54 age group will account for about 70 percent of the labor force by the year 2005 and the over-55 age group 14 percent. In 1992 these figures were 72 and 12 percent respectively. Perhaps the more important figures are the numbers of workers projected to be in each of these categories by 2005: 16–24 = 24 million; 25–54 = 105 million; 55 and over = 21 million. These numbers represent increases in these categories of 3.6 million, 13.9 million, and 5.9 million respectively when compared to the 1992 figures. While it is difficult to estimate the impact of these numbers on workers, businesses, and the economy generally, it may well be that the increases in larger numbers of people in the older categories will make it more difficult for younger workers to move into higher paying jobs because of increased competition from older workers who are often considered more reliable by employers.

Population growth is not uniform across the country. This is mainly the result of movement and relocation rather than significant regional differences in birth and death rates. The 1990 census shows 63 percent of the decade's total population growth accounted for by California, Arizona, Texas, and Florida. States such as West Virginia, Iowa, Wyoming, North Dakota, Illinois, Michigan, and Pennsylvania showed declines from almost 1 percent to over 8 percent.

Another expected change in the labor force is an overall increase in minority participation. While the proportion of African Americans will stay relatively stable at 11 percent of the work force, the proportion of Hispanic workers is expected to increase from 8 to 11 percent and Asians from 3.4 to 5.0 percent. As a result the proportion of Caucasian workers will decrease from 78 percent in 1992 to 73 percent in 2005. These figures represent increases in the numbers of Hispanics and Asians of 6.4 and 3.2 million respectively.

Immigration factors are even harder to predict. The Bureau of the Census assumes that documented immigration totals approximately 560,000 annually and emigration totals about 160,000 annually. The Immigration Reform and Control Act was fully implemented at the end of 1988, and this is expected to reduce undocumented immigration to about 100,000 per year by the late 1990s. This would result in a population increase by net immigration of approximately a half million per year. Many will compete for available jobs immediately.

A final aspect of population impact on occupations relates to the average age of workers in a specific occupation. Variation in average age between occupations can be produced by such situations as a large influx of workers within a short period when the occupation was established or when some factor created a sudden demand for workers. If the occupation then stabilizes, as most do, one sees this large cadre of single-age workers move through the working years together, with many withdrawing almost simultaneously at retirement time. Vacancies occur in occupations either because of growth that causes increased demand for workers or because of the need to replace workers who leave the occupation through resignation, retirement, or death. As the average age in an occupation increases, the replacement rate is also likely to increase.

Sociological Factors

The effect of sociological factors is sometimes more difficult to visualize than other causes of long-term trends. Social consciousness usually develops gradually, ultimately causing changes in ethical viewpoints and creating increased social pressures. This may, in time, result in officially sanctioned and enforced changes in human behavior. Even before official action occurs, there can be an observable influence on work and workers.

Forces that relate to lifestyle, social values, attitudes, and similar factors that change group behavior are classified in this group. Some of these factors may be expressed through legislation or by amendment or repeal of earlier legislation. For example, during the past two decades, concern for the environment has focused attention on the disposition of hazardous waste and on correcting conditions caused earlier by reckless handling of these materials. Similarly, concern for reducing the effects caused by acid rain can have an impact on jobs in the coal mines of the Midwest and in factories that use high-sulfur coal.

Efforts to reduce our dependence on foreign oil sparked the development of more fuel-efficient automobiles that are both smaller and lighter. The decrease in automobile size, as well as the use of lightweight materials, reduced the demand for steel and thereby the jobs related to steel production at the same time that demand for the substitute materials was increasing. Unfortunately, it is not easy to shift a steel mill or steelworkers to the production of aluminum and plastics.

One example of increased allegiance to the self-fulfillment ethic is greater participation in recreational activities. This interest has created demand for running shoes, warmup suits, and health club facilities as well as for camping equipment, boats, and recreational vehicles. Another example is the extended participation of women in the labor force, which has an effect far beyond the jobs they hold and the greater income those jobs produce. That participation influences living patterns for families—kinds of foods consumed and how they are prepared, household tasks and how they are managed, type of housing and transportation used, need for child care, and so on.

Changes in the educational attainment of the general population also affect occupations. The evidence is strong that the least educated have the greatest difficulty in securing and retaining employment and that those with the most educational background have the lowest rates of unemployment. The average amount of completed education is increasing for two reasons: First, older people withdrawing from work often have fewer years of education; and second, younger people entering work generally have completed more years of schooling.

The presence of adequate retirement programs for older workers also influences the number of workers who stay on the job. The average retirement age has declined steadily over the past two decades, but one in three retirees returns to some form of work within a year (Brown, 1995). It seems likely that more and more workers are likely to postpone retirement if the much discussed changes in Social Security and Medicare occur.

Economic Factors

In a totally free market, the supply and demand of workers and raw materials would greatly influence the number and nature of available jobs. In most societies, numerous controls have been developed that interfere with the free operation of the market. Many of these (e.g., minimum-wage laws, licensing requirements, and import controls) came into existence to regulate what had been seen as disruptive surges in that market. Although controls have subdued drastic and sudden fluctuations, there are still discernible trends suggesting upward or downward movements in the marketplace that bear on occupational opportunity.

Changes in capitalization requirements also influence jobs. Undoubtedly one cause of the consistent decline in employment in agriculture relates to this factor. Farming of almost every type now requires such an extensive investment in land and equipment that efficiency becomes the determining factor between success and failure. In other businesses, the constant search for mergers is often related to economic factors that are fundamentally based on productive efficiency—creating more goods with fewer workers. National fiscal policy also influences the number of jobs. Large national deficits create competition for investment dollars, making plant expansion more costly and hence slowing creation of jobs.

Technological Factors

Obvious factors that have a long-term influence on occupations are technological progress, invention, and discovery. Entire industries have come into existence as a result of the relentless march of technology. Sometimes the new discovery or invention creates a new market for itself as the public becomes familiar and accustomed to it. An example of this is air conditioning. Only a few decades old, this invention has brought with it thousands of jobs in the manufacture, distribution, sale, and maintenance of equipment. Similarly, television has created opportunities for vast numbers of workers not only in the fields just mentioned, but also in the broad entertainment and advertising aspects of that industry. For the most part, areas such as these have created entirely new occupations that were nonexistent before.

In many areas of modern life, technological progress (e.g., computers and word processors) has resulted in improvements and refinements, in the replacing of old methods and products with new and better ways. When this happens, some occupations may be drastically reduced and sometimes may disappear altogether, to be replaced by those related to the new technique or product. Examples include coopers, who were as prevalent as plumbers or pipefitters in the 1890 census but whose numbers had declined so much they were not listed in the 1940 census. Similar changes are occurring in many occupations and industries. The increased use of robots and automated equipment has reduced the number of production line workers in many fields. This is especially apparent in the U.S. automobile industry, where new plants use more machines and fewer workers.

Closely related to invention and discovery is our access to natural resources. The recognition of our dependence on outside sources for such crucial items as petroleum continues to produce vast changes in our lives and in occupational opportunities. The automobile industry has undergone a metamorphosis that, in turn, has affected the production of steel and other supplies. The search for oil has been accelerated, as has the search for alternative sources of energy.

Causes of Short-Term Trends

Several examples of factors producing short-term trends can be identified. Viewed objectively, these usually have less effect than do long-term trends. Nevertheless, to individuals who are caught in the crunch produced by transitory factors, the impact can be devastating. Some influences have a generalized effect across almost the entire economy; others may be more specific.

One of the most obvious causes of short-term trends is various types of calamities, either humanly caused or natural. Natural disasters such as earthquakes, floods, and volcanic eruptions can disrupt and change occupational patterns in the area for extended periods of time. Unexpected freezes in citrus-growing areas may not only destroy the current crop but also, if trees are seriously damaged, require new plantings that need several years to become productive.

Human disasters can be just as disruptive. War or the threat of war diverts large numbers of workers from civilian occupations to military assignments. It further affects others by switching manufacturing and other sectors to the production of military goods. It may create serious shortages of workers in fields that are considered less essential to the national welfare.

New directions in fashion, recreation, and other activities can also distort the occupational structure by creating new demands or reducing old ones. Changes in men's hairstyles in recent years have eliminated many barber shops. Similarly, changes in lapel width and hemline height can make clothing obsolete long before it wears out. Imitation of movie idols, popular athletes, or television stars can create demands where none previously existed. Some technological developments occasionally start as fads (e.g., video cassette recorders and personal computers).

Seasonal variations are also influential. Summers tend to increase demand for goods and services in mountain and seaside resorts; winters have the same effect on resorts located in warm areas. The back-to-school season includes buying in retail stores, for which manufacturers have been preparing. Planting time and harvest time change typical patterns in agricultural areas. The annual holiday shopping season creates demand for temporary sales workers, letter carriers, transportation workers, and other workers.

Short-term economic factors also exert an influence. Although the general business trend over long periods is either upward or downward, small segments of that larger trend will show considerable variation. Factors that create these short-term zigzags include strikes, unexpected surpluses or shortages of raw materials or processed goods, temporary market disruptions, fluctuations in access to short-term capital caused by changes in interest rates, inflationary pressures, changing tax laws, and sometimes even the anticipation of possible events.

The Occupational World through 2005

Having identified some of the factors most likely to create occupational change, we are now ready to look briefly at the world of work as it is today and as it may be in the near future. Our previous discussion pointed out the sudden changes that can occur. Major changes usually take some time to transpire; thus a projection based on recent trends is usually the safest estimate of what the near future is likely to hold. Most of our attention in this discussion focuses on the period between 1992 and 2005, for which Bureau of Labor Statistics estimates are available.

In the 1970s and early 1980s, much attention was focused on the changes that would occur as automation became more widespread. The word *automation* referred to the increased control of manufacturing processes by automatic machines directed by computerized programs. Now that automated processes are standard in many industries, we rarely refer to automation. Instead, we talk about high technology, or *high tech.*

The widespread application of high tech has had two massive effects on the world of work. First, automated equipment can operate only when it has been programmed to accomplish the various tasks to be performed. Thus many new openings have been created for individuals to process the information that must be programmed to make the machines work automatically. Second, as production workers have been replaced by machines, they have sought other areas for reentry to work. Only in the service area have jobs been expanding significantly, so many workers have shifted from relatively high-paying production jobs in manufacturing to much lower paying jobs with lower skill levels in service activities.

The exodus of many workers from manufacturing jobs has been intensified by the relocation of many manufacturing plants that are labor intensive to geographic sites where labor can be employed more economically. Within the United States, this has often meant relocation from the Northeast and North Central areas to the South and the West, where labor unions generally are weaker. In many cases, plants have been relocated to underdeveloped countries where pay rates are very low. High-tech equipment, involving computerized control coupled with worldwide communications systems, permits the home office to maintain its direction of operations just as easily as it did when the plant was "out back."

Industrial Grouping

In looking at today's world of work, we consider two perspectives: where the jobs are and what the jobs are. An *industry* is an establishment or group of establishments engaged in producing similar types of goods and services. In earlier paragraphs we referred to *manufacturing*—a term that is understood to mean the process of modifying and converting raw materials into finished, usable products. When we refer to the manufacturing industry, we are including all the establishments that make things. In Chapter 1 we defined *work* as the production of goods and services valued by others. Thus all work involves either goods or services, and all the places where people work must likewise be concerned with producing either goods or services. Goods-producing industries include agriculture, mining, construction, and manufacturing. Service-producing industries include transportation, communication, and public utilities; trade (both wholesale and retail); finance, insurance, and real estate; services; and government. These nine sectors, from both goods-producing and service-producing industries, provide the sites where all occupations are located. The reader should be aware that the term *service* is applied to two *industrial* categories as well as an *occupational* category. Service-producing industries are the industries not included in the goods-producing group, and they include the five sectors listed here. One of these sectors is also called the service sector and is described later. In addition, there are service occupations, and we consider this label later when we discuss other occupational groups. Understanding the statistics included in the tables in this chapter requires knowing which of these three images is applicable. For example, Table 4.1 (showing employment in the various industrial areas) lists the service-producing industrial area as probably having 109 million workers by the year 2005; of these, almost 34 million will be in the service sector of that broader industrial area. Most of these workers are not employed in service occupations. Table 4.2 shows that almost 42 million workers are expected to be in service occupations in the year 2005.

Table 4.1 provides specific information about the changes that have occurred in the industrial sectors between 1979 and 1992 and estimates of the changes expected to take place between 1992 and 2005. The projections include three sets of figures labeled "low," "moderate," and "high." The "low" column includes figures based on the most conservative estimate; the "high" column reflects the most optimistic data; the "moderate" column represents the average estimate and probably is the most realistic figure to use. We use the "moderate" estimate in our brief review of these data.

The labor force grew by approximately 20 million workers in the years from 1979 to 1992. It is expected to increase by another 16 million by 2005. The slower growth rate is, at least in part, due to the expectation of fewer available workers with expected declines in both the numbers of youth and women entering the labor market. We consider several of the categories listed in Table 4.1.

The *mining and petroleum* sector produces much of the raw material and energy sources used by industry and private consumers. Within the energy areas are coal mining and the finding and extraction of crude petroleum and natural gas. These industries account for approximately 75 percent of the workers in this sector. Other industries in this sector include iron mining; copper mining; mining of other metals such as gold, stone and clay mining and quarrying; and chemical and fertilizer mineral mining. This sector declined by approximately 30 percent from 1979 to 1992, and another decline of about 12 percent is expected to occur by 2005.

The *construction* sector includes jobs involved with building new homes, nonresidential building, public utilities, highways, as well as the maintenance and repair of existing structures. This sector employed 4.5 million workers, a figure that remained constant in 1992. However, some growth in construction jobs is projected by 2005 with the sector expected to add between 1 and 2 million jobs in this period. Most workers in this area are blue-collar workers, and more than half of the total group are craftspeople such as carpenters, plumbers, and electricians. Many of the other workers in this sector subcontract work from general contractors, while others are employed directly by general contractors on a variety of projects including everything from building a single-family home to heavy construction of a dam or superhighway.

Manufacturing is the second largest industrial sector, employing almost 18 million workers in 1992. This sector is expected to shrink slightly by 2005 and may employ as few as 16 million workers at that time. Manufacturing is made up of two broad categories: durable goods and nondurable goods. Durable goods are those that are expected to last 3 years or more such as steel, machinery, automobiles, and furniture. Nondurable goods are those items that are consumed in a rel-

TABLE 4.1 Employment by Major Industry Divisions, 1979, 1992, and for Low, Moderate, and High Projections to 2005 (numbers in thousands)

Industry	1979	1992	2005			Change, 1992–2005		
			Low	Mod.	High	Low	Mod.	High
Total	101363	121093	139007	147483	154430	17924	26390	33330
Nonfarm wage and salary	89491	107888	124931	132960	138944	17043	25072	31055
Goods-producing	26401	23142	21898	23717	26200	−1244	575	3058
Mining	958	631	510	562	690	−121	−69	57
Construction	4463	4471	5407	5632	6643	936	1161	2772
Manufacturing	21040	18040	15981	17523	18886	−2059	−517	820
Service-producing	63030	84746	102034	109243	112744	18287	24492	27512
Transportation and utilites	5136	5709	5909	6497	6763	200	788	1054
Wholesale trade	5221	6045	6641	7761	7761	596	1146	1716
Retail trade	14972	19346	22254	23777	24336	2908	4431	4990
Finance, insurance, and real estate	4975	6571	7585	7969	8078	114	1398	1507
Services	16779	28422	39808	41788	42766	11386	13365	14344
Government	15947	18653	20836	22021	23041	2183	3368	4385
Agriculture	3398	3295	5221	3325	3535	−74	−30	240
Private households	1264	1116	777	802	853	−339	−314	−263
Nonfarm self-employed and unpaid family	7210	8794	10078	10396	11098	1284	1602	2304

Source: DOL (1994). *The American work force 1992–2005.* Washington, DC: U.S. Government Printing Office.

atively short period of time such as paper, textiles, food products, and leather. Manufacturing is quite susceptible to both short- and long-term economic trends and so employment figures will vary considerably depending upon the economic picture in this country and in the world.

Some of the industries—motor vehicle and apparel, for example—are each larger than the entire mining and petroleum sector. In spite of the tremendous range of products created by the manufacturing sector, ten industries employ approximately 75 percent of all manufacturing workers:

Durable Goods	*Nondurable Goods*
Machinery, except electrical	Food products
Electrical and electronic equipment	Apparel and other textile products
Transportation equipment	Printing and publishing
Fabricated metal products	Chemicals
Primary metals	Rubber and miscellaneous plastic

As is true of the other sectors, manufacturing has its own unique composition of workers. Nearly two-thirds are blue-collar workers; of these the largest group consists of machine operatives, who account for about 40 percent of all manufacturing employees. The next largest section of blue-collar workers is the craft group, amounting to about 20 percent of all workers. Clerical workers (about 12 percent of the total) make up the largest group of white-collar workers, followed by the professional and technical workers, who fill about 10 percent of the jobs.

Transportation, communications, and public utilities provide quite different services and products but are often grouped together because they are considered to be public service activities and are either owned or regulated by governmental agencies. This sector is about the same size as the construction sector, including slightly more than 5.7 million workers in 1992. In addition to the obvious transportation systems—railroads, local and interurban buses, trucks, and air and water transportation—this category includes pipeline transportation and supporting services for each network. The communications area includes radio and television broadcasting and all other communications, the largest part being telephone systems. Utilities include electric, gas, and water and sanitation systems. Within transportation, the largest group of employees is operators, followed by craft and clerical workers. In communications the largest group is clerical workers, and in the utilities most employees are craft workers. The sector increased by about 2 million workers between 1979 and 1992 and will probably add another half million, or about 10 percent by 2005.

Wholesale trade is concerned with assembling materials from producers, sometimes recombining them in variously sized lots, and distributing them to retail stores and large users such as schools, hospitals, and industrial firms. The sector expanded by nearly one million workers in the 1979–1992 period and will likely grow by about 10 percent by 2005.

Retail trade sells goods or services directly to the consumers in stores, by mail and telephone, or through door-to-door contact. Although the customer ordinarily is most likely to have contact with a sales worker, sales jobs account for only about one-fifth of the jobs in this sector. Slightly smaller numbers are employed as managers, service workers, and clerical workers. This sector grew by about 30 percent between 1979 and 1992. It is expected to grow by about 15 percent more by 2005.

Finance, insurance, and real estate employed over 6.5 million workers in 1992 and will likely grow to 7.9 million by 2005, an increase of about 16 percent. The finance area includes banking, credit agencies, and financial brokers. The finance and insurance workers are mostly clerical employees. In the real estate section, sales workers predominate.

The *services* sector includes a wide spectrum of activities scattered across several large industries. It is the largest sector and will include one-third of the total work force. Under this heading one finds hotels and lodging places, barber and beauty shops, advertising agencies, automobile repair shops, amusements, health services, education, and other services. One-third of the workers in the service sector are professional and technical, the highest proportion in all the sectors. Other large groups of workers include service workers and clerical workers. Less than one-tenth of the employees are blue-collar workers.

The *government* sector employed about 18.5 million workers in 1992 and will probably increase to nearly 21 million by 2005. Only about one-sixth of the workers are employed by the federal government; most work in state or local units, including counties, cities, school districts, and similar governmental units. This sector does not include the military forces because they are not considered part of the civilian labor force. It does include public school teachers, who could justifiably be classified in the services sector.

The *agriculture* division includes farm jobs as well as relatively small numbers of workers engaged in forestry, fishing, hunting, and trapping. It does not include those workers engaged in what is often called agribusiness, who manufacture, sell, and repair the equipment and other materials used by farm workers. Large increases in productivity in agriculture have permitted fewer workers to produce more food and fiber, resulting in a continuing decline in the number of agricultural workers.

The *self-employed* sector includes those individuals who either work for themselves or are part of a self-contained, family-operated enterprise. The more than 20 percent increase from 1979 to 1992 is expected to slow somewhat by 2005.

Occupational Grouping

The previous section focused on where workers perform their tasks—the industrial sectors and the various industries. When we think of the various tasks performed by workers regardless of where they are accomplished, we think in terms of occupations. Technically, we use the term *occupation* to represent a set of tasks widely recognized as usually performed by a single worker—for example, a physician, secretary, tile setter, short-order cook, or bus driver.

Because we live in a technologically complex society, we have a very large number of occupations—so many, in fact, that it would be difficult to specify precisely how many there are. The number would depend on how very closely related sets of tasks are grouped or divided. Should one consider "high school teacher" as one occupation, or English teacher, foreign language teacher, biology teacher, chemistry teacher, mathematics teacher, physical education teacher, social studies teacher, and speech teacher as eight occupations? In some cases it is advantageous to group broadly; in others, specificity is best. Printed materials describing the world of work, occupational data, and other information about occupations use various grouping systems, often dependent on the source of the data. Therefore, it is essential that the career counselor be knowledgeable about each of these systems to help a client use information about alternatives in the decision-making process. We consider in detail several of these grouping systems in the next two chapters. Because in this discussion we are concerned only with the broad picture, we apply terminology drawn from two of these systems to describe frequently used occupational groupings. Because both systems cover the same territory, it is helpful to understand the similarity in structure. Although the names vary slightly, the similarity of the two systems is apparent immediately.

Bureau of Labor Statistics	*Dictionary of Occupational Titles*
Executive, administrative, managerial	Professional, technical, managerial
Professional specialty occupations	
Technicians and related support occupations	
Marketing and sales	Clerical and sales
Administrative support occupations including clerical	
Service occupations	Service occupations
Agricultural, forestry, fishing	Agricultural occupations
	Processing occupations
Precision production, craft, and repair	Machine trades occupations
Operators, fabricators, and laborers	Benchwork occupations
	Structural work occupations
	Miscellaneous occupations

Table 4.2 provides information on employment in the major occupational groups in 1992 and projected to 2005 based on the Bureau of Labor Statistics classification. Moderate alternative information is used for the projections.

Executive, administrative, and managerial occupations are involved in the operation and direction of organizations such as business. Examples include bank officers, buyers, credit managers, and managers of fast-food restaurants. Over 12 million workers were in this category in 1992. The group is expected to grow by approximately 26 percent by 2005.

Professional specialty occupations are concerned with the theoretical aspects of such fields as architecture, the sciences, medicine, education, law, theology, and art. Most of these occupations require lengthy educational preparation at college or other advanced levels. In 1992 there were nearly 16.5 million professional specialty workers, and the group is expected to increase by one-third by 2005.

TABLE 4.2 Employment in Major Occupational Groups, 1992, and Projected to 2005: Moderate Projections and Percentage Change (numbers in thousands)

Occupational Title	1992 Number	2005 Number	Percent Change 1992–2005
Total, all occupations	121,099	147,482	22
Executive, administrative, and managerial occupations	12,066	15,195	26
Professional specialty occupations	16,592	22,801	37
Technicians and related support occupations	4,282	5,664	32
Marketing and sales occupations	12,993	15,664	21
Administrative support occupations, including clerical	22,349	25,106	14
Service occupations	19,358	25,820	33
Agricultural, forestry, fishing, and related occupations	3,530	3,650	3
Precision production, craft, and repair occupations	13,580	15,380	13
Operators, fabricators, and laborers	16,349	17,902	10

Source: DOL (1994). *The American work force 1992–2005.* Washington, DC: U.S. Government Printing Office.

Note: The 1992 and 2005 employment data and the projected change 1992–2005 are derived from data from the industry–occupation matrixes for each year.

Technicians and support occupations is another rapidly expanding group, with a growth of nearly 32 percent expected in 2005. Workers in health technologies such as laboratory and X-ray technicians, workers in the engineering and science technologies, and computer programmers are examples of this cluster.

Marketing and sales occupations include those who attempt to influence customers in favor of a commodity or service and those workers closely related to this process. Workers are primarily employed in wholesale and retail trade or by manufacturing, insurance, or real estate companies. There were almost 13 million workers in 1992 and almost 16 million are expected by 2005, an increase that reflects average growth for the period.

Administrative support occupations, including clerical, are those workers who prepare, transcribe, systematize, or preserve written communications and records, distribute information, or collect accounts. Jobs included are computer operators, secretaries, stenographers, and clerical supervisors. This is the largest occupational group, including 22 million workers in 1992 and expecting another 2.3 million by 2005.

Service occupations are the second largest group, with over 19 million workers in 1992 and almost 26 million expected in 2005. This group is also growing rapidly. Examples of subgroups in this category include cleaning and building service jobs, food preparation and service, health service, personal service, private household workers, and protective service occupations.

Agricultural, forestry, fishing, and related occupations are concerned primarily with propagating, growing, caring for, and harvesting plant and animal products. The forestry and fishing sectors are both very small compared to the farm jobs. The area has been decreasing in number for some time, with the 3.5 million workers in 1992 expected to rise slightly by 2005.

Precision production, craft, and repair occupations are skilled jobs, including carpenters, tool-and-die makers, machinists, electricians, and mechanics. The area is expected to grow more slowly than the average for total employment from 1992 to 2005. Most of the additional million jobs expected to be added are in construction and service industry divisions.

Operators, fabricators, and laborers are mostly semiskilled and unskilled workers who run various machines or processes used primarily in the production of goods. Typical occupations include assemblers, production painters, transport workers, helpers, and laborers. There were about 17 million workers in 1992, and this number will increase by about one and one-half million by 2005.

Processing occupations are defined by the *DOT* as those concerned with refining, mixing, compounding, chemically treating, heat treating, or similarly working materials in solid, fluid, semifluid, or gaseous states to prepare them for use as basic materials, stock for further manufacturing treatment, or for sale as finished products to commercial users. Knowledge of a process and adherence to formulas or other specifications are required to some degree. Vats, stills, ovens, furnaces, mixing machines, crushers, grinders, and related machines and equipment usually are involved. The group includes occupations involved in processing metal ore, food, tobacco, paper, petroleum, chemicals, wood, stone, leather, and other materials.

Machine trades occupations include those concerned with the operation of machines that cut, bore, mill, abrade, print, and similarly work with such materials as metal, paper, wood, plastics, and stone. A worker's relationship to the machine is of primary importance. The more complicated jobs require an understanding of machine functions, blueprint reading, making mathematical computations, and exercising judgment to attain conformance to specifications. In other jobs, eye and hand coordination may be the most significant factor. Installation, repair, and maintenance of machines and mechanical equipment, and weaving, knitting, spinning, and similarly working textiles are included. Typical jobs in this group include machinists, grinders, punch press operators, automobile mechanics, typesetters, and cabinetmakers.

Benchwork occupations are those concerned with using body members, hand tools, and bench machines to fabricate, inspect, or repair relatively small products such as jewelry, record players, light bulbs, musical instruments, tires, footwear, pottery, and garments. The work is usually performed at a set position or station in a mill, plant, or shop, at a bench, worktable, or conveyor. Workers in more complex jobs may be required to read blueprints, follow patterns, use a variety of hand tools, and assume responsibility for meeting standards. Other jobs may only require workers to follow standardized procedures. Some occupations included in this group are jeweler, silversmith, watch repairer, television and radio repairer, piano tuner, assembler, stonecutter, glassblower, tailor, and shoemaker.

Structural work occupations include those occupations involved with fabricating, erecting, installing, paving, painting, and repairing structures and structural parts such as bridges, buildings, roads, motor vehicles, cables, internal combustion engines, girders, plates, and frames. Generally work is done outdoors, except for factory production line occupations. The worker's relationship to hand tools and power tools is more important than that to stationary machines, which are also used. Knowledge of the properties (stress, strain, durability, resistance) of the materials used (wood, metal, concrete, glass, clay) is often a requirement. Representative occupations include riveter, structural-steel worker, sheet-metal worker, boilermaker, rigger, test driver, electrician, paperhanger, bulldozer operator, carpenter, plumber, and chimney sweep.

Miscellaneous occupations are concerned with transporting people and cargo from one geographic location to another by various methods; packaging materials and moving materials in and around establishments; extracting minerals from the earth; producing and distributing utilities; modeling for painters, sculptors, and photographers; providing various production services in motion pictures and radio and television broadcasting; producing graphic art work; and other miscellaneous activities. Occupations include truck driver, barge captain, automobile service-station attendant, packager, hoist operator, stevedore, jack-hammer operator, miner, motion-picture projectionist, sign painter, photoengraver, bookbinder, and print-shop helper.

Present and Future Numbers

Table 4.3 shows the composition of the labor forces in 1979, 1992, and the projected composition for 2005. This table indicates that more than three-quarters of the men and 58 percent of the women age 16 and over were in the work force in 1992. The data provided in Table 4.3 also indicate that there is little variation in these numbers across ethnic groups with percentages varying from 57.3 to 64.4 percent for women and 69.7 to 76.4 percent for men.

During the 1992–2005 period the labor force is expected to increase from about 126 million to 150 million workers. Women's participation in the labor force is expected to increase faster than men's, especially in the 25–54 age group. As noted earlier, the relative number of Caucasians in the labor force will decrease, while relative numbers for African Americans will stay steady and will increase for Asians and Hispanics. The trend toward increased numbers of service jobs that has been in evidence for more than two decades will continue as we approach the year 2005. The numbers of professional specialty and technical jobs will also increase.

TABLE 4.3   Civilian Labor Force and Participation Rates by Sex, Race, and Hispanic Origin, 1979, 1992, and Moderate Growth Projection to 2005

Group	Participation Rate (thousands)			Level (thousands)			Change (thousands)	
	1979	1992	2005	1979	1992	2005	1979–1992	1992–2005
Total, 16 years and older	63.7	66.3	68.8	104,962	126,982	150,516	22,020	23,534
Men, 16 years and older	77.8	75.6	74.7	60,726	69,184	78,718	8,458	9,534
16 to 19	61.5	41.1	55.5	5,111	3,547	4,624	-1,564	1,077
20 to 24	86.4	83.3	84.4	8,535	7,242	8,111	-1,293	869
25 to 34	95.3	93.8	93.5	16,387	19,355	16,509	2,968	-2,846
35 to 44	95.7	93.8	93.5	11,531	18,162	19,645	6,631	1,483
45 to 54	91.4	90.8	90.2	10,008	12,101	18,065	2,093	5,964
55 to 64	72.8	67.0	69.7	7,212	6,701	9,560	-511	2,859
65 and over	19.9	16.1	14.7	1,943	2,077	2,203	134	126
Women, 16 years and older	50.9	57.8	63.2	44,235	57,798	71,798	13,563	14,000
16 to 19	54.2	49.2	52.4	4,527	3,204	4,222	-1,323	1,018
20 to 24	69.0	71.2	73.6	7,234	6,461	7,169	-773	708
25 to 34	63.9	74.1	80.7	11,551	15,748	14,839	4,197	-909
35 to 44	63.6	76.8	86.2	8,154	15,441	18,643	7,287	3,202
45 to 54	58.3	72.7	82.8	6,889	10,290	17,354	3,401	7,064
55 to 64	41.7	46.6	52.4	4,719	5,169	7,825	450	2,656
65 and older	8.3	8.3	8.8	1,161	1,485	1,747	324	262
White, 16 years and older	63.9	66.7	70.2	91,923	108,526	124,847	16,603	16,321
Men	78.6	76.4	77.2	53,856	59,830	66,007	5,974	6,177
Women	50.5	57.8	62.6	38,067	48,696	58,840	10,629	10,144
Black, 16 years and older	61.4	63.3	66.2	10,678	13,891	17,395	3,213	3,504
Men	71.3	69.7	70.5	5,559	6,892	8,355	1,333	1,463

TABLE 4.3 *Continued*

Group	Participation Rate (thousands)			Level (thousands)			Change (thousands)	
	1979	1992	2005	1979	1992	2005	1979–1992	1992–2005
Women	53.1	58.0	62.6	5,119	6,999	9,040	1,880	2,041
Asian and other, 16 years and older*	66.1	65.6	66.6	2,361	4,565	8,274	2,204	3,709
Men	76.6	74.6	74.1	1,311	2,462	4,355	1,151	1,893
Women	56.4	57.5	59.9	1,049	2,103	3,918	1,054	1,815
Hispanic, 16 years and older		(**)		(**)	10,131	16,581	(**)	6,450
Men		(**)		(**)	6,091	9,628	(**)	3,537
Women		(**)		(**)	4,040	6,953	(**)	2,913
Other than Hispanic, 16 years and older		(**)		(**)	116,851	133,935	(**)	17,084
Men		(**)		(**)	63,093	69,090	(**)	5,997
Women		(**)		(**)	53,758	64,846	(**)	11,088
White non-Hispanic, 16 years and older		(**)		(**)	98,819	109,753	(**)	10,934
Men		(**)		(**)	53,997	57,218	(**)	3,221
Women		(**)		(**)	44,822	52,535	(**)	7,713

*The "Asian and other" group includes (1) Asians and Pacific Islanders and (2) American Indians and Alaska Natives. The historical data are derived by subtracting "black" from the "black and other" group; projections are made directly, not by subtraction.

**Data for Hispanic origin is not available before 1980.

***Data are for 1980–1992.

The contrast between growth in numbers and percentage growth rate is an important factor when one examines specific occupations. Failure to discriminate between actual increases in the numbers of jobs and the percentage increase can lead to erroneous conclusions about where opportunities for employment are the greatest. For example, according to Figure 4.1 employment of home health aides, human services workers, and personal home care aides will increase by 130 percent or more in the 1992–2005 period. Figure 4.2, which shows the occupations with the largest numerical growth, does not list personal home care aides and indicates that there will be an increase of 479,000 home health aides and 256,000 human services workers. By contrast, it is projected that the numbers of retail sales workers will increase by 786,000 and that the number of registered nurses will increase by 765,000. Please note that neither of these jobs is listed among the fastest-growing occupations shown in Figure 4.1.

The reason for the apparent discrepancy between jobs that are listed as growing the fastest on a percentage basis and those jobs with the largest numerical increase is relatively simple. For example, there are relatively few systems analysts and thus a small numerical increase translates into a large percentage increase. Conversely, there are many retail salespeople and thus a large increase in numbers results in a relatively small percentage increase.

Although the expanding labor market generally suggests that most jobs will increase in numbers, the information in Figure 4.3 indicates that this is not true. As can be seen in Figure 4.3, farmers, sewing machine operators, cleaners and servants, farm workers, typists and word processors, and many other occupations are expected to decrease in numbers. In some instances, such as the one involving farmers and farm workers, the projected decreases are extensions of long-standing trends. For other jobs, such as typists and word processors and bank tellers, the decreases are a relatively new phenomenon resulting from automation, bank mergers, and increasing facility with computers and word processors by persons who used to defer their work to typists and word-processing specialists.

Sources of Information on Change and Structure

Whether one is assisting sixth graders to become more familiar with occupations generally, high school graduates to initiate job searches, workers with disabilities to move to compatible jobs, or structurally unemployed workers to find new directions, both helper and client need information about the present and future structure of the world of work as well as about likely change in the near and distant future. Current, useful information is available in a variety of publications.

Information about the current and projected national occupational structure is as close as the Internet. The Bureau of Labor Statistics website (http://bls.gov/) provides up-to-date information in both of these areas. However, many individuals will be more interested in state-level information, which is also available on the Internet. Most states maintain websites with current information and projections. Some website addresses (URLs) follow:

Louisiana	http://www.Idol.state.la.us/
New Mexico	http://wwwgsd.state.nm.us/dol/
North Carolina	http://www.esc.state.nc.us/lmi/index.html
Washington (state of)	http://www.was/gov/esd/lmea

Percent employment growth by occupation, projected 1992–2005

Occupation	Percent
Home health aides	138 percent
Human services workers	136
Personal and home care aides	130
Computer engineers and scientists	112
Systems analysts	110
Physical and corrective therapy assistants and aides	93
Physical therapists	88
Paralegals	86
Teachers, special education	74
Medical assistants	71
Corrections officers	70
Detectives except public	70
Travel agents	66
Childcare workers	66
Radiologic technologists and technicians	63
Nursery workers	62
Medical records technicians	61
Operations research analysts	61
Occupational therapists	60
Legal secretaries	57
Manicurists	54
Producers, directors, actors, and entertainers	54
Teachers, preschool and kindergarten	54
Flight attendants	51
Speech-language pathologists and audiologists	51
Guards	51
Insurance adjusters, examiners, and investigators	49
Respiratory therapists	48
Psychologists	48
Paving, surfacing, and tamping equipment operators	48

FIGURE 4.1   Fastest-Growing Occupations

Source: *Occupational Outlook Quarterly,* Fall 1993, p. 38.

Numerical employment growth by occupation, projected 1992–2005 (thousands)

Salespersons, retail	786 thousand
Registered nurses	765
Cashiers	670
General office clerks	654
Truckdrivers, light and heavy	648
Waiters and waitresses	637
Nursing aides, orderlies, and attendants	594
Janitors and cleaners, including maids and housekeeping cleaners	548
Food preparation workers	524
Systems analysts	501
Home health aides	479
Teachers, secondary school	462
Childcare workers	450
Guards	408
Marketing and sales worker supervisors	407
Teacher aides and educational assistants	381
General managers and top executives	380
Maintenance repairers, general utility	319
Gardeners and groundskeepers except farm	311
Teachers, elementary	311
Food counter, fountain, and related workers	308
Receptionists and information clerks	305
Accountants and auditors	304
Clerical supervisors and managers	301
Cooks, restaurant	276
Teachers, special education	267
Licensed practical nurses	261
Blue-collar worker supervisors	257
Human services workers	256
Computer engineers and scientists	236

FIGURE 4.2   Occupations with Largest Numerical Growth

Source: *Occupational Outlook Quarterly,* Fall 1993, p. 39.

Percent employment decline by occupation, projected 1992–2005

Occupation	Percent decline
Frame wirers, central office	−75 percent
Peripheral electronic data-processing (EDP) equipment operators	−60
Directory assistance operators	−51
Station installers and repairers, telephone	−50
Central office operators	−50
Portable machine cutters	−40
Computer operators except peripheral equipment	−39
Shoe sewing machine operators and tenders	−38
Central office PBX installers and repairers	−36
Job printers	−35
Childcare workers, private household	−35
Roustabouts	−33
Separating and still machine, operators and tenders	−33
Coil winders, tapers, and finishers	−32
Cleaners and servants, private household	−32
Billing, posting, and calculation machine operators	−29
Sewing machine operators, garment	−29
Signal or track switch maintainers	−28
Compositors and typesetters, precision	−27
Data entry keyers, composing	−26
Drilling machine tool setters and set-up operators, metal and plastic	−26
Motion picture projectionists	−26
Boiler operators and tenders, low pressure	−25
Statement clerks	−24
Telephone and cable TV line installers and repairers	−24
Watchmakers	−23
Tire building machine operators	−22
Packaging and filling machine operators and tenders	−22
Head sawyers and sawing machine operators and tenders	−22
Farmers	−21

FIGURE 4.3 Percent Employment Decline by Occupation, Projected 1992–2005

Source: *Occupational Outlook Quarterly,* Fall 1993, p. 41.

Information about states can also be obtained by accessing the website of the State Occupational Information Coordinating Committee (SOICC) website and then, through hyperlinks, accessing labor market information. The addresses (URLs) of some SOICCs follow:

Colorado	http://.aclin.org/other/jobs/cosoicc
Texas	http://www.soicc.capnet.state.tx.us/
Vermont	http://www.cit.state.vt.us/det/detmi/dervoicc

Fortunately, all SOICC websites can be accessed by going directly to the website of the National Occupational Information Coordinating Committee (NOICC) (http://www.noicc.gov/). Then, through the use of the hyperlinks provided on this site, SOICC websites can be accessed. Finally, information about the current structure and projections about the future of a given state can often be obtained through employment security websites such as the one in Virginia (Virginia Employment Commission (http://state.va.us/vec/vec.html). The website of ALMIS, America's Labor Market Information System (http://ecuvax.cis.ecu.edu/~lmi/lmi.html) contains links to state employment security sites.

State Employment Security Commission (SESC) reports on the Internet and in print form are typically the best sources of information about local and regional occupations. Analysts within these offices are responsible for the collection and collation of statewide occupational information. Their reports, which are disseminated within each state, become the basis for many of the regional and national publications regarding the occupational structure, as well as for the information located on websites.

Print materials regarding the occupational structure are also available from the Bureau of Labor Statistics and the Bureau of Industrial Economics in the Department of Commerce. A sample of these materials—national as well as state and local—is listed below. These publications can often be found in the local library. Some, like the *Occupational Outlook Handbook,* are available in the Career Resource Centers of high schools, community colleges, and universities.

National Sources

Occupational Outlook Handbook: Published biennially by the Bureau of Labor Statistics (BLS), this publication covers about 185 occupations, including data on job outlook.

Occupational Outlook Quarterly: Published quarterly, also by the BLS, this journal provides updated information related to the *Handbook* and other relevant outlook data.

Occupational Projections and Training Data: Published annually by the BLS, this publication provides data on employment prospects and on training requirements, so one can see not only the likely number of vacancies in an occupation but also the supply of trained individuals who can enter those positions.

U.S. Industrial Outlook: Published annually by the Bureau of Industrial Economics in the Department of Commerce, this publication provides a survey picture of current developments in each industry as well as long-range forecasts of what can be expected over the next decade.

State and Local Sources

Occupational Employment Survey Statistics: Published on a 3-year cycle by each State Employment Security Agency, the survey collects current data on wage and salary employment by industry on a sample basis, covering about 2000 occupations.

OES Employment Outlook: Published irregularly and updated as needed by the State Employment Security Agency, this material includes long-term projections on both occupations and industries and is produced through a federal-state cooperative arrangement.

Covered Employment, Wages, and Contributions: Published quarterly by the State Employment Security Agency, this report provides a detailed summary of employment and wage information for workers covered by state unemployment insurance laws.

Labor Market Information Newsletter: Published monthly by the State Employment Security Agency, this monthly summary shows significant changes in the labor force during the month and the year.

Summary

Although many people view the world of work as a rigid sociological structure, it is, in fact, a dynamic, constantly changing entity. Some of the influences causing long-term changes in the structure include population variables such as changes in birth rate and increasing longevity, and sociological and technological developments. Some events, such as calamities, human disasters, or seasonal variations, create either a beneficial or a depressing influence on a short-term basis.

Even though the work structure is subject to some continual changes, there is sufficient stability to permit classification and analysis. One approach to classifying work is based on an industrial view, that is, the work setting where the task is performed. Another approach is that of occupation—what the worker actually does.

Both industrial and occupational groups continue to change constantly. Nevertheless, the changes usually are not drastic and sudden. Consequently, numbers and trends can be predicted with a fair degree of accuracy, especially over short-term periods of 5 to 10 years.

References

Brown, D. (1995). *Choosing your job upon retirement.* Lincolnwood, IL: VGM Books.

DOL. (1993). *Occupational Outlook Quarterly* (Special issue on the American work force 1992–2005). Washington, DC: United States Department of Labor.

DOL. (1994). *The American work force: 1992–2005.* Washington, DC: U.S. Government Printing Office.

DOL. (1994–95). *Occupational outlook handbook.* Washington, DC: United States Department of Labor.

DOL. (1998). O*NET (http://www.doleta.gov/programs/onet/) Washington, DC: Author.

Important Websites

America's Labor Market Information System	http://ecuvax.cis.ecu.edu/~lmi/lmi.html)
Bureau of Labor Statistics	http://bls.gov/
NOICC	http://www.noicc.gov/
Occupational Outlook Handbook	http://www.bls.gov/ocohome.htm
U.S. Department of Labor	http://www/dol.gov/

5

The Dictionary of Occupational Titles, Guide for Occupational Exploration, and O*NET

Precise estimates of the number of different occupations depend on how one defines *different*, because many occupations have common factors and may differ only slightly. Nevertheless, it is commonly thought that the United States has more than 12,000 jobs sufficiently varied to be thought different. Many of these occupations may be known by more than one name in different regions, or even within a given region.

If one is to help individuals learn about occupations or develop an understanding of their relationship to the world of work, a broad knowledge of occupations is absolutely essential. Yet maintaining a good grasp of 12,000 constantly changing occupations is beyond the competence of most human minds. Some method of classification or grouping must be used to bring this array into manageable proportions.

Even though the number of occupations is large, many of them are related in various ways. Just as human families include brothers, sisters, and cousins, so too do many occupations show similar types of relationships. Classification systems are useful in understanding these relationships within the world of work.

Occupations can be grouped and classified by many systems, each of which has its own advantage or its unique contribution. Because the system that is best for a specific situation or purpose depends on the desired goal, there can be no single overall best method. The method that best achieves the goal is the best one to use. Because situations vary, the person involved in career education or career counseling must understand a variety of systems to make the best choice for the desired purpose. In this chapter and the next, we consider several of the commonly used classification systems. We first consider the *Dictionary of Occupational Titles* and those systems directly related to it, including O*NET. In the next chapter, we look at systems that are oriented in other ways.

Dictionary of Occupational Titles

Of all the publications related to counseling and teaching about occupations, the *Dictionary of Occupational Titles* has been the most widely used. It has provided classification systems for occupations, a basis for filing career materials, a method for relating beginning positions to jobs available for experienced workers, a system for identifying workers whose skills and abilities approximate those needed in fields with shortages, and a brief occupational description developed from job analysis reports.

Originally published in 1939, the *Dictionary of Occupational Titles* (DOL, 1991), usually called the *DOT*, was brought up to date by a second edition in 1949. The book was totally revised in 1965, with a new coding system and extensive new information provided in its structure. The fourth edition was published in 1977. A revision of the fourth edition was released in 1991. Plans for a fifth edition of the *DOT* were abandoned in favor of the publication of O*NET. This chapter uses the 1991 revision of the fourth edition. It consists of two volumes including 12,741 occupation descriptions, of which about one-fifth are new or revised. A further advantage of the 1991 revision is the incorporation of codes and information from the *Guide for Occupational Exploration (GOE)* and *Selected Characteristics of Occupations Defined in the Dictionary of Occupational Titles*. Both of these publications are discussed later in this chapter.

The *DOT* includes occupational groupings starting with "professional, technical, and managerial." These nine categories break into eighty-three occupationally specific divisions, such as various occupations in medicine and health in the professional category, or "mechanics and machinery repairers" in the machine trades category. The eighty-three divisions are further subdivided into 564 groups—for example, "dentists" or "registered nurses" in the medicine and health divisions and "motorized vehicle and engineering equipment mechanics and repairers" or "farm mechanics and repairers" in the mechanics and machinery repairer division.

Figure 5.1 presents typical *DOT* definitions and identifies the seven basic parts to be discussed next.

Occupational Code Number

The *DOT* code number assigned to each defined occupation consists of nine digits divided into three sections, with three digits in each part. The parts have a particular purpose and provide specific information about the occupation. In the first two parts, each digit supplies certain information.

The first three digits reveal the category, division, and group in which the occupation is classified. Figure 5.2 is a page from the *DOT* (p. xxix) listing the

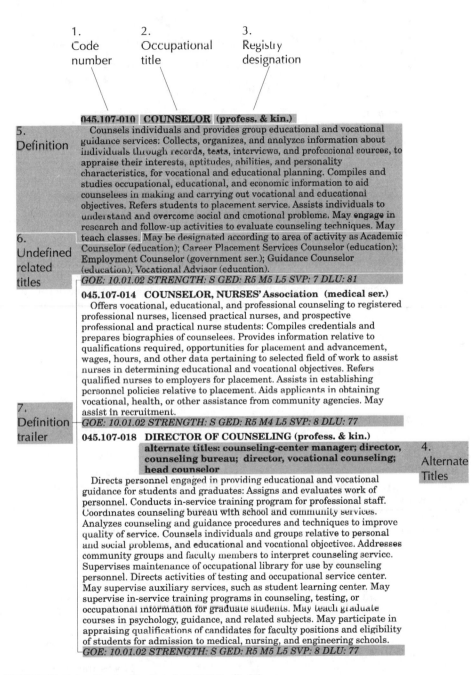

1.
Code
number

2.
Occupational
title

3.
Registry
designation

045.107-010   COUNSELOR   (profess. & kin.)

5.
Definition

Counsels individuals and provides group educational and vocational
guidance services: Collects, organizes, and analyzes information about
individuals through records, tests, interviews, and professional sources, to
appraise their interests, aptitudes, abilities, and personality
characteristics, for vocational and educational planning. Compiles and
studies occupational, educational, and economic information to aid
counselees in making and carrying out vocational and educational
objectives. Refers students to placement service. Assists individuals to
understand and overcome social and emotional problems. May engage in
research and follow-up activities to evaluate counseling techniques. May

6.
Undefined
related
titles

teach classes. May be designated according to area of activity as Academic
Counselor (education); Career Placement Services Counselor (education);
Employment Counselor (government ser.); Guidance Counselor
(education); Vocational Advisor (education).
GOE: 10.01.02 STRENGTH: S GED: R5 M5 L5 SVP: 7 DLU: 81

045.107-014   COUNSELOR, NURSES' Association   (medical ser.)
Offers vocational, educational, and professional counseling to registered
professional nurses, licensed practical nurses, and prospective
professional and practical nurse students: Compiles credentials and
prepares biographies of counselees. Provides information relative to
qualifications required, opportunities for placement and advancement,
wages, hours, and other data pertaining to selected field of work to assist
nurses in determining educational and vocational objectives. Refers
qualified nurses to employers for placement. Assists in establishing
personnel policies relative to placement. Aids applicants in obtaining
vocational, health, or other assistance from community agencies. May
assist in recruitment.

7.
Definition
trailer

GOE: 10.01.02 STRENGTH: S GED: R5 M4 L5 SVP: 8 DLU: 77

045.107-018   DIRECTOR OF COUNSELING (profess. & kin.)

**alternate titles: counseling-center manager; director,
counseling bureau; director, vocational counseling;
head counselor**

4.
Alternate
Titles

Directs personnel engaged in providing educational and vocational
guidance for students and graduates: Assigns and evaluates work of
personnel. Conducts in-service training program for professional staff.
Coordinates counseling bureau with school and community services.
Analyzes counseling and guidance procedures and techniques to improve
quality of service. Counsels individuals and groups relative to personal
and social problems, and educational and vocational objectives. Addresses
community groups and faculty members to interpret counseling service.
Supervises maintenance of occupational library for use by counseling
personnel. Directs activities of testing and occupational service center.
May supervise auxiliary services, such as student learning center. May
supervise in-service training programs in counseling, testing, or
occupational information for graduate students. May teach graduate
courses in psychology, guidance, and related subjects. May participate in
appraising qualifications of candidates for faculty positions and eligibility
of students for admission to medical, nursing, and engineering schools.
GOE: 10.01.02 STRENGTH: S GED: R5 M5 L5 SVP: 8 DLU: 77

FIGURE 5.1   Basic Parts of *DOT* Definition

Source: DOL (1991), p. 51.

FIGURE 5.2   Sample Page from *DOT* Illustrating Categories and Divisions

Occupational Categories, Divisions, and Groups

One-Digit Occupational Categories

0/1 Professional, technical, and managerial occupations
2 Clerical and sales occupations
3 Service occupations
4 Agricultural, fishery, forestry, and related occupations

5 Processing occupations
6 Machine trades occupations
7 Benchwork occupations
8 Structural work occupations
9 Miscellaneous occupations

Two-Digit Occupational Categories

0/1 Professional, technical, and managerial occupations
00/01 Occupations in architecture, engineering, and surveying
02 Occupations in mathematics and physical sciences
03 Computer-related occupations
04 Occupations in life sciences
05 Occupations in social sciences
07 Occupations in medicine and health
09 Occupations in education
10 Occupations in museum, library, and archival sciences
11 Occupations in law and jurisprudence
12 Occupations in religion and theology
13 Occupations in writing
14 Occupations in art
15 Occupations in entertainment and recreation
16 Occupations in administrative specializations
18 Managers and officials, n.e.c.
19 Miscellaneous professional, technical, and managerial occupations

2   Clerical and sales occupations
20 Stenography, typing, filing, and related occupations
21 Computing and account-recording occupations
22 Production and stock clerks and related occupations
23 Information and message distribution occupations
24 Miscellaneous clerical occupations
25 Sales occupations, services
26 Sales occupations, consumable commodities
27 Sales occupations, commodities, n.e.c.
29 Miscellaneous sales occupations

3   Service occupations
30 Domestic service occupations
31 Food and beverage preparation and service occupations
32 Lodging and related service occupations
33 Barbering, cosmetology, and related service occupations
34 Amusement and recreation service occupations
35 Miscellaneous personal service occupations
36 Apparel and furnishings service occupations
37 Protective service occupations
38 Building and related service occupations

4   Agricultural, fishery, forestry, and related occupations
40 Plant farming occupations
41 Animal farming occupations
42 Miscellaneous agricultural and related occupations
44 Fishery and related occupations
45 Forestry occupations
46 Hunting, trapping, and related occupations

5   Processing occupations
50 Occupations in processing of metal
51 Ore refining and foundry occupations
52 Occupations in processing of food, tobacco, and related products
53 Occupations in processing of paper and related materials
54 Occupations in processing of petroleum, coal, natural and manufactured gas, and related products
55 Occupations in processing of chemicals, plastics, synthetics, rubber, paint, and related products

FIGURE 5.2 *Continued*

56 Occupations in processing of wood and wood products

57 Occupations in processing of stone, clay, glass, and related products

58 Occupations in processing of leather, textiles, and related products

59 Processing occupations, n.e.c.

6 Machine trades occupations

60 Metal machining occupations

61 Metalworking occupations, n.e.c.

62/63 Mechanics and machinery repairers

64 Paperworking occupations

65 Printing occupations

66 Wood machining occupations

67 Occupations in machining stone, clay, glass, and related materials

68 Textile occupations

69 Machine trades occupations, n.e.c.

7 Benchwork Occupations

70 Occupations in fabrication, assembly, and repair of metal products, n.e.c.

71 Occupations in fabrication and repair of scientific, medical, photographic, optical, horological, and related products

72 Occupations in assembly and repair of electrical equipment

73 Occupations in fabrication and repair of products made from assorted materials

74 Painting, decorating, and related occupations

75 Occupations in fabrication and repair of plastics, synthetics, rubber, and related products

76 Occupations in fabrication and repair of wood products

77 Occupations in fabrication and repair of sand, stone, clay, and glass products

78 Occupations in fabrication and repair of textile, leather, and related products

79 Benchwork occupations, n.e.c.

8 Structural

9 miscellaneous

Source: DOL (1991), p. xxix.

occupational categories (first digit) and the divisions in the 0/1 to 7 categories. As one can see, the divisions involve two digits, always starting with the category number. Two numbers (0/1) are used for the "professional, technical, and managerial" category to allow sufficient space for the sixteen divisions included. This doubling up also happens twice at the division level, 00/01 and 62/63, for a similar reason. Only three categories (processing occupations, machine trades occupations, and benchwork occupations) use all the spaces that are available in each division. Unused two-digit codes (e.g., 06, 28, and 47) are left vacant to be used as new divisions of occupations emerge. For example, the 03 division was used for the first time in the 1991 revision for computer-related occupations.

Similarly, occupational groups are designated by the first three digits. Figure 5.3 presents a portion of page xxx of the *DOT* and lists the 00/01 to 14 divisions and their respective occupational groups. The sixteen divisions in the 00/01 to 19 range include 105 occupational groups ranging from "001—Architectural occupations" to "199—Miscellaneous professional, technical, and managerial occupations, n.e.c." (not elsewhere classified). Thus, we see that the first three digits for counselor, as shown in Figure 5.1, provide the following information:

Category	0	Professional, technical, and managerial occupations
Division	04	Occupations in life sciences
Group	045	Occupations in psychology

The second set of three digits in the code number provides the worker function ratings for the tasks performed in the occupations. The *DOT* assumes that all

FIGURE 5.3 **Examples of Occupational Divisions and Groups in the Professional, Technical, and Managerial Occupations**

Three-Digit Occupational Groups

Professional, Technical, and Managerial Occupations

00/01 Occupations in architecture, engineering, and surveying
001 Architectural occupations
002 Aeronautical engineering occupations
003 Electrical/electronics engineering occupations
005 Civil engineering occupations
006 Ceramic engineering occupations
007 Mechanical engineering occupations
008 Chemical engineering occupations
010 Mining and petroleum engineering occupations
011 Metallurgy and metallurgical engineering occupations
012 Industrial engineering occupations
013 Agricultural engineering occupations
014 Marine engineering occupations
015 Nuclear engineering occupations
017 Drafters, n.e.c.
018 Surveying/cartographic occupations
019 Occupations in architecture, engineering, and surveying, n.e.c.

02 Occupations in mathematics and physical sciences
020 Occupations in mathematics
021 Occupations in astronomy
022 Occupations in chemistry
023 Occupations in physics
024 Occupations in geology
025 Occupations in meteorology
029 Occupations in mathematics and physical sciences, n.e.c.

03 Computer-related occupations
030 Occupations in systems analysis and programming
031 Occupations in data communications and networks
032 Occupations in computer system user support
033 Occupations in computer systems technical support
039 Computer-related occupations, n.e.c.

04 Occupations in life sciences
040 Occupations in agricultural sciences
041 Occupations in biological sciences
045 Occupations in psychology
049 Occupations in life sciences, n.e.c.

05 Occupations in social sciences
050 Occupations in economics
051 Occupations in political science
052 Occupations in history
054 Occupations in sociology
055 Occupations in anthropology
059 Occupations in social sciences, n.e.c.

07 Occupations in medicine and health
070 Physicians and surgeons
071 Osteopaths
072 Dentists
073 Veterinarians
074 Pharmacists
075 Registered nurses
076 Therapists
077 Dietitians
078 Occupations in medical and dental technology
079 Occupations in medicine and health, n.e.c.

09 Occupations in education
090 Occupations in college and university education
091 Occupations in secondary school education
092 Occupations in preschool, primary school, and kindergarten education
094 Occupations in education of persons with disabilities
096 Home economists and farm advisers
097 Occupations in vocational education
099 Occupations in education, n.e.c.

10 Occupations in museum, library, and archival sciences
100 Librarians
101 Archivists
102 Museum curators and related occupations
109 Occupations in museum, library, and archival sciences, n.e.c.

FIGURE 5.3   *Continued*

11 **Occupations in law and jurisprudence**	137 Interpreters and translators
110 Lawyers	139 Occupations in writing, n.e.c.
111 Judges	
119 Occupations in law and jurisprudence, n.e.c.	**14** **Occupations in art**
	141 Commercial artists: designers and illustrators, graphic arts
12 **Occupations in religion and theology**	142 Environmental, product, and related designers
120 Clergy	
129 Occupations in religion and theology, n.e.c.	143 Occupations in photography
	144 Fine artists: painters, sculptors, and related occupations
13 **Occupations in writing**	149 Occupations in art, n.e.c.
131 Writers	
132 Editors: publication, broadcast, and script	

Source: DOL (1991), p. xxix.

occupations require the worker to be involved with data, people, or things (d-p-t) in some degree of complexity. The levels of relationship to data, people, and things are as follows:

Data (4th digit)	*People (5th digit)*	*Things (6th digit)*
0 Synthesizing	0 Mentoring	0 Setting up
1 Coordinating	1 Negotiating	1 Precision working
2 Analyzing	2 Instructing	2 Operating–controlling
3 Compiling	3 Supervising	3 Driving–operating
4 Computing	4 Diverting	4 Manipulating
5 Copying	5 Persuading	5 Tending
6 Comparing	6 Speaking–signaling	6 Feeding–offbearing
	7 Serving	7 Handling
	8 Taking instructions–helping	

As one can see from this list, the most complex relationships are assigned the lowest numbers; as complexity decreases, the numbers are higher. The levels are so arranged that, as one moves from the simplest level to the more complex, it is assumed that each succeeding level includes the previous level but is less complex than the next level above. The relationships that are significant in the performance of the occupation are used to evaluate the work, and those incidental relationships that are tangential to the performance of the job are disregarded. Definitions and explanations of each term can be found in the appendix to the *DOT*. Returning to our illustration in Figure 5.1, we now see that the 107 in the code number provides the following information:

4th DIGIT–DATA–1–*Coordinating* (Determining time, place, and sequence of operations or action to be taken on the basis of analysis of data; executing determination and/or reporting on events)

5th DIGIT–PEOPLE–0–*Mentoring* (Dealing with individuals in terms of their total personality in order to advise, counsel, and/or guide them with regard to problems that may be resolved by legal, scientific, clinical, spiritual, and/or other professional principles)

6th DIGIT–THINGS–7–*Handling* (Using body members, hand tools, and/or special devices to work, move, or carry objects or materials. Involves little or no latitude for judgment with regard to attainment of standards or in selecting appropriate tool, object, or material.)

Prediger (1981) contended that the data factor actually is a mixture of two antipodal components, "ideas" and "data." He suggests that *ideas* are intrapersonal, involving theories, knowledge, and insights, whereas *data* are impersonal—facts, records, files, and numbers. He combines the polarity of these two items with the earlier established concept of a people–things polarity to produce a two-dimensional classification system that we examine in the next chapter.

The last three digits of the code number have been assigned to permit differentiation of those occupations that share the same first six digits. At the time that these digits were assigned (several months before the fourth edition of the *DOT* was published), occupations with the same first six-digit code were arranged alphabetically and were then assigned an identifier code sequentially in multiples of four, starting with 010 for the first occupation in each six-digit code batch. The numbers for each batch run in this order: 010, 014, 018, 022, ... to the highest number needed. In our example, we see that "counselor" is the first occupation alphabetically among those occupations with the 045.107 code number. By examining *DOT* pages 51 and 52, where occupations with that code number are defined, we see that there are twelve other occupations that share the same first six digits with "counselor." The occasional exceptions to the sequencing are easily explained. For example, apprenticeships, not on the original list, are sometimes assigned a number two units higher than the occupation so that they will be located immediately after that occupation. A missing number in the sequence (010, 014, 022) suggests that the occupation originally assigned the identifier (018 in this case) was deleted after the list was established. An occupation with an identifier code higher than the alphabetical sequence suggests that it is probably one that was added to the list after the sequence had been assigned.

The *DOT* code number identifies and assembles closely related occupations in two ways. First, the initial three digits bring into the occupational group those occupations that share type or field of work within the occupational category. Thus the occupational division 68 brings together all the textile occupations, and within that cluster the occupational group 682 includes all the spinning occupations. The fourth, fifth, and sixth digits cluster occupations within each group according to the occupation's relationship to data, people, and things. Therefore, occupations sharing the same first six digits are closely related by type or field of work within a category and involve d-p-t activities at the same level of relationship. Further, other occupations with the same first three digits and very small differences in the second three digits are within the same field or type of work but have slightly different d-p-t relationships. As the differences between d-p-t codes grow larger, the differences between the jobs within the group grow larger.

Occupational Title

The occupational title appears in boldface uppercase letters immediately following the code number. This title, called the *base title,* is the name used most frequently for this specific job. Occupations that have more than one word in the base title will be listed in the index according to the key word in the title. Thus bridge carpenters, mine carpenters, rough carpenters, and ship carpenters are all listed together under "carpenter." On the other hand, career-guidance technician is listed alphabetically at "career" because there is no relationship between most of the various technicians. Alternative titles are synonyms for base titles and are listed in lower case.

Two other types of titles require some additional explanation: *master titles* and *term titles.* A *master title* is simply a means of conserving paper and space. It is used for those occupations that share a great many duties but that also have some specific duties. For example, in both retail and wholesale trade one can find many SALESPERSONS, usually named according to item or service sold, who share many duties in addition to some that relate uniquely to the item or service sold. The duties common to all salespersons are defined once as a *master definition.* Each base title definition then includes only the unique tasks and refers the reader to the master definition for the duties that are common to all salespersons. *Term titles* are common to a broad group of jobs that differ widely in the job knowledge required, the tasks performed, or the job location. The term title includes information about the jobs that are often grouped under this umbrella and suggests how to obtain the appropriate base title. For example, ENTERTAINER represents individuals who act, dance, sing, or perform feats of skill. Except for amusing audiences, they have little in common. The base title for each depends on the type of entertainment provided; thus examples of base titles would be ACTOR or ACTRESS, DANCER, SINGER, COMEDIAN, JUGGLER, and so on.

Industry Designation

Because occupations in different fields may share the same name but perform very different duties or tasks, the industry designation is a crucial part of the title. The industry designation may tell one or more of the following about an occupation:

Location of the occupation (hotel & rest.; mach. shop)
Type of duties associated with the occupation (clean; dye & press.)
Products manufactured (textiles; optical goods)

Processes used (electroplating; petrol. refin.)
Raw materials used (nonfer. metal alloys; stonework)

Some occupations occur in a large number of industries and are assigned an industry designation that reflects this dispersion. For example, clerical occupations that are found in almost every industry are labeled (clerical) and most professions are assigned (profess. & kin.). Several occupations are found in a number of industries but not as widely as others. These occupations usually carry an industry designation of (any ind.). A section of the *DOT* lists in alphabetical order all occupations in each industry designation. This listing is helpful when one knows the industry in which a worker is employed but does not know the proper title for the occupation. One can then identify possible titles from the list and check occupational definitions against the duties performed by the worker.

Alternate Title

An alternate title is a synonym for a base title. One might think of this as comparable to a nickname—John Smith may be known as "Jack" or "Smitty." Among the names used for a specific set of tasks, the one most widely used across the country has been selected as the base title, and the others are designated as alternate titles. A given job may have many alternate titles or none at all. Sometimes regional usage may focus on one of the alternate titles. The alternate titles are listed in lowercase type in the definition, in the alphabetical index, and in the listing according to industry designation. In the index and industry listing, alternate titles carry the code number of the base title. Therefore, regardless of the name used, either index or industry listing will refer the searcher to the base title via its code number.

Definition

The definition is a brief description of the job as it most commonly occurs. There are often minor variations from one work site to another in the duties performed by workers who mostly do the same things. It would not be possible to include all local variants in the definitions; therefore, the printed definition must be viewed as a composite or typical listing of duties.

The first sentence of the definition summarizes the essential information about the occupation. The remainder of the definition consists of task element statements that indicate what the worker does to accomplish the overall job purpose.

Some titles (including our illustration in Figure 5.1) contain additional statements introduced by the word *May.* These sentences describe duties that are frequently, but not universally, assigned to the worker.

Any technical terms used in the definition are printed in italics to alert the reader to the fact that the word has a special usage. Such italicized words are defined in the glossary included in the *DOT* following the coded definitions.

Sometimes different occupations within the same industry carry the same name. In earlier editions of the *DOT* this problem was solved by adding a Roman numeral following the industry designation. Although the d-p-t code numbers have eliminated the need for this in most cases, the practice is still continued.

Undefined Related Titles

Whereas an alternate title is a different name for the same job, an undefined related title is a name for a slightly different variant of the same job. It is so similar to the base title that it is properly grouped with it, yet different enough to require some separate recognition. It carries the same code number as the base title and is listed in the alphabetical index and industry listing.

Definition Trailer

The last line of the definition brings into the *DOT* five pieces of information that are most helpful to the user. The first piece ("a" in our illustration) refers to the *Guide for Occupational Exploration,* and the next three pieces (b, c, and d) relate to *Selected Characteristics.* Both of these publications are considered later in this chapter.

In Figure 5.1, the last line in the definition for counselor appears as follows:

GOE:10.01.02   Strength: S   GED: R5M5L5   SVP: 7   DLU:81

     a   b   c   d   e

The section marked "a" provides the *GOE* code to which this occupation relates.

The "b" piece indicates the amount of physical exertion required by the occupation.

The "c" code tells the amount of general education in reasoning, mathematics, and language required to perform the work.

The "d" section refers to the amount of specific vocational preparation demanded.

The "e" figure reveals the year in which the definition was last updated.

Information about how the material in the *DOT* is organized and how one can find an occupational title and code number is included in the introductory pages of the *DOT.* Readers who wish to develop some skill in using the *DOT* as a reference should read the introductory section carefully, examine each of the major parts of the book, and then attempt to find base titles and code numbers for a number of jobs with which they are already familiar.

Using the DOT

Experienced counselors and career development specialists will recognize at once that the *DOT* is not a panacea to solve instantly all the problems they encounter in career planning and counseling. In fact, the *DOT* alone probably will not solve even one problem. It is, however, a very important tool, the utility and value of which depend on the professional skill of the individual employing it.

The *DOT*, in its present form, has been developed and modified over many years to serve a wide range of users in many different situations. Not all these groups will use the book in the same way, or even for the same purposes. The neophyte should first attempt to understand how the tool is used in the function he or she wishes to perform and then develop skill and competence in this particular application. As one becomes more familiar with the book and its ramifications, additional insight into its other uses will ordinarily increase proficiency in using it for special purposes. Although the employment counselor will use the book often to ascertain a code number for a referred worker or to develop an entry code number for a person entering the labor market, most counselors will not be much concerned with this application.

Counselors and career development specialists will find the *DOT* helpful in the following ways:

1. It is a useful way of helping individuals, singly or in groups, to develop an understanding of the world of work. All people have some previously acquired knowledge of the world of work. The *DOT* can help them add to their knowledge in several dimensions. Classification systems can be used along with the *DOT* to show both scope and depth in various occupational areas. It is particularly valuable in introductory and exploratory activities in the classroom and in the counseling session. The coding structure and the data–people–things concepts are especially appropriate for helping a person to form some picture of the world of work, and are equally useful in helping to explore the relationship between an occupation and the rest of the working world.

2. The *DOT* clearly demonstrates the interrelationships that exist in the world of work. This is of great importance in working with individuals who may conceive of work as being organized into tight, unrelated compartments. The *occupational group arrangement* is directly related to the *field* concept of occupations and can be used to demonstrate this relationship. The *worker functions arrangement* clearly shows a *level* approach to occupations. Thus promotional routes and transfer lines can be demonstrated and studied so the individual can see the various avenues that lead from each occupation to other parts of the world of work. The industry designation provides further insight by relating each occupation to its industrial location.

3. Both the occupational group arrangement and the worker functions arrangement provide useful bases for filing career materials.

Guide for Occupational Exploration

Often one can see a similarity between the relationships that exist among jobs and the kinships that tie people together. In some ways the occupational groups of the *DOT* are like a nuclear family, closely related, sharing some common physical and personality characteristics, and often having the same name. There can be other individuals closely related to this group (half brothers and sisters, and cousins) who share in parts of the relationship but not in other parts. Thus listing those who share one element—a common surname, for example—may leave out much information that might be available if a different base were used. This is also true with occupations; therefore, we need several different systems, some of which may be closely coordinated, to see different types of relationships.

The Department of Labor published the *Guide for Occupational Exploration (GOE)* in 1979 as a companion volume to be used with the *Dictionary of Occupational Titles*. It includes an occupational grouping system based on extensive research with various well-known interest inventories. Droege and Padgett (1979) describe the research procedures followed in the development of the *GOE*. The *GOE* is particularly important to career counselors because it provides a useful bridge between interest inventory results and the *DOT*. A second edition, edited by Harrington and O'Shea (1984) is published by the National Forum Foundation and distributed by the American Guidance Service. A third edition, titled *Enhanced Guide for Occupational Exploration,* compiled by Maze and Mayall, was published by JIST Works in 1991. In 1993 a revised edition of the *GOE* was published (Farr, 1993).

The *GOE* grouping is based on twelve interest factors or very broad occupational clusters. Each of these is divided into variable numbers of work groups consisting of closely related activities. The work groups also are divided further into subgroups.

The *GOE* interest factors, briefly defined, are as follows:

1. *Artistic:* Interest in creative expression of feelings or ideas.
2. *Scientific:* Interest in discovering, collecting, and analyzing information about the natural world and in applying scientific research findings to problems in medicine, life sciences, and natural sciences.
3. *Plants and Animals:* Interest in activities involving plants and animals, usually in an outdoor setting.
4. *Protective:* Interest in the use of authority to protect people and property.
5. *Mechanical:* Interest in applying mechanical principles to practical situations, using machines, hand tools, or techniques.
6. *Industrial:* Interest in repetitive, concrete, organized activities in a factory setting.
7. *Business Detail:* Interest in organized, clearly defined activities requiring accuracy and attention to detail, primarily in an office setting.
8. *Selling:* Interest in bringing others to a point of view through personal persuasion, using sales and promotion techniques.
9. *Accommodating:* Interest in catering to the wishes of others, usually on a one-to-one basis.
10. *Humanitarian:* Interest in helping others with their mental, spiritual, social, physical, or vocational needs.
11. *Leading-Influencing:* Interest in leading and influencing others through activities involving high-level verbal and numerical abilities.
12. *Physical Performing:* Interest in physical activities performed before an audience. (p. 8)

The 12 interest areas are divided into 66 work groups that are further subdivided into 348 subgroups. The coding system uses a six-digit arrangement, with the first two digits representing interest area, the first four digits identifying the work group, and all six digits designating the subgroup. Each subgroup lists actual *DOT* occupational titles and code numbers so *DOT* information can be used when specific occupations are being considered. Figure 5.4 is a list of the interest areas and the work groups.

FIGURE 5.4 *GOE* **Interest Areas and Work Group Arrangement**

V. Area and Group Arrangement
01   Artistic
01.01 Literary Arts
01.02 Visual Arts
01.03 Performing Arts: Drama
01.04 Performing Arts: Music
01.05 Performing Arts: Dance
01.06 Craft Arts
01.07 Elemental Arts
01.08 Modeling
02   Scientific
02.01 Physical Sciences
02.02 Life Sciences
02.03 Medical Sciences
02.04 Laboratory Technology
03   Plants and Animals
03.01 Managerial Work: Plants and Animals
03.02 General Supervision: Plants and Animals
03.03 Animal Training and Service
03.04 Elemental Work: Plants and Animals
04   Protective
04.01 Safety and Law Enforcement
04.02 Security Services
05   Mechanical
05.01 Engineering
05.02 Managerial Work: Mechanical
05.03 Engineering Technology
05.04 Air and Water Vehicle Operation
05.05 Craft Technology
05.06 Systems Operation
05.07 Quality Control
05.08 Land and Water Vehicle Operation
05.09 Material Control
05.10 Crafts
05.11 Equipment Operation
05.12 Elemental Work: Mechanical
06   Industrial
06.01 Production Technology
06.02 Production Work
06.03 Quality Control

06.04 Elemental Work: Industrial
07   Business Detail
07.01 Administrative Detail
07.02 Mathematical Detail
07.03 Financial Detail
07.04 Oral Communications
07.05 Records Processing
07.06 Clerical Machine Operation
07.07 Clerical Handling
08   Selling
08.01 Sales Technology
08.02 General Sales
08.03 Vending
09   Accommodating
09.01 Hospitality Services
09.02 Barber and Beauty Services
09.03 Passenger Services
09.04 Customer Services
09.05 Attendant Services
10   Humanitarian
10.01 Social Services
10.02 Nursing, Therapy, and Specialized Teaching Services
10.03 Child and Adult Care
11   Leading-Influencing
11.01 Mathematics and Statistics
11.02 Educational and Library Services
11.03 Social Research
11.04 Law
11.05 Business Administration
11.06 Finance
11.07 Services Administration
11.08 Communications
11.09 Promotion
11.10 Regulations Enforcement
11.11 Business Management
11.12 Contracts and Claims
12   Physical Performing
12.01 Sports
12.02 Physical Feats

Source: Farr (1993), pp. v–vi.

Each work group area provides a general description of what workers in the group do and the settings where jobs are found. Additional information is provided as answers to five basic questions asked for each work group as follows:

What kind of work would you do?

What skills and abilities do you need for this kind of work?

How do you know if you would like or could learn to do this kind of work?

How can you prepare for and enter this kind of work?

What else should you consider about these jobs?

Most of the 1991 edition consists of descriptions of 2500 occupations selected as most important. Those included represent approximately 95 percent of the total work force. The two major criteria for inclusion were, first, "there is a significant labor market for the job," and second, "the occupation is an access point for people who have been working in other fields, or are just starting to work."

In addition to the 1977 *DOT* description of the occupation, several significant items are included in code form with code explanations in various appendices:

1. Office of Employment Statistics (OES) code number
2. General Educational Development code
3. Specific Vocational Preparation code
4. Academic code showing the degree or certification required and the amount of English usage skill
5. Work Field codes showing specific skills used in the job
6. MPSMS code telling what materials, products, subject matter, or services are used in the work
7. Aptitude codes as used with General Aptitude Test Battery (GATB)
8. Temperament codes showing personality characteristics required of the worker
9. Stress codes, listed where the work has a significant degree of stress
10. Physical codes, as used in *Selected Characteristics*
11. Work Environment codes, also from *Selected Characteristics*
12. Salary codes providing information on the average salary range to be expected
13. Outlook codes indicating how long it usually takes to find this type of job

One chapter provides a detailed explanation of how to use the book effectively, and another includes explanations of the various coding systems. Four of the appendices provide helpful lists, such as an alphabetical list of the occupations included in the book, an alphabetical list of industries, the grouping of the 2500 selected occupations by industry, and the selected occupations by educational level. Other appendices give further information about the OES, MPSMS, and Work Field codes.

The *GOE* has potential value for the career counselor because its foundation of interest areas provides such a useful device for helping clients translate assessment of their interests into relevant occupational fields. Further, information in each work group description about the skills and abilities required and about preparation programs also provides a base for relating the client's evaluation of aptitudes or general educational plans to appropriate occupational groups at the work group level. Those work group areas that appear to be related to client interests, aptitudes, or educational plans can be explored further by considering the narrative descriptions and coded information included in the 1991 edition. One must be aware that the narrative descriptions appear to be drawn from the 1977 edition of the *DOT*. Occupations that have changed extensively since that time are described more accurately in the 1991 revision of the *DOT*; consequently, caution is necessary if one uses the descriptions in the 1991 *GOE*.

Selected Characteristics of Occupations Defined *in the* Dictionary of Occupational Titles

In 1981 the U.S. Department of Labor published the third system in the series considered in this chapter: *Selected Characteristics of Occupations Defined in the Dictionary of Occupational Titles,* usually referred to simply as *Selected Characteristics.* The characteristics included are the physical demands, environmental conditions, and training time for all *DOT* base titles.

Occupations are listed in Part A according to *GOE* Work Subgroups (six-digit codes). Within each subgroup, occupations are grouped according to exertional level, and within these groups they are arranged by *DOT* code number. Other physical demands, the environmental conditions, and training requirements are listed for each entry. Each entry also includes the *GOE* subgroup code, the strength factor, the *DOT* base title, and the *DOT* industry designation. Because the data in *Selected Characteristics* are dated, no additional consideration will be given this document at this time. However, it is appropriate to say that *Selected Characteristics* and the *DOT* provided the foundation for the next system to be considered, O*NET.

O*NET and the Future of the DOT

A great deal of attention has been paid to the fourth edition of the *DOT* (DOL, 1991) in this chapter because it is currently the primary source of occupational information. However, in 1994 the Department of Labor (DOL) initiated an effort to replace the *DOT* with the *Occupational Information Network* or *O*NET.* The restructuring of American businesses in the early 1990s and the resulting layoffs of thousands of workers made it clear that the *DOT* had some serious shortcomings, not the least of which was the inability to assist people who were out of work to use the skills they had developed to identify potential jobs (Nottingham & Golec, undated).

The American Institute for Research (AIR) and several private and governmental agencies were charged with delivering O*NET. In developing O*NET, AIR,

DOL, and the other agencies involved hope to achieve three objectives. One of these objectives is to provide a common language that can be used to describe workers and the jobs they perform. The second objective is to develop a database about jobs that is relational in nature. The *DOT* tends to define and describe occupations as independent entities, with the result being over 12,000 occupational titles. It is anticipated that O*NET will include 1172 occupational units. The third objective of the effort to create O*NET is to provide the people who access the system with information about skills transferability as well as the ability to estimate the time it will take to retrain for related jobs (Nottingham & Golec, undated).

The content model adopted for O*NET can be seen in Figure 5.5. As can be seen in that figure, the content model of O*NET contains some of the data found in the *DOT* (e.g., general knowledge and education), some data that would normally be found in the *Occupational Outlook Handbook* (e.g., occupational outlook and wage information) and similar publications, information that is now located in the *Guide for Occupational Information* (e.g., data not currently included in current labor market and occupational information, such as cross-functional skills).

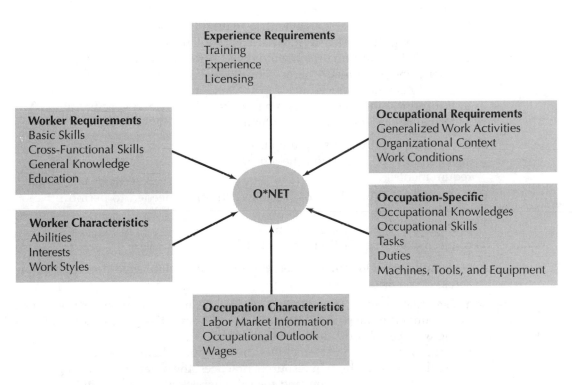

FIGURE 5.5 Conceptual Model of the O*NET

Source: Nottingham, J., & Gulec, J. (Undated). *Prototype development of the O*NET: The occupational information network.* Raleigh, NC: North Carolina Occupational Analysis Field Center.

The Content Model: Definitions

As can be seen in Figure 5.5, the content model of O*NET contains six domains of information, all of which will be defined here (Mumford & Peterson, 1995).

1. Worker characteristics—individuals' enduring characteristics that influence their motivation and capacity to function in an occupation. Three types of worker characteristics are included in O*NET:

   a. Abilities—characteristics needed to perform an occupation such as aptitudes.

   b. Occupational values and interests—values are preferences for certain types of occupational reinforcers such as autonomy; interests are likes and preferences.

   c. Work styles—characteristics that influence typical performance as well as the individuals' ongoing adaptation to and performance of work.

2. Worker requirements—individuals' attributes that influence occupational performance across a range of work activities:

   a. Basic skills—skills that facilitate the acquisition of new knowledge, such as reading.

   b. Cross-functional skills—skills that enable the worker to function across a broad range of work activities such as problem-solving and social skills.

   c. Knowledge—information about related principles and procedures that influence job performance across a number of work activities such as customer and personal service.

   d. Education—the amount and type (course of study and specific subjects) of formal education required to enter a job.

3. Experience requirements—prerequisite experiences in various types of jobs, specific job preparation, on-the-job training, and certification and licensure requirements:

   a. Training—highest level of specialized training needed to perform the job (related to 2.d, education, above).

   b. Experience—total time spent on a job.

   c. Licensing—specific licenses needed to perform the job.

4. Occupational requirements—job requirements established for individuals across domains of work:

   a. Generalized work activities—a cluster of similar occupational activities that underlie the performance of major job activities such as communicating with people outside the organization.

   b. Organizational context—includes the types of industry, the structure of the organization, the human resources practices, the organizational culture, the goals of the organization, and the roles expected of workers in the organization in which the work is performed.

   c. Work conditions—the physical, structural, interpersonal environment in which a particular occupation is conducted.

5. Occupation-specific requirements:
   a. Occupational knowledges—specific knowledges needed to perform the work.
   b. Occupational skills—specific job skills needed to perform the work.
   c. Tasks—specific tasks to be carried out by workers in the occupation.
   d. Duties
   e. Machines, tools, and equipment—specific machines, tools, and equipment used by workers on the job.
6. Occupation characteristics:
   a. Labor market information—information about the labor market context in which the job is performed.
   b. Occupational outlook—projections such as number of job vacancies due to growth and replacement of existing workers.
   c. Wages—amount of earnings and types of remuneration system.

Development of the Classification System

The O*NET database contains information regarding 1172 occupations and is designed so that new occupations can be added as they develop. The obvious question is: How were the nearly 11,761 occupations listed in the *DOT* reduced to 1172 titles? In the first step in this process, job analysts grouped the occupations in the DOT into the occupational clusters found in the Occupational Employment Statistics (OES) classification system used by the Bureau of the Census. This grouping was accomplished using two general criteria: belongingness and homogeneity. For an occupation to meet the "belongingness" criterion, the activities of the occupation had to match the definition of the OES. Homogeneity was determined by asking the question: Are the differences within the occupational category less than the differences within the category? Moreover, occupational categories had to have "skill transferability"; that is, the occupations within an occupational category had to have an overlap in the skills needed to perform the job. The specific criteria used in the occupational clustering process included information about aptitudes, temperament information; Specific Vocational Preparation information; the relationship of the occupations to data, people, and things; and information about the General Educational Development required for the occupation. Because not all of the occupations in the *DOT* met the general criteria of belongingness and homogeneity, additional aggregates of occupations had to be developed. The result of this aggregation was the development of 1,122 occupational units. Fifty occupational units were included as a result of additional analysis and input for a total of 1172.

Assigning Occupational Unit (OU) Codes

The starting point for the assignment of code numbers was the 1994 edition of the *Occupational Employment Statistics (OES) Dictionary*. The first five numbers of the

OU code are the same as the code found in this document, with a few exceptions. Thirteen of the codes were taken from the 1995 *OES Dictionary*, and four codes for private household occupations and one code for a military occupation were generated independently of the OES dictionaries. OU titles that contain five digits or letters are identical to those found in the OES dictionaries (e.g., Court Clerks 53702). Subdivisions within the OES codes were generated using letters (e.g., Stenotype Operators 55302A & Stenographers 55302B). Unlike the codes found in the *DOT*, which contained much information about the occupation, the O*NET codes provide little information by themselves. The exception to this is that the first number in the code identifies the major group in which the OU has been assigned. Finally, like all major taxonomies, the O*NET system has "holes" or spaces provided so that new occupations can be classified as they develop.

The occupational aggregation described above resulted in nine major subgroupings of occupations. These are listed below.

1. Executives, Managers, and Administrators
2. Professional and Support Specialists—Financial Specialists, Engineers, Scientists, Mathematicians, Social Scientists, Social Services Workers, Religious Workers, and Legal Workers
3. Professional Support Specialties—Educators, Librarians, Counselors, Health-Care Workers, Artists, Writers, Performers, and Other Professional Workers
4. Sales Workers
5. Administrative Support Workers
6. Service Workers
7. Agriculture, Forestry, and Fishing Workers
8. Mechanics, Installers, Repairers, Construction Trades, Extractive Trades, Metal and Plastics Working, Woodworking, Apparel, Precision Printing, and Food Processing Workers.
9. Machine Setters, Operators and Tenders, Production Workers, Hand Workers, Plant and System Workers, Transportation Workers, and Helpers

Development and Presentation of the Database

Once the classification system was developed, a far more rigorous task was pursued, determining the elements that would be included in the O*NET database and determining how these were to be presented. The point of departure for this effort were the domain and subdomains of the content model depicted in Figure 5.5. The committee charged with developing O*NET consulted existing models and, when appropriate, relied on these models to guide their decisions regarding the types of information that would be included. For example, Holland's (1997) model was used as the basis for collecting information about interests. The result of the deliberation was the identification of 445 data elements that would be included in the database. The O*NET database contains information about 10 basic skills, six social skills, eight complex problem-solving skills, twelve technical skills, and six systems skills (see Table 5.1 for examples of these skills).

TABLE 5.1   Examples of Skills in the O*NET Database

Elements	Basic Skills	Social Skills	Complex Problem-Solving Skills	Technical Skills	Systems Skills
Reading Comprehension	X				
Active Listening	X				
Critical Thinking	X				
Social Perceptiveness		X			
Persuasion		X			
Instructing		X			
Problem Identification			X		
Idea Generation			X		
Solution Appraisal			X		
Installation				X	
Programming				X	
Repairing				X	
Visioning					X
Mgmt. of Financial Resources					X
Mgmt. of Personnel Resources					X

Source: Mumford, M. D., Peterson, N. G., & Childs, R. A. (1997). Basic and cross-functional skills: Evidence for the reliability and validity of measures. In. N. G. Peterson, M. D. Mumford, W. C. Borman, P. R. Jeanneret, E. A. Fleishman, & K. Y. Levin (Eds.), *O*NET Final Technical Report Vol. I* (Figure 3.1). Salt Lake City, UT: Utah Department of Workforce Services.

The O*NET database also contains information about 33 knowledges (see Table 5.2), 13 generalized work experiences and work styles (see Table 5.3), 52 abilities (see Table 5.4), 39 work context variables and several subcontext items (see Table 5.5), seven dimensions of training, licensing, and work experience information with multiple subdimensions, 33 organizational context variables (see Table 5.6 for examples), six interests, and 21 values. Information about the occupation-specific tasks associated with each of the 1172 occupations in O*NET was also collected and is included in the database.

Once the elements to be included in O*NET were derived, workers or supervisors in the occupations contained in the classification system were surveyed to determine the relative importance of each of the elements in particular occupations. For example, workers were asked to rate the relative importance of certain specific job tasks and the frequency of performing those tasks. Work context information was collected by asking workers about the frequency of certain activities—such as meeting deadlines. Workers were also asked to rate the level of certain abilities needed to perform their jobs, and the importance of those abilities. The ratings

TABLE 5.2   Knowledges Contained in O*NET Database

1. Administration and Management	18. History and Archaeology
2. Clerical	19. Mathematics
3. Economics and Accounting	20. Design
4. Sales and Accounting	21. Building and Construction
5. Customer and Personal Service	22. Communication and Media
6. Personnel and Human Relationships	23. Public Safety and Security
7. Production and Processing	24. Law, Government, and Jurisprudence
8. Food Production	25. Sociology and Anthropology
9. Telecommunications	26. Chemistry
10. Foreign Language	27. Physics
11. English Language	28. Therapy and Counseling
12. Transportation	29. Medicine and Dentistry
13. Fine Arts	30. Biology
14. Philosophy and Theology	31. Computers and Electronics
15. Geography	32. Mechanical
16. Psychology	33. Engineering and Technology
17. Education and Training	

Source: Costanza, D. P., Fleishman, E. A., & Marshall-Mies, J. C. (1997). Knowledges: Evidence for the reliability and validity of measure. In N. G. Peterson, M. D. Mumford, W. C. Borman, P. R. Jeanneret, E. A. Fleishman, & K. Y. Levin (Eds.), *O*NET Final Technical Report Vol. I.* (Table 4.2). Salt Lake City, UT: Utah Department of Workforce Services.

TABLE 5.3   Samples of Generalized Work Experiences and Work Styles in the O*NET Database

Generalized Work Experiences	Work Styles
1. Getting information to do the job	1. Achievement orientation (effort, persistence, initiative)
2. Inspecting equipment, structures, etc.	2. Social influence (energy leadership)
3. Evaluating information for compliance to standards	3. Interpersonal orientation (cooperation, concern for others, social orientation)
4. Analyzing data or information	4. Adjustment (self-control, stress, flexibility/adaptability)
5. Making decisions and problem solving	5. Conscientiousness (dependability, attention to detail, integrity)
6. Scheduling work activities	6. Independence
7. Handling and moving objects	7. Practical intelligence (innovation, analytical thinking)
8. Interacting with computers	
9. Interpreting the meaning of information for others	
10. Performing administrative duties	

Sources: Borman, P. R., Jeanneret, P. R., Kubisiak, U. C., & Hanson, M. A. (1997). Generalized work activities: Evidence for reliability and validity of measures; and Borman, W. C., & Kubisiak, U. C. (1997). Work styles: Evidence for the reliability and validity of measures. In N. G. Peterson, M. D. Mumford, W. C. Borman, P. R. Jeanneret, E. A. Fleishman, & K. Y. Levin (Eds.), *O*NET Final Technical Report Vol. II & I* (Figures 6.2 & 11.1). Salt Lake City, UT: Utah Department of Workforce Services.

TABLE 5.4   Abilities Found in the O*NET Database

COGNITIVE ABILITIES

Verbal Abilities
Oral comprehension
Written comprehension
Oral expression
Written expression

Idea Generation and Reasoning Abilities
Fluency of ideas
Originality
Problem sensitivity
Deductive reasoning
Inductive reasoning
Information ordering
Category flexibility

Quantitative Abilities
Mathematical reasoning
Number facility

Memory
Memorization

Perceptual Abilities
Flexibility of closure
Perceptual speed

Spatial Abilities
Spatial orientation
Visualization

Attentiveness
Selective attention
Time sharing

PSYCHOMOTOR ABILITIES

Fine Manipulative Abilities
Arm–hand steadiness
Manual dexterity
Finger dexterity

Control Movement Abilities
Control precision
Multi-limb coordination

Response orientation
Rate control

Reaction Time and Speed Abilities
Reaction time
Wrist–finger speed
Speed of limb movement

Physical Strength Abilities
Static strength
Explosive strength
Dynamic strength
Trunk strength

Endurance
Stamina

Flexibility, Balance, and Coordination
Extent flexibility
Dynamic flexibility
Gross body coordination
Gross body equilibrium

SENSORY ABILITIES

Visual Abilities
Near vision
Far vision
Visual color discrimination
Night vision
Peripheral vision
Depth perception
Glare sensitivity

Auditory and Speech Abilities
Hearing sensitivity
Auditory attention
Sound localization
Speech recognition
Speech clarity

Source: Fleishman, E. A., Costanza, D. P., & Marshall-Mies, J. C. (1997). Abilities: Evidence for reliability and validity of measures. In N. G. Peterson, M. D. Mumford, W. C. Borman, P. R. Jeanneret, E. A. Fleishman, & K. Y. Levin (Eds.), *O*NET Final Technical Report Vol. II* (Figure 9.1). Salt Lake City, UT: Utah Department of Workforce Services.

TABLE 5.5   Work Context Taxonomy Found in O*NET

Work Context		
Interpersonal Relationships	**Physical Work Relationships**	**Structural Job Characteristics**
Communication	Work Setting	Criticality of Positions
Types of Role Relationships	Environmental Conditions	Routine vs. Challenging
Responsibility for Others	Job Demands	Competition
Conflictual Contact with Others		Pace and Scheduling

Source: Strong, M. H., Jeanneret, P. R., McPhail, S. M., & Blakely, B. R. (1997). Work context: Evidence for reliability and validity of measures. In N. G. Peterson, M. D. Mumford, W. C. Borman, P. R. Jeanneret, E. A. Fleishman, & K. Y. Levin (Eds.), *O*NET Final Technical Report Vol. II* (Figure 7.1). Salt Lake City, UT: Utah Department of Workforce Services.

received from workers, the analysis of these ratings to determine cross-occupational similarities, and data collected by various U.S. Department of Labor offices such as the Bureau of Labor Statistics are presented in the database.

Finally, a 1–12 point scale is used to indicate the educational level required for participation in the job with 1 indicating less than a high school diploma and 12

TABLE 5.6   Taxonomy of Organizational Context and Examples of Variables Found in O*NET

Type of Industry (organizational output)	**Social Processes**
Structural Characteristics	*Culture (organizational values)*
Organizational Structure	*Goals*
Organization and establishment size	*Roles*
Centralization and employee empowerment	Role conflict
Individual versus team structure	Role overload
Skill variety	Role negotiability
Task significance	*Leadership*
Autonomy	Task-orientation
Feedback	Visionary
Information sharing	Problem solving
Human Resources Systems and Practices	
Recruitment planning and operations	
Selection processes and methods used	
Group and individualized socialization	
Training topics/programs and methods	
Basis of compensation	
Benefits and compensation elements	

Source: Arad, S., Hanson, M. A., & Schneider, R. J. (1997). Organizational context: Evidence for reliability and validity of the measures. In N. G. Peterson, M. D. Mumford, W. C. Borman, P. R. Jeanneret, E. A. Fleishman, & K. Y. Levin (Eds.), *O*NET Final Technical Report Vol. II* (Figure 7.1). Salt Lake City, UT: Utah Department of Workforce Services.

indicating that some type of postdoctoral certification is required. The type of instructional program is designated using one of 42 categories, and specific subject matter education is identified using one of 15 descriptors. As noted in the content model description, licensure information is also included in O*NET. Earnings data similar to those now included in the *Occupational Outlook Handbook* also appear in O*NET along with labor market information regarding growth of occupations and supply and demand for workers.

The result of the data collection efforts engaged in by the O*NET development committee is a massive amount of information. The amount of data is so vast that, if the data for one occupation were inserted in this book, it would take several pages to print it in its entirety. Additionally, as can probably be surmised from examining the titles of the elements in the database, the data about occupations are somewhat redundant because factors such as the abilities and knowledges converge in several instances.

Using the O*NET Database

Unlike the DOT, O*NET was not developed to be for use in print form, although it seems likely that a print version will be available. However, because of the massiveness of the database, and because the domains and elements within it are interrelated, the most appropriate use of the database is via a computer, either online (http://www.doleta.gov/programs/onet/) or through the CD-ROM version that was scheduled for release in 1999. The data to be accessed will be dependent on the user. For example, an employer who wishes to write job descriptions based on O*NET might simply access the portion of the database dealing with specific occupational skills. A college student who wishes to explore the skills levels required for various occupations might first estimate his or her own skills using a checklist based on the O*NET list and then match ratings to the skills levels listed in the database. The search could then be broadened by looking at related occupations. A high school student can determine the entry-level skills required for occupations he or she is exploring. Students and adult workers could explore interest occupations that are commensurate with their interests or simultaneously look at occupations that are congruent with both their interests and skills. Displaced workers might search for jobs that utilize skills similar to those required on their former jobs. Another of the almost endless possibilities for the use of O*NET is that, after doing a careful evaluation of a client's physical attributes, rehabilitation counselors can search for occupational options based on physical characteristics. Educational policy makers may look at the skills and knowledges included in O*NET in order to set standards for their institutions, and business leaders may look at the data dealing with work and organization context as a source of information about high-performance workplaces (Borman, Hanson, & Kubisiak, 1997). Clearly all of these recommendations are speculative because O*NET has not had the comprehensive testing that allows career development specialists to draw final conclusions about its utility.

Summary

Each of the systems discussed here—*DOT, GOE,* and O*NET—serves a particular purpose and provides information not available in either of the other two volumes. The *DOT* is the basic reference that provides the definition, industry designation, occupational grouping, and worker functions information. One can also identify other occupations in the occupational group that have comparable or fairly similar worker functions.

The *GOE,* as its title indicates, was developed to provide assistance in the exploration process. Walker (1980) emphasizes its value for both school counselors and job service counselors. Because it provides brief information about basic questions—What do you do? What skills do you need?—it can be used by clients who are just beginning to match themselves against possible occupations. It is just as valuable for the displaced worker, the reentry worker, or the worker involved in midlife reassessment, who all usually need the same kind of information as they examine occupations for which they have limited knowledge. Grouping occupations, as occurs in the subgroup arrangement, provides a basis for widening horizons by suggesting closely related possibilities that were probably unlikely to be considered.

Although both the *DOT* and *GOE* are extensive occupational databases, O*NET is more comprehensive because of the number of elements included in it. If O*NET lives up to its promise, it is the occupational database of the future. On the face of it, a relational database about occupations that can be accessed using a computer through various "windows," depending on the needs of the workers, seems likely to be embraced by users and counselors alike. As we will see in Chapter 7, the number of online sources of career and labor market information is growing. As will be shown in Chapter 8, tens of thousands of individuals already use computers in their efforts to access career information. The publication of O*NET appears likely to accelerate the use of computers and online information in career planning and career development programming. This is, of course, dependent on continuing support to keep the system updated and vigorous efforts to teach career counselors and others to use it.

References

Arad, S., Hanson, M. A., & Schneider, R. J. (1997). Organizational context: Evidence for reliability and validity of the measures. In N. G. Peterson, M. D. Mumford, W. C. Borman, P. R. Jeanneret, E. A. Fleishman, & K. Y. Levin (Eds.), *O*NET Final Technical Report Vol. II* (Figure 7.1). Salt Lake City, UT: Utah Department of Workforce Services.

Borman, W. C., Jeanneret, P. R., Hanson, M. A., & Kubisiak, U. C. (1997). Issues in O*NET applications. In N. G. Peterson, M. D. Mumford, W. C. Borman, P. R. Jeanneret, E. A. Fleishman, & K. Y. Levin (Eds.), *O*NET Final Technical Report Vol. III* (pp. 15-1 to 15-21). Salt Lake City, UT: Utah Department of Workforce Services.

Borman, W. C., Jeanneret, P. R., Kubisiak, U. C., & Hanson, M. A. (1997). Generalized work activities: Evidence for reliability and validity of measures. In N. G. Peterson, M. D. Mumford, W. C. Borman, P. R. Jeanneret, E. A. Fleishman, & K. Y. Levin (Eds.), *O*NET Final Technical Report Vols. II & I* (Figures 6.2 & 11.1). Salt Lake City, UT: Utah Department of Workforce Services.

Borman, W. C., Hanson, M. A., & Kubisiak, U. C. (1997). Work styles: Evidence for the reliability and validity of measures. In N. G. Peterson, M. D. Mumford, W. C. Borman, P. R. Jeanneret, E. A. Fleishman, & K. Y. Levin (Eds.), *O*NET Final Technical Report Vol. II & I* (Figures 6.2 & 11.1). Salt Lake City, UT: Utah Department of Workforce Services.

Costanza, D. P., Fleishman, E. A., & Marshall-Mies, J. C. (1997). Knowledges: Evidence for the reliability and validity of measure. In N. G. Peterson, M. D. Mumford, W. C. Borman, P. R. Jeanneret, E. A. Fleishman, & K. Y. Levin (Eds.), *O*NET Final Technical Report Vol. I* (Table 4.2). Salt Lake City, UT: Utah Department of Workforce Services.

Department of Labor. (1977). *Dictionary of occupational titles* (4th ed.). Washington, DC: U.S. Government Printing Office.

Department of Labor. (1979). *Guide for occupational exploration.* Washington, DC: U.S. Government Printing Office.

Department of Labor. (1981). *Selected characteristics of occupations defined in the dictionary of occupational titles.* Washington, DC: U.S. Government Printing Office.

Department of Labor. (1991). *Dictionary of occupational titles* (4th ed., revised 1991). Washington, DC: U.S. Government Printing Office.

Droege, R. C., & Padgett, A. (1979). Development of an interest-oriented occupational classification system. *Vocational Guidance Quarterly, 27,* 302–310.

Farr, J. M. (Ed.). (1993). *The complete guide for occupational exploration.* Indianapolis, IN: JIST.

Fleishman, E. A., Costanza, D. P., & Marshall-Mies, J. C. (1997). Abilities: Evidence for reliability and validity of measures. In. N. G. Peterson, M. D. Mumford, W. C. Borman, P. R. Jeanneret, E. A. Fleishman, & K. Y. Levin (Eds.), *O*NET Final Technical Report Vol. II* (Figure 9.1). Salt Lake City, UT: Utah Department of Workforce Services.

Harrington, T. F., & O'Shea, A. J. (Eds.). (1984). *Guide for occupational exploration* (2nd ed.). Minneapolis: National Forum Foundation.

Holland, J. L. (1997). *Making vocational choices: A theory of vocational personalities and work environments* (3rd ed.). Odessa, FL: Psychological Assessment Resources.

Jones, L. K. (1980). Holland's typology and the new *Guide for occupational exploration:* Bridging the gap. *Vocational Guidance Quarterly, 29,* 70–76.

Maze, M., & Mayall, D. (1991). *Enhanced guide for occupational exploration.* Indianapolis, IN: JIST.

Mumford, M. D., & Peterson, N. G. (1995). Introduction. In N. G. Peterson, M. D. Mumford, W. C. Borman, P. R. Jeanneret, & E. A. Fleishman (Eds.), *Development of prototype occupational information network (O*NET) Content Model, Vol. I* (pp. 2-1 to 2-31). Salt Lake City, UT: Utah Department of Workforce Services.

Mumford, M. D., Peterson, N. G., & Childs, R. A. (1997). Basic and cross-functional skills: Evidence for the reliability and validity of measures. In N. G. Peterson, M. D. Mumford, W. C. Borman, P. R. Jeanneret, E. A. Fleishman, & K. Y. Levin (Eds.), *O*NET Final Technical Report Vol. II.* Salt Lake City, UT: Utah Department of Workforce Services.

Nottingham, J., & Golec, J. (Undated). *Prototype development of the O*NET: The occupational information network.* Raleigh, NC: North Carolina Occupational Analysis Field Center.

Prediger, D. J. (1981). Getting "ideas" out of the *DOT* and into vocational guidance. *Vocational Guidance Quarterly, 29,* 293–305.

Strong, M. H., Jeanneret, P. R., McPhail, S. M., & Blakely, B. R. (1997). Work context: Evidence for reliability and validity of measures. In N. G. Peterson, M. D. Mumford, W. C. Borman, P. R. Jeanneret, E. A. Fleishman, & K. Y. Levin (Eds.), *O*NET Final Technical Report Vol. II* (Figure 7.1). Salt Lake City, UT: Utah Department of Workforce Services.

Walker, M. J. (1980). Guide for occupational exploration. *Occupational Outlook Quarterly, 24,* 26–28.

6

Other Classification Systems

In Chapter 5, three comprehensive occupational classification systems were presented. Each of these systems was developed to meet specific needs. The first edition of the *DOT* was developed by the federal government in response to the Great Depression of the 1930s. Millions of people were searching for work, and agencies such as the Employment Security Commission needed a way to classify jobs and to estimate the potential of job seekers to fill various occupations. The *Guide for Occupational Exploration (GOE)*, which was developed by the U.S. Department of Labor and is now published by JIST Works (Farr, 1993), grew out of the need to relate interests, abilities, and values to the information in the *DOT*. Both the *DOT* and the *GOE* systems provide a basis for comparing occupations with regard to several criteria and are thus somewhat useful to career decision makers. O*NET (DOL, 1998) was commissioned partially in response to the fact that the information in the *DOT* was dated. It was also developed as a tool to help workers who had lost their jobs as a result of corporate restructuring or permanent changes in the occupational structure to identify occupations in which they could use their skills. However, the O*NET database is a much more dynamic system than either the *DOT* or *GOE* system because of the richness and extent of the information. Moreover, it should be more accessible, easier to use, and simpler to maintain than the earlier systems because it is on-line and computerized.

The major problem with the systems described in Chapter 5 is that they provide such a vast amount of information they may have limited utility with some client groups, particularly those at the early stages of occupational exploration. Moreover, agencies such as the Bureau of the Census require somewhat simpler classification systems than either the *DOT* or O*NET to parsimoniously describe the occupational structure of this country in their reports. The desire to provide simpler conceptual models has been one driving force behind the development of new classification systems. Another driving force that has led to the development of some occupational classification systems has been the need to link the results of interest and values to the occupational structure. Currently, most of the systems devised to link inventory results to occupations focus on the *DOT* system. However, it seems likely that this will change in the near future as O*NET assumes more importance as a source of occupational information. The result of these forces is that numerous alternative occupational classifications systems have been developed.

The purpose of this chapter is to introduce some of the more well-known alternative classification systems and to discuss their uses. In the section that follows, five classification systems will be presented that were developed primarily to help client groups better understand the occupational structure and to make better, more informed career choices as a result. These systems are the ones developed by Roe (1956), Holland's classification system (Gottfredson, Holland, & Ogawa, 1982; Gottfredson & Holland, 1996), the World of Work Map (Hanson, 1974; Prediger, Swaney, & Mau, 1993), and the *Minnesota Occupational Classification System III* (Dawis, Dohm, Lofquist, Chartrand, & Due, 1987) and the Cubic classification system (D'Costa & Winefordner, 1969). These presentations will be followed by discussions of two systems that were designed primarily for use by governmental agencies interested in classifying businesses and industries: the *Standard Industrial Classification* (OMB, 1997) and the *Standard Occupational Classification* (DOL, 1998) system.

Roe's Field and Level Classification System

The *DOT* and O*NET are complex systems that are not easily mastered by practitioners unless they are used on a daily basis. One of the earliest attempts to develop a classification system that is more user friendly than the *DOT* occupational classification system was undertaken by Roe (1957; Roe & Klos, 1972; Roe & Lunneborg, 1984). Roe's two-dimensional system classified occupations by field, or the focus of activity of the work, and level, which pertains to the responsibility involved and complexity of the work. Roe identified eight fields that constitute the rows in her classification system:

1. Service (e.g., social work, counseling, protective services)
2. Business contact (e.g., sales)
3. Organization (e.g., managerial occupations)
4. Technology (e.g., engineering, machine trades, transportation)
5. Outdoor (e.g., farming, fishing)
6. Science (e.g., physical, biological, and human sciences)
7. General culture (e.g., education, journalism, humanities)
8. Arts and entertainment (e.g., artists, dancers, actors)

The six levels of performance in Roe's (Roe & Klos, 1972) occupational classification system are based on the degree of responsibility, capacity, or skills required. These are listed below:

1. Professional and managerial I: Top-level administrators and managers
2. Professional and managerial II: Narrower, more circumscribed autonomy than managers in Level I
3. Semiprofessional and small business: low-level responsibility of others
4. Skilled: specialized training required
5. Semiskilled: some specialized training, but less skilled
6. Unskilled: no specialized training required

A fuller illustration of Roe's classification is shown in Table 6.1. The advantage of Roe's system, as compared to the *DOT*, O*NET, and other systems, is that it can provide clients with a quick overview of the entire occupational structure, some general ideas about the activities involved, an indication of the linkages that exist among jobs, and some basic understanding of the degree of responsibilities involved in various jobs. The obvious disadvantages of Roe's system are that it does not provide detailed descriptions of the duties performed in various occupations, lacks information about aptitudes required to acquire job-related skills, and tells us little about training time.

Holland's Classification System

In Chapter 2, Holland's Theory of Vocational Choice was presented. The most fundamental proposition of the theory is that, in order to be satisfied with their jobs, people must select occupations that are congruent with their personality types (Holland, 1997). In Holland's approach to career counseling, personality is determined by the administration of an instrument such as the Self-Directed Search (Holland, 1994a) or the Vocational Personality Inventory (Holland, 1997). These inventories yield scores for each of six types that were described in Chapter 2: realistic, investigative, artistic, social, enterprising, and conventional. Holland believes that all six dimensions of personality contribute to vocational choice making and satisfaction. However, he believes that the three types with the highest scores are most important; the type with the highest score being of primary importance, the type with the second highest score being of secondary importance, and the type with the third highest score being of tertiary importance.

Work environments also have "personalities" that can be determined by examining the Holland types (personalities) of the workers in those environments or by looking at the characteristics of the job analysis data to determine the functions performed by workers on the job (Gottfredson, 1991). Personalities of work environments can also be determined using the Position Classification Inventory (Gottfredson & Holland, 1991). In order to make choices that will result in satisfaction and enhance achievement, people must have access to data that permit them to compare their personality to the "personality" of the environment. In 1982 Gottfredson, Holland, and Ogawa published the *Dictionary of Holland Occupational Codes (DHOC)* that provided three-letter Holland codes for the 12,099 jobs listed in the third edition of the *DOT* (DOL, 1977). In 1989, Gottfredson and Holland published the second edition of the *DHOC* in an expanded version that attempted to

TABLE 6.1   Roe's Two-Way Classification of Occupations

Level	I Service	II Business Contact	III Organization	IV Technology

1
Professional &
managerial
(individual
responsibility)
	Personal
	  therapists
	Social work
	  supervisors
	Counselors
		Promoters	U.S. President &
			  cabinet officers
			Industrial tycoons
			International
			  bankers
				Inventive geniuses
				Consulting or chief
				  engineers
				Ship's commanders

2
Professional &
managerial
	Social workers
	Occupational
	  therapists
	Probation truant
	  officers (with
	  training)
		Promoters
		Public relations
		  counselors
			C.P.A.'s
			Business and
			  government
			  executives
			Union officials
				Applied scientists
				Factory managers
				Ship's officers

3
Semiprofessional
and small
business
	YMCA officials
	Detectives, police
	  sergeants
	Welfare workers
	City inspectors
		Salesmen;
		  auto, bond,
		  insurance
		Dealers, retail &
		  wholesale
		Confidence men
			Accountants,
			  average
			Employment
			  managers
			Owners, catering,
			  dry-cleaning,
			  etc.
				Aviators
				Contractors
				Foremen (*DOT* II)
				Radio operators

4 Skilled	Barbers Chefs Practical nurses Policemen	Auctioneers Buyers (*DOT* I) House canvassers	Cashiers Clerks Foremen, warehouse Salesclerks	Blacksmiths Electricians Foremen (*DOT* I) Mechanics

5
Semiskilled
	Taxi drivers
	General
	  houseworkers
	City firemen
		Peddlers	Clerks, file, stock,
			  etc.
			Notaries
			Runners
				Bulldozer operators
				Truck drivers

6 Unskilled	Chambermaids Hospital attendants Watchmen		Messengers	Helpers Laborers Wrappers Yardmen

TABLE 6.1 *Continued*

V Outdoor	VI Science	VII General Cultural	VIII Arts and Entertainment
Consulting specialists	Research scientists Univ., col. faculties Medical specialists Museum curators	Supreme Court justices Univ., col. faculties Prophets Scholars	Creative artists Performers, great Teachers, university equivalent Museum curators

Applied scientists
Land owners and
   operators, large
Landscape architects
	Scientists, semi-
	   independent
	Nurses
	Pharmacists
	Veterinarians
		Editors
		Teachers, high school
		   and elementary
			Athletes
			Art critics
			Designers
			Music arrangers

County agents Farm owners Forest rangers Fish, game wardens	Technicians, medical, X-ray, museum Weather observers Chiropractors	Justices of the peace Radio announcers Reporters Librarians	Ad writers Designers Interior decorators Showmen
Laboratory testors, dairy products, etc. Miners	Technical assistants	Law clerks	Advertising artists Decorators, window, etc. Photographers

Gardeners
Farm tenants
Teamsters
	Veterinary hospital
	   attendants
			Illustrators, greeting
			   cards
			Showcard writers
			Stagehands

Dairy hands
Farm laborers
Lumberjacks
	Nontechnical helpers
	   in scientific
	   organization		

Source: Reprinted with permission from *The Psychology of Occupations* by A. Roe, p. 151. Copyright 1956 by John Wiley & Sons, Inc., New York.

eliminate the contradictions between *DOT* data and Holland codes present in the first edition of the *DHOC*. In 1996, the third edition of the *Dictionary of Holland Occupational Codes* (Gottfredson & Holland, 1996) was published. This edition of the *DHOC* contains three-letter Holland codes for all occupations listed in the fourth edition of the *DOT* (DOL, 1991), and it has been revised in some other significant ways. As in earlier editions, *DOT* code numbers are provided so that users can go directly to that source for additional information. *Guide for Occupational Exploration* (*GOE*) (Farr, 1993) codes are also provided, but they have been placed in an appendix in the third edition. *GOE* codes have been replaced by *Occupational Outlook Handbook* codes in the main body of the *DHOC* as well as the college major (CIP) codes developed by the Department of Education. Occupational Employment Statistics (OES) codes are also provided in the third edition of the *DHOC*. These code numbers are used by the Census Bureau to classify occupations. Finally, in keeping with earlier editions, General Educational Development (GED) and Specific Vocational Preparation (SVP) data from the *DOT* are provided in the third edition of the *DHOC*.

The Occupations Finder is a miniversion of the *DHOC* and was developed by Holland (1994b) for use with the Self-Directed Search. The Occupations Finder contains three-letter Holland codes for well over one thousand occupations, along with *DOT* codes and GED information. The occupations in this publication are those that are most prevalent in our occupational structure. A few examples of the Holland environmental codes follow:

Carpenter	RIE
Bridge Inspector	RSI
Fashion Artist	AEI
Composer	ASE
Occupational Analyst	IES
Auditor, Internal	ICR
Psychologist, Counseling	SIA
Librarian	SAI
Career Counselor	SAE
Park Superintendent	ERA
Detective, Chief	ESC
Cashier	CSE
Programmer, Chief	CEI

Holland's classification has some limitations that should be taken into consideration before using it with clients. First, Holland recognizes that work environments are rarely homogeneous and suggests that the best approach is to help potential workers focus on that aspect of environment that will be most influential. For example, counselors are typically SAEs (social, artistic, enterprising), but they operate in many environments depending on their positions. Some counselors are involved with massive amounts of paperwork, must use computers, and are required to engage in extensive recordkeeping, all of which are more compatible with conventional or investigative personality types than they are with the preferences of SAEs. Holland also suggests that the size and complexity of the work environment, the relative power and influence of various people in the environment, and the perceptions of the worker also influence how the environment will affect the worker.

Holland's classification system (Gottfredson & Holland, 1996) is useful only to those practitioners who are interested in applying his theory in their work. However, because of the popularity of the Self-Directed Search, the use of Holland's theoretical constructs to organize the presentation of the data from the Strong Interest Inventory and the development of other inventories that measure Holland's constructs such as the Harrington–O'Shea Career Decision-Making Inventory, it is likely that most practitioners will encounter Holland's classification system. In fact, a classification system based to some degree on Holland's work will be considered next.

The World-of-Work Map

The current World-of-Work Map (ACT, 1995a) is based on a series of studies (Hanson, 1974; Prediger, 1976, 1981, 1982) and position papers (Prediger & Swaney, 1995; Prediger, Swaney, & Mau, 1993) and is an extension of Holland's hexagon, which was shown in Chapter 2. Prediger and associates (1993) suggest that the World-of-Work Map is more useful than the Holland's (1997) classification system because it is difficult to see relationships among the occupations within the three-letter codes used by Holland (Gottfredson & Holland, 1996). Therefore, when the Holland classification system is used to help identify potential occupational choices, it may not only be difficult to help clients identify all occupations that are related to their personality type, some choices that should be considered may be overlooked.

The World-of-Work Map shows the locations of the twenty-three job families based on their relationships to four primary work tasks: working with data, people, things, and ideas. The job families are also grouped according to six general areas of the world of work which are analogous to Holland types: business contact (enterprising), business operations (conventional), technical (realistic), science (investigative), arts (artistic), and social service (social). Holland types are designated on the map with the traditional R, I, A, S, E, C code letters. The World-of-Work-Map is shown in Figure 6.1 and the job cluster and job family list is presented in Figure 6.2. American College Testing distributes Job Family Charts (ACT, 1995b) that list over 500 occupations by job cluster, job family, and the level of preparation required.

The World-of-Work Map is an interpretive device and is used in conjunction with the Unisex Edition of the ACT Interest Inventory (UNIACT) (Swaney, 1995).

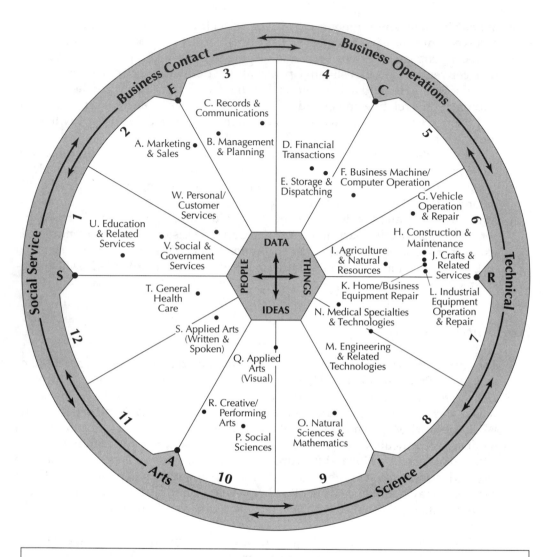

About The Map

- The World-of-Work Map arranges job families (groups of similar jobs) into 12 regions. Together, the job families cover all U.S. jobs. Although the jobs in a family differ in their locations, most are located near the points shown.

- A job family's location is based on its primary work tasks—working with DATA, IDEAS, PEOPLE, and THINGS.

- Six general areas of the work and related Holland types are indicated around the edge of the map. Job Family Charts (available from ACT) list over 500 occupations by general area, job family, and preparation level. They cover more than 95% of the labor force.

FIGURE 6.1   World-of-Work Map

Source: © 1995 by American College Testing (ACT), Iowa City, Iowa 52243. Used by permission of ACT.

FIGURE 6.2   Job Cluster and Job Family List

Business Contact Job Cluster

A. Marketing and Sales Job Family
Sales workers in stores; route drivers (milk, etc.); buyers; travel agents; sales workers who visit customers (real estate and insurance agents; stock brokers; farm products, office and medical supplies sales workers)

B. Management and Planning Job Family
Store, motel, restaurant, and agribusiness managers; office supervisors; purchasing agents; managers in large businesses; recreation/parks managers; medical records administrators; urban planners

Business Operations Job Cluster

C. Records and Communications Job Family
Office, library, hotel, and postal clerks; receptionists; computer tape librarians; office, medical, and legal secretaries; court reporters; medical record technicians

D. Financial Transactions Job Family
Bookkeepers; accountants; grocery check-out clerks; bank tellers; ticket agents; insurance underwriters; financial analysts

E. Storage and Dispatching Job Family
Shipping and receiving clerks; mail carriers; truck, cab, and airline dispatchers; cargo agents; air traffic controllers

F. Business Machine/Computer Operation Job Family
Computer console, printer, etc., operators; office machine operators; typists; word-processing equipment operators; statistical clerks

Technical Job Cluster

G. Vehicle Operation and Repair Job Family
Bus, truck, and cab drivers; auto, bus, and airplane mechanics; forklift operators; merchant marine officers; airplane pilots

H. Construction and Maintenance Job Family
Carpenters; electricians; painters; custodians (janitors); bricklayers; sheet metal workers; bulldozer and crane operators; building inspectors

I. Agriculture and Natural Resources Job Family
Farmers; foresters; ranchers; landscape gardeners; tree surgeons; plant nursery workers; pet shop attendants

J. Crafts and Related Services Job Family
Cooks; meatcutters; bakers; shoe repairers; piano/organ tuners; tailors; jewelers

K. Home/Business Equipment Repair Job Family
Repairers of TV sets, appliances, typewriters, telephones, heating systems, photocopiers, etc.

L. Industrial Equipment Operation and Repair Job Family
Machinists; printers; sewing machine operators; welders; industrial machinery repairers; production painters; laborers and machine operators in factories, mines, etc.; firefighters

M. Engineering and Other Applied Technologies Job Family
Engineers and engineering technicians in various fields; biological and chemical lab technicians; computers programmers; computer service technicians; drafters; surveyors; technical illustrators; food technologists

(continued)

FIGURE 6.2   *Continued*

N. Medial Specialties and Technologies Job Family
   Dental hygienists; EEG and EKG technicians; opticians; prosthetics technicians; X-ray technologists; medical technologists; dentists; optometrists; pharmacists; veterinarians

O. Natural Sciences and Mathematics Job Family
   Agronomists; biologists; chemists; ecologists; geographers; geologists; horitculturists; mathematicians; physicists

P. Social Sciences Job Family
   Marketing research analysts; anthropologists; economists; political scientists; psychologists; sociologists

Arts Job Cluster

Q. Applied Arts (Visual) Job Family
   Floral designers; merchandise displayers; commercial artists; fashion designers; photographers; interior designers; architects; landscape architects

R. Creative/Performing Arts Job Family
   Entertainers (comedians, etc.); actors/actresses; dancers; musicians, singers; writers; art, music, etc. teachers

S. Applied Arts (Written and Spoken) Job Family
   Advertising copywriters; disk jockeys; legal assistants; advertising account executives; interpreters; reporters; public relations workers; lawyers; librarians; technical writers

Social Service Job Cluster

T. General Health Care Job Family
   Orderlies; dental assistants; licensed practical nurses; physical therapy assistants; registered nurses; dietitians; occupational therapists; physicians; speech pathologists

U. Education and Related Services Job Family
   Teacher aides; preschool teachers; athletic coaches; college teachers; guidance/career/etc., counselors; elementary and secondary school teachers; special education teachers

V. Social and Government Services Job Family
   Security guards; recreation leaders; police officers; health/safety/food/etc., inspectors; child welfare workers; home economists; rehabilitation counselors; social workers

W. Personal/Customer Services Job Family
   Grocery baggers; bellhops; flight attendants (stewards, stewardesses); waitresses and waiters; cosmetologists (beauticians); barbers; butlers and maids

Source: ACT (1995). By permission of American College Testing.

ACT has developed several programs that include the UNIACT. These programs include (1) DISCOVER, which is a computer-based system that can be used to guide individual career planning; (2) The Career Planning Program (CPP) which is a paper and pencil program that involves UNIACT as well as several aptitude tests; (3) Vocational Interests, Experience, and Skill Assessment, an abbreviated version of CPP that substitutes self-ratings of ability for the battery of tests used in CPP; and (4) *Take Hold of Your Future,* a workbook used primarily in college-level career planning courses. Because UNIACT is included in all these programs, approximately 4.2 million people are exposed to the World-of-Work Map each year (Prediger & Swaney, 1995).

Minnesota Occupational Classification System III (MOC III)

MOC III (Dawis et al., 1987) was developed for use with the Theory of Work Adjustment (Dawis & Lofquist, 1984), which was presented in Chapter 2. As the name suggests, it is the third attempt at developing a classification system for this use. Both the first (Dawis & Lofquist, 1974) and the second (Dawis, Lofquist, Henley, & Rounds, 1982) classified relatively small numbers of occupations and had limited utility as a result. However, *MOC III* classifies all occupations in the third edition of the *DOT* (DOL, 1977) and is thus a comprehensive classification system worthy of consideration.

MOC III classifies occupations into sets of related occupations called taxons on the basis of abilities required to perform the job and the reinforcers available in the work environment. The authors suggest that the ability requirements for jobs can be divided into eight categories based on the perceptual, cognitive, and motor skills required to perform the tasks associated with the jobs. Moreover, they suggest that the reinforcements provided by occupations also fall into eight categories based on the extent to which they reinforce Internal values (achievement, autonomy, and status), social values (coworkers, social service, and moral), or environmental values (human relations, supervision, technical, activity, independence, variety, compensation, security, working conditions). The job abilities categories were developed using data from two sources: the Occupational Ability Patterns (DOL, 1979a) and job analysis data used in the development of the second edition of the *DOT* (DOL, 1965). The classification of workplace reinforcers is based on research by Shubsachs, Rounds, Dawis, and Lofquist (1978). It is based on the needs measured by the Minnesota Satisfaction Questionnaire (Weiss, Dawis, England, & Lofquist, 1967). The eight-by-eight classification system resulted in sixty-four taxons, which are shown in Table 6.2.

While the taxons listed in Table 6.3 represent the basic structure of *MOC III*, the authors went on to develop 729 subtaxons which include all occupations included in the third edition of the *DOT* (DOL, 1977). In Figure 6.3 is a sample page from *MOC III*. As can be seen, a great deal of data are presented in addition to the information about Occupational Requirements and Occupational Reinforcers. The occupations included in this subtaxon require average ability in the three occupational requirement areas, and they provide high levels of reinforcers for internal, social, and environment values. The nine-digit *DOT* code numbers for the occupations included in the subtaxon are broken down by group (GRP) and relationship to data, people, and things codes (DPT). The extended code (EC) is provided as well. Other data included on this page include interest (INT) information derived from the second edition of the *DOT* (DOL, 1965) as well as temperament (TMP)

TABLE 6.2 Structure of Primary Taxons in *MOCS III*

Ability Requirements	Occupational Reinforcers							
	Internal Social Environment	Internal Social	Internal Environment	Social Environment	Internal	Social	Environment	No Significant Reinforcers
Perceptual cognitive motor	1	2	3	4	5	6	7	8
Perceptual cognitive	9	10	11	12	13	14	15	16
Perceptual motor	17	18	19	20	21	22	23	24
Cognitive motor	25	26	27	28	29	30	31	32
Perceptual	33	34	35	36	37	38	39	40
Cognitive	41	42	43	44	45	46	47	48
Motor	49	50	51	52	53	54	55	56
No significant abilities	57	58	59	60	61	62	63	64

Source: Dawis, R. V., Dohm, T. E., Lofquist, L. H., Chartrand, J. M., Due, A. M. (1987). *Minnesota Occupational Classification System III*. By permission.

C

	DOT Title	Perceptual Abilities S, P, Q Average			Cognitive Abilities G, V, N Average			Job Des	Motor Abilities K, F, M Average							
		DOT Code			DOT Profile				Additional Data							
		GRP	DPT	EC	INT	TMP	PHY	DOT	OOH	FX	PR	OAP	SCH	ORP	ORC	INV
Internal AUT ACH High	Bookmaker bookie	187	167	014	56	059	L45	128	000	MOD	MOD	00	VI	NO		
	Gambling Dealer	343	467	018	56	059	L45	236	000	MOD	MOD	00	VI	NO		
STA	Office-Machine Servicer business-machine mechanic office-equipment mechanic office-machine inspector	633	281	018	190	OY	LMH 2346	553	371	LOW	MOD	21	FI	YES	C	
Social ALT High	Ring Conductor	159	367	010	56	059	L45	091	000	MOD	MOD	00	VI	NO		
	Sales Agent, Insurance insurance agent	250	257	010	26	579	L	204	255	MOD	MH	42	VI	YES	C	SK
	Sales Agent, Real Estate real estate agent	250	357	018	26	579	L	204	261	MOD	MH	43	VI	YES	C	SK
Environment COM SAF High	Sales Agent, Securities broker, securities registered representative securities advisor stockbroker	251	157	010	26	579	L	204	263	MOD	MH	60	VI	YES	C	

Occupational Reinforcers

GRP -- DOT (1977) Occupational Group (3-digit code)
DPT -- DOT (1977) Worker-Function Code for data, people, things
EC --- DOT (1977) extended code (last three digits)
INT -- Interests (DOT, Vol. II. Occupational Classification -- third edition 1965)
TMP -- Temperaments (DOT, Vol. II., Occupational Classification -- third edition 1965)
PHY -- Physical Demands (DOT, Vol. II., Occupational Classification -- third edition 1965)
DOT -- Page number for Occupational Description in the DOT (1977)
OOH-- Page number in the Occupational Outlook Handbook (1986-1987)
FX --- Estimated Flexibility of the Work Environment
PR --- Occupational Prestige Level
OAP -- Occupational Aptitude Pattern (where available)
SCH -- Schedule of Reinforcement
ORP -- Availability of Occupational Reinforcer Pattern
ORC -- Occupational Reinforcer Cluster (where available)
INV -- Interest Inventory Containing Occupational Scale (where available)

FIGURE 6.3   Taxon 057 from *MOC III*

and physical demands information from that same source (PHY). Page numbers from the 1977 *DOT* (DOL) and the 1986–1987 *Occupational Outlook Handbook* (*OOH*) are also provided. The *OOH* data are of little value today.

Other data provided include the estimated flexibility of the work environments, or the extent to which worker capabilities can deviate from job requirements (FX) (low, moderate, high), the occupational prestige (PR) (average, moderate, moderately high, high) of the occupations included in the taxon, the Occupational Aptitude Patterns (OAP) as determined from data from the General Aptitude Test Battery (DOL, 1979b), the schedule of occupational reinforcers (SCH) (fixed, variable, ratio, or interval) in the workplace, whether an occupational reinforcement schedule has been developed (ORP), the occupational reinforcer cluster to which the job belongs if it is available (ORC), and the interest inventory containing the occupational scale of the occupation when it is available (INV).

The authors of *MOC III* (Dawis et al., 1987) suggest that the classification system has many uses including helping people who have taken assessment devices locate work environments that correspond to their personalities. The comprehensiveness of the system poses an obvious advantage in this regard and a few disadvantages as well. The complexity of the system is a major disadvantage, and it is apparent that counselors using the system not only need to be conversant with the Theory of Work Adjustment, but they would have to be skilled in the use of the instruments employed within that system to measure constructs such as needs and values. The system also requires some familiarity with the General Aptitude Test Battery, but many career development practitioners have these competencies and, for those who do not, gaining this understanding is not an insurmountable obstacle. Perhaps the biggest problem with *MOC III* is that parts of it are based on information that is quite dated. For example, while the data in the various editions of the *DOT* stay relatively stable, each edition contains new titles, deletes some existing titles, and contains some new job analysis information. Because *MOC III* relies heavily on the second edition of the *DOT* (DOL, 1965), the utility of some of the information is questionable.

Standard Occupational Classification (SOC)

As was noted at the outset, most occupational classification systems were developed in response to a specific need. The *Standard Occupational Classification* (SOC) (U.S. Department of Commerce, 1980), which was published initially in 1977 and revised in 1980, was developed in response to the need for a unified system that could be used by a variety of state and federal agencies. In 1995, the Office of the Management of the Budget (OMB) indicated that the 1980 version of the SOC had not been fully utilized by federal agencies involved in gathering occupational information and announced its intention to revise the system. A Standard Occupational Revision Policy Committee (SORPC) was formed. This committee developed a set of guiding policies for the revision of the SOC that were, for the most part, similar to those that underpinned the earlier versions of the system. They can be found on the Internet at (http://stats.bls.gov/soc/sco%5Foct5.htm, p. 3).

1. The classification system should cover all occupations in which work is performed for pay or profit, including work performed in family-operated enterprises in which family members are not directly compensated. It should exclude occupations unique to volunteers.
2. The classification should reflect the current occupational structure of the United States and have sufficient flexibility to assimilate new occupations into the structure as they become known.
3. While striving to reflect the current occupational structure, the classification should maintain linkages with past systems.
4. Occupations should be classified based on work performed, skills, education, training, licensing, and credentials.
5. Occupations should be classified in homogeneous groups that are defined so that the content of each group is clear.
6. Each occupation should be assigned to only one group at the lowest level of the classification.
7. The size of an occupational group should not be a major reason for including or excluding it from separate identification.
8. Supervisors should be identified separately from the workers they supervise whenever possible. An exception should be made for professional and technical occupations, in which supervisors should be classified with the groups they supervise.
9. Apprentices and trainees should be classified with the occupations for which they are being trained, while helpers and aides should be classified separately, since they are not in training for the occupation they are assisting.
10. Comparability with the International Standard Occupational Classification of Occupations should be considered in the structure but should not be an overriding factor in it.

The SORPC used the Occupational Employment Statistics occupational classification system as their point of departure in the development of the new SOC. Information from O*NET and an automated version of the *DOT* were also used as sources of information in the developmental process. The result of the effort to revise the SOC is a classification system that contains four levels of aggregation of occupations. These are (1) major groups, (2) minor groups, (3) broad occupations, and (4) detailed occupations. There are 23 major groups, 98 minor groups, 449 broad occupations, and 810 detailed occupations in the system. The 23 major groups and their codes found in the new system are:

11-0000 Management Occupations
13-0000 Business and Financial Operations Occupations

15-0000 Computer and Mathematical Occupations
17-0000 Architecture and Engineering Occupations
19-0000 Life, Physical, and Social Science Occupations
21-0000 Community and Social Service Occupations
23-0000 Legal Occupations
25-0000 Education, Training, and Library Occupations
27-0000 Arts, Design, Entertainment, Sports, and Media Occupations
29-0000 Healthcare Practitioners and Technical Occupations
31-0000 Healthcare Support Occupations
33-0000 Protective Service Occupations
35-0000 Food Preparation and Serving Related Occupations
37-0000 Building and Grounds Cleaning and Maintenance Occupations
39-0000 Personal Care and Service Occupations
41-0000 Sales and Related Occupations
43-0000 Office and Administrative Support Occupations
45-0000 Farming, Fishing, and Forestry Occupations
47-0000 Construction and Extraction Occupations
49-0000 Installation, Maintenance, and Repair Occupations
51-0000 Production Occupations
53-0000 Transportation and Material Moving Occupations
55-0000 Military Specific Occupations

Each item in the classification system has been assigned a six-digit code. As can be seen above, the first two digits represent the major group. These numbers end in 0000. The third digit in the number represents the minor group. These numbers end with 000. The fourth and fifth digits in the system represent the broad occupation (these end with 0; e.g., Counselors) and the sixth digit represents the detailed occupation.

21-0000 COMMUNITY AND SOCIAL SERVICES OCCUPATIONS
  (major group)
21-1000 COUNSELORS, SOCIAL WORKERS, AND OTHER
  COMMUNITY (minor group) AND SOCIAL SERVICE SPECIALISTS
  21-1010 Counselors (broad group)
    21-1011 Substance Abuse and Behavioral Disorder Counselors
      (detailed occupation)
    21-1012 Educational, Vocational, and School Counselors
    21-1013 Marriage and Family Therapists
    21-1014 Mental Health Counselors
    21-1015 Rehabilitation Counselors
    21-1019 Counselors, All Other
  21-1020 Social Workers
    21-1021 Child, Family, and School Social Workers
    21-1022 Medical and Public Health Social Workers
    21-1023 Mental Health and Substance Abuse Social Workers

21-1029 Social Workers, All Other
21-1090 Miscellaneous Psychosocial, Community, and Behavioral
    Specialists
21-1091 Health Educators
21-1092 Probation Officers and Correctional Treatment Specialists
21-1093 Social and Human Service Assistants
21-1099 Psychosocial, Community, and Behavioral Specialists,
    All Other

21-2000 RELIGIOUS WORKERS
    21-2010 Clergy
        21-2011 Clergy
    21-2020 Directors, Religious Activities and Education
        21-2021 Directors, Religious Activities and Education
    21-2090 Miscellaneous Religious Workers
        21-2099 Religious Workers, All Other

Nines (9s) are used at three levels in the coding system to designate residual categories that are "left over" from the next *highest* aggregate of occupations. Residual categories are easily identified because they contain the words "Other," "Miscellaneous," or "All Other." Minor group residuals contain all occupations not included in the major group aggregates. These numbers end in 9000. The numbers used to indicate broad occupation residuals that include occupations not included in minor group aggregations end in 90, and the numbers for the residuals for detailed occupations end in 9 in the new SOC system. These designations are illustrated below.

51-0000 PRODUCTION OCCUPATIONS
    51-1000 SUPERVISORS, PRODUCTION AND OPERATING WORKERS
    51-2000 ASSEMBLERS AND FABRICATORS
    51-3000 FOOD PROCESSING WORKERS
    51-4000 METALWORKERS AND PLASTIC WORKERS
    51-5000 PRINTING WORKERS
    51-6000 TEXTILE, APPAREL, AND FURNISHINGS WORKERS
    51-7000 WOODWORKERS
    51-8000 PLANT AND SYSTEM OPERATORS
    *51-9000 OTHER PRODUCTION OCCUPATIONS (minor group residual)
    **51-9190 Miscellaneous Production Workers (broad group residual)
    ***51-9199 Production Workers, All Other (detailed group residual)

All of the 810 detailed occupations within the SOC also have job descriptions attached to them. For example, 11-3021 Computer and Information Systems Managers "plan, direct, or coordinate activities in such fields as electronic data processing, information systems, systems analysis, and computer programming." Exclude "Computer Specialist" (15-1011 through 15-1099). Another example is

21-1012 Educational, Vocational, and School Counselors who "counsel individuals and provide group educational and vocational guidance services."

The primary purpose of the new Standard Occupational Classification is exactly the same as the one that it will replace: to provide governmental agencies with a uniform system for classifying occupations so that the data collected by each agency can be compared to data collected by other agencies in a meaningful fashion. The Office of Management and Budget has said that all federal agencies, including the Bureau of the Census and the Department of Labor, are expected to use the new system and OMB has invited state agencies to adopt it as well. The complete SOC system was published in late 1998 in two volumes. Volume One contains a description of the classification system and detailed occupational descriptions such as the ones provided above. Volume Two contains a list of over 30,000 job titles and industries taken from the 1990 census and their new SOC classification. Both manuals are available in print and on the Internet (http://stats.bls.gov/soc/soc_home.htm). Career counselors and other users of occupational information are likely to encounter the new system as the overarching classification system in the *Occupational Outlook Handbook,* since the SOC has been used for this purpose historically.

North American Industry Classification System (NAICS)

In 1937, a committee was established to develop a classification system for industries that would classify them based upon their economic processes. The Standard Industrial Classification System (SIC), which was first published in 1939, was the product of this committee. Although the SIC was revised from time to time (e.g., 1980, 1987), changes in the global economy and the economic relationships among the United States, Canada, and Mexico prompted the Office of Management and Budget (OMB), in conjunction with agencies from Canada and Mexico, to commission a new classification system to replace the SIC. The result was the (NAICS). One of the major reasons for developing the NAICS was to provide a basis for collecting economic data in the three countries involved that could be compared in a meaningful fashion.

NAICS (OMB, 1997) is a system for classifying establishments. An establishment is "an operating unity for which records provide information of the cost of resources—materials, labor and capital—employed to produce units of output" (p. 16). Generally speaking, establishments operate out of a single site or location, although this may not be the case for construction, transportation, and communication establishments. Moreover, several establishments may operate out of the same geographic location. For example, an airport terminal, which is classified as Transportation and Warehousing in NAICS, may involve several establishments such as restaurants, clothing stores, bookstores, and so forth. Establishments are not to be confused with enterprises (companies). Enterprises often operate multiple establishments located in several geographic locations. For example, International Business Machines (IBM) operates establishments that (1) manage the operation, (2) manufacture the products sold by the company, (3) offer and deliver services such as consultation, and (4) conduct research and development work to name a few. The point here is that an establishment may exist for the sole purpose of supporting parts of a company or enterprise, it may produce a product, but it may not have receipts.

Establishments are classified within NAICS (OMB, 1997) using a six-digit code. The first two digits identify the sector to which the enterprise belongs, and the third digit identifies the subsector. The fourth and fifth digits designate the industry group and the NAICS group, respectively. The sixth digit in the code designates the national industry. If a zero (0) appears in the sixth place in the U.S. system, the national industry and the NAICS industry are identical. There are a total of 20 sectors, 96 subsectors, 311 industry groups, and 721 NAICS industries. There are 659 U.S. six-digit industries that are not identical to the NAICS designations and 511 that are, for a total of 1170 U. S. industries.

The 20 sector titles and code numbers are listed below.

11	Agriculture, Fishery, and Forestry
21	Mining
22	Utilities
23	Construction
31–33	Manufacturing
42	Wholesale Trade
44–45	Retail Trade
48–49	Transportation and Warehousing
51	Information
52	Finance and Insurance
53	Real Estate and Rental and Leasing
54	Professional, Scientific and Technical Services
55	Management Companies and Enterprises
56	Administrative and Support and Waste Management and Remediation Services
61	Educational Services
62	Health Care and Social Assistance
71	Arts, Entertainment, and Recreation
72	Accommodation and Food Services
81	Other Services (Except Public Administration)
92	Public Administration

NAICS contains the following information in addition to the six-digit classification designation.

- Lengthy sector and subsector descriptions in most instances.
- Brief descriptions of industry groups, NAICS industries, and U.S. Industries.
- A footnote system that designates whether the U.S. industry is equivalent to those in Mexico and Canada. For example, the following definition of a U.S.

industry includes the superscript CAN. This indicates that U.S. and Canadian Industries are comparable. Had US appeared after the six-digit code and title, it would have indicated that the industry is unique to the United States. If neither US nor CAN appears after the six-digit code and title, industries in the United States, Canada, and Mexico are viewed as comparable.

514191 On-Line Information Services.[CAN]   The U.S. industry comprises Internet access providers, Internet service providers, and similar establishments primarily engaged in providing direct access through telecommunication networks to computer-held information compiled or published by others.

Although, as noted above, the basis for classifying establishments is the production processes employed, industry codes (five- and six-digit codes) were assigned based upon the types of products or services produced. An example taken from Sector 22—Utilities may help to clarify this idea (OMB, 1997, p. 85)

Sector 22—Utilities

The Sector as a Whole.   The Utilities sector comprises establishments engaged in the provision of the following utility services: electric power, natural gas, steam supply, water supply, and sewage removal. Within this sector, the specific activities associated with the utility services vary by utility: electric power includes *generation, transmission,* and *distribution;* water supply includes *treatment* and *distribution;* natural gas includes *distribution;* steam supply includes *provision* and or *distribution,* and sewage removal includes *collection, treatment,* and *disposal* of waste through sewer systems or sewage treatment facilities (italics added to emphasize production processes).

221330 Steam and Air-Conditioning Supply.   This industry comprises establishments primarily engaged in providing *steam, heated air,* or *cooled air.* The steam distribution may be through mains (italics added to emphasize products provided).

NAICS is not a classification system that will be encountered frequently, if at all, by the typical career development specialist. It is included here for two reasons. First, NAICS illustrates one level of economic cooperation among nations, in this case the nations involved in the North American Free Trade Agreement. Second, NAICS brings the United States Canada, and Mexico one step closer to the adoption of a global classification system for industries. In 1990, the United Nations–sponsored International Standard Industrial Classification System (ISICS) was published. ISICS contains 17 broad sections, 60 divisions, 159 classes, and 292 classes. Although NAICS is not totally aligned with this system, attempts were made to calibrate the two systems. It seems likely that the future will bring greater congruence between them.

Summary

In this chapter several additional classification systems have been presented. All of them are widely used. None is ideal for every situation, and all have advantages as well as disadvantages. They are important to counselors and teachers, as well as to their clients and students, because classification systems provide a frame of reference that is helpful in understanding occupations and how they relate to one another.

References

ACT. (1995a). World-of-work map. Iowa City, IA: American College Testing.

ACT. (1995b). Job cluster and job family list. Iowa City, IA: American College Testing.

Dawis, R. V., Dohm, T. E., Lofquist, L. H., Chartrand, J. M., & Due, A. M. (1987). *Minnesota occupational classification system III*. Minneapolis: Vocational Psychology Research, University of Minnesota.

Dawis, R. V., & Lofquist, L. H. (1974). *Minnesota occupational classification system*. Minneapolis: Vocational Psychology Research, University of Minnesota.

Dawis, R. V., & Lofquist, L. H. (1984). *A psychological theory of work adjustment*. Minneapolis: University of Minnesota Press.

Dawis, R. V., Lofquist, L. H., Henley, G. A., & Rounds, J. B., Jr. (1982). *Minnesota occupational classification system II*. Minneapolis: Vocational Psychology Research, University of Minnesota.

D'Costa, A. G., & Winefordner, D. W. (1969). A cubist model of vocational interests. *Vocational Guidance Quarterly, 17*, 242–249.

DOL. (1965). *Dictionary of occupational titles* (2nd ed.). Washington, DC: U.S. Department of Labor.

DOL. (1977). *Dictionary of occupational titles* (3rd ed.). Washington, DC: U.S. Department of Labor.

DOL. (1979a). *Manual of the general aptitude test battery*. Washington, DC: U.S. Department of Labor.

DOL. (1979b). *General aptitude test battery*. Washington, DC: U.S. Department of Labor.

DOL. (1991). *Dictionary of occupational titles* (4th ed.). Washington, DC: U.S. Department of Labor.

DOL. (1998). O*NET (http://www.doleta.gov/programs/onet/) Washington, DC: Author.

Farr, J. M. (Ed.) (1993). *The complete guide for occupational exploration*. Indianapolis, IN: JIST.

Gottfredson, G. D. (1991, April). Using the Holland occupational-environment classification in research and practice. Paper presented at American Educational Research Association Conventions, Chicago, IL.

Gottfredson, G. D., & Holland, J. L. (1991). Position classification inventory. Odessa, FL: PAR.

Gottfredson, G. D. & Holland, J. L. (1996). *Dictionary of Holland occupational codes* (3rd ed.). Odessa, FL: PAR.

Gottfredson, G. D., Holland, J. L., & Ogawa, D. K. (1982). *Dictionary of Holland occupational codes*. Palo Alto, CA: CPP.

Hanson, G. (1974). *ACT research report 67: Assessing the career interests of college youth: Summary of research applications.* Iowa City, IA: American College Testing.

Holland, J. L. (1997). *Making vocational choices: A theory of vocational personalities and work environments* (3rd ed.). Englewood Cliffs, NJ: Prentice-Hall.

Holland, J. L. (1994a). *Self-directed search.* Odessa, FL: PAR.

Holland, J. L. (1994b). *The occupations finder.* Odessa, FL: PAR.

Nottingham, J., & Gulec, J. (Undated). *Prototype development of the O*NET: The occupational information network.* Raleigh, NC: North Carolina Occupational Analysis Field Center.

OMB. (1997). North American industry classification system. Washington, DC: Office of Management and Budget.

Prediger, D. J. (1976). A world-of-work map for career exploration. *Vocational Guidance Quarterly, 24,* 198–208.

Prediger, D. J. (1981). Getting "ideas" out of the *DOT* and into vocational guidance. *Vocational Guidance Quarterly, 29,* 293–306.

Prediger, D. J. (1982). Dimensions underlying Holland's hexagon: Missing link between interests and occupations? *Journal of Vocational Behavior, 21,* 259–287.

Prediger, D. J., & Swaney, K. B. (1995). Using UNIACT in a comprehensive approach to assessment for career planning. *Journal of Career Assessment.*

Prediger, D. J., Swaney, K. B., & Mau, W. C. (1993). Extending Holland's hexagon: Procedures, counseling applications, and research. *Journal of Counseling and Development, 71,* 422–428.

Roe, A. (1957). *The psychology of occupations.* New York: Wiley.

Roe, A., & Klos, D. (1972). Classification of occupations. In J. M. Whitely & A. Resnikoff (Eds.). *Perspectives on vocational guidance* (pp. 117–124). Alexandria, VA: American Personnel and Guidance Association (now ACA).

Roe, A., & Lunneborg, P. W. (1984). Personality development and career choice. In D. Brown & L. Brooks (Eds.), *Career Choice and Development,* 2nd ed. (pp. 68–101). San Francisco: Jossey-Bass.

Shubsachs, A. P. W., Rounds, J. B., Jr., Dawis, R. V., & Lofquist, L. H. (1978). Perceptions of work reinforcer systems: Factor structure. *Journal of Vocational Behavior, 13,* 54–62.

SORPC. (1997). Standard Occupational Classification Federal Register Notice: Part 1 SOC Classification Principles (*http://stats.bls.gov/soc/soc%5Foct5.htm*) Washington, DC: U.S. Department of Labor.

Swaney, K. B. (1995). *Technical manual: Revised unisex edition of the ACT interest inventory (UNIACT).* Iowa City, IA: American College Testing.

U.S. Department of Commerce, Office of Federal Statistical Policy and Standards. (1980). *Standard occupational classification manual.* Washington, DC: U.S. Government Printing Office.

U.S. Executive Office of the President, Office of Management and Budget. (1987). *Standard industrial classification manual.* Washington, DC: U.S. Government Printing Office.

Weiss, D. J., Dawis, R. V., England, G. W., & Lofquist, L. H. (1967). Minnesota satisfaction questionnaire. Minneapolis, MN: Vocational Psychology Research, University of Minnesota.

Winefordner, D. W. (1983). *Manual for interpreting Ohio vocational interest survey* (2nd ed.). San Antonio, TX: The Psychological Corporation.

7

Finding and Organizing Career and Labor Market Information

The rationale for increasing the emphasis on providing occupational information was established in Chapter 1. Surveys conducted by the National Career Development Association in conjunction with the Gallup Organization (e.g., Hoyt & Lester, 1995) have consistently found that approximately 70 percent of all workers would get more information about jobs if they were starting over. The career development theories presented in Chapter 2 strengthened the case for occupational information. For example, Gottfredson (1996) suggested that, without intervention, boys and girls would eliminate many appropriate career options. That intervention could and should be occupational data that suggest that gender is not a limiting factor in occupational success. This chapter focuses on two related types of information: career and labor market information. In 1976, members of Congress recognized the need for a better-organized and focused effort to collect and disseminate occupational information. They established the National Occupational Information Coordination Committee (NOICC) in that year. Nine federal agencies now cooperate in its operation. The purposes of the agency are to improve coordination, cooperation, and communication in the development of occupational information systems at the national and local levels; to standardize definitions, estimating procedures, and occupational classifications that meet common informational needs among various training programs; to assist state-level committees; to improve liaison between developers and users of occupational information; and to give special attention to young people's needs for labor market information. These goals, in simplest terms, are aimed at reducing overlap and preventing gaps in the development of occupational information and improving the quality and availability of materials.

The legislation that established NOICC also provided for similar organizations called State Occupational Information Coordinating Committees (SOICCs) in each state and territory. NOICC and the SOICCs, working cooperatively, embarked upon an extensive effort to develop Career Information Delivery Systems (CIDS). The intent of NOICC and the SOICCs is to provide better-quality occupational information to public school students, employment agencies, One Stop Career Centers, military bases, correctional institutions, libraries, and counseling centers at all levels. Their efforts include the development of statewide computerized networks of information about jobs and educational institutions. These are accessed by nine million users annually according to information on NOICC's home page (http://www.noicc.gov/). The SOICCs regularly publish "how-to-do-it" print materials for counselors and tabloids aimed at various client groups. Both NOICC and the SOICCs have provided extensive training in the use and delivery of occupational information. For example, NOICC, in cooperation with the National Career Development Association has engaged what are termed career development facilitators, who are sub–masters level practitioners who can deliver career development services in programs such as the welfare-to-work efforts. NOICC and many SOICCs also maintain websites so that potential users can readily determine the services available within their states. These sites can be accessed through the NOICC home page located at http://www.noicc.gov/. Finally, NOICC has developed and sponsored numerous publications including *Using Labor Market Information in Career Exploration and Decision Making: A Resources Guide* (NOICC, 1991). This guide has been used as the manual in countless seminars aimed at improving career counselor's and paraprofessional's ability to utilize various types of occupational information.

Two Types of Information

Career information includes educational, occupational, and psychosocial facts related to work. Although most of this chapter focuses on the location, organization, and delivery of career information, earlier chapters have laid the foundation for these discussions. Specifically, the discussions of O*NET, the *Dictionary of Occupational Titles (DOT)*, and the *Guide for Career Exploration (GOE)* in Chapter 5 have a direct relationship to the information that will be presented here. The *DOT* is related to this discussion because the material in that document serves as the underpinning of much current occupational information. The O*NET is related to this discussion because it represents the future basis of occupational information. All of the systems discussed in Chapter 5, including the *GOE*, have as their basic aim informing career decisions makers so that they can make better judgments regarding the suitability of careers.

Labor market information is also generated to provide career information to decision makers, but labor market information is collected and disseminated primarily for the purpose of informing policy makers. For example, the employment/ unemployment rate is of interest to individual decision makers because it may be one indictor of the difficulty or ease of the job search. However, Congress, the

United States Employment Security Commission, the Federal Reserve Committee, and a host of other agencies are interested in this figure because it may (1) indicate a need for legislation authorizing more or less funds for training and retraining programs, (2) suggest that the demand for employment placement services will increase or decrease, or (3) signal a positive or negative trend in the nation's economy. Labor market information includes data about the occupational structure and the trends that will shape it. For example, the Bureau of the Census collects and disseminates information about the numbers of people employed in various occupations. The Bureau of Labor Statistics collects data about the wages being paid to workers in various occupations and uses data from a variety of sources to make predictions about the future occupational structure as well as the demographic characteristics of the people employed in the labor market. In the future it seems likely that the Standard Occupational Classification, discussed in Chapter 6, will serve as the organizing scheme for reports from both of these agencies.

Not unexpectedly, given the differences in career information and labor market information, they are generated in decidedly different ways. Historically, information about specific careers was generated using job analysis techniques. Job analysis requires the observation of workers on the job to ascertain the functions they perform, the machines and tools required to perform their functions, the materials used on the job, the products produced, the nature of the work environment, and the worker traits (aptitudes, abilities, and temperaments) required to perform the job. The astute reader will recognize that the *DOT* contains elements that are the result of job analysis. As was noted in Chapter 5, the starting point for the development of the *DOT* was for the job analyst to cluster the 12,000 plus jobs in that system based on common characteristics. However, the developers of O*NET went one step further and asked workers in the jobs contained in the O*NET system to rate the nature of work they performed, the abilities needed to perform the job, and the nature of the work environment.

Labor market information is generated through various types of surveys ranging from those conducted by the Bureau of the Census to those conducted routinely by state Employment Security offices. A complete census is taken every 10 years, and thus these data on workers may be accurate for a relatively short period of time. However, state employment security agencies routinely collect labor market information within established geographic regions known as Standard Metropolitan Statistical Areas on a rotating three-year cycle. This provides relatively up-to-date-information about the labor market and the demographic makeup of the labor force on a regular basis.

Although, as stated, the primary focus of this chapter will be on career information, sources and types of labor information will also be discussed, particularly when the two types of information converge. For example, the *Occupational Outlook Handbook*, contains both labor market and career information in a format that is extremely useful to career decision makers. In addition to identifying different types of information, sections of this chapter deal with collecting, housing, and disseminating information.

Subtypes of Information

Over 30 years ago Kunze (1967) described a spectrum of occupational information that is, with a modicum of revision, still relevant today. In 1967 Kunze could not have anticipated the impact of technology on the access to and delivery of occupational information. Powerful personal computers using CD-ROM technology and the use of the Internet as a means of communication have begun to revolutionize the nature and use of occupational information. O*NET, a massive online database of career information has already been discussed. Other databases will be discussed in this chapter.

Kunze's (1967) spectrum, with revisions, can at once be construed to be a source of information by client-groups and as a delivery system by career development specialists. This spectrum includes:

1. Publications (print materials)
   a. Books and monographs that describe occupations
   b. Reports and brochures that contain labor market information
   c. Documents that contain both career and labor market information
2. Programmed materials
3. Audiovisual materials including films and videos
4. Computer-based, multimedia programs that contain interactive components, video clips, and graphics
5. Online storage and retrieval systems and publications
6. Simulated situations using CD-ROM technology, role play, mechanical trainers, and virtual reality job sites
7. Games
8. Occupational laboratories
9. Interviews with workers
10. Direct observation via field trips or job shadowing
11. Direct exploratory experiences such as work samples
12. Direct on-the-job tryouts using internships and part-time jobs

The Pros and Cons of Different Types of Information

Three criteria will guide the discussion in this section. These are (1) the cost of the material, (2) the nature of the involvement of clients when the material is utilized, and (3) the relative accessibility of the type of material.

Print materials include books, career monographs and bibliographies that describe workers and their careers in brief and in detail, occupational briefs that provide basic information about careers, governmental reports that provide information about occupational trends such as the *Occupational Outlook Handbook*, and related materials. At this time, print materials are still the most important source of occupational information because they are easy to reprint and devise. However, the placement of material on the Internet, the use of computerized systems to disseminate information, and the increasing availability of audiovisual material have already reduced the importance of print materials. Whether these forms of occupational information will become more important than print materials remains to be seen. Print materials are relatively easy to store in a media center or Career Resource Center, can be sent through facsimile machines, and can be scanned into computers and sent to users via e-mail. Two other important advantages of print materials are that they are portable, which increases their accessibility to users, and they are available for individuals at all stages of career development, including children and retirees.

Although print materials have several advantages, they also have a few disadvantages. One of these is that the reader is placed in the role of passive recipient of information. Also, some material, particularly that published by governmental agencies, is presented in an unattractive format. It should also be noted that these materials may not always be developed in a way that allows them to be highly useful for minority group members, despite guidelines for preparing print materials established by NCDA (1991b). Rodriguez (1994) found that, of the approximately 1000 pieces of print material submitted to the NCDA Information Review Service over approximately 10 years, only two pieces targeted minorities. She went on to describe a process that explored the best means of preparing materials for minorities. She concluded that material that contains specific job information as well as bibliographies of minorities in the occupation being discussed is the most effective when providing information to minorities.

Audiovisual materials such as videotapes and films are relatively expensive to acquire when compared to other types of information because of initial acquisition costs and the expense of acquiring and maintaining the equipment needed to view them. However, audiovisual materials have some distinct advantages that may offset the expense factor. The most obvious of the advantages is that audiovisual materials, such as videotapes, add sound and motion to the learning process as well visual images that may have greater impact than those provided in print material. Today it is possible to get high-quality materials that show workers from all ethnic groups of both sexes performing hundreds of jobs. In spite of the advantages of audiovisual materials, as stated previously, they place the learner in the role of a passive recipient of knowledge.

Computer-assisted career guidance systems (CACGS) may be quite expensive to acquire and maintain and may require that learners be given special instructions. CACGS do have several advantages when compared to other types of materials, however. One of these, as will be shown in a detailed discussion in Chapter 8, is that these systems can include several components such as assessment, career exploration, and occupational information. CACGS are interactive in nature and most CACGS incorporate CD-ROM technology. This technology allows sound and graphics to be added to the video presentation as well as greatly enhanced visual images.

Computers are revolutionizing the magnitude and accessibility of occupational information. Online database available from the SOICCs, commercial publishers, and governmental agencies make vast amounts of materials available to individuals who have Internet access. However, this serves as a major limitation of these materials unless users have a computer, an Internet service, and the proficiency needed to use the search strategies required. Moreover, the material stored in online systems and available in software packages is presented in on-screen text that has many similarities to print material. One advantage to some of these systems, when compared to print materials, is that they have built-in "search engines" that may allow a skilled user to get the information more easily. However, these search engines can be daunting to the unskilled Internet user.

Programmed print materials such as *Activities for Individualized Career Exploration and Planning* (AEL, 1994) include self-exploration exercises as well as career information. These materials are typically self-paced, are more interactive than print materials, relatively inexpensive, and are easy to store and maintain. These materials are not portable and are available to few client groups.

Simulations may range from simple role-playing exercises, where clients assume the role of the worker, to the use of highly sophisticated and expensive trainers such as those used in the training of airline pilots and astronauts. A middle ground between the simplistic role play and the sophisticated mechanical trainer is the simulations of rather complex work settings—such as in cities and hospitals—that are used in many public school career development programs. Recently, computer games such as SIMCITY have been produced using CD-ROM technology that, while not produced for this purpose, can be adapted to facilitate simulations. Simulations place clients in an interactive mode, can be developed to suit large groups, but may have limited accessibility. In the future, it seems likely that some career decision makers will have simulated access to work sites via virtual reality. Currently, the technology is available to produce these types of simulations, but the cost of doing so is prohibitive.

Games, such as the one based on *Jeopardy!* described later in this chapter, can be used at any age level, are inexpensive, and can be stored and maintained easily. Games, if properly used, can enhance motivation by making an activity that might otherwise seem boring exciting. Games can be used to help learners acquire occupational information, but they are not a substitute for observational or direct learning experiences.

Career laboratories are an interactive approach to providing occupational information. They can be used to provide simulations of simple work sites such as supermarket checkouts, auto tune-up stations, and nursing stations. Laboratories provide hands-on experiences and place the learner in an interactive role. Because of the expense involved in (1) providing and maintaining the space required for a laboratory, (2) acquiring the equipment needed, and (3) the supervision of the facility, laboratories have not been popular means of providing occupational information.

Direct contact with workers is another interactive approach to gaining occupational information. In some instances, workers can leave their work sites and come to schools or training centers to discuss their jobs. However, these experiences take away the learners' opportunities to observe the work environment. Direct observation of workers on their jobs is probably preferred to off-site interviews, but these experiences can add additional cost, particularly when the expenses associated with arranging these experiences is considered. Costs mount if transportation and supervision must be provided, which is usually the case when elementary, middle, and high school students are involved. Another problem that often presents itself when providing information through direct observation is the availability of a wide range of jobs to observe. Obviously, availability of a variety of jobs is greater in rural than in urban areas.

Job tryout in the form of work samples, short-term job trials, part-time work, and internships is probably the best way for a potential worker to gain knowledge about an occupation. Here again, the logistics involved in coordinating and supervising these types of programs make them costly. Availability of adequate opportunities for job tryouts can also be a problem, just as it is for providing observational experiences.

Effective programs for delivering occupational information will incorporate many of the approaches just described. What follows is a summary of some of the pros and cons of the subtypes of materials discussed.

Subtype	Cost	Learner Involvement	Accessibility
1. Print	Inexpensive	Passive	Easy
2. Programmed	Inexpensive	Interactive	Limited
3. Audiovisual	Expensive	Passive	Limited
4. CACGS	Moderate to expensive	Interactive	Limited
5. Online systems	Inexpensive	Passive	Limited*
6. Simulations	Inexpensive	Interactive	Limited
7. Games	Inexpensive	Interactive	Limited
8. Laboratories	Expensive	Interactive	Very limited
9. Interviews	Inexpensive	Interactive	Limited
10. Observation	Expensive	Passive	Limited**
11. Work samples	Expensive	Interactive	Limited**
12. Job tryouts	Expensive	Interactive	Limited**

* Easy if computer and Internet connection available
** Very limited in rural areas

In the sections of this chapter that follow, several examples of the subtypes of material will be presented, with a single exception. Because computer-assisted career guidance systems have expanded so rapidly in the past decade, the next chapter is devoted to that topic. In the final sections of this chapter, organizing and managing the career resource center are discussed.

Occupational: Print and On-Line

The National Career Development Association (NCDA, 1991a) identifies three general categories of publications: Vocational, Educational, and Career/Personal. These categories are then subdivided into several types as follows:

Vocational

A. Occupations (specific information about jobs)
B. Trends and Outlook
C. Job Training
D. Employment Opportunities

Educational

A. Status and Trends
B. Schools, Colleges
C. Scholarships, Fellowships, Grants, and Loans

Career/Personal

A. Planning (resumes, how to look for a job, career planning, etc.)
B. Adjustment (to work)
C. Theory
D. Assessment (interest, aptitude, testing, etc.)

NCDA (1991b) has also established guidelines for reviewing print materials. The general section of the guidelines suggest that the date of publications should be clearly identified, credit to all involved in the development of the material should be stated, information should be accurate, vocabulary used in the materials should be appropriate for the target audience, the intended use of the material should be delineated, bias and stereotyping should be avoided, and "graphics, when used, should enhance the value of the narrative information" (p. 3). The content guidelines provided by NCDA (1991b) suggest that occupational and career information should describe both the nature of the work and the work setting, identify the preparation required to enter the occupation including any special requirements, identify methods of entry into the occupation, present and future earnings profile, and discuss factors such as advancement opportunities, employment outlook, and opportunities for interested parties to explore the occupation through part-time and summer work. Finally the NCDA guidelines suggest that occupational information should identify occupations that are related to the one being discussed and provide sources of additional information.

A review of the types of occupational materials defined here reveals that some may be as brief as a single page, others as long as an entire book. Since each client or student has unique needs, career counselors will obviously require knowledge of a wide range of materials for many occupational fields. The student who is just beginning to explore the world of work is more likely to need access to a wide array of short descriptive statements such as those found in a brief or abstract. On the other hand, clients who are moving toward an appropriate choice may be anxious to read a lengthy description, such as a monograph, to answer specific questions about occupations.

Occupational information is processed and published by numerous agencies and companies—so many, in fact, that some categorization of these sources is essential in order to use them most effectively. This book does not attempt to provide an exhaustive list of either occupational materials or their sources. Major groupings of these sources include those discussed next.

Government Agencies

Many federal agencies publish materials relating directly to occupations. Free publications can be obtained directly from the agency that produces them. Most materials are sold and can be obtained either from the agency itself or from the Superintendent of Documents, U.S. Government Printing Office. The latter source is usually the better one.

Since the output of the U.S. Government Printing Office is so extensive, it is difficult to keep abreast of new items that might have value for counselors or clients. Many counselors find it convenient to be placed on the mailing lists of agencies that produce the major portion of occupational materials, or to obtain regularly the price lists of materials (available from either the agency or the Superintendent of Documents) published by those agencies. Many users will find it simpler to go directly to the Government Printing Office (GPO) home page (http://www.access.gpo.gov/). By clicking on the appropriate line, users can access government information and products, identify employment opportunities, search government databases, and gain entry to a host of other information sources. Publications can be ordered directly by (1) Clicking on the order icon that appears when documents of interest are identified, (2) completing the on-line order form, and (3) providing credit card information. Although the GPO publishes documents from all governmental agencies, a listing of those that are most involved in the publication of career and labor market information follows.

Department of Commerce. Many publications are available related to various aspects of business—both "business" in a broad sense and "business and commerce" in a narrow usage. Important materials for the counselor include the following:

1. *U.S. Industrial Outlook:* Published annually, this provides a survey of U.S. business, showing current developments in each industry as well as long-range forecasts.
2. *County Business Patterns:* Also published annually, this survey shows first-quarter employment and payroll data by industry in each county, SMSA, and state.
3. *Standard Occupational Classification Manual:* This classification system was discussed in Chapter 6.

Department of Defense.   Each of the armed services publishes handbooks and brochures describing career opportunities within that specific branch of service. Intended primarily for recruiting purposes, each book provides an indication of the relationship of each military specialty to civilian work.

The *Military Career Guide* (U.S. Department of Defense) is an example of armed services publications. Information provided includes typical work tasks, work environment, physical demands, training provided, helpful attributes, and special qualifications. Indexes included permit use of *DOT* numbers, *DOT* alphabetical listing, and information provided by the Armed Services Vocational Aptitude Battery (ASVAB).

The *Military Occupational and Training Data* (U.S. Department of Defense) publications are revised annually and provide comprehensive information on military occupations, both officer and enlisted. Information included parallels that described for the *Military Career Guide*.

Department of Labor.   Many sections of this large department publish materials crucial for counselors and teachers. The publication list would be a useful one to have available. Sample publications from this department include the following:

1. *DOT/GOE/OOH/O*NET/:* All these have been discussed in earlier chapters.
2. *Occupational Projections and Training Data:* Published annually, this volume provides information on employment prospects and related needed training. It includes a comprehensive supply–demand analysis for college graduates as well as other training programs.
3. *BLS Wage Surveys:* Published annually, these booklets supply data for occupations in seventy-six categories based on wage and salary information for workers in most industrial classifications, excluding public service and the relatively small areas of agriculture, mining, and construction.
4. Online Databases: America's Job Bank (also America's Career Info net (http://www.ajb.dni.us/) and America's Labor Market Information Systems Talent Bank (ALMIS) (http://www.mesc.state.mi.us.netrex.almishome.html). America's Job Bank is a computerized network that links a nationwide network of employment security offices. It typically contains hundreds of thousands of job listings and the resumes of tens of thousands of job seekers. It also contains information about employment outlook, earnings and training for specific occupations, and answers to questions about general job trends. It can be searched using a menu, keywords, or occupational code. There is no charge to job seekers or employers who list jobs. ALMIS is not fully developed at this time, but will eventually be a comprehensive talent bank and source of labor market information.

Many other federal departments and agencies publish materials that are useful in career development activities. Many items relate directly to the purpose of the agency. Obviously, the Department of the Interior provides information about jobs in national parks, and the Office of Personnel Management provides information about career jobs in the federal government. The home pages of these agencies can be contacted using keyword searches or through hyperlinks posted on the websites of agencies such as the Government Printing Office.

Commercial Publishers

Many commercial printing companies produce materials directly related to career development. Some concentrate their efforts on instructional materials, assessment instruments, counseling aids, and materials for special populations. The available materials range from occupational briefs of four to six pages to book-length items including fiction and biography. Several publishers have organized programs for varying age groups and grade levels as well as materials for individual counseling. The media specialist in the local school media center or public library is knowledgeable about the resources that identify these publishers and their materials.

Professional and Industrial Organizations

A variety of occupational materials is available from professional organizations and societies active in career fields. Some of these groups have prepared and published excellent monographs and other materials. The Department of Commerce has published a *Directory of National Associations of Businessmen,* which provides a list of most of the groups that can be classified under this heading. The Department of Labor publishes a similar directory of labor unions. Since the materials published by these groups may be designed to serve the special interests of the sponsoring group, the counselor should evaluate the materials carefully before using them.

Private Companies

A number of private companies in a variety of industries, such as retail merchandising, banking, steel production, and chemical production, publish occupational materials. Ordinarily, this is done by large nationwide corporations whose basic purpose is to use the materials in recruiting potential career workers; thus the publications tend to emphasize the benefits that accrue to the worker. On the other hand, the materials often include copious illustrations and information that make them very useful. The items available from these sources also vary widely, from brief pamphlets to substantial hardback books.

Educational Institutions

Many universities and other educational institutions have prepared materials that describe opportunities in career fields for which the specific school provides preparation. Some of these are brief, four-page abstracts; others are collections of such briefs; and a few are extensive publications covering several fields in depth.

Trade and technical schools often prepare descriptions of the fields for which they offer training; the materials tend to focus specifically on the area within which the school places most of its graduates. Many degree-granting schools prepare lists of occupations in which their graduates are employed. The home pages of many two- and four-year colleges and universities can be accessed via one of the following clearinghouses: College and University Home Pages (http://www.mit.edu:8001/people/cdemello/univ.html); College Board Online (http://www.collegeboard.org/); and CollegeNET (http://www.collegenet.com/).

Periodicals

One often encounters articles in popular national magazines that are pertinent to the field of career information. Many of these articles have been prepared as human interest or feature stories, but they may be highly useful in helping a student understand an occupational field.

Several professional journals regularly read by counselors include career information of value to counselors. Some of the journals primarily report research studies; some focus more on practical, how-to-do-it field reports; and some are factual, statistical reporting publications. Titles that the counselor should review include *American Vocational Journal, Career Development Quarterly, Journal of College Placement, Journal of Counseling and Development, Journal of Counseling Psychology, Journal of Employment Counseling, Journal of Vocational Behavior, Monthly Labor Review, Occupational Outlook Quarterly,* and *Work and Occupations.*

Indexes and Clearinghouses

Indexes published by commercial publishers, public service agencies, and professional organizations are a source of information. These indexes usually are printed at regular intervals and include lists of articles, pamphlets, or other material related to the field. Many counselors find this type of service especially helpful in locating materials from sources outside the channels they check routinely. The following are examples of indexes:

1. *Career Index.* Published by Chronicle Guidance Publications, Moravia, NY 13118. An annual listing of occupational and educational materials from many organizations.
2. *Educators Guide to Free Teaching Aids.* M. H. Saterstrom, editor. Published by Educators Progress Service, Inc., Randolph, WI 53956. An annual listing of free materials, including audiovisual materials as well as printed matter.
3. *Counselor's Information Service.* Published by B'nai B'rith Career and Counseling Services, Washington, DC 20036. Published four times yearly in newsletter form, this bibliography of current materials also identifies items useful with special populations—adults, aging, and people with disabilities.
4. *Clearinghouses.* Clearinghouses are on-line indexes or lists of other Internet sources. Several of the most important ones are The Definitive Guide to Internet Career Resources (http://phoenix.oakland.edu/career/internet.html); The Riley Guide: Employment Opportunities and Job Resources on the Internet

(http://www.jobtrak.com/jobguide/); What Color Is Your Parachute? Job Hunting Online (http://washingtonpost.com/parachute).

Indexes have few advantages when compared to on-line clearinghouse and will undoubtedly be replaced by them as the importance of the Internet grows. A webmaster can update a clearinghouse in a few hours and make the data instantly available to users. Published indexes take six months to a year to produce and thus are dated at the time of publication.

Educational: Print and On-Line

One might reasonably expect that occupational information would include explanations of the kinds of education or training needed to qualify for that work. This is often true, but there are at least two reasons for considering information about education and training opportunities separately. First, most occupational materials that include discussions of kinds of preparation needed for entrance and advancement do not identify specific schools or organizations where that preparation is available. Second, a large portion of high school graduates select a school for postsecondary education without first deciding what occupation they are preparing to enter. We consider sources of information for three types of postsecondary preparation: 2- and 4-year colleges and universities, technical and trade schools, and apprenticeship programs.

Colleges and Universities

Obviously, the most precise and up-to-date information about a specific school can be obtained from the institution itself. Colleges and universities, because of changes in enrollments, rapid advances in science and other fields of learning, fluctuating financial resources, and other factors, are in a state of constant change. Consequently, every other source of information, with the possible exception of the on-line data, must be considered as possibly obsolete because of modifications that might have occurred since the data were obtained. The schools are too numerous and the time required to obtain specific answers too long to consider individual contact with all higher educational institutions. Only when a prospective student has developed a tentative list of schools is such contact appropriate.

Careful reading and study of the catalog and other institutional publications is similarly impossible. However, one should recognize that, next to direct contact with the school itself, the catalog, on-line information, and other publications are probably the best sources of accurate data—barring changes that have occurred since publication. Further, even a carefully prepared catalog cannot answer many of the questions likely to occur to an investigating student.

Because of the scope of the problem, prospective students and their parents, teachers, and counselor often must rely on secondary sources of information about schools, at least during the early phases of the screening process. This inevitably leads to one of the guides or directories that offer condensed descriptions of the schools. Because up-to-date information is crucial, the latest edition always should be used—with the caution that even this may be out of date for a specific item concerning a particular school.

The list of directories in Table 7.1 includes several of those widely used. They are grouped by publisher and therefore cover both 2- and 4-year institutions. The listing is roughly alphabetical.

The college clearinghouses listed in the previous section can serve as a starting place for on-line searches.

Technical and Trade Schools

Obtaining accurate, usable information about a vocational school is often much more difficult than finding similar information about a degree-granting institution, for several reasons. Teachers and counselors, having been professionally prepared in colleges and universities, are more aware of the baccalaureate schools. Intercollegiate athletics and other activities publicize the colleges and universities locally, regionally, and nationally. Most of society's prestigious or high-status occupations require college educations and focus public attention on schools that provide such education. In addition, technical and trade schools usually offer

TABLE 7.1   Print Directories of Colleges and Universities

Directory	Publisher
Accredited Institutions of Postsecondary Education *American Universities and Colleges*	American Council on Education One Dupont Circle Washington, DC 20036
Barron's Profiles of American Colleges	Barron's Educational Series 250 Wireless Boulevard Hauppauge, NY 11788
The College Blue Book (5 volumes)	Macmillan, Inc. 866 3rd Avenue New York, NY 10022
The College Handbook *College Cost Book* *College Guide for Parents*	College Board Publications Box 886 New York, NY 10101
Comparative Guide to American Colleges	HarperCollins Publishers 10 East 53rd Street New York, NY 10022
Four-Year College Databook *Two-Year College Databook* *Financial Aid Guide*	Chronicle Guidance Publications Aurora Street Moravia, NY 13118

shorter training programs in less conspicuous quarters, have often been in existence for shorter periods, and rarely attract public attention.

The need for current, reliable, and useful information about vocational schools is apparent, but such information is difficult to obtain—although some SOICCs include this information in their database. Publications similar to the catalog or bulletin of a college, university, or community college are unusual rather than customary for vocational schools. Information often is provided in the form of brochures, briefs, flyers, or other sketchy statements. In vocational schools, new programs are established and old programs disappear more rapidly than in traditional 2-year and 4-year institutions; this affects routine publication of informational materials. Counselors who need current information about vocational schools may find it helpful to check with their state SOICCs about opportunities within their states. Another source of information includes the American Vocational Association in Washington, DC.

The directories listed in Table 7.2 provide information about many trade and technical schools. Because of the great diversity among these schools, directories often are less comprehensive than those that deal with traditional degree-granting institutions.

Apprenticeships

Printed material about specific apprenticeship opportunities is almost nonexistent. This is due partly to the nature of apprenticeship programs, in which national, state, and regional offices have mainly coordinating and liaison responsibilities and local offices have administrative and operating functions. Thus detailed information about actual training spaces and the process of filling those spaces usually must be obtained from a local office.

TABLE 7.2   Print Directories of Trade and Technical Schools

Directory	Publisher
American Trade Schools Directory	Croner Publications, Inc. 211-03 Jamaica Avenue Jamaica, NY 11428
Directory of the National Association of Trade and Technical Schools	Directory National Association of Trade and Technical Schools 2021 K Street, N.W. Washington, DC 20006
Directory of Postsecondary Schools with Occupational Programs, Public and Private	U.S. Government Printing Office Washington, DC 20402
Vocational School Manual	Chronicle Guidance Publications Aurora Street Moravia, NY 13118

General information about apprenticeship programs can be obtained from the Bureau of Apprenticeships, U.S. Department of Labor, Washington, DC 20210. Information about local and regional offices also can be obtained there. If the state government offices include a Department of Labor, that office can provide statewide information. In larger communities, local telephone directories will list numbers for local union representatives who can provide information about local programs for that union.

Audiovisual and Programmed Material

Until recently, AV material referred almost exclusively to films and filmstrips. These materials have been supplemented, and in many cases replaced, by videotapes and audiotapes. In addition, closely related to this field is an array of materials often called mechanized or programmed materials that use microfilm or systems of cards, charts, and similar visual material.

Videotapes, CD-ROMs, and Films

Audiovisual materials have tremendous advantages when compared to print material. These advantages are so obvious that some commercial publishers have switched their lists of materials almost entirely to these types of materials. Videotapes and films have the obvious advantage of sound and motion, but CD-ROMS allow the learner to interact with the material. Multimedia products such as *Occupational Outlook Handbook* and the *Multimedia Guide for Occupational Exploration* (available from Cambridge Education, Charleston, WV), and several other publishers allow individuals to access the materials in several ways. They may begin by answering a series of questions about their skills and interests and then be guided through the materials as they listen to a narrative, view video clips, and read text displayed on a screen. Individuals at the exploratory stage of career selection might begin by viewing video clips of the clusters of occupations in each of these products and then explore some of the areas in more detail. Third, users can access materials about occupations directly.

CD-ROM programs are relatively expensive to produce and purchase when compared to videotape. The result is that there are virtually thousands of videotapes available that show (1) most of the occupations in the work force, (2) interviews with workers, (3) how to develop resumes, conduct job interviews, conduct a job search on the Internet, and other employability skills, (4) how to succeed on the job, (5) how to increase one's self-awareness, and (6) a host of other development activities.

Finally, all schools own or have access to handheld video cameras that can be used to develop local materials. One school counselor asked pairs of students to conduct job interviews with workers, videotape the interviews, and play and narrate those videotapes for other students. These portable video cameras could be used to get information about dangerous jobs in the community, community help-ers, or to bring information to rural areas about jobs in distant locations.

Games

Miller and Knippers (1992), capitalizing on an idea first developed by Sandler (1990) used the format of the popular *Jeopardy!* quiz show to teach high school students occupational concepts ranging from Holland Types (Holland, 1997) to occupational information. They developed a *Jeopardy!* board using five catego-ries; Holland Types; Holland II; Self-Awareness; Occupational Information; and Potpourri. They then wrote questions of varying difficulty and divided their class into teams to compete by determining which team had acquired the most informa-tion. The Center on Education and work at the University of Wisconsin-Madison publishes two games, one aimed at helping students and adults learn to make on-the-job decisions. The other, Career Explorer, is a board game that helps stu-dents acquire occupational information.

Children's Materials

Almost all the material listed thus far has been useful for adolescents and/or adults. However, in Chapter 1 career development was defined as a lifelong pro-cess, and as we shall see later, many school districts have career development programs in their elementary and middle schools. Fortunately there are many ex-cellent print and nonprint materials available to support these programs. A list of these can be found below. Children can also benefit from interviews with workers, direct observation, and many of the approaches described in the subsequent sec-tions of this chapter.

Material	Publisher
The Children's Occupational Outlook Handbook (Print)	Ferguson
Children's Dictionary of Occupations (Print)	Ferguson
Kaleidoscope of Careers (AV–video)	Ferguson
Career Exploration Workbook (Programmed)	Center on Education & Work

Career Information Delivery Systems (CIDS)

As was noted earlier, in 1976 the Congress passed legislation establishing the Na-tional Information Coordinating Committee (NOICC). Subsequently, State Infor-mation Coordinating Committees (SOICCs) were established and charged with improving both the quality and delivery of occupational information. The result has been the establishment of CIDS in each state. These information delivery systems vary widely in their approaches, but engage in training activities and develop and disseminate tabloids and other printed materials, provide computer software to users, and provide material on microfiche; some operate telephone career information hotlines. Because Virginia VIEW (Vital Information for Education and Work) offers all of the services listed above, it will be discussed here.

Each year Virginia VIEW publishes two tabloids, *Career Hunt* and *VIEW Start*. *Career Hunt,* which is a seventy-two page newspaper, targets adolescents and adults. It contains labor market information, information about vocational education programs, information about specific careers, a guide that can be used to locate training opportunities for various careers within Virginia, and information about apprenticeship programs in Virginia. *VIEW Start,* which is also published in a newspaper format, is oriented to children and contains games, puzzles, and exercises that are aimed at stimulating self-understanding and the development of information about careers.

Most CIDS have purchased and modified some of the existing computer programs that will be discussed in Chapter 8. However, Virginia VIEW, as well as Arizona, Maryland and New Jersey, have developed their own computerized programs. *Interactive VIEW* contains *Occupations Search* and *College Search,* which are geared to occupational and college searches, respectively, within Virginia. Virginia VIEW also operates a hotline which responded to almost 43,000 calls over a 14-year period (McDaniels, Watts, Knoblich, Landon-Moore, & Tillerson, 1995). The types of information requested by callers vary widely and range from information on licensure for specific occupations to financial aid and educational information. A 1994 NOICC occasional publication provides description of hotlines in Rhode Island and Texas as well as the Virginia VIEW hotline.

Interviews with Workers

Every counselor or teacher has encountered problems of credibility when discussing career options outside the educational structure. Even the career counselor with many years of significant involvement in a noneducational field is likely to meet the attitude, "How can you know about that job—you're a teacher!" Attempting to dispel that point of view may be futile. Fortunately, a solution is available that is advantageous to all concerned. The logical step is to enlist the assistance of someone with that aura of credibility—someone working in the field and thereby automatically regarded as an expert.

Interviews with experts are appropriate experiences in the career development process at all steps, from the awareness level onward. Obviously, they should be adjusted to the level of development of the individuals involved, and other steps should be taken to make the experience valuable. In the awareness and early exploratory phases of career development, such interviews can be used best with groups of students. Career days and career conferences are examples commonly used in schools; we consider these shortly.

Career Day

On *career day* in most schools, groups of students are given an opportunity for direct contact with representatives of selected occupations. The career day program is designed to provide the students with pertinent and accurate information about specific fields of work. If properly organized, it can help them broaden their understanding of fields in which they have expressed an interest. It also gives them contact with at least one individual in the occupation from whom they may be able to obtain further information if their interest continues and expands.

Once the date has been set, the next question concerns the best part of the day for the program. Whether morning or afternoon is chosen depends largely on the local situation, the normal school schedule, and which portion of the day best lends itself to the objectives of the program. An evening program should be considered if the school wishes to include parents in the activity. There are many obvious advantages to a schedule that permits the maximum number of parents to be included, and this is more likely to occur outside the usual workday. Including parents in the career day is based on our assumption that the development of sound career plans involves the adults in the youth's immediate environment—parents, teachers, and counselors.

Career day programs have been criticized in some instances because the occupations included have not been representative of student interest. One way to prevent this is to begin planning with a survey of the students who will be involved in the program. Students may be asked to list the occupations they would most like included in a career day program. Sometimes a checklist is used, on which the student indicates from three to five preferences. The list can be compiled from a survey of occupations entered by students from the school or from a listing of the occupations most prevalent in the geographic area. Space should be provided on any checklist to add occupations not listed.

It is rarely possible to include all occupations listed by students in a single school. A tally of the checklists, however, will indicate areas in which student interest is sufficient to plan for one or more groups. Frequently one can meet specialized interests by grouping on a broader base than student response. For example, if only a few indicate interest in carpentry, stonemasonry, and painting, these logically can be grouped as construction trades. When student interest is too small to include the requested occupations, the students making the requests should be helped individually to obtain the desired information in other ways.

Once student interests have been inventoried and tallied, the occupations to be included can be identified. Every effort should be made to cover the entire range of student interests. Securing speakers for each occupation may be difficult and time-consuming. Members of the faculty may be able to suggest resources or speakers in some areas. Often local service clubs can suggest individuals who might discuss particular fields. Speakers for craft and manufacturing areas may be found by consulting local union representatives or employers.

Speakers should be sought who can present their occupations fairly to interested students. Years of experience in the field may not necessarily be a major concern, particularly of a field in which changes have occurred recently. Giving speakers appropriate materials well in advance can assist them in preparing for their participation. Pamphlets, booklets, pages from the *Occupational Outlook Handbook,* and similar materials may be useful in broadening the individual's perspective of his or her own field. Student groups—the advisory committee, perhaps—can prepare lists of questions that students are likely to ask in the actual program so speakers can anticipate some of the topics about which they might be questioned.

Since the program is basically a learning activity, students should be prepared properly for their part. If students are provided ample opportunity to read and study material about the occupations of interest before the career day program, they will be in a better position to ask appropriate questions and, thereby, make better use of the speakers' limited time. Groups of students can be encouraged to prepare questions in advance and to complete other preparatory steps that will increase the effectiveness of the program. Serious advance preparation also may help to alleviate the carnival air that sometimes surrounds career day programs.

Once students have indicated their interests on the inventory and the areas to be included in the program have been identified, it is possible to establish a schedule for each student and to see that groups where multiple sessions are needed can be balanced. Students should be informed in advance of their schedule for the day, and a duplicate copy of the schedule should be filed in case of forgetfulness. Rooms should be assigned with the sizes of the groups in mind.

Soon after the program has been held, it should be evaluated by all participants to determine whether such a program should be used in subsequent years and, if so, how it should be modified to improve its effectiveness. Ideally, evaluation should include reactions from students, faculty members, and occupational representatives. Most schools use a brief evaluation form for gathering reactions from students and speakers.

Follow-up is as crucial as preparation of students beforehand. Many opportunities for follow-up exist in every school situation; these should be identified and capitalized on. Several of the classes in which students are enrolled naturally lend themselves to further discussion of the topics in the program. Others, such as English classes, can be used for stimulating student thought and reaction through assigned papers, preparation of letters, role-playing interviews, and similar activities. Counselors should follow up with student interviews to help students obtain further information, discuss tentative career choices, arrange for visits to businesses, industries, or advanced schools; or schedule further activities that help develop career plans.

Career days are equally appropriate at all educational levels. Isaacson and Hayes (1980) describe an application of career day to an elementary school in which presenters were asked to show student participants what they did at work rather than using more abstract verbal explanations. It is also used at the college level either in the format described here or with various adaptations. Self and Lopez (1982) describe a seminar for college women in which presenters were women employed in nontraditional occupations. Because the seminar program scheduled one speaker each week, the format approximated the career conference, a plan that we consider next. Pate, Tullock, and Dassance (1981) describe an event that combines a career day with a postsecondary education day organized by a professional group for clientele drawn from several schools and the community at large.

Career Conferences

Some schools have used the career conference instead of scheduling a special career day. Arranging a special day obviously interrupts normal school activities and sometimes carries with it a holiday atmosphere that can interfere with its basic purpose. In some schools the career day is advantageous because it briefly concentrates the attention of the entire school, and sometimes even the community, on the school's commitment to career planning.

If a school prefers not to interrupt its schedule, a series of career conferences can be arranged within the framework of the regular school calendar. Basically, the career conference is a segment of the career day program in which an occupational representative is brought together with a group of interested students to discuss a specific field. Often a series of these, extending over a considerable period of time, can be strung together to provide the same coverage as the career day program.

Organizing and developing a series of career conferences involves the same steps as those described for the career day program. The major difference between the two activities is simply that the career day puts the whole program into a single day or portion of a day, whereas the career conferences may number one or two per day over a period of a month or more, depending on the number of occupations to be included.

The flexibility provided in a series of career conferences has certain definite advantages. Individual student scheduling is likely to be easy since students can be scheduled for the number of conferences in which they indicate an interest. Under the career day plan it is difficult to avoid the regimentation of scheduling all students for the number of sessions included in the program. Some students may be seriously interested in exploring only one or two areas, whereas others may wish to participate in five or six conferences. The students included in career conferences are more likely to be truly interested in the area being discussed, with the increased possibility that the session will be more profitable for them. The flexible schedule also may make it easier to obtain occupational representatives who can do the best job of presenting information about their fields.

Warrington and Method–Walker (1981) describe an adaptation of the career conference in which they used the campus radio station to broadcast a weekly interview with a guest resource person representing an occupational area affiliated with various collegial units within the university.

Follow-up and evaluation of the career conference are just as important as for the career day program. Usually the same techniques can be used.

Heppner (1981) describes the application of a program by a university counseling center where the job holders to be interviewed are university alumni volunteers. The program provides levels of intensity of contact, including taped interviews with the job holder, telephone contact with the job holder to acquire information, face-to-face interviews, and an externship extending from a half day to 3 days in length. The latter opportunity exceeds the usual range of interviews with experts, and we consider this type of contact later when we discuss shadowing. This type of career information is also usable in nonschool settings on a group or individual basis.

Post–High School Opportunity Programs

Many high schools have organized programs or special days labeled "College Day" or some similar title. These programs resemble the career day, except that speakers are drawn from educational institutions. Historically, these programs developed because school and college officials recognize that high school students need an opportunity to discuss post–high school educational plans with representatives of institutions in which they might be interested. Numerous high schools set aside a special day or time when the representatives of the various schools are invited to meet with interested students.

As the name implies, many schools invite only representatives of postsecondary educational institutions to participate in their programs. Since every school has students whose future plans do not include continuing their education, only a portion of the student group is served by such a program. Although many high schools have overlooked the importance of parental involvement in career days, they have often provided for them in programs related to colleges. Consequently, many of these sessions have been properly labeled "Postsecondary Opportunity Nights" and scheduled in the evening, to permit parents to attend with the youngsters. Scheduling both types of activities outside regular working hours might encourage greater participation by parents and result in a closer working relationship between school and parent. The format of these programs is similar to that used in career day programs, and the organization and development of such programs should be similar.

A further difficulty may be encountered in the typical postsecondary opportunity session. Student questions to the institutional representative can, of course, cover the entire range of the institution's program. It is difficult for any representative to be equally versed in all phases of an extensive educational program; consequently, the representative may not always be able to provide the precise information desired by the student.

Many schools have developed a modified version of the postsecondary opportunity program that is particularly advantageous. It involves asking recent alumni of the local school to be institutional representatives. The major advantages are obvious: (1) The former students arouse personal interest among the listeners, because they are probably known to them; (2) their experiences will be accepted by the student groups; and (3) the alumni concerns and problems will have meaning for the students.

Simulation of Work Environments

In this section, we discuss providing experiences, through artificial means, that are intended to help the student or client understand more completely the decision-making process or the nature of a work situation. This experience can often be encountered in the classroom or learning situation, but is by no means limited to the school setting. One type of simulation that everyone has experienced is role playing. Perhaps the simplest definition of simulation is that it is an artificial activity in an artificial setting that provides the participant some understanding of the real activity performed in a real situation.

Simulation has long been recognized as an effective means of teaching both simple and complex skills. Obviously, simulation offers counselors a comparable opportunity to transmit or develop insight into demands imposed on workers, the nature of the work environment, skills workers need to complete certain jobs successfully, and similar aspects of employment. Strangely, the procedure remains largely underdeveloped as it relates to counseling and career development activities.

A common example of simulation encountered by every elementary school pupil is the fire drill. The military services have used the technique extensively with infiltration courses, obstacle courses, and combat training. A more sophisticated example of simulation is the flight simulator, a device encountered by all who qualify for a commercial pilot's license.

Some high schools have developed "civil service commissions" (a student–faculty committee that assigns students to tasks in the school) of various types to provide students job experiences through various helper positions in classrooms, laboratories, and elsewhere in the school. These programs usually require completion of an application form, sometimes a job interview, supervisory reports from the responsible faculty member, and similar job-related experiences.

In an older but still relevant article, Fifield and Peterson (1978) describe the development and use of thirty simulation units with elementary school pupils. Each unit represents a realistic aspect of a job. For example, the auto brake repair unit includes an appropriately mounted car fender with backing plate and brake parts on a movable support. Units were developed locally at costs ranging between $200 and $400. Evaluation showed increased learning about occupations, improved attitudes, and greater interest in occupations. Cooperating teachers and parents also responded favorably.

The Singer Vocational Evaluation System, often used in vocational rehabilitation centers to evaluate the aptitudes of clients with disabilities, is another illustration of simulation. Some of the parts of the Vocational Evaluation System can be considered to be actual work samples, a technique we discuss in a later section.

Elementary teachers have used this technique frequently to enhance classroom learning activities; for example, the class establishes a "store" where class members acquire commonly used supplies such as paper, crayons, pencils, and paste, or perhaps a "bank" in which each student maintains a small savings account.

High school vocational education classes also have used the technique extensively to teach specific vocational skills. Many trade and industry departments assign construction craft students to a class project involving the complete building of a home that then is sold to provide the materials for next year's similar project. In the construction process, the students, under proper faculty supervision, actually do the work of a carpenter, an electrician, a plasterer, a plumber, a painter, a mason, and so on.

Almost every elementary and secondary counselor can find numerous work-related activities within the school that can be used effectively in career development. A little ingenuity and consultation with teachers will uncover unlimited possibilities.

Direct Experiences: Observation, Exploration, and Tryout

We now consider the use of direct contact with workers in natural work settings as the final form of career information media. The advantages of such a technique are immediately apparent. The credibility of reality is always difficult to contest. The student or client is able to see things as they are and to develop impressions and insights that would be impossible to foster in other ways. At the same time, this tremendous advantage also can operate in a negative fashion. Inexperienced observers and participants are not always able to see things as they really are, and misunderstandings can develop. Further, the specimen situation may be atypical for various reasons, so that misconceptions are created. Both difficulties can be counteracted by increasing the number and the time factor for direct contact; if this corrective measure cannot be applied, then the contacts used must be truly representative.

As the world of work has become more complex, many occupations have been removed from public view so that most students have little opportunity to go behind the scenes and actually see how and where certain types of work are performed. The perceptions they have may be developed on limited information and consequently may be unrealistic.

The field trip or industry tour provides many students their first chance to have direct contact with this side of the world of work. Such a trip can be highly motivating to students, encouraging them to explore further both the world of work and their own plans.

The group involved and the purposes to be accomplished are important in planning a field trip of this type. If the group consists of younger students and the purpose is to arouse interest and insight into how people earn their living, the tour probably should be limited to samples of occupations most frequently encountered in the local community. On the other hand, sophomores or juniors in the vocational curriculum will be interested in a different type of trip. They will be anxious to see working conditions, tools and equipment used, actual work processes, company organizations, and similar items that specifically relate to particular occupations. A high school class in occupations may be interested in exploring, but at a much different level from the elementary group.

The individual visit by a single student to a specific industry or business may offer one of the best opportunities to gain insight into a field in which the student is seriously interested. Such a visit often is arranged for an entire working day, and usually the visiting student is assigned to a worker with whom the entire day is spent. Such a visit provides maximum opportunity to see a variety of aspects of the job and to ask about what the worker does, as well as why and how. The student may have an opportunity to spend time with two or three workers in the course of the day. This provides a chance to become familiar with the workers' attitudes toward their work, opportunities for advancement, and work stability, among other things. This prolonged contact with one or two workers has become known as *shadowing.* Some schools have arranged for classes of elementary or middle school students to shadow a parent, other relative, or close family friend. High school or college students or nonschool adults usually would not require a personal acquaintanceship. Heppner's (1981) description of using alumni contacts to establish an externship of a day or more for college students is an application of the shadowing technique. A similar approach is reported by Sampson (1980) using local alumni. Tomlinson and DiLeo (1980) describe a field trip to local work sites as part of a seminar designed to assist college women considering careers in science. Herr and Watts (1988) describe shadowing as it is currently being used in Britain to help students learn about work.

The use of the individual industry visit is one way in which the career exploration program can be enhanced for many students. It should be restricted to students who would find a visit most helpful in developing plans. Arranging visits will be time-consuming for both school personnel and for the cooperating industry, but the benefits to the student are usually worth the effort.

Many colleges and universities have recognized the importance of such visits as part of the educational planning of high school students and have developed programs such as "Day on Campus," in which students from secondary schools are invited to participate in a day's program on campus. If a formal program is scheduled, it usually provides an opportunity to talk with representatives of the curricular areas in which the visitors are interested, to visit educational facilities and housing units, and to talk to one or two students from the visitors' home schools. Even though such a mass program has obvious disadvantages, it does at least permit the student to gain some feeling of the institution and its various programs.

The ideal campus visit occurs when prospective students are not part of a mass inundation, so they can see a typical cross-section of campus life. Individual school tours require more effort for the local counselor or teacher to arrange but usually can be handled without insurmountable problems.

Although the school visit is often considered in making plans for students who are college bound, it is just as important for students whose interests lie in other educational directions. The same arrangements can and should be made for students interested in vocational schools and other noncollegiate institutions. Many arguments can be raised that these visits are even more crucial; for example, many vocational schools provide limited facilities for student activities and housing, so a student may be forced to make individual arrangements to a greater extent than on many college campuses. Some preview of what is available may be helpful in making appropriate plans.

Work experience programs can be exploratory, general, or vocational preparatory. Exploratory programs aim at helping students understand various types of work, work settings, tools and equipment used by workers, demands placed on workers, and similar factors. General work experience programs are designed to assist students in the development of attitudes and skills that are not narrowly vocational in nature, including punctuality, dependability, acceptance of supervision, interpersonal relations, and similar characteristics that apply to all work situations.

Another example of direct on-the-job experience is the college-level cooperative program, usually associated with academic majors in many technical areas. In some fields these experiences are referred to as field practice or internship. Typically, all of these involve alternating periods of full-time study and work assignments. An experience of this kind usually comes late in the preparatory program and is designed to develop and sharpen work-related skills rather than to provide exploratory insight into the occupation. Nevertheless, it does offer a meaningful contact with work that the individual can use to confirm the appropriateness of an earlier choice or to begin the process of realigning plans.

Career Resource Centers

The increased availability of career materials—printed, audiovisual, programmed, and computer-based—has emphasized the need for an organized system to handle these items in an orderly way. The answer in most settings has been the development of a *career resource center*, also frequently called a *career information center*.

In the last decade there has been considerable growth of career resource centers. Such centers assemble materials and a professional and paraprofessional staff whose responsibility is to develop in-house and outreach programs. These activities are sometimes referred to as *career information delivery systems*. The combination of materials, staff, and programs provide the essentials for a career resource center.

There are many references to which the reader can turn for specific information on establishing a career resource center. Some of the more helpful references include Brown and Brown (1990); Cheshire (1988); Frederickson (1982); and Hubbard and Hawke (1987). Because there is such a great variability in clientele served, facilities and other resources available, and other relevant factors, our discussion focuses on general principles that are applicable across the variable factors.

Basic Criteria

At least four factors must be considered as plans are made to develop a career resource center: accessibility, attractiveness, ease of operation, and adaptability.

1. *Accessibility.* If career materials are conveniently located, more people will use them. If they are to be used in an educational setting, consideration should be given to student traffic flow and a location that is available to the greatest number of students for the maximum period of time. Although confidentiality is not a major consideration, it should be possible for the student or client to have access to career materials without feeling conspicuous.

In nonschool settings the problem of accessibility is likely to be a lesser one, because the number of individuals using the materials will probably be considerably fewer and the hours the materials are available will usually coincide with the operating hours of the agencies involved.

2. *Attractiveness.* The setting in which career information is maintained should be inviting to users and stimulate their interest. Furnishings should be tasteful and selected to encourage both casual browsing and serious study.

3. *Ease of operation.* Career materials probably will be used more if they are organized so the user can find items without help. If the filing system is easily understood and the materials so placed that users can be self-sufficient, they will likely sample what is available. If clients find that obtaining what they want is simple, they are likely to explore further. Perhaps the basic rule is to select the filing system that is easiest for the user and is compatible with the range and variety of available material.

4. *Adaptability.* It is important to collect career materials to fit the needs of the group that the resource center is intended to serve. The filing system also should be tailored to those needs. Because variations can be expected among various groups, the filing system should have enough flexibility to expand in areas that call for stretching and to contract in those areas in which the need is little or nonexistent.

Operational Decisions

In addition to the general criteria just discussed, several administrative factors bear directly on the development of a career resource center. Most of these must be considered and at least tentative answers obtained before a final decision on a filing plan or system can be reached. The following topics need attention:

1. *Responsibility.* One of the first decisions that should be made is who will be responsible for developing and maintaining the career resource center. In a non-school agency, this question is usually resolved easily by assigning responsibility to the person who takes leadership in the vocational counseling provided by the agency. If the agency is a large counseling center, each counselor may take primary responsibility for different phases of the program related to his activity, one of which would be the career resource center (others might be the testing program and the research activities).

Although one can generally assume that a collection of career information materials in a school media center has been developed to meet different uses than the materials found in the counselor's office, one cannot automatically assume that responsibility for the materials should be taken from the librarian or media specialist and given to the counselor. The decision should be based on all the factors in the local situation. One would expect the counselors, the media specialists, and the teachers to work together closely to find the best solution. Often some kind of joint responsibility will offer the best opportunity to provide the broadest service possible.

Because of increased decentralization on college and university campuses, the responsibility often gravitates to the student personnel division and usually to counseling center staff members. However, the staff should be familiar with resources and materials that may already exist in the library, or in offices of various academic divisions such as schools or departments, especially if those sections have traditionally held responsibility for scheduling and class selection. In non-educational settings, the responsibility usually can be assigned by administrative action.

2. *Staff.* Problems of staffing depend in part on the size and scope of the anticipated career resource center, the extent to which the clientele who will use the materials can operate independently, the volume of acquisitions, and the general usage of the materials and other factors. Professional people will be needed for at least part of the staff. Decisions about materials to be purchased, classification and evaluation, periodic review, and general supervision must all be put in responsible hands.

3. *Facilities.* The decision to develop a career resource center carries with it the assumption that necessary facilities and equipment can be provided. The following will be needed: a considerable quantity of shelf space, filing cabinets for unbound materials, furniture such as study tables and chairs, a table or desk for checking materials in and out and for processing new materials, small card files for recordkeeping, display racks for new booklets, and bulletin boards. Equipment that will be needed includes videocassette recorders, filmstrip viewers, slide projectors, and a copier. Centers should also include computer equipment and terminals with connections to on-line data banks.

Minimum space can be ascertained fairly easily if one visualizes the area required for initial and soon-to-be-acquired equipment, for staff to be assigned to the center, and for clients. In school and university settings, it may be difficult to operate with less than one large classroom or equivalent. In noneducational settings, with fewer clients using the space simultaneously, one might be able to operate in an area of about 500 square feet. The important factor is not number of square feet but what is to be done, how and with what it is to be accomplished, how many people will be involved at a time, and how much space this requires.

4. *Location.* Several factors bear on the location of the career resource center. Not the least of these is available space. The problem is likely to be simple when a new school is being opened. If adequate long-range planning has gone into the development of the building, a room has been set aside to meet this need. Ideally, there will be a room of adequate size, with direct access from the outer office of the guidance suite. Such a room can be readily available at all times to clients and others wishing to use the materials, as well as to counselors who desire to introduce counselees to the materials. Some supervision also is possible by the clerical or receptionist staff, whose work space is likely to be in the outer office.

5. *Security.* Every effort should be made to provide clients maximum access to the resources on file. The system for obtaining and using career information materials should be made as simple and as easy as possible. Without doubt, efforts to simplify the system may well result in some losses that could have been prevented by more stringent security measures. Generally, however, these losses will not be excessive and should be accepted as part of the operating costs.

6. *Budget.* Establishing an adequate career resource center involves considerable expense; additional funds are needed regularly thereafter to maintain and expand it. Unless the school or agency is willing to accept this double responsibility, it should think carefully before making the original investment. Because the amounts for both purposes depend on many factors, no particular amount can be specified as sufficient for the project.

Many schools find the support of the career resource center to be a project attractive to local service clubs seeking a worthwhile way to assist the school. It would probably be wise administrative policy to provide basic or minimal support within the regular school budget and to use such outside support for increased or expanded services. Because assurance of continued support may be difficult to obtain, provisions for continuity should probably be based on school support.

7. *Publicity.* A career resource center is meant to be used. Thus provision should be made to keep potential users continually informed of its availability. All agencies that work with adolescents are aware of the constant changes in their clientele as a result of maturation alone. Each school, for example, starts a new freshman class each year. This necessitates some plan for informing this group as well as familiarizing those who have been around before but who have not established contact. In most settings, the need for this communicative effort is continuous.

8. *Operating policies.* Many problems cannot be anticipated. Some person or group must be assigned the responsibility for solving problems as they arise. Even though the general operating framework of the career resource center can be determined ahead of time, there must be provision for flexibility and modification to fit the needs of the group served. Someone must be responsible for establishing procedures and for making changes as needed.

Collecting and Evaluating Materials

All agencies that work with adolescents and adults in the process of career choice and planning will need a wide range of print and AV career materials. Because the materials will be used with many clients and students, a collection of these items should be compiled in advance so they will be available for use as needed.

Among the changes that have occurred recently is the transformation of the school library into a learning resource center or media center. Technological developments have made possible the inclusion of much material in a variety of forms, both printed and nonprinted, as well as an assortment of equipment used in applying the materials. With increasing frequency, this vital area of the school is staffed by a highly competent, thoroughly trained media specialist.

Since many counselors work in nonschool settings and some work in schools without broadly trained media specialists, the remainder of this chapter is written on the assumption that the counselor must take either sole responsibility for or major leadership in developing and operating a career resource center.

Chapman and Katz (1981) report that the counseling staff has primary responsibility for career materials. Among the schools surveyed, 51 percent said the counseling staff had responsibility for replacing career materials and evaluating new material; 64 percent said counselors held responsibility for helping students find material or advising them where to look; and 57 percent said counselors must decide when to discard old and obsolete material.

Criteria for Collecting Material

Several factors must be considered in assembling the resources for the center:

1. *The group that will make major use of the materials.* Obviously, different materials would be used in a junior high school, where students are only beginning to ex-

plore concepts about the world of work, than in a vocational rehabilitation center for adults. Even where the differences are less extreme, materials should be appropriate to the specific group. Within a school, the grade levels to be served by the career resource center provide some basis for selection. If materials are to be used primarily by junior high school students, a different emphasis is needed than if students from grades 7 through 12 are expected to use the collection, or if only senior high school students are involved. The range of ability and interest in the group also influences the choice of materials.

Most nonschool agencies can almost automatically assume a broad range of interest, ability, and academic background in the clients they serve. These variations will necessitate planning to select as broad a range of career materials as needed. If the agency exists to serve a specific group, its needs must be considered in choosing materials.

2. *The nature of the community.* A knowledge of the community where the school or agency is situated will provide additional information about the group that will use the career resource center. Although the high mobility of Americans decreases the likelihood that they will remain within the community throughout their lives, the range and scope of occupations within the community may provide the framework for the evaluation and consideration of career fields by students and their parents. That is, it will be more difficult to stimulate students to consider a wide range of occupational choice if they have grown up in a stable community dominated by a single industry than if the town has many businesses and factories and the population is constantly changing.

The socioeconomic range within the community and the extent to which community attitudes encourage educational achievement and individual development are other factors to be considered.

3. *The staff that will apply the materials.* Logically, the materials to be used only by the counselor would differ from those to be used by group leaders or teachers. Use of some items—for example, the *Dictionary of Occupational Titles*—presupposes some understanding of the organizational structure of the world of work and of the volume itself, as well as the theoretical and philosophic basis for the book. If materials are purchased that lie beyond the competency of the staff that will use them, they will likely be misused or left unused unless a staff training program is provided.

4. *How the materials will be used.* Closely related to *who* uses the career resource center is the question of *how* the materials are to be used. If career materials will be used only in individual counseling concerning vocational plans, a wide range of items in single or duplicate copies will probably be most appropriate. On the other hand, if materials are to be used for instructional purposes in a group guidance or classroom setting, the range of materials will probably be narrowed to make available the number of copies needed for the entire group.

5. *Existing materials already available.* Even if a counselor were newly appointed in a school that had never previously had a counselor, it would usually be fallacious to assume that the school had no career material on hand. The only time this is likely to be true is when a new school is opened. Whether or not he or she finds a file of career information in the office, the counselor should check with the school librarian or media specialist to learn what pertinent materials are in the library or media center.

An additional reservoir of career materials may be found in the resource materials collected by teachers for their use in the classroom. Many teachers have encountered student inquiries concerning the relationship between subject area and possible career fields. The classroom bookshelves are a likely source of career materials.

6. *Auxiliary local resources.* Almost every community has agencies that work with youth or adults and hence might have materials that relate to their problems, including career materials. The local public library is an obvious location for materials of this type. Other local resources that may have materials would be 4-H clubs, youth centers, the YMCA, YWCA, and churches or other groups that operate active youth or adult programs.

7. *Funds available.* Obviously, plans for obtaining career information will be influenced by the amount of money available. Rarely does a school or any other agency have an unlimited budget; consequently, the development of a basic library of materials may have to be planned over a period of time. The individual responsible for developing the center should be sure that there are sufficient funds to make a reasonable start and that there will be continuing appropriations in future budgets for extending the project as well as replacing out-of-date items.

Initiating a Collection

As has been indicated throughout this section, the nature of the information collection will be dependent upon the clientele being served. A collection in a prison setting will be far different from a collection in a secondary school or a community college. As has also been indicated, the collection should contain a wide variety of materials including print, online, audiovisual, and other subtypes of materials. Finally, those materials that are needed most urgently by individuals in the institution should be collected first.

Once the counselor has collected the materials that are urgently needed to meet the most pressing needs apparent within the user group, it is logical to move toward the development of breadth of materials. The extent or range of materials to be considered is based on the range within the group. After these two needs have been met, at least minimally, one then may move toward acquiring materials related to specialized fields or adding depth to already selected areas.

The counselor should take the following steps, though not necessarily in this order, to gain familiarity with what is currently available:

1. Subscribe to some of the indexes listing occupational materials. Because these do not completely overlap, it often is wise to subscribe to at least two, if possible.

2. Request price lists from federal and state agencies that publish materials related to areas pertinent to the counselor's group. Also, listings of material from the Government Printing Office are available online.

3. Check recent professional publications, such as *Career Development Quarterly,* for appropriate materials.

4. Obtain price lists from commercial publishers who have materials related to occupations.

5. Ascertain from appropriate professional organizations and societies, private industries, industrial associations, and private companies what materials they have that are appropriate for the user group.

6. Contact educational institutions for publications. Many colleges and universities have career materials available, as well as such items as catalogs and bulletins.

7. Determine which general items or basic resource volumes are essential for immediate use. These might include one or more copies of the latest *Dictionary of Occupational Titles*, the *Guide for Occupational Exploration, Selected Characteristics*, the latest issue of *Occupational Outlook Handbook*, and annual subscriptions to *Occupational Outlook Quarterly* and appropriate educational directories.

Once counselors have completed these steps, they have the basic information needed to make appropriate purchases with the funds at hand. If funds are sufficient, they should hold some in reserve to purchase new materials as they appear or to obtain materials for special needs that develop during the year.

Evaluating materials is an integral part of building a good career resource center. Many of the factors discussed in the two previous sections impinge on decisions to acquire materials for the center. NCDA has established, and regularly revises, *Guidelines for the Preparation and Evaluation of Career Information Literature* (NCDA, 1991b). These will be helpful in the collecting process. A counselor always should keep in mind the needs of the group of clients or students who will use the materials. Further, one must remember the staff who will use the materials and the ways the materials will be used. Finally, one must remain aware of the costs of the desired items in relation to the funds available.

Additionally, each possible acquisition should be measured against these criteria: accuracy, currency, usability, appeal, and comprehensiveness.

1. *Accuracy.* Even if the item being evaluated meets all other criteria, it is valueless if it fails this one. The material must depict the occupation fairly and correctly if the reader is to draw inferences and conclusions that will help in understanding the field. Inaccuracies inevitably will be misleading and could lead to decisions based on fallacy rather than fact. The material should be forthright and honest and should describe the occupation as it is. The publisher who wants to serve both counselor and client will include within a publication information that will help the counselor judge its accuracy. As a minimum, this would include an indication of how the information was collected, the size of the sample on which it is based, its location and extent of dispersion, identification of the person who collected the information and prepared the publication, evidence of that person's competency in unbiased reporting, and the dates when the data were obtained.

Since most published data presumably are based on a fairly large geographic area, the counselor needs to check not only the general accuracy for the occupation across the country but also the degree of precision with which the local situation is depicted. When the information necessary to determine accuracy is not included, the counselor has little recourse other than to match the information against such sources as the *Occupational Outlook Handbook* and other Department of Labor publications that are based, for the most part, on careful job analyses with relatively large samples.

2. *Currency.* This criterion, though closely related to accuracy, is listed separately to emphasize its importance. *Accuracy* tends to stress precision; *currency* adds the time factor. In other words, as we evaluate career information, we must ask: Is it accurate *now?*

At any given point, an occupation either may be holding relatively constant or may be involved in very rapid, perhaps even extreme, change; or it may be someplace in between. For example, the present impact of technological modernization is producing extensive change in many of the manufacturing occupations.

It is difficult for the counselor to predict precisely or even to estimate the degree to which an occupation is caught up in this change at a given moment. The best basis for judgment probably lies in an unending effort to keep abreast of developments and anticipated changes across the entire spectrum of the world of work. Publications from the Bureau of Labor Statistics and the State Employment Security Agency will be of some help in this task, as will materials such as reliable weekly news magazines that keep the counselor informed of economic and technical developments.

3. *Usability.* At least during the preliminary period of collecting career materials, preference should be given to materials that concern the more common occupations, since these are usually of greatest interest to the greatest number.

Similarly, some materials are so organized and prepared that they are of value to a variety of students or clients whose purpose in using them may range from casual perusal to serious study. Certain publications can be used advantageously by a broader group of the staff and perhaps even in a wider variety of situations.

When this appears likely, first purchases should include those that have wide usability.

4. *Appeal.* Appeal varies with the type of material. However, no material will be appealing if it cannot be easily understood, is out-of-date, or is developmentally inappropriate. The appeal of computerized material is enhanced if the response to questions or commands is quick, if the graphics are clear and enhance the presentation, and if it is "user friendly," the current euphemism for "instructions are easy to follow." Computerized programs, audiovisual aids, and print material should be previewed before they are purchased to determine their appeal.

5. *Comprehensiveness.* Occasionally, in evaluating career materials for selection, a counselor will have a special purpose in mind and will be seeking material to fit that purpose. Ordinarily, however, the counselor is concerned with selecting materials that will have general application for the group using the resource center. In the latter case, comprehensiveness should be considered as material is evaluated.

To a large extent, this must be appraised in terms of the group that is to use the career resource center. Comprehensiveness is crucial for upper educational years and later, when users are seriously involved in actual choices and decisions. At this point the counselee or client should have available all information that depicts clearly the occupation considered.

Managing Materials

Selecting the management system for the information collection is a major decision. Many colleges and community colleges have career counselors who have as one of their duties oversight of the information collection. In these institutions the process of checking material in and out is typically handled by a clerical staff person. In some schools the collection is placed in the media center and thus is under the direction of the media director. In this system, career counselors should maintain primary responsibility for the selection of new material and the elimination of dated information. Businesses have used clerical staff persons who are specially trained to monitor the collection and have left the ordering of materials to their career development professions. There is no single management system that fits all institutions. Brown and Brown (1990) discuss this issue from the standpoint of a high school counselor. Smith (1983) describes a library management system called career key that utilizes a computerized system to track materials. This system, like many of those in place today, allows users to access the information using a search strategy and instantaneously to determine the types of materials in the collection and their immediate availability. There are obviously other systems available and in place. In most instances the management system will simply be an extension of what is already operating in the institution.

Filing Educational Materials

Most career information emphasizes either the educational and training aspects or the various occupations themselves. This book follows a similar approach, and we first consider the matter of filing educational materials. Three general topics are considered:

1. Training directories
2. School catalogs and bulletins
3. Miscellaneous educational materials and information

One essential ingredient in every career resource center is a collection of training or educational directories. The number and scope needed will vary with the age and educational range of the users and the breadth of their anticipated educational plans, but even a modest library should include at least one directory for each general educational level. Most centers, especially those serving senior high schools, should provide more than one.

Within the career resource center, the educational directories usually can be handled best by placing all directories together on a conveniently located shelf. If the center has several directories, it may help to divide this shelf according to educational level—for example, a section for college and university directories, one for trade and vocational schools, and so on. In some settings, it may be more appropriate to place the directories with other publications from the kinds of schools included in the directories; that is, the vocational school directories might be located with vocational school bulletins. Ordinarily, however, the centralized location will be more convenient and will permit more efficient use.

School catalogs and bulletins can be organized either on shelves or in filing cabinets. In either case, it is usually desirable to separate them according to broad categories of schools—professional schools, 4-year colleges and universities, community colleges, vocational–technical–trade schools, and others. Since most professional schools are related to a college or university, it may be advantageous to combine the first two categories. If it is anticipated that the range of schools regularly included will not be extensive, it may even be desirable to combine the first three categories so that only two groupings are used, with a general label such as "academic" for one group and "vocational–technical–trade" for the other.

Materials from the vocational–technical–trade schools can be arranged by either of the methods described for the academic institutions. In addition, another alternative is often preferred: These publications can be arranged according to the occupation for which training is provided. Since many schools of this type are likely to be single-purpose institutions, there is often an advantage in this system, which, for example, brings together in a single section all barber schools. When this system is used, the occupational headings are often arranged alphabetically or according to *DOT* number, with each school placed alphabetically within this category.

Unbound Occupational Materials

One major problem in establishing a career resource center is selecting a filing system for occupational materials. Since these materials make up a major portion of the total center, the filing system must be organized to meet the general principles already discussed. A decision about the filing system to be used should be reached before any attempt is made to collect materials so that all acquisitions can be incorporated into the file as soon as they arrive. Because no system yet devised serves all purposes ideally, a compromise is necessary. The selection should be made in terms of the factors most important in the local situation.

Most occupational materials are published as unbound pamphlets, briefs, or monographs. Obviously, these must be handled differently from bound items. Many attempts have been made to organize unbound materials into some meaningful system. Several systems are in use today, and no one method is generally preferred over others. We briefly discuss alphabetical, coded, and other systems.

Filing systems can be developed locally to meet the needs of a particular agency, or they can be purchased commercially. This decision depends on such factors as available funds, staff time, special local needs, and suitability of commercial systems. The commercial systems take a variety of forms. Some publishers, for example, sell a set of gummed labels and directions for developing the file; others supply printed folders with directions and cross-reference cards or a complete kit including the filing system and an assortment of occupational materials.

Alphabetical System

The simplest method of filing unbound occupational materials is in a series of folders, each labeled with the name of an occupation, arranged in alphabetical order. In schools or agencies where unorganized occupational materials have accumulated over a period of time, an alphabetical system is often an immediate solution.

A simple alphabetical system has certain obvious advantages. First, it is the easiest system to operate and therefore is usable at low educational levels or by clients whose educational background is limited. Second, an alphabetical system is totally adjustable to local conditions, since the number of folders included can be fitted exactly to the materials used in the file. As new materials are obtained on occupations not previously included, the file is expanded easily by simply labeling new folders with the names of the occupations to be added. Third, it requires no key or index to help find materials, which can be filed or found easily and rapidly. When it is expected that the ultimate size of the file will not exceed one or two file drawers, the alphabetical system is usually more efficient than any other method.

As the occupational file grows larger, the simple alphabetical system becomes less efficient. As the file expands, the problem of alternative titles becomes a serious one. The only feasible solution to the problem actually adds to its complexity. To be sure that clients will locate the material in the file, regardless of the title under which it is placed, it becomes necessary to set up folders for each title that they might use and organize a cross-reference system that will direct them to the folder or folders in which material can be found.

A further criticism of the simple alphabetical system is that it does not provide any way to identify occupational groups or families. Occupations that actually may be very closely related often are filed far apart because of alphabetical order.

Coded System

The *Dictionary of Occupational Titles* has served as a logical base for filing career materials since the first edition appeared in 1939. At one time, a system was proposed based on the literal translation of the *DOT* coding system into a filing plan. With more than 12,000 code numbers in the 1991 edition, it is obvious that such a plan is far too detailed for practical application. Nevertheless, the *DOT* provides an obviously useful base for filing career materials. Consequently, it has frequently served as the model for building filing systems, both privately developed and commercially prepared. One widely used plan of this type is the *Chronicle Occupational Library,* published by Chronicle Guidance Publications, Inc., Moravia, NY 13118.

The *Chronicle Library* includes a filing system of folders for approximately 700 occupational briefs and reprints. The user may select a basic filing system based on either the *Dictionary of Occupational Titles* or the *Guide for Occupational Exploration.* One advantage for this type of plan is its use of a widely used classification system. A second advantage is the ability to expand in areas where local circumstances suggest a need for more materials and to contract in areas of little interest or a paucity of material.

The major criticism aimed at such a plan relates to the first advantage listed. Some contend that the plan requires special knowledge and training to operate. Most individuals will find the system somewhat complicated at first encounter, especially if they are exploring on their own. But if we assume that most users will be introduced to the file system by a counselor or someone who understands it, this criticism is immaterial.

The *Careers Desk-Top Kit* published by Careers, Inc., Largo, FL 33540, is an attempt to provide a condensed supplement to the regular occupational file. It includes brief sketches of a fairly wide range of occupations organized in a portable box only 6 inches by 9 inches by 19 inches. The *Desk-Top Kit* can be used easily by the counselor, students, or clients. The material included is filed according to a system based on the *DOT.*

Other Systems

Through the years, a number of proposals have been made for other methods of filing unbound occupational information. Such plans frequently have been based on either areas of interest or academic subject areas. In the first case it has been fairly common to tie the filing system to an interest inventory, often Holland's Self-Directed Search. In the second case, either high school subjects or college major areas are used as a base for filing.

The major advantage of such plans is fairly obvious, since the filing plan is tied directly to a base that is easily understood by the users of the file. It is very simple to consider a Self-Directed Search profile, for example, to ascertain the area(s) of highest interest and then turn to a filing system that lists jobs in this same type of classification. On the surface, such a system appears to make sense and appeals to the user.

Such plans have two serious disadvantages, either of which can prevent their adoption. First, interest factors or academic subjects are unrealistic bases for classifying occupations, simply because most fields of work do not have or require a special or unique interest pattern that can be used to differentiate them from other fields. The second disadvantage is the danger that classification by either subject matter or interest area will mislead the user by placing undue emphasis on the base system (either interest or subject) as the primary factor in making a vocational choice.

Filing Bound Occupational Materials

Filing bound occupational information usually does not present the problems encountered with unbound materials. First, probably fewer items are published in bound form; second, counselors, teachers, and other personnel are more accustomed to working with bound materials.

If all occupational materials are to be located together—in the career resource center, for example—a simple plan for shelf filing usually can be developed to fit the system used for unbound materials. For most users it will be easier if the two types of materials are set up under the same general filing plan. Shelf space can be readily organized in this fashion. Because many of the bound items—such as the *Occupational Outlook Handbook*—include information that cuts across many occupations, a general shelf will have to be established in addition to the specific areas. The development of microfiche and computerized systems has changed the old card file plan for locating material, but has not eliminated the search for information. Sampson (1982) describes a computer-assisted index system for career materials used in a college setting. The system that best fits local conditions and the users is the ideal system to adopt.

Summary

The aims of this chapter were twofold: first to consider the various types of career information used in career development programs, and second to examine ways to organize and maintain that information in a career resource center so it can be used effectively in all career development activities.

All career-related information arises from two fundamental sources: either the person doing the work or the person for whom the work is being done. Career information coming from the two basic sources is acquired, processed, and distributed by various entities and organizations, such as government agencies, commercial publishers, professional organizations, private employers, and educational institutions. In addition to printed material, career information comes in many other forms, including audiovisual and computerized formats; interview sources; practice and artificial experiences; as well as direct exposure through observation, exploration, and tryout.

Establishing a resource center requires consideration of many problems beyond space, staff, equipment, funding, and maintenance. Among these considerations are the establishment of policies regarding who is to be served and how, and the setting up of operational policies. Before materials can be acquired, decisions about criteria for collecting and maintaining them must be made, as well as decisions about how materials will be stored and accessed.

References

AEL. (1994). *Activities for individualized career exploration and planning.* Bloomington, IL: Meridian.

Bradley, R. W., & Thacker, M. S. (1978). Developing local sources of career education. *Vocational Guidance Quarterly, 26,* 268–272.

Brown, S. T., & Brown, D. (1990). *Designing and implementing a career information center.* Garrett Park, MD: Garrett Park Press.

Chapman, W., & Katz, M. (1981). *Survey of career information systems in secondary schools.* Princeton, NJ: Educational Testing Service.

Cheshire, B. (1988). *A handbook for guidance counselors.* Statesboro, GA: School of Education.

Fifield, M., & Petersen, L. (1978). Job simulation: A method of vocational exploration. *Vocational Guidance Quarterly, 26,* 326–333.

Frederickson, R. H. (1982). *Career information* (pp. 48–65). Englewood Cliffs, NJ: Prentice-Hall.

Heppner, M. J. (1981). Alumni sharing knowledge (ASK): High quality, cost-effective career resources. *Journal of College Student Personnel, 22,* 173–174.

Herr, E. L., & Watts, A. G. (1988). Work shadowing and work-related learning. *Career Development Quarterly, 37,* 78–86.

Hoppock, R. (1970). How to conduct an occupational group conference with an alumnus. *Vocational Guidance Quarterly, 18,* 311–312.

Hubbard, M., & Hawke, S. (1987). *Developing a career information center.* Montreal, Quebec: Guidance Information Center, Concordia University.

Isaacson, L. E., & Hayes, R. (1980). Adapting career day to the elementary school. *Elementary School Guidance and Counseling, 14,* 258–261.

Johnson, W. F., Korn, T. A., & Dunn, D. J. (1975). Comparing three methods of presenting occupational information. *Vocational Guidance Quarterly, 24,* 62–66.

Kelly, E. W., Jr. (1978). Industrial shadow experiences: Career counseling from an experiential base. *Vocational Guidance Quarterly, 26,* 342–348.

Kelly, E. W., Jr., & Moore, P. R. (1979). Process analysis of industrial shadow experiences. *Vocational Guidance Quarterly, 27,* 244–249.

Kunze, K. R. (1967). Industry resources available to counselors. *Vocational Guidance Quarterly, 16,* 137–142.

Laramore, D. (1971). Counselors make occupational information packages. *Vocational Guidance Quarterly, 19,* 220–224.

McDaniels, C. M., Watts, G., Knoblich, M. A., Landon-Moore, M., & Tillerson, A. (1995). The Virginia VIEW career information hotline and 42,900 calls. *Virginia Counselors Journal, 23,* 40–48.

Miller, M. J., & Knippers, J. A. (1992). *Jeopardy:* A career information game for school counselors. *Career Development Quarterly, 41,* 55–61.

NCDA. (1991a). *Career and occupational literature rating form.* Alexandria, VA: Author.

NCDA. (1991b). *Guidelines for the preparation and evaluation of career and occupational information literature.* Alexandria, VA: Author.

NOICC. (1991). *Using labor market information in career exploration and decision making.* Garrett Park, MD: Garrett Park Press.

NOICC. (1994). *Career information hotlines sampler.* Washington, DC: National Occupational Information Coordinating Committee.

Pate, R. H., Jr., Tullock, J. B., & Dassance, C. R. (1981). A regional job and educational opportunities fair. *Personnel and Guidance Journal, 60,* 187–189.

Plotsky, F. A., & Goad, R. (1974). Encouraging women through a career conference. *Personnel and Guidance Journal, 52,* 486–488.

Reardon, R. C., & Minor, C. W. (1975). Revitalizing the career information service. *Personnel and Guidance Journal, 54,* 169–171.

Rodriguez, M. A. (1994). Preparing an effective occupational information for ethnic minorities. *Career Development Quarterly, 43,* 178–184.

Sampson, J. P., Jr. (1980). Using college alumni as resource persons for providing occupational information. *Journal of College Student Personnel, 21,* 172.

Sampson, J. P., Jr. (1982). A computer-assisted library index for career materials. *Journal of College Student Personnel, 23,* 539–540.

Sandler, S. B. (1990). *Jeopardy!* The counselor as a classroom teacher. *School Counselor, 38,* 65–66.

Self, C., & Lopez, F. (1982). Women in nontraditional fields: A career development seminar for college women. *Journal of College Student Personnel, 23,* 545–546.

Smith, E. (1983). Career key: A career library management system. *Vocational Guidance Quarterly, 32,* 52–56.

Tomlinson, E., & DiLeo, J. C. (1980). Broadening horizons: Careers for women in science. *Journal of College Student Personnel, 21,* 570–571.

U.S. Department of Defense. (1984). *Military career guide.* Washington, DC: Author.

U.S. Department of Defense, Office of the Assistant Secretary for Manpower, Installations, and Logistics. (1984). *Military occupational and training data.* Washington, DC: U.S. Government Printing Office.

U.S. Department of Labor, Manpower Administration. (1974). *Job analysis for human resources management: A review of selected research and development.* Manpower Research Monograph No. 36. Washington, DC: U.S. Government Printing Office.

Warrington, D. L., & Method-Walker, Y. (1981). Career scope. *Journal of College Student Personnel, 22,* 169–170.

Important Websites

NOICC	http://www.noicc.gov/
Government Printing Office	http://www.access.gpo.gov/
America's Job Bank	http://www.ajb.dni.us/
Colleges and Universities Home Page	http://mit.edu.8001/people/cdmello/univ.html
College Board Online	http://www.collegeborad.org/
CollegeNET	http://www.collegeNET.com/
The Definitive Guide to Internet Career Resources	http://phoenix.oakland.edu.career/internet.html
The Riley Guide: Employment Opportunities and Job Resources on the Internet	http://jobtrak.com/jobguide/
What Color Is Your Parachute? Job Hunting Online	http://washingtonpost.com/parachute

8

Computer-Assisted Career Guidance Systems (CACGS)

In Chapter 7, computer-assisted career guidance systems (CACGS) were identified as one of several methods of delivering career information and advancing the career development process. In fact, many current CACGS are capable of providing all the services normally offered in the career counseling process with the exception of developing a human relationship. Moreover, CACGS have far greater capacity to store and retrieve information than the counselors, and in some instances they replace career counselors in the career counseling process. One of the major purposes of this chapter is to explore the relationship that can and should exist between CACGS and career development specialists, including career counselors. This interrelationship will be discussed after a brief historical background of CACGS is presented. A second objective of this chapter is to provide an overview of some of the major CACGS in use in various types of institutions. Third, and finally, an overview of the current status and future possibilities for the use of CACGS will be provided.

Historical Background

Serious efforts were undertaken as early as the mid-1960s to relate computer technology to career counseling. Some of the early attempts are still operational today, although modernized and expanded. Jo Ann Harris-Bowlsby was instrumental in the planning that led to the Computerized Vocational Information System (CVIS), placed in operation in 1968. At the same time, Donald Super and Roger Myers of Columbia University were working with Frank Minor of IBM to create the Education and Career Exploration System (ECES), and David Tiedeman of Harvard and his colleagues were developing a system called Information System for Vocational Decisions (ISVD). CVIS provided a method for storing information about approximately 400 occupations arranged in the classification system originally developed by Roe (1956). The information file also included certain items of individual information for each student user, such as class rank, composite achievement and ability test scores, and interest inventory scores, thus permitting some comparison of prior data with requirements for entry and success in occupations. The system was primarily on-line information retrieval, and it effectively capitalized on the technology available at that time. It continued as a pilot program until 1972 and was then established as a demonstration center leading to widespread adoption of the system.

Both ECES and ISVD were more extensive efforts to computerize larger portions of the counseling process. Both provided for development and storage of self-descriptive information that would assist the client in better self-understanding; extensive data about future possibilities (in ECES this included occupations and educational files, and in ISVD these two areas were supplemented by files on military service and family); and procedures for clarifying and developing plans. Both reached the operational stage in the 1969–1970 period. The elaborate program incorporated in each system was theoretically sound, useful to clients, and technologically possible. Both, however, required such heavy use of computer time that they were ahead of reality in terms of cost-effectiveness, considering the developmental state of computers; consequently, neither has been widely adopted. Several of Tiedeman's colleagues on the ISVD project later turned to the development of a simpler system, which has become the Guidance Information System (GIS) in extensive use today.

During the early developmental years, essentially 1965 to 1980, computer technology was basically restricted to large, mainframe systems that were costly to operate both in terms of time and money. Harris-Bowlsby (1990) identifies eleven systems that were developed and put into usage during that period:

AUTOCOUN
CHOICES
CIS (Career Information System)
COIS (Computerized Occupational Information System)
CVIS (Computerized Vocational Information System)
DISCOVER
ECES (Education and Career Exploration System)
GIS (Guidance Information System)
ISVD (Information System for Vocational Decisions)
SIGI (System for Interactive Guidance Information)
TGIS (Total Guidance Information System)

One can deduce from the names of these early systems that two types of programs were being developed. One group emphasized information and focused on building systems in which one could search easily and rapidly for quality information about occupations and educational or training institutions. The other branch concentrated on the career planning process and provided use of self-information, decision-making strategies, and career development concepts. Very few systems were or are purely one type with total disregard for the other. The difference is primarily one of major emphasis. Recent years have shown movement toward the center; that is, inclusion of both branches. Two from each branch are discussed later in this chapter

Why Use CACGS?

Sampson (1997c) notes that the primary rationale for using CACGS is based on the fact that computers are more effective than people in handling certain repetitive tasks—such as storing and presenting information, administering and scoring tests and inventories, and matching information about the person to occupational characteristics. These repetitive tasks, if handled by CACGS, can free counselors to perform more complex tasks such as career counseling. However, it is undoubtedly the case that now and in the future many people will prefer to use computerized databases and CACGS in their career development activities. Although many career counselors are apprehensive about being left out of the career development process, it seems likely that, given the increasing importance of the Internet as a career development resource and the rise in the availability of CACGS, this may be the case. It therefore becomes incumbent upon career counselors to work to ensure that online resources and CACGS are designed in a manner that allows independent use. As will be shown in the next section, this may prove to be no easy task.

Who Can Benefit from CACGS?

Although it is somewhat of an oversimplification, the career development process can be summarized as (1) developing self-awareness, (2) developing an awareness of the occupations that may be suitable, (3) choosing an occupation, and (4) implementing the choice that is made. Implementation of one's career choice involves selecting an educational or training site, unless on-the-job training is provided by the employer. Implementation also includes developing the skills to find and secure jobs, and then using those skills in the job search. CACGS can be useful for *most* client groups in each of these steps. The question then becomes, "Who can benefit from the use of CACGS?" Sampson (1997a,b,c) has attempted to answer this question and provides the following guidelines for potential users of CACGS.

1. Users should have the verbal ability necessary to use the systems. Users who have low reading ability should probably be precluded from use of these systems or use them in conjunction with counselors or paraprofessionals.

2. Students with goal instability or low self-efficacy may not benefit from the systems and may need to engage in traditional career counseling or engage in what Sampson terms "supported use." Supported use of CACGS simply means that clients use them with the support of a professional or paraprofessional.

3. Poorly motivated clients—that is, clients who are not greatly concerned about getting more information about themselves or occupations or engaging in career planning—are unlikely to benefit from CACGS and thus should probably be involved in either traditional career counseling or supported use of CACGS.

4. Students with low self-esteem or negative thinking about careers or themselves are unlikely to benefit from CACGS. These individuals may distort the information they receive from CACGS and therefore must have this problem resolved prior to using one of these systems.

5. Anxiety and depression are barriers to effective decision making and need to be dealt with prior to accessing a CACGS.

6. Lack of information or misconceptions about CACGS are deterrents to effective use. Although these problems can be dealt with in brief interventions, it is inappropriate to allow people to use CACGS who are either unskilled in their use or under- or overestimate their potential to provide assitance.

7. People who have significant barriers, such as economic limitations or role conflicts, to making career choices or implementing those choices should not rely solely on CACGS. Counselor support is necessary for these clients.

Sampson (1997b) also raises the questions of the utility of CACGS for people who have intuitive (versus reflexive) decision-making styles and people who have Holland interest codes that are either social or enterprising. However, there seem to be no compelling data that would suggest that these people might not benefit from CACGS. Sampson (1997a,b,c) clearly believes that most people can benefit for some exposure to CACGS, but he differentiates between people who can use benefit by using CACGS as their sole source of support versus those who need support to gain maximum benefit from CACGS. He suggests that career development programs need to establish procedures for screening potential users of CACGS to ascertain who can take advantage of self-directed experiences versus those who cannot. Once this screening has been completed, various scenarios for helping clients can be established based on the conclusions reached in the screening process. Sampson's recommendations for these scenarios are summarized below, with some modifictions based on the recommendations of Brown and Brooks (1991).

Group A—Ready for independent use of CACGS: Individuals who are computer literate, and

1. have relatively simple questions such as the salaries or occupational duties of two or three occupations;
2. are motivated to use CACGS and are free from negative thinking, anxiety, depression, decisional anxiety, and role conflicts; and

3. have the reading skills needed to use the system.

Goup B—Ready for independent use of CCGA with orientation to the system:

1. All of group A who are not computer literate.

Group C—Not ready for independent use, but CACGS with support can be used without prior counseling interventions:

1. Individuals who have low reading ability, economic limitations.
2. Multipotentialed individuals.

Group D—Not ready for independent use, and counseling intervention should precede use of CACGS:

1. Individuals with low self-esteem, negative thoughts.
2. Individuals who have decisional anxiety.
3. Individuals who are highly anxious or depressed.

How Effective Are CACGS and What Are Their Benefits?

The literature regarding the effectiveness of CACGS is basically supportive of their use. Kapes, Borman, and Frazier (1989), Niles and Garis (1990), and Marin and Splete (1991) found that counselor intervention or counselors plus computers were more effective than CACGS alone, but in each case the researchers concluded that CACGS alone had a positive effect on clients. Earlier studies (e.g., Campbell, 1983; Garis & Harris-Bowlsby (1984) found no significant differences between the effectiveness of career counselors and CACGS.

Sampson (1997c) contended that the use of CACGS can produce numerous benefits for users and summarized 30 years of research to identify positive outcomes. The benefits include the generation of an increased number of occupational alternatives that are more related to personal characteristics, increased knowledge of occupations and labor market information, increased certainty regarding occupational choice, and increased career maturity. As noted earlier, it is also expected that individuals will receive better career development services and that the career development specialist will be freed from repetitive tasks. Sampson (1997c) goes ahead to suggest that when CACGS are presented using multimedia technology, other benefits such as increased motivation and opportunities for reality testing may result. As yet the impact of multimedia presentations have not been evaluated, however.

Ethical Considerations and CACGS Usage

All current codes of ethics (e.g., ACA, 1995) require that the use of any intervention, including CACGS, be appropriate given clients' needs and readiness, be fully explained to clients, and be followed up by counselors to determine problems or misunderstandings that may have arisen. Sampson (1997a) concluded that research is needed to determine the extent to which these guidelines are met in practice. However, to be in compliance, career development specialists must:

1. Purchase CACGS that have been designed and validated for independent use. CACGS, once purchased, should be kept up-to-date.
2. Screen to ascertain clients' needs and readiness. Clients who are not ready to uses CACGS should receive appropriate counseling or other services to ensure readiness.
3. Orient clients to the hardware and software used in the CACGS. Of particular importance is the need to make clients aware of the limitations of the software and the need for them to consider factors other than those included in the software package in their choice making.
4. Monitor the use of CACGS when clients do not meet the criteria for independent use.
5. Follow up with each CACGS user to ensure that no problems or misunderstandings develop.

Which CACGS? Components and Costs

Earlier in this section it was suggested that CACGS can provide assistance with each step in the career development process. Although at one time hardware and software costs for almost all CACGS precluded all but a few institutions from acquiring these systems, that is rarely the case at this time. Fairly sophisticated CACGS can be acquired through some SOICCs for as little as $125. Computers to run these systems are already available in all but the poorest institutions.

Although, as will be shown in the next section, CACGS vary widely, they may contain some or all of the following modules: (1) Assessment of users' needs and recommended use, (2) Self-assessment of interests, values, and abilities, (3) Information about occupations and training opportunities, (4) Search options that allow the matching of personal traits to occupations, (5) Employability skills modules that allow for resume development and that provide tips for other aspects of the job search, (6) Exploration of life-role relationships, and (7) external hyperlinks to Internet resources. The exact type of system needed will depend upon a number of factors including the ages of the potential users, the budget available to purchase and maintain the sytem, the amount of staff support available to use with the system, and the objectives that the career development specialists hope to achieve with the CACGS.

Widely Used Systems

Information about CACGS can be obtained from salespeople, technical manuals, catalogs, the state SOICC offices, and through hands-on tryouts. Probably the best source of information about CACGS is through direct, hands-on experiences, which can be gained at professional meetings where vendors may have set up demonstration systems, at SOICC sponsored workshops, and by traveling to sites that have the system of interest. Tables 8.1 and 8.2 contain listings of the most widely used CACGS in this country. Table 8.1 contains those systems that were designed for use with high school students and adults, and Table 8.2 contains a listing of the systems that were designed for use with middle school and junior high school age students. A comparison of selected components of the systems used with high school students and adults is shown in Table 8.3. The information in Table 8.3 was adapted from a comprehensive comparison of CACGS conducted at Florida State University (Sampson & associates, 1998). In addition to comparing the components of the systems, Sampson and his associates also looked at the user-friendliness of the system and the costs of securing and maintaining them. They found that the costs ranged from $250 to $1850 for the systems they compared. However, as has been noted elsewhere, some SOICCs such as Virginia VIEW provide the software needed for the state CACGS at no charge to the user.

In the sections that follow four of the most widely used CACGS are examined.

Career Information System (CIS)

CIS was developed as the Oregon state system under a 1969 grant from the U.S. Department of Labor directed by Dr. Bruce McKinlay. A separate organization, National CIS, now exists to coordinate the application of CIS in other parts of the country and to provide additional services in the development of software and the provision of training. CIS is the basic system in thirteen states and New York City. Most CIS state systems include the following two types of files, state or local files and national files. These include:

CIS State Files:

   1. Occupations—descriptions of at least 320 occupations are included in this file. These descriptions include the duties performed, aptitudes required to perform the job, the nature of the work setting, wages earned, and local labor market information including occupational outlook information, and licensing and training information.

   2. Programs of Study—lists in-state preparation programs for specific occupations including 2- and 4-year colleges and public and private vocational schools. This file contains information about entry requirements, costs, and sources of additional information.

TABLE 8.1   Widely Used Computer-Assisted Career Guidance Systems Adolescents and Adults

System	Publisher
Career Information System	Career Information System National Office, Eugene, OR
Career Visions	Wisconsin Career Information System, Madison, WI
*CareerWays**	Wisconsin Career Information System, Madison, WI
*Choices**	Careerware: ISM System Corp. Ottawa, Ontario (Canada)
Modular C-Lect	Chronicle Press, Moravia, NY
COIN	COIN Educational Products Toledo, OH
Discover: Colleges and Adults* High School Students* Military*	American College Testing Hunt Valley, MD
Visions Plus	American College Testing for Maryland SOICC
Guidance Information System: II & III*	Riverside Publishing Co. Chicago, IL
SIGI Plus	Educational Testing Service Princeton, NJ

*Available in multimedia format

TABLE 8.2   CACGS for Elementary and Middle/Junior High Students

System	Publisher
Choices Jr. (Middle)	Careerware
C-Lect Jr. (Middle)	Chronicle Press
COIN JR (Middle)	COIN Educational Products
Visions (Middle)	American College Testing for Maryland SOICC
Discover for Middle/Junior	American College Testing
GIS Jr. (Middle)	Riverside Publishing
Career Trek (4 through middle)	Career Information System

TABLE 8.3   Comparison of Selected Components of Most-Used Adult and High School Computer-Assisted Career Guidance Systems

Abbreviations Used:

CI	=	Career Information System	DC =	DISCOVER—high school and adult versions for Windows
CV	=	Career Visions	GI =	Guidance Information System III
CH	=	Choices	SP =	SIGI Plus
CL	=	C-Lect	VI =	Visions
CO	=	COIN		

Components	Included
1. Overview of systems	CI, CH, CO, CL, DC, SP, VI
2. Recommended pathway based on user characteristics	GI and SP
3. Assessment information	
A. Readiness for career choice	DC
B. Clarify life roles	DC colleges and adults
C. In-put of paper and pencil inventories possible	All but SP & DC
D. Administer inventories on-line	CV, CL, CH, DC, GI
4. Basis for selecting occupational alternatives	
A. Abilities/skills	CI, CV, CH, DC, GI, SP
B. Aptitudes	CI, CV, CH, DC, GI
C. ASVAB scores	CI, CH, GI
D. Training	All
E. Majors/course of study	CV, CI, DC, GI
F. Salary	CI, CH, CV, CO, DC, GI, SP
G. Values	CI, DC, GI, SP
5. Occupational information	
A. Capacity to compare two occupations on selected characteristic	CV, CH, CO, DC, SP
B. Crosswalks to other files from occupations files	All
C. Multiple sources of information used	All
D. Beginning income	All
E. Income range	CI, CV, CH, CL, CO, DC, SP, VI
6. Educational opportunities	
A. Apprenticeship search	DC, VI
B. Voc–tech schools	All
C. 2 and 4 year college search	All
D. Financial aid search	CI, CH, CL, CO, DC, SP, VI
E. Crosswalks from education files to others	DC, GI
7. Decision-making model described on-line	DC, SP
8. Employment planning	
A. Books (resources)	CI
B. Networking	CI, DC, SP, VI
C. Job applications	CI, DC, VI
D. Job interviewing	CI, DC, VI
E. Resume writing	CI, DC, VI

Source: Adapted from Samson, J. P., Jr., and others (1998). *A differential feature-cost analysis of seventeen computer-assisted career guidance systems* (Tech. Rep. No. 10). Tallahassee, FL. Center for the Study of Technology in Counseling and Career Development (pp. 13–32).

3. In-State Schools—entrance requirements, housing information, costs, for colleges, graduate schools, proprietary schools, and other schools included in this file.

4. Local Financial Aid—state and local sources of financial assistance are included in this file.

5. Job Search File—includes how to apply for jobs, develop a resume, interview for a job.

6. OWN—has tips for planning and owning your own business.

7. Industry—describes industries, the type of work provided, and industry outlook information.

8. Special files—the Georgia CIS helps users identify skills that may be transferable to another job.

CIS National Files:

1. National Schools—contains information about more than seven hundred 2- and 4-year colleges in the United States.

2. National Financial Aid—contains information about 1000 scholarship sponsors and 59,000 scholarships.

3. Military Occupations and Worklife—provides information about jobs in the military.

4. Special files—for example, Georgia CIS helps users define their skills that are transferable to other jobs.

Users of CIS may access the information files in one of the following ways:

1. Quest—user answers a series of questions about interests and work preferences and is provided a list of occupations.

2. Link—user enters test scores such as those from the Armed Services Aptitude Battery or Self-Directed Search and is provided a list of occupations based on scores.

3. School Sort—user answers a series of questions about types of schools desired and is given a list of potential schools.

4. Aid Sort—user answers questions about school plans and needs and is given a list of potential sources of aid.

CIS represents one type of CACGS, one that is oriented to providing occupational information, not career guidance. The system is not designed to engage users in decision making to help them narrow their lists of choices that are generated either as a result of Quest or the entry of results from various assessment devices. CIS contains no on-line tests or inventories at the current time, and this would be considered a limitation by many. It is, however, one of the least expensive of the CACGS available and can be individualized to meet the specific needs of a state or city. The New York City schools provide information about jobs in New York State and the metropolitan New York City area through a CIS called MetroGuide.

Kjos (1987) studied one hundred people drawn from a population of 3000 unemployed workers from south Chicago. Seventy percent of the group had been unemployed for an average of 3 years. The purpose of the study was to determine if the list of occupations generated as a result of Quest directly or indirectly matched the prior work experience of the people being studied. Kjos concluded that the occupations generated were generally reflective of past work experience regardless of the work history, educational attainment, or age of the subjects.

Guidance Information System (GIS)

GIS is another of the widely used CACGS. It provides access to ten possible files:

1. Occupational Information—contains information about 489 general occupations and 1000 specialized occupations.
2. Armed Services Occupations—over 200 military careers are cross-referenced with civilian jobs.
3. Two-Year College File—over 1700 two-year colleges are included.
4. Four-Year College File—includes descriptions of 1700 colleges from across the country.
5. Graduate and Professional School File—contains descriptions of 1850 professional and graduate schools.
6. Financial Aid File—descriptions of more than 650 sources of financial aid.
7. Majors and Career File—provides a crosswalk between college majors and jobs.
8. Interest Inventory Score Entry—permits entry of Career Decision-Making Inventory, Career Assessment Inventory, Strong Interest Inventory, and Self-Directed Search scores to be used to identify occupations.
9. Career Decision-Making System—optional on-line interest inventory.
10. State Vocational School Files—optional listing of state-level vocational schools.

Information in the files is arranged according to groups of characteristics or attributes. For example, the occupations file includes data on interests (11 characteristics), aptitudes (10 characteristics), physical demands (12 characteristics), work conditions (9 characteristics), lifestyle (16 characteristics), salary (12 characteristics), employment potential (5 characteristics), education and training (21 characteristics), and other qualifications (5 characteristics). The 4-year college file is arranged according to academic program (approximately 450 characteristics), location (68 characteristics), type of institution (14 characteristics), undergraduate enrollment (11 characteristics), control (2 characteristics), religious affiliation (5 characteristics), accreditation (5 characteristics), faculty (2 characteristics), admissions information (13 characteristics), academic characteristics of first-year students (22 characteristics), admissions policies (15 characteristics), calendar plan (6 characteristics), degree requirements (3 characteristics), student body data (5 characteristics), annual costs (24 characteristics), residence policies (11 characteristics), financial aid (13 characteristics), special programs (27 characteristics), ROTC (4 characteristics), campus life (25 characteristics), athletic programs (129 characteristics), and athletic scholarships (86 characteristics).

Users can obtain general or detailed information about occupations or schools in which they are interested. The PRINT command can be used to obtain general information about a specific occupation or school or about several occupations or schools. The ITEMIZE command can be used similarly to obtain detailed information either about a single occupation or school or about several. If desired, detailed information about specific sets of characteristics can be obtained without itemizing all the information in the file. This request for general or detailed information about one or more occupations or schools is labeled the *direct method*. Obviously, it is most useful when the client has an occupation or school in mind and wants to obtain information about it. The armed services file works only with this method. All other files can also be approached in this way.

The *search method* is probably used more frequently. This approach is designed to help the user who wants to know what occupations or schools would meet characteristics or requirements she might have in mind. Local worksheets for the various files are usually arranged so that they list brief identifiers for each of the characteristics included in the file. The user is asked first to identify those characteristics to be included, those to be excluded, and those that can be combined on an either/or basis. Next the user is asked to arrange these marked items in a hierarchy with the most important item, either inclusion or exclusion, listed first. Summary sheets are often provided for this ranking. The ADD command is used to enter those characteristics to be included, and the SUBTRACT command is used for excluded items. If combined items exist on the list, the EITHER/OR command tells the computer to include any occupation or college that has at least one of the listed characteristics. Starting with all occupations or schools in the file being searched, the system reports after each entry the number that remain. As each ADD or SUBTRACT is made, the number qualifying dwindles. When those occupations or schools remaining in the list number twenty-five or fewer, the user can ask for the names of those remaining. This list can then be used with the PRINT or ITEMIZE commands described earlier. If the user enters a command that reduces the list too drastically, or if the user changes her mind about the characteristics, the DELETE command eliminates that characteristic from the search. The user has great flexibility in organizing the search and can capitalize on personal preferences as well as change directions during the process. The user also can move from one file to another easily—for example, from the occupations file where possible jobs were identified to one of the school files to explore information about relevant preparatory programs.

Efficient use of computer time requires the user to give prior consideration to those characteristics that are personally important. This can be done either independently or with the counselor, and many GIS sites have locally developed worksheets that facilitate identifying the characteristics the user wants to include. As the various characteristics are entered, the computer immediately responds with the number of occupations or schools remaining on the list; thus the user can see at once the impact of that particular characteristic. If the user previously has identified the characteristics he or she is most interested in, the required terminal time is usually not more than 10 or 15 minutes.

The *User's Guide* is a handbook that explains how the system operates and includes a description of each characteristic included in the national files. The *Guide* is revised regularly and distributed to centers using GIS. In addition to the *User's Guide*, there are indexes for each of the national files. Each index is most useful for the user who wishes to apply the direct method. For example, the *Occupations Index* arranges occupations according to three different systems: general occupations, *DOT*-based descriptions, and occupational clusters. Additional supplementary materials are available.

A recent GIS format change for microcomputer users permits the presentation of characteristics of all files on screen so that the user can select them from there rather than from the *Guide* or a local worksheet. The major search commands are visible at the bottom of the screen at all times, and a user can type HELP followed by a command letter to obtain an on-screen explanation of how to use that command. In addition, a change has been made in the use of interest inventory data. The Harrington–O'Shea Career Decision-Making System is available on-line; after completing the inventory (including items on occupational preference, school subject preferences, future educational plans, job values, and self-reported abilities), the user is presented with titles of career clusters related to the responses. It is also now possible to enter results from other interest inventories.

Most clients will want and/or need counselor help both before and after terminal use. Although the characteristics included in the various files are clear and easily understood, their relationship to the client's psychological world becomes more apparent in a counseling session. Similarly, the final printout of the narrowed list of occupations or schools may well leave the user without a sense of closure. The counselor can help the user consider exploratory steps to acquire additional information on the listed items that will lead to decision making and subsequent planning.

DISCOVER

The development of DISCOVER has been largely the work of Jo Ann Harris-Bowlsby and, in part, is an extension of her previous effort on CVIS, one of the earliest systems that gained widespread usage. DISCOVER was developed as a systematic career guidance program to assist in career development activities at the secondary school level. From its earliest days, its emphasis has been on the career planning process. Harris-Bowlsby (1990) stresses that competitive pressures among the various systems require updating and redevelopment on a regular basis. ACT has followed such a pattern and has been very successful in anticipating market needs.

In 1998 ACT offered five CACGS: DISCOVER for high schools; DISCOVER for colleges and adults; VISIONS for middle schools and VISIONS Plus both of which were developed for the Maryland SOICC; and DISCOVER for the Military.

The middle/junior school version, designed for students in grades 6 to 9, is focused toward helping them plan for high school. The conceptual approach, based on the ACT World-of-Work Map (described in Chapter 6), is intended to give students a start in career exploration with an overview of the world of work and identification of personal characteristics. The middle/junior high version has an entry/exit section and three major modules. The individual may choose to use any one or all three of the modules.

Entry/Exit

This section explains how to use the system and collect identifying information in order to store student records, and it explains the career planning process used in the modules. When ready to sign off, students can save the results for later use or reference. The modules are as follows:

1. *You and the World of Work:* This module uses the ACT World-of-Work Map described in Chapter 6. Users can participate in a World-of-Work Map game that requires identifying basic work tasks involved in nine job-related activities. They are required to become familiar with basic work tasks (working with people, data, things, or combinations of these) and examples of typical activities for each. Users are asked to identify whether they would enjoy the activity, thus beginning awareness of their reactions to work activities.

2. *Exploring Occupations:* In this module students systematically explore occupations using the World-of-Work Map and Holland's typology. Students can enter their scores on any of several achievement tests, grades earned in selected courses, or self-ratings in several ability areas, to relate specific achievement or ability to various occupational clusters. Occupational information can be accessed by adding the anticipated educational level students hope to attain before going to work.

3. *Planning Your High School Program:* This module uses the student's tentative career and educational aspirations to plan a high school program of studies. If desired, schools can incorporate local graduation requirements and course offerings in this section.

The high school version places primary emphasis on career direction and thereby proposes to offer help to both students whose plans are beginning to crystallize and students who are still undecided or uncertain. This version provides modules at each step of the career planning process. There are seven in all, and each is divided into subparts that can be used independently if desired. Several activities (e.g., interest assessment) are available either on-line through the computer or in paper-and-pencil format not requiring computer time. The seven modules are as follows:

1. *Beginning the Career Journey:* In this module the user checks his level of career decision-making maturity to determine which later modules will be most useful. A 36-item inventory, taken either on- or off-line, is keyed to the remaining modules and provides a list of modules most likely to be helpful.

2. *Learning about the World of Work:* This section presents the ACT World-of-Work Map and explains the concepts of work tasks, map regions, clusters, and job families.

3. *Learning about Yourself:* This module helps the user acquire information about self through a series of exercises, including interest assessment and other devices that also can be completed on- or off-line. Factors besides interest include abilities, work-related values, and experiences. The module can also accept data from a range of previously completed interest and aptitude measures.

4. *Finding Occupations:* This module generates lists of occupations for consideration and exploration. The user can select suboptions from an array of categories such as employment outlook, job setting, work hours, amount of supervision, job pressure, and education needed.

5. *Learning about Occupations:* This module provides detailed information about any of the 458 occupations included in the file. Information is updated annually. As new occupations become significant in the labor market, they are added to the file. DISCOVER claims that the 458 occupations represent 95 percent of the employment opportunities in the United States.

6. *Making Educational Choices:* This module presents information on educational preparation leading to the occupations identified in Module 5. Appropriate majors or programs of study are also listed for chosen occupations.

7. *Planning Next Steps:* This module provides information about postsecondary educational opportunities. The file includes 2921 vocational-technical schools, 1458 two-year colleges, 1731 four-year colleges, 1241 graduate schools, 144 external degree programs, and 212 military programs.

The college and adult version of DISCOVER consists of modules 1 through 7 of the high school version, with two additional modules:

8. *Planning a Career:* This module is designed for adults in transition or others beyond the college age group. It uses Super's Life/Career Rainbow (1990) as the basis for exploring the various roles in each person's life. Users can apply the module to plan for changes in their future.

9. *Making Transitions:* This module helps users understand career transitions that are increasingly common, the pressures and tensions that one encounters in such transitions, and how to deal with and control these factors.

Roselle and Hummel (1988) report a study of twelve college students to examine the relationship between intellectual development and effective use of

DISCOVER. Students with higher scores on the Measure of Intellectual Development showed higher ability to use DISCOVER as one more tool in career planning, to adapt easily to the system, and to show greater self-knowledge. This suggests that most users will need assistance in using the system for maximum advantage in reverse proportion to intellectual development. Shahnasarian and Peterson (1988) report that having students view a brief videotape explaining Holland's typology improved their thinking about occupational possibilities; however, those who did not view the videotape felt more certain of their vocational choices. Fukuyama, Probert, Neimeyer, Nevill, and Metzler (1988) report that completion of the college system resulted in higher self-efficacy scores for undergraduates. The students who had completed the system were much more certain of their occupational plans than students who had not used DISCOVER. Garis and Niles (1990) report a study using DISCOVER and SIGI with career planning courses matched against students taking the courses without access to CACG. Their results do not show significant increases when computer systems are added.

System of Interactive Guidance and Information (SIGI)

SIGI, now known as SIGI PLUS, is the product of developmental effort by a research group led by Martin Katz at Educational Testing Service. Katz (1990) describes the early activities that resulted in SIGI. It was originally intended for use by students in or about to enter 2-year colleges. It is now applied more broadly, including usage in 4-year schools and with out-of-school adults in a variety of settings.

The philosophic basis for SIGI proposes that values identification and clarification are basic to an effective career decision process involving evaluation of the rewards and risks that accompany each option. The system covers the major aspects of career decision making, using nine separate modules or sections. Each module provides an array of user activities that can be used selectively or entirely. The introductory section can recommend specific pathways based on user-provided personal information about present career status. Like DISCOVER, the system provides a means of storing client records that permits the client to recall information from previous system usage. Included in the following brief descriptions of the nine modules is a question that indicates the purpose of the section, a description of what the client can do, and some of the special features built into the module.

1. *Introduction* *What is in SIGI PLUS?*

   Included: An overview of SIGI PLUS and a recommended pathway based on client-provided information.

   Features: Clear explanation; directs clients to sections that apply to them; permits requests for additional information about subsequent parts.

2. *Self-Assessment What do I want? What am I good at?*

Included: Work-related values and personal choices of most importance; choice of main interest fields; consideration of work activities and evaluation of likes and what one does well; a game to help clarify values.

Features: Chance to clarify personal values, interests, and skills; helps identify what's most important personally; maintains emphasis on personal values; uses an activities inventory that links interests and skills; relates these to everyday life.

3. *Search What occupations might I like?*

Included: Identification of preferred work features; identification of work features client wishes to avoid; creates a list of occupations having the preferred features.

Features: Helps client develop a personal list of occupational alternatives; allows any combination of values, interests, skills, level of education, and features to be avoided; permits exclusion of occupations client does not want to consider; explains which factor eliminated a specific occupation not on the list.

4. *Information What occupations might I like?*

Included: Selection of one or two occupations at a time to match against information such as skills required, advancement possibilities, potential income, national employment outlook, and educational requirements.

Features: Answers twenty-seven questions about each selected occupation, gives alternate job titles, provides sources for additional information, possible to add local information.

5. *Skills Can I do what's required?*

Included: Lists specific skills required for any listed occupation; self-rating on skills required.

Features: Selection of any included occupation; shows how work skills are applied in the specific occupation, provides examples of how these skills are applied in everyday life; includes information on managerial and supervisory skills.

6. *Preparing Can I do what's required?*

Included: Shows typical preparatory paths, estimates client's likelihood of completing preparation.

Features: Links career planning to preparatory programs; shows typical preparation for each specific field, including courses and course descriptions if desired; considers factors related to acquiring preparation such as finding time, finding money, handling the difficulty, staying motivated.

7. Coping *Can I do what's required?*

Included: Suggestions on dealing with issues related to preparation such as finding time and money; arranging care for others; obtaining school credit for present knowledge; learning to handle preparation-related worries.

Features: Provides specific suggestions for time management and financing alternatives; responds to common preparation worries; provides information on establishing academic credit; permits addition of local information.

8. Deciding *What's right for me?*

Included: Client can match three occupations at a time for rewards, anticipated employment, chances for entrance and success, overall evaluation.

Features: Summarizes information from previous sections; provides a decision-making strategy; permits comparison of occupation with possible new careers; introduces basis for graphic comparison of alternatives.

9. Next Steps *How do I put my plan into action?*

Included: Clients can start toward career goal by planning short-term goals such as more education or training; developing new skills; proving they can do the work; building a network of contacts; writing a resume; overcoming obstacles.

Features: Helps identify specific steps; provides concrete suggestions, tips, and models for resume writing; prompts planning immediate first steps.

Mazel and Cummings (1982) report that the average user spends 3.5 hours to complete the process. This time is all computer-connect and terminal use time and therefore is relatively costly under present conditions. SIGI software has been developed for use with a variety of computers of all three sizes.

Like other systems, SIGI's strengths and weaknesses depend on how those characteristics are valued by user sites. SIGI is based on a clearly conceived theoretical position. It emphasizes the importance of values, and some will see it as underplaying other important attributes. It focuses on an educationally related clientele, so some will see it as serving other groups less adequately. It requires the user to progress methodically through its conception of the career decision process, so some will see it as more rigid and less flexible than systems that do not adhere to a clear philosophic position.

Other Systems

Two other systems are used widely in the United States. CHOICES (Computerized Heuristic Occupational Information and Career Exploration System), originally developed for Canadian users, has been adopted by a number of states plus the District of Columbia. *Although largely aimed toward information access and retrieval, CHOICES does include aspects of career exploration.*

Information about included occupations is divided into four categories, namely, identification data, descriptive data, coded attribute data, and similar occupations data. The coded attribute data section includes seventeen *topics,* such as education, work sites, physical demands, temperaments, earnings, aptitudes, and interests. The Explore Route permits the user to hunt for occupations compatible to her evaluation of the personal importance of these topics. The Information Route permits the user either to obtain specific coded attribute information about a particular occupation or to compare two occupations simultaneously on the attributes.

Information about 2400 two- and four-year colleges is structured in parallel fashion. The general categories of information, again called *topics,* include geographic location, programs, institutional types, tuition, enrollment, community size, athletic programs, and on-campus housing. As with occupations topics, users are asked to complete a personal profile that reports their priority for the topics as well as personal preferences within each one. These responses can then be used to search for institutions that match personal preferences or to obtain specific information about institutions for which they desire further details.

C-LECT (Computer-Linked Exploration of Careers and Training), marketed by Chronicle Guidance Publications, also includes identification of personal temperament and interest patterns in addition to occupational and educational information. Both CHOICES and C-LECT are designed for general use in the career development process and, thereby, are used mainly in educational settings. C-LECT is quite brief compared to the more extensive programs described earlier and usually requires less than an hour to complete.

Some programs or systems are designed for either special purposes or special clientele. Two of these are described briefly as representative of a field that can be expected to expand rapidly.

Career Navigator is a software system designed specifically to assist job seekers, particularly new entrants interested in business and professional careers. The system has been developed by Drake Beam Morin Inc., a consulting firm that has specialized in outplacement—a process of helping discharged employees to find new opportunities elsewhere. The package includes four computer diskettes and a 200-page manual that has quizzes, worksheets, short case studies, examples of resumes, letters, and interview sessions. Sections of the program include the following: Start the Program, Know Yourself, How to Communicate, Develop Your Job Search Tools, Conduct Your Job Search Campaign, and Land the Job. Each section includes a sequence of related activities, skill-developing tasks, time schedules, and so forth. Garis and Hess (1989) report a study of College of Business juniors and seniors using Career Navigator with a comparable group enrolled in a course dealing with professional development and a control group with access to neither. The Career Navigator group scored higher on a questionnaire related to confidence and progress in career implementation and on a questionnaire about their knowledge of the job search process.

Finally, two new CACGS were published in late 1995 that target specific audiences. *CareerWays*, which is published by the Wisconsin Career Information System, was developed to help high school students with educational and career planning. As noted in Table 8.1, this CACGS is available in a multimedia format as well as the traditional diskette version. It contains the following modules:

1. *CareerWays* Tutorial (helps students learn to use system)
2. Self-Portrait (helps students process educational and life experiences)
3. Class Planner (assists students in planning high school curricula)
4. Resume (assists students in developing resumes)
5. Lifestyles (helps students develop personal budgets)

The other system published in 1995 was developed by the Department of Defense to assist high school age students interested in exploring military careers. To use this system students must first complete the Armed Services Vocational Aptitude Battery (ASVAB) and Interest-Finder (IF), a newly published interest inventory based on the Holland's theory. This system, the Armed Services Career Exploration System (ACES), will be distributed free of charge to high schools throughout the country.

Present Status of CACGS

The most important recent technological breakthrough in the offering of CACGS is the use of CD-ROM technology. The use of CD-ROMs allows the addition of sound and video to the systems. Users can be guided through a system such as DISCOVER via auditory instructions and can view clips of individuals in the workplace. This has the distinct advantage of providing various models (e.g., females in male-dominated occupations) to users. One problem that has arisen in the use of CD-ROMS is that the more comprehensive systems such as DISCOVER use multiple compact disks (CDs). The data on the CDs can be downloaded to the hard drive of a computer if the computer has substantial memory. The memory requirement and the need for more powerful computers increases the overall cost of using DISCOVER and similar systems. The use of video clips also introduces a problem heretofore associated with print materials. Images, like data, become dated. Dated images can deter potential users, even if the information contained in the system is up-to-date.

CACGS have become an important feature in many career development programs in the United States and Canada, as well as in several other countries such as Australia, France, Hungary, Luxembourg, Belgium, and the Netherlands. Not surprisingly, given this international interest, CACGS are available in several different languages. Choices, Choices CT, and Career Futures are available in Canada in both French and English, and Choices is available in Dutch, Flemish, and Hungarian to accommodate these countries (Sampson et al., 1998). In the United States, twelve states have developed and maintain their own systems, 30 states and Guam have a state version of Choices and Choices CT, and 13 states have adopted Career Information Systems (CIS) as their official state CACGS. DISCOVER and COIN are also widely used systems (Sampson et al., 1998).

In 1990, Harris-Bowlsby pointed out that less than 10 percent of the potential users of CACGS have access to them. Although availability has increased dramatically since her observation, it is still the case that many users do not have access to CACGS. Historically K–12 schools have been the primary users of CACGS, with correctional institutions, vocational-technical schools, community colleges, Employment Security Service Offices, and four-year colleges and universities also making systems available to users in some instances (McKinlay, 1990). At one time, cost was a major barrier to the acquisition of CACGS, but as noted earlier, this is no longer the case. It is likely that the major barrier to the purchase and use of CACGS is the reluctance of many counselors to use computers (Gysbers, 1990). This is undoubtedly because counselor preparation programs' training in this area has not kept abreast of the technological development.

Future Possibilities

Participants in an international teleconference produced a series of recommendations for improving both design and usage of CACG systems. Sampson, Reardon, Lenz, and Morgenthau (1990) summarize and group these proposals into six broad categories. These topics and brief descriptive statements include the following:

1. *Improved design and use of CACG is primarily dependent upon improved training systems.* Better training programs should be directed toward preservice training in counselor education; better materials and procedures for training support; attention to operational use of CACG systems; better training for paraprofessionals, administrators, and support personnel; dissemination of validated training materials; and identification of training as a priority activity by all involved personnel.

2. *Differential effects and programming of systems for varied client groups, career guidance environments, and levels of counselor support.* Systems should be intentionally designed for, and used with, special populations, such as unemployed youth and adults, children, ethnic minorities, and disabled persons.

3. *Increased local funding, legislative support, and public information for career guidance in general and CACG systems in particular.*

4. *Conceptualizing effective use of CACG within the context of a comprehensive system of career guidance services.*

5. *Needed improvements in software.* This includes better client record keeping, use of videodisc technology, more demonstrated validity in self-assessment and search procedures, and improved career information databases.

6. *Improved dissemination of information about comparative system features, successful implementation models, and outcome studies on the effects of CACG systems.* (pp. 100–102)

Summary

In less than half a century the importance of CACGS for career development specialists has changed from novelty to an important part of many career development programs. The promise of these systems remains unfulfilled because many counselors have not embraced them. This is partially due to the fact that counselors have received substandard training in the use of CACGS in some instances and an aversion to technology and computers in others. When evaluating CACGS career development, specialists need to recall that computerized systems offer the potential to (1) deliver information more quickly and accurately because software is easier to update than most forms of information, (2) extend their services to students who increasingly use computers in their lives, and (3) reduce the amount of time spent on routine tasks such as test administration. However, it is also clear that computers must be used in conjunction with the support of career development specialists in most instances.

References

ACA. (1995). *Code of ethics and ethical standards.* Alexandria, VA: American Counseling Association.

Brown, D., & Brooks, L. (1991). *Career counseling techniques.* Boston: Allyn & Bacon.

Campbell, R. B. (1983). *Assessing the effectiveness of DISCOVER in a small campus career development program.* York, PA: Career Development and Placement Center (ERIC Document Reproduction Service NO. ED 253–782).

Fukuyama, M. A., Robert, B. S., Neimeyer, G. J., Nevill, D. D., & Metzler, M. A. (1988). Effects of DISCOVER on career self-efficacy and decision-making of undergraduates. *Career Development Quarterly, 37,* 56–62.

Garis, J. W., & Harris Bowlsby, J. (1984). *DISCOVER and the counselor: Their effects upon college student career planning progress.* Research Report #85. Hunt Valley, MD: American College Testing.

Garis, J. W., & Hess, H. R. (1989). Career Navigator: Its use with college students beginning the job search process. *Career Development Quarterly, 38,* 65–74.

Garis, J. W., & Niles, S. G. (1990). The separate and combined effects of SIGI or DISCOVER and a career planning course on undecided university students. *Career Development Quarterly, 38,* 261–274.

Gysbers, N. C. (1990). Computer-based career guidance systems: Their past, present, and a possible future—A reaction. In J. P. Sampson, Jr., and R. C. Reardon (Eds.), *Enhancing the design and use of computer-assisted career guidance systems.* Alexandria, VA: National Career Development Association.

Harris-Bowlsby, J. (1990). Computer-based guidance systems: Their past, present, and future. In J. P. Sampson, Jr., & R. C. Reardon (Eds.), *Enhancing the design and use of computer-assisted career guidance systems.* Alexandria, VA: American Counseling Association.

Kapes, J. T., Borman, C. A., & Frazier, N. (1989). An evaluation of SIGI and DISCOVER microcomputer-based career guidance systems. *Measurement and Evaluation in Counseling and Development, 22,* 126–136.

Katz, M. R. (1990). Yesterday, today, and tomorrow. In J. P. Sampson, Jr., & R. C. Reardon (Eds.), *Enhancing the design and use of computer-assisted career guidance systems.* Alexandria, VA: National Career Development Association.

Kjos, D. L. (1987). QUEST: Work experience and the results of an occupational search questionnaire among unemployed adults. *Career Development Quarterly, 35,* 326–336.

Marin, P. A., & Splete, H. (1991). A comparison of the effect of two computer-based counseling interventions on the decidedness of adults. *Career Development Quarterly, 39,* 360–371.

Mazel, M., & Cummings, R. (1982). *How to select a computer assisted guidance system.* Madison, WI: Wisconsin Vocational Studies Center.

McKinlay, B. (1990). Information systems in career development: History and prospects. In J. P. Sampson, Jr., & R. C. Reardon (Eds.), *Enhancing the design and use of computer-assisted career guidance systems.* Alexandria, VA: National Career Development Association.

Niles, S., & Garis, J. W. (1990). The effects of a career planning course and a computer-assisted career guidance program (SIGI PLUS) on undecided college students. *Journal of Career Development, 16,* 237–248.

Roe, A. (1956). *The psychology of occupations.* New York: Wiley.

Roselle, B. E., & Hummel, T. J. (1988). Intellectual development and interaction effectiveness with DISCOVER. *Career Development Quarterly, 36,* 241–250.

Sampson, J. P., Jr. (1997a). Ethical delivery of computer-assisted career guidance services: Supported vs. stand-alone system use. Paper presented at the National Career Development Association Convention, Daytona Beach, FL, January 9–11, 1997.

Sampson, J. P., Jr. (1997b). Helping clients get the most from computer-assisted career guidance systems. Paper presented at the Australian Association of Career Counselors 7th National/International Conference, Brisbane, Australia, April 4, 1997.

Sampson, J. P., Jr. (1997c). Enhancing the use of career information with computer-assisted career gudance systems. Paper presented at symposium "The Present and Future of Computer-Assisted Career Guidance Systems in Japan" Tokyo, Japan, October 8, 1997.

Sampson, J. P., Jr., & Reardon, R. C. (Eds.). (1990). *Enhancing the design and use of computer-assisted career guidance systems.* Alexandria, VA: National Career Development Association.

Sampson, J. P., Jr., Reardon, R. C., Lenz, J. G., & Morgenthau, E. D. (1990). North American conference recommendations. In J. P. Sampson, Jr., & R. C. Reardon (Eds.), *Enhancing the design and use of computer-assisted career guidance systems.* Alexandria, VA: National Career Development Association.

Sampson, J. P., Jr., Reardon, R. C. Reed, C., Rudd, E., Lumsden, J., Epstein, S., Folsom, B., Herbert, S., Johnson, S., Simmons, A., Odell, J., Rush, D., Wright, L. G., Lenz J. G., Peterson, G. W., & Greeno, B. P. (1998). A Differential Feature-Cost Analysis of Seventeen Computer-Assisted Career Guidance Systems: Technical Report Number 10 (Eighth Edition). Tallahassee, FL: Center for the Study of Technology in Counseling and Career Development, Florida State University.

Super, D. E. (1990). A life-span, life-space approach to career development. In D. Brown, L. Brooks and Associates, *Career choice and development* (pp. 121–178). San Francisco: Jossey-Bass.

9

Systematic Career Development Programming: Application to Elementary and Middle Schools

Historical Background

It has long been theorized that career development is a lifelong process (Ginzberg, Ginzburg, Axelrad, & Herma, 1951; Super, 1957) and that crucial aspects of this development occur during the school years. Over the past 3 decades there have been numerous educational thrusts aimed at promoting career development in elementary, middle, and high schools. The most ambitious of these programs was the career education movement that developed during the Nixon administration under the leadership of then Secretary of Education Sidney Marland. Many prominent counselor educators, including K. B. Hoyt, were prominently involved in this movement, which saw the establishment of extensive programs to help children and adolescents broaden their career horizons, learn decision making skills, acquire vocational skills, and generally develop an appreciation for themselves. Hoyt (1977, p. 5) defined career education as follows:

> *Career education is an effort aimed at refocusing American education and the actions of the broader community in ways that will help individuals acquire and utilize the knowledge, skills, and attitudes necessary for each to make work a meaningful, productive and satisfying part of his or her way of living.*

Marland (1974, pp. 100–102) describes the eight elements of career education as identified by the Center for Research in Vocational Education at Ohio State University:

1. Career Awareness—knowledge of the total spectrum of careers.
2. Self-Awareness—knowledge of the components that make up self.
3. Appreciations, Attitudes—life roles; feelings toward self and others in respect to society and economics.
4. Decision-Making Skills—applying information to rational processes in order to reach decisions.
5. Economic Awareness—perception of processes in production, distribution, and consumption.
6. Skill Awareness and Beginning Competence—skills in ways in which man extends his behavior.
7. Employability Skills—social and communication skills appropriate to career placement.
8. Educational Awareness—perception of the relationship between education and life roles.

By the mid-1980s, most of the remnants of the career education movement had been swept from American schools by the back-to-basics educational movement. Advocates of back to basics were particularly critical of career education in elementary schools that focused children's attention on workers, developing skills with tools through hands-on approaches, and field trips to work sites because these activities took time away from core subjects. However, the failure of career education in the elementary school cannot be laid solely at the doorstep of the back-to-basics movement. Many mistakes were made in the design and implementation of those programs, including (1) they were funded with monies external to the school district with no plans to provide internal financial support once external funding was withdrawn; (2) they added to the workload of an already overloaded group: teachers; (3) the term *career education* was negatively associated with vocational education by many middle-class parents, who were concerned that their children might be diverted from the college preparatory curriculum; and (4) local political support among educators, parents, and the business community was not carefully developed in many instances.

Even though the career education movement of the seventies has largely dissipated, Hoyt (1985) is still a vigorous advocate for the concept. Interestingly, at about the time of Hoyt's reaffirmation of the viability of career education in our nation's schools, the National Occupational Information Coordinating Committee (NOICC) was funding the first phase of what has become the National Career Development Guideline Project, which resulted in four extensive publications of guidelines for establishing career counseling and guidance programs in elementary schools, middle and junior high schools, high schools, and postsecondary educational institutions (NOICC, 1989a, b, c, d). These were revised and consolidated in 1996 (Kobylarz, 1996).

The National Career Development Guidelines Project and companion initiatives have revitalized career development programs in some but not all schools. This revitalization comes at a time when many efforts have been launched to rejuvenate the public educational system and to increase student achievement levels in the process. The crosscurrents in the school reform movement sometimes work in favor of and sometimes discourage efforts aimed at improving career development programs. One factor that bodes well for the latest attempt to improve career development services within public schools is public support. Nearly 60 percent of the adults in this country favor increases for career development programming, with African Americans being somewhat more supportive than white Americans (Hoyt & Lester, 1995). The latest data support the results of earlier studies (Brown & Minor, 1989, 1992), which yielded similar percentages.

Programming for Career Development

As noted earlier, several strategic errors were made in the establishment of career development programs, not the least of which may have been to label them *career education,* because that term was associated with vocational education in the minds of many. However, the focus of current efforts to establish career development programs is to avoid the mistakes of the past while building on the positive experiences from that era. Perhaps the clearest message that came out of the experiences of the 1960s and 1970s was that programs need to be carefully conceptualized, planned, implemented, and evaluated. In this vein, Walz and Benjamin (1984) list several characteristics of what they term a systemic career development program. To paraphrase Walz and Benjamin, the program

1. Is organized and planned by a team of knowledgeable professionals, parents, and representatives from the community.
2. Includes materials and learning experiences that are appropriate for the developmental stage of the students. The delivery of the program is carefully articulated across educational levels.
3. Is based on the needs of the students.
4. Is designed around a set of measurable objectives that are clearly stated at the outset.
5. Has an evaluation plan that includes the measurement of the extent to which goals are achieved and determines the value of the various processes involved in the program.
6. Is delivered by highly skilled personnel who use a wide variety of resources and strategies to achieve program objectives.

The remainder of this chapter includes a general discussion of the principles of change and the steps involved in the development of a comprehensive career development model. A discussion of the NCDG model is presented, as is a review of some of the unique aspects of developing a career development program in elementary and middle schools.

Program Development and Change

Whether a new program is being devised or an old program is being renovated, program planners are engaged in a change process that should follow certain principles. These principles have been set forth by various authors (e.g., Brown, Pryzwansky, & Schulte, 1998; Lippitt & Lippitt, 1986). Perhaps the primary principle that should be followed when initiating a change process is that the rationale for the change must be clearly communicated to those involved. Two corollaries to this principle are that the people affected by the change process must be involved in designing the changes and their support for them must be engendered. Developing support for change is not an easy task, particularly if there is satisfaction with the status quo or when people involved in the change process see the personal costs (e.g., time spent to bring about the changes) as exceeding the value of the changes. Therefore, it is necessary to assess the extent to which the people most affected by the change are invested in the current program and to develop an approach to change that will not overburden them. In addition, planners often set up resistance to the change process by failing to consider some of the psychological forces that are set in motion by change. One of these is that people who perceive themselves as competent in the current program may be concerned that they will not have the skills they need to be competent in the new program. Program planners must assure those people involved in developing new programs that they will have opportunities to develop needed skills. Finally, program changes need to be endorsed by the educational leaders, and these individuals must systematically reinforce change efforts. Without support and encouragement from the "top," change efforts are likely to be unsuccessful.

Conceptualizing Career Development Programs

Herr and Cramer (1996) suggested that there are a number of conceptual bases for career development programs. Two of the obvious ones can be characterized as theoretical and rational. Career development theories such as Super's (1990) can be used as the conceptual basis for designing a career development program. We might, for example, want all elementary students to develop a vocational self-concept, be aware of the major groups of occupations available to them as workers, develop an awareness of the need to plan for their future occupations, become aware of the types of occupational information, and develop basic decision-making skills. All of these areas would be in line with Super's theoretical propositions.

Another approach to developing a conceptual base for a career development program would be to rationally and/or empirically determine what career development skills and attitudes are needed by students and workers and set up a K–12 program to develop those competencies. We know that women have increasingly entered the work force and will continue to do so in the future, and thus girls and young women should develop those skills and attitudes necessary to enter and succeed in a career. As a result of this same trend, boys and girls need to overcome stereotypes that suggest that some jobs are "women's jobs" and others are "men's jobs." For the most part, those people engaged in conceptualizing career development programs have taken the rational/empirical approach and have tried to ascertain on an a priori basis what students and workers need and then have logically set about to build programs based on their assumptions. This is not to suggest that career development theory has not influenced the conceptualizing of career development programs. Almost all programs include ideas such as enhancing self-concept and developing an awareness of interests, work values, and aptitude—ideas that are derived directly from career development theory.

Developing a Program Philosophy

The conceptual basis of a career development program suggests in general terms what the program planners hope to accomplish (e.g., produce students with marketable skills). The statement of philosophy tells why the program planners believe that a career development program is important (Herr & Cramer, 1996). In a sense, the philosophy statement is a statement about values. A school district can be committed to a host of educational values, some of which may be mutually exclusive, complementary and overlapping, and/or conflicting. Some people see focusing on career development as antithetical to fostering academic achievement because career development activities detract from the amount of time that can be spent on academic pursuits. Other educators see career development programming as complementary to the idea that schooling should first and foremost be preparation for life. They also believe that career development programming enhances the achievement of students by illustrating the relevance of education to work and thus to students' futures. The philosophical statement clarifies these beliefs.

Typically, program philosophy statements are succinct. The following statement might reflect the philosophy of a school district:

> *The ultimate goal of education is to enrich the lives of students by providing them with the skills they need to lead happy, productive lives. In modern society quality of life is dependent on having the educational skills needed to participate fully in our society, including those skills required for the citizenship role, the worker role, the family role, and the leisure role. The career development program is aimed at helping students realize the importance of education, to identify personally relevant career options, and to develop the personal, interpersonal, educational, and vocational skills needed to enter and advance in their careers.*

Establishing Needs

School districts located in rural West Virginia, suburban Indianapolis, inner-city Chicago, and Chapel Hill, North Carolina, will have different types of students and thus the need for different types of career development programs. Many of the students in rural West Virginia will go directly into the military or the civilian workplace, as will the students in inner-city Chicago. However, students in rural West Virginia will probably have to relocate to another geographic area within the state or even outside of the state to find suitable employment. If the students from an inner city are minority students, they are likely to be confronted with varying degrees of discrimination. It is likely that large numbers of students from the Chapel Hill and suburban Indianapolis school districts will attend some form of postsecondary educational institution, and therefore their initial career decision process will be somewhat more protracted. However, all these students need to be able to incorporate career planning into their educational planning processes. To determine the type of program that will best serve the students in these school districts, it is imperative that a full understanding of the characteristics of students and their families be developed. The process of developing this profile is usually termed *needs assessment.*

Data about the needs of students are available from a variety of sources, including demographic data about the community, the results of achievement testing, information about the dropout rate, follow-up of studies of graduates and dropouts, and direct surveys of students, teachers, business leaders, and parents. The questions to be answered through needs assessment are (1) Who are our students? (2) What are their needs as they relate to the career development process? and (3) What seems to be the best approach to meeting the needs that are identified? (Herma, Morris, & Fitz-Gibbon, 1987). When data from needs assessment devices such as the one shown in Figure 9.1 are combined with information such as that collected from graduates and business leaders as well as other sources, planners can begin to get a sense of the type of program that needs to be delivered.

The needs assessment may be directed by a steering committee as suggested in the *NCDG Handbook* (Kobylarz, 1996). However, it is more likely that the needs assessment will be directed by a school counselor, the districtwide director of school counseling services, or a representative from the vocational education division. Steering committees are typically put into place once needs are established and top-level administrative support is gained. Once the need for the career development program has been documented, two courses of action are possible. One of these is to appoint an advisory committee that will lobby for the program. The second is for the person or persons who conducted the needs assessment to use the data gathered about the needs of the students to gain approval from school administrators and the school board. Regardless of how it is sought, an administrative endorsement of the program should be secured before launching a full-scale planning process.

FIGURE 9.1   Needs Assessment Survey Form—Elementary School

The (Steering Committee/School Counseling Staff) is assessing the career development needs of our students and we need your help. The goals of a career development program in the elementary school are to help students develop an awareness of the occupational structure, an appreciation for the relationship between school and work, and the interpersonal skills needed to be successful in life and at work. This survey lists the knowledge, skills, and abilities needed by elementary school students if we are to accomplish these goals.

Please rate the importance you personally attach to each of the items in the survey using a scale of 1 to 3. By circling a 1 you are indicating that you believe the item is of little importance; if you circle a 2 you are indicating that you believe that the item is of moderate importance, and by circling a 3 you are indicating that you believe the item is of great importance. **Thank you for your help in this very important matter.**

	Level of Importance		
	Little	**Moderate**	**Great**
Self Knowledge: Students will develop			
Knowledge of the importance of a positive self-concept	1	2	3
Skills to interact positively with others	1	2	3
Awareness of need for continued emotional growth	1	2	3
Educational and Occupational Exploration: Students will develop			
Awareness of the importance of educational achievement	1	2	3
Awareness of the relationship between work and learning	1	2	3
Skills to understand and use career information	1	2	3
Awareness of the importance of personal responsibility and good work habits	1	2	3
Awareness of how work relates to the needs and functions of society	1	2	3
Career Planning: Students will develop	1	2	3
Understanding of how to make decisions	1	2	3
Awareness of the interrelationships among life roles	1	2	3
Awareness of the changing roles of men and women in the work force	1	2	3
Awareness of the career-planning process	1	2	3

Source: Adapted from Kobylarz, L. (Ed.). (1996). *National career development guidelines: K–adult handbook.* Stillwater, OK: Career Development Training Institute, p. A.3.

After the Needs Assessment

The *NCDG Handbook* (Kobylarz, 1996) indicates that, once administrative support is obtained, it is important to appoint a program coordinator. This is an obvious step if the program is to be districtwide. However, career development programs can flourish in individual schools if the school counselor or another professional is willing to assume the role of coordinator. Whether the program is for an entire district or a single school, getting the endorsement of teachers is as important as getting an endorsement from administrators. Without the support of teachers, career development programs in schools are unlikely to succeed. If administrators are supportive, a lead person is in place, and the faculty of the school endorses the concept of a career development program, the process of program development can proceed.

The *National Career Development Guidelines* (Kobylarz, 1996) also contain the suggestion that two committees should be appointed as the process of program development moves into the planning stage: a steering committee and an advisory committee. The purpose of the steering committee, according to the *Guidelines,* is to manage the development and implementation of the program, whereas the role of the advisory committee is to provide input and review the program. This arrangement seems unnecessarily bureaucratic, and thus it is suggested that a steering committee be appointed that would subsume the roles of both the committees. The steering committee should be made up of administrators, teachers, counselors, students, parents, representatives from business and industry, and citizens from the community. This committee would prioritize the needs identified in the needs survey, make certain that the program develops in accordance with school policies, conduct public relations regarding the program, and develop a budget. Identifying ways to integrate the program with the school counseling and instructional programs, determining the staff training needs, and overseeing the evaluation of the program would also be the responsibility of the steering committee. Moreover, the committee would work to develop a productive interface between the career development program and the business community. If necessary, the steering committee should also engage in seeking funds from external sources to support the career development program.

Writing Goals, Objectives, and Establishing Criteria for Successes

Although the steering committee for a districtwide program should establish goals, specific program objectives should be established for each school. Goals are usually stated in rather broad terms such as, "Students will increase their knowledge of the types of careers available to them." Broad goal statements are then broken down into their behavioral objectives, which are sequenced chronologically.

Behavioral objectives contain four components: who will accomplish, what they will accomplish and to what degree they will accomplish it, by when they will accomplish it, and by what means they will accomplish it (Burns, 1972; Morris, Fitz-Gibbon, & Lindheim, 1987). The following is an example of a series of behavioral objectives that might be written for the aforementioned goal:

Goal: Students will increase their knowledge of the careers available to them.

K—By the end of kindergarten, students will be able to identify their parents' jobs and be able to list at least three of the duties they perform on those jobs, as a result of homework assignments to interview their parents about their jobs.

1st grade—By the end of grade 1, all students will be able to identify three community helpers and three of their duties as a result of a speakers' program featuring community workers.

2nd grade—By the end of grade 2, all students will be able to identify three workers who work in their county along with two tasks they perform and how they use reading on their jobs, as a result of classroom unit titled "Workers in Our County."

3rd grade—By the end of grade 3, all students will be able to identify five workers employed by the state, identify their major responsibilities, and tell two ways they use mathematics on their jobs, as a result of a field trip to the state capitol and follow-up activities.

4th grade—By the end of grade 4, all students will be able to identify five workers who are unique to the Southeast, describe their major job responsibilities, and tell how they use information learned in at least two school subjects on their jobs, as a result of completing an out-of-class assignment "Workers in Our Region."

5th grade—By the end of grade 5, all students will be able to identify ten U.S. workers who hold jobs outside of the Southeast, the major duties they perform, and how they use information from school on their jobs, as a result of writing an essay on jobs in America, viewing filmstrips at a workstation established for this purpose, and class assignments.

Middle school—By the end of grade 8, students will have identified three jobs that may be of interest to them in the future, determined what academic skills are needed to enter those jobs, and analyzed how their aptitudes and academic performance may prepare them for or provide a barrier to entering those jobs, as a result of the following activities:

6th grade—Students learn about careers in our hemisphere and the world as a result of infusion in all classes. Students complete an English essay "If I Could Be Anything." Counselor-led monthly seminars will feature speakers who represent international careers.

7th grade—Students complete an interest inventory and then participate in counselor-led groups to discuss the sources of interests and how interests influence career choice making.

8th grade—Students complete a 9-week class on choosing a career that focuses on decision making and using occupational information along with data about self to make career choices. The culminating experience is to select three careers of interest and to do a self-analysis regarding potential to enter those careers and to lay out an educational path to the most desired career.

High school—Each student will make a preliminary career choice along with an alternative choice and construct educational plans to enter those careers, as a result of counselor-directed activities such as career seminars, individual planning sessions, bibliotherapy, job shadowing, participation in career day, interest and aptitude assessment, and so forth.

The construction of behavioral objectives for each facet of the career development program is a laborious task. However, these specific objectives serve as the road map that tells which activities are going to be performed and when and with what expected result. With this type of information, it is relatively easy to design an evaluation of the program.

Program Evaluation

Burck (1978) states that "the aim of [program] evaluation is to establish worth, effectiveness, and efficiency" (p. 179) after reviewing more than half a dozen definitions of the process. Burck's position is endorsed in the current version of the National Career Development Guidelines (Kobylarz, 1996). He also concludes that evaluation consists of determining the outcomes that have been achieved, examining the processes by which these outcomes were achieved, and finally judging the value not only of the total program but the components of the program as well.

Process and Product Evaluation
Program evaluation can and should be conducted on two dimensions of the program: product and process. Product or summative evaluation attempts to answer the question, "What were the outcomes of our program?" or, put somewhat differently, "What new skills and attitudes (learning) resulted from students participating in our program?" Process or formative evaluation attempts to answer the question, "Why did students learn (or fail to learn) the things that they did?" In other words, "What contributed to the observed product or outcome?" Traditionally, schools have been more concerned with outcomes and less concerned with why the outcomes occurred. It is important to note that these two types of evaluations are conducted for different reasons. Product evaluation allows us to ascertain that we have accomplished what we set out to do (i.e., influence student career development) and allows us to be accountable to ourselves and our public.

Process evaluation gives us the information that we need to make changes in our programs. As suggested earlier, we need to know why programs are successful or unsuccessful so we can alter or delete those parts of programs that are not contributing to the outcomes and perhaps intensify those efforts that are contributing to outcomes.

There are a number of approaches that may be used in evaluating a program (Stecher & Davis, 1987). One of these is to establish an experimental design which allows program developers to compare the outcomes of their program to those in a school that has no program. When establishing this type of evaluation design, it is important that the demographic characteristics of the "control" school be as similar to the one in which the career development program is being developed as possible. The goal-oriented approach to evaluation, which is the primary approach recommended here, focuses on the extent to which specific goals are attained. Often, in a goal-oriented approach to evaluation, the multitude of goals that are inevitably developed will have to be prioritized because it will be impossible to evaluate all of them in a single evaluation effort. Decision-oriented approaches to evaluation may also be conducted to inform key decision-making processes (What type of professional functions most effectively in the program?). User-oriented evaluation focuses on the human factors in the program, such as staff rapport. Responsive evaluation is a more qualitative approach to evaluation and focuses on what various people have at stake in the program and their points of view about it. When this type of evaluation is conducted, the evaluator spends a great deal of time interacting with the program staff and observing various types of program activities. Stecher and Davis (1987) point out that comprehensive evaluations include several of the aforementioned evaluation approaches.

One of the objectives set forth in a preceding subsection was that each high school student should establish a career goal, develop an alternative goal, and construct an educational path to reach the goals that have been established. If our evaluation indicates that we have achieved this goal, we would want to know which of our activities contributed to goal attainment. Similarly, if our evaluation suggests that we have not attained our objective, we would want to ask which activities had contributed to students' planning and which had not. Process evaluation allows us to keep and strengthen those aspects of our programs that contribute to product (goal) attainment and to delete or alter those that do not.

Establishing Criteria

One issue that must be addressed in goal-oriented evaluation involves establishing the criteria by which success will be judged. For example an objective states that all students will make a career choice, choose an alternative, and then develop an educational plan that would allow them to implement their choices. The word *all* suggests that to be successful, 100 percent of the students must complete the activity, which is one aspect of the criterion. A second part of the criterion issue concerns what constitutes a career choice and an educational plan to implement the choice. Many students have career choices that are unrealistic for a variety of reasons. Perhaps the objective should state that the choice should be attainable, but then the question needs to be posed, "How do we know that the career goal is attainable?" The objective could read that each student will establish a career goal that is attainable as judged by the counselor and in doing so establish that all students will establish an attainable career goal that the counselor perceives to be realistic. It must also be determined how the educational plan mentioned in this objective is constructed so that students will advance toward their goals.

When program objectives are established, they constitute the basis for product evaluation if they are properly written. Thus objectives need to be constructed carefully. It is also important that program objectives are within reach of the staff's ability to attain them. All students may select career options, but it would be unrealistic to expect that all students would prepare for and enter those options. A more realistic objective might be that 50 percent of the students in school would prepare for and enter either their primary or secondary career choice within 6 years of their graduation from high school as determined by a follow-up study of graduates. In this objective, a reasonable criterion has been established along with a time frame in which the objective is to be accomplished and a means of evaluating the extent of goal attainment (student self-reports in a follow-up study). The career development competencies listed in the *National Career Development Handbook* (Kobylarz, 1996) can be incorporated into behavioral objectives as indicators of program success (see Table 9.1). Are the components listed in Table 9.1 the ones that should be targeted by public schools?

Freeman (1994) conducted a national study of school counselors to determine whether they agreed that the competencies advanced by NOICC in the *National Career Development Guidelines (NCDG)* are important. She found that counselors overwhelmingly endorsed the following competencies for elementary school students: strengthening self-concept, developing interpersonal skills, increasing children's awareness of growth and change, developing an awareness of the importance of education, accepting personal responsibility, and understanding the decision-making process. School counselors were only moderately supportive of the following competencies: career planning awareness, awareness of work in our society, skills in using career information, and gender-role changes and their impact on work. Counselors who responded to Freeman's study (1994) also rated the importance of the *NCDG* competencies for middle school students. Once again they were of the opinion that knowledge of self-concept, interpersonal skills, understanding the relationship of education to work, and decision-making skills are important to engender in middle school students. They were also highly supportive of the idea that middle school students need to understand the interrelationship of life roles. Respondents were in agreement that the other competencies advanced for middle school students in the *NCDG* are important, but their overall endorsement level was lower.

TABLE 9.1   Career Development Competencies

Elementary School

1. Knowledge of the importance of a positive self-concept to career development
2. Skills for interacting with others
3. Awareness of the importance of emotional and physical development on career decision making
4. Awareness of the importance of educational achievement to career opportunities
5. Awareness of interrelationship of work and learning
6. Skills for understanding and using career information
7. Awareness of the interrelationship of personal responsibility, good work habits, and career opportunities
8. Awareness of how careers relate to needs and functions of society
9. Understanding of how to make decisions and choose alternatives related to tentative educational and career goals
10. Awareness of the interrelationship of life roles and careers
11. Awareness of changing male/female roles in different occupations
12. Awareness of career planning process

Sample Indicators That Competency Has Been Developed
Student Can:

1. Describe positive characteristics about self
2. Demonstrate skills in resolving conflicts
3. Identify ways to express and deal with feelings
4. Implement a plan of action for improving academic skills
5. Describe how one's role as a student is like that of an adult worker
6. Describe jobs in his/her community
7. Describe the importance of cooperation among workers for accomplishing a task
8. Describe how careers can satisfy personal needs
9. Describe how decisions affect self and others
10. Identify the value of leisure activities for enriching one's lifestyle
11. Describe the changing roles of men and women in the workplace
12. Describe the importance of planning

Middle School/Junior High School

1. Knowledge of the influence of positive self-concept on career development
2. Skills for interacting with others
3. Knowledge of the importance of emotional and physical development on career decision making
4. Knowledge of the relationship of educational achievement to career opportunities
5. Skills for locating, understanding, and using career information
6. Knowledge of skills necessary to seek and obtain a job
7. Understanding of the attitudes necessary for success in work and learning
8. Understanding how careers relate to needs and functions of the economy and society
9. Skills in making decisions and choosing alternatives in planning for and pursuing tentative educational and career goals
10. Knowledge of the interrelationship of life roles and careers
11. Understanding of changing male/female roles
12. Understanding of the process of career planning
13. Understanding the relationship between work and learning

Student Can:

1. Describe personal likes and dislikes
2. Demonstrate an appreciation for similarities and differences in people
3. Identify internal and external sources of stress and conflict
4. Relate one's aptitudes and abilities to broad occupational areas
5. Identify various ways occupations can be classified
6. Compile a job application form in a satisfactory manner
7. Demonstrate effective learning habits and skills
8. Discuss the variety and complexity of occupations
9. Describe one's current life context as it relates to career decisions
10. Describe the interrelationships among family, career, and leisure
11. Describe problems, adjustments, and advantages of entering a nontraditional career
12. Identify tentative life and career goals
13. Demonstrate effective learning habits

Source: Adapted from Kobylarz, L. (1996). *National career development guidelines: K–adult handbook.* Stillwater, OK: Career Development Training Institute.

In addition to student competencies, the *NCDG* developers have enumerated forty-nine skills and competencies needed by school counselors regarding guidance and counseling generally, including the utilization of information, program implementation, individual and group assessment, management and administrative consultation, and working with special populations. For example, counselors need to have the ability to identify appropriate role models, understand career paths and patterns, identify assessment resources, and help parents assist students to explore career options and alternatives for their children according to the guidelines (Kobylarz, 1996; NOICC, 1989a). Earlier we listed the ways that career development activities could be delivered to elementary and middle school students. Clearly the *NCDG* are set up to focus on one of these options: delivery by the school counselor.

Program Implementation

After the needs assessment has verified the need for the program, support has been gained for it, objectives have been clearly stated, and an evaluation model selected, it is time to implement the program. There are 10 different processes or delivery strategies that can be employed to deliver the program. These are listed below.

1. Classroom instruction
2. Counseling
3. Assessment
4. Career information
5. Placement
6. Consultation
7. Referral
8. Outreach
9. Follow-up
10. Work experience

The following list is presented as a means of demonstrating how these processes might be employed in the development of student competencies. Some of these processes presuppose that a counselor will be present in the school. However, many of the processes can and probably will involve teachers.

Elementary School Competencies to Be Developed:

1a. Identify positive and negative ways to express and deal with feelings
1b. Implement plan of action for improving academic skills

Processes Used to Develop Competencies

Consultation:

1a. Parent consultation
1b. Parent/teacher consultation

Classroom Instruction:

1a. Classroom activity; my emotions
1b. Study skills units

Assessment:

1a. Informal assessment of outcomes
1b. Informal

Career Information:

1a and 1b not used with these competencies

Counseling:

1a. Individual counseling for students having problems
1b. Individual and group counseling for students with low achievement

Placement:

1a. Not used with this competency
1b. Place cross-grade tutoring program

Referral:

1a. More severe problems referred to Community Mental Health Center (CMHC)
1b. Referred private groups that provide remedial tutoring work program

Middle School Competencies to Be Developed:

1a. Identify skills that are transferable from one occupation to the other
1b. Identify strategies used in decision making
1c. Describe changing life roles of men and women in the family

Processes Used to Develop Competencies

Consultation:

1a. Teacher consultation
1b. Teacher consultation
1c. Teacher consultation

Classroom Instruction:

1a. Units on occupational clusters
1b. Units on decision making
1c. Units on male/female relationships

Assessment:

1a. Informal
1b. Informal
1c. Informal

Career Information:

1a. Cluster information
1b. Not addressed
1c. Information on nontraditional careers

Counseling:

1c. Small group guidance on male/female roles

Placement:

1a. Placement for job shadowing activities
1b, c. Not used for these competencies

Referral/Outreach/Work Experience/Follow-Up

Not used for these competencies

The Institutions

At one point in educational history, it was decided that the middle years of schooling should be preparatory for high school, and the junior high school was established to emulate the high school. Less than a decade ago, when numerous educational problems began to manifest themselves, the junior high school came under fire and middle schools became more prevalent. These schools typically enroll students in grades 6, 7, and 8 and are fashioned along lines similar to elementary schools. Elementary schools and middle schools are intended to provide a nurturing atmosphere where students can receive emotional and educational support. In the early elementary school years, self-contained classrooms are not uncommon. In these classrooms one teacher provides most of the basic instruction, with support in some instances from art, music, physical education, and special education teachers and in some instances from counselors.

As students progress in school, typically in the intermediate years (grades 3 and 4), they are exposed to a number of teachers who possess specialized knowledge in areas such as mathematics, science, social studies, and so forth, in addition to music and physical education teachers, special education teachers, and counselors. At the upper elementary and middle school levels, the pattern remains essentially the same although middle schools are typically larger; specialization in instruction occurs and the curriculum becomes more diverse. For example, some students may be taking algebra in the eighth grade while others are enrolled in pre-algebra and general mathematics courses.

Career development activities in elementary and middle schools may be delivered in several ways: by the teacher in regular units much like social studies; by the teacher through infusion into the curriculum (e.g., careers related to science may be discussed in each science unit); by special teachers who teach careers, usually on a day, week, or semester basis; by counselors who teach special units on careers and plan activities such as career days, when workers representing various occupations visit the school and meet with students to discuss their jobs; through parent-directed activities typically designed by school counselors; and by personnel external to the school (usually from the central administrative offices of the school district) who perform some combination of the foregoing activities. The exact nature of the program, including its staffing and delivery, will depend on the philosophy of the school district, the availability of personnel, and the financial resources available to support various activities.

The Students: Elementary School

Elementary school youngsters bring to the classroom attitudes and ideas that have developed as a result of the interaction of their background or environment and their experiences (Super, 1990). Since both are necessarily limited in the early years of elementary school, they reflect primarily attitudes of the adults with whom students have contact. Thus in many ways their ideas and concepts may be a generation out of date. During each generation, tremendous changes occur, especially in areas such as the world of work.

Early in the elementary school, each child should be helped to grasp the idea that much of what happens to her in the future will be of her own making and will depend to a large extent on how she uses abilities in the opportunities encountered. Long before entering school, every child will have made fantasy occupational choices such as teacher, police officer, mechanic, or secretary. During the early school years, the child will have matured to the point of recognizing that these are fantasy choices and nothing more. As this realization develops, children can begin to comprehend what factors are involved in the choices faced as they complete an educational program. Children need to understand the extent to which all choices—recreational activities, hobbies, reading materials, clubs, and others—ultimately influence major choices and decisions. They should also realize that career choice is always evolving and changing, throughout the entire life span.

In other words, if elementary school students are helped to develop an awareness of the world of work and to develop a more acute sensitivity to themselves as individuals with differing interests, abilities, and motivations, we may reasonably expect some understanding of how they as individuals function. Two opposing dangers exist that underscore the importance of focusing attention on this goal at the elementary level. One danger is assuming that an automatic connection between work and self will be made; this leaves too much to chance. The other danger is that elementary students may attempt to move too far toward closure and make definite choices prematurely. The goal lies between these two extremes. Students should be taught early that they do make decisions that affect their lives. This involves at least two aspects—namely, how decisions are made and how, once made, those personal choices influence their lives.

Programming Ideas for K–5: Awareness

Nelson (1980) describes the CREST program as a technique that helps elementary children become aware of the choices they make and the impact of these choices in establishing insight. Since self-understanding is fostered early, the pupils benefit not only in establishing better relationships with others but in many other ways. For example, as self-understanding improves, the child is likely to understand others better. It is an easy step from understanding self and others to understanding how different kinds of people can make different contributions to their groups as a result of special knowledge, skill, or experience.

Simulations were identified as an important means of providing occupational information in Chapter 7. Catlett (1992) describes how she simulated an automobile assembly line which she dubbed the Yontiac Motor Company. In this project children completed job applications, signed worker contracts, and assumed roles on an assembly line designed to build an 8-inch-long paper car with plastic wheels. The children assumed jobs such as design engineers, adhesive specialists, and salespeople for which they were paid in scrip redeemable at the Yontiac Store. In addition to assuming occupations, the children were engaged in decision-making processes when the teacher introduced various "corporate" problems such as poor sales for the Yontiac they were producing. Stein (1991) also employed many of the strategies described in Chapter 7 to introduce her children to various occupations including the use of children's occupational information. She also asked her children to make costumes and engage in role plays that illustrated five characteristics of one occupation and to develop scrapbooks that identified each of Holland's types.

Using career-oriented materials in the elementary classroom may help many children build positive self-concepts. Too often success in the classroom may be based on activities that are academically oriented but have less direct relationship to the world of work. Of course, it is important for academically able youngsters to experience success; but all youngsters should have those experiences. Learning that is related to the real world and solving problems in that world is likely to have greater value for the child than an activity that is carried out to please the teacher.

Over 30 years ago, Hansen (1972) proposed a career development model that can be incorporated into the school curriculum. She assumed that career development is self-development—in other words, a process of developing and implementing a self-concept satisfying both the individual and society. By providing for exploration of self, particularly in educational and vocational pursuits, the system suggests that vocational maturation will develop. Hansen identifies objectives for this approach that will parallel those we have been considering. These goals propose that students will

1. Be aware of their own preferred lifestyles and work values.
2. Exercise some control over their own lives through conscious choice and planning.
3. Be familiar with the occupational options available to them.
4. Know the educational paths to preferred occupations and the financial requirements for entry.
5. Be familiar with the process of career decision making.
6. Know the major resources available in the school and community and be able to use them.
7. Be able to organize and synthesize knowledge of self and the world of work and to develop strategies. (p. 244)

McGee and Silliman (1982) describe a group of activities for fourth-, fifth-, and sixth-grade students using an interest-related inventory. Although there is general agreement that interests at these grade levels are very immature, they can still be used as a basis for increasing an awareness of individual differences and of one's own characteristics at this time.

Wernick (1972) describes the use of an adult from the community as a nucleus for building classroom activities that not only involve basic learning skills but also develop attitudes toward a wide range of occupations. The T4C project in New Jersey places a complete set of hand tools in the elementary school classroom along with a set of learning guides for forty-seven different learning episodes (Leonard, 1972). These experiences help the child feel the role of the various workers who use those tools in their jobs. Rost (1973) relates the building of a "career pyramid" by selecting any occupation suggested by an elementary class member and then constructing the pyramid of jobs, identified by the class members, that support that job.

Thompson and Parker (1971) report a study in which fifth graders were taught a unit based on learning objectives related to occupations. They found that the youngsters gained insight and knowledge of work from the unit. After completing the unit, they could identify better reasons for working and could identify a broader range of occupations, thus apparently understanding better the system by which individuals move into occupations.

Healthy attitudes toward work also require the recognition and elimination of gender-role stereotypes. Miller (1977) found that gender-role stereotyping already existed among 9-year-olds. Navin and Sears (1980) and Wolleat (1979) confirm the early appearance and restrictive results of such attitudes. Hageman and Gladding (1983) studied the attitudes of third- and sixth-grade students, and found that there was increasing stereotyping as youngsters advanced in school and that a majority of girls at both grade levels did not feel free to pursue nontraditional careers. The elementary school years provide a time to build open attitudes in both boys and girls through exposure to role models, field trips where both sexes can be seen in positions that might easily be stereotyped, and similar experiences.

Many myths and attitudes impede the development of respect for all kinds of work. Unfortunately, the school has sometimes contributed to these fallacies rather than helped to overcome them. This is not surprising because teachers are drawn primarily from the middle class and bring to the classroom ideas and concepts typical of the middle class. The family backgrounds and previous experiences of teachers have made them more familiar with white-collar workers than with skilled and semiskilled workers. The youngsters with whom they work in the classroom, however, may be drawn from a much wider sociological spectrum, with attitudes and viewpoints quite different from those of the teacher. Teachers should avoid developing or supporting biases and prejudices toward various types of work. Instead, they should teach that all work is important and that the worker who uses unique skills and abilities effectively in any field makes an important contribution to all members of society.

Several studies have looked at the vocational values held by elementary school children. For example, Cooker (1973) reports differences across both grade level and gender on values concerning altruism, control, and money. He reports fourth-, fifth-, and sixth-grade girls scoring higher on altruism as a vocational value and boys in those grades scoring higher on control and money. Hales and Fenner (1973) report similar differences across gender but no differences across social classes.

Bailey and Nihlen (1989) report that many children are quite willing to ask questions about careers after being exposed to nontraditional occupational role models and conclude that "elementary school children are indeed interested in the world of work" (p. 143). They suggest that elementary school career development contain the following elements:

1. Information about the responsibilities of various occupations
2. Opportunities for children to share their knowledge of and experience with work
3. Opportunities to interact with workers and to find out how workers feel about their jobs
4. Activities that counteract gender-role stereotyping

Interestingly, the Bailey and Nihlen (1989) study, which was done with elementary school children, supports at least one of the findings of Rubinton (1985), who concludes that middle school children benefit from activities that allow them to engage in self-expression and share their own experiences and concerns.

Seligman, Weinstock, and Owings (1988) conclude, on the basis of their research with young children, that "promoting a positive home environment as well as strong parent-child relationships is critical not only for its own sake but as a determinant of the children's career development" (p. 229).

The Students: Middle School

The increasing academic skills required in most occupations have further persuaded the general public that all youth should be encouraged to continue their education as far as possible. The trend toward greater percentages of our youth completing secondary school is clear. Minimum school-leaving-age requirements and employment restrictions keep almost all youth in school at least through the middle school years. One can expect that present pressures to keep them in school for longer periods not only will continue, but will increase, with the result that very few youth will withdraw before completing high school.

For most youth, the middle school years are stormy and hectic as students enter adolescence and move toward greater independence and self-direction. Self-awareness becomes more pronounced, and the youth's concept of self as an individual independent of parents and family takes shape. As this distinctiveness of self becomes more apparent, the adolescent inevitably moves toward a view of self in terms of the world of work. Many of the career information activities of the middle school must be keyed to this transitional phase, to provide the adolescent an opportunity to try out self-concept and to modify, refine, and expand his view of self as a person. The middle school came into being largely as an effort to provide this opportunity for tryout and exploration, and it is at this level in most school systems that the pupil encounters the first opportunity to make educational choices. In addition to the curriculum, middle schools provide clubs and other activities that serve the purpose of exploration.

Most pupils entering middle or junior high school are still many years removed from full-time activity in the world of work. Similarly, the majority are still many years away from such activity when they move on to high school. Nevertheless, they are on their way toward the world of work, and during these years most become aware of this and develop a greater concern with the occupational world and their personal relationship to it. Although they are, for the most part, still concerned with work in the future, the realization of that future involvement enhances their awareness of it and focuses their attention on it to a much greater extent than previously. Students who are likely to be school dropouts may already have passed this point and may be concerned with thoughts of work in an immediate and specific sense.

By middle or junior high school age, most youngsters have had casual work experiences such as babysitting and newspaper routes. Even though these occasional bits of employment have little direct vocational significance, they do provide further contact with the world of work. Incidental employment not only helps youngsters gain some insight into why and how people earn a living, but also makes them more aware of an ultimate relationship to work. This new awareness usually stimulates concern for information about occupations generally. Often involvement in casual work provides an opportunity to encounter some of the experiences of adult workers—for example, receiving a paycheck and deciding how to use the money.

Jessell and Boyer (1989) surveyed 5464 seventh and eighth graders to determine the extent to which educational and vocational plans have been developed. They found that 94 percent of those surveyed expected to finish high school, 14 percent expected to enroll in vocational–technical school after high school, and 67 percent said they intended to complete college. Many of these same students had made career decisions. Twenty-six percent said they had made a decision and were reasonably confident that the decision was final. An additional 41 percent reported that they had made a decision but suggested that it might change later. Only 6 percent of the students in the survey reported that they had given career choice no consideration.

McDonald (1989), also studying seventh- and eighth-grade students, concluded on the basis of the results from 857 students that level of self-esteem, capacity to interpret complex occupational information, being female, of relatively high socioeconomic status, and coming from a family with two parents present were favorably related to positive attitudes toward careers. Obviously, the school can only have an impact on two of these variables, self-esteem and the interpretation of information. Finally, Luzzo and Pierce (1996) found that DISCOVER, a computer-assisted career guidance system could be used to produce significant positive changes in the career maturity of middle school students.

Programming Ideas: Middle School

To avoid redundancy in activities, the overall organization of the program needs to be organized around a theme. A common theme used in elementary schools could be characterized as proximity—that is, activities are designed initially to focus on workers who are closest to the child, gradually expanding as the child grows older. An example of this organizational theme would be as follows:

> Kindergarten: Workers at home and in my neighborhood
> First grade: Workers in my community
> Second grade: Workers in my county
> Third grade: Workers in my state
> Fourth grade: Workers in my nation
> Fifth grade: Workers of the world

The middle school then could be a continuation of the proximity or geographic theme simply by regarding the process and focusing on jobs of interest to the student in the neighborhood, community, state, and so on. It is more likely that middle school activities will be organized around an occupational theme, however. Some school districts give an interest inventory and then organize their programs around the occupations suggested by the inventory. The 23 major occupational groups listed in the Standard Occupational Classification System (see Chapter 6) could be used as the basis for the organization of the middle school program. This system is comprehensive and is linked to the *Occupational Outlook Handbook (OOH)*. As noted in Chapter 7, the *OOH* is available in print, online, and multimedia formats.

Whether the middle school decides to organize its program around Holland's (1985) interest categories (realistic, investigative, artistic, social, enterprising, conventional), the SOC classification system, or some other system, it is important to make sure that students are given a comprehensive, realistic look at the occupations available to them. It is also important that the program be integrated and fully coordinated with the elementary school and high school programs. Once an organizational theme has been selected, activities must be designed within the organizational theme to meet the objectives of the program. The following are some activities that might be used to develop various career development competencies.

Competencies of Elementary School Students

Be able to describe work of mother and father (if both in home)

Geographic Theme
Grade Activities

K. "What do you do, mother?"

1. Spend half an hour observing a community worker and give verbal report

2. Write brief report and give verbal report

Identify skills learned in school that are used in jobs

3. Class telephone call using speaker phone to "visible" (e.g., governor) state official

4. Analyze jobs of congressional representative

5. Study educational skills of workers in industrialized versus nonindustrialized countries

Competencies of Middle School Students	*Interest Theme*
Demonstrate understanding of self	6. Have students estimate interests; then give interest inventory with follow-up discussions
Identify at least five changes in society that affect work	7. Bring in old copies of *USA Today* and have small groups compete for number of trends that can be identified
Identify sources of employment in the community	8. Have job service counselor or personnel manager speak

It is also possible to organize the activities "vertically" (that is, by grade level) so that certain vital competencies and attitudes are developed.

Competency to Be Developed	*Grade Activities*
Students will understand gender-role stereotyping and broaden their own view of their potential in nontraditional occupations.	K. What kind of jobs do men and women hold? Start with mom and dad. Spontaneous discussion focusing on community.
	1. Cut pictures out of old magazines that show men and women working. Discuss stereotyping. Build collage to show nontraditional careers.
	2. Men and women working in our county. Discuss why men and women hold certain types of jobs. Bring in some nontraditional role models.
	3. Focusing on state government, look at the number of men and women in government. Discuss reasons.
	4. Focus on roles of women and men in national government. Why have we never had a woman president? What factors limit women in politics?
	5. Get figures for males and females in various jobs throughout the world. Why the discrepancy? What is the impact on men and women?

6. Study social occupations. Why are they predominantly made up of women? Also look at realistic occupations. Why are they predominantly made up of men? Bring in nontraditional role models. What problems/rewards have resulted in holding nontraditional jobs?

7. Using the interest inventory as a guide, have each person identify three or four nontraditional occupations. Do in-depth papers about one or two.

8. Identify potential nontraditional career options. Assign job shadowing, filmstrip review, or interviews with workers in that field. Have students ask friends, "What would you think of me if I entered _____ (nontraditional career option)?" Have students discuss rewards of their traditional and nontraditional jobs.

Once all activities are developed for all competencies at each level, the result will be substantial. Typically these guides are organized by grade level; identify the objectives that are to be achieved, specify how attainment of each objective is to be measured, provide a detailed outline of the activities that are to be employed to accomplish that objective, and list the materials such as books and filmstrips that are to be associated with the activities. Some school districts have comprehensive guides that counselors and others can use when planning a program for an individual school. Other districts have prescribed minimal programs that must be delivered by counselors.

The literature suggests that the opportunities to integrate career awareness and exploration with other learning experiences abound.

Donahue and Woodcock (1985) describe how eighth-grade students interviewed workers and prepared occupational profiles for thirty local occupations in the process of preparing a career-oriented mathematics book. Workers were asked how they used math in their everyday work and to provide samples of the kinds of problems they solved. The result was a ninety-two-page workbook used as a supplementary textbook. Hill (1981) describes a shadowing experience in a group of stores in a nearby mall. Staley and Mangieri (1984) provide a bibliography identified by level (K–3, 4–6, 7–9) for each of the fifteen career clusters of the U.S. Office of Education and discuss strategies for using books to help elementary students increase their career awareness. Innis (1982) provided sixth graders experience in obtaining jobs, working, and receiving "pay" by developing an "employment service" within the school. Christopher and Blocker (1980) describe using a fourth-grade social studies unit on the environment to acquaint students with environmental- and recycling-related occupations using AV materials, interviews with experts, and field trips. Both Montimurro (1980) and Isaacson and Hayes (1980) describe adaptations of the career day format used with elementary-age students.

As noted in the section on elementary school students, sex-typing of occupations occurs early, and by the time students arrive in the middle school these stereotypes are well entrenched (McKenna & Ferrero, 1991). Rea-Poteat and Martin (1991) found that their 80-hour summer program designed to orient young girls to occupations seemed to have only a limited impact in this area. The Broadening Horizons Project (Okey, Snyder, & Hackett, 1993) project was designed specifically to offset the impact of early sex-typing of occupations, particularly with regard to occupations involving mathematics and computers. They found that eighth graders in the program did significantly increase their career and academic self-efficacy and suggested that the program had attained its objectives. Speight, Rosenthal, Jones, & Gastenveld (1995), while not directly attempting to offset the results of occupational sex-typing, did find that a 3-day simulation called Medcamp increased self-efficacy regarding completion of medical school and the tasks associated with the practice of medicine for the thirty-five girls and ten boys enrolled in the camp.

Role Relationships

As most people realize, elementary and middle schools are made up of three types of personnel: administrators, teachers, and support personnel. The question that arises is Which of these groups will be responsible for the development and delivery of the career development program? The *National Career Development Guidelines* (Kobylarz, 1996) and *The National Standards for Counseling Programs (NSCP)* (Campbell & Dahir, 1997) make it very clear that one of the elementary and middle school counselors' responsibilities is the development and delivery of a career development program. The following statement was taken from the *NSCP*.

> *A comprehensive school-counseling program is developmental and systematic in nature, sequential, clearly defined, and accountable.—More specifically, school counseling programs employ strategies to enhance academics, provide career awareness, develop employment readiness, encourage self-awareness, foster interpersonal communication, and impart life success skills for all students. (p. 9)*

The foregoing statement does not imply that school counselors are responsible for actually providing all the services that are part of the school counseling program.

School counselors collaborate with teachers, community members, and others as they develop and deliver services.

What if there is no school counselor in a particular school? Is it still possible to develop and deliver a comprehensive program? Probably not! Teachers have neither the expertise nor the time needed to perform all the duties that were outlined throughout this chapter. Although the standards for school counseling programs emphasize that the school counseling program is more than what counselors alone can deliver, the fact is that the nation's schools are still in the throes of a twenty-year-long effort to improve themselves. The agenda of improving the quality of education in public schools seems likely to continue into the foreseeable future. Although a case can be made that a career development program promotes academic achievement (see the *NCDG* competencies), it seems unlikely that teachers will replace academic activities with career awareness and exploratory activities unless school counselors encourage them to do so.

Helping Parents Understand and Accept Their Role in Career Development

We would be remiss if we did not add to the list the involvement of the family as an important aspect of the program. Young (1994) suggests that parental influence on career development will be most effective if it is intentional, planned, and goal-directed. He suggests that many parents see the choice of an occupation as a child's right and thus do not wish to infringe on that right by actively working to influence the choice. He also reports some of his earlier research (Young, Frieson, & Pearson, 1988) that suggests that parents may treat their male and female children differently when they do engage in behavior aimed at influencing career development. His research suggests that, when helping male children, parents tend to be more understanding and affirming than they are when helping their female children. What is unsaid in Young's article is that, whether intentional, planned, or goal-directed, parents are one of the primary sources of influence in career development. Career development specialists need to make them more fully aware of their influence, develop an awareness that they may inadvertently be interacting differentially with their male and female children, and help them engage in effective facilitative behavior.

Parental ambition for a youngster may affect how he or she looks at the world and at occupations specifically. Deprecating one's own work in an effort to motivate the child toward something "better" may not help the youngster develop a base for decision making where crucial factors can be weighed objectively. Parental pressures that push a child of limited ability toward academically competitive areas are just as harmful and wasteful as those that encourage academically able children to leave school and go to work as soon as possible. Similarly, parental attitudes toward various occupational fields may influence the child's view of these fields. This is particularly true of attitudes that certain jobs are "men's work" or "women's work."

Earlier, we considered the use of parents as an information resource to help youngsters learn about occupations. Almost every elementary teacher already uses the variety of job holders within the parental group in this way. Bearg (1980) discusses the use of parents as role models in developing career awareness, by using parents as classroom visitors to explain their occupations. The value of this simple activity should not be discounted. It provides an opportunity for the other children in the class to learn about a particular job by listening to Johnny's mother and Mary's father tell about what they do, how, and why. It also may help Johnny and Mary see their parents' work from a different viewpoint than the random, end-of-the-day remarks that may have been the major basis for their view. Many peripheral values in school–home relationships may accrue from such an activity. There are, of course, numerous ways in which the school can involve parents in classroom activities as well as in school functions outside the classroom. If these are organized to maximize contact between the participating parents and children, both their own and others, many opportunities to learn adult roles, attitudes, and values will ensue.

Counselors can help parents see the unlimited opportunities within the home for children to learn about work. Unfortunately, many parents have developed the attitude that parental success is accomplished by making the life of their children easier than the life they experienced as children. Such a distorted view prevents capitalizing on home-based circumstances to learn about work. The assignment of regular home tasks to each child helps the child learn necessary work-related attitudes such as punctuality, reliability, efficiency, and responsibility. It also helps children learn the rewards of work—satisfaction in a job well done, service to others, a feeling of worth and accomplishment, and comradeship with fellow workers. Some families have found it helpful to develop family projects such as do-it-yourself home improvements, gardening projects, or similar tasks that also teach much about work and create family togetherness.

Parents sometimes are unaware of the attitude toward work that they reflect in the family setting. Counselors can help parents identify the extent to which they emphasize the negative aspects of their jobs—boredom, weariness, discontent, conflict, pressure, competitiveness—during family conversations. If only these aspects are revealed, the child will have difficulty in seeing the positive values that the job provides. Children whose classroom view of work seems heavily negative may be reflecting parental comments and behavior of this type, although the parents may be unaware of the impact of their words and actions. Elementary-age youngsters are not yet mature enough to recognize that for every job holder the advantages of the job exceed the disadvantages. This is especially true if they are taught only the disadvantages. Parental work values are the primary base on which the youngster begins to build a personal view of work.

The family also can provide many decision-making experiences that will help the child build these essential skills. Parents can help the child build self-confidence as well as responsibility by encouraging the child to make choices rather than usurping decisions. As the child makes decisions, she learns the consequences of good and bad choices. Study after study has consistently shown that parents exercise more influence on the eventual educational and vocational choice of children than any other adults. If parents view occupations in limited ways, the child is likely to do so as well. Parents who see only a few occupations as suitable for their daughters limit girls' ability to see wider opportunities. Parents who insist that their children follow parental patterns or ambitions may build frustration, dissatisfaction, and failure.

Summary

The elementary and middle school years are crucial in the career development process, particularly since crucial attitudes, values, and stereotypes are developing. Career development programming must be geared to broaden students' views of themselves as their perceptions relate to careers, as well as to enhance their self-esteem. However, because of the diversity of institutions, students, and personnel each school must develop its own program to accommodate these factors. Since each school functions in the context of a larger system, the school district, it is essential that the program be articulated with other schools at levels within the system. The final result should be a program that addresses the needs of the students, that is endorsed within the school and by the school district, and that involves parents and the community in which the school is located.

References

Bailey, B. A., & Nihlen, A. S. (1989). Elementary school children's perceptions of the world of work. *Elementary School Guidance and Counseling, 24,* 135–145.

Bearg, E. (1980). Parental role modeling as a career awareness tool. *Elementary School Guidance and Counseling, 14,* 266–268.

Brown, D., & Minor, C. W. (Eds.) (1989). *Working in America: A state report on planning and problems.* Alexandria, VA: NCDA.

Brown, D., & Minor, C. W. (Eds.) (1992). *Career needs in a diverse workforce: Implication of the NCDA Gallery Survey.* Alexandria, VA: NCDA.

Brown, D., Pryzwansky, W. B., & Schulte, A. (1998). *Psychological consultation: Introduction to theory and practice* (4th ed.). Boston: Allyn & Bacon.

Burck, H. D. (1978). Evaluating programs: Models and strategies. In L. Goldman (Ed.), *Research methods for counselors: Practical approaches in field settings* (pp. 177–197). New York: Wiley.

Burns, R. W. (1972). *New approaches to behavioral objectives.* Dubuque, IA: Wm. C. Brown.

Campbell, C. A., & Dahir, C. A. (1997). *The national standards for school counseling programs.* Alexandria, VA: American School Counselors Association.

Catlett J. L. (1992). The dignity of work: School children look at employment. *Elementary School Guidance and Counseling, 27,* 150–154.

Christopher, C., & Blocker, J. (1980). Career awareness through school and community activities. *Elementary School Guidance and Counseling, 14,* 281–285.

Clapsaddle, D. K. (1973). Career development and teacher inservice preparation. *Elementary School Guidance and Counseling, 8*, 92–97.

Cooker, P. G. (1973). Vocational values of children in grades four, five, and six. *Elementary School Guidance and Counseling, 8*, 112–118.

Donahue, M., & Woodcock, G. (1985). Project math-co. In C. L. Thompson (Ed.), Idea exchange column. *Elementary School Guidance and Counseling, 199*, 238–240.

Freeman, B. (1994). Importance of career development guidelines to school counselors. *Career Development Quarterly, 20*, 224–228.

Ginzberg, E., Ginzburg, S. W., Axelrad, S., & Herma, J. L. (1951). *Occupational choice: An approach to a general theory.* New York: Columbia University Press.

Hageman, M. B., & Gladding, S. T. (1983). The art of career exploration: Occupational sex-role stereotyping among elementary school children. *Elementary School Guidance and Counseling, 17*, 280–287.

Hales, L. W., & Fenner, B. J. (1973). Sex and social class differences in work values. *Elementary School Guidance and Counseling, 8*, 26–32.

Hansen, L. S. (1972). A model for career development through curriculum. *Personnel and Guidance Journal, 51*, 243–250.

Herma, J. L., Morris, L. L., & Fitz-Gibbon, C. T. (1987). *Evaluators handbook.* Beverly Hills, CA: Sage.

Herr, E. L., & Cramer, S. H. (1996). *Career guidance and counseling through the life span: Systemic approaches* (5th ed.). Glenview, IL: Scott, Foresman and Co.

Hill, P. L. (1981). Career education at Meadowbrook Mall. In H. H. Splete (Ed.), Career guidance in the elementary school. *Elementary School Guidance and Counseling, 16*, 47–50.

Holland, J. L. (1985). *Vocational choices: A theory of vocational personalities and work environment* (2nd ed.). Englewood Cliffs, NJ: Prentice-Hall.

Hoyt, K. B. (1977). *A primer for career education.* Washington, DC: Office of Career Education.

Hoyt, K. B. (1985). Career guidance, educational reform, and career education. *Vocational Guidance Quarterly, 34*, 6–14.

Hoyt, K. B., & Lester, J. N. (1985). *Learning to work.* Alexandria, VA: National Career Development Association.

Innis, J. (1982). Operation employment: A taste of the world of work. In C. L. Thompson (Ed.), Idea exchange column. *Elementary School Guidance and Counseling, 16*, 235–240.

Isaacson, L. E., & Hayes, R. (1980). Adapting career day to the elementary school. *Elementary School Guidance and Counseling, 14*, 258–261.

Jessell, J., & Boyer, M. (1989). *Career expectations among Indiana junior high and middle school students: A second survey.* Terre Haute, IN: Indiana State University.

Kobylarz, L. (1996). *National career development guidelines: K-adult handbook.* Stillwater, OK: Career Development Training Institute.

Leonard, G. E. (1972). Career guidance in the elementary school. *Elementary School Guidance and Counseling, 7*, 234–237.

Lippitt, G. L., & Lippitt, R. (1986). *The consulting process in action* (2nd ed.). La Jolla, CA: University Associates.

Luzzo, D. A., & Pierce, G. (1996). The effects of DISCOVER on the career maturity of middle school students. *Career Development Quarterly, 45*, 170–172.

Marland, S. P., Jr. (1974). *Career education.* New York: McGraw-Hill.

McDonald, J. (1989). *The influence of selected variables in career attitudes and perceived abilities of young adolescents* (doctoral thesis in preparation). Terre Haute, IN: Indiana State University Department of Counseling.

McGee, L., & Silliman, B. (1982). Interest measurement as a basis for elementary career awareness activities. *Elementary School Guidance and Counseling, 16,* 172–179.

McKenna, A. E., & Ferrero, G. W. (1991). Ninth-grade students' attitudes toward nontraditional careers. *Career Development Quarterly, 40,* 168–181.

Miller, J. V. (1977). *Career development needs of nine-year-olds: How to improve career development programs.* Washington, DC: National Advisory Council for Career Education.

Montimurro, T. (1980). A career day for elementary school students? *Elementary School Guidance and Counseling, 14,* 263–265.

Morris, L. L., Fitz-Gibbon, C. T., & Lindheim, E. (1987). *How to measure performance and use tests.* Beverly Hills, CA: Sage.

Navin, S. L., & Sears, S. J. (1980). Parental roles in elementary career guidance. *Elementary School Guidance and Counseling, 14,* 269–277.

Nelson, R. C. (1980). The CREST program: Helping children with their choices. *Elementary School Guidance and Counseling.*

NOICC. (1988). *National career counseling and development guidelines: Elementary schools.* Washington, DC: Author.

NOICC. (1989a). *The national career development guidelines: Local handbook for elementary schools.* Washington, DC: Author.

NOICC. (1989b). *The national career development guidelines: Local handbook for high schools.* Washington, DC: Author.

NOICC. (1989c). *The national career development guidelines: Local handbook for middle/junior schools.* Washington, DC: Author.

NOICC. (1989d). *The national career development guidelines: Local handbook for postsecondary institutions.* Washington, DC: Author.

Okey, J. L. Snyder, L. M., & Hackett, B. (1993). The broadening horizons project: Development of a vocational guidance program for eighth-grade students. *The School Counselor, 40,* 218–222.

Rea-Poteat, A. E., & Martin, P. F. (1991). Taking your place: A summer program to encourage nontraditional career for adolescent girls. *Career Development Quarterly, 40,* 182–188.

Roberts, N. J. (1971). Establishing a need for a vocational guidance program at the elementary and middle school level. *Elementary School Guidance and Counseling, 6,* 252–257.

Rost, P. (1973). The career pyramid. In G. E. Leonard (Ed.), Career guidance in the elementary and middle school level. *Elementary School Guidance and Counseling, 8,* 50–53.

Rubinton, N. (1985). Career exploration of middle school youth: A university school cooperative. *Vocational Guidance Quarterly, 33,* 249–255.

Seligman, L., Weinstock, L., & Owings, N. (1988). The role of family dynamics in career development of 5-year-olds. *Elementary School Guidance and Counseling, 22,* 222–230.

Speight, J. D., Rosenthal, K. S., Jones, B. J., & Gastenveld, P. M. (1995). Medcamp's effect on junior high school students' medical career self-efficacy. *Career Development Quarterly, 43,* 285–295.

Staley, N. K., & Mangieri, J. N. (1984). Using books to enhance career awareness. *Elementary School Guidance and Counseling, 18,* 200–208.

Stecher, B. M., & Davis, W. A. (1987). *How to focus an evaluation.* Beverly Hills, CA: Sage.

Stein, T. S. (1991). Career exploration strategies for the elementary school counselor. *Elementary School Guidance and Counseling, 26,* 153–157.

Super, D. E. (1957). *The psychology of careers.* New York: Harper & Row.

Super, D. E. (1990). Career and life development. In D. Brown, L. Brooks, & associates, *Career choice and development* (2nd ed., pp. 197–261). San Francisco: Jossey-Bass.

Thompson, C. L., & Parker, J. L. (1971). Fifth graders view the work world scene. *Elementary School Guidance and Counseling, 5,* 281–288.

Walz, G. R., & Benjamin, L. (1984). Systemic career guidance programs. In N. C. Gysbers (Ed.), *Designing careers* (pp. 336–360). San Francisco: Jossey-Bass.

Wernick, W. (1972). The ABLE model. In G. E. Leonard (Ed.), Career guidance in the elementary school. *Elementary School Guidance and Counseling, 7,* 150–155.

Wolleat, P. L. (1979). School-age girls. *Counseling Psychologist, 8,* 22–23.

Young, R. A. (1994). Helping adolescents with career development: The active role of the parents. *Career Development Quarterly, 42,* 198–203.

Young, R. A., Frieson, J. D., & Pearson, H. M. (1988). Activities and interpersonal relations dimensions of parental behavior in the career development of adolescents. *Youth and Society, 20,* 29–45.

10

Career Development in the High School

In Chapter 9, a general model for creating career development programs was delineated along with the National Career Development Guidelines model. In this chapter, some of the specific aspects of creating a career development program at the high school level are discussed, along with some strategies that may be useful in fostering the career development of high school students. However, before discussing program development, some background information and some of the unique characteristics of high schools and high school students are presented.

Background

The idea of individual differences suggests that each person will grow at his or her own pace. Therefore, we must expect some variation in the rate of career development that we encounter in our schools. The U.S. educational system provides considerable latitude for this diversity of growth; nevertheless, the passage of time and progression through the grades bring all individuals to certain crucial points in their educational experience. Decisions must be made, and the individual must pursue the consequences of each decision.

Nearly twenty-five years ago, Mitchell (1977) reported the results of the survey of the career development of 17-year-olds. Briefly, the data revealed the following:

1. Most had discussed future plans, twice as often with parents as with counselors.
2. Most could match five out of nine occupations with the physical characteristics or skills required, but less than 10 percent could do all nine correctly.

3. Only 2 percent saw school and academic areas as activities that would be useful for a job.
4. Most recognized that at least one course taken in high school might be useful on a job; most named a vocational subject.
5. Most felt that the best way to find out job requirements was by observation.
6. Nearly all had thought about the job they would like to hold in the future.
7. When identifying important elements of a letter applying for a job, most failed to include educational and training qualifications.

Several more recent studies provide evidence to support Mitchell's findings. Noeth, Engen, and Prediger (1984) found that a group of 1200 college-bound high school juniors reported that interesting classes and their own families (92 percent and 90 percent) were most helpful in terms of assistance with career decisions. Next highest were grades (86 percent) and friends (73 percent). Counselors and out-of-school activities ranked at the bottom (52 percent and 53 percent) in terms of providing assistance with career decision making. Lee (1984) studied 520 rural tenth graders and found that parental influence varied by ethnic group but was the major factor in career development. McNair and Brown (1983), in a related study of 259 tenth graders, also found parental influence to be stronger than any other factor in the career development of this group. Dillard and Campbell (1981) found that parental aspirations for their high schoolers' careers influenced aspirations among African Americans and Puerto Ricans but not Anglos. These studies appear to emphasize the importance of an effective career guidance program in the school that involves parents.

Unfortunately, helping students plan for their work roles after high school seems to be a low priority in high school guidance programs. Moles (1991), reporting the results of a national survey of guidance program directors, indicates that helping students with academic achievement, planning postsecondary schooling, and promoting personal growth all receive more emphasis than career development activities. Not surprisingly, this emphasis is in agreement with the wishes of school counselors according to these program leaders. Moles's findings suggest that school counselors spend approximately 9 to 13 percent of their time in activities that are directly related to career development. These activities include career days, career seminars featuring speakers from specific occupations, visits to job sites, promoting the use of career information, and placement for exploratory work experience.

A fundamental goal of the high school career guidance program should be to alert the student to each impending decision sufficiently far enough in advance to permit the student, and parents when appropriate, to prepare for a wise choice. Only rarely do elementary or middle school students face educational and career decisions of major importance. These situations ordinarily begin to occur near the end of middle or junior high school and then appear with increasing frequency for the next several years. In Chapter 9, we discussed the importance of developing readiness for decision making among elementary and middle school students. The interaction of human development and educational organizations coincides in a way that confronts high school-age students with a continuous network of situations in which decisions must be made.

Decision making during the high school years can only be as good as the information on which the process is based and the students' ability to interpret and use this information. Students, parents, teachers, and counselors will all need access to comprehensive career information centers stocked with current, accurate information. Career information, its collection, storage, and dissemination have been discussed extensively in Chapter 7 and elsewhere, and here we reinforce the importance of information in the overall career development program. Apparently, most schools have "an abundance of occupational information available to U.S. high school students if they want it" (p. 73), according to a survey by Chapman and Katz (1983). These authors concluded that students do not access the information available to the extent they should. Nearly 20 percent of the students studied had never used reference books, 33 percent had not used occupational books, and in those schools having computerized systems, 50 percent of the students had not used them. Clearly career development programming is needed to change this situation.

A meta-analysis of eighteen career development programs by Baker and Popowicz (1983) suggested that, generally speaking, career development programs can be effective. The developers of the *National Career Counseling and Guidance Guidelines* for high schools (NOICC, 1988; Kobylarz, 1996) concluded that these programs would have several positive outcomes—on students, their parents, and their schools—based on the literature reviews of Campbell, Connell, Boyle, and Bhaerman (1983), Crites (1987), Herr (1982), and Spokane and Oliver (1983). These benefits are listed in Table 10.1.

While there may not be unanimous agreement that career development programs in high schools will produce the outcomes identified in Table 10.1, there is widespread agreement that the high school years are crucial and that many activities that occur routinely in the high school lend themselves to fostering career planning and development. For example, students are confronted with numerous curricular choices, and it is not unusual for counselors to engage students in consideration of the occupational implications of their educational courses. Certain entire programs of study, such as auto mechanics, business education, and construction trades, have dramatic implications for career choice making, and the choice of these curricula is typically accompanied by a discussion of the occupational consequences of the choice. Similarly, students' desires to get part-time jobs and make postsecondary educational plans have tremendous implications for career choice making.

Continuation of the exploratory activities initiated at earlier levels should be maintained, with major attention during the high school years on narrowing and clarifying students' goals. Identification of specific career options should not be expected for most high school students; and those students who are likely to pursue a baccalaureate degree may be least inclined to engage in career planning. The refining of choice to the point of naming a specific goal is not a function of age, grade level, or ability but rather should be directly related to the imminence of entry into the world of work or into a specific preparatory program. That choice

TABLE 10.1   Expected Benefits of High School Career Development Programs

Student Benefits
Decreased dropout rates
Higher self-esteem and self-concept
Improved school attendance
Better social adjustment
Lower rates of delinquency, truancy, and running away
Understanding of the relationship between education and employment
More competent decision making
Improved information-seeking and information-use skills
Awareness of changes in the world of work
Greater independence in decision making
Improved academic achievement
Increased appreciation for the value of education
Increased motivation resulting from personal career goals
More realistic selection of courses of study

Benefits to Parents
Greater parental involvement in students' career planning
Increased parental satisfaction with students' career plans

Benefits to Schools
Program goals stated in terms of student outcomes (thus accountability enhanced)
Student achievement assessed regularly
Program components evaluated in relationship to student outcomes
Student outcomes and program components clearly specified at each level
Reinforcement of learning from previous levels
Student competency assessment that provides basis for individualized
    career-planning assistance
Individualized career plans that provide continuity of career planning
    at various levels

should precede the entry point by sufficient time for the student to acquire the specialized training that the chosen occupation requires. For example, the scientific and technical professions generally require a specific, detailed baccalaureate program for admission. College prep for these fields often specifies a program heavily loaded with high school mathematics and science. A decision to move toward occupations in this general cluster would have to be made early enough in high school to ensure completion of these preparatory courses. On the other hand, some professional occupations require specialization only in the final year or two of college. In these fields, the student could remain unfocused until the college sophomore year and still encounter no delay in preparation.

Teachers and counselors have a crucial responsibility in the career development process: to help students develop awareness of the prerequisites for entry. Unless the students are willing to sacrifice the time needed to make up missed prerequisites, the opportunity to choose an area (e.g., engineering) is lost when the student passes the point at which the first required prerequisite (e.g., introductory algebra) ordinarily is started.

High School Students

As suggested earlier, high school students undergo a number of transitions including preparing for the transition from high school to work. Unfortunately, as many as 25 percent leave school prior to graduation. Although 40 percent of these return to school through alternative high school programs, community college programs, and other means, the economic consequences for those who do not are dramatic. For example, in 1996 workers who had finished high school earned over $7000 per year more than students who had not, according to the U.S. Census Bureau Current Population Survey (U.S. Census Bureau, 1997).

Students who are planning to graduate from high school are also making important educational decisions that have economic, psychological, and sociological consequences. In 1995, 14.3 million students were enrolled in an institution of higher education, up from 12.2 million in 1985. The enrollment of African American students in 4-year institutions increased from 9 percent to 11 percent in the 1980–1995 period. With the exception of Native Americans, the percentage of enrollees of other minorities increased during this period as well. College graduates can expect to earn $450,000 more than high school graduates and $700,000 more than high school dropouts over their lifetime (NCES, 1997).

Minorities face a particularly difficult situation if they leave school prematurely since there is every indication that they generally fare less well in the labor force than their white counterparts. Unemployment data have consistently suggested that the employment ratio of minority youths is approximately 2.5:1.

A study by Post-Kammer (1987) shows that eleventh-grade girls' work values tended to run contrary to gender stereotypes in some instances. For example, girls valued achievement and variety to a higher extent and security to a lesser extent than did boys. However, boys valued management, economic returns, and independence more highly, and girls valued altruism and way of life more highly, which is in accordance with traditional gender stereotypes. These values and their implications for career planning need careful consideration, particularly for young women. Substantially more young women enter the labor force early and remain there longer than they did a generation ago. Moreover, both the entry rate and the proportion remaining in the labor force indefinitely will increase probably to the point that it approximates that of men (W. T. Grant Foundation, 1988).

During their high school years many students will gain their first experiences as workers. In 1986, 41 percent of 16- and 17-year-old students were in the labor force (W. T. Grant Foundation, 1988), and there is no reason to believe this percentage has diminished in the past 15 years. Most of the jobs held by young workers are entry-level service jobs such as those in fast-food restaurants. These work experiences provide students with valuable (if sometimes negative) work experiences that can be capitalized on when exploring career options.

We also know that students with various types of disabilities enter high school. The number of students enrolled in special education programs from kindergarten through high school is approximately 5.6 million. Students with learning disabilities make up the largest group whereas students with speech and language disabilities constitute the second largest group (NCES, 1997). The consequences of not maximizing these students' educational potential and failing to make well-considered career plans is potentially more disastrous for students with disabilities than for any other group because of the biases that exist in our society regarding the potential of these students as workers.

As noted earlier, parents are an important influence in the career development of adolescents. Many adolescents do have difficulty communicating with their parents, according to a study of 11,000 eighth, ninth, and tenth graders (Bensen, Mangen, & Williams, 1986). Only 25 percent of these students said they would go to their parents if they were having trouble with alcohol or sex. However, it seems clear that many students do talk directly to parents about careers or are influenced indirectly by them. What is not clear is whether parents are maximizing their impact, but it is unlikely that this is occurring.

The Institution

High schools are more diverse than either elementary or middle schools. For example, there are comprehensive high schools that offer a wide variety of programs including academic, vocational, and general courses of study. However, some high schools are specialized with regard to curricular offering. For example, it is not unusual to find vocational–technical high schools, high schools that emphasize the arts (music, dance, etc.), and mathematics and science preparatory schools. So-called alternative high schools may offer daytime or evening programs for potential dropouts or reentry opportunities for students who have already left school.

Types of students and their backgrounds will be major determiners of the career development program, as will the philosophy and objectives of the school itself. In the next section, we consider the unique aspects of developing a comprehensive career development program in a high school.

Developing the Program

In Chapter 9, the process of developing a comprehensive career development program was outlined, a process that is identical for each level. What varies are the competencies that are to be developed for the high school. These are listed in Table 10.2 (NOICC, 1989b; Kobylarz, 1996) along with some sample indicators.

As was the case with the guidelines for elementary and middle schools, the competencies and indicators shown in Table 10.2 are general guidelines, and it is expected that school staffs will develop their own competencies and skills based

TABLE 10.2   Competencies to Be Developed in High School Students and Sample Indicators

Competencies	Sample Indicators: The student will
1. Understanding of the influence of a positive self-concept on career development	1. Demonstrate the ability to manage her/his behavior in developing and maintaining a healthy self-concept
2. Interpersonal and social skills required for positive interaction with others	2. Describe appropriate employee–employer interactions in varying situations
3. Understanding of the interrelationships of emotional and physical development and career decision making	3. Exhibit behaviors that are important to good physical and mental health
4. Understanding of the interrelationship between educational achievement and career planning, training, and placement	4. Identify essential learning skills required in the work environment
5. Positive attitudes toward work and learning	5. Demonstrate positive work ethic and attitude
6. Skills for locating, evaluating, and interpreting information about career opportunities	6. Describe the impact of factors such as population, climate, and geographic location on local job opportunities
7. Skills for preparing for, seeking, obtaining, maintaining, and advancing in a job	7. Develop skills in preparing a resume and completing a job application
8. Understanding of how societal needs and functions influence the nature and structure of work	8. Demonstrate an understanding of the global economy and how it affects each individual
9. Skills in making decisions and choosing alternatives for and pursuing educational and career goals	9. Project and describe factors that may influence educational and career decisions
10. Understanding of the interrelationships of life roles and career	10. Describe the ways career choice may influence lifestyle
11. Understanding of the continuous changes in male/female roles and how they relate to career decisions	11. Develop attitudes, behaviors, and skills that contribute to the elimination of sex stereotypes and sex bias
12. Skills in career exploration and planning	12. Develop career plans that include the concept that a changing world demands lifelong learning

Sources: *National career development guidelines: Local handbook for high schools.* (1989). Washington, DC: NOICC, pp. 5–6.

on the needs of the students. Obviously, the competencies outlined in Table 10.2 will need to be translated into a series of specific objectives and programs or delivery mechanisms developed to achieve these objectives. Delivery mechanisms are discussed later in this chapter.

One task involved in planning and implementing a comprehensive career development program for an individual school not discussed in Chapter 9 is articulation. Articulation can be roughly defined as the process of coordination both within and across program levels (NOICC, 1988). The obvious purposes of program articulation, whether it be within a school or among school levels, are to ensure that the districtwide program is comprehensive and free from unneeded redundancy, and to plan so activities will be sequenced properly. In Chapter 9, we briefly discussed articulating the elementary school career development program with curricular offerings as well as sequencing activities so they will add to students' knowledge and skill level in a logical fashion. As was stated at the outset of this chapter, the elementary and middle school programs should prepare the student for career development activities in the high school. Numerous states have developed comprehensive, carefully sequenced, and articulated models of career development programs that can be used as models in this planning process.

Delivery Mechanisms

The processes identified in the local handbooks for the *National Career Development Guidelines* for elementary and middle/junior high schools (NOICC, 1989a, c) were presented in Chapter 9. The discussion that follows identifies processes that can be used to develop career development competencies in high school–age students.

As noted in Chapter 9, Freeman (1994) surveyed school counselors to determine the extent to which they are in agreement with the competencies identified in the *National Career Development Guidelines* (NOICC, 1989; Kobylarz, 1996). With the exception of helping students understand the impact of work on society, counselors responding were strongly supportive of the competencies identified for high school students. They were only moderately supportive of developing high school students' understanding of the impact of work on society as an outcome of career development programming.

Classrooms and Groups

Let us first consider educational situations, in which the teacher is likely to be responsible for the career development program. We focus most of our attention on classroom and group-related activities. When considering the teacher's involvement in career development, however, one must not think only of the classroom, nor should one think that only the teacher works with students in groups. The counselor often may teach a class or lead a group, and the teacher often is involved with students out of class in career exploration activities such as field trips and visits to training programs.

The development of the self-concept is a continuing, lifelong process that begins with the individual's first awareness of self as a person. Continuous though this process is, there are periods of particular intensity. The secondary and post-secondary school years comprise one of these periods, in which the individual is deeply involved in learning to understand the self in relationship to others and to the world.

The school provides the principal setting in which the elementary and early secondary student encounters the world outside the close family circle. In this setting, the student usually establishes the first prolonged contacts with adults and with peers who are not a part of the family group. It is entirely normal to select some of these people as models and ideals. As the student experiments with the different roles perceived as possibilities, he encounters varying degrees of gratification and satisfaction. Some of the roles played may be at variance or even in conflict with the roles that would be encouraged and approved within the family circle. Thus, inevitably, the school setting helps students to broaden their development.

Most secondary and postsecondary schools attempt to assist students in the career development process by using portions of regular academic classes for special units related to the general topic of educational and vocational planning. There are certain obvious advantages to this approach. First, the administrative difficulties of staffing and scheduling are reduced since the work is simply incorporated into a regular course. Second, if a required course is used, all students at a given grade level are reached automatically, thus providing the broad coverage that the administrator usually desires. Third, the use of certain courses for special units leads to involvement of those teachers in the guidance program.

These advantages, unfortunately, have corresponding disadvantages. Attaching a special unit to a subject-matter class may solve the staffing problem, but in an unfortunate way. The subject-matter teacher may lack preparation or background for such teaching, with the result that he or she will feel both unhappy and threatened. Subject-matter teachers, naturally, have an affinity for their own subject area and see so much in their own field that they need to teach students that they are often reluctant to give up any sizable portion of that subject time for a special unit. Similarly, even though scheduling problems are resolved by the special unit, designating time in one subject area for a special unit may cause difficulties with accrediting agencies or may result in student deficiencies in that subject area.

Even though a career development unit in freshman English will reach all freshmen enrolled in that course, this may not be the best or most appropriate time to present the unit to all freshmen. Individual differences in development and in personal plans may make the unit appropriate for some students, but perhaps premature for others. Placing the course arbitrarily at a given grade level may meet the needs of the average students but may fall seriously short for the others.

Balancing the advantages and disadvantages of using subject-matter time for career development units must be resolved by the administrator. Resolving the problem requires careful consideration of many factors, including assessment of student needs, teacher abilities and interests, guidance staff utilization, and various other components.

Career development units incorporated into regularly scheduled courses may be either general or specialized in nature. A general guidance unit usually is complete in itself, with little or no direct connection to the subject area into which it is inserted. A specialized guidance unit usually has a direct relationship to the subject area.

General career development units may be found at any grade level of the secondary school. Because of the desire to reach all students at that level, they are usually attached to courses such as English or social studies. The objectives of these courses are usually broad enough, especially in content, to make them more amenable to such adaptation.

At the upper junior high and lower senior high levels, the general units most frequently are related to such broad topics as orientation to school, educational and vocational planning, or personal adjustment. In the upper grades they may, instead, deal with selecting a college, applying for a job, military service, or some similar topic appropriate for the person about to complete high school work. The duration of units may vary from 1 to 4 weeks.

The purposes of career development units vary considerably. Usually the purpose is to encourage and stimulate occupational exploration and to help students see the relationship between school and later careers. When the purpose is limited in this way, there is usually a reasonable chance that the unit will be successful. If, on the other hand, the school attempts to meet its total obligation for career development through such a unit, the project is doomed to failure, since the total process is too large to be handled in such a manner. Close cooperation between teacher and counselor is essential, so the counselor can assist the teacher in developing and presenting the unit and so the unit can lead to individual counseling for students for whom it is appropriate.

Specialized units frequently focused on career opportunities that relate to specific areas. Such units logically are a part of courses that have obvious career implications. They also may be relevant in courses that have broader, fundamental, general education value, since few occupations are filled any longer by workers with only a specialized preparation. Too often in the past such specialized units have concentrated on the related specialties and have overlooked the broader application that each subject may have. Thus, non-college-bound students may feel that, because college preparation is necessary to become a chemist or a physicist, science holds no opportunity for them. Understanding the interrelationships of occupations should help the teacher see the broader implications and provide an opportunity for students to grasp the vast range of openings at various levels in all fields. Career-oriented units not only assist the student in career development but also serve a special purpose in stimulating interest in a specific course. Close cooperation between teacher and counselor will be helpful to both and will provide maximum value to the student.

Historically, career education advocates (e.g., Hoyt, Pinson, Laramore, & Mangum, 1973) staunchly support the idea of teacher involvement in the career development process. They contend that the activities just described inevitably include a degree of artificiality because the unit is laid on the ordinary subject-matter instructional efforts of the teacher. They propose that more could be accomplished if the attention to career-related aspects were totally infused into the day-to-day classroom activities. This would require the teacher continually to relate subject matter to the world of work, to use illustrations from work whenever possible, and to orient classroom learning to postschool plans of the students. While one can argue against this position in theory, most high school teachers never adopted this approach. Its successful implementation necessitates major curricular revision and joint effort by teacher, counselor, and administrator. Because curricular revision is not in the offing, the classroom teacher can use career units advantageously.

For many years, a number of schools have included regular courses in their curriculums, under various titles, often "Careers" or "Occupations." They are sometimes taught at the ninth-grade level. Grade placement of such a course always has presented a difficult problem. Placement in the ninth grade permits maximum opportunity for educational planning after that grade, but students of ten feel so far removed from the world of work that motivation may be difficult. If the course is taught at the twelfth-grade level, students are more likely to see its pertinence to their own lives, but the course may come too late in the educational career to permit capitalizing on it effectively. The difficulties at either level can be met best if the course is developed to meet the needs of the students involved. Obviously, the ninth grader is likely to be more concerned with exploring occupations broadly, as they affect educational planning for the years ahead, whereas the senior is more apt to be confronted with the specifics of job seeking and preparation for entrance into the world of work. Ideally, it should be a required course and carry credit.

Organized classes in careers permit more extensive consideration of the topic than is possible in the short unit studied in another class. Nevertheless, any course will not be of limited value to the student if it is approached in textbook fashion with the aim of thorough familiarization with the world of work. The goal of such a course should be to maximize self-actualization through the development of concepts appropriate to the student's level of maturity and proximity to the world of work.

One advantage of an organized course in "Occupations" or "Careers" is that it can be closely tied to the school's total guidance program and properly staffed. In some schools the course is taught by a member of the counseling staff, whose academic preparation may be more appropriate for teaching such a course than is that of a subject-area teacher. Even though this arrangement gives the counselor contact with students, it also reduces the time available for individual counseling and other activities.

A regularly scheduled course taught by a counselor may offer the best opportunity to meet the individual needs of the students enrolled. It should be possible to relate class activities to individual counseling and to develop an approach based on both group procedures and individual counseling, with the student being involved in both phases to whatever extent is appropriate. When this dual approach can be arranged, the student will have the maximum opportunity to benefit.

The adoption of an organized course may cause a school faculty to assume that it has met its responsibility for helping students in the career development process. When this happens, the course becomes a one-shot effort, and the basic axiom that career choice and development should start in the early years and continue throughout one's life is disregarded. Two- and four-year colleges often adopt this view by offering an elective course called "Life and Career Planning" or "Career Exploration." Although the course is useful to those who enroll, it is not enough to meet the needs of all students.

Another aspect of this problem occurs when the careers course is organized on the premise that each participating student will make a career choice during the course. This approach disregards the developmental aspect of career development and may lead the student to the unwarranted view that a vocational choice is static and permanent rather than dynamic and flexible. Even in adulthood, the possibility of modification and revision of choice—because of change in self-concept, technological developments, and other factors—is so likely for most people that any implication of early permanent choice is not only misleading, but also likely to make later adjustment difficult. A much more realistic approach is to help the student see vocational choice as a continuing series of choices, each of which is likely to be revised, thus leading to a new choice that may similarly be modified.

A final disadvantage can exist in the regularly scheduled careers course if it focuses only on the occupational aspects and disregards the educational factors. Educational and vocational planning and development are so closely interrelated, both during formal schooling and later, that it is inappropriate to consider one without the other. This is especially important in a society in which we can expect increasing numbers of adults to need continuing education and retraining beyond the regular school years to prepare them for occupations that did not exist when they were in school. As technological changes eliminate and modify existing occupations and create new ones, more adults become involved in further education to fit them for new jobs. The school can serve this group better if it helps them accept and understand the inevitability of change rather than leading them toward a specific niche as a definite and final goal.

Concern for the career development of the individual should have a natural and normal place within any classroom. Each member of the instructional staff has a responsibility in this area of student growth and maturity. This responsibility probably can be met best by an awareness by all staff members and a concerted effort by all, led by the administration and the guidance staff, to develop an approach that permeates the school program with sufficient breadth and depth to meet the varying needs of all students.

Small Groups

Group procedures may enable the school or other agency to work with all or many of these individuals collectively on certain aspects of their development. The commonality of the problem may make it easier for more students to become involved with members of their peer group in seeking information or understanding that will help them resolve their problems. This attitude may also lead them to accept suggestions and reactions from the peer group that they would be inclined to resist from others. The recognition that their peers face similar problems and uncertainties may help them obtain a different perspective on their own concerns, and this may encourage more independence and initiative on their part in seeking information and solution. In addition, an inevitable sharing of knowledge and information leads to a broader foundation for ultimate decision making.

Certain disadvantages or limitations exist in group procedures, and care must be taken to ensure the accrual of advantages and the avoidance of negative experiences. One individual within the group may be ahead of the others in personally acquiring the information or resolution that the group is seeking. Even though no loss may result from being part of the group, this individual's personal progress may be slowed by group participation. It also is possible for specific individual problems to be overlooked or sidetracked while the group focuses on a broader, more general concern. Thus either the individual does not acquire what he or she had hoped to gain, or the rest of the group marks time while attention is given to the individual's specific concern. Finally, there is always the possibility of loss of status by an individual within the group, since it may be difficult to develop a totally accepting group.

Even though a school goes to great pains to provide career information in class situations, it should not disregard out-of-class group activities led by the counselor. Class activities usually are oriented toward the general needs of the class, even in schools that make every effort to individualize instruction. Within each class, one can expect to find individuals whose particular needs scatter around the general mean for the class. Some individuals will obviously be farther from the mean than others. For those whose needs are quite different from those of the majority, the general class activity will have less significance. In many situations, these special needs can be met more adequately by out-of-class groups. For example, students already planning to terminate their formal education shortly confront quite different questions than do students who anticipate continuing to graduation or beyond. A senior class unit on how to apply for a job is of no help to the early dropout who expects to be gone from school before then. Unless he or she can be helped before leaving school, the unit is wasted. Further, the student may need help in acquiring information about specific job opportunities available locally to young workers with limited education. However, exploration of this topic in sufficient depth to be meaningful to a potential dropout may not be of crucial importance to the rest of the group.

Group career development activities may be quite varied. For example, it is possible to hold career seminars where a representative of an occupation such as insurance sales or over-the-road truck driving can discuss the nature of the job, the training, requirements, hiring requirements, lifestyle advantages and disadvantages, and so forth with a small group of interested students. Groups can also be organized for exploratory purposes, to focus on the career decision-making process, or for field trips to explore hospitals, industrial sites, and so forth.

Dropout prevention groups that center on career development activities are increasingly popular. In *Dropping Out or Hanging In* (Brown, 1998), which is a manual for students to use in dropout prevention groups, students are first taken through a series of self-awareness activities. These are followed by activities designed to teach decision-making skills, and then students are encouraged to practice using their skills in setting career, education, and other life goals. The culmination of these small groups is preparing students to "drop into" school if they do drop out and decide that they have made an error.

Prior to involving students in a group activity, a screening interview should be held to determine the students' objectives, degree of motivation, and the extent to which they will work collaboratively with other group members. Unmotivated students and potential discipline problems may be precluded from groups unless the counselor feels that the problems can be corrected in the group setting.

Life Planning Classes and Groups

The focus throughout much of this chapter has been on career exploration experiences. However, there is increasing support for broader career experiences that involve integrating career planning with other life roles. Brown (1980) outlines what he terms a life planning workshop for high school students, which consists of seven components: (1) understanding human behavior, (2) conceptualizing one's self as a winner, (3) the importance of fantasy in planning, (4) matching fantasy and reality, (5) setting goals, (6) short-term planning, and (7) long-term planning.

Amatea, Clark, and Cross (1984) evaluated a 2-week course for high school students, called Lifestyles, aimed at (1) increasing students' awareness of their values and their preferences for various life roles, (2) increasing students' awareness of the costs and benefits associated with various lifestyles, and (3) helping students establish life role priorities. They found that their course did seem to increase students' decisiveness about their career choices. They also found that, at the end of the group sessions, males and females did not vary in their attitudes toward the family role.

Resources for Classes and Groups

It seems appropriate to review various resources that can be used with groups, with major emphasis on awareness and exploration objectives. We briefly consider publications, resources within the school, and community resources. Sources of occupational information have already been discussed in Chapter 7.

Publications

The school newspaper offers almost unlimited opportunity for passing information to students, arousing their interest, informing them of services that are available, or in other ways involving them in acquiring career information. It has many built-in advantages and should be used regularly to communicate with the student body.

The news columns of the newspaper can be used to inform the students of career conferences, scheduled field trips, visits to the school by industrial or educational representatives, and other newsworthy events that relate to career information. Feature pages are logical spots for stories such as reports from recent graduates or reviews of new career books available. Many aspects of career information lend themselves to a regular column presentation; for example, nearby colleges can be described in a continuing series, as can jobs available locally or nearby nonacademic training programs.

Special issues can be used to inform students of a major activity such as a Career Day. Details of the event and supplementary information about the topics to be included in the program can be published so students may participate more intelligently in the event.

Local daily newspapers provide additional access to student readers. Already rich with information about what is happening in the community, many also carry special business or financial pages that feature stories about employment opportunities or new and expanding businesses or industries. The classified advertisements, a convenient barometer of job openings in the community, can be used to build realistic concepts of the local world of work.

Besides being an excellent source of local information, the newspaper usually provides some coverage of school activities. This offers a means of keeping parents and other school patrons aware of the school program of career education and information. Special events in the school always warrant coverage in the local press. Keeping the community informed in this way can lead to closer cooperation between school, students, and parents.

Many schools regularly prepare a student handbook. Intended basically as an orientation device for new students, it has considerable potential as an instrument for transmitting educational information and materials about services available to students. Most handbooks include a section that presents the various curricula offered in the school. To be of maximum utility for students and parents, this section should include the educational and vocational goals to which each curriculum leads. Examples of employment opportunities, further schooling available, and future advanced career fields should be discussed here. A brief survey of occupational fields related to each subject should be discussed here as well as a brief survey of occupational fields related to each subject.

The handbook is probably more practical if arrangements are made for its use in a series of orientation sessions for new students, either within the framework of regularly scheduled classes or in special groups created specifically to help students adjust to their new environments. Group discussion of the contents should emphasize the importance of the information in the book.

School Resources

Even the most circumscribed and isolated school often has resources of which most staff members are unaware. This is especially true of career information resources, often because no one has attempted to determine and evaluate the information existing beyond the career resource center.

Useful resources include the educational and occupational experiences of the school staff. A simple inventory of the institutions attended by staff members probably will reveal a fairly adequate representation of many nearby colleges and universities—often including the schools in which most of the college-bound students ultimately will enroll. Obviously, a staff member who has attended "school

X" can help students who are interested in the institution. Impressions of types of students, institutional goals and standards, student life, living accommodations, standards of dress, major activities, and similar information that usually cannot be assessed accurately from the printed page are particularly helpful.

Similarly, the typical school staff will have experienced a wide variety of part-time or full-time work during their high school and college years and later. In addition to their direct experiences, one is likely to find additional occupations with which they have had indirect contact through family, close friends, or other personal contact.

Another often overlooked built-in resource is the student body itself. Many young people have had opportunities to observe or experience a specific occupation, or they have become knowledgeable in some other way.

Community Resources

Outside the school, but within the local community, are many resources that can build insight into and understanding of career fields. Almost everyone is a potential resource who can be used to help students. Many local agencies recognize a responsibility in this area and are willing to assist the school in activities related to career choice.

Schools that maintain a file of community resources will have on hand an extensive listing of agencies and individuals that can be used in a variety of ways. Schools that do not have such a file may want to consider some of the following nearby resources.

In most cases, local businesses and industries already have close ties with the school. They have a continuing interest in the students of the local school, which is often their main source of employees, particularly for positions that do not require post-high-school training. Because of this natural relationship, they are usually interested in cooperating in any way possible to improve the quality of those students. This provides the school with an entree to representatives of local businesses and industries, who may be able to inform students about their fields of activity. Local professional groups may also be eager to render the same kind of service to interested students.

Local service clubs, whose members are drawn from local businesses, industries, and professions, are also frequently eager to provide assistance to the school or to specific students in problems related to career information. They can be helpful in organizing career day conferences or community occupational surveys. Members often are encouraged to make themselves available to students to discuss career opportunities in their fields.

Local labor union representatives or officials can provide information on training requirements, apprenticeship programs, employment opportunities, membership requirements, and benefits. Government offices located in the community, at the local, state, or national level, often can provide information that will assist students. Government service opportunities and requirements are areas that can be covered by such representatives. Agencies such as county extension offices and employment services already are involved, by the nature of their work, in career information activities.

Every community includes some social agencies that are involved in career information activities. Particularly likely to be involved are agencies whose services are directed primarily at youth, such as Boy Scouts, Girl Scouts, YMCA, YWCA, and 4-H clubs. Many of these serve the same young people as the school. Special career information projects that they may develop can be of genuine assistance to the school. They may also have access to information in specialized fields that can help the school in its career information program.

Many churches organize special activity programs for school-age youth. Often these programs focus on the concerns and problems of the age group involved; for teenagers, this inevitably includes career-related problems. Many churches support or maintain church-related colleges or other educational institutions that may be of particular significance to members of the church's youth group. A number of churches operate summer camping programs for school-age youth, thus providing an additional means of reaching young people.

The importance of the local library to the career information program already has been mentioned. Cooperation with the library often will lead to a more comprehensive collection of career information materials as well as to the development of special services that will be of assistance to school-age youth.

Many resources cut across more than one of the categories we have considered. In many ways, these may be the most valuable of all. Counselors and teachers may find it advantageous to establish networks involving contact with as many school and community resources as possible so that each of those contacts can provide information on new resources.

Internships and Youth Apprenticeships

As was noted in Chapter 7 there are many approaches to providing occupational information that involve hands-on experiences including internships and part-time work. Hoyt (1994) noted that these approaches are now being referred to as work-based learning by some advocates of this approach. He also notes that there are calls for what are termed youth apprenticeships which are experiences for students that would move from career exploration activities for middle school students, to increasing amounts of time spent on the job for high school students, and either full-time employment or further education for high school graduates. It is undoubtedly the case that various work-based approaches such as internships will continue to be important components of high school career development programs. It may also be that some students will find their way into youth apprenticeship programs of the type described by Hoyt. It seems unlikely, given the educational demands placed on students in the modern high school, that large numbers of student will be spending one-quarter to one-half their time in youth apprenticeships, however.

Other Interventions

Career Counseling

The career counseling process is discussed in detail in Chapter 14. However, it is worth noting that career counseling with high school students typically involves *initial* choice as opposed to adjustment within the current occupation or job loss. Many students who come to counselors for career counseling have little or no work experience, have developed few if any salable skills, may have a very limited understanding of their interests, values, and aptitudes, and probably have a very limited understanding of the skills needed to acquire and successfully perform a job. As a consequence of their limited exposure to the real world and often to other types of career information, experiences that can be provided through various types of information, including job shadowing, interviews with established workers, print, and audiovisual materials, are very important.

Career planning, as opposed to career counseling, may also be (and probably will be) a longer-term process. Many high schools require that counselors discuss current career interests as they relate to current educational objectives each time counselors meet with students to engage in course selection or longer-term educational planning. Career counselors need to be prepared to work with a wide variety of situations including various mental and physical disabilities, being mentally or artistically gifted, lack of motivation or educational achievement, and so forth.

As mentioned earlier, the label *talented* need not be restricted to students with high levels of academic ability. Dayton and Feldhusen (1989) identify two types of talented students enrolled in vocational educational programs; academically talented and vocationally talented. "Vocationally talented students are students who demonstrate exceptional capability within one of more vocational areas" (p. 357). Vocational education directors surveyed identified a number of special needs of both the academically and vocationally talented students, including the need for self-evaluation, in-depth career development activities, seminars, use of community resources, and the ability to interact with others who have similar intellectual capacities and interests.

In Moles's (1991) study of high school counseling programs, he found that helping students with academic achievement and planning for postsecondary schooling were the areas most emphasized by high school counselors according to program directors. It is suggested here that these two activities be integrated with career planning. As students are seen for course planning activities, counselors can explore interests and perceptions of aptitudes, review achievement test information, and discuss the implications of this information and the courses that are being selected for career choice. Students and counselors may wish to complete an Individual Career Plan using a form such as the one shown in Figure 10.1 (NOICC, 1989b, pp. 81–87).

FIGURE 10.1   Individual Career Plan Form: High School Level

This activity suggests a technique to help staff monitor and strengthen student achievement of the career guidance and counseling competencies and to assist in developing an educational and career plan.

Instructions

1. It is recommended that an Individual Career Plan be maintained for each student throughout the high school experience.
2. The counselor or counselors to whom a student is assigned will be responsible for meeting with that student to develop, review, revise and implement the plan.
3. As product evaluation is completed, an individual profile of student attainment of the standards will be added to the plan.

Name _____
　　　　　　Last　　　　　　　　　　　　First　　　　　　　　　　　　Middle

School _____

1. My interests are:

9th Grade	10th Grade	11th Grade	12th Grade
_____	_____	_____	_____
_____	_____	_____	_____
_____	_____	_____	_____

2. My abilities and skills are:

9th Grade	10th Grade	11th Grade	12th Grade
_____	_____	_____	_____
_____	_____	_____	_____
_____	_____	_____	_____

3. My hobbies and recreational/leisure activities are:

9th Grade	10th Grade	11th Grade	12th Grade
_____	_____	_____	_____
_____	_____	_____	_____
_____	_____	_____	_____

4. The school subjects in which I do best are:

9th Grade	10th Grade	11th Grade	12th Grade
_____	_____	_____	_____
_____	_____	_____	_____
_____	_____	_____	_____

5. I have explored careers in the following occupation clusters:

9th Grade	10th Grade	11th Grade	12th Grade
_____	_____	_____	_____
_____	_____	_____	_____
_____	_____	_____	_____

(continued)

FIGURE 10.1   *Continued*

6. I have worked part time or had some experience with the following jobs or work tasks:

9th Grade	10th Grade	11th Grade	12th Grade
_____	_____	_____	_____
_____	_____	_____	_____
_____	_____	_____	_____

7. My tentative career goal(s) is (are):

9th Grade	10th Grade	11th Grade	12th Grade
_____	_____	_____	_____
_____	_____	_____	_____
_____	_____	_____	_____

8. I have chosen the following curriculum to study in high school. Courses are outlined on my high school studies plan, which is part of my cumulative record.
   (20) Credit Diploma _____
   (22) Credit Diploma _____
   Other _____

9. I plan to pursue further training beyond high school in the following programs, schools, or colleges:

   _____
   _____
   _____
   _____

OR

   I plan to obtain work in one of the following jobs (businesses, industries):

   _____
   _____
   _____
   _____

10. I have attained the indicators specified in the local student career development standards. If not, I have met with my counselor to determine activities I can do to strengthen each indicator that I have not attained. Also attach individual profile summarizing student attainment of indicators each year.

Competency	Grade			
	9th	10th	11th	12th
Understanding the influence of a positive self-concept.	___	___	___	___
Skills to interact positively with others.	___	___	___	___
Understanding the relationship between educational achievement and career planning.	___	___	___	___
Understanding the need for positive attitudes toward work and learning.	___	___	___	___
Skills to locate, evaluate, and interpret career information.	___	___	___	___
Skills to prepare to seek, obtain, maintain, and change jobs.	___	___	___	___
Understanding how societal needs and functions influence the nature and structure of work.	___	___	___	___
Skills to make decisions.	___	___	___	___

FIGURE 10.1 *Continued*

	Grade			
	9th	10th	11th	12th
Understanding the interrelationship of life roles.	___	___	___	___
Understanding the continuous changes in male/female roles.	___	___	___	___
Skills in career planning.	___	___	___	___

Signatures:
Student_____
Parent_____
Counselor _____

Source: *National career development guidelines: Local handbook for high schools.* (1989). Washington, DC: NOICC, pp. 81–87.

Involving Parents

A number of studies were cited at the outset of this chapter that strongly suggest that parents should be an integral part of the career development process. Another example of this type of information came out of a study by Palmer and Cochran (1988), who found that the Partners Program—which consists of the *Parent Career Guidance Manual* (Cochran, 1985), three workbooks that help parents facilitate self-awareness and the development of occupational information, and a planning manual—improved career development scores as measured by the *Career Development Inventory.*

The outcome of the *Going Places* program described by Amatea and Cross (1980) was not as carefully evaluated as that of the Partners Program, but it had similar components. These components were compiling self-evaluation data (awareness), systematically exploring careers, developing the skills to acquire occupational information, matching self and occupational information, exploring educational alternatives, and developing decision-making skills. However, unlike the self-directed Partners Program, students and parents were involved in six 2-hour counselor-led sessions to consider each of the careers mentioned. Evaluation data suggested that students and parents approved of the group format and appeared to benefit from the program.

Programs for Special Students

Gifted

It is probably a truism that counselors consistently underestimate the needs of students who are gifted, or as Pask–McCartney and Salomone (1988) termed them, multipotentialed students, because they have so many avenues to pursue. It is also the case that having so many career avenues open is a curse of sorts. Post–Kammer and Perrone (1983) report that over 30 percent of the gifted students in their study felt unprepared to make career decisions when they left high school. It is probably the case that the types of programs needed by these students do not vary dramatically from those required by their less talented counterparts, although a report by Borman, Nash, and Colson (1978) suggests that the gifted students in their program did not like the testing component. It is certainly possible that these students have been tested so extensively that they are alienated from the formal assessment process.

In a study that has implications for career development programming for gifted boys and girls, Gassin, Kelly, and Feldhusen (1993) found that in middle school there was no difference between the certainty of career choice between gifted girls and boys. However, as they matured, girls became progressively less certain about their career choices, perhaps because they were beginning to consider their roles as spouse and mother in their plans. Interestingly, girls were more involved in career planning than boys during the high school years. This study suggests that efforts directed toward girls may need to focus on identifying the factors that lead to uncertainty and help them deal with them, while efforts may need to be mounted to stimulate career planning among high school boys.

Physically Challenged

As Lombana (1979, 1980) aptly noted, the main barrier to entrance to various careers for students with visual and auditory limitations is not their disability; it is the mistaken beliefs of employers, teachers, counselors, family members, and members of the general public regarding the potential of these clients. Her statement can be extended to all but students with the most severe disabilities. These students need the typical career development program, including activities to foster self-awareness and information about work. However, the career development program must be extended to include building self-confidence and the remediation of the negative attitudes of others (Lombana, 1980).

Students with physical limitatons, like other students, need to have an opportunity to observe models similar to themselves. These observations can come through discussions for visually impaired students (Lombana, 1979, 1980) or through firsthand observations for students with physical limitations who are not visually impaired. Self-esteem development can be facilitated by making sure that the environment in which the students go to school has been adapted to meet their needs and that learning opportunities are developed and taught so these students can experience success. Counselors may need to become more actively involved in the career placement process so they can work to offset the negative attitudes of employers.

Emotionally and Mentally Limited

Levinson (1984) suggested that career development programs for emotionally disturbed students will necessarily have to be more extensive and intensive than those for typical students. He suggests that a comprehensive program would involve a simulated employer–employee program in the school in which the student would have the opportunity to try out several jobs, be evaluated, and receive pay in the future of a better job for adequate performance, academic training, vocational skills development, and the development of work adjustment skills. Work adjustment skills include occupational social skills and the development of work habits (Levinson, 1984) such as punctuality, following through, and meeting performance standards.

School counselors are routinely faced with assisting students with mental limitations in career planning. Their potential, like that of students with physical limitations, is often misunderstood by teachers, parents, and employers. They need assistance in maximizing their educational skills, developing an awareness of their potential as workers, and developing occupational social skills, employability skills, and some basic life skills such as budgeting, planning, and decision making. With the possible exception of occupational social skills, students who can be mainstreamed into regular classroom environments need programs similar to those required by other students. However, counselors may need to be more involved in the job placement process and assist in combating negative attitudes against these students, who are potentially very valuable workers. It may also be the case that the intensity and duration of some aspects of the program, such as the development of employability skills, may need to be increased.

Roessler, Johnson, and Schrimmer (1988) summarized the characteristics of effective programs for all students with limitations, which they characterize as enhancing vocational potential by developing good basic educational skills, developing career awareness, and developing marketable skills by carefully coordinating the Individualized Educational Plan required by PL 94–142 (and some state statutes) and the Individualized Written Rehabilitation Program, which focuses on job skills, employability skills, and the ability to interact with nondisabled peers. Roessler (1988) recommends that schools adopt Brolin and Kokaska's (1979) Life-Centered Career Education program by focusing on daily living skills, personal/social skills, and career development. Among the daily living skills addressed in this curriculum are raising children, managing a household, citizenship, and using recreational facilities and leisure time. Developing self-confidence, interpersonal skills, and making good decisions are among the areas covered in personal social skills. Finally, finding a job, applying and interviewing for a job, maintaining occupational adjustment, meeting competitive standards, and knowing how to make a job adjustment or career change are considered in the career development component of the curriculum.

Learning Disabled

Biller and Horn (1991) have suggested that career development specialists may need to tailor their efforts if they are to be helpful to students with learning disabilities (LD). Biller and Horn admonish counselors to consider the possibility that LD students may not be as ready as their peers to engage in career planning and that, because of lower reading levels, they may have more difficulty absorbing information from printed material, reading instructions on computer screens, and completing assessment devices. Also, Humes (1992) found that LD students have somewhat different career interests than other students and suggests that counselors need to be prepared to assist them explore careers related to those interests.

Roessler (1988) identifies several barriers to the implementation of a comprehensive program for career development for students with disabilities: "assessment, planning, curriculum materials, generalization and maintenance (from the school to the community), and system commitment" (p. 24). The processes outlined in the *National Career Development Guidelines* (Kobylarz, 1996; NOICC, 1989b) could be used as a guide to overcoming the planning and school system commitment barrier if applied appropriately. Measures for assessing the occupational potential of students with disabilities are improving steadily, and Roessler and his colleagues (Roessler et al., 1988) validate materials that can be used in the assessment of students with disabilities. Roessler also concludes that the Life-Centered Career Education curriculum materials may solve the previous deficit in this area.

Part-Time Job Placement

Formal job placement activities are discussed in detail in Chapter 16. However, it is worth mentioning that many high schools operate rather informal job placement services where a secretary or volunteer accepts job orders from businesses and citizens from the community, posts these on bulletin boards, and circulates them to counselors and teachers. For example, the Youth Employment Service and Chapel Hill High School operate on this informal basis. The school asks the potential employer to identify the nature of the job, the skills required to perform the job, the salary, the dates/hours when the job is to be performed, and the name, address, and telephone number of the potential employer. This information is recorded on job order forms and circulated. The job placement service, whether formal or informal, can be a useful means of promoting career development by providing work experience.

Assessment

Standardized tests are given to school-age youngsters often beginning in kindergarten as a part of the screening process for first grade. Achievement testing typically begins in the third grade and continues through high school. Some schools administer special aptitude tests, such as those designed to measure clerical speed and accuracy or spatial relations, in the late middle school years or the early high school years so the data will be available to these students as they engage in career and educational planning. Interest inventories may also be included as a part of this overall assessment process, again being administered as a stimulus for career and educational planning. Additionally, high school students may be given tests and inventories selected to meet their special needs. Finally, thousands of students take a variety of specialized tests, such as the Scholastic Aptitude Test (SAT), American College Test (ACT), and the Armed Services Vocational Aptitude Battery (ASVAB), that may provide information both to the student and a college admissions office (in the case of the SAT and ACT) or a military recruiter (in the case of the ASVAB).

Tests and inventories administered by schools serve two basic purposes: monitoring educational progress and promoting self-awareness. Tests given to groups of students often ignore the fact that few students possess the psychological readiness needed to use the data generated. It is common practice in some school districts to administer an interest inventory *and* a special aptitude battery in the eighth grade so students and parents can use the information provided as one basis for selecting a high school curriculum and begin to engage in some preliminary planning. However, high school counselors report that few students actually remember what their scores were or how they related to careers, primarily because they were unready to engage in meaningful career planning at the time the tests were administered.

Counselors can and should engage in awareness activities that may promote readiness in students to use information about themselves, such as offering units on the changing work force, decision making, or the importance of self-awareness. Chapter 13 presents a more in-depth look at the types of tests and inventories available and how these might be used.

Consultation

The *National Career Development Guidelines: Local Handbook for High Schools* (NOICC, 1989b) as well as the updated version (Kobylarz, 1996), suggest that consultation is a skill to be used to facilitate career development. Given the importance of parents and teachers in the career development process, it seems that consultation with teachers and parents is indeed an essential aspect of the program. Teachers may require assistance in finding and using occupational information or in discovering the implication of their subject matter for careers. Parents often need assistance in facilitating the career exploration of their children and helping them make well-considered educational and career choices. Munson and Manzi (1982) suggest that young children first be involved in watching and listening, then in assisting, then in participating, and then in performing jobs. It seems reasonable to suggest that this same approach might also be used with adolescents. Mangum (undated) also suggests that parents need to be made aware of their influence and be taught labor market information and decision-making skills so these can be passed on to their children.

Summary

The high school career development program's central aim is to continue the developmental processes begun in the preceding grades. However, because many students are nearing the end of their educational careers, the process takes on a new urgency as a result of the need to help students make the transition from school to work. For some students this means formulating concrete educational plans and developing the skills to implement them. For others it means setting educational goals and adopting preliminary career goals based on the educational plans that have been laid out. Careful and comprehensive planning is required if career development competencies are to be developed in the diverse students who attend our schools. Although it is difficult to identify a single group of students as the neediest, high school dropouts and minorities have traditionally fared the least well in the workplace and are perhaps the most deserving of attention. Certainly, any student who is without a supportive home environment should be targeted in a career development program.

References

Amatea, E. S., Clark, J. E., & Cross, E. G. (1984). Life-styles: Evaluating a life role planning program for high school students. *Vocational Guidance Quarterly, 32,* 249–259.

Amatea, E. S., Cross, E. G. (1980). Going places: A career guidance program for high school students and their parents. *Vocational Guidance Quarterly, 28,* 274–287.

Baker, S. B., & Popowicz, C. L. (1983). Meta-analysis as a strategy for evaluating effects of career education interventions. *Vocational Guidance Quarterly, 31,* 178–186.

Bensen, P. L., Mangen, D. J., & Williams, D. L. (1986). *Adults who influence youth: Perspectives from 5th and 12th grade students.* Minneapolis: Search Institute.

Biller, E. F., & Horn, E. E. (1991). A career guidance model for adolescents with learning disabilities. *The School Counselor, 38,* 279–286.

Borman, C., Nash, W., & Colson, S. (1978). Career guidance for gifted and talented students. *Vocational Guidance Quarterly, 27,* 72–76.

Brolin, D. L., & Kokaska, C. J. (1979). *Career education for handicapped children and youth.* Columbus, OH: Merrill.

Brown, D. (1980). A life-planning workshop for high school students. *Vocational Guidance Quarterly, 29,* 77–83.

Brown, D. (1998). *Dropping out or hanging in* (2nd ed.). Lincolnwood, IL: National Textbook Center.

Campbell, R. E., Connell, J. G., Boyle, K. K., & Bhaerman, R. D. (1983). *Enhancing career development: Recommendations for action.* Columbus, OH: NCRVE, Ohio State University.

Chapman, W., & Katz, M. R. (1983). Career information systems in secondary schools: A survey and assessment. *Vocational Guidance Quarterly, 31,* 165–177.

Cochran, L. (1985). *Parent career guidance manual.* British Columbia, Canada: Bachanan–Kells.

Crites, J. O. (1987). *Evaluation of career guidance programs: Models, methods, and microcomputers.* Columbus, OH: NCRVE, Ohio State University.

Dayton, J. D., & Feldhusen, J. F. (1989). Characteristics and needs of vocationally talented high school students. *Career Development Quarterly, 37,* 355–364.

Dillard, J. M., & Campbell, N. J. (1981). Influences of Puerto Rican, Black, and Anglo parents' career behavior on their adolescent childrens' career development. *Vocational Guidance Quarterly, 30,* 139–148.

Freeman, B. (1994). Importance of national career development guidelines to school counselors. *Career Development Quarterly, 42,* 224–228.

Gassin, E. A., Kelly, K. R., & Feldhusen, J. F. (1993). Sex differences in the career development of gifted youth. *The School Counselor, 41,* 90–95.

Herr, E. L. (1982). The effects of guidance and counseling: Three domains. In E. L. Herr & N. M. Pirson (Eds.), *Foundations of policy in guidance and counseling* (pp.22–64). Alexandria, VA: American Association of Counseling and Development (formerly APGA).

Hoyt, K. B. (1994). Youth apprenticeship "American style" and career development. *Career Development Quarterly, 42,* 216–223.

Hoyt, K. B., Pinson, N. M., Laramore, D., & Mangum, G. L. (1973). *Career education and the elementary school teacher.* Salt Lake City, UT: Olympus.

Humes, C. W. (1992). Career planning implications for learning disabled high school students using the MBTI and SDS. *The School Counselor, 39,* 362–368.

Johnson, W. F., Korn, T. A., & Dunn, D. J. (1975). Comparing three methods of presenting occupational information. *Vocational Guidance Quarterly, 24,* 62–67.

Kobylarz, L. (Ed.). (1996). *National career development guidelines: K–adult handbook.* Stillwater, OK: Career Development Training Institute.

Lee, C. C. (1984). Predicting the career choice attitudes of rural black, white, and native American high school students. *Vocational Guidance Quarterly, 32,* 177–184.

Levinson, E. M. (1984). A vocationally oriented secondary school program for the emotionally disturbed. *Vocational Guidance Quarterly, 33,* 76–81.

Lombana, J. H. (1979). Facilitating career guidance of deaf students: Challenges and opportunities for counselors. *Vocational Guidance Quarterly, 27,* 350–359.

Lombana, J. H. (1980). Career planning with visually handicapped students. *Vocational Guidance Quarterly, 28,* 219–224.

Mangum, G. L. (undated). *Youth transition from adolescent to the world of work.* Washington, DC: W. T. Grant Foundation Commission on Work, Family, and Citizenship.

McNair, D., & Brown, D. (1983). Predicting the occupational aspirations, occupational expectations, and career maturity of black and white male and female 10th grade students. *Vocational Guidance Quarterly, 32,* 29–36.

Mitchell, A. M. (1977). *Career development needs of seventeen year olds: How to improve career development programs.* Washington, DC: National Advisory Committee for Career Education.

Moles, O. C. (1991). Guidance programs in American high schools: A descriptive portrayal. *School Counseling, 38,* 163–175.

Munson, H. L., & Manzi, P. A. (1982). Toward a model of work task learning in the home. *Vocational Guidance Quarterly, 31,* 5–13.

Noeth, R. J., Engen, H. B., & Prediger, D. (1984). Making career decisions: A self-reporting of factors that help high school students. *Vocational Guidance Quarterly, 32,* 240–248.

NCES. (1997). *Digest of education statistics.* Washington, DC: U.S. Department of Education.

NOICC. (1988). *The national career counseling and guidance guidelines: High schools.* Washington, DC: Author.

NOICC. (1989a). *The national career development guidelines: Local handbook for elementary schools.* Washington, DC: Author.

NOICC. (1989b). *The national career development guidelines: Local handbook for high schools.* Washington, DC: Author.

NOICC. (1989c). *The national career development guidelines: Local handbook for middle/junior high schools.* Washington, DC: Author.

Office of Special Education and Rehabilitative Services. (1988). *OSEP state reported data, 1986–1987 school year.* Washington, DC: U.S. Office of Education.

Palmer, S., & Cochran, L. (1988). Parents as agents of career development. *Journal of Counseling Psychology, 35,* 71–76.

Pask-McCartney, C., & Salomone, P. R. (1988). Difficult cases in career counseling III: The multipotentialed client. *Career Development Quarterly, 36,* 231–240.

Post-Kammer, P. (1987). Intrinsic and extrinsic work values and career maturity of 9th and 11th grade boys. *Journal of Counseling and Development, 65,* 420–423.

Post-Kammer, P., & Perrone, P. (1983). Career perceptions of talented individuals: A follow-up study. *Vocational Guidance Quarterly, 31,* 203–211.

Roessler, R. T., Johnson, J., & Schrimmer, L. (1988). Implementing career education: Barriers and potential solutions. *Career Development Quarterly, 37,* 22–30.

Spokane, A. R., & Oliver, L. W. (1983). The outcomes of vocational interventions. In W. B. Walsh & S. H. Osipow (Eds.), *Handbook of vocational psychology.* Hillsdale, NJ: Lawrence Erlbaum and Associates.

U.S. Bureau of Labor Statistics. (1986). *Employment and earnings.* Washington, DC: U.S. Department of Labor.

U.S. Census Bureau. (1997). *Current population survey.* Washington, DC: Author.

W. T. Grant Foundation. (1988). *The forgotten half.* Washington, DC: Author.

Wetzel, J. R. (1987). *American youth: A statistical snapshot.* Washington, DC: W. T. Grant Foundation Commission on Work, Family, and Citizenship.

11

Career Development in Four-Year Colleges, Community Colleges, and Vocational–Technical Schools

Over half of the students who graduate from high school attend some form of postsecondary educational institution, including 4-year colleges, community colleges, or vocational–technical schools. Whereas one of the primary reasons for pursuing a college education is to train for a career, only approximately 54 percent of college graduates report being in their present career as a result of following a conscious plan. Of those adults who either did not finish college or attended a 2-year institution, about 35 percent followed a conscious plan into their current careers. Approximately one-quarter of those who attended some form of postsecondary education never used occupational information (Hoyt & Lester, 1995). This study plus an earlier study by Hatcher and Crook (1988) suggest that certain aspects of the career development of students are not being addressed. They surveyed graduates of a small liberal arts institution to determine what surprises they had encountered on their jobs. They found that students were better workers than they expected they would be, they perceived themselves to be criticized for poor work more than expected, and the organization's demand for good work was greater than they had anticipated. They also found that when expectations regarding work did not coincide with reality, particularly if that was a negative reality, students expressed intentions to leave their current jobs.

While not every student pursuing postsecondary education does so for the sole purpose of preparing for a career, many expect this to be a product of their educational experience. It is important that the career development needs of these students be met. Healy and Reilly (1989) tried to determine if career development needs of vocational–technical students enrolled in ten California community colleges varied by age level. Older students indicated that they had less need to set career goals, become certain of career plans, explore career-related goals, select courses relevant to career goals, develop employability skills, and/or obtain a job than did younger students. However, about 25 to 50 percent of all age groups studied rated these needs of major concern. They also rated knowing more about their interests and abilities as an important need. The authors reported that the finding that older students have less need for career development activities was not unexpected. However, one suspects that the reason that more younger respondents did not rate their needs for career development activities higher was because of lack of awareness of the problems encountered by college graduates.

Sixty-four percent of college graduates would try to get more career information if they were starting over. This may be because only 54 percent of adults who attended or graduated from college believe that their skills are being fully utilized on their current job. Moreover, approximately 6 percent of this group expected to be forced out of their jobs within 3 years after the 1993 NCDA survey (Hoyt & Lester, 1995). Finally, while it is expected that the number of jobs requiring a college education will increase in the next decade, it is also forecast that unemployment and underemployment will increase among college graduates because of a mismatch between their skills and the demands of the workplace (Johnston & Packer, 1987).

The Students

The stereotype of the community college and college student is that they are 18 to 22 years old and pursuing their first postsecondary educational experience. However, it is now projected that as many as two-thirds of the students entering postsecondary education will be nontraditional students (deBlois, 1992; Healy & Reilly, 1989). Nontraditional students fall into several categories including those older than 22, those who are reentering school because of previous academic failure, those who have been displaced from their marriages or jobs, or students who have decided to change careers.

However, the influx of older than average students into postsecondary institutions is not the only change that has occurred in the demographic make up of student bodies. The diversity of college students increasingly reflects the diversity of our society. Minorities representing almost all ethnic groups make up sizeable portions of the enrollments of most community and 4-year colleges. The American Disabilities Act has made it mandatory that all educational institutions provide access to people regardless of the nature of their disability. This has made it possible for students with physical limitations such as visual impairment and students

with learning disabilities such as dyslexia to avail themselves of a college education. Two other groups present on campuses of postsecondary institutions, gays
and lesbians, also present challenges to career development specialists who hope
to meet the needs of their students.

Many authors have suggested that many of the students enrolled in postsecondary institutions need specialized career development services. For example, Leong (1993) suggested that both the content and the process of career
counseling must be altered to accommodate the interpersonal styles, cultural values, attitudes, and beliefs of Asian students. Padula (1994) and Luzzo (1995) have
both addressed the special needs of college women, with Padula focusing more on
reentry women and Luzzo on gender differences in career maturity. Luzzo's research identified a recurring theme in the literature dealing with women's career
choice making: conflicts between career and other life roles, as did Padula's literature review. Belz (1993) indicates that assuming a homosexual identity may have
to be addressed concurrently with career development concerns when working
with gay and lesbian students. Student athletes are another group that may require some special attention because of their failure to set academic and career
goals (Blan, 1985; Lanning, 1982; Petrie & Russell, 1995). Wilkes, Davis, and Dever
(1989) outlined a joint planning effort between the career planning and placement
office that attempted to address these problems. This litany of special needs could
be extended to each group of students present on today's campuses, and these
needs will be addressed in more detail in Chapter 12.

It would be easy to conclude that career development programs must be tailored to each student and there is more than a grain of truth in this conclusion.
However, Griff (1987) indicates that there are common needs among groups of
students, and the career development services available to students should include some or all of the following:

1. Career and self-awareness activities.
2. Exploration of interests, values, goals, and decisions.
3. Realities of the job market and future trends.
4. Practical, accurate information about careers.
5. Workshops that deal with special needs such as risk taking, resume development, interviewing, and so forth.
6. An academic advising system that makes it possible for students to get the assistance they need in academic planning.

The Institutions

Three general types of institutions are of concern here. The first of these, vocational–
technical colleges, are extensions of high school vocational education programs and
provide skills training in a variety of careers ranging from semiskilled to professional
(such as heating and air conditioning equipment installation and maintenance,

licensed practical nurses, registered nurses, and drafters). Because of the vocational nature of these programs, students often select an area of study at the time of entry and pursue it to completion. In many instances the necessity to make an early decision has led to mistakes.

Community colleges often have a vocational–technical component along with a college transfer program. In many states the college transfer program is coordinated with the programs in colleges and universities so that students transferring to 4-year institutions do so as "junior transfers." Students select community colleges because of financial reasons (they can live at home and thus save money), because of the need for remedial study to make up for academic deficits, because they want to explore whether post–high school study is actually something they want to pursue, and for a variety of other reasons. Students who have had academic difficulty may also regain their eligibility to reenroll in 4-year institutions by demonstrating their competencies in community college courses. A remarkable aspect of community colleges is their open-door admissions policy, which enables students to begin at their academic competency level and advance their education. This open-door policy does not extend to all programs offered in these institutions, however. Vocational–technical programs as well as programs such as nursing, accounting, and others have established standards that must be met prior to entry.

Four-year colleges and universities are nearly as diverse as vocational–technical schools and community colleges. Highly prestigious colleges such as Harvard, Stanford, Yale, Williams, and Brown turn away hundreds and in some instances thousands of highly qualified applicants while some other colleges are barely able to attract sufficient numbers of minimally qualified applicants to maintain their enrollments. Some colleges are predominantly female, while others are comprised largely of males. Predominantly African American colleges such as Howard University have led the way in providing quality education to African American students, while Gallaudet has focused on students with hearing impairments. Enrollments range from a few hundred to over 50,000, and the cost can vary from $6,000 a year to over $30,000 a year. Not surprisingly, the curriculums can vary widely. Some colleges emphasize liberal arts preparation, which focuses on the arts, sciences, and humanities, while others may concentrate on technical areas such as engineering or on preparing people for educational careers.

Resources, philosophy, mission, size and characteristics of the student body, curriculum offerings, location, and a variety of other factors influence the career development program. Career development specialists in liberal arts institutions must be prepared to help students choose careers that appear to have little relevance to their majors. Law schools give preferential treatment to English majors, all other things such as grades and Law School Aptitude Test (LSAT) scores being equal. Psychology majors may be able to use their skills in a variety of related areas, but they will need to know that personnel officers, human services workers, and researchers draw on psychological principles in their work.

Career Development Programs

Johnson and Figler (1984) suggested that there are many issues confronting career development specialists as they plan programs for postsecondary institutions. Among these are philosophical issues of whether to (1) emphasize counseling or placement, (2) send clients out on their own to collect information, (3) focus students on the "vocational" aspects of their training, (4) involve significant others such as parents in the career planning process, and (5) emphasize risk taking or security in the career planning process. They also suggest that in the future the demand for career development services will increase and that services will expand. Dealing with the issues identified by Johnson and Figler and planning to meet new demands will require programming decisions that must be considered carefully.

The National Career Development Guidelines for postsecondary institutions (Kobylarz, 1996; NOICC, 1989) lay out a process for developing a comprehensive program which is quite similar to the processes outlined in Chapters 9 and 10 for building or improving programs in elementary, middle, and high schools. In the document *The National Career Development Guidelines: Local Handbook for Post-Secondary Institutions*, two sets of competencies are laid out: those for young adults and those for adults. The 1996 version of the *National Development Guidelines* (Kobylarz, 1996) consolidated the adult and young adult competencies into a single set of competencies. A combination of the 1989 and 1996 competencies for adults is shown in Table 11.1. As can be seen in that table, the Guidelines emphasize that adults need to (1) identify a positive self-image, (2) be able to identify career information and use that information to make informed career decisions, (3) engage in lifelong learning, (4) prepare for transitions in their careers, (5) understand the interaction of career and other life roles, (6) understand the changing roles of men and women in our society, and (7) understand the interrelationships that exist between the needs of society and the world of work.

Developing the Program

As noted in Chapters 9 and 10, organizing and developing the career development program is essentially a five-step process: organizing for program development, establishing expected student outcomes for the institution, acting to improve the existing program by determining strengths and making additions or deletions as needed, implementing the new program, and evaluating the outcomes (Kobylarz, 1996; NOICC, 1989).

It is expected that the career development plan will contain a statement of the purpose of the program as well as the competencies that are to be developed as a result of the program. Like the elementary, middle/junior high school, and high school plans, the processes (e.g., counseling, placement) that will be employed in the program along with specific activities should be included in the plan, along with the staff who are expected to deliver the activities and a time line for delivery (Kobylarz, 1996; NOICC, 1989).

TABLE 11.1 Adult Competencies and Indicators

Competency	Sample Indicator: The Adult Will
1. Maintenance of a positive view of self in terms of potential and preferences and assessment of their transferability to the world of work.	1. Identify achievements related to work, learning, and leisure and state their influence on his/her perception of self.
2. Ability to assess self-defeating behaviors and reduce their impact on career decisions.	2. Understand physical changes that occur with age and adapt work performance to accommodate these.
3. Skills for entering, adjusting to, and maintaining performance in educational and training situations.	3. Document prior learning experiences and know how to use their information to obtain credit from educational institutions.
4. Skills for locating, evaluating, and interpreting information about career opportunities.	4. Assess how skills used in one occupation may be used in other occupations.
5. Skills required for seeking, obtaining, keeping, and advancing in a job.	5. Develop a resume appropriate for an identified career objective.
6. Skills in making decisions about educational and career goals.	6. Develop skills to assess career opportunities in terms of advancement, management styles, work environment, benefits, and other conditions of employment.
7. Understanding of the impact of careers on individual and family life.	7. Describe how family and leisure roles affect and may be affected by career roles and decisions.
8. Skills in making career transitions.	8. Accept that career transitions (e.g., reassessment of current position, job changes, or occupational changes) are a normal aspect of career development.
9. Skills in retirement planning.	9. Recognize the importance of retirement planning and commit to early involvement in the retirement planning process.
10. Understand how the needs and functions of society influence the nature and structure of work.	10. Recognized economic trends that influence workers.
11. Understanding the continuing changes in male and female roles.	11. Identify changes in the job and family roles held by men and women.

Source: Kobylarz, L. (Ed.). (1996). *National career development guidelines: K–adult handbook.* Stillwater, OK: Career Development Training Institute; and NOICC. (1989). *The national career development guidelines: Local handbook for postsecondary institutions.* Washington DC: Author.

Conducting a needs assessment is the first step in developing local standards. Evans (1985) compared two general approaches to needs assessment in postsecondary educational institutions: interviews and questionnaires. Within these general categories, Evans also tried to discern whether questionnaires and interviews based on developmental theory were superior to needs assessment procedures that had been empirically derived. She concluded that questionnaires provided a more efficient means of collecting and tabulating data about needs while interviews produced a richer database that provided more insight into the individual's concern. However, data for all the approaches suggested the same areas of need, including academic performance, career and lifestyle concerns, and issues relating to personal identity.

Once needs are identified, indicators should be selected and then standards of performance established. This process is as follows:

Needs Assessment: Sixty percent of sophomores uncertain about the relationship between their educational and career plans

↓

Develop Competency 3

Ability to relate educational and occupational preparation to career opportunities

Indicators	*Processes Involved*	*Activities*	*Standard*
1. Assess education and training alternatives and selected field of study or training post	Information	Advising begins at matriculation	100% by end of sophomore year
2. Identify education or training requirements of specific occupations that are related to field of study	Classroom instruction	Required class on careers	100% will select appropriate occupation
3. Develop an action plan to achieve educational goal	Classroom instruction	Required class on careers; counseling	100% will develop action plan
4. Not chosen			
5. Develop long- and short-range plans to achieve identified career goals	Classroom instruction; counseling information	Required class; counseling, advising	100% will develop short- and long-range plan

Develop Competency 6

Skills in making decisions about educational and career goals

Indicators	*Processes Involved*	*Activities*	*Standard*
1. Establish personal criteria for making decision about educational and career goals	Classroom instruction	Required class on careers	100% will meet criteria
6. Make and implement effective career and educational decisions	Classroom instruction, information counseling	Career Resource Center (CRC) advising, career counseling, required class	100% will complete

The actual competencies to be developed in the career development program, the processes to be used, and the specific activities will be dependent on the overall philosophy and the nature of the school itself. Because students in vocational–technical schools begin specific vocational preparation immediately, it is important that their ability to relate educational and occupational preparation to career opportunities (Competency 3) and use skills in making decisions about educational career goals (Competency 6) be developed early, perhaps prior to beginning the training program. Orientation, initial advising, and perhaps screening devices might be relied on to develop these competencies. Some suggested activities that may be used in conjunction with each of the processes identified in the postsecondary career development guidelines (Kobylarz, 1996; NOICC, 1989) are listed in Table 11.2.

Specific Activities

Advising

Advising is the backbone of the educational planning process in postsecondary institutions, and it appears that the quality of this process varies greatly. If competencies dealing with the integration of educational and career planning are to be developed, it seems logical that one goal must be the development of an outstanding advising system. Dailey (1986) suggests that advisors use decision trees to aid in the academic/career planning process at the time the student must select a major. A decision tree is little more than a graphic representation of life decision points, with the branches of the tree representing options. The process of decision making using a decision tree approach is illustrated in Figure 11.1. Dailey believes that the decision tree approach may be particularly applicable for use with business majors because they have probably been oriented to this approach in their courses. However, use of the tree concept should not be limited to business.

Advisors need to be oriented to the implications of educational programs for careers. This can be done through consultation (if advisors are open to this process). However, advisors need data from follow-up studies that examine the career success of graduates. They also need information from recruiters who come on campus. Recruiters should be invited to provide seminars for advisors that focus on the criteria used by their institutions to make difficult admissions decisions. Finally, advisors should receive information regularly about the jobs entered by graduates of various programs.

Courses

As noted in Table 11.2, there are numerous approaches to delivering career exploration courses to students, including modules, credit courses, and noncredit courses. Quinn and Lewis (1989) found that certainty of career choices was increased by inserting career-related material into a traditional academic course.

TABLE 11.2 Processes/Approaches to Career Development

Outreach

1. Career seminars in housing units
2. Informal rap sessions in housing units to establish contacts
3. Activities designed for special groups delivered at their meetings (e.g., international students)
4. Mentoring programs using alumni or upper-classmen
5. Parent involvement such as career development seminars

Classroom Instruction

1. Required classes for credit
2. Optional classes for credit
3. Noncredit, short-term classes
4. Employability skills training classes
5. Units in regular classes dealing with careers

Counseling

1. Individual career counseling
2. Group career counseling
3. Employability skills groups
4. Special programs for alumni such as group counseling activities
5. Support groups for job hunters

Assessment

1. Screening examinations given at entry to focus on career/decision making
2. Ongoing assessment offered to students in counseling/career planning and placement center
3. As part of career counseling
4. Computer-assisted services
5. Self-directed assessment (e.g., Self-Directed Search)
6. Needs assessments

Information

1. Orientation sessions/information
2. Catalogs
3. Advising information/careers
4. Career information center
5. Articles in student newspapers
6. Computer-assisted systems
7. Handouts that relate educational programs to career opportunities
8. Alumni newsletters

Placement

1. Regular job placement activities for students
2. Job fairs to link employers and workers

Work Experience

1. Internship programs
2. Placement for part-time work
3. Cooperative educational/work programs
4. Work-study programs

(continued)

TABLE 11.2 *Continued*

Consultation

1. With faculty advisors to make them aware of education–career connection; needs of certain students
2. With residence hall assistants and directors to provide assistance
3. With instructors who wish to infuse more career information
4. With club/social activities advisors to suggest career-related activities

Referral

1. To workers in the community for career information
2. To mental health professionals to get assistance with personal problems blocking career-related decisions

---

Savickas (1990, p. 278) designed and field-tested a career exploration course that tried to develop the following attitudes and concepts: (1) Become involved now, (2) explore your future, (3) choose based on how things look to you, (4) control your future, (5) work: A problem or opportunity, (6) view work positively, (7) conceptualize career choice, (8) clear up career choice misconceptions, (9) base your choice on yourself, and (10) use four aspects of self as choice bases. He found support for the idea that the course generally had a positive impact on ability to engage in career decision making and on long-term time perspective, with students enrolled in the course being somewhat more oriented to a future

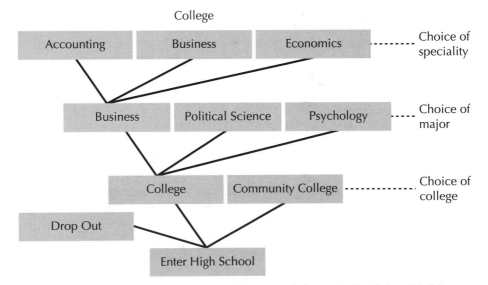

FIGURE 11.1 Decision Tree of College Sophomore's Decision-Making Process

time perspective. Savickas's findings generally support the earlier research of Lent, Larkin, and Hasequa (1980), who found that a 10-week career planning course focusing primarily on technical and scientific careers was helpful in facilitating career planning.

The availability of career planning classes is widespread. Typically, these courses focus on career exploration and development, career decision making, employability skills, and to a lesser extent on careers for special groups, field experiences, and self-assessment. Allyn (1989) described a departure from this traditional curricular approach. She tried to "focus on the learning styles associated with the left and right hemispheres" (of the brain) (p. 281) and to apply the 4MAT System, which attempts to capitalize on learning styles using an experiential approach. The objectives of her course were to have students learn more about themselves, discover their support system, and learn about careers that might be of interest. The first step in the course was to have students deal with the *why* of the course goal (e.g., "Why is this important?"). Then she focused on the *what* question, that is, "What is the content of the course?" After the *what* question is answered, students engaged in hands-on activities to determine how they would answer the question, "How will I fit into the world of work?" The *if* question was answered next, that is, "What if the information I have learned applies to me (or doesn't), what are the consequences?" The content of Allyn's (1989) course does not vary greatly from that covered in other courses described earlier, but the techniques employed, which include guided imageries, are worth serious consideration.

Finally, the results of a study by Johnson and Smouse (1993) found no significant increase in career decidedness, knowledge of occupations, and certainty of occupational choices among students who completed a career planning course versus a control group. They suggest that in order for these courses to be effective they must be developed to meet the specific needs of the students who are enrolled in them.

Brief Interventions

Goodson (1982) found that relatively short interventions, such as workshops and seminars, were available on 87 percent of the campuses surveyed. Pickering and Vacc (1984) reported, after a review of the literature on career-related interventions, that the most commonly researched areas were those with six sessions or less, including a variety of activities. They also reported that longer-term interventions (more than five sessions) were usually more effective than short-term interventions. However, in a recent study, Buescher, Johnston, Lucas, and Hughey (1989) reported that a brief intervention consisting of a 1.5-hour meeting with a career counselor, the completion of an occupational card sort, a discussion of career options, and a tour of the career center resulted in positive changes for undecided students.

Kahnweiler and Kahnweiler (1980) reported on a dual-career-family workshop that has particular relevance given the likelihood that married couples are likely to face this situation. The workshop was divided into didactic input, models of dual-career families, and discussion. In the didactic phase the benefits (e.g., extra income) and liabilities (e.g., gender-role conflicts) were presented. In the modeling section the workshop leaders, who were involved in a dual-career marriage, discussed the pros and cons of their relationship. Finally, students were engaged in a discussion focusing on their backgrounds and the problems they might have with dual-career marriages.

Unfortunately, many career seminars and other more didactic career interventions are not evaluated systematically. However, if the needs of the target audience are clearly identified and seminars and other experiences are carefully designed to meet these needs, these approaches can be highly effective for students who do not have decisional anxiety or other personal problems that preclude them from benefiting from the experience.

An example of a carefully designed and evaluated seminar that addressed specific student needs is presented by Robbins and Tucker (1986). Their concern, like that of many career counselors, was career goal instability, and they tried to discern whether small groups that were primarily self-directed were more effective than those involving leader-directed interaction. They found that students with high and moderate goal instability engaged in greater numbers of career information–seeking behaviors as a result of the interactional groups than those who participated in the self-directed groups. On the other hand, the type of group appeared to make little difference on the information-seeking behaviors of students with low goal instability. Students enrolled in the groups that were interactionally oriented were more satisfied with their groups than those where the leaders emphasized self-direction.

Self-Directed Activities

Many colleges provide opportunities for students to engage in self-directed activities including assessment, computer-assisted career exploration, and career exploration books. Pickering (1984) compared the results of a career planning seminar run by career counselors, a similar seminar run by peer tutors, and a self-directed group where students were oriented to using a career exploration workbook. The analysis of the outcome yielded no significant differences among the treatment groups. Unfortunately, Pickering did not include a no-treatment control group in the design. However, Pickering concluded that the self-study method was the most cost-effective method, an inference that must be interpreted very cautiously since Pickering and Vacc (1984) had earlier concluded that self-help approaches were the least effective approaches based upon their review of the research literature.

For those individuals who wish to establish a self-help section in their career information centers, Nachreiner's (1987) description of the material housed in the University of Wisconsin–Madison Center is instructive. Their materials are placed in four color-coordinated stations:

Station I: Who Am I—Includes materials about life transitions, values, interests and skills

Station II: Job Search—Includes information about employability skills, such as resume development

Station III: Education and Career Research—Includes study skills information as well as educational and career information

Station IV: Bibliographies—Includes lists of readings on various topics

Information

Chapters 7 and 8 were devoted to discussions of various informational approaches, including types of information and the establishment and operation of a career information center. That discussion is not duplicated here. However, the *Career Line* approach developed at Michigan State University is worth consideration (Forrest & Backes, 1988). *Career Line* is a weekly career information column that appears in the student newspaper at Michigan State. It is a 300- to 400-word column that appears weekly and addresses such topics as planning for summer jobs, various types of careers, and related topics. One by-product of the program has been the development of a *Career Line* booklet that includes some of the better columns.

Consultation

Spokane (1991) discusses career development consultation and prevention together, and while he does not link them directly, he suggests that both are linked to promoting career competence. Brown, Pryzwansky, and Schulte (1996) go one step beyond Spokane's position and link consultation to the prevention process, asserting that consultants can be instrumental in preventing problems from arising if they can effectively intervene in programs and activities that promote developmental processes. As suggested in Table 11.2, consultation from internal consultants can be offered to advisors, residence hall advisors, instructors who wish to make their courses more career relevant, and the advisors of students who may wish to promote career development. Campus activities from the ski club to the student newspaper can have relevance to career and lifestyle decisions and should be pursued by career development consultants.

Career development specialists have numerous opportunities to engage in consultation with faculty members, club sponsors, resident assistants, and others to assist them in planning programs that will facilitate career development. However, one variant on this is to use alumni to consult with students about their career options. Willamette College developed such a program by creating a file of alumni who would be willing to consult with students and then providing their names to interested students (Bjorkquist, 1988). The staff at Willamette College also uses this alumni file as a basis for securing speakers for on-campus seminars. Ohio State University has also developed a program of this type.

Career Counseling

Chapter 14 is devoted entirely to the career counseling process, and thus this discussion is brief. However, many colleges and universities now offer career counseling services to alumni and some, like the University of South Carolina, devote a great deal of attention to this area. It is also noteworthy that some colleges and universities have developed cooperative arrangements with other institutions to provide counseling and informational services when geographic location makes it impossible for alumni to return to their alma mater.

Career counseling is probably the most widely offered of the career-related services (Goodson, 1982). Typically, career counseling services are offered through specialized agencies called career planning and placement, the university counseling center, or both. Magoon (1989) reports that over one-fifth of the counseling centers offered no career counseling, while 40 percent of the counseling centers in large universities and 53 percent of the centers in small universities reported sharing the responsibility of offering career counseling with another agency on campus. Career counseling is offered exclusively at the remaining counseling centers (30 percent of the large and 24 percent of the small centers). If Stone and Archer (1990) are correct, there is decreasing interest among the counselors and counseling psychologists who have traditionally offered career counseling in university counseling centers. This may result in career counseling services being offered more frequently through career planning and placement centers.

Career counseling is offered in three modes: individual, group, and computerized services. Some career counselors would take exception to including computerized services in this listing, and perhaps they have a legitimate case since career counseling is an interpersonal process between two or more people aimed at solving a career-related problem. However the CACGS discussed in Chapter 8 do approximate traditional career counseling, and Hoyt and Lester (1995) report that 10.6 percent of adults in their nationwide survey who attended college reported that they had used one of these systems. However, 48 percent of the adults who had attended community colleges and 52 percent of the college grads reported that they had consulted a professional counselor about their career choices at some point in their lives. In all likelihood this consultation occurred on a one-to-one basis.

Some agencies that provide career counseling services have developed intake procedures in an effort to identify the best approach to dealing with students' problems. Intake interviews are conducted by counselors to determine students' needs and expectations. After this interview, students are referred variously to a psychometrician for testing, individual counseling, group counseling, or group guidance activities such as developing employability skills. The goal of the intake process is to deliver career development services effectively and efficiently.

Group career counseling has not received the same degree of investigation or discussion that individual career counseling has, although Oliver and Spokane (1988) concluded after a review of the literature that group interventions are as effective or more effective than other types. However, Butcher's (1982) suggestion that students be carefully screened prior to group counseling seems appropriate. She recommends that students need to be ready to engage in counseling, by which she means they are prepared to accept the responsibility of the process. She also suggests that some determination be made as to whether students have pervasive decisional problems (they are indecisive), because students who have decisional problems must have that concern addressed prior to engaging in the decision-making process.

One additional suggestion should be added to those advanced by Butcher: Students placed in groups should be at the same relative developmental level. For example, students who are just beginning to explore the relationship between educational and career goals should not be placed in the same groups with English majors who are determining potential career paths growing out of their major. However, a senior majoring in English who has decided that he made an error in choosing English as a major might very well be at the same place developmentally as a freshman or sophomore exploring all possibilities.

Butcher (1982) indicates that career counseling groups move through three distinct phases—exploration, transition, and action—and that understanding these stages along with the dynamics associated with them is a prerequisite for leading groups. It seems likely that not all counselors possess the skill to fully assess career maturity (readiness) or decisional problems (indecisiveness) or to lead groups, which requires a full understanding of group dynamics as well as career development issues. This suggests that some differential staffing may be required when deciding who should conduct career counseling.

Kivlighan (1990) reviewed the literature to determine whether the therapeutic factors believed to be necessary in group therapy had been studied in group career counseling studies. He concluded that the role of "self disclosure, catharsis, guidance, universality, altruism, vicarious learning, cohesion, interpersonal learning, self understanding, and instillation of hope" (p. 64) in the change process had gone largely unexamined. He also concluded that males and females come to career groups with different expectations, react differently to the group experience, and have different outcomes. Women seem to broaden their career horizons as a result of the group experience, while men tend to get confirmation for their plans. Finally, Kivlighan reported that two variables that have long been viewed as important factors in group therapy—group composition and leadership style—have been largely unexamined as factors in career group outcomes.

Career Resource Centers

Reardon, Zunker, and Dyal (1979) surveyed 4-year institutions of higher learning to investigate whether institutions had a separately budgeted career resource center. At that time, 51 percent responded affirmatively. This number has grown dramatically in the time since the survey, although exact percentages are not available. However, it is noteworthy that college graduates list the college career center as the second most often used source of information about careers, followed by newspapers. Nearly 48 percent of the college-educated adults in a Gallup poll (Gallup

Organization, 1989) indicated that they had used the College Career Center, as it was termed in the survey. Clearly, the career resource center is the key to the dissemination of career information on the campus.

Major Fairs

Elliot (1988) described a Pennsylvania State University program aimed at fostering educational planning. Undecided students, along with faculty representatives of various academic programs, were invited to attend an evening program in which students and faculty could interact about major areas of study. While no formal evaluation was conducted, those involved believed that the program was an effective way to stimulate educational exploration.

Peer Counseling Programs

Postsecondary institutions facing personnel shortages have at times turned to peer programs of various types, including tutorial and counseling programs. As Holly (1987) notes, careful screening and training of counselors is an essential aspect of a successful program. Screening criteria should include motivation, psychological openness, freedom from psychological concerns, communications skills, and interpersonal style. The nature of the training program will be dependent on the goals of the program, but with proper supervision, peer counselors might orient students to computer-assisted career planning systems, assist students to locate and interpret occupational information, train students in job shadowing and information interviewing, and answer questions about self-directed self-assessment devices. It is imperative that supervisors be available to answer immediate questions and that regular, ongoing supervision is established to protect both the client and the peer counselor. It is also important to note that serving as a peer counselor can provide a valuable career development experience for students who aspire to careers in the mental health field. The University of Maryland, Cornell University, and Dickinson College have developed exemplary peer counseling programs (Johnson & Figler, 1984).

Assessment

Many of the indicators that competencies have been developed require self-knowledge. For example, one indicator that the young adult is maintaining a positive view of self in terms of potential and preferences in the world of work is the ability to identify factors such as interests and values and to indicate how they influence choice making. In some instances, this competency could be partially developed by the administration and interpretation of interest and values inventories as part of an ongoing career counseling process. In other instances, self-directed assessment may be all that is required and thus a student might take either a paper and pencil or computer-administered form of an interest inventory or a values survey.

Postsecondary institutions offer career-related assessment in numerous ways, including the aforementioned approaches. However, some include interest and personality inventories and aptitude tests as part of the orientation programs. Others support psychometric centers where students can go to take various types of inventories, usually after an intake interview. Students who enroll in career classes or volunteer for career groups are also likely to find that assessment plays a prominent role in the process of these experiences.

Program Evaluation

Evaluation of the outcomes of career development programs was discussed in Chapters 9 and 10. We have provided the findings of studies evaluating the impact of career development intervention throughout this chapter. Obviously, the success of a program will depend on the extent to which students attain the competencies listed in Table 11.1. The indicators listed are measured separately and collectively as a means to infer competency acquisition. The standards associated with these indicators tell us in a relative sense how well the program has succeeded. For example, if all students are expected to understand the uses and limitations of occupational outlook information (Table 11.1, Competency 4), we must establish criteria by which to judge that success. We might, for example, use a paper and pencil test where students are asked to identify the three uses and three limitations of occupational outlook information and expect that 100 percent of the students would be able to answer this question correctly. If only 80 percent do answer it correctly, we can either accept this result, judge our programs accordingly, or reteach the competency. What is actually done will depend on resources and the importance attached to the competency. As the reader may recall from previous chapters, this type of evaluation is called product or outcome evaluation.

Mines (1985) suggested that measuring certain developmental phenomena poses difficulty because students do not "develop" at the same rate, even given identical experiences and backgrounds, and because students respond to their experiences differentially. For example, all students may participate in a course on career development, but because readiness (developmental stage) varies, the course will have differential impact. Also, because of learning styles and environmental variables (e.g., parent's demands), students will absorb the material at differential rates.

As noted in Chapter 9, process evaluation looks at decision making, staffing, resources, management variables, and other program process variables that may contribute to, or detract from, attainment of program goals. If these processes are perfect (which they will not be) and if the programs themselves are perfectly designed (which they will not be), some failure will occur because of the interaction of development and the environment. An example of the results of a process evaluation is presented by Reardon and Regan (1981). The objective of their evaluation was to determine student reactions to a career development course at Florida State University. The course, which consisted of three units (Self and Environmental

Analysis, Decision Making, and Job Acquisition), was evaluated by two types of student rankings and by looking at academic records. Reardon and Regan found that students learned about the course from friends, faculty advisors, and the schedule of classes. They also discovered that students enrolled in the class to develop a fuller understanding of the career planning and decision-making process, to increase their motivation to engage in career planning, to find out more information about careers, and to determine how careers and majors are linked. Finally, they found that students valued the organization of the course and the level of instructor–student interaction. Reardon and Regan concluded that the information resulting from their evaluation was helpful in determining how the course could be marketed and as an aid in course redesign.

Summary

Career development activities in postsecondary educational institutions can assist students to crystallize their career plans and begin the process of implementing them by linking education and career. However, not all students perceive that they need these activities; many hold the opposite view. In some instances, students do not need career development activities, but in others it is just as obvious that students' perceptions of the relevance of career development activities is based on naivete, not information. It is also clear that students enrolled in postsecondary institutions are diverse, both by virtue of their development and because of their age, ethnicity, and reasons for being in college. Good programming requires that these needs be carefully considered and attempts be made to meet them. It is likely that only those programs that use multiple approaches—including information, career counseling, classes, small groups, and units in classes—and that link advising and career planning will be successful.

References

Allyn, D. P. (1989). Application of the 4MAT model of career guidance. *Career Development Quarterly, 37,* 280–288.

Belz, J. R. (1993). Sexual orientation as a factor in career development. *Career Development Quarterly, 41,* 197–200.

Bjorkquist, P. M. (1988). Creating an alumni career consultant program in a liberal arts college. *Journal of College Student Development, 29,* 77–78.

Blan, F. W. (1985). Inter-collegiate athletic competition and students' educational and career plans. *Journal of College Student Development, 26,* 115–118.

Brown, D., Pryzwansky, W. P., & Schulte, A. (1996). *Psychological consultation: Introduction to theory and practice* (2nd ed.). Boston: Allyn & Bacon.

Buescher, K. L., Johnston, J. A., Lucas, C. B., & Hughey, K. F. (1989). Early interventions with undecided college students. *Journal of College Student Development, 30,* 375–377.

Butcher, E. (1982). Changing by choice: A process model of group counseling. *Vocational Guidance Quarterly, 30,* 200–209.

Dailey, M. J. (1986). Using decision trees to assist students through academic and career advising. *Journal of College Student Development, 27,* 457–458.

deBlois, C. S. (1992, July). *The emerging role of the female nontraditional education student-family and professional development.* Paper presented at the annual meeting of the Association of Teacher Educators, Orlando, FL.

Elliot, E. S. (1988). Major fairs and undergraduate student exploration. *Journal of College Student Development, 29,* 278–280.

Evans, N. J. (1985). Needs assessment methodology: A comparison of results. *Journal of College Student Development, 26,* 107–114.

Forrest, L., & Backes, P. (1988). CareerLine: Career resources delivered to students. *Journal of College Student Development, 29,* 165–166.

Gallup Organization. (1989). A Gallup survey regarding career development. Princeton, NJ: Author.

Goodson, W. D. (1982). Status of career guidance programs on college campuses. *Vocational Guidance Quarterly, 30,* 230–235.

Griff, N. (1987). Meeting the career development needs of returning students. *Journal of College Student Development, 28,* 469–470.

Hatcher, L., & Crook, J. C. (1988). First-job surprises for college graduates: An exploratory investigation. *Journal of College Student Development, 29,* 441–448.

Healy, C. C., & Reilly, K. C. (1989). Career needs of community college students: Implications for theory and practice. *Journal of College Student Development, 30,* 541–545.

Holly, K. A. (1987). Development of a college peer counselor program. *Journal of College Student Development, 28,* 285–286.

Hoyt, K. B., & Lester, J. N. (1995). *Learning to work: The NCDA Gallup survey.* Alexandria, VA: NCDA.

Johnson, C. A., & Figler, H. E. (1984). Career development and placement services in postsecondary institutions. In N. C. Gysberg (Ed.), *Designing careers* (pp. 458–481). San Francisco: Jossey-Bass.

Johnson, D. C., & Smouse, A. D. (1993). Assessing a career planning course: a multidimensional approach. *Journal of College Student Development, 34,* 145–147.

Johnston, W. B., & Packer, A. E. (1987). *Workforce 2000: Workers and work for the twenty-first century.* Indianapolis, IN: Hudson Institute.

Kahnweiler, J. B., & Kahnweiler, W. M. (1980). A dual-career workshop for college undergraduates. *Vocational Guidance Quarterly, 28,* 225–230.

Kivlighan, K. M. (1990). Career group therapy. *The Counseling Psychologist, 18,* 64–79.

Kobylarz, L. (Ed.). (1996). *National career development guidelines: K–adult handbook.* Stillwater, OK: Career Development Training Institute.

Lanning, W. (1982). The privileged few: Special counseling needs of athletes. *Journal of Sports Psychology, 4,* 19–23.

Lent, R. W., Larkin, K. C., & Hasequa, C. S. (1980). Effects of a "focused" interest career counseling approach for college students. *Vocational Guidance Quarterly, 34,* 151–159.

Leong, F. T. L. (1993). The career counseling process with racial-ethnic minorities: The case of Asian Americans. *Career Development Quarterly, 42,* 26–40.

Luzzo, D. A. (1995). Gender differences in college students' career maturity and perceived barriers in career development. *Journal of Counseling and Development, 73,* 319–322.

Magoon, T. M. (1989). *The 1988/1989 college and university counseling center data bank.* College Park, MD: University of Maryland Counseling Center.

Mines, R. A. (1985). Measurement issues in evaluating student development programs. *Journal of College Student Personnel, 26,* 101–106.

Nachreiner, J. A. (1987). A self-help education and career planning resource for adult students. *Journal of College Student Development, 28,* 277–278.

NOICC. (1989). *The national career development guidelines: Local handbook for postsecondary institutions.* Washington, DC: Author.

Oliver, L., & Spokane, A. R. (1988). Career intervention outcome: What contributes to client gain? *Journal of Counseling Psychology, 35,* 447–462.

Padula, M. A. (1994). Reentry women: A literature review with recommendations for counseling and research. *Journal of Counseling and Development, 73,* 10–16.

Petrie, T. A., & Russell, R. K. (1995). Academic and psychosocial antecedents of academic performance for minority and nonminority college football players. *Journal of Counseling and Development, 73,* 615–620.

Pickering, J. W. (1984). A comparison of three methods of career planning for liberal arts majors. *Career Development Quarterly, 35,* 102–111.

Pickering, J. W., & Vacc, N. A. (1984). Effectiveness of career development interventions for college students: A recovery of published research. *Vocational Guidance Quarterly, 32,* 149–159.

Quinn, M. T., & Lewis, R. J. (1989). An attempt to measure a career-planning intervention in a traditional course. *Journal of College Student Development, 30,* 371–372.

Reardon, R., & Regan, K. (1981). Process evaluation of a career planning course. *Vocational Guidance Quarterly, 29,* 265–269.

Reardon, R., Zunker, V., & Dyal, M. A. (1979). The status of career planning programs in career centers in colleges and universities. *Vocational Guidance Quarterly, 28,* 154–159.

Robbins, S. B., & Tucker, K. R., Jr. (1986). Relation of good instability to self-directed and interactional career counseling workshops. *Journal of Counseling Psychology, 33,* 418–424.

Savickas, M. L. (1990). The career decision making course: Description and field test. *Journal of College Student Development, 38,* 275–284.

Spokane, A. (1991). *Career interventions.* Englewood Cliffs, NJ: Prentice-Hall.

Stone, G. L., & Archer, J. A., Jr. (1990). College and university counseling centers in the 1990s: Challenges and limits. *The Counseling Psychologist, 18,* 539–607.

Wilkes, S. B., Davis, L., & Dever, L. (1989). Fostering career development in student athletes. *Journal of College Student Development, 30,* 567–568.

12

Career Development Needs of Special Groups

The goal of this chapter is to consider some of the groups for whom circumstances or conditions require a modification in the usual career development process. We have assumed that career development is a unique, individualized process for every person, and it depends on all of an individual's personal attributes and characteristics interacting with the environment, the times, and the people who make up that person's world. Nevertheless, within that uniqueness one can find certain commonalities that are generally shared by others, and this provides the basis for the group activities that are used to educate, civilize, and socialize the person. Ideally, these are supplemented with personal experiences that aid people to maximize their total development.

Many types of classification could be used to identify representative groups that face somewhat different circumstances in career development experiences. This chapter considers five of these groups without any claim that these are all-inclusive; rather, they have been chosen because they are representative of groupings to which career information and counseling can be related in special ways. We consider the following groups:

1. Special-needs groups, particularly those that are often described as disabled or disadvantaged
2. Culturally different groups, including minority ethnic groups, the geographically or socially isolated, and immigrants
3. Delayed entrants, such as displaced homemakers or those who elect to enter or return to work later than the usual entry time, returning military personnel, and criminal offenders

4. Midlife changers, including those who either voluntarily or involuntarily change careeers.
5. Older workers—those who reach or approach the retirement period with a desire to continue some kind of relationship with work

A second purpose of this chapter is to raise readers' awareness of the distinct characteristics that influence the career development process. Some of these characteristics, such as physical limitations, may be quite obvious. Others, such as learning disabilities and cultural values, may be less obvious. Although few well-trained career counselors and career development specialists would assume that all clients are alike, they might overlook some of the subtle differences that exist. Because it will not be possible to provide detailed descriptions of the groups considered in this section, additional readings are listed through each discussion. These books and articles are readily available to professionals and should be accessed to expand the basic information provided here.

Special-Needs Groups

In the truest sense, every individual qualifies for this category because each person does have special needs that make him or her unique. Here, however, the term is applied in a slightly different way. Only two groups are considered in this category: those individuals who have a physical or mental disability and as a result encounter handicaps, and those individuals who are disadvantaged because of education, language, or economic factors. For this chapter's discussion, the terms *disabled* and *disadvantaged* are restricted to those individuals for whom the disability or disadvantage clearly intrudes on the career development process to a degree that demands special attention to that characteristic.

Physically and Mentally Challenged Clients

In the past, people in this category were referred to as physically and mentally disabled. However, the term *disability* is often misunderstood and misused. The *Chartbook on Disability in the United States* (Kraus & Stoddard, 1989) recommended the definition adopted by the World Health Organization; that is, "a disability is any restriction or lack (resulting from an impairment) of ability to perform an activity in the manner or within the range considered normal for a human being." Hadley and Brodwin (1988) and Grealish and Salomone (1986) discussed the impact of imprecise terminology on the lives of people with disabilities. We often incorrectly use the terms *disabled* and *handicapped* synonymously. Fagan and Wallace (1979, p. 216) distinguished between the two terms as follows:

The disability may be considered as the person's observable, measurable characteristic that is judged to be deviant or discrepant from some acceptable norm. In

*contrast, the handicap may be considered as the barriers, demands, and general
environmental press placed on the person by various aspects of his or her environment, including other persons. Thus the absence of legs is a disability, whereas
the presence of stairs, as the only means of access to a goal, is a handicap.*

This definition suggests that a physical or mental condition becomes a handicap or impairment when the disability limits one or more major life activities.
Public Law 93-112 defines a handicapped person in this way, and further states
that physical or mental impairment means

*any physiological disorder or condition, cosmetic disfigurement, or anatomical
loss affecting one or more of the body systems: neurological, musculoskeletal; special sense organs; respiratory—including speech organs; cardiovascular; repro-
ductive; digestive; genitourinary; hemic and lymphatic, skin or endocrine; or any
mental or physical disorder, such as mental retardation, organic brain syndrome,
emotional or mental illness, and specific learning disability.*

One result of the consideration of the terms used to describe people with mental and physical limitations has been to change the descriptors for these groups
from physically and mentally disabled to physically and mentally challenged.
These new descriptors affirm that, while people with physical and mental limitations may experience some problems in the various arenas of their lives, they can
overcome them, particularly if they receive the right type of assistance. Because
our attention is directed toward career and career development, we are concerned
only with impairment as it limits or interferes with work-related activities—in
other words, vocational handicap. To return to the original differentiation proposed by Fagan and Wallace, a disability is a handicap only if it limits or impedes
the person's work involvement. Thus their illustration of disability—the absence
of legs—is a handicap if legs are necessary for successful work involvement.
Therefore, a paraplegic desk worker might not be handicapped, whereas a similarly disabled mail carrier definitely would be handicapped.

Kraus and Stoddard (1989) reported that an estimated 14.1 percent of the 231.5
million noninstitutionalized U.S. residents have an activity limitation. Of these,
8.8 million are unable to perform their major activity, 13.6 million are limited in
the kind and amount of major activity they can perform, and 10.1 million are limited in other activities. Of the 13.3 million people who are considered to have a
work disability, 33.6 percent are in the labor force and 15.6 percent are unemployed; thus roughly half of those with a work disability are outside the work
structure (neither employed nor classified as unemployed). These figures contrast
with the population without disability, where 78.5 percent are participating in the
labor force and less than 5.0 percent are unemployed.

The term *rehabilitation* is gradually being broadened in concept to apply to
the overcoming of many kinds of disabling human problems, including physical
disability, mental illness, mental retardation, alcoholism, drug addiction, delinquency, and crime. Specifically, rehabilitation may refer to special services such as

education, physical functioning, psychological adjustment, social adaptation, vocational capabilities, or recreational activities.

Vocational rehabilitation traditionally has referred to the process of returning a disabled worker to a state of reemployability. In at least two major ways, however, this concept is unnecessarily narrow. First, it implies that a person must have acquired certain marketable skills before eligibility for help can be established; second, the idea of employability as a product of the service may make ineligible for help those for whom employability may be uncertain or unlikely. Fortunately, there has been some movement toward reducing both of these restrictions, so that people who face handicaps but have never worked may qualify and even those for whom assistance may result in greater self-esteem and self-satisfaction without clear certainty of employment may be included. More recognition is now being given to the impact of disability on family life as well as on the individual. This has placed greater emphasis on the need for independence, self-regard, and integration within the total society rather than on separation and isolation from it.

Public Law 93-112, the Rehabilitation Act of 1973; Public Law 94-142, the Education for All Handicapped Children Act (1975); Public Law 95-602, the Rehabilitation, Comprehensive Services, and Developmental Disabilities Amendments of 1978; Public Law 101-476, the Education of the Handicapped Amendments of 1990; and Public Law 101-336, the Americans with Disabilities Act of 1990 have reinforced and expanded existing laws to produce greater public concern for disabled individuals as well as more adequate programs of assistance. One result has been an increasing quantity of helpful material in the professional literature.

Literature on the general topic of vocational rehabilitation ranges from articles in professional counseling journals to special issues of those journals to journals that focus on rehabilitation to professional books on the topic. Examples of the first type (articles in professional journals) include articles by Chubon (1985), Curnow (1989), Dahl (1982), Hagner and Salomone (1989), and Roessler (1987). A special issue of the *Journal of Counseling and Development* (November/December 1989) devotes forty pages to "Counseling Persons With Disabilities: A 10-year Update." Journals that concentrate on rehabilitation topics include *Career Development for Exceptional Individuals, Journal of Applied Rehabilitation Counseling,* and *Rehabilitation Counseling Bulletin.*

Rehabilitation services are provided by a number of professions—counseling, medical, nursing, psychological, social work, and others. Career counseling services are most frequently provided by rehabilitation counselors, whose counseling preparation has also usually included the medical and social aspects of various disabilities and their relationship to work. There are presently about 175,000 educational and vocational counselors in the United States according to the most recent version of the *Occupational Outlook Handbook.* Rehabilitation counselors make up a substantial portion of this group. In addition to the state vocational rehabilitation offices, they are employed in a number of national, state, and local public and private social agencies. Among the well-known organizations involved in vocational rehabilitation are Goodwill Industries, Jewish Vocational Service, and the Department of Veterans Affairs. Public schools play a significant role, especially for those of school age. Postsecondary schools are also involved in providing not only educational services but other types of programs as well.

Like other federal and state programs, public vocational rehabilitation programs exist in every state and are operated by state personnel under state policies within broad guidelines and provisions established by the federal agency. Funding for state services is provided on a shared or matching basis, with the formula used being a four-to-one ratio of federal to state funds. In other words, within the limits established by congressional authorization, for every $20 provided by state funds, the federal government matches with $80. The state first must make its funds available, and then federal dollars are allocated. Despite the generous matching formula, many states do not appropriate enough money to claim all the federal funds available to them. In these circumstances, unclaimed funds are reallocated to other states that are willing to provide additional matching monies. The obvious result is considerable variation in the quality and scope of public rehabilitation services from state to state. Costs vary greatly from one rehabilitation case to another, with some simple cases requiring small amounts of money to resolve the problem, while other cases require much time and money. In general, data from annual federal reports show that the average age for rehabilitants stays under 40, and the average client pays in federal income taxes within 3 years as much as the rehabilitation services cost. Thus an overwhelming case could be made in support of rehabilitation services on economic terms alone.

Fagan and Jenkins (1989) report the number of rehabilitation cases successfully closed in 1985 by type of disability. Of the more than 424,000 cases, almost 54 percent were individuals who were blind, 11 percent lacked an extremity, 9 percent were cases of alcoholism, 7 percent had epilepsy, 3.5 percent were drug abuse victims, and the other disabilities were each less than 2.5 percent of the cases. A word of caution is necessary to emphasize that these figures include only successfully completed cases; often these numbers were served in various ways by the state and federal rehabilitation program.

Thomas and Berven (1984) describe the career counseling process for clients with disabilities. They propose a sequence consisting of assessment, occupational exploration and choice, vocational training, placement, and follow-up. The presence of a disability may require adjustment of some of the steps.

The purpose of assessment is to help the individual (and the counselor) understand the client as completely as possible. As with any client, tests and other techniques are used to obtain needed information not readily available. Also as with any client, the counselor must determine the appropriateness of the test for the specific client and judge the likelihood that the needed information can be obtained in this way. Guidubaldi, Perry, and Walker (1989) stressed the importance of proper assessment procedures with students with disabilities. Zunker (1986) describes a number of assessment devices appropriate for many clients with disabilities. There are several indicators that nontest techniques may be more useful for clients with disabilities; for example, the disability may have isolated the client from experiences customary for his or her age group, or the impact of the disability on the client's physical and mental abilities may be such that psychometric measurement is inappropriate or produces imprecise results. The use of interview procedures with the client or with physicians and therapists may provide better evaluation of the disabling condition and its effect on the client. Work samples and job tryouts may be much more significant in evaluating the individual than in ordinary circumstances. Evidence of what the client *can* do, such as strength factors or aptitudes, is even more important than accurate identification of what he or she cannot do.

The occupational exploration process is similar to that followed by clients without disabilities except for greater emphasis on identifying occupations that meet the client's physical and mental abilities. O*NET, described in Chapter 5, promises to be a useful tool for helping clients relate their abilities and aptitudes to specific jobs. Some of the computer-based career guidance systems (for example, Guidance Information System, described in Chapter 8) include evaluations of physical demands and environmental conditions of occupations. Visits to work sites and actual tryout experiences may often be of special significance because client and counselor would be dealing with reality rather than conjecture. In the past, workers with disabilities were often restricted to narrow segments of the world of work by the interaction of public attitudes and their own self-image. Nevertheless, the range of suitable work for workers with disabilities should be nearly as wide as the universe of jobs.

When selecting from among the training options available, accessibility becomes a major consideration. Most educational institutions have modified their facilities to provide access for students with physical limitations in response to the American Disabilities Act. Students with and without disabilities in high school will find increasing opportunities for career training in tech–prep programs, which are coordinated efforts between high schools and community colleges that encourage students to select technical careers in high school, begin their preparation at that level, and complete their training after graduation from high school. The number of disabled students in vocational–technical training programs in community colleges rose from 6 percent of all enrollees in 1990–1991 to 8 percent in 1993–1994 according to a survey conducted by the General Accounting Office (GAO, 1995). Perhaps a more encouraging sign was that community colleges are increasingly offering support services for students with disabilities according to this same survey. The GAO found that 98 percent of the community colleges they surveyed offered remediation in basic skills, 82 percent provided an interpreter for hearing-impaired students, and 84 percent provided a reader for vision-impaired students. Although no similar surveys could be found for 4-year colleges, it is likely that the proportion of these institutions that provide support services for impaired students equals or exceeds the community college percentages.

Much of the literature dealing with the career development of the physically or mentally challenged student focuses on adapting existing practices to meet the special needs of these groups. For example, Skinner and Schenck (1992) stress the importance of helping the learning disabled (LD) locate colleges that offer specialized services for LD students and the need to develop compensatory study skills that will help them succeed. Stern and Dubois (1994) drew on the expertise of 286 people with disabilities to craft recommendations for students with visual, hearing, and mobility impairments interested in science careers. She focused on using assistive technology, communicating needs, and linking to faculty members as keys to success. Finally, Mather (1994) warned people working with the visually impaired not to allow their clients to become too dependent on technology.

Placement services for workers with disabilities, described in more detail in Chapter 16, involve more complexity than those for workers without disabilities. The added complications arise from attitudes of employers and fellow workers, as well as those of the client. Job club techniques, also described in Chapter 16, are appropriate. When the disability is severe, job modification may be necessary to permit full participation in work.

Follow-up activities with recently placed workers with disabilities provide a service similar to that performed by the work experience coordinator. The major function is to facilitate satisfactory adjustment between the worker and the work site. When identified early and solved rapidly, problems tend to be less severe and less disruptive. Sometimes minor adjustments in the work site are all that is needed to ensure that the worker can be as productive as workers without disabilities.

Economically Disadvantaged Clients

Fitzgerald and Betz (1994) raised a provocative question: Is career development a meaningful term in the lives of a majority of the population? (p. 104). They make the point that, for many people including the unemployed, discouraged workers who have given up looking for jobs, and marginally employed workers who teeter on the edge of poverty, work is not psychologically central to their lives. However, most of these people realize that meaningful employment is their way out of their current existence, and it becomes incumbent on career development specialists to finds ways to facilitate this escape and to make career development a meaningful term for them.

The term *disadvantaged* can be interpreted very broadly, in its usual dictionary sense, to include everyone who is in an unfavorable economic or social circumstance. Certainly almost everyone in the category just discussed would fit this description, as would many members of minority groups, women, the poor, dropouts, and several other large segments of the population; even left-handed individuals occasionally find themselves in awkward social circumstances. It can also be applied very legitimately in a restricted or narrow sense, as Miles (1984) used it to describe the economically disadvantaged, equating the term with *economically deprived* or *poor*. Typically, two subgroups are included under this label because their circumstances often assign them here. These include those with limited education (in either quantity or quality) and those caught in geographic dislocation (often rural poor or urban unemployed who have moved elsewhere searching for something better).

Miles (1984) stated that three groups make up the economically disadvantaged:

The Chronically Poor: *These are individuals born into poverty and raised in families with inadequate resources to meet basic needs.*

The Unemployed or Newly Disadvantaged: *Some unemployed can bridge brief periods of unemployment by using savings and other available resources. It is probably fair to assume that unemployment, sooner or later, puts each victim in the disadvantaged group. The structurally unemployed are in the greatest danger because they no longer have a job to which they can ultimately return. The cyclically unemployed can also be hurt if the economic recession outlasts their available resources.*

The Underemployed: *Miles calls these the working poor because they are found mainly in low-wage, marginal jobs that involve little skill. Their wages are not sufficient to exceed poverty standards. One unfortunate result of plant closing and plant exporting is likely to be a rapid increase in this category as structurally unemployed skilled workers settle into low-paying unskilled jobs. Miles states that approximately one sixth of the working population earn incomes that only barely exceed the poverty level; hence this group is constantly on the margin of falling into the poverty group. (pp. 386–389)*

Some of the major problems faced by the disadvantaged in career planning may be lack of basic educational skills, unsuccessful vocational adjustment at early career entry stage, inability to obtain vocational training, low income level, incongruity between self-concept and previously held low-level jobs, and periods of unemployment. Because of these needs, disadvantaged people often need career development programs that address both short-term and long-term goals. The counselor will need to involve the client in short-term planning accompanied by rewards and reinforcement to help the client reach a point where long-range goals and plans appear feasible.

It would appear that many of the career-related problems of the economically disadvantaged could be confronted with a four-part program including the following:

1. Access to basic adult education
2. Personal and/or career counseling
3. Information about the world of work
4. Access to appropriate vocational training and placement

Individuals with limited educational background are almost automatically relegated to the most marginal work opportunities. Literacy training, basic mathematics, and language proficiency are minimal essentials for almost every job in our society. Adult education programs exist in almost all metropolitan areas; however, individuals may be unable to capitalize on these services because of lack of transportation or unfamiliarity with local transportation systems, lack of child care, time schedule problems, and so forth. It is fairly safe to say that until basic educational skills are acquired, the individual has very little to sell to a prospective employer.

Personal counseling may be needed prior to career counseling by disadvantaged individuals to clarify self-concept as well as to understand their circumstances. Several authors have emphasized the devastating impact that job loss has on feelings of self-worth. The chronically poor are likely to carry an even heavier feeling of worthlessness. The so-called American dream suggests that one's success in life is the product of hard work—the harder one works, the more one reaps in material rewards, status, and self-satisfaction. One frequent product is the feeling of guilt and failure by those without jobs or with only marginal jobs. Marshall (1983), Shifron, Dye, and Shifron (1983), and Havercamp and Moore (1993) described ways to help such clients deal with feelings and values that may interfere with everyday life and often result from forces outside the individual's control.

Realistic and practical information about the world of work can be used to help the disadvantaged to see potential opportunities to break out of what is frequently viewed as a hopeless morass. Interviews with workers, work samples, plant visits, and synthetic work situations may help the person to understand the job, to relate that job to self, to see attainable goals, and perhaps to acquire usable role models.

Access to realistic skill training is necessary for all jobs but those at the lowest skill level. One problem is that many disadvantaged students withdraw from school before they reach the grade level where vocational skills are taught. This situation limits their access to skill training, to Job Training Program Administration (JTPA) programs, or to similar efforts provided at the local level. Compared with the numbers of people who truly need such preparation, the few training positions available are far too limited. Miles (1984) suggested that counselors must become change agents and assist clients in changing the system if this deficit is to be overcome.

One encouraging note came from the General Accounting Office (GAO, 1995) survey cited in the previous section. Researchers found that the percentage of economically disadvantaged students enrolled in vocational education courses in community colleges and vocational–technical schools had increased slightly in the 1990–1991 to 1993–1994 period. This group of students comprised 29 percent (versus 28 percent in the earlier period) of all students enrolled in these courses in the 1993–1994 school year according to the GAO. Less positive was the finding that the percentage of students who were enrolled in vocational education courses with limited English proficiency had declined during this same period. Limited proficiency with English may limit career choices and potential earnings.

Cultural, Racial, and Ethnic Minorities

Recent projections by the Bureau of Labor Statistics (BLS, 1997) suggest that, by early in the twenty-first century, 29 percent of the labor force will be made up of workers from cultural, ethnic, and racial minorities. African Americans and Hispanics will make up the largest portion of this group, each accounting for about 12 percent of the workers. Asian Americans, Native Americans, and others will make up about 5 percent of the work force by 2006, with Asian Americans constituting most of this latter group. Career development specialist must be prepared to deal with the unique worldviews and values held by these groups, some of which will have a dramatic impact on the career choice making process. They must also be ready to cope with language barriers, histories of hardship and discrimination, and other variables that may have influenced workers' views of work. The first step in preparing for cross-cultural interactions—whether it be between white, European American counselors and minority clients, or between minority clients and majority clients or clients from other minorities—is the development of a thorough understanding of the culture of the client. This quest for understanding cultural differences should probably begin by looking at the cultural values of clients (Brown, 1997). It is particularly important to understand clients' orientation to time (future oriented, present oriented, or oriented more to recurring natural events), social relationships (the wishes of individuals are most important versus the wishes of the group or tribe are most important), and problem solving (it is important to do something about problems that arise versus immediate responses to problems are unnecessary). The traditional values of white, European Americans have been to value a future time orientation, individual social relationships, and a doing or immediate response to problem resolution.

Career development specialists should also be knowledgeable about the history, religion, customs, and traditions of the cultural groups of their clients. This information, along with the knowledge about the typical values of various minority groups, can serve as a point of departure in designing and delivering career development services. However, even if the cultural group of the client is well understood, culturally sensitive career development specialists should realize that there is much variation within each cultural group, and they should be careful to consider the "internal" culture of the client as opposed to external, demographic characteristics (Ho, 1995). For a fuller discussion of the issues that arise when providing career development services to minorities, Leong's (1995) edited book, *Career Development and Vocational Behavior of Ethnic Minorities*, should be consulted. However, some of the most salient special needs of the major ethnic groups will be presented here.

Until recently, African Americans were the largest minority group in this country. Currently, their numbers and the numbers of Hispanics in the United States are approximately the same, a fact reflected in the work force statistics presented in the introduction to this section. Most African Americans can trace their history to slavery in the South, although there are some African Americans who immigrated to this country from Africa in the past few years. Historically, African Americans have been disadvantaged in the workplace because of discrimination and limited educational opportunities. The result of this has been lower earnings, higher unemployment rates, and growing family instability because of economic uncertainty. Some strides have been made in the education area in recent years, which are reflected in the statistics that indicate that the high school completion rate of African Americans is roughly equivalent to that of white, European Americans (Brown, 1998). However, occupational segregation of African Americans in lower paying, less rewarding occupations remains high (Hotchkiss & Borow, 1996). The values of African Americans approximate those of white, European Americans, although there may be greater variability regarding the social relationships value within this group (Carter, 1991). Available evidence suggests that African Americans are more likely to endorse collateral social relationships than are white, European Americans. African Americans, like all the groups discussed here, are tremendously diverse, particularly with regard to socioeconomic status.

Casas and Arbona (1992) and Arbona (1995) described the career-related issues confronting Hispanics. Many of these issues have to do with recency of immigration, limited proficiency in English, substandard educational backgrounds, culture shock and alienation, and adapting to a new culture. Arbona (1995) also suggested that Hispanics of African origin may be the subject of greater discrimination because of their skin color. Savickas (1991) noted that career development requires a future time orientation. Hispanics may be more oriented to the present than the future. They may also be less inclined to solve career development problems because of their being activity oriented, which may make them more inclined to accept the current situation (Sue & Sue, 1990). Finally, many Hispanics hold a collateral social value, which means they are more inclined to put the group's wishes ahead of their own. One implication of this is that family members and godparents may need to be involved in the career planning process of youthful Hispanics.

Hispanics are racially diverse and may in fact be descended from European, Africans, or Asian ancestors. They also come from diverse geographic backgrounds (Casas & Arbona, 1992). Large subgroups within this ethnic group include those of Mexican origin, Puerto Ricans, Central and South Americans, Cubans, and other Hispanic groups. The groups vary from a racial perspective, comprised of individuals who are of Caucasian, Mongoloid, and Negroid descent. There is also wide diversity within and across Hispanic subgroups in factors that can be labeled demographic, sociohistorical, sociopolitical, socioeconomic, and sociopsychological. Some of the subgroups, even though dispersed across the country, have high concentrations in certain areas. For example, Mexican Americans are numerous in the Southwest, many Cuban Americans are found in south Florida and near New York City, and many of Central American background are found in New York City, Los Angeles, and San Francisco.

Similarly, Fukuyama (1992) discusses Asian Americans and career development. This ethnic minority includes a wide range of national origins, including Asian Indian, Pakistani, Thai, Chinese, Japanese, Filipino, Vietnamese, Laotian, Cambodian, Hmong, Hawaiian, Samoan, Guam, Korean, and others. Obviously, the cultural diversity within and across these national subgroups is wide.

Many Asian Americans have values that are markedly different than those of White, European Americans. Their time orientation is more likely to be past future than is that of the other ethnic groups, although other time orientations will be found among the members of this highly diverse group. Some of the members (e.g., Chinese Americans) have a collateral value that may mean that they place the wishes of the group ahead of their own concerns. In other cases, Asian Americans may hold what is termed a lineal social value and thus may allow elders or parents to make career decisions for them. A frequently occurring scenario in counselors' offices is conflicts between students who have begun to adopt an individualism social value and their parents who still hold lineal social values.

Native Americans are perhaps the most diverse of all cultural groups in the United States. Currently there are over 450 recognized tribes (Casas & Arbona, 1992) in this country. The stereotype of Native Americans that has evolved in the literature is that they do not intervene directly in the career development process of other tribal members, but individuals are socialized to respect tribal values, traditions, and expectations. However, the research literature (Carter, 1991) indicates that some tribes have values that are similar to those of European Americans, which suggests that they might have different expectations of individuals (i.e., might be accepting of individual action) than those tribes that subscribe to a collateral value. Because of the potential of making an erroneous assumption about the values structure of Native Americans, career development specialists should be careful to assess these beliefs accurately.

Although some Native Americans may choose either not to participate in the workforce or to minimize their efforts because of the wish to ascribe to the norms of their tribes, other problems are probably more serious barriers to their career development. Poverty, historic patterns of discrimination, geographic isolation, lack of occupational information, and geographic relocation resulting in loss of family and tribal support are major barriers to successful participation in the workforce. So is a time orientation that focuses on natural events as opposed to the mechanical monitoring of time. As noted above, Savickas (1991) suggested that individuals who are successful in their careers look ahead and attempt to anticipate the future. Perhaps more importantly, participation in the workplace requires punctuality and attending to matters in a "timely" fashion. An orientation that does not include mechanical monitoring of time using clocks and calendars may lead to serious problems for the Native American worker. So may tribal customs that dictate that some religious and other ceremonies are scheduled spontaneously by healers or tribal elders, thus interfering with the schedule of the worker.

Because of the increasing diversity of our society, career counselors and others engaged in providing career development services will increasingly be involved in providing services to many of the groups listed above. Fortunately, increasing attention is being given to preparing counselors to work with culturally different clients. Karayanni (1987) reports on the impact of modernization pressures on the vocational interests in a traditional-minded population. Articles by Ross (1984) and Webb (1983) focus on broad cultural factors such as adult development in different cultures and awareness of cross-cultural differences. Within the counseling literature one can find many articles that discuss the general problems produced by this impact of ethnicity and different cultural backgrounds on the counseling relationship and many articles that deal with preparing counselors to meet these challenges. Typical of articles that focus on cultural factors are those by Ahia

(1984); Cheatham (1990); Giles (1990); Gim, Atkinson, and Kim (1991); Heinrich, Corbine, and Thomas (1990); Lee (1984); Leong and Hayes (1990); Sue & Sue (1990); and Sundal-Hansen (1985). Articles that stress counselor preparation for work with culturally diverse clients include those by Arrendondo–Dowd and Gonsalves (1980), Rosser–Hogan (1990), and Sue and associates (1982).

We must assume that culturally different clients have all the problems faced by other clients, problems that may be increased by the cultural variances. Sue and Sue (1990) suggested a framework that can help counselors organize their approach to the counseling relationship, based on a two-dimensional concept with locus of control serving as the horizontal axis and locus of responsibility as the vertical axis. Thus the four quadrants represent the different combinations of internal-external control and internal-external responsibility. Sue and Sue believe that the internal control/internal responsibility quadrant represents the typically American outlook, reinforcement of behavior is primarily a product of our own behavior, and success or failure is primarily the result of our own skill and adequacy. This view also is basic to most philosophies of counseling. Many culturally different clients, however, would classify themselves in one of the other quadrants because of traditions and values. Understanding this difference, especially the factor of values, and adjusting one's approach appropriately may be the secret to successful counseling with these clients.

In addition to those factors that can be clearly labeled as cultural differences— such as importance of family group among Hispanics, unquestioning respect for elders and authority among some Asians—other problems are faced by many in these groups. One of these is language and communication. Even the well-educated foreign graduate student often may find American vernacular and slang incomprehensible. Further, nonverbal communication is very different; for example, eye contact with a respected elder (the counselor, maybe), body contact such as handshaking, or the use of a negative may be considered rude or very difficult. A second difficulty arises from unfamiliarity with the system—not knowing how to do certain things that we take for granted. Sue and Sue (1990) recommended that cross-cultural counselors maintain an open attitude that allows them to be aware of their cultural heritage and its values and biases, to recognize the differences that exist between counselor and client, and to be sensitive to the client's needs.

Clearly the counselor must bridge the chasm of cultural difference before career counseling or the use of career information can be effective. Counseling culturally different clients is discussed further in Chapter 14.

Delayed Entrants

Many factors lead to delayed entrance into the civilian labor force. Traditionally, many women have elected to assume the role of housewives after completing their education. Although fewer women elect this route today, some women and men still elect to stay home and provide child care as well as caring for the household. Another reason for delaying entrance into the workforce is the decision to enter one of the armed services or the merchant marines. People who select this option serve from four to thirty or more years before deciding to embark upon a civilian career. Another group, people who are incarcerated because they commit a crime, also delay entering employment because of a very different set of circumstances. Regardless of the reason for delaying entrance into the workforce, people in this situation are faced with some unique challenges.

Late-Entry Women

One group of women includes those who have acquired significant work experience before interrupting that work to devote their time to homemaking and mothering, and who after a period of time deliberately return to work. For the most part, these women are not the center of our concern in this section because they have both occupational skills and a career plan. Two other groups do exist that we consider here. One group, often referred to as *displaced homemakers,* includes those women who have considered themselves primarily to be homemakers but now, perhaps even unexpectedly, find that circumstances necessitate their working for pay. Their reasons vary: widowhood, divorce, illness or unemployment of spouse, abandonment, unexpected economic circumstances, and so on. The crucial aspect is the relatively sudden and unexpected—or at least unplanned—necessity of entering the labor market. The second group includes women who have deliberately planned to enter employment at a later time, after their children are all in school, or all in college, or all on their own, or when their parents no longer require full-time attention.

Melamed (1995, 1996) concluded that the fact that women make approximately two-thirds as much as men can be attributed to three factors: initial career selection, workforce participation, and discrimination. Women who plan to interrupt their career after marriage or the birth of their children often select careers that require skills that can rather easily be updated such as those found in some health care occupations, education, and clerical jobs. Unfortunately, these are not among the higher paying occupations. Even women who are in occupations that are potentially high paying limit their potential earnings when they "stop-out." Finally, women, whether delayed entrants or not, face a problem that is analogous to one faced by minorities—discrimination in the workplace. Perhaps the best illustration of direct discrimination can be found in comparative salaries between men and women working in the same job in the same industry. Although women have made strides, they are still not as well paid as men when these types of comparisons are drawn (Hotchkiss & Borow, 1996). The career counselors' job is to make women aware of the consequences of selecting traditional, female-dominated careers as well as of the decision to interrupt their careers. They also need to prepare women for discrimination in the workplace and to make them aware of the services provided by the Equal Employment Opportunity Commission (EEOC) when they have complaints about their employers. EEOC receives complaints of discrimination, investigates those complaints, and authorizes legal action if their investigation supports the allegations. Finally, career counselors need to make women aware of their rights when confronted with sexual harassment in the workplace. Technically, sexual harassment occurs when a member or members of one sex create a hostile environment that either precludes, or limits, the functioning of a member of the opposite sex. EEOC also investigates complaints of sexual harassment.

There is literature in the field for the counselor who assists women with work-related problems. More articles appear to be focused on the reentry worker than on the delayed entrant. Examples of available materials include articles by Ekstrom, Beier, Davis, and Gruenberg (1981); Farmer (1985); Gerson and Lee (1982); McGraw (1982); Pickering and Galvin–Schaefers (1988); Read, Elliott, Escobar, and Slaney (1988); Robinson, Rotter, and Wilson (1982); and Zawada (1980). More specialized discussions can be found in Bowen (1982), who describes career counseling with abused women; and Chusmir (1983), who describes women whose vocational choices are nontraditional. Slaney and Dickson (1985) have studied the effect of indecision on career exploration for reentry women workers, and Wade and Bernstein (1991) have examined counselor race and cultural sensitivity in dealing with African American female clients.

The displaced-homemaker group will often need personal counseling because of the drastic, sudden, and sometimes traumatic events that have displaced them before they are ready for career counseling. Unfortunately, some decide that if they can leap into a full-time job or training program, their other problems will shrink or go away. Those other difficulties, however, must be resolved at least in part before any intelligent planning about education and/or work can take place.

Frequently, one of the problems that needs prior attention is the modifying of self-concept so the person can assume responsibility for decisions that previously may have been made jointly or by the absent partner. This may require both self-confidence building and access to basic information and knowledge needed for sound decisions. In some marriages, items often relegated to males include maintenance of property or living quarters, automobile purchase and care, and legal or financial matters. If these and other important areas are unfamiliar to a female client, she must either acquire that competence or deal with the problem in another way.

Displaced homemakers often face serious financial problems, either short term or long term. Referral to competent financial advisors may be necessary to resolve acquisition or disposition of property, relocation of residence, financial planning to cover a period of education or training, and so on.

A further common problem for the displaced homemaker is identifying and cultivating support systems to replace those that may have been lost (Eby & Buch, 1995). The counselor may be able to help the client explore the types of systems she needs and desires, how she might develop them, and specific groups and organizations that might facilitate this aspect.

After some of these problems have been sorted out or at least are headed toward solution, career problems can be considered. One issue that is likely to arise early is whether the woman is considering immediate employment only or is contemplating entry into some preparatory program. All the factors that bear on this decision for a teenager apply here, along with several additional ones—costs in time, effort, and money; whether the payback will justify those expenditures; opportunity; individual energy and psychological resources; and so on. If the person is thinking primarily of work, without specialized preparation, the counselor must help identify existing skills and ascertain the extent of job search skills. Identification of skills is obviously related to available or potentially available jobs; and occupational information, especially local labor market information, may be crucial in the early planning stages. The materials available in the career resource center may be particularly useful at this point along with referral to an agency that operates a job club that may offer experience in job interviews, help in searching, and other job-getting experiences. Kahn (1983) described an employment counseling service that serves this group of reentry women.

The deliberate returner does not necessarily face the same problems that confront the displaced homemaker. Her decision is voluntary, although she may feel that economic factors or the desire for self-fulfillment require her to work. The basic support systems of family, friends, and organizations probably are intact, although the role she anticipates assuming may necessitate adjustments in all of these. Undoubtedly changes in lifestyle will and must occur, but they generally can be resolved without the pressure, grief, and uncertainty that confront the displaced person. Problems that are likely to be constant across both groups are those that relate to self-concept, development of independence, and assertiveness. The deliberate returner can undertake career planning more rapidly because she does not face the massive difficulties of her displaced counterpart. Financial pressures may be less, so the possibility of appropriate educational or training programs can be considered. Timing may be easier to handle, and often gradual reentry to work or preparation can be arranged.

Former Military Personnel

Individuals who return to civilian life after a period of military service can be divided into three groups: (1) those who have served their full time of 20 to 30 years and are now retiring from military duty and will draw pension benefits, (2) those who have incurred a disability that prevents continuing in military service and will now draw disability benefits, and (3) those who are leaving after a relatively brief period (often a single enlistment of 3 to 6 years). We consider the first group in the section "Midlife Changers." The second group, if they attempt to enter civilian employment, qualify for rehabilitation benefits as described earlier. Hence our concern here is primarily with the person who delays entrance into the civilian work force because of a period of military service long enough to justify the label of delayed entrant.

In addition to the customary reasons of patriotism and long-range career plans, many young people volunteer for military service for quite different purposes. The majority of voluntary enlistees are probably recent high schools graduates. Some, recognizing that they have no clear-cut educational or occupational plan, decide to enlist to give themselves time to decide what they want to do. Some, unable to obtain acceptable civilian employment because of either economic factors or the lack of salable skills, enlist as an alternative course of action. Others may volunteer to escape an array of problems—difficult family situations, unsatisfactory living conditions, or a desire for affiliation and belonging. Still others may have clearly formed long-range civilian goals in mind and may enlist to acquire specialized training that they expect to use in a civilian position, or to accrue educational benefits that will permit later completion of civilian college programs.

Many military occupations have equivalent civilian counterparts, and individuals who have acquired these skills in military service can transfer with little difficulty from one to the other, just as other workers move from one employer to another. There are, however, many other military occupations for which transferability of learned job skills is impossible.

Service personnel who elect not to reenlist or are not eligible to do so, and who have had military assignments where no transferable skill was acquired, are most likely to need career counseling. Like displaced homemakers, many in this group view themselves as disadvantaged because they are competing against younger individuals for entry-level jobs. Similarly, they may have only vague ideas about work values and occupational goals and may fail to see that, although they lack specific transferable skills, they may have generalized skills that employers value highly. Further, as a result of having lived in a tightly structured and directed environment, some will need help in assuming responsibility for decision making.

Whenever counselors identify the existence of problems involving self-concept, values, interpersonal relations, attitudes toward work and society, and similar personal attitudes or viewpoints, they must help the client focus on these factors first before proceeding to career choice. Added complications are sometimes encountered in former service personnel because they often feel that they are in a hurry to catch up with their age cohorts who have been in civilian jobs while they were in service, or because some fail to realize the extent of differences between life in military and civilian settings. Further, those who enlisted because of vocational uncertainty or various personal problems may find those difficulties still unresolved.

Those individuals who have completed periods of obligated service have usually incurred the obligation by accepting financial support from military sources for some portion of their advanced educational training—for example, scholarship support for advanced ROTC at the undergraduate level or a stipend or scholarship for completion of a professional school graduate program. Few of these people will need career counseling because the acquired preparation is ordinarily highly transferable. Those who have participated in such programs usually did so because they anticipated military careers or originally planned to transfer to civilian activity after satisfying the obligated period of service. Occasionally, a client who has followed this path may decide that the original choice of field was inappropriate or is no longer desirable and may wish to move to some other kind of work.

Many governmental agencies maintain special programs of assistance for former military personnel. Clients are sometimes unaware of the help that is available to them through various community resources. Among the best known of these programs are state service officers, state employment security agencies, state and federal civil service and personnel agencies, and the Department of Veterans Affairs.

Prior Offenders

Individuals released from penal institutions face the problems encountered by displaced homemakers and returning military personnel plus some others that are unique to their situation and previous experiences. It is probably safe to say that this group is at highest risk, and studies of recidivism show that overwhelming numbers soon find themselves incarcerated again.

State and federal penal institutions vary widely in fundamental philosophy with respect to the goal of rehabilitation versus custodial care. The range of variation is probably even greater when one examines the services actually provided in these two areas. Many prison officials confirm that even in those institutions that emphasize rehabilitation programs, the primary attention is still given to security and custody. One must conclude that very few inmates acquire significant occupational training during their imprisonment. Wendt (1980) pointed out that vocational programs in correctional institutions are aimed at inmates with low-level educational backgrounds and assume that any type of job, even broom pushing, is sufficient to keep the ex-inmate on the straight and narrow. Deming and Gulliver (1981) described an exemplary program in five New York correctional facilities aimed at helping inmates begin or complete college-level training that will prepare them for professional careers. There is an obvious need nationwide for vocational preparatory programs ranging from secondary through university level that can use the period of incarceration to help inmates acquire salable skills.

Most prior offenders will need extensive personal counseling before effective career counseling can be initiated. In many cases, the factors that originally led the person into difficulty may still exist. These have often been compounded by the experiences of confinement, producing an explosive mixture of hostility, anger, and frustration.

The former inmate faces new challenges and difficulties on release. Few communities provide any type of reentry assistance such as halfway houses or other organized social services. Prospective employers or educational institutions often react negatively to the individual on learning about the prior record. Probation and parole officers are usually overloaded and often provide only cursory assistance. The resources available to assist in this difficult transition are generally very few, frequently of limited quality, and rarely able to overcome the opposing pressures.

Many would agree that prior offenders can often be described as the most disadvantaged of all groups that might carry that label. Individuals in the disadvantaged group often encounter barriers such as poor job qualifications, conflicts with others, legal and/or financial difficulties, and emotional problems. Each, if it exists, must be dealt with in the counseling process before serious career counseling can be successful. Some of these problems can be relieved by focusing first on establishing a series of short-term goals, finding appropriate role models, and building self-directedness and personal responsibility.

Midlife Changers

In Chapter 2 Super (1990) posited that people move through a maxicycle consisting of five stages: growth, exploration, establishment, maintenance, and decline. He also suggests that many people pass through several minicycles made up of these same stages as they change jobs throughout their lives. Bejian and Salamone (1995), drawing on the work of Murphy and Burck (1976), suggested that a sixth developmental stage occurs during the 35–45 age period, a stage they call midlife career renewal. Career renewal is a transitional stage and is a time for reevaluation and self-analysis that may lead the individual to change careers or to reaffirm his or her original career direction. The developmental tasks to be performed during the renewal stage are (1) reconsideration of the original career choice, (2) dealing with the polarities that may have developed in the personality, and (3) modifying the structure of one's life to fit the conclusions reached. Bejian and Salamone (1995) proceed to provide support for the validity of adding a sixth career development stage for both men and women. It should be noted that while the idea of a sixth developmental stage is relatively new, the tasks described by Bejian and Salamone parallel the substages of the minicycle posed by Super (1990). However, while Murphy and Burck suggest that renewal occurs within a certain period (midlife), Super suggests that a recycling of the career choice process (the minicycle) can occur several times throughout the life cycle.

The idea of a sixth developmental stage advanced by Bejian and Salamone, along with the ideas of Super (1990), certainly seem to provide viable explanations of what we will call voluntary midlife career change in this review. However, the first half of the decade of the nineties saw an unprecedented number of people at midlife who were forced to change jobs because of structural changes in the labor market, competition from foreign businesses, and many other factors. These workers, along with other groups that will be discussed in this section, are involuntary midlife career changers who are often involved with outplacement specialists and career counselors. Brown (1995a) suggests that these clients may need dramatically different types of assistance than voluntary changers because of the trauma associated with the job loss and the lack of planning for change. Midlife career change has increasingly been the subject of research, especially during the last decade. Several authors consider causes and emerging patterns, including Schlossberg's (1984) book. Articles that deal more briefly with the topic include

Armstrong (1981), Brown (1984), Kanchier and Unruh (1988), and Perosa and Perosa (1987). Stark and Zytowski (1988) provide a brief case study of a midlife counseling client's search for satisfying work. Finnegan, Westerfeld, and Elmore (1981) describe a workshop approach to helping midlife changers. Helping midlife individuals deal with job loss is discussed by Davenport (1984), Mallinckrodt and Fretz (1988), and Schlossberg and Leibowitz (1980).

In a previous section we contrasted the problems encountered by displaced homemakers with those of women who deliberately decide to go to work. One of the crises faced by the first group is recognition of tremendous life change brought about by factors over which they had little or no control. It seems logical to consider midlife changers as being somewhat similar to these two groups of women. Some find themselves faced suddenly, often unexpectedly, by change they would like to have go away; others, often with careful thought and planning, initiate change by their own intentional action. We discuss the two groups separately because they appear to face quite different problems.

Voluntary Changers

The deliberate decision to redirect one's career goals can be caused by many factors. Some of these reflect increased maturity and self-understanding, clearer identification of values and goals, changing needs, or perhaps the appearance of new opportunities. Levinson and associates (1978) found that most of their sample reviewed their past during the early forties and began to make new plans or confirm already developed plans.

One aspect that is likely to transpire in a period of reevaluation is matching earlier dreams and aspirations against present and potential realities to judge the possibility of reaching those early goals. When the discrepancy seems insurmountable, change is likely to occur. Thomas (1979) found that many of his sample gave up high-status positions to search for "more meaningful" work. Closely related to this is the recognition of change in interest and needs within the individual: The youthful desire for travel may become less intense after years on the road; the need to maintain an income may become less pressing once the mortgage is paid off, the children are independent, and investments begin to pay dividends.

Changing circumstances in one's work may also lead the worker to consider change. For example, revision of one's assignment, changes in company management, failure to win a desired promotion, relocation of the work site, anticipated changes in process or quality, and similar factors can produce a desire for change. Feelings of dissatisfaction may lead the worker to look for other options. Sometimes those new opportunities appear even when the worker feels content with the present position—for example, when a new industry moves to town or new educational opportunities make options available that previously appeared closed. Snyder, Howard, and Hammer (1978) indicate that an occupational change will occur when the attractiveness of the new opportunity plus the expectation of successful entry exceeds the pressure to remain in the current position.

A further factor might be called an *enabling option.* The increase in the number of two-income families, with approximately half of U.S. wives now employed for pay, decreases the financial pressure that previously deterred many men from contemplating any type of occupational change. The presence of the second income allows some room for risk taking. Also, a spouse who finds self-satisfaction and fulfillment in work may encourage the partner to look for similar compensations.

Most counselors would concur that individuals who are motivated by factors such as these are mostly acting from positions of strength and are likely to need limited help, if any. Clarification of personal values, needs, and goals may help some, especially the worker who feels dissatisfied and has not focused on the causes of discontent. Some may desire information about job requirements and opportunities or educational preparation needed to qualify in a particular occupation. Others may want information about job search procedures or how to start a business.

Vaitenas and Wiener (1977) reported some causes of midcareer change that may be less healthy than the aforementioned situations. They compared career changers and nonchangers in two age groups—a younger group (median age 29.4) and an older group (median age 43.0). They found significant differences between changers and nonchangers but not between age groups. The changers had less stable interest patterns, more emotional problems, and greater fear of failure. These results suggest that some changers are running away because of lack of self-understanding, inconsistent interest patterns, or concern that they will be unable to succeed in their jobs. Where these behavioral patterns are evident, there is need for personal counseling aimed at expanding self-understanding before any attention is given to career counseling (Bejian & Salomone, 1995).

Involuntary Changers

Like displaced homemakers, some workers suddenly find themselves in totally unexpected situations that they have never dreamed possible—their job is gone. Essentially, there are two conditions that account for most of the involuntary changers and a third, closely related, situation that we include here.

One example of involuntary change is that faced by the suddenly discharged worker. Some workers are fired because of incompetence or inability to meet the requirements of the job. Four out of five discharged workers are released because of their inability to get along with supervisors or fellow workers. Closely related to the discharged worker is the one who realizes that discharge is imminent and quits before the boss can announce the termination.

A second group of involuntary changers includes those whose job disappears because of technological change (structural unemployment), plant closing, or plant relocation. Whether the worker is fired from an ongoing job or caught in one that simply melts away, the result for the worker is the same.

Sandler (1988), responding to an earlier article by Kjos (1988), discussed her experiences with a 2-week workshop dealing with dislocated workers who ranged in age from 20 to 65. Although the workshop content focused on job-seeking skills and activities, one might reasonably expect that participation with a group in such activities might help to relieve some of the traumatic effects that job loss has on individuals. Hurst and Shepard (1986) described the experience as an emotional roller coaster ride for the dislocated worker. They identified grief, anger, panic, depression, and denial as typical feelings experienced by the worker caught in a plant closing and resultant displacement.

A third group of involuntary changers includes those engaged in what might be called early leaver occupations. These include many of those who participate in professional athletics, where the physical strength and stamina of youth is a crucial component and one is an oldtimer before age 40. Occupations in the public safety area involve high physical risk and therefore usually carry early compulsory retirement. Representative of these are occupations such as firefighter, police officer, and the military positions mentioned previously. Typically, workers in these positions qualify for retirement after 20 years of service, often by the time they reach 40. Although retirement may not be compulsory, and those who have advanced to managerial positions do stay on, the pension program is structured so that workers in lower-level positions cannot afford to continue.

Workers in early leaver occupations have ample opportunity to anticipate departure from the job. Many plan their careers in patterns similar to those of the voluntary changers by anticipating when the event will occur, preparing for the change by developing educational or other transitional activities, and moving on easily to the next stage of their lives.

Change and readjustment are most difficult for the worker confronted with unexpected job loss. Not only must the grief process be managed, but the suddenness of the event must be handled (Eby & Buch, 1995). Further, not anticipating such a drastic change probably means that one is totally unprepared for the whole affair of choosing a new field, perhaps preparing for it, engaging in the job search task, and reestablishing oneself again. The available options are quite narrow for most involuntary changers, who frequently are not prepared to make the decisions required to resolve the dilemma. The choices include only the following:

1. Find a comparable job at another local establishment using the same skills.
2. Relocate to a site where there is a demand for the worker's skill.
3. Seek a job locally that involves other skills, usually at a lower level, possessed by the worker. (This is what happens to most structurally unemployed manufacturing workers who gain reemployment in low-paying service jobs.)
4. Enter an educational or training program that will create new salable skills.
5. Remain unemployed.

The counselor must help the involuntary changer to work through grief, blame, self-accusation, and defeat and then assist in the process of identifying appropriate options and developing plans to pursue those options.

Older Workers

What is an older worker? The maxicycle described in Super's (1990) developmental model suggests that deceleration typically begins at age 60 with disengagement from work following thereafter. His model suggests that age 60 may be the line of demarcation between older and younger workers. However, the average 60-year-old male has a life expectancy of 17 years, and females the same age can expect to live an additional 25 years. However, many 60-year-olds are at the peak of their careers and do not consider themselves to be older workers.

The Age Discrimination in Employment Act adopted in 1967 and amended in 1986 prohibits discrimination against workers older than 40, and thus anyone who is 40 or older is legally an older worker. Age, like beauty, is very much in the eye of the beholder. For purposes of this discussion we have arbitrarily adopted Super's (1990) idea that one becomes an older worker at about age 60.

The stereotype of older workers spending their golden years playing golf, fishing, traveling, and grandparenting is as faulty as most stereotypes. According to the Bureau of Labor Statistics (BLS, 1997), more than 3.8 million people over age 65 are in the labor force. Moreover, there are 8.7 million workers over the age of 55 in the labor force and this is projected to grow to 11.7 million by 2005.

It is worth noting that some older workers who are in the labor force are reentry workers. Many of them have retired at least once and found it to be an unsatisfactory experience. One in three workers who retire return to work within a year (Brown, 1995b). While the median age of retirement has decreased steadily to 62 since 1950 when it was 67, it may well be that a greater proportion of older workers will remain in the labor force beyond this age in the future. Changes in Social Security and Medicare benefits will make it mandatory that more workers stay in the work force to protect their economic well-being. The elimination of compulsory retirement in all but a few occupations will also contribute to people staying in the labor force beyond the traditional retirement age. However, the decision to stay in the labor force is not purely an economic one. Most older workers continue in their careers for the same reasons that younger workers do: financial need, desire to improve the quality of their lives and the lives of others around them, fellowship with other workers, social status, desire to make a contribution to society, maintaining a sense of self-worth, and simply having something to do. A study by Soumerai and Avorn (1983) found that retirees who engaged in part-time work reported higher levels of happiness, better health, and greater overall satisfaction with their lives than did a nonworking control group. Cahill and Salamone (1987) suggested that there is not enough research to establish a link between working and life satisfaction for older workers, but judging by the outcomes of the Soumerai and Avorn research and the fact that tens of thousands of older workers return to some form of work after retirement, we can conclude that for may older workers engaging in some form of work is important to their well-being.

This section focuses on the process of helping older workers change careers. Books such as Marsh's (1991) *Retirement Careers* attempt to help "working retirees" combine work and pleasure by identifying new careers that provide flexible schedules. This book, along with others (e.g., Brown, 1995b), has identified some of the problems associated with changing careers later in one's life. One problem older workers experience is age discrimination (Cahill & Salamone, 1987). The American Association of Retired Persons has sponsored two studies that explore the extent of age discrimination in the workplace. In the first of these studies the Gallup Organization polled 1300 workers over the age of 40. Six percent of the respondents reported experiencing age discrimination directly (AARP, 1989). In the second study, Bendick, Jackson, and Romero (1993) sent nearly identical resumes of two fictional workers, one 32 years old and one 57 years old, to a randomly selected national sample of 775 large firms and employment agencies. They concluded that the older worker with identical job qualifications received less favorable responses approximately one-quarter of the time than did the "younger" counterpart. The researchers also concluded that job application strategies that de-emphasize age and that emphasize the youthful qualities of the applicant are superior to strategies that emphasize the importance of experience and maturity in the job hunt for older workers.

While two studies do not offer conclusive evidence that age discrimination exists, it does support the long-held belief that employers respond less positively to older workers. The number of age discrimination suits filed in federal and state courts indicates than an increasing number of older workers are less inclined to accept discrimination. In 1980, 11,397 suits were brought against employers for age discrimination. In 1990 this number had risen to 24,110 (EEOC, 1989).

Career development specialists must prepare workers to deal with the following myths (AARP, 1993; Brown, 1995b):

1. Older workers have more health problems; they have higher absentee rates.
2. Older workers are inflexible.
3. Older workers are less productive than younger workers.
4. Older workers are likely to be unhappy in jobs for which they are "over-qualified."
5. Older workers will be unhappy working for a younger supervisor.
6. Older workers have diminished strength and learning capacity.

Of the six beliefs listed above, only one has any basis in fact. It is true that the older the worker the greater the likelihood that major health problems will occur. For this reason Brown (1995b) suggested that older workers who wish to change jobs (1) focus on improving their appearance by losing weight, (2) go on an exercise program that includes both lower-body and upper-body exercise, (3) have a physical examination and take the results with them to job interviews as one means of preempting this concern, and (4) use health insurance benefits from previous employment to offset the cost of insurance on a new job when possible. Older workers also need to know that, as a group, they have the lowest incidence of all mental health problems except depression, and thus the costs associated with mental health problems will be lower for them than for younger workers. Finally, older workers have better attendance records than younger workers who often have to miss work because of dependents.

With regard to the the misconceptions listed above, the unfortunate thing is that many older workers have internalized them. Therefore, the first task for the career counselor to undertake may be to help the older clients identify and eliminate some of their own beliefs about themselves. In order to counter their own stereotypical thoughts, older workers need to know the following (AARP, 1993; Brown, 1995b):

1. As we age our personality traits do become more fixed; however, if we were flexible as a young person we become more flexible as an older person. The point is that the traits that make us good young workers as well as poor young workers become more salient as we age.

2. Older workers are as productive as younger workers, and in some instances more productive.

3. Being overqualified for a job may be a source of unhappiness for an older worker. However, because older workers sometimes take jobs to supplement existing income such as Social Security or pensions, they may be more interested in factors such as flexibility of schedule than their qualifications to do the job.

4. The characteristics of the supervisor will be the most important determinant of the supervisory relationship, not the age of the supervisor.

5. There is evidence that brain cells are destroyed as we age. However, unless older workers have Alzheimer's disease or dementia, they learn just as well as younger persons, primarily because they have developed successful learning strategies as they aged.

6. Strength decline is more a function of lack of exercise than it is of age, at least up to a point. However, few jobs in our labor force require unusual strength, and thus the absence or presence of strength is typically not a limiting factor.

7. It is true that some of the senses, namely sight and hearing, decline with age. Compensatory devices make these losses of negligible importance in the performance of all but a few jobs.

The process of changing careers or reentering the work force is little different for older workers than it is for younger workers, with the possible exception that consideration of other life roles in the job selection, particularly leisure, may be more important (Brown, 1995b). Once choices are made, many older workers will require substantial assistance with the development of employability skills because they may have not been involved in a job hunt for many years. For example, older workers may have developed the skills and personal flexibility needed to hold several jobs and they may need several resumes as a result. Fortunately in this day of personal computers this is easy to accomplish. They also need to develop interviewing skills that will help them counteract the misconceptions about older workers listed earlier in this section. AARP (Stern, 1993) has been quite active in providing assistance to the older job hunter, both in the development of materials and in the sponsorship of workshops for employability skills development. Books such as Schwarz's (1993) *Successful Recareering,* Brown's (1995b) *How to Choose a Job upon Retirement,* and materials developed by AARP (1992) such as *Returning to the Job Market: A Woman's Guide to Employment Planning* can also serve as valuable sources of information for the older job hunter.

Job clubs, which have been mentioned throughout this section, may be a useful means of helping older workers find jobs. Hitchcock (1984) describes a report by Gray (1983) of the results of using a job club with elderly job seekers. He worked with a group of 46 males and females, about half of them between 50 and 62, and half older than 62. The job club operated in the usual fashion. Individuals established concrete personal job goals, explained their goals to the group, reported regularly on achievement or failure in the search process, and maintained support from the group throughout their search. Gray reported that, at the end of the experiment, job club members had significantly higher employment rates than the control group, who had been referred to the state employment security agency.

Of course, a job club is not the automatic answer to placement of older workers. It is, instead, only one technique that is possible. The point is that older workers, like any other group of individuals who want to work and have usable skills, can be helped to find employment that is satisfying to them and to society.

Summary

The focus in this chapter has been on several groups for whom the usual career development pattern does not apply. Consideration has been given to why the individual differs, as well as to how the career development helper can assist the individual.

Clients with physical or other restrictions find some occupations inaccessible because the work requires a physical act they are unable to perform. Vocational rehabilitation services can assist the person in preparing for activities that do not require that particular physical act. Economically disadvantaged clients can obtain training or other services to compensate for the restriction they are experiencing.

Individuals with different cultural backgrounds need counselors who can understand and help bridge the cultural differences, and who can assist the individual in recognizing and understanding the cultural climate of the workplace.

Some individuals enter the workplace at a later time in life than typical members of their age group. Examples include the woman who devoted her early posteducation years to homemaking and childrearing, the individual who spent some years in military assignments before moving to civilian life, and the individual who has been released from a penal institution. All must be helped to understand the world of work as it exists at the time of their entrance into it. They also usually need help in dealing with the age differential between themselves and other entering workers.

Other workers face major occupational change at midcareer periods. Those who initiate such changes voluntarily need primary help in the transitional process. Those who find themselves unexpectedly switching jobs may need help in dealing with factors related to the change process: grief over loss of the old job; readjustment to a new, undesired situation; and learning how to seek and find a new position.

The final group considered in this chapter was those who are approaching or have reached the usual retirement age, but who either wish to or are forced to continue to work. They may need help in developing realistic plans that fit their physical, emotional, and economic conditions.

Every person seeking career development help can be best served when attention is focused on the interaction between personal characteristics and the total environment in which that person exists.

References

AARP. (1989). *Work and retirement: Employees over 40 and their views.* Washington, DC: American Association of Retired Persons.

AARP. (1992). *Returning to the job market: A woman's guide to employment planning.* Washington, DC: American Association of Retired Persons.

AARP. (1993). *America's changing work force: Statistics in brief.* Washington, DC: American Association of Retired Persons.

Ahia, C. E. (1984). Cross-cultural counseling concerns. *Personnel and Guidance Journal, 62,* 339–341.

Arbona, C. (1995). Theory and research on racial and ethnic minorities: Hispanic Americans. In F. T. L. Leong (Ed.), *Career development and vocational behavior of ethnic and racial minorities* (pp. 37–66). Mawah, NJ: Lawrence Erlbaum.

Armstrong, J. C. (1981). Decision behavior and outcome of midlife career changers. *Vocational Guidance Quarterly, 29,* 205–212.

Arrendondo–Dowd, P. M., & Gonsalves, J. (1980). Preparing culturally effective counselors. *Personnel and Guidance Journal, 58,* 657–661.

Bejian, D. V., & Salamone, P. R. (1995). Understanding midlife renewal: Implications for counseling. *Career Development Quarterly, 44,* 52–63.

Berkell, D. E., & Brown, J. M. (Eds.). (1989). *Transition from school to work for persons with disabilities.* New York: Longman.

Bendick, M., Jr., Jackson, C. W., & Romero, J. H. (1993). *Employment discrimination against older workers: An experimental study.* Washington, DC: Fair Employment Council of Greater Washington, Inc.

BLS. (1997). News: United States Department of Labor. Washington, DC: Bureau of Labor Statistics.

Bowen, N. H. (1982). Guidelines for career counseling with abused women. *Vocational Guidance Quarterly, 31,* 123–127.

Brown, D. (1984). Mid-life career change. In D. Brown, L. Brooks, & associates (Eds.), *Career choice and development.* San Francisco: Jossey-Bass.

Brown, D. (1995a). A values-based approach to facilitating career transitions. *Career Development Quarterly, 44,* 4–11.

Brown, D. (1995b). *How to choose a career upon retirement.* Lincolnwood, IL: VGM Books.

Brown, D. (1997). Brown's values-based theory of career and life-role choice and satisfaction: A revision focused on the work role. Chapel Hill, NC: Unpublished manuscript.

Brown, D. (1998). *Dropping out or hanging in: What you should know before you leave school, Leader's manual* (2nd ed.). Lincolnwood, IL: NTC Publishing.

Brown, D., & Minor, C. W. (Eds.). (1992). *Report of second Gallup survey: Focus on minorities.* Alexandria, VA: NCDA.

Bureau of National Affairs. (1986). *Source work and family—A changing dynamic.* Washington, DC: Author.

Cahill, M., & Salomone, P. R. (1987). Career counseling for worklife extension: Integrating the older worker into the labor force. *Career Development Quarterly, 35,* 188–196.

Carter, R. T. (1991). Cultural values: A review of empirical research and implications for counseling. *Journal of Counseling and Development, 70,* 164–173.

Casas, J. M., & Arbona, C. (1992). Hispanic career related issues and research: A diverse perspective. In D. Brown & C. W. Minor (Eds.), *Report of second Gallup survey: Focus on minorities.* Alexandria, VA: NCDA.

Cheatham, H. E. (1990). Afrocentricity and career development of African Americans. *Career Development Quarterly, 38,* 334–346.

Chubon, R. A. (1985). Career-related needs of school children with severe physical disabilities. *Journal of Counseling and Development, 64,* 47–51.

Chusmir, L. H. (1983). Characteristics and predictive dimensions of women who make non-traditional vocational choices. *Personnel and Guidance Journal, 62,* 43–47.

Curnow, T. C. (1989). Vocational development of persons with disability. *Career Development Quarterly, 37,* 269–278.

Dahl, P. R. (1982). Maximizing vocational opportunities for handicapped clients. *Vocational Guidance Quarterly, 31,* 43–52.

Davenport, D. W. (1984). Outplacement counseling: Whither the counselor. *Vocational Guidance Quarterly, 32,* 185–191.

Deming, A. L., & Gulliver, K. (1981). Career planning in prison: Ex-inmates help inmates. *Vocational Guidance Quarterly, 30,* 78–83.

Eby, L. T., & Buch, K. (1995). Job loss as career growth: Involuntary career transitions. *Career Development Quarterly, 44,* 26–42.

EEOC. (1991). *Fiscal year 1991 report.* Washington, DC: A U.S. Equal Employment Opportunity Commission.

Ekstrom, R. B., Beier, J. J., Davis, E. L., & Gruenberg, C. B. (1981). Career and educational counseling implications of women's life experience learning. *Personnel and Guidance Journal, 60,* 97–100.

Fagan, T. K., & Jenkins, W. M. (1989). People with disabilities: An update. *Journal of Counseling and Development, 68,* 140–144.

Fagan, T. K., & Wallace, A. (1979). Who are the handicapped? *Personnel and Guidance Journal, 58,* 215–220.

Farmer, H. S. (1985). Model of career and achievement motivation for women and men. *Journal of Counseling Psychology, 32,* 363–389.

Finnegan, R., Westerfeld, J., & Elmore, R. (1981). A model for midlife career—Decision-making workshop. *Vocational Guidance Quarterly, 30,* 69–72.

Fitzgerald, L. F., & Betz, N. (1994). Career development in a cultural context. In M. L. Savickas & R. W. Lent (Eds.), *Convergence in career development theories* (pp. 103–118). Palo Alto, CA: CPP Books.

Fox, J. H. (1985). Continuities in the experience of aging. In E. B. Palmore (Ed.), *Normal aging III.* Durham, NC: Duke University Press.

Fukuyama, M. A. (1992). Asian-Pacific Islanders and career development. In D. Brown and C. W. Minor (Eds.), *Report of second Gallup survey: Focus on minorities*. Alexandria, VA: NCDA.

GAO. (1995). *Vocational education: 2-year colleges improve programs, maintain access for special populations*. Washington, DC: General Accounting Office.

Gerson, B., & Lee, S. (1982). Women and career competence: A theoretical and experiential model. *Personnel and Guidance Journal, 61*, 236–238.

Giles, H. C. (1990). Counseling Haitian students and their families: Issues and interventions. *Journal of Counseling and Development, 68*, 317–320.

Gim, R. H., Atkinson, D. R., & Kim, S. J. (1991). Asian-American acculturation, counselor ethnicity and cultural sensitivity, and ratings of counselors. *Journal of Counseling Psychology, 38*, 57–62.

Ginzberg, E. (1983). Life without work: Does it make sense? In H. S. Parnes (Ed.), *Policy issues in work and retirement*. Kalamazoo, MI: W. E. Upjohn Institute for Employment Research.

Gray, D. (1983). A job club for older job seekers: An experimental evaluation. *Journal of Gerontology, 38*, 363–368.

Grealish, C. A., & Salomone, P. R. (1986). Devaluing those with disability: Take responsibility, take action. *Vocational Guidance Quarterly, 34*, 147–150.

Guidubaldi, J., Perry, J. D., & Walker, M. (1989). Assessment strategies for students with disabilities. *Journal of Counseling and Development, 68*, 160–165.

Hadley, R. G., & Brodwin, M. G. (1988). Language about people with disabilities. *Journal of Counseling and Development, 67*, 147–149.

Hagner, D., & Salomone, P. R. (1989). Issues in career decision making for workers with developmental disabilities. *Career Development Quarterly, 38*, 148–159.

Harris, L., & associates (1981). *Aging in the eighties: America in transition*. Washington, DC: National Council on the Aging.

Haverkamp, B. E., & Moore, D. (1993). The career-personal dichotomy: Perceptual reality, practical illusion, and workplace integration. *Career Development Quarterly, 42*, 154–160.

Heinrich, R. K., Corbine, J. L., & Thomas, K. R. (1990). Counseling native Americans. *Journal of Counseling and Development, 69*, 128–133.

Hitchcock, A. A. (1984). Work, aging, and counseling. *Journal of Counseling and Development, 63*, 258–259.

Ho, D. Y. F. (1995). Internal culture, culturocentrism, and transcendence. *The Counseling Psychologist, 23*, 4–24.

Hotchkiss, L., & Borow, H. (1996). Sociological perspective on work and career development. In. D. Brown, L. Brooks, and Associates. *Career choice and development* (3rd ed., pp. 281–336). San Francisco: Jossey-Bass.

Humes, C. W., & Hohenshil, T. A. (1985). Career development and career education for handicapped students: A reexamination. *Vocational Guidance Quarterly, 34*, 31–40.

Hurst, J. B., & Shepard, J. W. (1986). The dynamics of plant closings: An extended emotional roller coaster ride. *Journal of Counseling and Development, 64*, 401–405.

Kahn, S. E. (1983). Development and operation of the Women's Employment Counseling Unit. *Vocational Guidance Quarterly, 32*, 125–129.

Kanchier, C., & Unruh, W. R. (1988). The career cycle meets the life cycle. *Career Development Quarterly, 37*, 127–137.

Karayanni, M. (1987). The impact of cultural background on vocational interests. *Career Development Quarterly, 36*, 81–90.

Kjos, D. L. (1988). Job search activity patterns of successful and unsuccessful job seekers. *Journal of Employment Counseling, 25,* 4–6.

Kraus, L. E., & Stoddard, S. (1989). *Chartbook on disability in the United States.* Washington, DC: U.S. National Institute on Disability and Rehabilitation Research.

Lee, D. J. (1984). Counseling and culture: Some issues. *Personnel and Guidance Journal, 62,* 592–597.

Leong, F. T. L. (Ed.). (1995a). *Career development and vocational behavior of ethnic minorities.* Mahwah, NJ: Lawrence Erlbaum.

Leong, F. T. L., & Hayes, T. J. (1990). Occupational stereotyping of Asian Americans. *Career Development Quarterly, 39,* 143–154.

Levinson, D. J., Darrow, C. N., Klein, E. B., Levinson, M. H., & McKee, B. (1978). *The seasons of a man's life.* New York: Knopf.

Levinson, E. M. (1984). A vocationally oriented secondary school program for the emotionally disturbed. *Vocational Guidance Quarterly, 33,* 76–81.

Mallinckrodt, B., & Fretz, B. R. (1988). Social support and the impact of job loss on older professionals. *Journal of Counseling Psychology, 35,* 281–286.

Marsh, D. L. (1991). *Retirement careers.* Charlotte, VT: Williamson.

Marshall, J. (1983). Reducing the effects of work oriented values on the lives of male American workers. *Vocational Guidance Quarterly, 32,* 109–115.

Mather, J. (1994). Computers, automation and the employment of the blind and visually impaired. *Journal of Visual Impairment and Blindness, 88,* 544–549.

McGraw, L. K. (1982). A selective review of programs and counseling interventions for the reentry woman. *Personnel and Guidance Journal, 60,* 469–472.

Melamed, T. (1995). Career success: The moderating effects of gender. *Journal of Vocational Behavior, 47,* 295–314.

Melamed, T. (1996). Career success: An assessment of a gender-specific model. *Journal of Occupational and Organizational Psychology, 69,* 217–226.

Miles, J. H. (1984). Serving the career guidance needs of the economically disadvantaged. In N. C. Gysbers & associates (Eds.), *Designing careers.* San Francisco, CA: Jossey-Bass.

Murphy, P., & Burck, H. (1976). Career development of men at midlife. *Journal of Vocational Behavior, 9,* 337–343.

Parker, R. M. (Ed.). (1987). *Rehabilitation counseling: Basics and beyond.* Austin, TX: Pro-Ed.

Perosa, S. L., & Perosa, L. M. (1987). Strategies for counseling midcareer changers: A conceptual framework. *Journal of Counseling and Development, 65,* 558–561.

Pickering, G. S., & Galvin–Schaefers, K. (1988). An empirical study of reentry women. *Journal of Counseling Psychology, 35,* 298–303.

Ponterotto, J. G., & Casas, J. M. (1991). *Handbook of racial/ethnic minority research.* Springfield, IL: Thomas.

Read, N. O., Elliott, M. R., Escobar, M. D., & Slaney, R. B. (1988). The effects of marital status and motherhood on the career concerns of reentry women. *Career Development Quarterly, 37,* 46–55.

Robinson, S. L., Rotter, M. F., & Wilson, J. (1982). Mothers' contemporary career decisions: Impact on the family. *Personnel and Guidance Journal, 60,* 535–537.

Roessler, R. T. (1987). Work, disability, and the future: Promoting employment for people with disabilities. *Journal of Counseling and Development, 66,* 188–190.

Ross, D. B. (1984). A cross-cultural comparison of adult development. *Personnel and Guidance Journal, 62,* 418–420.

Rosser-Hogan, R. (1990). Making counseling culturally appropriate: Intervention with a Montagnard refugee. *Journal of Counseling and Development, 68,* 443–445.

Rubin, S. E., & Roessler, R. T. (1987). *Foundations of the vocational rehabilitation process* (3rd ed.). Austin, TX: Pro Ed.

Rubin, S. E., & Rubin, N. M. (Eds.). (1988). *Contemporary challenges to the rehabilitation counseling profession.* Baltimore: Brookes.

Sandler, S. B. (1988). Dislocated workers: A response. *Journal of Employment Counseling, 25,* 146–148.

Savickas, M. L. (1991). Improving career time perspective. In D. Brown & L. Brooks, *Career Counseling Techniques* (pp. 236–249). Boston: Allyn & Bacon.

Schlossberg, N. K. (1984). *Counseling adults in transition: Linking practice with theory.* New York: Springer.

Schlossberg, N. K., & Leibowitz, Z. (1980). Organizational support systems as buffers to job loss. *Journal of Vocational Behavior, 17,* 204–217.

Schwarz, J. A. (1993). *Successful recareering.* Hawthorne, NJ: Career Press.

Shifron, R., Dye, A., & Shifron, G. (1983). Implications for counseling the unemployed in a recessionary economy. *Personnel and Guidance Journal, 61,* 527–529.

Skinner, M. E., & Schenck, S. J. (1992). Counseling the college bound student with a learning disability. *School Counselor, 39,* 369–376.

Slaney, R. B., & Dickson, R. D. (1985). Relation of career indecision to career exploration with reentry women: A treatment and follow-up study. *Journal of Counseling Psychology, 32,* 355–362.

Snyder, R., Howard, A., & Hammer, T. (1978). Mid-career change in academia: The decision to become an administrator. *Journal of Vocational Behavior, 13,* 229–241.

Soumerai, S. B., & Avorn, J. (1983). Perceived health, life satisfaction, and activity in urban elderly: A controlled study of the impact of part-time work. *Journal of Gerontology, 38,* 356–362.

Stark, S., & Zytowski, D. G. (1988). Searching for the glass slipper: A case study in midlife career counseling. *Journal of Counseling and Development, 66,* 474–476.

Stern, L. (1993). Modern maturity report: How to find a job. *Modern Maturity, 36,* 24–43.

Stern, V., & Dubois, P. (1994). *A career planning guide for college students with disabilities and the advocates who work with them* (2nd ed.). Washington, DC: American Institute for Research.

Stumpf, S. A. (1984). Adult career development: Individual and organization factors. In N. C. Gysbers & associates (Eds.), *Designing careers.* San Francisco, CA: Jossey-Bass.

Sue, D. W., Bernier, J. E., Durran, A., Feinberg, L., Petersen, P., Smith, E. J., & Vasquez–Nutall, E. (1982). Position paper: Cross-cultural counseling competencies. *The Counseling Psychologist, 10* (2), 45–52.

Sue, D. W., & Sue, D. (1990). *Counseling the culturally different* (2nd ed.). New York: Wiley.

Sundal-Hansen, L. S. (1985). Work-family linkages: Neglected factor in career guidance across cultures. *Vocational Guidance Quarterly, 33,* 202–212.

Super, D. E. (1990). A life-span, life-space approach to career development. In D. Brown, L. Brooks, & associates, *Career choice and development* (2nd ed.). San Francisco: Jossey-Bass.

Thomas, K. R., & Berven, N. L. (1984). Providing career counseling for individuals with handicapping conditions. In N. C. Gysbers & associates (Eds.), *Designing careers.* San Francisco: Jossey-Bass.

Thomas, L. E. (1979). Causes of mid-life change from high status careers. *Vocational Guidance Quarterly, 27,* 202–208.

Thomason, T. C. (1995). Introduction to counseling American Indians. Flagstaff, AZ: American Indian Rehabilitation Research and Training Center.

Vaitenas, R., & Wiener, Y. (1977). Development, emotional, and interest factors in voluntary mid-career change. *Journal of Vocational Behavior, 11,* 291–304.

Wade, P., & Bernstein, B. L. (1991). Culture sensitivity training and counselor's race: Effects on black female clients' perceptions and attrition. *Journal of Counseling Psychology, 38,* 9–15.

Webb, N. M. (1983). Cross-cultural awareness: A framework for interaction. *Personnel and Guidance Journal, 61,* 498–500.

Wendt, J. A. (1980, February 21). "Going straight" means bumpy road. *APGA Guidepost,* pp. 1, 7.

Zawada, M. A. (1980). Displaced homemakers: Unresolved issues. *Personnel and Guidance Journal, 59,* 110–112.

Zunker, V. G. (1986). *Using assessment results in career counseling* (2nd ed.). Monterey, CA: Brooks/Cole.

CHAPTER 13

Testing and Assessment in Career Development

The original model of vocational development set forth by Frank Parsons in 1909 emphasized the importance of "personal analysis" to promote individual self-understanding. The trait and factor model of vocational development, which was built on Parsons's tripartite model, focused the science of psychology on the development of tests and inventories to promote personal analysis and became such a pervasive influence on vocational counseling that they became inextricably linked.

In 1972 Goldman observed that the marriage between testing and counseling had failed and that it was time to look for other approaches to facilitating growth and development. Specifically, Goldman raised concerns about the use of tests and inventories to predict vocational success and/or satisfaction. Goldman's criticism had been voiced earlier by Crites (1969) and has been rehashed since by Ivey (1982) and Weinrach (1979). However, Prediger (1974) took a different path. He discussed how the "failed marriage" between tests and inventories could be revived by using comprehensive assessment programs, providing test results to help those being tested bridge the gap between the tests results and career choice implementation, and relying more on self-administered and self-interpreted instruments.

More recently, Healy (1990) contended that the traditional trait and factor approaches to testing and assessment have had certain shortcomings that are inconsistent with the goal of promoting client growth and development. One of these inconsistencies is that people being assessed are placed in a dependent role because, typically, the assessment devices are selected by counselors. Healy also contended that trait and factor approaches to assessment do not strengthen clients' abilities to assess their own strengths and weaknesses, which he believes is inconsistent with the ideal of promoting independence. Moreover, relying on tests and inventories as the principal personal assessment tool denies the influence of environmental and contextual (e.g., work setting) variables, such as qualities of supervision, that may interact with clients' characteristics. Finally, Healy criticizes traditional approaches to assessment because they emphasize helping clients find careers that "fit" them rather than actively involve them in identifying and implementing a career choice.

Healy enumerates certain remedies for the problems he sees with traditional approaches to assessment. For example, he suggests that clients be prepared to act as collaborators in the appraisal process by giving them more information about appraisal and its potential use in career choice and implementation. Counselors should also accentuate the development of self-assessment skills such as the ability to estimate aptitudes. Not surprisingly, Healy advocates that clients be made more aware of how their characteristics interact with workplace variables and how these interactions may influence their performance and ultimately their success or failure. Healy believes that in addition to the foregoing reforms in the appraisal process, there is a need to design new approaches to appraisal devices that will not only improve decision making but the implementation of decisions as well.

The degree to which clients are involved as collaborators engaged in developing self-evaluation skills, including the utilization of assessment data to make as well as implement choices, will depend on a number of variables. For example, one application of career development assessment is to facilitate exploration and planning over a period of time, as opposed to providing information for decision making at a specific point in time (Prediger, 1974). In the former, assessment is used to promote readiness by developing self-awareness, whereas in the latter the use of assessment data is to inform decision making and implementation of decisions once made. Prediger (1974) also pointed out that counselors may use assessment devices to diagnose various aspects of students' (and presumably nonstudents') career development for the purpose of designing programs to meet career needs. For example, counselors might give an interest inventory to ninth graders to stimulate self-awareness. This inventory might be selected, administered, and interpreted by counselors because only the most preliminary career decisions are being made at the time the inventory is administered and assessment of large numbers of students precludes the use of highly individualized strategies. On the other hand, a career counselor working with a college senior who is deciding among various career options could implement all of Healy's (1990) suggestions.

As noted above, criticisms of the philosophy and practice of traditional assessment have been prevalent. Goldman (1972, 1982) has criticized tests because they are mechanistic and reductionistic. Tyler (1978), another early proponent of tests, criticized them because they encourage competition rather than foster development. Tests and inventories have also been criticized because of gender and racial bias (Cronbach, 1984; Lonner, 1988) and for a host of other reasons. However, as Lonner concluded, psychologists, counselors, and others have developed a large number of appraisal devices that are constantly being used to measure not only values, aptitudes, and personality variables but a host of other variables. The challenge is to be aware of the issues surrounding tests and use them for the benefit of those being served.

Types of Assessment

Assessment procedures used in career development programming and career counseling can be classified as objective, qualitative, and clinical. In clinical assessment the counselor synthesizes data from various assessment sources and makes diagnoses and/or predictions. Clinical diagnoses are often based on a combination of objective and qualitative assessments as well as the counselor's hunches or intuition about the client (Goldman, 1961). In this chapter, only objective and qualitative assessment approaches are discussed, primarily because understanding these approaches is basic to career counseling and development. Clinical assessment is discussed in Chapter 14.

Objective assessment devices are those most familiar to readers because they have taken achievement tests, the Scholastic Aptitude Test, or other similar tests as they progressed through public schools. Most readers will also have completed inventories that measure interests, values, or personality. These are also objective assessment devices. Tests are presumed to be measures of maximum or optimal performance, while inventories are presumed to measure typical performance. However, both tests and inventories have standardized administration and scoring procedures. Typically, tests are time-limited, although power tests are not timed. Inventories are usually not time-limited.

Tests and inventories may be paper-and-pencil tests or may have been adapted for computer administration and/or scoring. Today even paper-and-pencil versions of tests and inventories are typically "machine" scored and the profile of results is computer generated. Sampson (1990) identified a number of distinct trends as they relate to computer applications in testing. Among the most salient of these are the use of computer-based interpretational systems to support the interpretations made by practitioners, the use of computers to generate cutoff scores when aptitude tests are used as the basis for job or educational placement decisions, and the use of computer-controlled videodisc technology to reduce dialectic and language barriers in the interpretation process. Sampson also notes that adaptive devices such as braille keyboards are being used to enable some people with disabilities to take tests with relatively little assistance.

Qualitative assessment approaches, in contrast to objective approaches, are bound by less rigid parameters. For example, there may be no standardized set of directions and the "scoring" is more subjective; in fact, often there is no scoring at all. The results of these devices are not profiled, and they are interpreted ideographically as opposed to normatively. Goldman (1990) points out that qualitative assessments tend to involve clients more actively than standardized or objective tests and inventories since the objective approach gives the client very little voice in where or how the instrument will be administered and scored. Goldman goes on to identify several qualitative assessment devices including card sorts, values clarifications exercises, simulations such as the use of work samples, and observations.

Some of the "qualitative" devices identified by Goldman (1990) can be developed into objective approaches to assessment. For example, Jones (1981) has developed a card sort, *Occ-U-Sort,* to measure Holland's (1985) personality types that has a well-defined set of instructions and scoring procedures. Similarly, behavioral psychologists have developed highly sophisticated observational systems, as well as procedures for establishing interobserver reliability, that are as standardized as any test or inventory.

Throughout the history of the career counseling and development movement, objective or standardized tests have been emphasized (Brown, 1990). However, some of the earliest writings (e.g., Williamson, 1939) about career counseling also discussed qualitative methods of assessment such as job shadowing, which was used to help individuals "assess" their potential interests in, and aptitude for, a particular occupation. Perhaps what is different is that there are currently more qualitative assessment approaches available than ever before. Role play, self-efficacy assessment, and cognitive assessment are all strategies. Some of these qualitative assessment devices are potentially very useful.

Assessment is a major field of academic study with many facets. There are literally hundreds of quantitative and qualitative assessment approaches that could be included in this chapter. The question is, "What to include?" A few of the most useful qualitative assessment devices are discussed in this chapter. The qualitative assessment devices discussed were selected on the basis of the authors' perceptions of the utility of these devices in career development programming and counseling. The tests and inventories included were selected to a large degree on the basis of three surveys (Engen, Lamb, & Prediger, 1982; Kapes & Mastie, 1988; Zytowski & Warman, 1982). These authors examined the professionals' use and perceptions of various instruments used to assess interest, aptitudes, career development, and values. A few inventories that did not surface on any of these lists are also discussed, as are some instruments that may be useful in assessing certain decisional problems, such as career indecisiveness.

Qualitative Assessment Devices

As noted earlier, qualitative assessment devices are those that do not possess a standardized set of directions and are not objectively scored. They are an extension of the counselor's clinical skill and to some extent require clinical skill to interpret. Four qualitative assessment devices are discussed in this chapter: (1) self-efficacy measurements, (2) role playing, (3) card sorts, and (4) the genogram.

Self-Efficacy Measurements

Self-efficacy is the individual's judgment regarding ability to perform a task at a certain level (Bandura, 1977). These self-efficacy cognitions mediate action with the result that individuals avoid tasks or activities that they believe are beyond their capabilities and engage in those that they judge themselves capable of performing (Bandura, 1986). Betz and Hacket (1981, 1986) were the first to emphasize the importance of self-efficacy expectations on career decision making and, drawing on Bandura's work (1977, 1986), set forth a model of career decision making based primarily on this construct. Self-efficacy has traditionally been measured by first identifying a task to be performed (e.g., complete algebra successfully), then asking clients to estimate the degree of difficulty of the task and the extent of their confidence that they can perform the task, and then estimating their performance in related situations (range) (Bandura, 1986).

The following is an example of how self-efficacy expectations might be assessed during career counseling.

Counselor: We have been discussing engineering as a possible career option for you. On a one-to-ten scale, with one being extremely difficult, how would you rate the difficulty of engineering?

Client: A ten—definitely a ten.

Counselor: Then how confident are you that you can complete an engineering curriculum with at least a 2.5 GPA, again using the one-to-ten scale, with one being very confident and ten being extremely confident?

Client: That's tough. Probably a seven. I'm pretty good in math and science.

Counselor: OK, just one more rating. We've discussed several options that are related to engineering, such as engineering technology, architecture, and industrial relations. Using the one-to-ten scale, how would you rate your confidence that you can enter and complete courses of study in these areas?

Client: Engineering technology a ten, definitely, architecture, a five or a six. I'm just not sure I can do some of the things that are needed. Industrial relations probably a nine or a ten.

Self-efficacy ratings can be used on an ongoing basis to assess the clients' perceptions of their ability to find information about jobs, complete interviews with workers, or even complete career counseling successfully.

It is possible to measure self-efficacy more objectively, as Rotberg (1984, pp. 96–98) did. As can be seen in Figure 13.1, individuals were asked to rate their perceived ability to perform certain types of careers. The instrument shown in Figure 13.1 contains careers that are traditionally female, male, and androgenous; that is, occupations that have a balance of males and females in them. This type of assessment device could be used to determine if people perceive themselves in a stereotypical fashion.

FIGURE 13.1   A Career Self-Efficacy Rating Scale: Certainty of Performing Job Duties

Please complete the following by indicating how certain you are that you could, if you elected to do so, perform the duties involved in the following occupations by circling a number on the scale provided. One (1) indicates that you are very uncertain that you could perform the task and five (5) indicates that you are very certain that you could perform the task.

1. *Secondary School Teacher:* Instructs junior or senior high school students, usually in a specific subject.

1	2	3	4	5
Very Uncertain		Somewhat Certain		Very Certain

2. *Psychologists:* Concerned with the collection, interpretation, and application of scientific data to human behavior.

1	2	3	4	5
Very Uncertain		Somewhat Certain		Very Certain

3. *Pharmacist:* Mixes and dispenses medicines, gives medication advice to health practitioners and the public.

1	2	3	4	5
Very Uncertain		Somewhat Certain		Very Certain

4. *Dental Hygienist:* Provides dental treatment, gives instruction on teeth care, takes x-rays, and assists dentists.

1	2	3	4	5
Very Uncertain		Somewhat Certain		Very Certain

5. *Buyer, wholesale or retail:* Purchases merchandise from manufacturers or wholesales merchandise that is then sold to the public.

1	2	3	4	5
Very Uncertain		Somewhat Certain		Very Certain

6. *Sales Manager:* Directs staffing and training of sales staff, and develops and controls a sales program.

1	2	3	4	5
Very Uncertain		Somewhat Certain		Very Certain

7. *Primary School Teacher:* Teaches elementary school students, teaching several subjects and supervising various activities.

1	2	3	4	5
Very Uncertain		Somewhat Certain		Very Certain

FIGURE 13.1 *Continued*

8. *Stocks and Bonds Salesperson:* Gives information and advice in the buying and selling of stocks and bonds.

1	2	3	4	5
Very Uncertain		Somewhat Certain		Very Certain

9. *Editor:* Assigns, stimulates, prepares, accepts or rejects, and sometimes writes articles for publication.

1	2	3	4	5
Very Uncertain		Somewhat Certain		Very Certain

10. *Registered Nurse:* Administers nursing care to the ill and injured, using skills, experience, and education.

1	2	3	4	5
Very Uncertain		Somewhat Certain		Very Certain

11. *Engineer:* Uses practical applications of mathematics, physics and chemistry to solve applied problems dealing with construction, use of chemicals, machine design, etc.

1	2	3	4	5
Very Uncertain		Somewhat Certain		Very Certain

12. *Personnel Relations:* Hires and assigns people to jobs that they can do, to benefit themselves and their employer.

1	2	3	4	5
Very Uncertain		Somewhat Certain		Very Certain

13. *Laboratory Technician:* Works with other health professionals in the laboratory analysis of biological materials.

1	2	3	4	5
Very Uncertain		Somewhat Certain		Very Certain

14. *Designer:* Creates original designs for new types and styles of clothing, leather goods, and textiles.

1	2	3	4	5
Very Uncertain		Somewhat Certain		Very Certain

15. *Librarian:* Maintains library collections of books and other materials, and aids people in using library material.

1	2	3	4	5
Very Uncertain		Somewhat Certain		Very Certain

Source: Rotberg, H. L. (1984). *Career self-efficacy expectations and perceived range of career options in community college students.* Unpublished doctoral dissertation. Chapel Hill: The University of North Carolina at Chapel Hill, pp. 96–98. Reprinted with permission.

Role Playing

Role playing can be used as both an intervention and an assessment strategy, and while this discussion focuses largely on assessment, a brief description of the uses of role playing as an intervention is also presented. Role playing involves acting out a social situation to demonstrate how one would, or has, performed. For example, a career counseling client may report that she "blew her last job interview." The counselor needs to determine why the interview was blown and ask the client to report verbally what occurred. Verbal reports may be enlightening, but situations involving social skills are rarely described accurately.

Role playing represents an alternative to verbal descriptions. The career counselor may begin by asking the client to describe the interviewer or, better still, to imitate the interviewer's behavior. Once the counselor has a relatively full understanding of how the interview went, the client is asked to reenact the job interview with the counselor acting as the interviewer. If the client agrees to reenact the interview, she should be asked to illustrate through her behavior how she actually performed in the job interview. Then the role playing begins.

During the role-playing situation, the counselor observes the client, making mental notes about strengths and weaknesses. After the interview is completed, these observations may be shared with the client, or if the counselor wishes to "clench" the assessment, he may engage in role reversal. In role reversal, the counselor assumes the role of the client and the client assumes the role of the job interviewer, and the interview is repeated. Once completed, the interviewer asks the client if he has accurately depicted the client's behavior. If the answer is yes, then the client is asked to evaluate her own performances as observed in role reversal. The counselor then may provide any additional evaluations, and the client and the counselors can construct a list of interviewing strengths and weaknesses. Intervention follows. It usually entails presenting models of desired behaviors, practice through behavioral rehearsal, and feedback. Role playing can be used to assess clients' social skills in a wide variety of areas such as job interviews, telephone contacts, and employee–employer interactions (e.g., asking for a raise).

Card Sorts

Card sorts are devices that are typically designed by the counselor to assess a variety of variables such as values, interests, job skills, and lifestyle preferences. The potential options may be placed on 3" by 5" cards, and clients are asked to sort them into three to five stacks. For example, the following lifestyle variables could be placed on cards:

1. Ballet available
2. Symphony available
3. Theater available

4. Skiing within commuting distance
5. Short commute to work
6. High-quality schools for children
7. Golf courses nearby
8. Educational opportunities available for myself
9. Warm climate
10. Cold climate
11. Moderate climate (has all four seasons)
12. Close to parents
13. Intramural sports program for children
14. Near a large city
15. Near recreational water

The client could then be asked to sort these fifteen cards into stacks of no importance, some importance, or of great importance while discussing the reasons for the selections with the counselor. Tyler (1961), Dolliver (1967), and Dewey (1974) pioneered the use of card sorts to measure interests. Gysbers and Moore (1987) provided a detailed discussion of how to construct card sorts.

Genogram

The genogram was developed for use in family therapy, and McGoldrick and Gerson (1985) have written an excellent book on its use with families. Essentially, in career counseling the genogram is used first to get a graphic representation of the careers of a client's family or a client's origin, namely grandparents, parents, aunts, uncles, and other relatives who might have influenced the client's career-related attitudes. If used correctly, it can be used to assess sources of self-limiting stereotypes, expectations about the outcomes of various career choices, and the sources of career values and interests (Brown & Brooks, 1991; Okiishi, 1987).

The construction of a total genogram, as outlined by McGoldrick and Gerson (1985), is quite time-consuming, but because the use of this device in career counseling has somewhat more limited objectives, an abbreviated version can be developed. Typically, generations of the family are listed on different lines with grandparents listed on line 1, parents and their brothers and sisters on line 2, influential cousins on line 3, and siblings on line 4. This organization is shown in Figure 13.2. It is also possible to add to this family tree other individuals outside the immediate family who had a significant impact on the "career thinking" of the client, such as teachers, early employers, and so forth.

Once the "family is placed on an organizational chart, occupations of each person (including homemaking) should be listed. Then clients should be asked to report how their relatives felt about their occupations, what values they tried to engender in the client, and why they believe each person in the chart influenced them either positively or negatively.

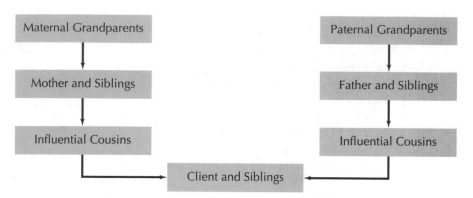

FIGURE 13.2   Organization of a Career Genogram

Support for Use of Qualitative Devices

Of the qualitative devices discussed here, only the use of self-efficacy measurement has been studied widely. Studies have demonstrated that self-efficacy is positively related to academic achievement (Lent, Brown, & Hackett, 1996; Lent, Brown, & Larkin, 1984), range of career options considered (Betz & Hackett, 1981; Lent, Brown, & Larkin, 1986; Rotberg, Brown, & Ware, 1987), and persistence in technical and scientific majors (Lent, Brown, & Larkin, 1984, 1986). To reiterate, self-efficacy expectations regarding one's ability to complete the academic and/or job requirements should be used at various stages of career counseling with some confidence that they will yield useful data. Empirical support for the use of the other devices discussed in this chapter is not as compelling, although there is widespread support for the use of card sorts (e.g., Gysbers & Moore, 1987) and role playing (e.g., Brown & Brooks, 1991).

Quantitative and Objective Assessment Devices

Needs and Work Values Inventories

Needs and values are sometimes confused in discussions, or the differences simply are not addressed. Similarly, values and interests are sometimes equated, although they are actually two separate constructs (Rokeach, 1979). Some needs are assumed to stem from the physiological functioning of the individual (e.g., need for air and water), and unless they are met the individual perishes. Psychological needs also stem from the functioning of the individual, and unless they are met the individual's development is arrested with various consequences (Rokeach, 1973, 1979). Values, on the other hand, are learned or may grow out of needs and are assumed to be a basic source of human motivation. Values may have either a positive or negative valence; that is, individuals are assumed to either seek or move toward values with a positive valence and away from those things that hold negative valences (Rokeach, 1973, 1979). Interests typically are viewed as less basic and as growing out of values (Holland, 1985; Rokeach, 1979). The following is a description of four work values inventories that may be helpful in identifying areas for client exploration.

Minnesota Importance Questionnaire (MIQ)
David J. Weiss, René V. Davis, and Lloyd H. Lofquist

Background/purpose: The MIQ grew out of the trait and factor tradition and was designed to measure sources of worker satisfaction. It measures twenty worker needs and the six values associated with them. The needs scales include Ability Utilization, Achievement, Activity Advancement, Authority, Composing Policies and Practices, Compensation, Coworkers, Creativity, Independence, Moral Values, Recognition, Responsibility, Security, Social Service, Social Status, Supervision—Human Relations, Supervision—Technical, Variety, and Working Conditions. The values measured are Achievement, Altruism, Autonomy, Comfort, Safety, and Status Validity.

Target population: Males and females 16 years of age and older; reading level approximately fifth grade. Individuals' scores are compared to the ratings of supervisors and workers in 185 occupations (predominantly blue collar) to determine whether they might be satisfied in those occupations.

Dates of publication: User's manual, 1981; technical manual, 1971; counseling uses, 1975.

Publisher: Vocational Psychology Research, University of Minnesota, N620 Elliot Hall, 75 East River Road, Minneapolis, MN 55455.

Values Scale (VS)
Donald E. Super and Dorothy D. Nevill

Background and purpose: The VS is designed to measure what its authors term intrinsic and extrinsic values. Intrinsic values are those that are satisfied by actually performing the activity. Extrinsic values are those to be satisfied as an outcome of performing an activity. The scales of the VS are Ability Utilization, Achievement Advancement, Aesthetics, Altruism, Authority, Autonomy, Creativity, Economic Rewards, Lifestyle, Personal Development, Physical Activity, Prestige, Risk, Social Interaction, Social Relations, Variety, Working Conditions, Cultural Identity, Physical Prowess, and Economic Security.

Target population: Grade 8 and up. Norm samples include high school students, college students, and adults.

Date of publication: Manual for VS, 1986.

Publisher: Consulting Psychologists Press, 577 College Avenue, Palo Alto, CA 94306.

Salience Inventory (SI)
Dorothy D. Nevill and Donald E. Super

Background and purpose: The SI was developed to measure the extent of participation in, the degree of commitment to, and the values expectations attached to study (education), work, homemaking, leisure, and community service. It was designed to help clients and counselors answer one question: "What is the relative importance attached to these roles at this time?" The authors contend that the SI will help clients and counselors understand the readiness of the client to make certain decisions at a given time. Scale scores are provided for each of the five life roles for three areas: participation, commitment, and values expectations.

Target population: Grades nine and up. Norm samples include high school students, college students, and adults.

Date of publication: Manual for the SI, 1986.

Publisher: Consulting Psychologists Press, 577 College Avenue, Palo Alto, CA 94306.

Life Values Inventory (LVI)
R. Kelly Crace and Duane Brown

Purpose: The LVI was developed both as a measure of values that guide normal behavior and as an intervention to assist clients to crystallize and prioritize their values within life roles. It measures fourteen values including Belonging, Concern for Others, Creativity, Prosperity, Dependability, Health and Activity, Scientific Understanding, Privacy, Spirituality, Loyalty to Family or Group, Achievement, Concern for the Environment, and Humility.

Target population: Grades nine and up

Date of publication: 1996

Publisher: Life Values Resources, 620 Bayberry Dr., Chapel Hill, NC 27514.

Support for the Use of Values Inventories

Cochran (1983) asked high school students to (1) generate and rank order a list of ten occupational alternatives, and (2) to study and rank-order a list of value-laden career constructs (e.g., higher salary). He concluded that their explicit ranking of career values did not correlate well with their implicit values that seemed to guide their selection of career alternatives. Pryor and Taylor (1980) also studied high school students in an effort to determine whether it was beneficial to use both values and interests measures. Their conclusion was that counselors are justified in using both. Their findings also support the conclusion of Knapp and Knapp (1979) that values and interests are two separate constructs. However, as we see in the next section, interest measures are the most widely used career counseling tools. This is probably because instruments measuring values have not received as much attention as have interest inventories.

Most practitioners use crude devices such as the checklists employed in Cochran's (1983) study to "measure" values, or they are measured using values clarification exercises or imagery (Brown & Brooks, 1991). Some practitioners may also infer values clinically from verbal reports. These approaches, as well as the use of psychometric instruments, appear useful as long as the limitations of the approaches used are kept clearly in mind.

Interest Inventories

Literally hundreds of thousands of interests inventories are administered each year. Regardless of the theoretical or empirical origin of these scales, they are presumed to measure liking or preferences for engaging in certain specific occupations.

Once scores on interest inventories are obtained, they may be compared to those of others in a reference or norm group, compared to some absolute criterion such as the interest levels of other pilots, or interpreted as raw scores (Blocher, 1987). Typically, inventories used in career development programs to promote awareness use either the normative or the raw score approach. For example, the individual's scores or the Strong Interest Inventory are compared to a series of norm groups of successful workers in managerial, technical, and professional occupations. On the other hand, the raw scale scores on the Self-Directed Search (Holland, 1994) are used to construct a scale profile that is used to locate jobs of interest. Whether a normative approach is superior to a raw score approach to scoring and interpretation has been a hotly debated area (for a detailed discussion as this relates to the Self-Directed Search, see Weinrach, 1984).

Career Occupational Preference System (COPS)
R. R. Knapp and L. Knapp

Purpose: The COPS was designed to reveal preferences for job activities in the following areas: Science Professional, Science Skilled, Technology Professional, Technology Skilled, Consumer Economics, Outdoor, Business Professional, Business Skilled, Clerical, Communication, Arts Skilled, Service Professional, and Service Skilled.

Target audience: Junior high through college. Norm groups include junior high, high school, and college students.

Date of publication: Copysystem technical manual, 1990.

Publisher: EDITS, PO Box 7234, San Diego, CA 92107.

Self-Directed Search (SDS)
John Holland

Purpose: The SDS was developed to be a self-administered, self-scored, and self-interpreted instrument to measure Holland's types: Realistic, Investigative, Artistic, Social, Enterprising, and Conventional. Depending on the form, the inventory yields two- or three-letter personal profiles that can be used with an Occupations Finder to locate a career that should be of interest to the individual.

Target audience: Junior high through adult. Raw scores are reported. Inventory was developed using high school and college students as well as adults.

Dates of publication:
    Form R 1994
    Form E 1990
    Form CP 1990
    Manual 1994
    Occupations Finder 1994
    Educational Opportunities Finder 1994

Publisher: Psychological Assessment Resources, PO Box 998, Odessa, FL 33556.

Career Decision-Making System (CDM)
Thomas F. Harrington and Arthur O'Shea

Purpose: The CDM is based on Holland's theory of occupational choice and yields six scores that are analogous to his types: Crafts (Realistic), Scientific (Investigative), the Arts (Artistic), Business (Enterprising), Clerical (Conventional), and Social (Social). The raw scores in the highest two or three interest scales are assessed to identify career clusters for exploration. Self-estimates of abilities, work values, future plans, and preferences for school subjects are incorporated into the overall career decision-making system.

Target audience: Junior high through adult. Norms drawn from junior high schools and senior high schools from across the country.

Dates of publication:
    Self-scored and machine-scored versions, 1992
    User's guide, 1992
    Technical manual, 1993
    College finder, 1991

Publisher: AGS, Publishers Building, Circle Pines, MN 55014.

Strong Interest Inventory (SII)
E. K. Strong, Jr., Jo-Ida C. Hansen, and David P. Campbell

Purpose: The SII was originally developed to help people interested in managerial, technical, and professional careers identify career options. It is now widely used in business and industry and adult counseling centers to assist people interested in making career changes as well as initial career choices. The SII yields a wealth of data including basic interest scales, general interest scales, general occupational themes, as well as administrative indices and special scales (e.g., Extroversion–Introversion). The 23 basic interest scales and 6 general occupational themes (GOT) are organized around Holland's types

(RIASEC), and the 207 occupational interest scales (OIS) are also reported in this context.

Target audience: Late adolescents and adults. Norm groups for OIS were drawn from successful and satisfied people; those for GOTs were composed of women and men from each of six Holland types and from various educational levels.

Dates of publication: Latest revision form, 1994; manual, user's guide, 1994.

Publisher: Consulting Psychologists Press, 577 College Avenue, Palo Alto, CA 94306.

Kuder Occupational Interest Survey Form DD (KOIS)
G. Frederick Kuder

Purpose: The purpose of Form DD is to provide data on 104 occupational scales, 39 college major scales, 10 vocational interest estimates, as well as eight experimental scales to be used in educational and career planning, using norms based on successful workers or graduating students.

Target audience: Grade 10 through adult. Norms provide for males and females on occupational and educational scales.

Dates of publication: Latest revision inventory, 1985; manual 1991.

Publisher: Science Research Associates, 155 N. Wacker Drive, Chicago, IL 60606.

Jackson Vocational Interest Survey (JVIS)
Douglas N. Jackson

Purpose: This inventory is designed to assist in educational and career planning. The thirty-five basic interest scales include work role dimensions and work style scales. Scores on ten general occupational themes, similarity to seventeen educational major fields, and a ranking of thirty-two occupational clusters are available if the inventory is computer scored.

Target audience: High school to adult. Norm groups drawn from colleges and universities, students admitted to Penn State University, and a university in Ontario, Canada.

Dates of publication: Latest revision of inventory, 1978; manual, 1977.

Publisher: Sigma Assessment Systems, 4110 Military Street, PO Box 984, Port Huron, MI 48061.

Reading—Free Vocational Interest Inventory—Revised (RFVII)
Ralph L. Becker

Purpose: The purpose of the revised RFVII is to determine the interests of mentally retarded and adolescents and adults with learning disabilities. It was developed to help these groups identify jobs in which they might gain proficiency and have productive lives. It yields scale scores in the following: Automotive, Building Trades, Clerical, Animal Care, Food Service, Patient Care, Horticulture, Housekeeping, Personal Service, Laundry, and Materials Handling.

Target audience: 13- to 60-year-old people with mental retardation and learning disabilities. Norms drawn from mentally retarded; learning disabled; sheltered workshop adults; environmentally disadvantaged adults.

Dates of publication: Inventory, 1981; manual, 1988.

Publisher: Elbern Publications, PO Box 09497, Columbus, OH 43209.

USES Interest Inventory (II)
United States Employment Service

Purpose: The II is used to identify areas highest of interest to focus career planning activities. It is typically given together with the General Aptitude Test Battery by employment counselors. The II yields scores in the following areas: Artistic, Scientific, Plants and Animals, Protective, Mechanical, Industrial, Business Retail, Selling, Accommodatory, Humanitarian, Leading–Influencing, and Physical Performing. The scores are used in conjunction with the *Guide to Occupational Exploration* to identify specific occupations.

Target audience: Grade 9 through adulthood. Extensive normative data are available including information on high school seniors, adults in occupational training programs, college students, and out-of-school job applicants.

Publication dates: All documents, 1982.

Publisher: United States Employment Service, 200 Constitution Avenue, N.W., Washington, DC 20210.

Campbell Interest and Skill Survey (CISS)

Purpose: The CISS was developed to measure career interests and self-estimates of skills. The instrument yields interests and skill scores on seven Orientation Scales, twenty-nine Basic Interest and Skill Scales, and three special scales. The Orientation Scales include Influencing, Organizing, Helping, Creating, Analyzing, Producing, and Adventuring. The Basic Interest and Skill Scales are subscales of the orientation scales. The special scales include Academic Focus, Extraversion, and Variety.

Target audience: 15-year-old students and up.

Publication date: 1992

Publisher: National Computer Systems, Inc., PO Box 1294, Minneapolis, MN 55440.

Ashland Interest Assessment (AIA)
Douglas N. Jackson and Connie W. Marshall

Purpose: The AIA consists of 144 pairs of work-related items and yields scores in 12 interest areas. These are Arts and Crafts, Personal Services, Food Service,

Clerical, Sales, General Service, Protective Service, Health Care, Mechanical, Construction, Plant or Animal Care, and Transportation. It is written at a third-grade reading level and is printed in larger type than most inventories. At this time it uses Canadian norms and thus must be evaluated carefully by U.S. users.

Target Audience: Adults or older adolescents who have learning disabilities, developmental handicaps, limited use of English, limited education, brain injury, or a chronic emotional or psychiatric condition. Also useful for students who do not wish to finish high school. The instrument can be hand-scored, can be mailed in to the publisher for scoring, or users can purchase software that will administer, score, and provide an interpretive report.

Date of Publication: All materials, 1997

Publisher: Sigma Assessment Systems, Inc., 4110 Military Street, PO Box 984, Port Huron, MI 48061.

Interest Assessment On-Line

The popularity of the Internet has resulted in a number of instruments being placed online. Many of these instruments appear to have little empirical support. However, there are exceptions—one of which is the Career Key. It is described in the following section, along with a much less well-developed, but potentially useful, approach.

Career Key (A free public service to help people make sound career decisions)
Lawrence K. Jones

Internet Address: http://www4.ncsu.edu/unity/lockers/users/l/lkj/index.html

Key Word Search: Career Key (Exact Phrase)

Purpose: The purpose of the Career Key is to provide a free interest inventory to Internet users. The inventory, which is taken and scored automatically if directions are followed properly, yields Holland (RIASEC) scale scores. The website also includes an occupations locator so that students and adults can identify occupations that match their Holland codes. The occupations locator is linked directly to the *Occupational Outlook Handbook (OOH)* via hyperlinks. Simply by clicking on occupation of interest, users can access the *OOH.*

Target Audience: Middle school students (a separate version of the inventory is provided for this group) through adulthood.

Date of Publication: 1997

Publisher: Lawrence K. Jones, North Carolina State University.

Michigan Occupational Information System (MOIS)
Self-Assessment Career Survey
MOIS

Internet Address: http://www.mois.org/moistest.html

Purpose: The purpose of the inventory is to provide a free, quick assessment of interests by having users check subjects they like best, tasks they would enjoy, and job titles of interest. The inventory is scored online and three job clusters are identified. Users can click on the cluster name and receive a list of occupations (over 2000 occupations are included in the system) that can be explored. By clicking on job titles they will be linked to a job description. If users wish to identify institutions within Michigan that provide training related to the occupation they are exploring at the time, hyperlinks to lists of institutions are embedded within the occupational descriptions.

Target Audience: High school students (primarily) through adults in Michigan. However, this assessment device could be used by others.

Publisher: MOIS, 2630 West Howell Road, Mason, MI 48854.

Support for the Use of Interest Inventories

Tittle and Zytowski (1980) estimated that 3.5 million people take interest inventories each year, and although there are no current estimates of the number, it seems unlikely that this number has decreased. Studies and opinion articles on the use of interest inventories abound. It also comes as no surprise that the Strong Interest Inventory (SII), earlier called the Strong Campbell Interest Inventory (SCII), and the Self-Directed Search (SDS) are the object of much of this research since the SII is the oldest (and perhaps best) of the currently published inventories and the SDS is one of the most popular. Some of these studies are reported here.

Hansen and Swanson (1983) studied the validity of the SCII as a predictor of college majors and concluded that it was valid for this purpose, although slightly less so for males than females. Johnson and Hoese (1988) also studied the SCII and concluded that it cannot be used as the sole career planning device since many of the college students in this sample had a wide variety of personal and career development problems. The SCII was *not* developed as a stand-alone career planning instrument. Galassi, Jones, and Britt (1985) also studied the SCII along with six other inventories to determine to what degree they suggest nontraditional options for women. The instruments studied, in addition to the SCII, were the Kuder Occupational Interest Survey (KOIS), Career Assessment Inventory (CAI), Harrington–O'Shea Career Decision-Making Systems (CDM), the Self-Directed Search (SDS), Non-Sexist Vocational Card Sort (NSVCS), and the Occ-U-Sort. The SCII suggested 46 nontraditional occupations, while the Occ-U-Sort guide suggested 382 jobs, the SDS Job Finder 327, the CDM 164, the KOIS 65, the CAI 50, and NSVCS 41. In another comparative study, the SCII was compared to the Vocational Card Sort (VCS) in order to compare expressed and inventoried interests of college women. Slaney and Slaney (1986) found that 42 percent of the expressed and inventoried interests were incongruent. They found that interests as measured by the VCS were more highly related to expressed interests than those of the SCII, suggesting that the VCS may be a superior means of measuring interests, at least for some groups. Finally, Borgen's (1988) comments on the SCII are noteworthy. He states that the latest revision of the SCII provides the counselor with even greater confidence and utility for the Strong.

The Self-Directed Search, as an interest inventory, has also been explored extensively. For example, Gottfredson and Holland (1975) studied the predictive validity of the SDS and found it to be a moderately efficient predictor of choices for both men and women. However, the section of the SDS that asks for expressed career choice proved to be the best predictor of career choice. Numerous studies (e.g., Holland, Gottfredson, & Baker 1990; Noeth, 1983) have supported this finding.

Maddux and Cummings (1980) compared the test–retest reliability of the SDS and the SDS Form E (Easy) with high school students with learning disabilities and found that the Form E may be more appropriate because test–retest reliabilities are higher for the Form E for this group. In another comparative study, Jones, Gorman, and Schroeder (1989) compared the utility of the SDS with the Career Key (CK) in helping undecided college students choose academic majors. Students rated the CK more positively than the SDS and spent more time exploring career resources after testing than those taking the SDS. Finally, Gault and Meyers (1987) compared the SDS with the Vocational Interest, Experience, and Skills Assessment (VIESA) to determine which would best serve college and adult populations. In this study the SDS was rated more positively and as being more effective.

An argument arose about 20 years ago about the validity of using raw scores, particularly with women (e.g., Holland, Gottfredson, & Gottfredson, 1975; Prediger, 1981). This debate continued for nearly a decade and is still unresolved. For example, in 1981 Prediger questioned the validity of the SDS for females. His meta-analytic research suggested that using raw scores instead of normative scores restricted the range of occupations suggested for women and had less construct validity than when normed scores were reported. The crux of Prediger's arguments rests on the relative value of construct versus predictive validity. Holland (1982) asserted the importance of predictive validity in his reply, suggesting that "the depreciation of predictive validity [by Prediger] is a step backward" (p. 197).

The SII and the SDS are not the only instruments that have received attention from researchers. For example, the Harrington–O'Shea has been shown to have moderate predictive validity for a high school student's choice of a college major in a longitudinal study (Brown, Ware, & Brown, 1985). Generally speaking, research supports the continued use of these inventories.

Personality Inventories

Few personality inventories have captured the interest of career counselors, perhaps because many of those available were developed to measure abnormal behavior. As a result, only two personality inventories are discussed here.

Myers-Briggs Type Indicator (MBTI)
Isabel Briggs Myers and Katharine C. Briggs

Purpose: The MBTI was developed to provide a measure of Jung's types and yields scores of four dipolar scales: Extroversion–Introversion; Sensing–Intuition; Thinking–Feeling; and Judgment–Perception. A profile is constructed based on the person's highest score on each of the scales (e.g., ENTJ).

Target audience: High school students through adults. Norms available on junior high, high school, college, and various adult groups.

Dates of publication: Standard Form (6), 1977; Revised Form (F), 1985; Abbreviated Form (AV), 1985, Manual 1998.

Publisher: Consulting Psychologists Press, 577 College Avenue, Palo Alto, CA 94306.

Sixteen P. F. Personal Career Development Profile (16PFQ)
Verne Waller

Purpose: The interpretive profile (Personal Career Development Profile) provides an interpretation of personality and its potential influence on career choice and development. The profile is in actuality a computer-generated, occupationally oriented interpretation of the sixteen personality factors measured by the Sixteen Personality Factor Questionnaire developed by Cattell (1969).

Target audience: High school through adult. Norms available for high school, college, and general adult population.

Dates of publication: 16 PFQ, 1969; 16 manual, 1980; PCDP manual, 1985.

Publisher: IPAT, 1801 Woodfield Drive, Savoy, IL 61874.

Support for the Use of Personality Inventories

Willis and Ham (1988) reviewed the MBTI and suggested that it has utility (1) in helping clients build a cognitive framework for organizing career information, (2) in work adjustment counseling, and (3) as a self-assessment device. They also provided some cautionary notes. For example, they suggested that the MBTI is not a comprehensive personality test and that it would be a mistake to overestimate the utility of the information gained from the scales. However, it is worth noting that the manual of the MBTI lists data on over 180 occupations. Perhaps the most striking feature of these tables is that most types are found in most occupations.

Wholeben (1988) suggested that the PCDP, which derived from the 16PF, "is an excellent tool for career awareness in the high school curriculum and occupational exploration of adults" (p. 241). However, little construct or predictive validity information has been developed and, thus, much caution is in order.

It seems likely that the MBTI will receive increasing use in career counseling, although other personality inventories may not fare so well.

Multiple Aptitude Test Batteries

Theoretically, aptitude tests measure one's potential to acquire a skill or learn some specialized knowledge. In reality, they measure what has already been learned, which is an indicator of future performance. Unfortunately, not everyone has had the opportunity to acquire knowledge and/or skill to the same degree. However, when taken as *one* indicator of potential aptitude, tests can be of assistance to clients attempting to make career plans or can be simply one way of promoting self-awareness.

Differential Aptitude Test (DAT)
G. K. Bennett, H. G. Seashore, and A. G. Wesman

Purpose: Yields data that are potentially useful in the career/educational planning process. The subtests on the DAT are Verbal Reasoning, Numerical Ability, Abstract Reasoning, Clerical Speed and Accuracy, Mechanical Reasoning, Space Relations, Spelling, and Language Use.

Target audience: Grade 8 through adult. Norms for grades 8–12.

Date of publication: Latest edition of all documents, 1990; 1991.

Publisher: The Psychological Corporation, 655 Academic Court, San Antonio, TX 78204.

Armed Services Vocational Aptitude Battery (ASVAB)
Department of Defense

Purpose: This test provides data that may be useful to counselors and students in planning a military career. It is also used by military recruiters to determine applicants' potential for military careers. The ASVAB yields seven composite scores: Academic Ability; Math; Verbal; Mechanical and Crafts; Business and Clerical; Electronics and Electrical; and Health, Social, and Technology; as well as ten subtest scores in General Science, Word Knowledge, Paragraph Comprehension, Numerical Operations, Arithmetic Reasoning, Math Knowledge, Auto and Shop Information, Mechanical Comprehension, Electronics Information, and Coding Speed.

Target audience: High school (10–12) and adults. Norms available for target groups.

Dates of publication: Counselor's manual, 1990; ASVAB test manual, 1984; student workbook, 1987.

Publisher: U.S. Military Entrance Processing Command, 2500 Green Bay Road, North Chicago, IL 60064.

General Aptitude Test Battery
United States Employment Service

Purpose: This battery measures nine vocational aptitudes including General Learning Ability, Verbal Aptitude, Numerical Aptitude, Spatial Aptitude,

Form Perceptions, Motor Coordination, Finger Dexterity, and Manual Dexterity. The inventory yields fifty-nine Occupational Aptitude Patterns.

Date of publication: Most recent, 1982.

Publisher: United States Employment Service, 200 Constitution Avenue, N.W., Washington, DC 20210.

Support for the Use of Aptitude Batteries

Support for the use of all aptitude tests is probably summed up best by Anastasia's (1988) discussion of the Differential Aptitude Test (DAT). She observes that the support for the predictive validity of the DAT is relatively high when the criterion variable is success in high school, academic, and/or vocational education programs and quite modest when used to predict success in specific occupations. Ghiselli (1973) reviewed research prior to 1965 and concluded that the average correlation between test scores and educational performance was in the order of .30 and for occupational proficiency about .20. However, as Hogan, DeSoto, and Solano (1977) noted, average correlations are of little value, and in some instances validity coefficients for occupational performance reach .60. Career counselors should carefully inspect validity studies to determine whether the test being used has adequate predictive validity generally and whether the norm groups are sufficiently representative to include the client with whom they are working. It is also important to keep in mind that even if a validity coefficient approaches .60, only 36 percent of the variance associated with performance is being accounted for by the test, and thus a combination of other variables such as work or study habits, motivation, family support, and person–environment are likely to be more important to the success of the individual than aptitude.

Diagnostic Inventories

A number of inventories have been developed to measure certain career development "problems." These inventories are often used in research but also have reliability in determining problems that may limit or retard the career development or career decision-making process.

Career Decision Scale (CDS)
Samuel H. Osipow

Purpose: The CDS was developed to provide explanatory information regarding failure to make career decisions. The CDS yields two scale scores: Certainty and Indecision. The scales provide an estimate of indecision; they also provide data regarding the antecedents of indecision.

Target audience: High school through adult. Norms available on high school students, college students, continuing education students, returning adults.

Date of publication: Most recent edition, 1987.

Publisher: Psychological Assessment Resources, PO Box 998, Odessa, FL 33566.

My Vocational Situation
John L. Holland, Denise C. Daiger, and Paul G. Power

Purpose: My Vocational Situation was developed primarily to identify lack of vocational identity, but it also provides information about lack of information and environmental or personal barriers to occupational choice. Three scale scores (Vocational Identity, Occupational Information, and Barriers) provide evidence regarding these areas.

Target audience: High school age through adult. Norm groups made up of high school through adult.

Date of publication: All information, 1980.

Publisher: Psychological Assessment Resources. P.O. Box 998, Odessa, FL 33566.

Career Development Inventory (CDI)
Donald Super, Albert S. Thompson, Richard H. Lindeman, Jean P. Jordaan, and Roger A. Myers

Purpose: The CDI was developed as a general measure of readiness to engage in career decision making and yields eight scale scores: Career Planning; Career Exploration; Decision Making; World of Work Information; Knowledge of Preferred Occupational Group; Career Development—Attitudes; Career Development—Knowledge of Skills; Career Orientation—Total.

Target audience: Eighth graders through college age. Norms for high school students and college students.

Date of publication: School form, 1979; college form, 1981; user's manual, 1981.

Publisher: Consulting Psychologists Press, 577 College Avenue, Palo Alto, CA 94306.

Career Beliefs Inventory
John D. Krumboltz

Purpose: To assist individuals to identify problematic self-perceptions and world views.

Target audience: High school through adults.

Publication date: All documents, 1988.

Publisher: Consulting Psychologists Press, 577 College Avenue, Palo Alto, CA 94306.

Support for the Use of Diagnostic Inventories

The aforementioned diagnostic inventories fall into two categories: those that can be used to measure normal development, such as the Career Development Inventory, and those that can be used to diagnose some aspect of abnormal development, such as the Career Decision Scale. Psychologists and counselors have generally been concerned with both of these areas, although recent research has focused on diagnosing decisional difficulties.

Super and Thompson (1979) report that the CDI has three major uses: (1) to evaluate the outcomes of career development programs, (2) as a survey instrument to determine extent of information about careers and the sources of information being utilized, and (3) in individual counseling to determine decision-making problems or clients' knowledge of occupational information. What has not been demonstrated to this point is that this inventory is the most efficient means of collecting data about career development. The same is true of the various other instruments that purport to measure normal development and, thus, at least for the time being, their utility should probably be restricted to evaluation and research studies (Savickas, 1984).

With one exception, the diagnostic inventories described should probably not be used for any purpose other than research, since their authors and others have failed to produce the necessary empirical support to justify their usage. The exception to the recommendation is the *Career Decision Scale* (CDS). Numerous studies (Fuqua, Blum, & Hartman, 1988; Hartman, Fuqua, & Blum, 1984; Hartman, Fuqua, & Hartman, 1983b) have demonstrated that the CDS may be a useful tool when used as a preliminary screening device to differentiate undecided clients, who can benefit from traditional career counseling strategies such as testing and the provision of occupational information, and indecisive clients, who have decisional difficulties that must be addressed prior to the use of traditional strategies. Recent studies (Fuqua, Blum, Newman, & Seaworth, 1988; Larsen, Heppner, Harm, & Dugan, 1988; Vondracek, Hostetler, Schulenberg, & Shimiza, 1990), as well as some of the earlier studies, suggest that the constructs *undecidedness* and *indecisive* have correlates in other personality variables such as anxiety and locus of control; they have not provided evidence that the CDS may not be useful to practitioners.

Multipurpose Tests and Inventories

Most tests and inventories are designed to measure a single construct (e.g., career interests) or dimensions of a construct (e.g., aptitudes). However, a few tests and inventories have been developed to measure more than one construct (e.g., interests and aptitudes). A few of the potentially useful ones are presented here.

Occupational Aptitude Survey and Interest Schedule (OASIS)
Randall M. Parker

Purpose: The OASIS was developed to help junior and senior high school students engage in career planning. The instrument yields scores in twelve interest scales (Artistic, Scientific, Nature, Protestive, Mechanical, Industrial, Business Detail, Selling, Accommodating, Humanitarian, Leading–Influencing, and Physical Performing) and provides measures of five aptitudes (General Ability, Perpetual Aptitudes, Spatial Aptitudes, Numerical Aptitudes, Verbal Aptitudes).

Target audiences: Eighth through twelfth graders. Norm groups made up of twelfth graders.

Date of publication: All documents, 1983.

Publisher: PRO-ED, 5341 Industrial Oaks Boulevard, Austin, TX 78735.

McCarron-Dial System (MDS)
Lawrence T. McCarron and Jack G. Dial

Purpose: The MDS was developed for use with special education and rehabilitation groups. It yields five scores: Verbal–Spatial–Cognitive, Sensory, Motor, Emotional, and Integration–Coping. The basic purpose of the MDS is to predict how clients will be functioning after training, and the instrument can be used in counseling or placement activities. The actual subtests included in the battery are The Peabody Picture Vocabulary Test, Bender Visual Motor Gestalt Test, Behavior Rating Scale, Observational Emotional Inventory, Haptic Visual Discrimination Test, and McCarron Assessment of Neuromuscular Development.

Target audience: Learning disabled, emotionally disturbed, mentally retarded, cerebral palsied, head injured, socially disadvantaged. Norms are available for target groups.

Date of publication: User's manual, 1986.

Publisher: McCarron–Dial Systems, PO Box 45628, Dallas, TX 75245.

Valpar 17-Pre-Vocational Readiness Battery (PVRB)
Valpar International Corp.

Purpose: The PVRB has four subtests—Development Assessment, Workshop Evaluation, Interpersonal/Social Skills, and Money Handling Skills—and was designed to measure functional skills that may transfer to educational or occupational settings. Its basic purpose is to identify people who may have functional problems as a preliminary step to in-depth diagnosis.

Target audience: High school age and adult. Learning disabled, educably mentally retarded, and trainable mentally retarded. Norms are available for people living in sheltered independent living groups and students in schools for exceptional children.

Date of publication: Most recent test, 1986.

Publisher: Valpar, PO Box 5767, Tuscon, AZ 85703.

Support for Using Multipurpose Tests and Inventories

Multipurpose inventories were developed for specific purposes and typically for use with special populations. Test manuals should be consulted to determine whether the inventory is appropriate for one's client(s) and if the psychometric characteristics of the inventory justify its use.

Selecting Assessment Devices

Career counselors may select from among hundreds of tests, inventories, and qualitative assessment strategies. For some of these, such as standardized tests and inventories, criteria have been developed that can be useful in the process. At present, only the ethical principles developed by the American Counseling Association (ACA) and APA guide the selection of qualitative assessment approaches. Specifically, counselors must be competent in the use of any assessment device selected, the welfare of the client must be maintained as the uppermost consideration when selecting an assessment strategy, and cultural and gender issues must be carefully weighed prior to using an assessment approach with a client. Of course, these same ethical guidelines must be adhered to in the use of standardized inventories as well. However, the additional guidelines alluded to are outlined below. These criteria are based to some degree on earlier discussions by Womer (1988) and Prediger and Garfield (1988).

Technical Qualities

The reliability, validity, and representativeness of the norm group (standardization) are of utmost importance in the selection of tests and inventories. The exact type of reliability (test–retest vs. internal consistency will, to some degree, be determined by the type of test or inventory, but test–retest reliability is generally preferred when measuring those traits of importance in career planning.

Both predictive and construct validity are of concern to career counselors, although the degree of importance of each will be determined by the purpose of the test. If the test is to be used for screening purposes or placement, predictive validity is of utmost importance. Construct validity becomes particularly important when one purpose of the assessment is to promote self-awareness. For example, the Self-Directed Search was developed by Holland (1994) to measure his theoretical personality types. These types and their descriptions became important aspects of the way students and adults see themselves, and thus any inventory puporting to measure Holland types should have construct validity. These inventories should also have predictive validity, but construct validity is the first consideration.

Not all inventories and tests compare the scores of the person tested to a norm sample. The SDS uses raw scores to determine a personality subtype without regard to how the individual compares to others. For those tests that do use norm-referenced comparisons, the representatives of the group become important. Obviously, in career planning and placement, the best comparison groups would be people with whom the client would be working or competing. When specific norm groups are unavailable, the value of the test is weakened.

Gender and Culture Bias

Gender and culture bias have received widespread attention in the counseling literature. For example, Tittle and Zytowski (1980) provided a full discussion of gender issues in assessing interest. More recently, Lonner (1988) discussed the cross-cultural issues in testing and assessment. At the center of these discussions is the question: Do the tests used by career counselors produce information that may mislead either the person taking the test or persons (e.g., personnel managers) who may use tests to make a decision? (Sundberg & Gonzalez, 1981, p. 222).

It is probably fair to say that tests and inventories are biased to some degree, but that most counselors attempt to use these products in a nondiscriminatory fashion. There are of course a number of legal prohibitions against the use of tests in a discriminatory manner, of which the most important is the Equal Employment Opportunity Act (Title VII of the Civil Rights Act of 1964 and its subsequent amendments) (Anastasia, 1988). Professional standards regarding the use of tests have also been developed and published.

Obviously, career development workers need to avoid using inventories and tests that have not been developed properly. However, even given the safeguards built into the development of tests and the legal prohibitions against using them inappropriately, subtle forms of bias do exist in the use of tests and inventories, particularly as they relate to minorities. The following concerns must be addressed in the assessment process if this is to be avoided.

The test or inventory itself: The relevance of the content of the assessment device is a major concern when assessing minorities and women and clients who are culturally isolated, such as those from certain parts of Appalachia. If the following question is posed—Are you more interested in going to an art gallery or reading quietly at home?—a number of clients will have had no experience with art galleries, may never have had a quiet place to read, and as a result may begin to see the entire process as irrelevant to them. Similarly, if the question Would you rather repair a small engine or complete a crossword puzzle? is posed, not many females have been accorded the opportunity to repair a small engine, and those people who do not receive newspapers may have had little opportunity to do crossword puzzles. Careful examination of the content of tests and inventories as well as a thorough knowledge of the people to whom the devices are to be given is perhaps the only way to avoid this subtle form of bias.

The testing process: Anastasia (1988) pointed out a number of factors that contribute to bias in the assessment process, including lack of previous experience with assessment, lack of motivation to do well or to present a representative picture of self, and the inability of the test administrator to establish rapport, particularly with culturally different people. However,

Anastasia states, "By far the most important consideration in the testing of culturally diverse groups—as in all testing—pertains to the interpretation of the test scores" (p. 66). The interpretation process is discussed in detail later in this chapter, but good test interpretation requires a thorough knowledge of the test or inventory and an awareness of the characteristics of the people taking the test, and how these might interact with the counselor and the assessment device.

In summary, when an inventory includes questions that are oriented to middle-class whites it is culturally biased (Fouad, 1993; Lonner, 1988). There are numerous other sources of cultural bias, including language used and making assumptions about the motivation to take the test. The possibility that the norm group used is inappropriate because of underrepresentation of minorities (Lonner, 1988) can also be a problem. Moreover, when items are selected that are outside the experiences of females or, because of gender-role socialization, interact negatively with past experiences, the test or inventory is gender-biased.

Other Issues

The time needed to take the test or inventory, the cost, the reading level, the availability of computerized or hand scoring, and the counselor's preference are all factors to take into consideration when selecting tests or inventories. Prediger and Garfield (1988) suggest that career counselors need a high level of expertise in measurement and statistics as well as a thorough knowledge of various types of tests prior to using tests to promote career development.

Interpreting Results

Goodyear (1990) reported, after an extensive review of the literature on career test interpretation, "Counselors can have some confidence that the interpretation of test results has a positive effect. Moreover there is little evidence that outcomes are differently affected by one treatment [interpretational approach] over another, although clients seem to *prefer* individual interpretations, and self-administered/interpreted measures offer a substantial cast scoring" (p. 246). He also reported that subjects in research studies tend to accept positively worded test results better than those that are couched in negative terms and that there seems to be no gender difference in the acceptance of results of generalized personality interpretations. Goodyear's summary probably represents the extent of empirically based knowledge about test interpretation. However, clinical experience and common sense provide some additional guidelines.

Tinsley and Bradley (1986, 1988) present a four-stage approach to test interpretation. The first stage, counselor preparation for test interpretation, involves counselors taking the time to make certain that they are thoroughly familiar with the test or inventory, the meaning of the scores, how the results can be integrated with other data such as educational history and family situation; determining the order of presentation if more than one assessment device is to be interpreted; and reviewing briefly interpretation plans.

All of the steps in the interpretation process stages are important, but one part that should receive particular attention is the integration of the data gained from more formal assessment devices with other sources of data. Do these data agree or conflict with other data (Tinsley & Bradley, 1988)? What are the implications of the agreement or disagreement? How will these implications be addressed?

The second stage involves preparing clients for test interpretation. As Tinsley and Bradley (1988) noted, people who have taken tests are typically eager to get the results; however, it may be useful to review the purpose of the assessment device, how they "experienced it" when they were taking it, and ask clients to speculate scores or profiles.

During stage three, the actual delivery of information, counselors are advised to keep the goals of the assessment in mind, to report scores but to explain measurement error, to avoid jargon, and to encourage reactions to the test results. Tinsley and Bradley also suggest that defensiveness should be minimized when providing "bad news." They suggest that one may do this by leaving the door open that the scores may not be totally accurate but, more importantly, by focusing on the meaning of the scores rather than the scores themselves. For example, a lower than expected score on an aptitude test may mean that the client will have to exert more effort than other individuals, not necessarily that the client is precluded from a field of study. It is also worth mentioning Goodyear's (1990) conclusion that clients more readily accept results that are positively phrased.

After the formal interpretation, stage four, the counselor may wish to discuss the results in follow-up sessions, continue to check client's understanding of the results, and continue to help them integrate what they learned from formal assessment with informal data.

Finally, Bradley in a still-relevant article (1978) suggested that we use what he calls a "person referenced" approach to test interpretation. In this approach the counselor first determines whether the test is valid for the individual. This would be particularly useful when tests and inventories are administered to women, minorities, and people with disabilities. The counselor also determines, with the client, the strengths and weaknesses of the client's performance and determines means of dealing with the weaknesses. The counselor should also assist the client to determine how the information gained can be useful in decision making. The counselor and client should also look at the client's norm-referenced score if one is available. This approach to test interpretation fits with Healy's (1990) recommendation for reforming career assessment, discussed at the outset of this chapter.

The Internet as a Resource in the Assessment Process

In two provocative papers, Sampson (1998a, b) outlined how the Internet might serve as a resource in the career development process. His assertions regarding each step in the process are outlined below:

1. Selection: Sampson suggests that password protected websites could be researched with regard to specific client needs, the reliability and validity of available measures, and other factors to aid the selection process. Unfortunately these websites are unavailable at this time.

2. Orientation of clients to testing: Sampson suggests that websites that contain information about inventories and tests could be used to orient clients to instruments prior to the assessment process. He also suggests that e-mail can be used to communicate with clients about tests. A review of test publishers' websites indicates that there may be enough information on these sites to orient clients to some inventories. Some practitioners now correspond with their clients via e-mail on a variety of topics. Chat rooms could also be used for this purpose and might provide a more satisfactory interaction with clients. In the very near future, many practitioners will be able to interact directly with clients via voice and video on the Internet. Virtual orientation sessions can replace face-to-face sessions when the situation dictates.

3. Test administration: As has been noted, some types of tests can be administered and scored via the Internet. As Sampson noted (1998a, b,) timed tests do not lend themselves to Internet administration because of the need to ensure that a proper climate exists for maximum performance on these inventories and that they are administered properly.

4. Test interpretation: As noted earlier in the discussion of specific tests and inventories, many companies make software available to practitioners that provide interpretive reports. These can be delivered via the Internet. Videoconferencing can be used in conjunction with these reports to enhance the process (Sampson, 1998b), but the question to be raised is How can difficult issues such as resistance and the delivery of "bad news" be handled in this type of interpretive session? At this time, there are no satisfactory answers to this question.

The Internet has great potential as an aid in the assessment process, but its use raises a number of ethical questions. Specifically, how will standards be maintained in the assessment process, how will confidentiality be ensured, and how will the welfare of clients be protected? The National Board for Certified Counselors (NBCC, 1997) and the National Career Development Association (NCDA, 1997) have established guidelines for providing services on the Internet that can help answer these questions.

Summary

Assessment is an essential ingredient in career counseling and other career development activities. However, unlike some activities associated with career development, the appropriate use of tests requires a high level of expertise that must be gained by careful training and supervision. It is inappropriate for untrained people to use tests and inventories for any purpose.

The two approaches to assessment discussed in this chapter, qualitative and quantitative, are both important and have long been used by career counselors. It may be that the effective use of qualitative assessment procedures requires a higher level of clinical skill because fewer guidelines are provided to guide this work. However, both qualitative and quantitative approaches require counselors to be sensitive to issues related to race, ethnicity, gender, and socioeconomic status if they are to be used appropriately. Moreover, if these approaches are to be used effectively with the counseling process for any group, a high level of counseling skills is a prerequisite to administering and interpreting tests and inventories.

References

American Association of Counseling and Development. (1988). *Ethical standards.* Alexandria, VA: Author.

Anastasia, A. (1988). *Psychological testing* (6th ed.). New York: Macmillan.

Bandura, A. (1977). Toward a unifying theory of behavior change. *Psychological Review, 89,* 191–125.

Bandura, A. (1986). *Social foundations of thought and action: A social–cognitive theory.* Englewood Cliffs, NJ: Prentice-Hall.

Betz, N. E., & Hackett, G. (1981). The relationship of career-related self-efficacy expectations to perceived career options in college women and men. *Journal of Counseling Psychology, 28,* 399–410.

Betz, N. E., & Hackett, G. (1986). Applications of self-efficacy theory to understanding career choice behavior. *Journal of Social and Clinical Psychology, 4,* 279–289.

Blocher, D. H. (1987). *The professional counselor.* New York: Macmillan.

Borgen, F. H. (1988). SCII review. In J. T. Kapes & M. M. Mastie (Eds.), *A counselor's guide to career assessment instruments* (2nd ed., pp. 121–126). Alexandria, VA: National Career Development Association.

Brown D. (1990). Trait and factor theory. In D. Brown, L. Brooks and associates (Eds.), *Career choice and development* (2nd ed., pp. 13–36). San Francisco: Jossey-Bass.

Brown, D., & Brooks, L. (1991). *Career counseling techniques.* Boston: Allyn & Bacon.

Brown, D., Ware, W. B., & Brown, S. T. (1985). A predictive validation of the career decision-making inventory. *Measurement and Evaluation in Counseling and Development, 18,* 81–85.

Bradley, R. W. (1978). Person-referenced test interpretation: A learning process. *Measurement and Evaluation in Counseling and Development, 10,* 201–210.

Cattell, R. (1969). *The Sixteen Personality Factors Questionnaire.* Savoy, IL: IPAT.

Cochran, L. (1983). Implicit versus explicit importance of career values in making a career decision. *Journal of Counseling Psychology, 30,* 188–193.

Crites, J. O. (1969). *Vocational psychology.* New York: McGraw-Hill.

Cronbach, L. J. (1984). *Essentials of psychological testing.* New York: Harper & Row.

Dewey, C. R. (1974). Exploring interests: The non-sexist card sort. *Personnel and Guidance Journal, 52,* 348–351.

Dolliver, R. H. (1967). An adaptation of the Tyler Vocational Card Sort. *Personnel and Guidance Journal, 45,* 916–920.

Engen, H. B., Lamb, R. R., & Prediger, D. J. (1982). Are secondary schools still using standardized tests? *Personnel and Guidance Journal, 60,* 287–290.

Fouad, N. A. (1993). Cross-cultural vocational assessment. *Vocational Guidance Quarterly, 42,* 4–13.

Fuqua, D. R., Blum, C. R., & Hartman, B. W. (1988). Empirical support for the diagnosis of career indecision. *Vocational Guidance Quarterly, 36,* 363–373.

Fuqua, D. R., Blum, C. R., Newman, J. L., & Seaworth, T. B. (1988). *Journal of Counseling, 35,* 154–158.

Galassi, M. D., Jones, L. K., & Britt, M. N. (1985). Nontraditional career options for women: An evaluation of career guidance instruments. *Vocational Guidance Quarterly, 34,* 124–130.

Gault, F. M., & Myers, H. H. (1987). A comparison of two career-planning inventories. *Career Development Quarterly, 35,* 332–336.

Ghiselli, E. E. (1973). The validity of aptitude tests in personnel selection. *Personnel Psychology, 26,* 461–477.

Goldman, L. (1961). *Using tests in counseling.* New York: Appleton-Century-Crofts.

Goldman, L. (1972). Tests and counseling: The marriage that failed. *Measurement and Evaluation in Guidance, 4,* 213–220.

Goldman, L. (1982). Assessment in counseling: A better way. *Measurement and Evaluation in Guidance, 4,* 213–220.

Goldman, L. (1990). Qualitative assessment. *The Counseling Psychologist, 18,* 205–213.

Goodyear, R. K. (1990). Research on the effects of test interpretation: A review. *The Counseling Psychologist, 18,* 240–257.

Gottfredson, G. D., & Holland, J. L. (1975). Vocational choices of men and women: A comparison of predictors from the self-directed search. *Journal of Applied Psychology, 22,* 28–34.

Gysbers, N. C., & Moore, E. J. (1987). *Career counseling: Skills and techniques for practitioners.* Englewood Cliffs, NJ: Prentice-Hall.

Hansen, J. C., & Swanson, J. L. (1983). Stability of interests and predictive and concurrent validity of the 1981 Strong–Cambell Interest Inventory for college majors. *Journal of Counseling Psychology, 30,* 194–201.

Hartman, B. W., Fuqua, D. R., & Blum, C. R. (1984). A path-analytic model of indecision. *Vocational Guidance Quarterly, 33,* 231–240.

Hartman, B. W., Fuqua, D. R., & Hartman, P. T. (1983a). The construct validity of the career decision scale administered to high school students. *Vocational Guidance Quarterly, 31,* 250–258.

Hartman, B. W., Fuqua, D. R., & Hartman, P. T. (1983b). The predictive potential of the Career Decision Scale in identifying chronic career indecision. *Vocational Guidance Quarterly, 32,* 103–108.

Healy, C. C. (1990). Reforming career appraisals to meet the needs of clients in the 1990s. *The Counseling Psychologist, 18,* 214–226.

Hogan, R., DeSoto, C. B., & Solano, C. (1977). Traits, tests, and personality research. *American Psychologist, 32,* 255–264.

Holland, J. L. (1982). The SDS helps both females and males: A comment. *Vocational Guidance Quarterly, 30,* 195–197.

Holland, J. L. (1985). *Making vocational choices: A theory of vocational personalities and work environments* (2nd ed.). Englewood Cliffs, NJ: Prentice-Hall.

Holland, J. L. (1994). *Manual—Self-Directed Search.* Odessa, FL: Psychological Assessment Resources.

Holland, J. L., & Gottfredson, G. D. (1975). Predictive value and psychological meaning of vocational aspirations. *Journal of Vocational Behavior, 12,* 290–296.

Holland, J. L., Gottfredson, G. D., & Baker, H. G. (1990). Validity of vocational aspirations and interest inventories, extended, replicated, and reinterpreted. *Journal of Counseling Psychology, 37,* 337–342.

Holland, J. L., Gottfredson, G. D., & Gottfredson, L. S. (1975). Read our reports and examine the data: A response to Prediger and Cole. *Journal of Vocational Behavior, 7,* 253–259.

Ivey, A. E. (1982). Toward less of the same. Rethinking the assessment process. *Measurement and Evaluation in Guidance, 15,* 82–86.

Johnson, R. W., & Hoese, J. C. (1988). Career planning concerns of SCII clients. *Journal of Career Development, 36,* 251–258.

Jones, L. K. (1981). *Professional manual: Occ-U-Sort.* New York: McGraw-Hill.

Jones, L. K., Gorman, S., & Schroeder, C. G. (1989). A comparison of the SDS and career key among undecided college students. *Career Development Quarterly, 37,* 334–344.

Kapes, J. T., & Mastie, M. M. (1988). *A counselor's guide to career assessment instruments* (2nd ed.). Alexandria, VA: National Career Development Association.

Knapp, R. R., & Knapp, L. (1979). Relationship of work values to occupational activity interests. *Measurement and Evaluation in Guidance, 12,* 71–76.

Larsen, L. M., Heppner, P. P., Harm, T., & Dugan, K. (1988). Investigating multiple subtypes of career indecision through cluster analysis. *Journal of Counseling Psychology, 35,* 439–446.

Lent, R. W., Brown, S. D., & Hackett, G. (1996). A sociocognitive theory of career development. In D. Brown, L. Brooks & associates, *Career choice and development* (3rd ed.). San Francisco: Jossey-Bass.

Lent, R. W., Brown, S. D., & Larkin, K. C. (1984). Relationship of self-efficacy to self-efficacy expectation to academic persistence and achievement. *Journal of Counseling Psychology, 31,* 356–362.

Lent, R. W., Brown, S. D., & Larkin, K. C. (1986). Self-efficacy in the prediction of academic performance and perceived career options. *Journal of Counseling Psychology, 33,* 265–269.

Lonner, W. J. (1988). Issues in testing and assessment in cross-cultural counseling. *The Counseling Psychologist, 18,* 599–614.

Maddux, C. D., & Cummings, R. E. (1980). Alternate form reliability of the Self-Directed Search—Form E. *Career Development Quarterly, 35,* 136–140.

McGoldrick, M., & Gerson, R. (1985). *Genograms in family assessment.* New York: Mortin.

NBCC. (1997). Standards for the ethical practice of webcounseling. Greensboro, NC: National Board for Certified Counselors.

NCDA. (1997). NCDA guidelines for the use of the Internet for the provision of career information and planning services. Alexandria, VA: National Career Development Association.

Noeth, R. J. (1983). The effects of enhancing expressed vocational choice with career development measures to predict occupational field. *Journal of Vocational Behavior, 22,* 365–375.

Okiishi, R. W. (1987). The genogram as a tool in career counseling. *Journal of Counseling and Development, 66,* 139–143.

Parsons, F. (1909). *Choosing a vocation.* Boston: Houghton Mifflin.

Prediger, D. J. (1974). The role of assessment in career guidance. In E. L. Herr (Ed.), *Vocational guidance and human development* (pp. 325–349). Boston: Houghton Mifflin.

Prediger, D. J. (1981). A note on Self-Directed Search validity for females. *Vocational Guidance Quarterly, 30,* 117–129.

Prediger, D. J., & Garfield, N. (1988). Testing competencies and responsibilities: A checklist for counselors. In J. T. Kapes & M. M. Matie (Eds.), *A counselor's guide to career assessment instruments* (2nd ed., pp. 47–54). Alexandria, VA: National Career Development Association.

Prediger, D. J., & Hawson, G. R. (1976). It's time to face some issues: A response to Holland, Gottfredson, and Gottfredson. *Journal of Vocational Behavior, 1,* 261–263.

Pryor, R. G. L., & Taylor, N. B. (1980). On combining scores from interest and value measures for counseling. *Vocational Guidance Quarterly, 34,* 178–187.

Rokeach, M. (1973). *The nature of human values.* New York: Free Press.

Rokeach, M. (1979). *Understanding human values: Individual and societal.* New York: Free Press.

Rotberg, H. L. (1984). *Career self-efficacy expectations and perceived range of career options in community college students.* Unpublished doctoral dissertation. Chapel Hill, NC: University of North Carolina–Chapel Hill.

Rotberg, H. L., Brown, D., & Ware, W. B. (1987). Career self-efficacy expectation and perceived range of career options in community college students. *Journal of Counseling Psychology, 34,* 164–170.

Sampson, J. P., Jr. (1990). Computer-assisted testing and the goals of counseling psychology. *The Counseling Psychologist, 18,* 227–234.

Sampson, J. P., Jr. (1998a). Using the Internet to enhance test selection, orieantation, administration, and scoring. Paper presented at the American Association for Assessment in Counseling, Indianapolis, IN, March 1998.

Sampson, J. P., Jr. (1998b). Using the Internet to enhance test interpretation. Paper presented at the Assessment '98 Conference, St. Petersburg, FL, January 18, 1998.

Savickas, M. L. (1984). Career maturity: The construct and its measurements. *Vocational Guidance Quarterly, 32,* 222–231.

Slaney, R. B., & Slaney, F. M. (1986). Relationship of expressed and inventoried vocational interests of female career counseling clients. *Career Development Quarterly, 35,* 24–33.

Sundberg, N. D., & Gonzales, L. R. (1981). Cross-cultural and cross-ethnic assessment: Overview and issues. In P. McReynolds (Ed.), *Advances in psychological assessment* (Vol. 5, pp. 475–491). San Francisco: Jossey-Bass.

Super, D. E., & Thompson, A. S. (1979). A six-scale, two-factor measure of adolescent career or vocational maturity. *Vocational Guidance Quarterly, 28,* 6–15.

Tinsley, H. E. A., & Bradley, R. W. (1986). Test interpretation. *Journal of Counseling and Development, 64,* 462–466.

Tinsley, H. E. A., & Bradley, R. W. (1988). Interpretation of psychometric instruments in career counseling. In J. T. Kapes & M. M. Mastie (Eds.), *A counselor's guide to career assessment instruments* (2nd ed., pp. 37–46). Alexandria, VA: National Career Development Association.

Tittle, C. K., & Zytowski, D. G. (Eds.). (1980). *Sex-fair interest measurement: Research and complications.* Washington, DC: Institute of Education, U.S. Government Printing Office.

Tyler, L. E. (1961). Research explorations in the realm of choice. *Journal of Counseling Psychology, 8,* 195–202.

Tyler, L. E. (1978). *Individuality.* San Francisco: Jossey-Bass.

Vondracek, F. W., Hostetler, M., Schulenberg, J. E., & Shimiza, K. (1990). Dimensions of career indecision. *Journal of Counseling Psychology, 37,* 98–106.

Weinrach, S. G. (1979). Trait and factor counseling: Yesterday and today. In S. G. Weinrach (Ed.), *Career counseling: Theoretical and practical perspectives.* New York: McGraw-Hill.

Weinrach, S. G. (1984). Determinants of vocational choice: Holland's theory. In D. Brown, L. Brooks, and associates, *Career choice and development* (pp. 61–93). San Francisco: Jossey-Bass.

Wholeben, B. E. (1988). Sixteen PF personal career development profiles: Review. In J. T. Kapes & M. M. Mastie (Eds.), *A counselor's guide to career assessment instruments* (2nd ed, pp. 238–242). Alexandria, VA: National Career Development Association.

Williamson, E. G. (1939). *How to counsel students.* New York: McGraw-Hill.

Willis, C. G., & Ham, T. L. (1988). Myers–Briggs Type Indicator: Review. In J. T. Kapes & M. M. Mastie (Eds.), *A counselor's guide to career assessment instruments* (2nd ed., pp. 228 233). Alexandria, VA: National Career Development Association.

Womer, F. B. (1988). Selecting an instrument: Choice or challenge. In J. T. Kapes & M. M. Mastie (Eds.), *A counselor's guide to career assessment instruments* (2nd ed., pp. 25–36). Alexandria, VA: National Career Development Association.

Zytowski, D. G., & Warman, R. E. (1982). The changing use of tests in counseling. *Measurement and Evaluation of Guidance, 15,* 147–152.

14

Career Counseling

Background

It is likely that some type of career counseling has been available in this country since colonial times (Picchioni & Bonk, 1983). However, in this chapter the current status of career counseling will be examined, beginning with a fuller exploration of the definitions of the process than has been previously offered. The process of career counseling will also be explored. Client groups served by career counselors, techniques employed by career counselors, and the issue of credentialing career counselors will also be discussed.

Career Counseling Defined

The earliest approaches to career counseling were based on trait and factor ideas. E. G. Williamson (1939, 1965) defined career counseling as a six-step process including (1) analysis, or collection of data about the individual; (2) synthesis or summarizing the data that have been gathered; (3) diagnosis of the career problems (no choice; uncertain choice; unwise choice; discrepancy between interests and aptitudes); (4) prognosis or forecasting how successful the person will be if she has established goals; (5) counseling, which occurs if the person has not made a "good choice"; and (6) follow-up, which entails determining if the course of action taken as a result of the process is a viable one. If the choice turns out to be nonviable, the entire career exploration process needs to be recycled.

The National Career Development Association (NCDA) published a definition of career counseling which, like Williamson, focuses on career but expands on his ideas considerably. The authors stated (NCDA, 1988):

> *Vocational/career counseling consists of those activities performed or coordinated by individuals who have credentials to work with other individuals or groups of individuals about occupations, life/career, career decision making, career planning, career pathing, or other career development related questions or conflicts. (p. 3)*

Obviously, the NCDA definition adds a wider array of career-related activities to the career counseling process than did Williamson's. It also alludes to, but does not spell out, that career counseling focuses on the interaction of career and other life issues and notes that counselors who conduct career counseling should be appropriately credentialled. The NCDA definition does not mention the relationship between career counseling and personal counseling, which are viewed by some as separate processes.

However, Crites (1981) noted the need for a rapprochement between counseling that focuses on career issues and personal counseling and suggests that career counseling not only facilitates career development but enhances personal development as well. Crites (1981) also suggested that career counseling is more difficult than therapy and that, in fact, career counselors need to be experts in psychotherapy as well as in career counseling. Many authorities who write about career counseling have agreed with at least one of Crites's positions: It is time to eliminate the dichotomy between career and personal counseling.

Yost and Corbishley (1987) stated, "In the course of pursuing a career choice, clients often clarify values unrelated to careers, reassess general life goals, learn new interpersonal skills, and increase their self esteem" (p. 24). They pointed out that emotional constraints such as guilt and behavioral constraints such as nonassertiveness and cognitive constraints voiced in the form of "I can't," "I won't," "I shouldn't" statements all surface in the course of career counseling and must be dealt with if the process is to be successful.

Gysbers and Moore (1987) took a position similar to that of Yost and Corbishley (1987). They indicate that career counseling involves two phases, namely client goal or problem identification and resolution of the problem that has been identified. In phase 1 (goal or problem identification) they list the following subphases:

1. Establishing a working relationship and defining roles
2. Developing an understanding of the client's characteristics and environment
3. Making a diagnosis of the client's problem

In the problem resolution phase, the following subphases are listed (Gysbers & Moore, 1987):

1. Making an intervention
2. Evaluating the impact of the intervention
3. Terminating if the intervention is successful

On the surface, these phases and subphases appear somewhat analogous to Williamson's (1939) stages. However, Gysbers and Moore made it clear that career counseling involves such activities as identifying and eliminating irrational beliefs that may preclude career exploration, planning, or the establishment of career plans or distorted thinking that may result from filtering information (e.g., hearing only the negative or positive). They also provide guidelines for lifestyle analysis and looking at decisional problems that may grow out of faulty cognitions.

In what appears to be a radical departure from the traditional definitions of career counseling that focus on career choice, Kivlighan (1990) outlines a process that he refers to variously as career group therapy and career group counseling. He suggests that the same therapeutic factors that operate in therapy groups may be the curative factors in career group counseling as well. He also suggests that therapy and career counseling are analogous processes. However, he concludes that at this time we possess only rudimentary knowledge of the role of therapeutic factors and other group process variables in career counseling groups.

Brown and Brooks (1991) defined career counseling as a process aimed at facilitating career development that involves choosing, entering, adjusting to, and advancing in a career. They also suggested that career development occurs over the life span and interacts with the development of other life roles (e.g., child, student, or leisurite). They defined career problems as including areas such as undecidedness, indecisiveness (the inability to choose), work performance, incongruence between the person and the work role, job stress, and inadequate integration of work with other life roles.

The process of career counseling, according to Brown and Brooks (1991), involves establishing a relationship followed by evaluating the extent to which a client is able objectively to assess his or her personal characteristics and how they relate to potential occupations, and the client's motivation to engage in career counseling. If the counselor determines that cognitive clarity is lacking (inability to assess objectively self and environment), personal counseling may be necessary. If motivation is lacking, emphasis may need to be placed on preparing the client for the career counseling process. If cognitive clarity and motivation are present, the counselor can proceed with career counseling.

As stated at the outset, many career counselors see the relationship between personal and career problems. It is also the case that many career counselors adopt counseling approaches that integrate personal and career counseling aimed at helping their clients integrate work with other life roles. There are times when the counseling process focuses only on career choice or adjustment within the existing career. However, even in these moments, career counselors are alert to the possible impact of other life roles and/or mental health problems on work. It is also equally true that a process initiated ostensibly to correct career-related problems may have to be interrupted while personal problems are addressed. Finally, clients who come for personal counseling may actually need career counseling. For example, incongruence between people and their jobs and roles may result in job stress. This tension may in turn manifest itself as headaches, depression, insomnia, and lower back pains that may be treated by the novice as mental health problems (Brooks & Brown, 1986; Brown, 1985).

The career counseling definitions posed by Yost and Corbishley (1987), Gysbers and Moore (1987), and Brown and Brooks (1991) have focused to some degree on the relationships between mental health and career problems, work, and other life roles. These authors view career counseling as an interpersonal process aimed at fostering career development by identifying and eliminating mental health problems, if necessary, and by facilitating the development of personal awareness by eliminating cognitive and emotional barriers to self-exploration as well as enhancing knowledge of occupations, occupational mobility, the social and economic influences on careers, and the context in which people work (businesses, professions, etc.). It is also implicit in most definitions and explicit in two (Crites, 1981; NCDA, 1988) that career counseling requires specialized training in areas such as assessment and use of occupational information in addition to basic training in personal counseling.

Theoretical Bases

Early in this volume, several theories of occupational choice and career development were presented (see Chapter 2). Because of the rather brief treatment of these theories, it may not have been apparent that they would serve as a basis for career counseling. However, when many of the leading theorists were asked to apply their theories to a case description, most were able to do so without difficulty (Brown & Brooks, 1991). However, as Srebalus and associates (1982) pointed out, the study of theory in most instances is meant to be a stimulus for the trainee to develop her own personal theory. They also suggest that theories of occupational choice and career development may need to be integrated with general counseling theory, personality theory, and behavior-change theory, a recommendation that seems justified given the stage of evolution of theories of occupational choice and career development.

Most career counselors have developed their own approach to career counseling. Srebalus and associates (1982) suggested that the following factors should be considered as the counselor–trainee develops an approach to career counseling: foundation, description of clients, statements about client problems or goals, a conceptualization of career counseling clients, conceptualizations of the counseling relationship, beliefs about how problems are diagnosed, development of counseling strategies that will engender change, and approaches to evaluating counseling outcomes.

The foundation of most counselors' "theories" probably stems from two sources: formal theory and informal theory of human functioning (Strohmer & Newman, 1983). All trainees come to counselor preparation programs with a set of beliefs about how people develop and change, although these may not have been carefully articulated. At the outset of most training programs, trainees are exposed to numerous theories including those that attempt to explain human development, personality formation, learning, change via counseling and therapy, and occupational change and career development. In well-conceptualized training programs, students are then assisted to integrate these formal theories with their personal belief systems to develop their own models of counseling. More often, students are left to their own devices to develop personal approaches to counseling. It is suggested here that prospective career counselors begin to formulate their own models of career counseling by answering the following questions:

1. What are my personal beliefs about human nature? Are people essentially energetic and self-motivated or by nature lazy and in need of external motivation? What are the forces that cause people to grow and change? What retards that process?
2. With regard to formal theories of human development, how does normal development occur? What leads to abnormal functioning? How can abnormal behavior be changed? What circumstances may result in normal people becoming abnormal?
3. How do interests and work values develop? Why do they change? How can I measure them?
4. What are the indications of abnormal behavior? Why do they change? How can I measure them?
5. How does the work role interact with other life roles? How can they be interrelated? What happens when conflict between life roles occurs? How can the work role and other roles be brought into harmony?
6. How do I establish relationships with my clients?
7. How do I use information from tests and inventories in counseling?
8. How do I assess work satisfaction? How can I facilitate the process?
9. How do I motivate unmotivated clients?
10. What are the potential problems in providing career counseling to clients from other cultures? How can these be avoided? Remedied if they are used?
11. How can I evaluate the outcomes of my work?

To answer these questions adequately, career counselors need the following competencies (NCDA, 1991, unnumbered).

Individual and Group Counseling Skills
Individual and group counseling competencies considered essential to effective career counseling.
    Demonstration of:

1. Ability to establish and maintain productive personal relationships with individuals.
2. Ability to establish and maintain a productive group climate.

3. Ability to collaborate with clients in identifying personal goals.
4. Ability to identify and select techniques appropriate to client or group goals and client needs, psychological states, and developmental tasks.
5. Ability to plan, implement and evaluate counseling techniques designed to assist clients to achieve the following:
   a. Identify and understand clients' personal characteristics related to career.
   b. Identify and understand social contextual conditions affecting clients' careers.
   c. Identify and understand familial, subcultural and cultural structures and functions as they are related to clients' careers.
   d. Identify and understand clients' career decision-making processes.
   e. Identify and understand clients' biases toward work and workers.
   f. Identify and understand clients' biases toward work and workers based on gender, race, and cultural stereotypes.
6. Ability to challenge and encourage clients to take action to prepare for and initiate role transitions by:
   a. Locating sources of relevant information and experience.
   b. Obtaining and interpreting information and experiences.
   c. Acquiring skills needed to make role transitions.
7. Ability to support and challenge clients to examine the balance of work, leisure, family, and community roles in their careers.

Individual/Group Assessment

Individual/group assessment skills considered essential for professionals engaging in career counseling.
Demonstration of:

1. Knowledge about instruments and techniques to assess personal characteristics (such as aptitude, achievement, interests, values, and other personality traits).
2. Knowledge about instruments and techniques to assess leisure interests, learning style, life roles, self-concept, career maturity, vocational identity, career indecision, work environment preference (e.g., work satisfaction), and other related lifestyle/development issues.
3. Knowledge about instruments and techniques to assess conditions of the work environment (such as tasks, expectations, norms, and qualities of the physical and social settings).
4. Ability to evaluate and select instruments appropriate to the client's physical capacities, psychological states, social roles, and cultural background.
5. Knowledge about variables such as ethnicity, gender, culture, learning style, personal development, and physical/mental disability which affect the assessment process.

6. Knowledge of and ability to effectively and appropriately use computer-assisted assessment measures and techniques.
7. Ability to identify assessment [procedures] appropriate for specified situations and populations.
8. Ability to evaluate assessment [procedures] in terms of their validity, reliability, and relationships to race, gender, age, and ethnicity.
9. Ability to select assessment techniques appropriate for group administration and those appropriate for individual administration.
10. Ability to administer, score and report findings from career assessment instruments.
11. Ability to interpret data from assessment instruments and present the results to client and to others designated by client.
12. Ability to assist client and others designated by the client to interpret data from assessment instruments.
13. Ability to write a thorough and substantiated report of assessment results.

Information/Resources
Information/resource base and knowledge essential for professionals engaging in career counseling.
Demonstration of:

1. Knowledge of employment information and career planning resources for client use.
2. Knowledge of education, training, and employment trends; labor market information and resources that provide information about job tasks, functions, salaries, requirements and future outlooks related to broad occupational fields and individual occupations.
3. Knowledge of the changing roles of women and men and the implications for work, education, family and leisure.
4. Knowledge of and the ability to use computer-based career information delivery systems (CIDS) and computer-assisted career guidance systems (CACGS) to store, retrieve and disseminate career and occupational information.
5. Knowledge of community/professional resources to assist clients in career/life planning, including job search.

Career Development Theory
Theory base and knowledge considered essential for professionals engaging in career counseling and development.
Demonstration of:

1. Knowledge about counseling theories and associated techniques.
2. Knowledge about theories and models of careers and career development.

3. Knowledge about differences in knowledge and values about work and productive roles associated with gender, age, ethnic and race groups, cultures and capacities.
4. Knowledge about career counseling theoretical models, associated counseling and information techniques, and sources to learn more about them.
5. Knowledge about developmental issues individuals address throughout the life span.
6. Knowledge of the role relationships to facilitate personal, family, and career development.
7. Knowledge of information, techniques, and models related to computer-assisted career guidance systems and career information delivery systems and career counseling.
8. Knowledge of the information, techniques, and models related to career planning and placement.
9. Knowledge of career counseling theories and models that apply specifically to women or are inclusive of variables that are important to women's career development.

Special Populations

Knowledge and skills considered essential in relating to special populations that impact career counseling and development processes.

Demonstration of:

1. Knowledge of the intrapersonal dynamics of special population clients while understanding resistances and defenses that may occur naturally during the counseling process.
2. Sensitivity toward the developmental issues and needs unique to minority populations.
3. Sensitivity toward and knowledge of various disabling conditions and necessary assistance and requirements.
4. Ability to define the structure of the career counseling process to accommodate individual cultural frames of reference and ethnic and racial issues.
5. Ability to distinguish between the special needs of the culturally different, immigrants, the disabled, the elderly, persons with the AIDS virus, and minority populations.
6. Ability to find appropriate methods or resources to communicate with limited-English-proficient individuals.
7. Ability to identify alternative approaches to career planning needs for individuals with specific needs.
8. Ability to identify community resources and establish linkages to assist clients with specific needs.
9. Ability to assist other staff members, professionals, and community members in understanding the unique needs/characteristics of special

populations with regard to career exploration, employment expectations, and economic/social issues.

10. Ability to advocate for the career development and employment of special populations.
11. Ability to deliver and design career development programs and materials for hard-to-reach special populations.

Ethical/Legal Issues
Information base and knowledge essential for the ethical and legal practice of career counseling.
Demonstration of:

1. Knowledge about the code of ethical standards of the American Association for Counseling and Development, the National Career Development Association, NBCC, CACREP, and other relevant professional organizations.
2. Knowledge about current ethical and legal issues that affect the practice of career counseling.
3. Knowledge about ethical issues related to career counseling with women, cultural minorities, immigrants, the disabled, the elderly, and persons with the AIDS virus.
4. Knowledge about current ethical/legal issues with regard to the use of computer-assisted career guidance.
5. Ability to apply ethical standards to career counseling and consulting situations, issues, and practices.
6. Ability to recognize situations involving interpretation of ethical standards and to consult with supervisors and colleagues to determine an appropriate and ethical course of action.
7. Knowledge of state and federal statutes relating to client confidentiality.

The Career Counseling Process

As can be seen from the preceding listing of competencies, career counseling involves much more than matching a person to an occupation. Career counselors need to be prepared to identify "psychological states," understand cultural variables that may influence both career choice and the counseling relationship, and help clients consider career options in the context of other life roles. However, in the most simplistic terms, the career counseling process consists of five stages: (1) establishing a counselor–client relationship and structuring the relationship, (2) diagnosing the problem, (3) goal setting, (4) intervention, and (5) evaluation. As we have already seen from the definitions provided, some people writing about career counseling would elaborate on these stages (e.g., Crites, 1981; Brown & Brooks, 1991) but most would accept this framework. In this section, the process of career counseling is described using these stages as the basic framework for the process.

Relationship/Structure

In this stage of career counseling, several tasks must be accomplished. Chief among these is the development of an open, trusting relationship based on mutual respect. Literally dozens of "how to" books have been written about how these steps are to be accomplished (e.g., Carkhuff, 1983; Hutchins & Cole, 1997) and these should be consulted for further information. Structuring the career counseling process occurs simultaneously with relationship development and, although it is a separate process to some degree, is an integral part of the relationship development process. Yost and Corbishley (1987) indicated that the first task in structuring career counseling is to give the client a clear statement regarding the counseling process including goals, procedures to be used, risk to the clients, limitations of the process, possible outcomes, and cost if a fee is to be charged. Clients also have a right to know about the qualifications of the counselor and the role the counselor will assume.

One or two more aspects of structuring should probably be added to the Yost and Corbishley (1987) list. For example, in addition to making disclosures about the responsibilities of the counselor, some discussion of the counselor's expectations of the client are also in order (Brown & Brooks, 1991). For example, early in career counseling, perhaps in a discussion of the procedures to be used, the counselor will want to establish expectations about the client's responsibility in taking tests and inventories, homework assignments, interviewing workers or job shadowing, and disclosure of information about self.

Embedded in Yost and Corbishley's (1987) statement about counselor responsibility is a statement about confidentiality. In most states, the clients of licensed counselors, psychologists, and social workers are accorded privileged communication in the laws that establish licensure requirements. The codes of ethics of all mental health professionals require practitioners to keep in confidence information disclosed in the course of counseling. Therefore clients' disclosures are protected both legally and ethically with certain limitations, namely if clients pose a threat to themselves or to others. These limitations should be explained along with the legal and ethical constraints on the counselor.

Structuring the career counselor relationship also involves establishing a time and place to meet and developing some preliminary expectations about how long the process is likely to take. Most career counselors working in college counseling centers have experienced the situation with the sophomore who, when confronted with the necessity of deciding a major in her sophomore year, concludes that she should also decide on her life's work. As one sophomore put it, "I only have 3 weeks until I meet with my advisor and I want to have both a major and a job picked out." It may be possible that a career can be selected in 3 weeks, but most career counselors find that it takes longer and should communicate to the client that the process may not be completed in 3 weeks.

Assessment

In Chapter 13, the general topic of assessment in career development was addressed. The primary focus of that chapter was on the use of tests and inventories to identify assessment strategies that may have relevance to career development. Certainly, formal assessment procedures will be employed to help clients develop an increased awareness of their interests, values, aptitudes, personality traits, and decisional style. However, much of the assessment that occurs in the career counseling process is based on the informal observations of the counselor. As noted in Chapter 13, this assessment is referred to as clinical assessment.

Clinical assessment of the client begins at the first contact and continues throughout the career counseling process. For many counselors, clinical assessment involves developing, and at times discarding and redeveloping, a hypothesis about the nature of the client's problem. In many instances, informal observations made during the course of the counseling interview are supplemented with data from the tests and inventories described in Chapter 13. If the hypothesis developed by the counselor suggests that a health problem may be involved, a physician may be consulted and the client may be asked to have a physical examination. The conclusion arising from all of the data gathered in the assessment process is the diagnosis.

Williamson's (1939) diagnostic system classified clients as having no choice, an uncertain choice, an unsure choice, or having a discrepancy between interests and aptitudes. Crites (1969) developed a comprehensive diagnostic system for career counselors that looked at interests and aptitudes as they related to three variables: adjustment, indecision, and realism. According to Crites, the adjusted person is in a field with appropriate interests and aptitudes and may simply come to career counselors for assurance. Maladjusted individuals are in neither a field of interest nor one that is commensurate with their aptitudes. Multipotentialed individuals may have many occupations that interest them and may have the aptitudes to pursue them all, while undecided individuals have no choice. Unrealistic individuals have a field of interest but do not have the aptitude to pursue that field. Unfulfilled clients have a field of interest, but it is below their measured potential. Coerced individuals are in an occupation where they can succeed because of aptitude, but they are not interested in it.

Contemporary career counselors are less likely to establish distinct nosological categories, choosing to look at certain distinct variables instead. Brown and Brooks (1991) identify cognitive clarity, informational deficits, client motivation, suitability of work environment (worker fit), interrelationship of work and other life roles, health factors, and the flexibility of significant others, such as spouses, as factors that should be assessed. Super (1990) suggested assessing autonomy, time perspective, self-esteem, interests, vocational preferences, occupational self-concept, and a variety of other factors. Yost and Corbishley (1987) simply divided assessment into two spheres: psychological problems and work-related concerns. Regardless of the assessment categories, the end result is a diagnosis of the client's problem by the counselor. This diagnosis is shared with the client and, if there is consensus, goal setting occurs.

Goal Setting

Gysbers and Moore (1987) described the goal-setting stage as goal *or* problem identification, clarification, and specification, since they believe that having a counseling goal does not necessarily mean that the client has a problem. They refer specifically to clients who come to career counseling for self-improvement, not to solve problems. The term *goal setting* has been adopted here because it subsumes both situations where problems are to be resolved and where the client wants to pursue self-improvement.

Well-developed career counseling goals should be specific, feasible, desired by the client, and not dictated by the wishes of others and, if the counselor is to continue, compatible with the skills of the counselor (Brown & Brooks, 1991). Typically, clients pursue multiple goals during the process of career counseling. If it becomes apparent that this is going to be the situation, potential goals should be identified and prioritized. In many instances, circumstances dictate the priorities. Individuals who have lost their jobs will probably want to focus on getting another one, particularly if they have limited financial resources. Once a new job is secured, other more suitable occupations may be explored and additional choices pursued.

Intervention

Once goals are selected, the counselor suggests interventions that may be useful in helping the client attain the goal that has been set. It is undoubtedly true that all of the techniques explored in counseling are potentially useful in career counseling. However, a few of those techniques that are often used in career counseling are discussed here.

Gathering Occupational Information

Many clients who come for counseling simply lack occupational information. Others have the information but do not know how to use it in job planning. Twenty-five percent of American adults report that they have never used any form of occupational information (Brown, Minor, & Jepsen, 1991).

Occupational information can be used to clarify occupational alternatives, to generate new alternatives, or to eliminate some of the occupations currently being considered by the client. It can also be used to familiarize inexperienced clients with various occupations and to eliminate stereotypical perceptions of occupations and the people who hold various jobs. Occupational information can be used to motivate clients to make career choices by showing them the rewards associated with various careers (Brown & Brooks, 1991). Finally, occupational information is often used as a way to help individuals engage in reality testing by exposing them to the skills, aptitudes, and training required to prepare for and enter an occupation and the working environment for different types of jobs.

Identifying Transferable Skills

Displaced homemakers reentering the work force, students, people who have lost their jobs because of job termination, and many others find it necessary to find different jobs. Often career counselors engage in helping clients identify skills that have been acquired in their current jobs or in other jobs that will transfer to other jobs. These skills are typically not technical competencies, such as drafting, but are more general in nature (e.g., writing, communication, managing, scheduling, public speaking, fund raising).

Counselors typically use checklists (Figler, 1979), card sorts (Hampl, 1983), and logs of activities performed over a period of time (Yost & Corbishley, 1987) and then help the client organize them into clusters or patterns, perhaps using something like the Holland typology (RIASEC) as the basis for the organization (Brown & Brooks, 1991)

Multicultural Considerations

Many of the competencies listed in the section of the NCDA competencies labeled Special Populations pertain to counseling the culturally different. In this section, some of the legal and ethical issues surrounding the career counseling process will be discussed. Not the least of the ethical concerns is that career counselors must possess the skills and sensitivities needed to provide counseling to minority clients. To put the matter plainly, it is unethical to use models and approaches to career counseling, or any of the processes associated with it (e.g., assessment), based on Eurocentric cultures—with one caveat. This exception is that clients who are from different races and ethnic backgrounds who are acculturated, that is, those who have adopted Eurocentric values regarding social relationships, time, activity, and self-control, probably will benefit from a traditional approach to career counseling. What follows is a brief set of guidelines for providing career counseling to people who are culturally different.

1. Be aware of your stereotypes and avoid acting on them. Ho (1995) suggested that counselors should be aware of the internal culture of their clients and not concern themselves with external characteristics that may or may not be indicators of culture. The entire career development movement has been predicated on a respect for individual differences and providing career counseling to cultural, racial, and racial minorities to continue this tradition. In order to ascertain the internal culture of the clients, it is necessary to assess their cultural identity. During the process of enculturation, certain values are learned that result in views about role relationship and beliefs about what is appropriate and inappropriate behavior.

The client's values, behavior, expectations, and beliefs are indicators of their cultural identity (Okun, Fried, & Okun, 1999). Unless the client's values and worldview are fully understood, the likelihood that career counseling will be successful is greatly diminished.

2. Consider the client's values regarding time when scheduling appointments. As was noted by Okun, Fried, and Okun (1999), people who do not have a future time orientation may see their activities and the people involved in them as more important than being on time for an appointment. Moreover, the idea of being on time varies from culture to culture. In Eurocentric culture, being five minutes late for a meeting is acceptable. In other cultures, being 30 to 45 minutes late is considered being on time. In Eurocentric culture, being late is considered to be rude, but this is not always the case in other cultures.

3. Before proceeding with career counseling, identify the decision maker. For many career counselors who hold the Eurocentric social value individualism, the student or adult is the decision maker and thus the client. In many subgroups of Asian Americans (e.g., Koreans, Japanese, Asian Indians) the father, parents, or other individuals within the family unit will be the decision makers and should thus be included in the counseling process. Leong (1991) found that Chinese American college students in his sample preferred a dependent decision-making style, and it is likely that this finding would be replicated in many other Asian subgroups.

4. Consider the issue of face when providing career counseling. Loss of face occurs when a client feels that the counselor does not show the proper respect or insults him or her, with the result that the client's identity is challenged (Okun, Fried, & Okun, 1999). Few counselors would insult or show disrespect for a client intentionally, but they might do so inadvertently. An example of this occurred when a counselor who was meeting with a Korean father and high school student suggested to the father that he consider career options other than medicine for his son, who had lower-than-average grades. The father, who clearly saw himself as the decision maker, felt that the counselor had not been respectful and had caused him to lose face with his son.

5. Vary counseling techniques to fit the preferred verbal and nonverbal preferences of the clients. Many Native American clients prefer not to disclose their feelings; thus, the use of reflection of feelings or questions that ask how clients feel may be inappropriate. Additionally, questions that ask for disclosures about family members when the client has a collateral value (e.g., many Asian Americans and Native Americans) may be too intrusive. This is because, in contrast to individuals who hold Eurocentric values, concerns about privacy extend beyond the individual to the family. Nonverbal counseling techniques must also be varied for some cultural group. One excellent example of this concerns contact. In Eurocentric culture, eye contact is expected, and lack of it may be seen as lack of respect or disinterest. However, in many Asian cultures (e.g., Vietnamese) direct eye contact is seen as a sign of aggression. Among some African Americans, the preferred approach to eye contact is to look at individuals when they are speaking and to look away when others are speaking to them. There are

also considerable differences in how pauses or silences are viewed among various cultures. For example, African Americans and white European Americans are often uncomfortable with silent periods in conversations, but long silences characterize the conversations of many Native Americans (Srebalus & Brown, 1998). Many other differences in the verbal and nonverbal communications styles of various cultures could be provided. However, hopefully the foregoing illustrations should be sufficient to alert career counselors that these differences are important.

6. Do not assume that individuals who have developed a functional use of the language have vocabularies that are sufficiently well developed to deal with the jargon and language found in occupational information and on various assessment devices. Many indigenous people and some newly arrived immigrants have sufficient command of the English language to operate in our society. However, for many people, English is their second language, and they may not have the technical understanding necessary to understand the language that is used daily by career development specialists and that can be found on assessment devices and in occupational information. It is incumbent upon career counselors to ascertain that clients understand the language used. In fulfilling this obligation, counselors may need either to make referrals to counselors who speak the client's language or to secure the services of an interpreter.

Facilitating Decision Making

Career decision making, whether it be making an initial choice, choosing a new career, or making an adjustment in one's current career, involves posing and answering a series of questions. To assist decision makers in dealing with the vast amount of data that is involved in the decision-making process, counselors often introduce decision-making aids that are generally of two types.

The first type is lateral decision-making aids. These were designed to increase both the quality and quantity of information available, by looking creatively at information that is available, and to create new ways of looking at job situations, even those that are satisfying. The lateral thinking techniques developed by de Bono (1970, 1985) can be used for these purposes.

While space does not permit an extensive discussion of de Bono's many and varied decision-making aids, his "six thinking hats" technique illustrates many of his ideas. When using this technique, the career decision maker is advised that creative decision makers wear six thinking hats: blue, white, red, black, yellow, and green. The counselor then suggests that the client wear each of the following hats:

White: Looks at only facts about self and careers

Red: Relies on intuition; follows unjustified hunches (e.g., I feel like I'd be a good mechanic)

Black: Figures how, why things do not work; is pessimistic and critical

Yellow: Is optimistic; figures out why things will work

Green: Brainstorms new alternatives, looks at problems differently

Blue: Is rational

The data generated by the client while wearing each hat are examined to determine what new or additional data about career choices are needed.

De Bono (1985) suggests that lateral thinking techniques are useful, but ultimately decision makers may need to turn to rational (wearing the blue hat) approaches. The several types of decision making that counselors offer are decision aids using rational procedures. These aids are, for the most part, based on scientific method: Identify the problem, generate alternatives, gather data, select an alternative based on the data, select and test the alternative, and recycle if necessary. However, many are much more complex.

The balance sheet decision-making aid (Janis & Mann, 1977) is an example of a fairly complex but highly useful decision-making aid. In this approach, the decision making begins by thoughtfully generating three to five career alternatives. Then the client makes a list of personal gains (e.g., money status) and losses (e.g., would be unable to participate in favorite leisure pursuit). These gains and losses are then weighted from +5 to –5. Lists of other gains and losses (e.g., spouse) that would accrue are then made and weighted in a similar fashion. This same procedure is followed with sources of self-approval and disapproval and with sources of social approval and disapproval. A brief version of the balance sheet technique is shown in Table 14.1.

TABLE 14.1   Career Alternatives

	Mechanic	Engineer
Personal Gains & Losses		
Training time	4	–5
Status	–3	4
Others Gains & Losses		
Girlfriend—I go away to school	1	–5
Parents' expenses	1	–5
Sources of Self-Approval/Disapproval		
Work with my hands	5	1
Can see finished product	5	2
Sources of Social Approval or Disapproval		
Parents' pride	0	5
Friends	4	2
Total	+17	–1

Once the totals in the balance sheet are compiled, the career decision maker examines the information that has been generated and, if appropriate, reevaluates the weights. Obviously, the balance sheet should not dictate the final occupational choice but may be helpful in weighing alternatives.

Improving Time Perspective

Clients may come to career counselors with three time perspectives: past, present, and future. It is essential to career planning that, at least with regard to career orientation, they have a future orientation (Savickas, 1991). It is also imperative, according to Savickas, that the "future" be viewed optimistically and that the future have density, that it is filled with a variety of events (e.g., choosing a career, completing preparations for the chosen career, getting hired, getting the first promotion).

Savickas recommended that techniques such as a birth-to-death lifeline be employed to assist clients to differentiate the future from the past and to anticipate future events and duties in the future to be established for anticipated events. Guided fantasy, a technique described in the next section, can also be used to "transport" the career client into the future and to have him or her "experience," via fantasies, certain events.

Guided Fantasy

Guided fantasy is a process that is structured and directed (guided) by the career counselor to enhance self-awareness, to help the client develop appreciation for his or her masculine and feminine side, to generate career alternatives, and, just as importantly, to solve anticipated problems.

Counselors design guided fantasies to fit client needs. Some clients, perhaps as many as 25 percent, have difficulty participating in guided fantasy (Richardson, 1981), and therefore it is imperative that before guided fantasy is employed that same exploration be conducted within the fantasy about the appropriateness of the procedure. However, once this is determined, the counselor should design the fantasy so that it relates to the goals being pursued. Some examples of fantasies that might be employed are shown in Table 14.2.

TABLE 14.2   Design of Fantasy for Career Clients

Problem	Fantasy
Cannot decide between two goals, one set of values or outcomes	A winding path, one leading to the other to a second set
Stuck in an appropriate career; designs a way out	Client treads into tar pit
Client fearful about job change, but also fearful of outcomes of risk taking	Fantasy involves tasks of old job, pleasant tasks of new job

After the suitability of guided fantasy has been determined, induction to fantasy should occur. This involves introducing the concept of fantasy to the client, gaining permission to use it, and providing an overview of the fantasy with statements such as, "After I get you relaxed, we are going to take a trip into your future where you will encounter some surprises. None of these will be unpleasant, but they may be perplexing." Clients should also be told that fantasy is natural: Almost everyone fantasizes; some people fantasize in color; others in black and white; you are in control of your fantasies; and it is possible that even the most innocuous fantasy will arouse powerful emotions (Brown & Brooks, 1991).

Induction is followed by relaxation (e.g., deep breathing), the fantasy itself, reorientation to the here and now, and processing what was experienced in the fantasy. Of these stages, reorientation is most critical. The client may be reoriented by touching objects in the immediate surrounding and perhaps doing mild physical exercise. Failure to reorient the client properly can have negative effects (e.g., feeling that the counselor is still in control; Heikkinon, 1989).

Homework

One of the most often used techniques in career counseling is homework. Homework assignments are developed collaboratively by the client and counselor (Brown & Brooks, 1991) and generally are engaged in to extend the learning that has begun in the counselor's office. For example, clients may be assigned to interview workers after developing a tentative job choice.

According to Shelton and Ackerman (1974), homework assignments should be specific in that they include what is to be done and how it is to be done. Homework assignments should also include components of where and when (e.g., "Please interview two nurses this week, in their work settings if possible, and try to determine why they selected their jobs, how they trained for them, what their duties are, the satisfying and dissatisfying aspects of their work, and where they hope to be in 5 years careerwise"). Brown and Brooks (1991) adopted the following formula for remembering the components of a well-designed homework assignment: 3 W H S S (what is to be done, where it is to be done, when it is to be done = 3W; how often it is to be done = H; self-statements = SS). Self-statements are self-reinforcing statements that are included when the client finishes her work. An example might be, "I feel good because I completed my homework assignment!"

There are literally dozens of other techniques that can be employed during the course of career counseling. Books by Gysbers and Moore (1987), Yost and Corbishley (1987), and Brown and Brooks (1991) should be consulted for a more elaborate discussion of the techniques listed in this section as well as discussions of other techniques.

Clients

The foregoing discussion was intended to serve as a general orientation to career counseling regardless of the clients involved. However, all groups of clients require special considerations, preparation, and sensitivity. This section presents a brief overview of some of the special needs of various client groups.

Women

Women bring approximately the same general types of career problems to counselors as do men, with a few exceptions. For example, because of socialization influences, women have had lower career aspirations than men (Kerr, 1983), have entered a more restricted range of careers (Astin, 1984; Brooks, 1988; Hansen, 1984), and tend to put family concerns before career issues (Coombs, 1979; Di Benedetto & Tittle, 1990). Career counselors must be aware of the self-limiting stereotypes that restrict women's choices and be sensitive to the importance placed on families. They should also be aware that certain life experiences, such as sexual and physical abuse, may have severely lowered some women's self-esteem (Bowen, 1982). This is not to suggest that counselors must accept these stereotypes or should let the consequences of putting family ahead of career go unexplained. In short, good counseling strategy dictates that self-limiting stereotypes and inability to attribute success to one's own efforts (Stonewater, Eveslage, Dingerson, 1990) should be challenged and the impact of placing the family first in life planning should be fully explored. It also means accepting and supporting the decisions that are needed. Career counselors should also be prepared to accept various lifestyles and to explore the potential impact on careers of remaining single, lesbian relationships, single parenthood, and cohabitation. Career counselors also need to be aware of career options for women in the military (Lange, 1982), high-level government service, consulting, self-owned businesses, and occupations where telecommuting is possible.

Men

Even a casual observer of male–female relationships is aware that role relationships are changing, with men filling many of the roles that women have filled when women enter the work force out of choice and necessity. Just as women must plan for multiple roles, so too must men, even though there is some evidence that men are still planning careers without consideration of their family role (Di Benedetto & Tittle, 1990). Unfortunately, there is also some evidence that mental health professionals impose negative stereotypes on men who might opt for these nontraditional roles (Robertson & Fitzgerald, 1990). Again, career counselors must be prepared to challenge the self-limiting stereotypes of men, to explore the interaction of work and other life roles, and to examine alternative lifestyles (e.g., never marrying, gay relationships, cohabitation, and single parenthood).

The selection of, and adjustment to, nontraditional careers may increasingly be a reality for men as women fill spots in occupations traditionally held by men.

Chusmir's (1990) review of the literature in this area suggests that men who have selected nontraditional careers in the past possess many of the same characteristics of women in those careers and are comfortable with their masculinity. However, his review also suggests that there are strong negative perceptions of men in occupations such as nursing, child care, and early childhood education, although there appears to be some evidence that attitudes are changing.

Minorities and Majorities

White counselors often find themselves faced with the prospect of assisting people with cultural backgrounds and value systems quite different from their own. Conversely, career counselors from various minority groups may find themselves dealing with a person who has adopted the values and customs of the dominant culture. While little attention has been given to the latter issue (Sue & Zane, 1987), the problems involving white counselors and minority clients have been discussed at length. For example, Bowman (1993) tried to design culturally appropriate intervention for Hispanics, American Indians, African Americans and Asian Americans. Leong (1993) made suggestions aimed at white counselors working with minorities, but they are appropriate for any career counselor involved in cross-cultural career counseling. He suggested that the counseling process, which includes all aspects of communication, as well as relational issues between counselor and client(s) needs to be culturally appropriate. For example, it may be inappropriate to engage in direct, confrontive interactions with Asian Americans (Leong, 1993), but this communication style would be quite appropriate when counseling many people who have Eurocentric values. Other examples of the numerous pitfalls befall career counselors engaged in cross-cultural issues, but perhaps it will suffice to say that a prerequisite to being successful in cross-cultural career counseling is for the counselor to understand the values, goals, and communication and decisional styles of each client and to translate these understandings into action in the counseling process.

Minorities, like women, are concentrated in a restricted range of occupations, are more likely to be unemployed, earn less, and consequently are more likely to live in poverty (Arbono, 1989, 1990). Even the "model" minority, Asian Pacific Islanders, find themselves stereotyped as good at science and math, nonassertive, and nonexpressive, with the result that they are underrepresented in top-management positions (Fukuyama, 1992). Career counselors need to be aware of their own stereotypes of minorities, be sensitive to the cultural norms of each minority group, and be prepared to deal with the anger, frustration, and even apathy that may result from being discriminated against and living in poverty (Brown & Brooks, 1991).

Smith (1985) makes a number of more specific suggestions for counseling minority clients. She suggests that the process should begin by identifying the sources of stress being experienced by the client, particularly those that are resulting from the minority status, and the client's reaction to these stressors particularly if it has led to social isolation and alienation.

For example, Palacios and Franco (1986) suggest that family conflict, interpersonal relationships, absence of working skills, low problem-solving ability, and low stress tolerance may contribute to the problems of Hispanic women, while Asamen and Berry (1987) suggest, on the basis of their research, that perceptions of prejudice may be more problematic for Japanese Americans than for Chinese Americans.

Once stressors associated with racial status have been determined, stress related to work and family roles should be assessed (Smith, 1985). When these and other stressors are identified, the counselor should help clients develop a sense of internal control and develop a support network. In designing specific strategies, the counselor must take into consideration the values pattern of the client's culture, the extent to which the client has adopted the values pattern of the dominant culture, and the points of conflict between mainstream values and the client's values, and then work with the client to resolve values clashes.

People at Midlife

Bradley (1990) observes that relatively little is known about the actual number of people at midlife who are engaged in making career transitions and cites one estimate that approximately 10 percent of adults between 30 and 44 are in transition. The latest Gallup poll (Hoyt and Lester, 1995) commissioned by the NCDA sheds some light on this question. For example, 22.7 percent of the 26- to 40-year-olds surveyed indicated that they would choose to change jobs in the 3 years subsequent to the poll, and nearly 6 percent believed that they would be forced to change jobs within 3 years. These figures for the 41–55 age group were 13.8 (choose to change) and 6.2 (will be forced to change) percent. While neither of these groups matches Griffin's 30–44 category, they indicate that the estimate that 16 percent of people at midlife are involved in some type of career transition is probably conservative.

The midcareer changer who chooses to change jobs presents a somewhat different problem than the worker who is forced to change jobs, particularly if the worker's job has been terminated suddenly. As Bradley (1990) notes, "Psychologically, the loss of a job can be devastating, as a job is closely linked to one's identity, self esteem, and self worth" (p. 7). Typically, career counseling for this group begins with providing emotional support, but it may turn quickly to finding immediate employment, depending on the financial circumstances of the client.

People who are electing to change jobs are less likely to be experiencing stress than are clients who are forced to change jobs. This is not to suggest that some of those career changers who are electing to change jobs do not feel the same sense of urgency as that experienced by their counterparts who have lost their jobs and, if retraining is involved, have many of the same concerns.

Counselors working with midlife career changers need to be prepared to help develop (1) employability skills (e.g., job search, job interviewing, etc.) and (2) time management skills, particularly if the client will have heavy child care or family responsibilities, and to utilize those techniques already described in this chapter. If clients are depressed, angry, or frustrated because of the loss of their jobs, the counselor must also be prepared to deal with those concerns (Newman, 1995).

Adolescents and Young Adults

Many career counselors are engaged in helping high school and college students make initial career choices. Career development programs to help these groups are discussed in more detail in subsequent chapters. However, these clients usually need a great deal of emphasis on developing self-awareness, exploring career options, acquiring employability skills, and matching educational options to career choices. It is also true that this group needs to reorient its time perspective from the present to the future in many instances. Another common problem that arises when working with younger clients is that they have no well-articulated set of interests or work values. This problem is often related to lack of experience with career-related activities; psychological problems such as low self-esteem and perceived environmental constraints ("I'll never be able to get an education because we are poor") can also be at the heart of this problem (Brown & Brooks, 1991).

Interventions for clients who lack experience include the use of occupational information (bibliotherapy), interviews with workers, visits to job sites to observe workers (shadowing), and attending career seminars. When the problems are based on psychological problems, these will need to be addressed prior to, or simultaneously with, career exploration.

Multipotential Clients

Multipotential clients are those that, because of superior intellect, physical ability, artistic or other talents, have a variety of viable career options open to them. Perhaps the most publicized of these people are the few athletes who have the potential to pursue two or more professional careers. However, there are literally thousands of gifted individuals who can enter and succeed in almost any career of their choice. This potential, while apparently a blessing, can be quite frustrating.

Pask-McCartney and Salomone (1988) suggested that, in dealing with multipotential clients, the counselor should begin by ascertaining that the client is truly multipotential. This process may begin with the administration of an interest inventory but must ultimately be determined by "measures" of aptitudes. These measures are most readily available in the intellectual areas. Artistic and physical attributes will in all likelihood have to be determined by experts since there are no objective measures that can accurately predict who will be a star athlete or a ballerina.

Kerr (1988) also asserted that believing that you have too many options can be a problem and suggests that a program be used such as the one developed at the University of Iowa (Kerr, Hood, & Wollison, 1987), which helps clients identify careers that are aligned with their values, interests, and abilities and ultimately helps them make career choices on the basis of their values. It may also be useful to advise these types of clients that being multipotentialed means they do in fact have multiple pathways to successful careers.

Clients with Disabilities

Clients with physical, emotional, or mental disabilities present the career counselor with a series of challenges. As Zunker (1991) noted, these clients may have limited interpersonal skills because they have limited (or others have limited) their social lives to interactions with other people with disabilities. They may also have lowered self-esteem, limited skills for independent living (perhaps because of a desire to be dependent), and limited career options, perhaps because of employers' perceptions of how well they can perform in various careers.

The career counseling process for clients with disabilities will involve addressing all of the aforementioned issues and may very well begin with an extensive psychological and vocational assessment (Zunker, 1991). The purpose of the psychological assessment will be to pinpoint debilitative psychological problems so these can be ameliorated and do not interfere with career planning or functioning on the job. Vocational assessment may involve routine interest, value, and aptitude testing along with involvement in work samples from various careers. In many instances, actual preparation for careers may take place in the same institutions as it does for clients without disabilities. In other instances, specialized training programs, sheltered workshops, and carefully supervised on-the-job training experiences will be necessary.

Finally, career counselors who work with clients with disabilities will need to stay apprised of the technological breakthroughs (e.g., scanners that can read and "verbalize" written documents) that open up increasing numbers of educational and career opportunities for people with disabilities every year.

Dual-Earner and Dual-Career Clients

Technically speaking, dual-career couples are those where both the husband and wife have a high level of commitment to work and where work is continuous for both parties. Dual-earner (Rapoport & Rapoport, 1971) or dual-work families are those where one spouse, typically the mother, works primarily for economic reasons and has a lower commitment to work (Gilbert & Rachlin, 1987). In the 1970s and 1980s, the dual-career/dual-earner family replaced the traditional family, where one spouse, typically the husband, was the sole wage earner. For a number of reasons, these families present unique problems for the career counselor.

Perhaps the major problem confronting dual-earner and dual-career families is role differentiation. Gilbert and Rachlin (1987), drawing on Peplau (1983), suggested that there are three types of role relationships that may be assumed by these families: traditional, modern, and egalitarian. Gilbert (1985) studied dual-career families and found three types of role relationships, which she labeled traditional, participant, and role sharing. These categories correspond quite closely to those established by Peplau (1983) and can be described as follows:

Traditional: Female spouse adds the work role to her traditional role; male role little affected

Participant: Parenting role is shared; woman retains responsibility for household chores

Egalitarian: Gender has no impact; specialization eliminated

The specific problems growing out of dual-career and dual-earner families involve (1) role overload, more typically for the wife; (2) individual and couple role conflicts often revolving around caring for the children and careers; (3) secondary importance attached to wife's career by husband; (4) competition between spouses; (5) deciding when (or whether) to have children; and (6) occupational mobility (Gilbert & Rachlin, 1987).

Helping clients from dual-career families often requires that the couples be seen together, thus requiring the counselor to have some knowledge of couples counseling. More specifically, career counselors need to do the following:

1. Help spouses examine their assumptions about their roles (Parker, Peltier, & Wolleat, 1981; Wilcox–Mathews & Minor, 1989)
2. Engage in role adjustment such as renegotiating work role to increase role compatibility (Thomas, 1990)
3. Identify strategies for coping with stress (Gilbert & Rachlin, 1987)
4. Help couples plan and implement career goals and job shifts (Wilcox–Mathews & Minor, 1989)
5. Reduce role overload by redistributing work (Sunby, 1980; Wilcox–Mathews & Minor, 1989)
6. Teach time management skills
7. Foster basic marital communication skills
8. Help African American couples who live in predominantly white areas deal with feelings of social isolation (Thomas, 1990)
9. Help African American couples deal with feelings of guilt because they have achieved a higher level of affluence than relatives (Thomas, 1990)
10. Help lesbian (Hetherington & Orzek, 1989) and gay couples deal with issues such as whether to acknowledge the relationship and, if so, how best to handle the situation

Case Study

The *Career Development Quarterly* sometimes publishes case studies of a career counseling client in each issue and then asks two or three career counselors to react to
that case by telling how they might approach the counseling process with that client. The case of Jessie, which follows, is one of those cases (Kearney, 1988, pp. 5–8).

*Jessie was referred to a rehabilitation counselor working in a mental health clinic.
The clinic social worker felt that Jessie needed vocational counseling and, because
she was unemployed, Jessie was amenable to such services.*

*The counselor's first impression of Jessie (in September, 1987) was that
she was poor, not well educated, and personable. She appeared to be her stated
age of 45. Her hands were black from picking walnuts, her hair was somewhat
disheveled, and her polka-dotted pants did not match her striped blouse. When
she spoke, she would sometimes misuse a word; for example, she said "insex"
for incest.*

*During the first session, Jessie indicated that she would like to finish her sec-
ond year in a food preparation course at a small vocational training school. She
felt that she needed to learn how to use commercial ovens and how to cook large
quantities of food for groups of people. She was convinced that without additional
training no employer would hire her.*

*Jessie noted that even though she received a grade of 80 in her first year at the
training school, she was told that she could not return to complete the program.
Jessie stated that she did not get along with the other students because they were
young and immature. She alleged that these students took her shoes and other
items from her locker. (At that time, she was 42 and most of the other students
were in their late teens.) Jessie also indicated that she often had car problems and,
as a result, was absent from school 20 days and was late 38 days during the school
year.*

*When the rehabilitation counselor called the school (with Jessie's permis-
sion), the cooking instructor implied that Jessie's behavior was improper because
she would often compete with the teacher in conducting the class. The instructor
felt that Jessie was trying to prove that she knew more than did the teacher. Also,
she stated that Jessie's marginal personal hygiene was not appropriate for a cooking class.*

*In the next session, Jessie talked about her husband. She married John in
1965 and they have four children: three girls and a boy. Jessie declared that her
husband was often unfaithful to her and that she still resented the physical abuse
and personal mistreatment experienced in her marriage. She is still seeking advice
from her legal assistant (who works for a community legal agency) regarding the
separation from her husband in 1982 because she is not convinced that they were
legally divorced in 1985. Because she has never received alimony payments, she is
convinced that her husband bribed the lawyer. (Because they live in a rural area in
the Northeast, somehow they both had the same lawyer.) Jessie stated that she
went before a legal grievance board to complain about the quality of the legal ser-*

vices she had received, but one of the lawyers who had previously represented her was a member of the board. She is still trying to contest the negative alimony decision.

When Jessie reviewed her work history, she noted that following her high school graduation in 1960, she worked for 5 years in a garment factory (in a small town) as a seamstress. She enjoyed the work and felt that she developed a valuable skill. She did not work out of the home for many years after she was married.

Recalling an incident when she made her first pie, she said that her husband took a bite and immediately discarded it because of the displeasing taste. Afterwards, she learned how to bake and began to improvise with some of her recipes. She also grew some of the necessary baking ingredients (e.g., rhubarb) from her own garden.

In 1980, she started specializing in baking small pies and selling these to a local business. Jessie noted that she prospered in this situation until her husband became involved. She indicated that John wanted her to sell the pies for more money and that this action resulted in the termination of the business relationship between Jessie and a store owner in town. Two years later, Jessie started working with the store owner again, but her husband interfered and damaged her friendly association with the owner.

In a later session, Jessie indicated that she would like to start her own baking business and not give all of her profits to a "middle man." She expressed fear, however, that her ex-husband might jeopardize her future business dealings by his malicious gossip.

After giving further thought to her occupational plans, Jessie decided not to go back to the vocational school, but to consider starting a baking business within the next few months. Her plan was to sell her usual baked goods, special breads, and other foods (such as canned pickles) at farmer's markets, flea markets, and other shows. She realized that she would have to pay entrance or space fees, but she was pleased with the prospect of keeping the total profits.

Noting that because she had sold some of her baked goods at the local farmer's market 2 years ago, Jessie had learned to estimate the prices for which she could sell her goods. She stated that she had a large freezer for the storage of baked goods and that she had an adequate baking oven. Jessie thought that she needed to take a bookkeeping course because she did not know how to keep financial records.

In a later session, she indicated that she would also want to sew children's clothes and sell them at the various markets. Jessie preferred to set her own pace by having a baking and sewing business rather than working for someone else. Eventually, she would like to buy a specialized van out of which she could sell her goods or start a catering business.

The rehabilitation counselor spoke with Jessie's case manager to inquire about her community reputation regarding her bakery products. The case manager, who lived in the same area as Jessie, stated that Jessie was highly regarded for her baking. She remarked that the store owner, with whom Jessie had worked, had commented favorably about Jessie's baked goods.

Jessie's social worker indicated, in case notes, that Jessie is having difficulty coping with the stresses of being a single parent and managing a household. She also seeks assistance from service providers in the department of social services, at the legal assistance agency, and from a pastor. She continues to have numerous conflicts with her ex-husband, but has some emotional support from her mother and mother-in-law. She has a case manager helping her to locate a new living situation.

From Jessie's viewpoint, the immediate problem is her health. When she first saw the rehabilitation counselor, she complained of back pain. She visited an orthopedist but was not satisfied because, she said, he could not find anything wrong with her. She went to a neurologist for a second opinion because she also had numbness and tingling sensations in her arms and legs, especially in her right hand. When the counselor telephoned Jessie following her medical examinations, she read the results of her tests. She had plantar spurs on both feet and arthritic degeneration of the lumbosacral spine at C5–C6, and C6–C7. These physical conditions, Jessie indicated, are the reasons that she wants to work in her own home. She implied that she would be able to rest when needed and would have the help of her oldest daughter, if necessary.

Jessie defined another problem as not living in an adequate home. She would like to rent a three-bedroom apartment with a kitchen (in a frame house) that would be approved to standard health and commercial regulations. Her current apartment has not been so approved. Jessie was adamant that she would not leave the local area even though there are few apartments available. She was approved by HUD (Housing for Urban Development) for reduced rental payments in government-sponsored housing. She was advised by her case manager, however, to improve the condition of her current apartment substantially. According to her case manager, her home is disgraceful. Her porch and front yard are cluttered with junk and the inside is "total chaos." Jessie has a poor reputation as a tenant in her small town and, apparently, no apartment owner is willing to rent to her.

Jessie has been applying for Social Security disability benefits because of her physical condition. She has been denied benefits twice and recently had a hearing to determine if she is eligible. She is currently receiving social services assistance.

The clinic rehabilitation counselor has referred her to the Office of Vocational Rehabilitation, and they are currently reviewing her medical condition to determine service eligibility. If she is accepted, the OVR counselor has indicated a willingness to help Jessie learn bookkeeping for her new business venture. Jessie stated that she would also like help from OVR to purchase some of her business equipment.

Jessie sees the clinic rehabilitation counselor about twice a month and occasionally speaks to the counselor by phone. Jessie's always open to suggestions from the counselor and follows through on any assignments given to her. Her goals are that she will (a) discover what is wrong with her physically, (b) have an apartment soon, and (c) be accepted for services by OVR and be able to start baking and sewing by spring 1988—in time for the opening of the local farmer's market.

MacKinnon-Slaney (1988) was one of the career counselors who outlined the approach that she would use with this client. She suggests that the information provided in the case study would need to be supplemented with additional information, such as a history of sexual or physical abuse, an assessment of her coping strategies, and information about why she is not receiving alimony.

In approaching the case, MacKinnon-Slaney suggested that, through assessment, she would want to provide Jessie with a greater awareness of her general strengths and weaknesses as well as a heightened sense of her vocational personality. The goal of this assessment would be to confirm Jessie's expressed choice as well as develop a greater sense of self-awareness.

Other interventions suggested by MacKinnon-Slaney (1988) would involve helping Jessie improve her management skills, perhaps through a mentoring program, assist her to gain the capital she needs to start her business and to gain the knowledge she needs to succeed at that business. In related interventions, Jessie would need to improve her own housekeeping and personal hygiene skills.

Ursprung (1988), also reacting to the case of Jessie, emphasized the need to give Jessie feedback about her personal hygiene and appearance, simply because to be successful Jessie must convince others that she will produce clean products. In addition, Ursprung suggests that more information is needed about Jessie's current situation (e.g., medical state), that she requires supportive counseling as a means of helping her overcome her feelings of low self-esteem, and that she needs assertiveness training and work adjustment counseling to develop job survival skills (e.g., time management and punctuality).

Two important points need to be made about the reactions to Jessie. First, while there are similarities in the reactions, there are also differences in the approaches. Second, even though the present problem is a career problem, the personal concerns relating to self-esteem and family relationships would be addressed in the context of the counseling process.

Credentialing Career Counselors

Increasingly, the credentials of people who are providing career counseling services are questioned. Whether or not one accepts Crites's (1981) assertion that career counseling is more difficult to conduct than psychotherapy, it should be apparent that specialized training is required if career counseling is to be delivered competently. Some mental health professionals, such as school counselors, mental health counselors, rehabilitation counselors, and counseling psychologists, routinely receive training in career development theory and career counseling practice. Typically, this training is restricted to a single didactic course and may or may not be accompanied by supervised field work involving actual career counseling. In 1981, the National Career Development Association established a certification program for career counselors as a means of recognizing individuals who meet minimum training, knowledge, and skill requirements to practice career counseling. This certification, Nationally Certified Career Counselor (NCCC), has been administered by the National Board of Certified Counselors (NBCC, 1995) in Greensboro, North Carolina, since 1985 and remains as the single credential designed for career counselors. The qualifications for the NCCC are outlined in Figure 14.1. At the time of this writing, other forms of credentialing for career counselors, such as specialty provisions for licensed counselors, are being discussed and at least one state, Maryland, has a provision in its licensing law for counselors that has not been activated. Psychologists must be licensed in their states before they can practice career counseling presently. Unfortunately, NBCC certification and licensing laws for counselors and psychologists do not preclude untrained people from offering career counseling services. Credentialing is discussed in more detail in Chapter 16.

Summary

Until recently, trait and factor approaches to career counseling dominated. Increasingly, career counselors are rejecting this simplistic approach in favor of models that incorporate theoretical constructs and techniques from personal counseling. These new approaches call for the use of more diverse assessment strategies that allow the counselor to determine the presence of mental health problems simultaneously with the determination of career development problems. These new models demand that career counselors first be skilled in personal counseling and then develop a set of additional skills to deal with career concerns.

At the time when career counseling practice is changing, the demand for the service is increasing and is likely to continue to do so. Unfortunately, this has led to the entrance of some poorly trained professionals into practice. For the moment *caveat emptor,* or let the buyer beware, is the watchword. The future is likely to bring new credentialing requirements for career counselors, however. The standards established by the National Board for Certified Counselors and the National

FIGURE 14.1   1996 Criteria for Certification as a National Certified Career Counselor (NCCC)

1. Complete a graduate degree in counseling with at least 48 semester hours or 72 quarter hours of credit.

   A. Must include 3-hour course dealing with career and lifestyle development and a 3-hour course that focuses on assessment.

   B. Complete practicum with 25 percent of time devoted to school counseling.

2. Pass both the National Counseling Examination and the National Career Counseling Examination.

3. Two years of professional experience of at least 20 hours per week.

Source: National Board for Certified Counselors.

Career Development Association for Nationally Certified Counselors seem to be the most viable at this time.

References

Arbono, C. (1989). Hispanic employment and the Hollonil typology of work. *Career Development Quarterly, 37, 267–268.*

Arbono, C. (1990). Career counseling research and Hispanics: A review of the literature. *The Counseling Psychologist, 18,* 300–323.

Asamen, J. K., & Berry, G. L. (1987). Self-concept, alienation, and perceived prejudice. Implications for counseling Asian Americans. *Journal of Multicultural Counseling and Development, 15,* 146–160.

Astin, H. S. (1984). The meaning of work in women's lives: A sociopsychological model of career choice and work behavior. *The Counseling Psychologist, 12,* 117–126.

Bowen, N. H. (1982). Guidelines for career counseling with abused women. *Vocational Guidance Quarterly, 31,* 123–127.

Bowman, S. L. (1993). Career intervention strategies for ethnic minorities. *Career Development Quarterly, 42,* 14–25.

Bradley, L. J. (1990). *Counseling midlife career changers.* Garrett Park, MD: Garrett Park Press.

Brooks, L. (1988). Encouraging women's motivation for nontraditional career and lifestyle options: A model for assessment and intervention. *Journal of Career Development, 14,* 223-241.

Brooks, L., & Brown, D. (1986). Career counseling for adults: Implications for mental health counselors. In A. J. Palmo & W. J. Weikel (Eds.), *Foundations of mental health counseling* (pp. 95–114). Springfield, IL: Charles C. Thomas.

Brown, D. (1985). Career counseling: Before, after, or instead of personal counseling. *Vocational Guidance Quarterly, 33,* 197–201.

Brown, D., & Brooks, L. (1985). Career counseling as a mental health intervention. *Professional Psychology: Research and Practice, 16,* 860–867.

Brown, D., & Brooks, L. (1991). *Career counseling techniques.* Boston: Allyn & Bacon.

Brown, D., Minor, C. W., & Jepsen, D. (1991). The opinions of minorities about preparing for work. *Career Development Quarterly, 40,* 5–19.

Carkhuff, R. R. (1983). *The art of helping* (5th ed). Amherst, MA: Human Resource Development Press.

Chusmir, L. H. (1990). Men who make nontraditional career choices. *Journal of Counseling and Development, 69,* 11–16.

Coombs, L. C. (1979). The measurement of commitment to work. *Journal of Population, 2,* National Institute of Education.

Crites, J. O. (1969). *Vocational psychology.* New York: McGraw-Hill.

Crites, J. O. (1981). *Career counseling: Models, methods, and materials.* New York: McGraw-Hill.

de Bono, E. (1970). *Lateral thinking: Creativity step by step.* Boston: Little, Brown.

de Bono, E. (1985). *Six thinking hats.* Boston: Little, Brown.

DiBenedetto, B., & Tittle, C. K. (1990). Gender and adult roles: Role commitment of women and men in a job family trade-off context. *Journal of Counseling Psychology, 37,* 41–48.

Farmer, H. (1980). *The importance of family and career roles for high school youth.* Paper presented at a symposium. APA annual convention, Montreal.

Figler, H. (1979). *The complete job-search handbook.* New York: Holt, Rinehart & Winston.

Fukuyama, M. (1992). Report of the 1989 NCDA Survey. In D. Brown & C. W. Minor (Eds.), *Working in America.* Alexandria, VA: National Career Development Association.

Gilbert, L. A., (1985). *Men in dual career families: Current realities and future prospects.* Hillsdale, NJ: Lawrence Erlbaum.

Gilbert, L. A., & Rachlin, V. (1987). Mental health and psychological functioning of families. *The Counseling Psychologist, 15,* 7–49.

Gysbers, N. C., & Moore, E. J. (1987). *Career counseling: Skills and techniques for practitioners.* Englewood Cliffs, NJ: Prentice-Hall.

Hampl, S. P. (1983). The skills sort: A career planning tool. *Journal of College Student Personnel, 24,* 463–464.

Hansen, L. S. (1984). Interrelationships of gender and career. In N. C. Gysbers & associates (Eds.), *Designing careers* (pp. 216–247). San Francisco: Jossey-Bass.

Heikkinon, C. A. (1989). Reorientation from attend states: Please, more carefully. *Journal of Counseling and Development, 67,* 520–521.

Hetherington, C., & Orzek, A. (1989). Career counseling and life planning with lesbian women. *Journal of Counseling and Development, 68,* 52–57.

Ho, D. Y. F. (1995). Internal culture, culturocentrism, and transcendence. *The Counseling Psychologist, 23,* 4–24.

Hoyt, K. B., & Lester, J. L. (1995). *Learning to work: The NCDA Gallup survey.* Alexandria, VA: National Career Development Association.

Hutchins, D. E., & Cole, C. G. (1997). *Helping relationships and strategies* (3rd ed.). Monterey, CA: Brooks/Cole.

Janis, I. L., & Mann, L. (1977). *Decision making: A logical analysis of conflict, choice, and commitment.* New York: Free Press.

Kearney, D. (1988). Poverty and Its Manisfestations: The Case of Jessie. *Career Development Quarterly, 37,* 5–8.

Kerr, B. A. (1983). Raising the career aspirations of gifted girls. *Vocational Guidance Quarterly, 32,* 37–43.

Kerr, B. A. (1988). Career counseling for gifted women and girls. *Journal of Career Development, 14,* 259–268.

Kerr, B. A., Hood, A., & Wollison, A. (1987). *Attracting and retaining academically talented students.* American College Personnel Association Convention, Chicago.

Kivlighan, D. M., Jr. (1990). Career group therapy. *The Counseling Psychologist, 18,* 64–79.

Kuney, D. (1988). Poverty and its manifestations: The case of Jessie. *Career Development Quarterly, 37,* 5–8.

Lange, S. (1982). Ten-hut! Careers for women in the military. *Vocational Guidance Quarterly, 31,* 118–127.

Leong, F. T. L. (1991). Career development attributes and occupational values of Asian American and White high school students. *Career Development Quarterly, 39,* 221–230.

Leong, F. T. L. (1993). The career counseling process with racial–ethnic minorities: The case of Asian Americans. *Career Development Quarterly, 42,* 26–40.

MacKinnon-Slaney, F. (1988). Overcoming poverty: Female persistence and determination. *Career Development Quarterly, 37,* 9–12.

NBCC. (1995). *National Directory of Certified Counselors,* Alexandria, VA: National Board of Certified Counselors.

NCDA. (1988). *The professional practice of career counseling and consultation: A resource document.* Alexandria, VA: National Career Development Association.

NCDA. (1991). *Career counseling competencies memograph.* Alexandria, VA: Author.

Newman, B. K. (1995). Career change for those over 40: Critical issues and insights. *Career Development Quarterly, 44,* 64–66.

Okun, B. F., Fried, J., & Okun, M. L. (1999). *Understanding diversity: A learning as practice primer.* Pacific Grove, PA: Brooks/Cole.

Palacios, M., & Franco, J. N. (1986). Counseling Mexican-American women. *Journal of Multicultural Counseling and Development, 14,* 124–131.

Parker, M., Peltier, S., & Wollcat, P. (1981). Understanding dual career families. *Personnel and Guidance Journal, 60,* 14–18.

Parsons, F. (1909). *Choosing a vocation.* Boston: Houghton Mifflin.

Pask-McCartney, C., & Salomone, P. R. (1988). Different cases in career counseling III: The multipotentialed client. *Career Development Quarterly, 36,* 231–240.

Peplau, L. A. (1983). Roles and gender. In H. H. Kelley, E. Berscheid, A. Peplau, & D. R. Peterson, *Close Relations* (pp. 220–264). New York: Freeman.

Picchioni, A. P., & Bonk, E. C. (1983). *A comprehensive history of guidance in the United States.* Austin, TX: Texas Personnel and Guidance Association.

Rapoport, R., & Rapoport, R. N. (1971). *Dual career families.* Middlesex, England: Penguin Books.

Richardson, G. E. (1981). Educational imagery: A missing link in decision making. *Journal of School Health, 51,* 560–564.

Robertson, J., & Fitzgerald, L. F. (1990). The (mis) treatment of men. Effects of client gender role and life-style on diagnosis and attribution of pathology. *Journal of Counseling Psychology, 18,* 352–357.

Savickas, M. L. (1991). Improving career time perspective. In D. Brown & L. Brooks (Eds.), *Career counseling techniques* (pp. 236–249). Boston: Allyn & Bacon.

Shelton, J. L., & Ackerman, J. M. (1974). *Homework in counseling and psychotherapy.* Springfield, IL: Charles C. Thomas.

Smith, E. M. J. (1985). Ethnic minorities: Life stress, social support, and mental health issues. *The Counseling Psychologist, 13,* 537–580.

Srebalus, D. J., & Brown, D. (1998). Counseling strategies for culturally diverse clients. Morgantown, WV: School of Education and Human Resources, West Virginia University.

Srebalus, D. J., Maranelli, R. P., & Messing, J. K. (1982). *Career development: Concepts and procedures.* Monterey, CA: Brooks/Cole.

Stonewater, B. B., Eveslage, S. A., & Dingerson, M. R. (1990). Gender differences in career helping relationships. *Career Development Quarterly, 29,* 72–85.

Strohmer, D. C., & Newman, J. L. (1983). Counselor hypotheses testing strategies. *Journal of Counseling Psychology, 30,* 557–565.

Sue, S., & Zane, N. (1987). The role of culture and cultural techniques in psychotherapy: A critique and reformulation. *American Psychologist, 42,* 37–47.

Sunby, D. Y. (1980). The career quad: A psychological look at some divergent dual-career families. In C. F. Derr (Ed.), *Work, family and career* (pp. 329–353). New York: Praeger.

Super, D. E. (1990). A life-span, life-space approach to career development. In D. Brown, L. Brooks, & associates (Eds.), *Career choice and development* (pp. 197–261). San Francisco: Jossey-Bass.

Thomas, V. G. (1990). Problems of dual-career black couples: Identification and implications for family interventions. *Journal of Multicultural Counseling and Development, 18,* 58–67.

Ursprung, S. L. (1988). Counseling toward clarification and skill building: The case of Jessie. *Career Development Quarterly, 37,* 13–16.

Wilcox-Mathews, L., & Minor, C. W. (1989). The dual career couple: Concerns, benefits, and counseling implications. *Journal of Counseling and Development, 68,* 194–198.

Williamson, E. G. (1939). *How to counsel students.* New York: McGraw-Hill.

Williamson, E. G. (1965). *Vocational counseling: Some historical, philosophical, and theoretical perspectives.* New York: McGraw-Hill.

Yost, E. B., & Corbishley, M. A. (1987). *Career counseling: A psychological approach.* San Francisco: Jossey-Bass.

Zunker, V. G. (1991). *Career counseling: Applied concepts of life planning* (2nd ed.). Monterey, CA: Brooks/Cole.

CHAPTER 15

Preparing for Work

Training time can be divided into two broad types, general education and specific vocational preparation. The first includes all the general academic preparation that develops reasoning and adaptability; ability to understand and follow directions; and basic tool skills such as mathematics, language, reading, and writing. Acquisition of these skills starts no later than an individual's first day of school and, in most cases, many months earlier. Although much general education is acquired outside the classroom and supplements the school curriculum, most is learned in school.

Specific vocational preparation, on the other hand, is training directed toward learning techniques, knowledge, and skills needed for average performance in a specific job–worker situation. In general, an individual is concerned with obtaining specific vocational preparation after a tentative career decision has been made and the person recognizes (usually in the planning period) that she must acquire certain skills and knowledge to implement the decision.

Every occupation requires some combination of these two types of preparation. Continued attendance in the formal school setting inevitably exposes the person to general education development. On the other hand, specific vocational preparation must usually be sought out, although it can be obtained in a number of different sites. In this chapter, we consider those situations where the person obtains the combination of preparation that the selected occupation requires. For some students, the preparation is included in the high school program; others elect to leave school before graduation and enter a training program; many select a nonclassroom training program that follows high school graduation; and some go on to postsecondary educational programs that may or may not include a college degree.

High School Preparation for Work

School enrollment statistics in every state show us that a sizable fraction of students who enter high school will discontinue their education before they graduate, and nearly half of those who do graduate will seek no further education immediately. Obviously, if the goal of making work possible and meaningful is to be met for these two groups, it must be done within the high school years. Many believe that no one should complete grade 12 without being ready to enter higher education or enter useful and rewarding employment. We consider those going on to higher education in later sections of this chapter. At the moment we are concerned with those who plan no further training and must acquire specific vocational preparation during their high school years. We discuss briefly two types of high school preparation—vocational education and work experience programs.

Vocational Education

The direct antecedents of the modern high school, the grammar schools and the academies, were started for the explicit purpose of preparing students to enter and succeed in the institutions of higher education. Thus, at least presumably, all students were college bound. As the modern, publicly supported high school appeared a century ago, it enabled many non-college-bound individuals to extend their educations beyond grade school level. Many schools soon added a general curriculum to meet the needs of this noncollegiate group. A few years later, some schools began to offer vocational courses, and national legislation during the World War I era established vocational education in the high school curriculum across the country.

This long history has established vocational education solidly in practically every high school in the nation. State departments have provided support staff and funding programs as well as many other advantages. The need for high-quality work-preparation programs to serve almost every student is overwhelmingly obvious, and career education principles have emphasized that need even further. Many factors and events have interfered to prevent vocational education from being a broadly based program that can be used advantageously by most of the students. Instead it has often been narrowly defined and rigidly limited to a small portion of the student body. These restrictive influences have sometimes been self-imposed by vocational educators; but more frequently they have been introduced by other school staff (including counselors and administrators), local school boards, community attitudes, state-level regulations, occupational groups, or other sources.

The point to be emphasized here is that there is a clear need to revamp vocational education and its role in the U.S. high school so that it can serve effectively all students without clearly established postsecondary educational plans and most of that other group as well. One might reasonably expect all individuals by high school graduation to have encountered realistic contact with work to an extent that permits them to develop career plans for themselves, as well as acquire usable, salable skills that adequately qualify them to participate in meaningful and satisfying work experiences. The logical place for this to occur is in the high school vocational education program. Beale and Jacobs' (1982) 20-year-old observation is still accurate: Cooperation between school counselors and vocational educators to facilitate maximum student development is important.

Tech Prep

Tech Prep is a relatively new option for high school students that developed as a result of the awareness that preparation for the jobs of the future required more rigorous training in science, math, and English. This curricular offering parallels to some degree the college-prep curriculum, and students enrolled in it are preparing for highly technical occupational training in community colleges or vocational technical schools.

Work Experience Programs

Many secondary schools include in their curricula some opportunities for students to combine study in the classroom with experience in an employment situation. These opportunities vary slightly from school to school and are known by a range of titles—cooperative work experience, distributive education, office practice, job experience, diversified training. The programs are usually incorporated into the school's vocational curriculum.

The general purpose of the program is to prepare selected students for employment while they complete their high school education. As a result of successful participation, a student graduates with her class, completing a basic general education and being prepared for full-time employment in her chosen occupation.

Operationally, these programs depart somewhat from traditional high school instructional procedures. Often the students in the group are involved in widely varied occupations; in fact, one of the titles used for this type of program—Diversified Cooperative Education—stresses the variety. The program requires cooperation of the high school and local employers, who divide instructional and supervisory responsibilities to assist the student in gaining occupational competence. In general, then, this is a school–community program of vocational instruction that uses the training and educational resources, facilities, and personnel of both the local school and the community.

The program is expected to accomplish the following:

1. The student establishes an occupational objective consistent with abilities and interests.
2. The student develops skills necessary for full-time employment as a worker or as an apprentice in a chosen occupation.
3. The student acquires related and technical information necessary for intelligent occupational practice.
4. The student develops appropriate attitudes and personal characteristics enhancing adjustment, success, and progress in the occupational field.
5. The student becomes increasingly mature in her relationship to school, economic, social, and home life.

The specific objectives can be thought of in terms of (1) the job skills that the student will need to master, (2) the knowledge that must be gained to perform the work with intelligence and judgment, and (3) the personal and social traits one must develop to get along well on the job and in the community.

The instruction in job skills is provided by the employer under actual employment conditions, according to the program developed jointly by the school representative and the employer. Students usually work a minimum of 15 hours a week, mostly scheduled during the regular school day.

The typical program permits a student, usually in the junior or senior year, to attend classes half-time and work in an assigned employment position the other half. In a few large city systems, the student spends 1 week in school and the following week at work, alternating with a fellow student who is on a reverse schedule. The most common situation, however, has the student in school in the morning and on the job in the afternoon. The student is supervised by the employer in the work assignment, but a school staff member serves as liaison agent between the school and the employer and maintains close contact with both the student and the employer. The student earns academic credit for the work assignment as a part of the school's vocational curriculum.

All participants are enrolled in a related study class that meets for at least one regular class period each school day. The class is conducted by the school staff member responsible for the program—usually designated as a coordinator. Most of the instruction is technical and has a direct relationship to the student's work assignment. The study provides the trainees with information that will help them in their work. Because the students are usually involved in a wide range of occupational assignments, they have a similar variety of individual training plans; so the class work is necessarily provided on an individual basis, using special instructional materials.

General information for beginning workers is included in the study class. Subjects covered usually include units on employer–employee relations, Social Security provisions, money management, income tax problems, personality and work, and labor organizations. This material is usually provided to all students in the program and often is called *general related* instruction. Some schools arrange the program so that each day includes one period of general related instruction and another period of specialized or individualized instruction.

The development of desirable personal–social traits needed by young workers is more difficult to approach directly. Although the general related instruction helps meet this objective, direct contact with the employment assignment also contributes. Finally, the coordinator aids the development of the desired traits through individual contacts with the student.

Work experience is totally realistic—it has every characteristic of a regular job, including pay. The student has an opportunity to face the same situations that every worker encounters, with the added advantage of having a coordinator to assist in making adjustments or solving the problems encountered in the position.

Students who enroll in the work experience program are normally placed in an assignment appropriate to their vocational aims. Because of limited placement

possibilities, distances involved, or other factors, the relationship between assign
ment and vocational goal may be only indirect. Even in such a situation, participation in the program has many advantages for youth not contemplating further
formal education. They are provided an opportunity to gain insight into the working situation and their responsibility in it. They must adjust to the employer, fellow workers, the public related to the job, and the demands of the work situation.
They learn the importance of punctuality, cooperation, responsibility, paths for advancement, and similar factors that lie beyond simple vocational skill. It is not
unusual for participants, on completing their schooling, to accept full-time employment with the companies in which they were placed for work experience,
even when such an arrangement was not planned in the original placement.

The major advantages of the work experience program are immediately obvious. The experience is totally realistic, with none of the artificialities thought by
students to exist in the school setting. There is a direct relationship between school
and work, with the study course serving as the connecting link. The participant
gains an additional advantage later, since one can claim actual experience when
seeking full-time placement.

Inevitably, the program also has some disadvantages. It is not always possible
to arrange the ideal placement that would provide the maximum in training and in
experience. Some employers are primarily concerned with obtaining inexpensive
workers, when they should be fundamentally interested in training them. Similarly, students may enter the programs principally for the financial benefits rather
than for vocational preparation. Some communities have no available employment
settings that offer a wide range of experiences. Some programs have such strict admission requirements that the student who most needs assistance is ineligible to
participate. Because of the time consumed in field supervision, consultation with
employers, and observation of student workers on the job, each coordinator can
handle effectively only a limited number of students; consequently, the program is
rarely as extensive as it should be to meet the needs of most non-college-bound students in a given high school.

Though rarely used to the fullest extent, the work experience program appears to offer an opportunity for most secondary schools to render a service to
both students and community by helping students prepare themselves realistically for postschool employment. Closer cooperation between the coordinator and
the school counselor should bring more effective selection and placement in the
program and more satisfying results to the student, school, and community.

Career development advocates point to the work experience program as illustrative of the close school–community cooperation considered essential for effective career education. They suggest that all students, from high school entrance
onward, should have related experience in the work setting. This should be part-
time, perhaps even intermittent, not necessarily for pay, but clearly significant and
participatory. Early assignments would be expected to be essentially exploratory
in purpose, whereas later assignments would be considered more preparatory in
nature, providing a practical laboratory experience with maximum realism. Extending over several school years and incorporating a variety of work assignments,

such a program would clearly provide students with a better understanding of the world of work as well as with a set of marketable skills. Inevitably, the school and local employers would be drawn together into cooperative relationships of mutual benefit.

Implementation of a full-scale program involving all upper-level students would necessitate major changes in the educational program, but fundamentally that is what career education is all about. Other countries have already adopted versions of this kind of activity with obvious benefits for participating students. Several high-level leaders of government and industry have suggested that child labor laws should be revised and possibly modified to encourage and permit more work participation by school-age individuals. One can only agree that exploration and preparation would be strengthened if students could share actively in work experiences.

Outside the Classroom—No Diploma Required

Few if any school systems succeed in retaining all students until they graduate. The group usually referred to as high school dropouts includes many who might more appropriately be labeled "pushouts" or "lost-outs." Some individuals decide that the school program has nothing to offer them and voluntarily leave when they reach the legal age or shortly thereafter. Others, confronting difficult problems—poverty, parental discouragement, lack of family, pregnancy, personal adjustment or behavioral problems, addiction, and so forth—do not receive sufficient help from the school to overcome the difficulties they face. With some obvious exceptions, most of those who leave before graduation are likely to face the greatest problems in finding, obtaining, and keeping a job. At the same time, the least amount of help is usually available for this group. Often these individuals have no career plan or goal, no specific vocational preparation, and only marginal general education. Unfamiliarity with the world of work makes them ignorant of how to seek work, what kinds of jobs might fit their qualifications, and where those jobs are. Those who find their way to state employment security agencies are helped by referral to other local agencies that may be able to provide some of the needed services or by referral to employers who are seeking unskilled entry-level workers. In general, two possibilities are available for this group—on-the-job training, or skill acquisition through programs such as the Job Training Partnership Act.

On-the-Job Training

Some employment situations require neither specialized educational preparation nor specific vocational experience as a prerequisite. The absence of such requirements usually means that the work either can be learned readily during a brief demonstration period or is such that only a minimal general education is sufficient to prepare the worker. Such a conclusion is not always precise. The employer may prefer, for a variety of reasons, to hire inexperienced workers who can be trained as desired.

Frequently, large companies employ training directors and extensive staffs who operate elaborate programs, including class instruction, to prepare new employees for their future assignments. Such companies prefer to start with totally inexperienced workers so that they can be taught the exact procedure to follow on the job. Previous experience may have taught the worker different techniques or methods that the employer wishes to avoid. The employer prevents such "contamination" by providing a training program. In some cases, such a supervised training program may be quite lengthy and detailed and may require at least a high school diploma.

More commonly, employers offer on-the-job training when the essentials of production can be learned in a relatively brief period of time, so that the worker is soon assigned to the task for which he was employed. Where the basic operation is performed by a team or crew of skilled workers, the new employee may be assigned to a skilled worker or to a team as a helper, where he learns a complex task by observing and assisting skilled practitioners for a specified period. Some employers may rotate the beginner's assignment so that he serves a period with several teams involved in different aspects of the work, thus becoming familiar with several phases before assignment to a specific job. Frequently, however, the rotation does not give the trainee comprehensive preparation for all parts of the work.

This type of training is sometimes found in occupational fields that also involve apprenticeship. On-the-job training frequently lacks the careful organization involved in apprenticeship, thus producing workers who may not have the thorough preparation that goes with the latter.

Job Training Partnership Act (JTPA)

Since World War II, the United States has attempted to develop a system for training or retraining workers needed in certain parts of the economy. The Manpower Defense Training Act served this purpose during the war years to train workers to fill positions in rapidly expanding defense and war-related industries. This was followed by the Manpower Development and Training Act (MDTA) to provide workers with skills needed in new and expanding industries. Training was aimed especially at unemployed or underemployed individuals. Next, the Comprehensive Employment and Training ACT (CETA) was developed to provide a decentralized program in which state and local units of government could develop training programs to meet local conditions and the needs of prospective employers as well as those of unemployed or underemployed workers. CETA was replaced by the Job Training Partnership Act in 1982.

The major differences between CETA and JTPA are that JTPA provides for more input from prospective employers in the private sector concerning the kind of job training to be provided locally. Second, those obtaining training or education under JTPA are not paid during the learning period, as trainees were under

CETA. One intent of JTPA is to shorten the training time and to direct it toward specific occupations.

JTPA provides authority for state-level officials to designate "service delivery areas," geographic regions that consist of contiguous counties or other political units that constitute a "labor market." Within each service delivery area a Private Industry Council is created, consisting primarily of representatives of businesses or industries in the area, with responsibility for policy guidance and administrative oversight of job training in the area. The Private Industry Council and local government officials must concur on the local plan and its administration; this local plan then must be approved by the state governor's office. The law requires that 70 percent of the funds available to a service delivery area be spent on training. Each state, through the governor's office, is required to monitor programs in the service delivery areas.

The program authorizes a wide range of training activities aimed at economically disadvantaged youth and adults to prepare them for unsubsidized employment. Programs may include on-the-job training, classroom training, remedial education, basic skills training, job search assistance, and exemplary youth programs. At least 40 percent of the funds must be spent for disadvantaged youth between the ages of 16 and 21. Ninety percent of the participants must be economically disadvantaged. The other 10 percent must have identifiable labor market disadvantages, and might include individuals with disabilities, prior offenders, displaced homemakers, older workers, teenage parents, and others.

JTPA authorizes a state-administered program to assist dislocated workers, including workers from permanently closed plants, those unlikely to be returned to previous employment, and the long-term unemployed who have little prospect of obtaining local employment. Services provided may include job search assistance, retraining, prelayoff assistance, and relocation.

The law, as passed in 1982, provides for continuation of the Job Corps program. The Job Corps was originally established under provisions of the Economic Opportunity Act of 1964 to assist the most underprivileged youth by providing training and supportive services in residential sites where they could be assisted in a transition to a productive life. It was primarily intended for those youth who had dropped out of school and were in the greatest need of remediation to become employable. Some Job Corps centers have operated essentially as civilian conservation centers in national parks and forests; others have been located near large urban areas. Educational and vocational programs have covered a number of occupations. Both residential and nonresidential centers have been operated. All centers provide the following services:

1. Intensive individual and group counseling intended to improve the enrollee's self-concept and to raise motivation and expectation
2. Medical attention and fundamentals of personal health care
3. Remedial education for enrollees, 45 percent of whom are either illiterate or poor readers on enrollment

4. Vocational training geared to realistic standards, which prepare enrollees for employment on completion
5. Activities designed to develop behavior patterns that will improve the enrollee's chances of obtaining and keeping a job
6. Courses leading to a high school equivalency certificate
7. Opportunities for learning and assuming the responsibilities of a contributing member of society

The educational program is organized to meet the needs of enrollees and comprises reading, mathematics, the "world of work," an advanced general education program, and health education. Some centers offer supplementary programs of physical education, driver education, language and study skills, English as a second language, home and family living, and tutorial programs. The advanced general education program provides the information and knowledge required to pass the High School General Education Development test for high school equivalency. The vocational preparatory program provides instruction and practical experience and may include on-the-job training.

Programs established under CETA for Native Americans and for migrant and seasonal farm workers have been continued under JTPA. The amount of funding for this portion of the program is very small.

Information about JTPA programs must be obtained within the local service delivery area because there is no state or national pattern. This is also true for on-the-job training.

Outside the Classroom—High School Diploma Preferred or Required

High school graduates, of course, have access to on-the-job training, and in some situations they may also be eligible for certain training programs under JTPA. In addition, there are at least two other types of nonclassroom training situations where a high school diploma increases the likelihood of qualifying. Both provide some opportunities for the person without a diploma, but it is safe to say that many more opportunities are available for high school graduates. We consider apprenticeship programs and military training.

Apprenticeship Programs

The use of apprenticeships for transmitting knowledge and skills to new workers dates back at least to the Middle Ages. The various guilds of skilled craftsmen developed the regular practice of indenturing young workers to master craftsmen. During the period of indenture, often 7 years, the young worker served or worked for the master; in return, the master provided food and lodging for the boy, usually in the master's own home, and taught him the skills and secrets of the craft.

On successful completion of the indenture, the worker was accepted by the guild as a journeyman or independent craftsman. As the practice of his craft grew and expanded, he in turn later became a master and took into his shop apprentices to whom were taught the necessary skills.

The general use of apprenticeships has continued since those early days. The experience of Ben Franklin, an apprentice printer under his older brother, is part of our own colonial history. During the 1800s, as our industrial development mushroomed, thousands of workers were attracted to the United States from Europe. Many were skilled craftsmen, and for nearly a century immigration was the major source of the mechanics and craftsmen needed to operate our growing industries. Following World War I, changes in immigration laws seriously restricted the movement of many European skilled workers to this country, thus necessitating the development of other sources of labor that this country needed in increasing numbers.

The National Apprenticeship Program was established by Congress in 1937 with the support of both labor and management organizations. The Fitzgerald Act authorized the Secretary of Labor to set up standards to guide industry in employing and training apprentices; to bring management and labor together to work out plans for training apprentices; to appoint such national committees as needed; and to promote general acceptance of the standards and procedures agreed on.

The agency now known as the Bureau of Apprenticeship and Training was created to put the program into effect. A committee representing management, labor, and government was appointed, known as the Federal Committee on Apprenticeship, to develop standards and policies.

A basic policy of the Bureau of Apprenticeship and Training has been that programs for employment and training of apprentices should be jointly developed by and mutually satisfactory to both employers and employees. Because apprenticeship programs exist in a wide range of trades, the standards recommended by the Federal Committee on Apprenticeship are quite general, thus permitting the employer and employee groups in the various trades to work out the details for the training programs. Under the provisions of the Bureau of Apprenticeship and Training, an apprentice is a person at least 16 years of age (most programs require 18 years of age) who works under a written agreement registered with the state apprenticeship council (or with the Bureau of Apprenticeship and Training if there is no state council). The regulation provides for a specified period of reasonably continuous employment for the person, and for her participation in an approved schedule of work experiences supplemented by at least 144 hours per year of related classroom instruction.

The bureau has established certain basic standards under which an apprenticeship program can function:

1. An apprenticeable occupation usually requires from 1 to 6 years of employment to learn. Most last about 4 years.
2. The employment must be organized into a schedule of work processes to be learned so that the worker will have experience in all phases of the work in

the apprenticeship. This prevents assignment to only one or a few specific details for the period of training, and is intended to ensure the development of skill and knowledge in all aspects of the work.

3. There should be a progressively increasing wage scale for the apprentice, starting at about half the regular journeyman's rate.
4. Related classroom instruction should amount to at least 144 hours per year.
5. A written agreement, including the terms and conditions of employment and training of each apprentice, is registered with the State Apprenticeship Council.
6. The State Apprenticeship Council provides review of local apprenticeships.
7. Programs are established jointly by employer and employees.
8. Adequate supervision and records are required for all programs.
9. Full and fair opportunity to apply for apprenticeship is provided, with selection made on the basis of qualifications alone without discrimination.
10. Periodic evaluation of the apprentice's progress is made, both in job performance and in related instruction.
11. Recognition of successful completion is provided.

There are a number of easily identified advantages in apprenticeship programs:

1. They provide the most efficient way to train all-around craftspeople to meet present and future needs.
2. They ensure an adequate supply of skilled tradespeople in relation to employment opportunities.
3. They assure the community of competent craftspeople, skilled in all branches of their trades.
4. They assure the consuming public of those high-quality products and services that only trained hands and minds can produce.
5. They increase the individual worker's productivity.
6. They give the individual worker a greater sense of security.
7. They improve employer–employee relations.
8. They eliminate close supervision because the craftsperson is trained to use initiative, imagination, and ability in planning and performing work.
9. They provide a source of future supervision.
10. They provide the versatility necessary to meet changing conditions.
11. They attract capable young people to the industry.
12. They generally raise skill levels in the industry.

State departments of labor were asked to establish apprenticeship councils at the state level. Such councils were intended to serve as liaison agencies between federal local levels and to encourage cooperation of state agencies and employers and employee groups with the state. Where formed, these groups include an equal number of representatives of employers and employees, and representatives from appropriate state agencies. The state organization, using standards recommended by the federal committee as guides, sets up state standards and procedures to be followed by industry in employing and training apprentices. Once established and recognized by the bureau, the state council becomes a part of the national apprenticeship program.

In some industries, national employer groups and national trade unions have appointed apprenticeship committees. These committees meet as joint management–labor groups to develop national apprenticeship standards and to encourage the establishment of training programs in accordance with the adopted standards. These organizations grow out of specific industries and are concerned with programs within the specific industry; they are, therefore, independent of the Bureau of Apprenticeship and Training. The usual practice has been for a close relationship to develop between the national committees and the federal bureau, with each assisting the other through the sharing of information and consultation.

Both the federal and the state organizations are primarily concerned with the establishment and development of standards. The actual employment and training of apprentices occur at the local level. Local joint apprenticeship committees are established to organize the development of standards for employment and training for all apprentices in the specific trade by employers who are members of the local groups and other employers who subscribe to the program.

Qualifications for employment, such as age, education, aptitude, wages, hours of work, the term of the apprenticeship, the schedule of job processes, and the amount of class time required, are usually spelled out in detail in the local standards. Also included are procedures for executing and registering the agreement and methods of supervising apprentices at work and at school. The classroom instruction is provided by local and state vocational schools. The local committee often serves as an advisory group in developing an appropriate program of instruction.

Admission requirements are set by the local apprenticeship council in compliance with general standards set at the state and national level. Considerable variation can be found from trade to trade and even within a particular trade among geographic regions. Although the majority of apprenticeships require a high school diploma, some programs require less. The number of applicants usually far exceeds the number of vacancies. For example, in the construction trades, applicants usually exceed openings about 8 to 1.

There are nearly 35,000 registered programs for apprenticeships in over 800 occupations (BAT, 1998). The precise number of occupations involved is difficult to ascertain because, like occupational names, some general names in one locality may be broken into several more specific titles elsewhere. Table 15.1 provides a partial list of apprenticeable occupations. Though not comprehensive, the list does show the range of programs that can be included.

The Bureau of Apprenticeship and Training (BAT, 1998) indicates that there were 367,700 registered apprentices at the end of 1996, 27 percent of which were filled by minorities and 8 percent of which were filled by females. The largest numbers of apprentices were in the construction trades of electrician, carpenter, and plumber. There are women and minorities in *almost* every apprenticeship, although women in particular are decidedly underrepresented in most groups. For example, there were no women in the apprenticeship program for horticulturist,

TABLE 15.1   Examples of Apprenticeable Occupations

	DOT Code
1. Airframe-and-Power Plant Mechanic	621.281-014
2. Automobile-Body Repairer	807.381-010
3. Automobile Mechanic	620.261-010
4. Baker	313.281-010
5. Biomedical Equipment Technician	719.261-010
6. Boatbuilder, Wood	860.381-018
7. Boilermaker I	805.261-014
8. Boiler Operator	950.382-010
9. Butcher, Meat	316.681-010
10. Bricklayer	861.381-018
11. Cabinetmaker	660.280-010
12. Car Repairer (Railroad)	622.381-014
13. Carpenter	860.381-022
14. Cement Mason	844.364-010
15. Compositor	973.381-010
16. Computer-Peripheral-Equipment Operator (Clerical)	213.382-010
17. Construction-Equipment Mechanic	620.261-022
18. Cook	313.361-014
19. Coremaker	518.381-014
20. Cosmetologist	332.271-010
21. Dairy Equipment Mechanic	629.281-018
22. Dental Laboratory Technician	712.381-018
23. Drafter, Architectural	001.261-010
24. Drafter, Mechanical	007.281-010
25. Drilling-Machine Operator	007.281-010
26. Electrician	824.261-010
27. Electrical Repairer	829.281-014
28. Electronics Mechanic	828.281-010
29. Electronics Technician	003.161-014
30. Emergency Medical Technician	079.374-010
31. Environmental-Control System Installer–Servicer	637.261-014
32. Farm Equipment Mechanic I	624.281-010
33. Fire Fighter	373.364-010
34. Fire Medic	373.364-014
35. Furniture Finisher	763.381-010
36. Glazier	865.381-010
37. Heavy Forger	612.361-010
38. Instrument Mechanic	710.281-026
39. Insulation Worker	863.364-580
40. Legal Secretary	201.362-010
41. Line Erector	821.361-018
42. Line Maintainer	821.261-014
43. Machine Repairer, Maintenance	626.281-010

(continued)

TABLE 15.1 *Continued*

44. Machinist	600.280-022
45. Maintenance Machinist	600.280-042
46. Maintenance Mechanic	638.281-014
47. Medical Laboratory Technician	078.381-014
48. Millwright	638.281-018
49. Mine-Car Repairer	622.381-030
50. Miner I	939.281-010
51. Model Maker	693.361-010
52. Mold Maker Die Casting & Plastic Molding	601.280-030
53. Office-Machine Servicer	633.281-018
54. Offset-Press Operator I	651.482-010
55. Ornamental-Ironworker	809.381-022
56. Painter	840.381-010
57. Patternmaker, All-Around	693-280-560
58. Patternmaker, Wood	661.281-022
59. Pipefitter	862.381-018
60. Plumber	862.381-030
61. Powerhouse Mechanic	631.261-014
62. Precision Lens Grinder	716.382-018
63. Programmer, Business	020.162-014
64. Programmer, Engineering and Scientific	020.167-022
65. Refrigeration Mechanic	637.261-026
66. Sheet-Metal Worker	804.281-010
67. Shipfitter	806.381-046
68. Shoemaker, Custom	788.381-014
69. Stationary Engineer	950.382-026
70. Structural-Steel Worker	801.361-014
71. Television and Radio Repairer	720.281-018
72. Tool Maker	601.281-042
73. Tool-and-Die Maker	601.280-046
74. Water Treatment-Plant Operator	954.382-014
75. Welder, Combination	819.384-010
76. Welding-Machine Operator, Arc	810.382-010

Source: USDOL. (1987). *The national apprenticeship program* (pp. 5–9). Washington, DC: Author.

chef, welder–fitter, and office machine services, which are all small apprenticeship programs. Moreover, women make up less than 5 percent of the apprenticeships for electrician and carpenter and only about 2 percent of the apprenticeships in plumbing. Minorities, on the other hand, make up slightly less than 15 percent of the apprentices in the largest building trades and are overrepresented in apprentices such as correction officer, cook, and radio station operator, with about 50 percent of these apprentices coming from minority groups. Unfortunately, the ethnicity and race of the apprentices were not identified (BAT, 1990, 1991).

Information about apprenticeships can be obtained from several sources. Locally, labor unions can provide information about programs in their occupation, and local offices of the state employment security agency can usually provide names, addresses, and telephone numbers of nearby resources. The state or regional office of the Bureau of Apprenticeship and Training (usually listed in the directory of state offices) can provide information on programs within the state or region. The national office (Bureau of Apprenticeship and Training, U.S. Department of Labor, Washington, DC 20210) (http://smiley.xpandcorp.com/bat/bat.html) can provide national information.

Military Training

In this section, opportunities for occupational training within the military services are considered. Although there are a number of specialized occupations that actually exist only within the military—infantryman is a prime example—there are many more military occupations that have civilian counterparts to which military training and experience are directly transferable. Of the approximately 3500 occupational specialties in the military services, 2600 have civilian equivalents. Those that do not have civilian counterparts are primarily combat specialties.

Several military programs may be especially important for some individuals. One of these is college-level training, either in one of the service academies where a 4-year program leads to both a commission and a degree, or in a civilian college or university, where a 4-year ROTC (Reserve Officer Training Corps) program can produce the same results. A second option is a matched savings program in which enlisted personnel can designate pay set-asides that are supplemented by additional two-for-one grants from the military to pay for college education after completing the military enlistment.

The third option is enlistment. Enlistment periods can be as brief as 2 years in the Army, 3 years in the Navy, and 4 years in all other branches. Six years is the maximum commitment in all branches except the Coast Guard, where the ceiling is 4 years. Pay and allowances are uniform through the branches. High school graduation is highly preferred for all recruits and is required for all Coast Guard recruits, and for some training programs in the other branches of the service. Some high school seniors who want to acquire specialized occupational training in a specific occupation can assure themselves of this by participating in the delayed-entry program, in which they enlist for a specific training program with reporting to active duty delayed until high school graduation is completed.

Typically, new enlistees complete a basic training program that ranges from 6 to 10 weeks and consists of rigorous physical training along with classroom study and fieldwork on weapons, military law, drill, and so on. After completing basic training, the person enters the training program for the selected occupation. This is usually a classroom-based program, but it may combine classwork with field experience or may even be primarily practical training. Table 15.2 lists the occupations for which apprenticeships are available in the military services.

In addition to job-oriented training, the military services provide several other educational advantages. These include tuition assistance (up to 90 percent)

TABLE 15.2   Apprenticeable Occupations in the Military

Apprenticeships in the following occupations are offered in the military. All are available in the Army unless otherwise indicated

Air-traffic communication technician (Marine Corps only)

Air-traffic control radar technician (Marine Corps only)

Air-traffic navigational aids technician (Marine Corps only)

Aircraft electrical mechanic

Aircraft engine mechanic (turbine)

Aircraft mechanic, armament

Airplane mechanic

Artillery repairer

Automatic equipment technician

Automobile body repairer and painter

Automobile mechanic (Marine Corps only)

Automotive electrical systems repairer

Baker (Marine Corps only)

Cable splicer

Camera repairer (Navy only)

Carpenter (Marine Corps only)

Central office telephone installer and repairer (Marine Corps only)

Construction equipment mechanic (Marine Corps only)

Cook (Marine Corps and Navy)

Drafter (architectural)

Electrical instrument repairer

Electrical mechanic (aircraft)

Electrical repairer (Marine Corps also)

Electrician (Marine Corps and Navy)

Electrician, radio

Electromechanical technician

Electronic mechanic (Marine Corps also)

Electronic mechanic (radar)

Electronic technician

Electronic technician (communications)

Electronic technician (radar)

Electronic technician (radio/TV)

Electronic warfare intercept systems repairer

Field engineer (microwave)

Fire control instrument repairer

Fire control system repairer

Firefighter

Fuel systems repairer

Grading and paving equipment operator

Heavy-duty equipment mechanic

Heavy-duty repairer (construction equipment)

Helicopter mechanic

Hydraulic equipment mechanic

Illustrator

Industrial electrician/repairer

Industrial welder

Instrument repairer (electronic)

Laboratory technician (petroleum)

Land surveyor (Marine Corps only)

Line installer/repairer

Lithographer (offset press operator)

Lithographer platemaker (Navy only)

Machinist (Navy also)

Maintenance mechanic (Navy only)

Maintenance mechanic, hydraulic equipment (aircraft)

Marine heavy-duty mechanic (heavy-duty mechanic—diesel)

Marine hull repairer, ironworker (boatbuilder—steel)

Meteorologist (Navy only)

Molder (Navy only)

Office machine servicer (Navy also)

Offset press operator (Marine Corps only)

Ordnance artificer

Photograph interpreter

Photographer, motion picture

Photographer, still (Navy also)

Photographic equipment maintenance technician

Plant equipment operator

Plumber (Marine Corps only)

Plumber, pipefitter

Powerhouse electrician/repairer

Production coordinator (radio/TV broadcasting)

Pumper–gauger (petro-chemical)

Radio communications technician

Radio mechanic (Marine Corps also)

Radio operator

Radio/television repairer

Refrigeration/air-conditioning repairer/servicer

Refrigeration mechanic (Marine Corps only)

Rigger

Sewing machine repairer

Sheet-metal worker (aircraft)

Small weapons repairer

Station installer/repairer (wire systems)

Stationary engineer (Navy only)

Surveyor (artillery)

Surveyor, engineering

Telegraphic-teletypewriter operator

Television cable installer

Truck mechanic

Universal equipment operator (construction equipment)

Welder, combination (Marine Corps only)

for off-duty study at accredited schools, payment of fees for tests that establish college credit such as CLEP or SAT, independent study courses, and similar programs.

Information is easily obtained from recruiting offices that exist throughout the country. There are also toll-free telephone numbers that can be used, and information regarding the branches of the military and the military academies is also available on the Internet (e.g., http://www.army.mil).

Postsecondary Nondegree Schools

Career education advocates envision education as a lifelong process with the individual moving back and forth from classroom to work to classroom to work again, and even combining the two at times. Certainly most astute viewers of the U.S. scene would argue that the old concept of *commencement* as the end of education and the beginning of life is gone forever. The increasing complexity of life in our society, especially the impact of technological developments, requires that every worker keep abreast of change in some way. Furthermore, the changes are broader and require more than just routine updating—new jobs appear, old fields melt away or are combined with others. Workers who need education to qualify originally for employment also must continue education to maintain their qualification, to master new procedures or developments, and to move to new fields that offer greater opportunity.

The greatest change in U.S. education since the end of World War II has been the expansion of postsecondary schools offering programs shorter than the traditional baccalaureate degree. The expansion has occurred in both the trade/vocational/technical schools and community/junior colleges. We consider both groups.

Trade, Vocational, and Technical Schools

One by-product of the increased emphasis on career education and alternative educational programs has been the focus of greater attention on vocational preparation. During periods of economic downturn, high unemployment rates, and general uncertainty, there is a frequent upsurge in vocational school enrollment. Some of this is a search for security or a grasping for any help that might ensure employment or even an opportunity for employment.

A technical society, growing constantly more complex, underscores a continuing need for expanded opportunities for such preparation. The increasing emphasis on more varied forms of postsecondary education and the continuing technological thrust of our society undoubtedly will encourage many youth and adults to seek specialized education of one sort or another, often in vocational and technical schools, either public or private.

In many states, the expansion of the community college program or the establishment of publicly supported technical schools has met the major need in specialized education. Such expansion has not been uniform across the nation, however. Some states have established public area vocational schools; other states have established programs of postsecondary public specialized education through contractual arrangements with local secondary schools, universities, or other agencies equipped to offer vocational training to groups of students. Part of the impetus producing these rapid changes has come from the Vocational Education Amendments enacted by Congress, which broadened and redefined vocational education.

We are concerned here with schools whose programs generally are shorter than those offered by community colleges. Obviously, there is considerable overlap, since one type of program offered by 2-year schools is the short-course program to meet local needs. Some schools within the group are publicly supported by local, regional, or state tax units. Most, however, are private, proprietary schools; the extent of this aspect of education is often surprising.

Obtaining accurate, usable information about a vocational school is often much more difficult than finding similar information about a degree-granting institution, for several reasons. Teachers and counselors, having been professionally prepared in colleges and universities, are more aware of the baccalaureate schools. Intercollegiate athletics and other activities publicize the colleges and universities locally, regionally, and nationally. The prestigious or high-status occupations in society mostly require a college education and focus public attention on schools providing such an education. In addition, vocational schools usually offer shorter training programs in less conspicuous quarters, have often been in existence for shorter periods, and rarely attract public attention. Private proprietary vocational schools, like any other type of business, can include establishments that do their best to deliver a high-quality product for the lowest possible price, shoddy merchandise at exorbitant prices, or something between these two extremes.

The counselor who needs current information about vocational schools may find it helpful to check with the state office of education or SOICC about opportunities with her state. Now that almost every state career information delivery system incorporates current data about education opportunities within the state, this resource can be very helpful to the person interested in trade or technical schools. Information can also be found on the website Yahoo!/Peterson's College Search (http://features.Yahoo.com/college/search.html).

Community Colleges and Junior Colleges

Junior colleges have existed in this country for many years. Some states—California, for example—have included community colleges as an integral part of the statewide education program for over 50 years. Of more recent origin is the community college now found in most states. The two institutions are increasingly serving the same purposes and are therefore largely synonymous.

The junior college originally was developed essentially as a downward thrust of the college or university. Often established in populated areas not conveniently close to baccalaureate institutions, the junior college provided a means of delivering the first 2 years of several degree programs to students who, for varying reasons, could not attend a residential college or university. Since the curriculum consisted largely of introductory, or at least lower-level, college courses, it needed neither elaborate facilities nor senior faculty members. Costs were often considerably less than those charged at 4-year campuses. The underlying idea was that the increased accessibility and the lesser costs would permit greater numbers of high school graduates to undertake baccalaureate programs, which could then be completed by transfer.

For 20 years or more after World War II, the expanded interest in college programs added further pressure for the development of new postsecondary opportunities for education. Changing interests, vocational goals, and lifestyles as well as increased mobility, new teaching procedures, and other factors led to the creation of an institution somewhat different from the junior college. The junior college function of bringing the college or university to "Main Street" was usually incorporated in the structure, but ordinarily as only one part of a broader program serving a much wider segment of the community population. Thus the community college often is considered to be an upward thrust of the secondary school, incorporating extensive offerings not necessarily leading to the traditional baccalaureate degree. Instead, many community college programs are designed to be terminal in nature, sometimes vocationally oriented, but also based on local needs and interests. Many junior colleges have moved to meet more effectively a wider range of local needs; hence the two titles are now often used almost interchangeably, and one would be hard pressed to establish clear-cut differential criteria. Probably they are now more commonly known as community colleges or as 2-year colleges.

Whether called community college or junior college, most of the public institutions, as well as most of the independent schools, provide a four-part program that includes the following:

1. The traditional college-related program for students who plan to transfer to a 4-year institution to complete a baccalaureate degree
2. A technical–terminal program to prepare students to enter employment on completion of the 2-year, or shorter, curriculum
3. Short courses of various sorts needed locally for retraining or further education
4. An adult education program of either formal or informal courses

Church-supported schools normally include the first two types of programs, but less often the latter two. A few of the private schools offer only a 2-year liberal arts program that provides for transfer to another institution.

Among the four types of programs, the greatest expansion has been in the technical–terminal area. This growth of the occupationally oriented part of the curriculum will increase the significance of the institution as a part of the educational plans for students who are not interested in the formal 4-year degree programs of the traditional baccalaureate institution. Its significance in the educational structure will be further increased as the concepts of career education are more widely adopted. It is entirely logical that this school can be expected to become the local skills center that will provide basic employment competencies through training and/or retraining programs. In some geographic areas, it will assume the role of the area vocational school. The place of the 2-year school in U.S. education is now firmly established; one should not expect, however, that these schools will assume a uniform organization, curriculum, or clientele. One of their greatest advantages may well be the flexibility that permits them to respond to local needs and interests.

The 2-year transfer programs and those technical–terminal programs that extend over two academic years often provide for the granting of an Associate in Arts degree on satisfactory completion. Programs that ordinarily are completed in less than this amount of time recognize successful completion with a certificate or other credential.

As with baccalaureate institutions, variation in admission requirement is common. Schools offering only college-related programs may establish entrance requirements parallel to those used by the schools to which their graduates transfer. Technical–terminal programs are more likely to have skill-based or experience-based requirements and are unlikely to specify particular academic records as prerequisites for admission. Terminal programs and adult education programs often operate on a totally open admission plan within the community served by the school. As a generalization, admission requirements usually are less stringent in the 2-year schools than in the 4-year schools, in keeping with the broader education function of the 2-year school.

Some students will have a special interest in certain 2-year schools with college-related programs for many different reasons—church affiliation, family ties, special programs available, geographic location, or other reasons. In these situations, the student may need the same kind of assistance in planning the other college-bound students require. Often, however, the choice is based on local accessibility or a similar factor, and obtaining the information needed to aid the student may be easy.

Responsibility for accreditation of 2-year schools rests primarily with state and regional agencies. Originally, accreditation was focused on the state department of education, the state university, or an organization of colleges within the state. In recent years, there has been a trend toward establishing regional accreditation, and most schools are moving toward such recognition if it has not already been acquired.

Financial aid at institutions that basically emphasize college-related programs is usually structured in a fashion similar to that at 4-year schools. Schools that emphasize other programs often have different plans for financial aid of students. Because students who attend 2-year schools often reside at home, one of the biggest expenses in college attendance is drastically reduced. Furthermore, because many schools are tax supported, tuition and fees are frequently modest. Some programs that lead to specific employment opportunities may be further subsidized with private, local, state, or federal funds.

The most reliable source of information about any school is the school itself. Direct contact with appropriate officials is most likely to result in up-to-date, correct answers to questions. The next best source of information is the bulletin or other publications of the school—also subject to the inevitable time lag and the danger that change has occurred. Because data in most state Career Information Delivery Systems (CIDS) are revised at least annually, these materials may be more current than institutional publications. A directory, Information, about 2-year schools is also available on-line at U.S. Universities and Community Colleges (http://www.utexas.edu/world/univ/).

Colleges and Universities

From the early colonial beginnings of this country, there has been a continuing and increasing emphasis on the acquisition of as much formal education as possible. The history of our national development is studded with events that demonstrate this trend—including the founding of colleges almost with the beginning of the colonies, the "old deluder Satan" act of the Massachusetts Bay Colony establishing compulsory schooling in the towns, the Northwest Ordinance providing land for support of local schools, the Morrill Act establishing land grant colleges and universities, the Kalamazoo decision endorsing tax support for secondary schools, and the GI Bill, which has sent thousands of veterans on to higher education—to name only a few.

As our society has increased in complexity and become more dependent on technological development, the need for education beyond minimal levels also has become more apparent. Although the legal school-leaving age is still set at 15 or 16 in most states, the majority of youngsters now stay in school beyond this point. The proportion completing high school has increased steadily, doubling almost every decade in recent years. Not too long ago, the high school graduate was considered to have a very real educational advantage on entering the labor market, and many employers gave priority in hiring to such individuals. More recently, high school graduation is considered as minimal educational preparation, and the person who wishes to be in a position of advantage in the labor market now thinks of further preparation beyond high school.

We can expect the school-leaving age to continue to rise in all industrialized societies, since the increasing complexity of living makes more education imperative for the typical citizen. Further, the ideal of completing one's education with graduation from high school or college is now obsolete. The impact of technology on the world of work will emphasize a pattern in which individuals regularly return to school for either new or refresher training. For example, the rapid development of new scientific knowledge and its application is sometimes reputed to make an engineer's preparation obsolete within 5 years of graduation.

In times of drastic social and scientific change, the traditional degree-granting higher educational institutions find themselves between a rock and a hard place. The need for improved facilities, better programs, and higher-quality faculty comes at the same time as leveling or declining enrollments, increasing costs, decreasing funding, and greater competition from other educational options. Eurich

(1985) reported that educational programs operated by various U.S. corporations and associations for their employees are now educating almost as many people (8 million) as the number of students enrolled in 4-year colleges and universities in the United States. Further, the budget for these special educational programs amounts to about $40 billion per year, about two-thirds of the total budgets for colleges and universities. Increasing numbers of these corporate programs are gaining accredited status from the same regional accrediting associations that evaluate the colleges and universities. Eurich reported that in 1984 there were eighteen business-operated colleges that granted degrees, and plans were under way by eight other companies to have an additional nineteen degree programs operational by 1988, and these programs have continued to expand. Some programs are as brief as 1 to 7 weeks in length and are highly job-oriented; others parallel traditional baccalaureate programs, with a special company-aimed emphasis; and several are graduate programs.

In addition to competition from the new corporate educational programs, 4-year schools also risk losing students to the vocational and technical schools and the 2-year schools that we have considered in previous sections. We focus the remainder of our discussion on the degree-granting colleges and universities.

Kinds of Programs

The variety of degree programs in colleges and universities has developed in many ways from numberless roots. Some of these simply developed; others originated from legislated prescriptions, pressures of professional groups, public insistence, or national emergencies. Higher education in the United States has followed a pattern permitting more flexibility and more breadth than is ordinarily encountered in the rest of the world. One result has obviously been greater variations in the nature and quality of educational programs and in the size and organization of the institutions. Because of this dispersion, any general statement is subject to exceptions in one or many schools.

Unlike most of the rest of the world, U.S. colleges and universities view college study as a cumulative process, with students earning credits, course by course, on a time-period base that may be a quarter, semester, term, or trimester. Degrees are most frequently granted when the requisite number of credits have been attained with a satisfactory level of quality. Most institutions use a letter-grading system; some use a numerical system; and a very few, usually small colleges, use a narrative report system. The pass/fail grading system has been adopted by very few schools on an across-the-board basis; many schools, however, use it as an adjunct or supplementary plan, permitting students to take a restricted number of hours, ordinarily outside of their basic program, with pass/fail grades.

Programs may range from the broad, liberal arts option originally developed to produce the "educated person" in early American colleges to the narrow, intense, professional preparation requiring almost all of the student's allotted schedule. Most matriculations fall between these extremes and provide that part of the student's time be devoted to broad, foundational, or enriching study and part of the work be focused on a subject or area major or professional specialty. Except in those programs controlled by law, licensure or certification requirements, or professional organizations, the degree of variation is probably greater than most people realize. The plan used at one's own alma mater is not necessarily the universally accepted one.

Admissions Requirements

The restriction of admission by a school, either because of its desire to maintain a student body size that it considers desirable or because it wishes to limit its faculty or facilities, at once creates a competition among applicants. If the school has a generally favorable reputation, the competitiveness is accentuated and the school's prestige is enhanced. Unfortunately, many prospective applicants and their parents assume that limitation of enrollment automatically reflects a high-quality educational program. Often one can find academic opportunities of equality at nearby public or private institutions that have not yet enforced limited admission policies.

Again, generalizations are risky. Different institutions are moving in opposite directions on admission policies for various reasons. Some schools are establishing enrollment ceilings as a means of maintaining what the school views as an ideal size for its purpose, faculty, and facilities. Often, when such ceilings are set, admission requirements may become more specific to narrow the range of clientele served by the school. Other institutions have moved in exactly the opposite direction, with some schools now adhering to a policy of open admissions, under which anyone with a high school diploma or other basic qualification may be permitted to enroll. Many institutions, even before the recent emphasis on career education, had established means by which individuals whose schooling had been interrupted at high school graduation or earlier could qualify for admission on the basis of signficiant employment, examination results, or other criteria.

For many years, most institutions have asked applicants to support the usual application data and transcript of high school or preparatory school record with admissions test data. Colleges and universities require test scores for many reasons. Most large schools serve students from wide geographic regions, often nationwide or worldwide. In such a broad area, considerable difference in academic standards of high schools can be anticipated; as a result, high school grades are difficult to compare, and the college or university may elect to require test scores in order to provide some uniform basis on which applicants' potential ability can be compared. Other schools may seek to serve a particular type of student. For example, they may choose to focus on the development of writing skill; such schools would be anxious to identify those students with high verbal skill. Some schools, in which enrollment restrictions limit the number of students, may wish to give priority only to the most able students; such a school may feel that a uniform testing program will provide the information it needs to select the students it wishes to admit. On the other hand, a school may wish to diversify the group it admits and may use test results as an additional means of ensuring the variety it wishes to include in its student body. Many schools base their financial aid programs partly on consideration of ability and therefore require scholarship applicants to submit test scores for this purpose.

Most degree-granting schools now require applicants to submit, with their application materials, scores obtained on either the College Entrance Examination Board (CEEB), Scholastic Aptitude Test (SAT), or the American College Testing Program (ACT). Most schools specify the test they require, but many institutions now accept any one of the three. Both tests are now so widely used and are so generally available in U.S. high schools that they require no special discussion here. Some colleges and universities using SAT scores also may ask applicants to submit scores on achievement tests in subject areas relevant to the field the applicant plans to study.

The College Level Examination Program is one method used by many colleges and universities to determine if an applicant qualifies for advance standing and college credit. The program consists of a group of achievement tests more difficult than those we have just discussed. The basic assumption of this program is that there are many ways in which an applicant might acquire the knowledge or competencies taught in beginning-level college courses. Many high schools now provide advanced study for highly motivated students; some students undertake self-teaching projects because of interest or other reasons; tutorial assistance may push other students beyond the levels usually accomplished in high school; and some students may acquire these skills through travel, employment, or other out-of-school activity. Assuming that many colleges would willingly recognize such claims for advance standing as legitimate if properly documented, the CEEB established the CLEP plan. This program enables the student to move ahead to an appropriate level in those areas in which advanced skill has been developed and to obtain credit for the bypassed courses. CEEB reports at least two separate studies demonstrating that students given CLEP advanced standing do as well or better in advanced courses as students who have completed the usual prerequisite courses.

The Financial Aid Form is another program operated by the CEEB. This service is designed to simplify the process of providing family financial information to colleges and universities by applicants for financial aid. It provides a Parents' Confidential Statement that the applicant's parent completes, describing the family's financial situation. The report is analyzed, and a copy of the form and the analysis are forwarded to the schools specified by the applicant. A comparable form, the Family Financial Statement (FFS), is provided by the American College Testing Program. These forms are used by scholarship program sponsors as well as by financial aid officers in colleges and universities, and they are available online.

Factors to Consider in Choosing a College

School administrators, teachers, and counselors can anticipate a greater demand for accurate, usable information about college preparation. Inevitably, concerned students and parents will expect greater effort by the secondary school to assist its graduates in preparing for college and in gaining admission. This will likely require planning over a longer period as well as developing more extensive information about available institutions and greater staff involvement in the transitional process.

Since institutions of higher education come in an almost limitless variety of size, kind, and purpose, one can find almost as many individual differences here as among people. One can properly conclude, then, that specific schools will better fit the particular needs of certain students than will others. If an appropriate matching process is to occur, accurate information is imperative.

Many high school students assume that there is one perfect college that exactly fits their needs and personality. Such a romantic notion is comparable to similar ideas on finding the one perfect mate that often are prevalent in the same age group. It is more likely that for most individuals there are several colleges or universities that will suit them equally well.

Even students who are motivated to make careful educational plans may feel frustrated when confronted with an array of educational institutions numbering in the thousands and varying in many important characteristics that can have tremendous effects on their future. Just as the occupational world is too vast to consider job by job, so too is the range of colleges and universities. Some methodical approach is necessary to help the student understand the educational world. Since it can be assumed that it is impossible to study every school, some procedure must be applied that will help identify certain institutions for careful consideration.

Although the selection of a few schools for final consideration by a specific student depends on a great many factors, several general characteristics can be used in reducing the number of schools to be studied in detail. Among these are the following:

1. *Type and compatibility of program:* Does the college offer the major that the student intends to study in a package that matches the student's plans and expectations?
2. *School environment:* The geographic location and the size of the community should meet the student's needs.
3. *Admission requirements:* Can the student meet the institution's demands, and do they reflect the level of rigor desired?
4. *Size:* Many students have preferences for a general category such as small, medium, or large.
5. *Type of school:* A school may be tax supported, church supported, or independent; each type may offer particular advantages desired by the student.
6. *Type of student body:* Several factors need to be considered here, such as gender, geographic range, cultural homogeneity, and degree of competitiveness.
7. *Expenses and financial aid:* Costs vary extensively, with public schools usually less expensive than private institutions; however, financial aid may help balance some of these differences.

8. *Student activities, social, and cultural life:* If desired by the student, are these other aspects of college life available?
9. *Campus facilities:* Are the facilities adequate to provide the program and educational experience desired?

The student can consider many factors in the preliminary selection process. In some cases, such items as the availability of military training, extent of campus housing, fraternities and sororities, placement facilities, and success of graduates may be of greater importance than the items enumerated here. Certainly there are particular items that may be of relatively less importance to a specific student. Probably one of the first factors for a student to decide is the type of education desired; then he or she should decide which of these items, or others, apply to the situation. These selected factors then can be used in completing the preliminary screening.

Accreditation

Much of our time is spent in a world in which regulation and control are very obvious—speed limits, building permits, Social Security numbers, consumer protection agencies. We sometimes forget the ancient warning, *caveat emptor.* The commitment to a college education, in terms of time, effort, and money, is so great that both student and parent need to be assured that value will be received. Accreditation is one means by which the potential purchaser of a college education can have some assurance about the quality of the purchase.

Accreditation of colleges and universities is usually accomplished by two different kinds of organizations. In some academic areas, programs are evaluated by established groups of agencies formed by the appropriate professional organization into which graduates of the program ultimately will be received. The second type of accrediting agency is an association of educational institutions organized on a geographic basis, either national or regional. The National Council for the Accreditation of Teacher Education (NCATE) is an example of the first type, and the North Central Association of Colleges and Secondary Schools is an example of the second type.

Many prospective students or their parents raise questions about the ranking of a college or university or of a specific department or section within the school. It is often difficult to convince them that such rankings are not made by the accrediting agencies or other national groups. Generally, the accrediting groups simply list schools that meet certain levels of standards. Occasionally, this listing is arranged into appropriate groupings related to the scope of the program, the areas included, or similar factors, but a numerical listing in order of quality is seldom made. The variety of programs among schools, even in highly specialized subject areas, precludes the possibility of such ranking in terms of quality.

Public conviction that such rankings exist stems primarily from two sources. Many loyal alumni remember their alma mater as "the best in the country," "tops in such and such," or "highly recognized." Such evaluation is, of course, subjeclive and not based on comparative criteria. Second, many popular magazines, newspapers, and Sunday supplements run feature stories based on the judgment of a single person or a panel of so-called experts who often purport to evaluate institutions in various subject fields or by type of school. Again, the published judgments may be made by highly knowledgeable individuals who have a wide acquaintance with many schools; nevertheless, these reports are subjective in nature and are not based on detailed study of the type and scope that would justify a precise ranking.

Accreditation must be understood by the prospective student. The accreditation process is usually quite involved, relatively expensive, and highly demanding of faculty time to prepare materials, reports, and other studies for review. If a school has been accredited by a recognized agency, this indicated that the school has demonstrated to the satisfaction of that agency that it meets the minimum standards established by the agency. If the school is not accredited, one cannot automatically assume that it falls short of the minimum standards. There are sometimes valid reasons that a school with high quality and standards is not accredited, including the desire of the school to maintain a position of independence, the newness of the program, or a reluctance to expend the time and funds required to establish accreditation. An applicant should ascertain that nonaccreditation is for some reason other than quality of program.

Financial Aid

As the costs of higher education increase steadily, many students and their families need accurate information about the sources and extent of financial assistance available. Frequent change in federally funded and state-funded programs not only affects specific programs included in federal and state support but impinges on all other aid programs as well. Consequently, the basic data needed for planning are seldom available far enough in advance to permit broad publication of the information. Even the institution's financial aid office often encounters difficulty in answering questions about next year's aid.

There are a number of directories about financial aid and scholarships available that can be placed in career resource centers or in counselor's offices. Students should be alerted to the changes that occur with respect to financial help and the need for direct contact, at an early date, with the financial aid office in the institution they are planning to attend. Directories provide useful *general* and *supplementary* information. Examples include the following:

1. *Meeting College Costs: A Guide for Students and Parents,* The College Scholarship Service, College Board Publications Orders, PO Box 2815, Princeton, NJ 08541.
2. *Scholarships, Fellowships, Grants and Loans,* Macmillan Information, Division of Macmillan, 866 3rd Avenue, New York, NY 10022.
3. *Scholarships, Fellowships and Loans* (6 volumes), Bellman Publishing Co., PO Box 164, Arlington, MA 02174.
4. *Student Aid Annual,* Chronicle Guidance Publications, Inc., Moravia, NY 13118.

Information about financial aid is also available on the Internet. For example, FastWEB (http://www.fastweb.com/) is a comprehensive database that provides information about scholarships, fellowships, and grants. Information about federally and state subsidized grants and loans can be obtained at the website, Grants and Scholarships Provided by Federal and State Sources (http://www/ashland.edu/fedg.html). Both of these sites provide links to other on-line sources of information.

Sources of Information

Historically, one of the major tasks of U.S. high schools has been preparing students to continue their education at a degree-granting institution. Because of that historical tradition, one might expect the high schools to have information about colleges and universities in sufficient depth, breadth, and currency to meet the needs of most students. Unfortunately, this is only partly true. The importance of this kind of information was discussed in Chapter 8, along with the listing of commonly used directories that provide brief sketches and basic information on many schools. As mentioned previously, most state CIDS have at least statewide educational information, and many systems include national educational information. If these files are updated frequently (many are revised on an annual basis), the computerized information may well be more current than shelved copies of college catalogs and far more current than the directories. It is certainly the case that the websites that most colleges and universities have developed will be more up-to-date than catalogs or other print material, in most cases. A clearinghouse that will allow students to access the websites of many colleges and universities can be found at http://www.eapp.com.

Continuing Education

Because of the rapidity with which jobs change in today's dynamic workplace, preparation for work continues throughout most workers' lives. When a national sample of employed adults was asked, " Do you think you will need more formal training or education to maintain or increase your earning power during the next few years?" 56 percent answered "yes." Not unexpectedly, the percentage of workers who expected to need more training to maintain or improve their earnings in the 18–25 year group was highest (83 percent said yes) and the 66+ age group lowest (17 percent said yes). Also, more blacks than whites (66 percent vs. 51 percent) indicated that they would need additional training in the years ahead if they were to maintain or improve their income. When these workers were asked where they expected to go to get the training they needed over 30 percent said 4-year colleges, 23 percent indicated that they would enroll in courses offered by their employers, 13 percent said they would enroll in community colleges, and a like percentage expected to enroll in business or technical schools. Smaller percentages of employed adults expected to engage in training activities in adult education courses, special courses offered by their professional associations or trade unions, or some form of public job training program (Hoyt & Lester, 1995).

Perhaps the only thing surprising about the survey results cited above is that the percentages were low. Except for those jobs requiring only minimal skills, continuing education is a fact of life for almost all workers, even if they stay with their current job. Job changes, whether within the current business or changing employers completely, inevitably involve additional training. As noted in Chapter 1, over 25 percent of the workers surveyed in the NCDA Gallup Poll expect either to change voluntarily or be forced to change jobs (Hoyt & Lester, 1995). This figure does not account for the number of people who make either lateral changes or are promoted to jobs with greater responsibility within their current workplace. Neither do these figures account for the continuing education required of workers when changes such as computer hardware or software packages, new accounting systems, new production strategies, and so on, occur. We suspect the percentages would have been much higher if the question posed had been Do you expect to be involved in additional training either to maintain your ability to perform a job at a satisfactory level or because of a change in your current job status?

Summary

Students and adults have a variety of educational options open to them once they make a career choice. Choosing from among these options may in fact be as bewildering as choosing a career itself. The ultimate option chosen will depend on a variety of factors including the career chosen, the wishes of the student, the ability of the student to finance his occupation, the academic record of the individual, and so forth. A carelessly chosen preparation program can lead to personal dissatisfaction and even to a change in career plan. Thus it becomes incumbent on career counselors to be fully abreast of educational information and to develop the skills necessary to facilitate educational exploration, because career and educational choices are inextricably linked.

References

Apprenticeship. (1983). *Occupational Outlook Quarterly, 27*(4), 18–30.

BAT. (1990). *National apprenticeship statistics ranked by DOT* (mimeographed). Washington, DC: USDGL Bureau of Apprenticeship and Training.

BAT. (1991). *Registered apprentices on workload of Bureau of Apprenticeship and Training (BAT) and State Apprenticeship Councils (SAC)* (mimeographed). Washington, DC: USDOL.

BAT. (1998). Home Page Bureau of Apprenticeship and Training—http://smiley.xpandcorp. com/bat/bat.html). Updated 10/19/98.

Beale, A. V., & Jacobs, B. C. (1982). Hand in hand or a fist in the teeth: Counselors and vocational educators working together. *Vocational Guidance Quarterly, 31,* 21–27.

Eurich, N. (1985). *Corporate classrooms: The learning business.* New York: Carnegie Foundation.

Hoyt, K. B., & Lester, J. N. (1995). *Learning to work: The NCDA Gallup survey.* Alexandria, VA: National Career Development Association.

USDOL. (1987). *National apprenticeship program.* Washington, DC: USDOL Employment and Training Administration.

Important Websites

Apprenticeships

Bureau of Apprenticeship and Training   http://smiley.xpandcorp.com/bat/bat.html

Colleges and Universities

Colleges and Universities   http://www.cciu.k12.pa.us/aColleges

College Search and Financial Aid: http://www.collegeview.com/
   Search for Colleges and Universities

Fast WEB   http://www.fastweb.com/

Grants and Scholarships Provided by   http://www/ashland.edu/fedg.html
   Federal and State Sources

Yahoo!/Peterson's College Search   http://features.yahoo.com/colleges/search.html

U.S. Universities and Community   http://www/utex.edu/world/univ/
   Colleges

Vocational Schools by State   http://www.rwm.org/rwm/states.html

Military Careers

Army's Home Page   http://www.army.mil/

Navy's Home Page   http://www.navy.mil/

Air Force's Home Page   http://www.airforce/mil/

CHAPTER 16

Job Placement, Outplacement, and the Job Search Process

In this chapter, two vital aspects of the career development process will be addressed: gaining initial employment and becoming reemployed after leaving or losing a job. Each year, millions of workers enter the labor force for the first time. The most obvious groups of new workers are high school and college students, but as was shown in Chapter 12, many older workers such as displaced housewives can be found among the first-time job seekers as well. These groups, plus the people who are seeking reemployment after voluntarily or involuntarily leaving their jobs, spend millions of dollars each year on a myriad of self-help materials designed to provide them with the skills they need to be successful in the job search. The demand for resources concerning the job hunt suggests that many individuals feel unprepared to find jobs in the modern workplace. These feelings may be intensified as job seekers are faced with searches involving the use of the Internet.

Individual job hunters are not the only ones who spend money on the job search. Tens of millions of dollars are spent each year to staff high school, college, and public job placement offices that offer free services designed to support individuals who are seeking employment. Employers pay large sums of money to private employment agencies, head hunters, and others to facilitate the process of locating workers. Businesses also pay large sums of money to outplacement firms to assist individuals, whose jobs have been eliminated, to find new careers. The vast amount of money spent on the job search and job placement processes attests to the importance placed on them by individuals and institutions alike.

The reason that individuals spend large sums of money and devote much time and energy to job seeking is obvious. Most people must work in order to maintain their current standard of living, or the one to which they aspire. There are also psychological reasons that will be discussed in the next paragraph. Institutions—particularly colleges, community colleges, and vocational–technical colleges—invest in job placement services for both altruistic and self-serving reasons. The altruistic reasons relate to the perception that it is incumbent on institutions, particularly educational institutions, to facilitate the transition from education to the next life stage, which is typically work. The self-serving motive is that inevitably institutions are evaluated on the basis of their services to students, particularly services related to success in life. Businesses also have altruistic and selfish reasons for hiring private employment agencies to assist them to find employment agencies and outplacement firms to assist their employees who have been dismissed from their jobs. Private employment agencies can cut personnel recruiting costs and increase profits by doing so. Outplacement firms help corporations maintain their public images as caring institutions, assuage corporate guilt, and reduce certain costs, such as levies for unemployment insurance.

The job search process is fraught with anxiety for job seekers, whether they are seeking their first job or looking for a new job. Gaining employment not only assures economic stability, it validates the individuals' worth to some degree. Those who have lost their jobs due to economic downturns, technological advances, or other reasons may have already suffered blows to their self-esteem (e.g., Lopez, 1983) and thus success in the job search process may become even more important for these job seekers. Social support may offset some of the anxiety experienced by job seekers and amplify their potential for success. The point here is that career development specialists engaged in facilitating the job search must attend to psychological issues and the emotional state of the job seeker (Subich, 1994).

This chapter is divided into three sections. The first section deals with job placement services; the second addresses the skills needed by job seekers as they venture into the process of locating employment; the third section deals with executing the job search. In each section, the increasing importance of the Internet in finding and getting jobs will be emphasized.

Job Placement Services

A few individuals may have no contact with placement services at any time in their working life. Most, however, will use these services several different times. At least four types of placement services are generally available, and we consider all of them: public agencies, private agencies, school-based services, and on-line placement centers.

Public Employment Services

Every state has a state employment security agency (SESA). In some states it is called the Job Service; in others it is referred to as the Employment Service. It is a state-operated service that works within the general structure, regulations, and operating procedures established by the United States Employment Service (USES).

Public employment services in the United States have a history that spans over a century and a half. New York City organized a municipal service as early as 1834, and San Francisco established programs before the turn of the century. Ohio did so in 1890, Montana in 1895, New York in 1896, Nebraska in 1897, and Illinois and Missouri in 1899. The federal government entered the scene in 1907 with the formation of the United States Employment Service to help arriving immigrants find jobs across the country. During World War I, its task was changed to assist all unemployed people seeking work and to help employers find needed workers. After the war, many local offices were closed; and the agency was relatively inactive until the impact of the Great Depression in the 1930s resulted in reestablishment of a federal system of state offices. These state offices were nationalized during World War II and returned to state control in 1946. They are still the most-used source of assistance by people who lose their jobs (Ports, 1993)

Because each SESA is state operated, one finds some variation in structure and in operating procedure from state to state. Overall, however, there are far more similarities than differences, and most SESAs offer parallel services. Most states have established local offices in all metropolitan areas and conveniently located regional offices that serve less populated areas. The services usually provided include the following:

1. *Placement:* Applicants are registered, classified, selected, and referred to prospective employers. Orders for workers are received, and applicants' qualifications are matched with the employers' specifications so that referrals can be made.
2. *Counseling:* Applicants without previous work records or with inadequate experience are provided assistance through aptitude testing and counseling, so that appropriate classification and referral can be made.
3. *Service to veterans:* Each office is charged with providing special assistance to veterans seeking employment.
4. *Service to applicants with disabilities:* Each office is also responsible for providing placement assistance to people with disabilities.
5. *Collection of labor market information:* Changes and trends in the local employment situation are assessed regularly; pooling this information at the state and federal levels increases the services available to those seeking work and provides a current picture of employment across the nation.
6. *Cooperation with community agencies:* The local office helps keep the public informed, attracts applicants and possible employers, and maintains close contact with local employment conditions.

In addition to the foregoing, the SESA handles the registration and processing of unemployed workers who qualify for unemployment compensation payments. It also cooperates in the operation of the Job Bank, a computerized listing of hard-to-fill jobs across the nation. Further, in those states where the state Career Information

Delivery System (CIDS) has incorporated statewide job vacancy information, it provides the basic input and monitors the recency of these data.

Because of the specific responsibilities assigned to the local public employment agency, it offers many services and advantages to the person attempting to obtain employment. Liaison with other local offices through the state provides useful information to workers on employment opportunities at both a statewide and nationwide level. The services of the local office are available without charge to applicants seeking work, who will be served by a professional staff concerned with matching applicants' abilities to employers' needs.

Besides providing direct service to the individual job seeker and the unemployed worker, the SESA is a prime source of information that can be used by counselors and those in charge of career resource centers. Because the SESA is the basic collecting unit for local labor market information, its staff is usually more knowledgeable about local job conditions and trends than any other agency. Since local data are pooled at the state level and, in turn, at the national level, the SESA has access to the latest available data on the employment situation at these broader levels as well. Most state offices issue regular labor market information reports as part of the occupational employment survey; and local, current data are available in frequently published newsletters and in radio and television reports in some cities. The career resource center should maintain a file of recent copies of both local- and state-level publications.

Private Employment Agencies

Probably every metropolitan area has several private employment agencies. A quick survey of the telephone directory's yellow pages will usually reveal more listings than most people would expect. Because they have many different purposes, it is difficult to provide a simple classification system. Some are regular profit-seeking businesses. Some serve the general public; others limit their clientele to a particular occupational group. Some work primarily for the job seeker; others serve the employer. Some list only regular, full-time positions; others handle only short-term, temporary jobs.

For-profit job placement organizations serve a role similar to the agent who represents a popular entertainer. The agency contracts with the job seekers to assist them in finding a satisfactory position with the understanding that a fee will be charged for the service if the person accepts a job. Some businesses contract with for-profit agencies to screen prospective employees and thereby reduce the load on the company's personnel office. When this arrangement exists, the employer often pays the fee charged by the private agency. As with any other group of businesses, the quality of service ranges widely. Lilley (1978) describes some of the problems that arise from involvement with unethical private placement agencies, and during the 1980s and 1990s thousands of complaints were lodged against some of these agencies. However, it would be unfair to label all agencies as fraudulent. Fees may be on a sliding scale, with higher-paying positions carrying a decidedly heavier fee. As a rough rule of thumb, most fees will approximate at least

1 month's pay, due in full the moment the individual accepts a position. The exact fee should be determined in advance.

Special-purpose placement agencies may restrict their clientele to a specific occupational or professional group. For example, some agencies serve only technical occupations at the professional or subprofessional level; others may handle only educational positions such as teachers, school administrators, and related jobs. Closely related to this type of placement agency is the union hiring hall, which serves only members of the organization, or the professional registry, like those found in some metropolitan areas for nurses who accept private cases.

A few placement agencies limit their activities to what they label as executive searches, or what others may call head-hunting. These companies are employed by organizations to find a person for a specific position rather than the more customary reverse situation. The position to be filled is usually top-level management or some particularly sensitive position where those most qualified would be reluctant to be identified as candidates because of the impact that information would have on their present positions. Fees are typically paid by the employing organization for these services.

Secondary and Postsecondary Placement Services

The most obvious time for individuals to need placement assistance is at the point when they complete their preparatory programs. Thus, logically, one would expect placement services to be an automatic adjunct of the educational system. We consider school involvement in terms of both secondary and postsecondary institutions.

Schools have several options available in organizing a placement service, ranging from transferring full responsibility to the local public employment security office to retaining total responsibility within the school itself. We consider each option briefly.

The major arguments for full use of the local public employment agency to meet the placement needs of the local school usually are as follows:

1. The state employment service, including the local office, is set up uniquely for placement services, with a trained staff, close contact with employers, and current and accurate local information on the labor market.
2. It is uneconomical to operate two parallel systems.
3. Development of a competing placement service within the school would arouse ill will among the public, who would oppose duplication.
4. The state employment service is where workers go to get a new job, so this facility might just as well be available in looking for a first job.

In spite of the foregoing points, a strong argument can be made in support of job placement services within the school. Advocates of this position usually argue as follows:

1. Our educational institutions are responsible for the adjustment of the individual. Changing from the classroom to the job is part of the adjustment of the
   individual.
2. Placement, to be best, should be made with consideration of the individual's
   previous experience and abilities. The educational institution is in the best position to know these.
3. If the school provides vocational education, it should logically include placement as part of the total process.

Of special importance in school-based placement activities is the opportunity
to help students obtain part-time and vacation employment. Valuable experience,
as well as a more realistic understanding of the relationship of worker to job, can
be acquired by teenagers and young adults who engage in work after school
hours, on weekends, or during vacations. These experiences can be helpful to students in their career planning. Often, part-time placements can be arranged that
give students exploratory experiences that have a direct relationship to career
fields. Even when this is not possible, the student can expect to profit in various
ways from participation in work experience, such as becoming familiar with supervisory styles.

Some of the reasons that high school students and recent graduates encounter
failure in obtaining positions include unsatisfactory appearance, attitude, and behavior; unrealistic wage demands; insufficient training; insistence on the job
though unqualified; impatience and unwillingness to adapt to entry requirements; insistence on own concept of job duties; and ignorance of labor market
facts. Many of these problems, prevalent in many young, inexperienced job seekers, can be reduced or even eliminated by an effective combination of counseling
and placement. The recognition and eradication of possible problems is more
likely to occur in the school setting, where the young person is better known and
where time for counseling is available.

If the school assumes that the student needs special assistance as major
changes are encountered in the educational experience, such as moving to junior
high school and on to senior high school, it is certainly logical to expect that help
will be needed in moving from school to job. The school can strongly contend that
the student will learn most effectively if the change from school to job is correlated
with experiences in the school that have been organized to prepare and assist in
making the transfer. A school placement program would presumably provide this
assistance. The discussion of the work experience program in an earlier chapter
pointed out that a major advantage of the program was the availability of the coordinator as a liaison between school and employer, thus helping the student adjust to the demands of the work situation. A school placement officer can serve
this function for students not enrolled in the school's work experience program.

Another argument for providing placement services within the school is the
basic philosophic position that must be taken by each agency to perform its responsibility to society. The employment service has a primary responsibility for
meeting the communities' needs for workers. The school, however, to meet its

share of the responsibility, must give preeminence to the long-range development of the individual. It must consider the individual as a unique person with particular needs and goals, and its efforts should be to maximize the development of that person.

To some extent, the question of whether the school should be involved in placement services is an academic one, because inevitably, the school is involved. In every school, staff members are contacted by employers seeking applicants for positions. Probably this happens most frequently in the vocational departments of the school, where commercial and shop teachers are asked to recommend possible candidates for existing vacancies. The basic question is whether the school wishes to continue an informal, unorganized placement service or whether it prefers to recognize a responsibility to all students who may seek work, regardless of the curriculum in which they are enrolled, and to organize a program to meet the needs of all students.

School districts that elect to provide placement services to their students have several options available. They can create a decentralized system, a centralized program, a combination of the two, or a cooperative program with the local SESA office.

The decentralized plan places responsibility at the lowest functional level. In a small school system involving only one high school, this probably would simply extend the informal placement efforts in which teachers or school departments already engage. In large school systems with more than one high school, placement would operate at the school level. The advantages are that students are in familiar surroundings, with staff members who probably already know them well, so little or no delay is involved in the referral process. The disadvantages of such a system are also obvious. The program serves a smaller group of students and may not be able to supply the best applicants; little time is available for developing employer contacts and conducting follow-up; there is duplication of effort and competition among the schools in the system; and employers are uncertain about which school staff member to contact or must make several calls to reach the proper person without a central clearinghouse.

In a centralized program, a single office is established that develops pertinent information about students desiring placement and employers who may send notification of job openings. The advantages of this approach are convenience and efficiency, with the likelihood of better staff, uniform policies, and better community relations. The disadvantages are that student records are not as readily available to placement, and the staff usually does not know the student personally.

Larger school systems may find it advantageous to develop some combination of the two basic systems, in order to capitalize on local situations or to meet particular needs. For example, a school system might establish a central office for employer contacts but use separate school offices for developing student records, or a central office might be used to coordinate the activities in the various schools.

A cooperative program involving both a school placement service and the local public employment service may provide the best opportunity to secure the advantages of each and to minimize the disadvantages. Several variations are possible in building such a service. The appointment by both agencies of liaison persons, who work together to accomplish the desired goals, is probably the first step. Both offices can focus on those parts of the work they can handle best, information can be shared as needed, and skills can be developed mutually. The likelihood of having a program that meets local needs seems greater when the two agencies effectively combine their efforts.

Postsecondary schools are involved in placement, and many of them operate placement offices for their students and alumni. Typically, these offices operate as part of the services provided by the educational institution and charge either no fee or a very modest registration charge. Two types of placement offices can be seen on most university campuses.

Many university placement offices operate placement activities in a way that might be compared to a dating bureau, where the major objective is to facilitate the meeting of two people—the student and an employer's representative. In these situations the agency focuses its attention on inviting employer representatives to campus and establishing interviewing schedules so that as many students as time permits can have an opportunity to meet with that representative. Minimal student records are maintained, at most a resume, and more likely only a registration card. When they register, students may be asked to identify type of company or industry, geographic preference, or occupational goal. Then a notification system alerts students when representatives of companies that relate to their indicated preferences will be on campus, and a sign-up system provides an opportunity to register for an interview.

On-Line Job Placement Centers

The most recent innovation in job placement is on-line or virtual job placement centers. As is the case with other centers, some of these are privately operated and require a fee for their services. Others, primarily those operated by governmental agencies, are free to both employers and job seekers. Both the private and public placement centers allow resume and job postings by job seekers and employers, respectively. They may also allow employers to conduct a resume search in order to identify prospective workers; create a hyperlink between their websites and the websites of businesses that have posted jobs; and provide e-mail addresses so that employees can contact employers directly, resume screening to ensure that the information on resumes is correct, and user support services to provide assistance when problems are encountered. The fees charged by these private job placement centers vary and in some instances no fees are charged to job seekers who wish to post their resumes on their websites. Some examples of private on-line job placement services and their Internet addresses follow:

JobCenter   http://www.jobcenter.com/quality.asp
Career Mosaic   http://www.careermosaic.com/

CareerWeb	http://www.cweb.com/
CareerSite	http://careersite.com/
Internet Career Connection	http://iccweb.com/Default.asp
Monster Board	http://monster.com:80/
Best Jobs in the USA Today	http://www.bestjobsusa.com/
JobBank USA	http://www.jobbankusa.com/

Although the private on-line job placement agencies list large numbers of jobs (over 50,000 in some instances), the public agencies have larger listings. For example, in early 1999, America's Job Bank (http://www.ajb.dni.us/) listed more than 900,000 and included the resumes of over 220,000 job seekers. Another example of a public, on-line job placement center is Federal Job Bank (http://www/fapac.org/fed.htm).

Job hunting on the Internet has one major advantage: efficiency. Resumes can be posted on websites that cover vast geographic areas while sitting at a personal computer. This approach to job seeking may have the advantage of lower cost as well. Resumes are posted on-line, thus bypassing development and printing costs. Transportation costs are eliminated as well. These costs must be weighed against the fees charged by the placement agency, however. Given the rapid expansion of on-line job placement centers, it seems reasonable to expect that future job seekers will need to be aware of these services and include them in their overall plans to gain employment.

Outplacement Services

Outplacement involves providing assistance to workers whose jobs have been terminated because of technological advances, business mergers, relocation of businesses outside this country, the need to increase competitiveness by reducing costs, employee dismissal for poor performance, or a number of other reasons. Outplacement services are most often provided to exempt employees (salaried; not reimbursed for overtime) but are also provided to nonexempt (salaried; reimbursed for overtime) and hourly workers. One study (Bohl, 1987) found that almost 55 percent of the companies sampled offered some form of outplacement service to their employees.

The source of assistance with outplacement can come from an external consulting firm such as Drake Beam Morin, The Redford Group, or Hickey & Associates, or from within as an extension of the career development program. Outplacement firms typically charge a fee equal to 15 to 25 percent of the employee's salary and are therefore generally more expensive than internally located services (Bohl, 1987). However, Morin and York (1982) argued that externally located services have higher prestige and signal to employees that a serious effort is being made on their behalf. They also suggest that externally located services may be better able to gain the confidence of the employee who is to be outplaced, since they are not employees of the company that has terminated them.

Whereas some companies offer internally located outplacement services and others contract with external outplacement firms, still others offer what they term assistance for displaced workers, which includes paid time off for conducting job searches, relocation opportunities with other units in the company, job fairs, job market data, liaisons with public employment agencies such as SESA, and opportunities to network with other managers to develop job opportunities. None of these activities meets the specific requirements of a comprehensive outplacement program.

Morin and York (1982) suggested that a comprehensive outplacement counseling service should be aimed at diffusing the employee's feelings of frustration, depression, and anger, establishing a contract with the employee to proceed with a job search, helping employees develop a job search plan and the skills to implement it, and following up with employees as they search for a job. Brammer and Humberger (1984) offer a similar outline, although they place more emphasis on assisting workers to engage in self-assessment strategies as prerequisites to establishing career goals, than did Morin and York (1982).

The intensity of the outplacement process is reflected in Brammer and Humberger's (1984) observation that a counselor may spend 30 to 65 hours for each candidate for outplacement. The counselor may spend 5 hours orienting the candidate to the process of outplacement; 20 hours helping the candidate conduct a self-assessment of interests, values, and attitudes; and 40 more hours helping with job selection and mounting the job search campaign. Brammer and Humberger (1984) note that the candidates may spend 310 hours on these same activities.

Brammer and Humberger suggested that much of outplacement work is necessary because adequate counseling services regarding career opportunities, retirement, performance, and similar topics is not provided on an ongoing basis. Regardless, the process begins soon after the termination conference, and in some instances immediately after the conference. After an initial period of shock, ventilation of feelings often occurs followed by a typical career counseling process including assessment, goal setting, the development of employability skills, and the job search.

If the outplacement program is internally located, the resources to support it are probably already on hand. These resources include occupational and training information, duplication equipment, telephones, training space, and access to a computerized database. If an external placement firm is involved, these facilities may have to be created, sometimes at a substantial cost to the firm.

Finally, offering an outplacement service is not a guarantee of a job, only the guarantee of assistance in finding a new position. The quality of the personnel and the availability of a full support system including stationery, clerical help, occupational information, message services, and other similar services seem to be the most important features involved when outplacement agencies are being selected. Having a full support service and the quality of the experience will be key factors in the success of these programs.

Employability Skills

Job hunters need a wide range of employability skills ranging from locating jobs to interviewing. Historically, groups ranging from classroom size to small groups have been employed in the development of these skills. For example, Eden and Avarim (1993) designed an 8-week workshop that employed cognitive strategies to increase jobs hunters' self-efficacy and job search activity. They found that their intervention was more helpful for people who had low self-efficacy at the outset and that reemployment increased dramatically for this group. Platt, Husband, Hermalin, Cater, and Metzger (1993) also used cognitive behavioral approaches in an attempt to increase the reemployment of drug abusers on methadone mainte-nance. They found that African American clients in the treatment groups were far more likely to be employed than their counterparts in the control groups, but they found no significant difference in the employment of white clients in the experi-mental and control groups.

Whereas the two studies described above illustrate that group interventions can be useful in the development of employability skills, two other observations can also be made on the basis of the results of these studies. First, the treatments did not work equally well for all groups involved, suggesting the need to tailor the types of interventions used to the needs of the clients. Second, in the study conducted by Platt and associates (1993), only 15 percent of the people in the ex-perimental groups had jobs after 1 year. This suggests that employability skills training cannot overcome other obstacles to employment such as substance abuse or inadequate preparation for the job. Not surprisingly, Eck (1993) found, in his study, a direct link between the education of the people hired and the education required to do the job.

Finally, employability skills training and initial employment and reemploy-ment may be tempered by another variable, social support. Rife and Belcher (1993) found that workers who had the greatest degree of social support for their job-hunting activities spent more hours searching for jobs and made more employer contacts. Unemployed friends were judged to be better sources of support than employed friends and relatives in this study. This finding provides direct support for many of the group-oriented activities such as job clubs described later in this section.

The present Job Training Partnership Act (JTPA) includes provisions for sup-plying *transitional activities*—a term that includes teaching and helping individu-als to find and obtain jobs. JTPA programs are in a position to provide this type of group help to disadvantaged individuals, including school dropouts, displaced homemakers, dislocated workers, and some others. Obviously, secondary and postsecondary institutions are in a position to provide such help to enrollees who are about to complete their educational programs. Community agencies often sponsor support groups or directly operate programs that provide this assistance to other members of the community who need and want such help.

The principal difference among these various settings is that in educational in-stitutions the emphasis is on teaching skills and techniques for application in the future—usually short range, from 6 to 12 months in advance. In JTPA and community agencies, the emphasis is on an immediate problem: Enrollees are trying to find a job *now.* The difference is deeper than appears on the surface. In the school setting the process is somewhat abstract and future-oriented, whereas in the community the participants are in crisis, often accompanied by personal concerns and financial emergencies that can affect the process.

At the high school level, units on job search techniques can be incorporated into several courses established as electives or offered as special activities during or outside regular school hours. The content is usually based either on a brief textbook or, more often, on a workbook or manual. Examples of the materials available for this purpose include those by Bloch (1989); Wegman, Chapman, and Johnson (1989); and Farr (1989). The range of materials available for use with college-level students is much broader than that aimed at high school students. Many of these publications can be used by higher education students either on an individualized self-help basis or in a workshop or elective-course setting.

One development that is being used in JTPA and community groups to help those actually engaged in the job search process is job clubs (Azrin & Besadel, 1979; Murray, 1993). They propose the formation of a group that not only provides support and encouragement but also helps members to improve their interview skills through role playing; clarifies and sharpens their goals through group efforts; shares tips with other members as possible leads appear; and seeks group solutions to problems facing individual members—child care, transportation, and so on. The more obvious advantages to this approach are found in the support group whose members face a common problem, in the resolution of those problems that frequently cause failure in the job search, in improved access to information about possible openings through networking, and in skill building in job-seeking techniques. The approach is clearly appropriate not only for the so-called disadvantaged groups but also for dislocated workers, the structurally unemployed, and late entrants.

Local labor market information is particularly useful with job clubs because members are seeking jobs within the local area. Some communities have formed advisory committees consisting of representatives of local employers who are able to add further realism to job club activities in several ways, such as role-playing application interviews, alerting members to potential vacancies, and helping members know what employers look for in applicants.

People with Disabilities

When considered in general terms, the process of placing people with mental and physical disabilities is essentially the same as that for those without disabilities. However, when clients with disabilities have limited potential for competitive employment, two options exist. One is to develop sheltered workshops that subcontract with other businesses to produce various products. The second alternative is to develop job skills through supported work programs that include job-site training, job coaching, placement, and long-term follow-up to determine work adjustment. In both types of programs extensive assessment, including medical and psychomotor, intellectual, academic, interests, interpersonal skills, and work skills (Kanchier, 1990) must be conducted. This is followed by training, coaching, counseling, observation, and evaluation. People in supported work programs typically work in restaurants, motels, hospitals, and similar situations (Lam, 1986). Lam found that the supported work program is a more cost-effective means of servicing clients with mental retardation, while sheltered workshops may be more cost effective with those clients with moderate to severe mental retardation.

When clients with disabilities have the potential for competitive employment, such as is the case with many individuals with physical disabilities, additional support in the form of counseling, training, and work with employers to overcome stereotypes will be necessary, much as it is for clients with mental disabilities (Jones, Ulicny, Czyzewski, & Plante, 1987).

Executing the Job Search

The first step is essentially one of inventory taking—that is, establishing what one has for sale. If the counselor has been working with the client in a career counseling process, this step has already been identified and clarified. If the counselor or helper is starting at the job search stage, some backtracking is necessary to be sure that the client does know self thoroughly and accurately and can identify personal strengths and weaknesses. Identifying personal skills and strengths may be difficult for the individual with limited work experience. For example, the displaced homemaker may discount or overlook skills that were used in homemaking responsibilities but did not produce a paycheck. The period devoted to clarifying self-knowledge should be expanded to include consideration of goals and longer-range views of self in order to provide a rationalization against which possible openings can be evaluated. Though often postponed until later, a basic resume can be prepared at this stage, because, fundamentally, the resume is simply an inventory of personal characteristics and accumulated experiences that relates to what one wants in work. Zunker (1990) suggests that a client can use self-estimates to classify work skills as functional, adaptive, or technical and, then, to identify the types of positions for which he is best qualified.

The second step is to identify the individual's job market. Here we are concerned first with circumscribing a geographic area and, second, with identifying information sources within that specified territory. An individual's labor market area ordinarily must be described in terms of personal factors. Influencing items include one's access to transportation; how long and far one is willing to travel to and from the work site; whether restricting factors such as geographic, personal, or family barriers exist; and similar items that relate to the individual. Next the person can begin to identify how he can obtain information about possible job openings. Actually there are several sources available to the individual, who may often overlook some of the possibilities. One source, often disregarded, is the hidden job market that exists almost everywhere. The jobs consist of vacancies that are about to develop, perhaps through promotion, retirement, reorganization, or some similar influence. The individual who can capitalize on this situation is the one who has access to learning about such positions before they become public knowledge. Perhaps the basic question for many might be: How well do you know what is happening inside the companies you are interested in?

The second source of information is closely related to the hidden market and consists of the network of acquaintances in the local area where a job is sought. Those who are employed in businesses that are potential sites for a client may know the hidden job market in their company. They may also know what trends are beginning to influence their industry and how competing companies plan to respond. Job clubs, which were first described by Azrin in 1979, still operate in many parts of the country. These clubs have traditionally emphasized the importance of networking in the job search. Silliker (1993) found that networking, primarily with relatives and friends, was the primary way that unemployed workers over 50 found new jobs if they were in Conventional, Enterprising, or Realistic occupations. People in Social, Artistic, and Investigative occupations were more likely to find jobs through agencies or by consulting newspaper advertisements. In a related study, Ports (1993) studied trends in job seeking beginning in 1970 and found that more and more workers use newspaper articles as a means of locating jobs.

Pencom, an employee recruiting firm, surveyed personnel officers to determine what they considered the most effective means of recruiting new workers. The results were as follows: 36.4 percent of the personnel officers favored the use of professional recruiters, 32.3 percent found that getting referrals from other workers or acquaintances (networking) worked best for them, and 10.1 percent preferred to retrain existing workers for new positions. Other preferred methods of recruiting workers listed by the personnel officers included newspaper advertisements (9.1 percent), Internet postings (6.1 percent), and job fairs (6.0 percent). These findings have many implications for the job hunter, perhaps the most important one being that job hunters are going to have to consult many sources of job listings if they are to be successful (Eisenstadt, 1995).

The Internet

As has already been noted, the Internet is potentially an invaluable tool if the job seekers elect to take advantage of the on-line job placement centers. However the Internet can also be used as a means of identifying job openings by traditional job seekers. The four Internet websites listed below, along with their addresses, may be useful to several types of job seekers. Additionally, most major newspapers have websites that include the jobs listed in their classified advertisements.

Information about Jobs for People with Disabilities
Careers On-Line   http:www.disserv.stu.umn.edu/TC/Grants/COL/

Information about Jobs for Students in Colleges
Riley's Guide   http://www.jobtrak.com/jobguide

Information about Jobs Listed in Newspapers in 25 cities
CareerPath   http://www.careerpath.com/

Information about Civilian Jobs in the Military
Government Job Openings   http://usgovinfo/tqn.com.blmiljob.htm

The third step in the job search process is developing a strategy for selling one-self to prospective employers and polishing the skills needed to complete this phase. The appropriate strategy depends on many factors and must be developed essentially according to rules set by the employer. If the potential position has been identified, a properly written, well-stated letter containing a resume should be sent to the employer. If the advertisement asks applicants to telephone for an appointment, telephone manners may become quite important. The immediate goal is to secure an interview; the long-range goal is to complete that interview in a way that produces a job offer. Clients may need assistance in translating want ads in order to understand what is being said about the job. Clients almost certainly will need help in preparing letters of application, resumes, and interviewing skills. Many job applicants, especially first-timers, may be unaware of the influence of such items as personal grooming, appropriateness of attire, eye contact, proper grammar and self-expression, how one sits, and the ability to explain what one can give to a job and what one expects in return. Role playing and practice interviews are the most common techniques for sharpening these skills. Many of the workbooks listed earlier include sample questions that are likely to be asked in the interview.

The job-hunting process is generally outlined as we have done here: establish career goals; develop employability skills such as resume development, letter writing, networking, and interviewing; and finally wage the job search campaigns. However, both research and the experience of job hunters give us some additional clues about how to make this process more successful. For example, Helwig (1987) surveyed career and placement specialists to rate what they perceived as the most important information needed by job hunters. The fifteen items rated (1–7 scale) most important and fifteen rated least important information needed (out of ninety-nine items) can be seen in Table 16.1. Perhaps the most obvious finding, as Helwig noted, is that all items in his questionnaire were viewed as at least somewhat important by the respondent.

Yates (1987) took a somewhat different approach in her research than Helwig in that she asked job seekers to rate the information and skills they needed during the job search. She found that generally among job hunters self-assessment skills, decision-making skills, and job-hunting knowledge and skills were considered most important, while occupational and educational information were considered less important. The top ten needs of job seekers, according to their own ratings, are (1) selling yourself, (2) preparing for a typical interview, (3) writing a resume, (4) self-assessment skills, (5) salary information, (6) budgeting until a job is found, (7) legal and illegal questions that may be posed by interviewers, (8) understanding the career decision-making process, (9) how to use skills acquired

TABLE 16.1 Counselors' Perceptions of Most and Least Important Information Needed by Job Seekers (*N* = 1121)

Most Important:
1. Ability to identify one's aptitudes (6.35)
2. Ability to identify one's skills (6.34)
3. Ability to identify one's interests (6.31)
4. Knowledge of the importance of personal appearance and hygiene in getting a job (6.29)
5. Ability to sell one's skills to get a job (6.28)
6. Awareness of the importance of a properly completed application (6.28)
7. Ability to relate one's skills, interests, aptitudes, and values to a job (6.26)
8. Knowledge of how to participate in a job interview (6.23)
9. Ability to prepare for an interview (6.18)
10. Knowledge of the personal characteristics that are considered important by employers (6.17)
11. Knowledge of the importance of proper language and dress in the workplace (6.13)
12. Knowledge of the importance of personal responsibility in finding a job (6.11)
13. Ability to understand the employer's expectations for a specific position (5.99)
14. Knowledge of the steps in job hunting (5.97)
15. Knowledge of where to find job openings (5.97)

Least Important:
1. Knowledge of military information (4.01)
2. Knowledge of labor organizations (4.27)
3. Knowledge of the regional history of employment changes and attitudes (4.28)
4. Knowledge of how the natural environment influences the jobs that are available (4.40)
5. Knowledge of seasonal jobs (4.52)
6. Information about starting one's own business (4.58)
7. Knowledge of the relationship between work and leisure time (4.58)
8. Knowledge of the General Educational Development (GED) certificate (4.63)
9. Knowledge of how cycles in the economy affect the number of job openings (4.63)
10. Knowledge of the different parts of a cover letter (4.67)
11. Knowledge of how public transportation may affect job choice (4.74)
12. Knowledge of how family and friends may influence occupational choice (4.74)
13. Ability to use the *Dictionary of Occupational Titles* and the *Occupational Outlook Handbook* (4.75)
14. Ability to ascertain employer differences regarding worker benefits (4.76)
15. Knowledge of illegal questions that may occur during the interview (4.78)

in past jobs in a new occupation, and (10) information about entry-level requirements of various jobs.

The interview has also been the focus of some important and enlightening research. Atkins and Kent (1988, p. 102) asked 95 business recruiters at West Virginia University to rate the most important variable involved in the job interview. The recruiters' rankings can be seen in Table 16.2.

Riggio and Throckmorton (1987) examined the nature of errors in oral communication committed during the mock job interviews and found that the most common problem was responses that failed to provide enough information. Other errors identified were extreme difficulty in answering a question, complaining about either their employers or the quality of their education, providing negative personal information, lack of emphasis on their careers, too much emphasis on salary, inability to communicate skills, and poor grammar. Often oral communication problems included answers that were too long, too vague, or bizarre such as thinking of committing suicide. Riggio and Throckmorton (1987) also found that students who received a 40-minute lecture on interviewing skills did no better in their oral communication than did those who had not been exposed to the lecture.

Some empirical guidelines for resume and cover letter preparation have also come forth. Helwig (1985) surveyed seventy-one recruiters from fifty corporations and found that they had a clear preference for a resume that was one page in length, was clearly labeled, had headings on the left side, used action verbs in describing work experience, and looked uncluttered as opposed to other one- and two-page resumes. Neatness, use of proper English, and correct spelling have also been found to be important to corporate recruiters, as has the order of presentation of data (Stephens, Watt, & Hobbs, 1979).

In a particularly significant study, Ryland and Rosen (1987) found that 230 personnel professionals preferred the functional resume format as compared to the standard chronological format (see Figure 16.1). Ryland and Rosen also found that functional resumes are particularly helpful when applying for highly skilled careers.

Apparently, personnel managers want to see education listed first and work experience second, whereas they have mixed opinions about the presentation of personal data, according to Stephens and associates (1979). How should the resume be structured? With regard to the importance attached to items on the resume, current address, past work experience, major in college, job objectives, permanent address, tenure on previous jobs, colleges attended, and specific physical limitations were rated as the most important items to include on the resume,

TABLE 16.2   College Recruiters' Rankings of the Most Important Considerations in the Employment Interview

1. Overall oral communication skills	11. Overall appearance
2. Enthusiasm	12. Assertiveness
3. Motivation	13. Manners
4. Credentials	14. References
5. Degree	15. Preparation or knowledge of employer
6. Career maturity	16. Sense of humor
7. Initiative	17. Report-writing skills
8. Grade-point average	18. Summer or part-time job experience
9. Listening skills	19. Ability to resolve conflict
10. Punctuality	20. Extracurricular activities

Jane E. Taylor
105 Oakdale Road
Columbus, Ohio 45710
614-554-3934

JOB OBJECTIVE: Sales representative for large pharmaceutical company

SALES
Sold merchandise in busy neighborhood store, handled purchase orders for stocks, and trained three other successful sales clerks.

MANAGEMENT
Assisted store manager of large discount department store with maintaining stock, supervising sales clerks, ordering inventory, developing displays for new merchandise, and handling customer returns and complaints.

Founded amateur photographers' club, increasing membership to 103 in one year. Coordinated convention for national photographers' organization, and organized and implemented photo show, featuring 30 artists.

ADMINISTRATION
Evaluated jobs for manufacturer office furniture and supplies, determined job grading system, gathered wage survey data, determined and justified merit increases and adjustments, approved job descriptions, established salary ranges, and counseled employees.

Studied jobs, categorized positions, interviewed prospective applicants, conducted exit interviews, assisted with annual employee attitude surveys and with administration of pension programs.

EDUCATION AND EXPERIENCE:

1980 to present	APEX OFFICE FURNITURE AND SUPPLY COMPANY Wage and Salary Specialist
1976–1980	Apex Office Furniture and Supply— Personnel Assistant
1974–1976	$-Mart Department Stores—Assistant Store Manager
1971–1973	ABC Drugstores—Sales Clerk (summers)
1970–1974	B.A. in Business Administration, Florida State University
INTERESTS:	Tennis, Photography

References available upon reqest   Willing to relocate

FIGURE 16.1   Two Resume Formats

Jane E. Taylor
105 Oakdale Road
Columbus, Ohio 45710
614-554-3934

JOB EXPERIENCE: Sales representative for large pharmaceutical company

WORK EXPERIENCE:
1980 to present: APEX OFFICE FURNITURE AND SUPPLY COMPANY
Wage and Salary Specialist: Evaluate jobs for manufacturer office furniture and supplies, determine job grading system, gather wage survey data, determine and justify merit increases and adjustments, approve job descriptions, establish salary ranges, and counsel employees.

1976–1980   APEX OFFICE FURNITURE AND SUPPLY COMPANY
Personnel Assistant: Studied jobs, categorized positions, interviewed prospective applicants, conducted exit interviews, assisted with annual employee attitude survey and with administration of pension programs.

1974–1976 $-MARK DEPARTMENT STORES
Assistant Store Manager: Assisted store manager with maintaining stock, supervising sales clerks, ordering inventory, developing displays for new merchandise, and handling customer returns and complaints.

1971–1973   ABC DRUGSTORES
Sales Clerk (summers): Sold merchandise in busy neighborhood store, handled purchase orders for stock, and trained three other successful sales clerks.

EDUCATION: B.A. in Business Administration, Florida State University
  1974

INTERESTS: Tennis, Photography

References available upon reqest   Willing to relocate

FIGURE 16.1   Continued

Source: Ryland, E. K., & Rosen, B. (1987). Personnel professionals' reactions to chronological and functional resume formats. *Career Development Quarterly,* p. 231. By permission.

while religious preference, race, personal data on parents, high school transcripts, photograph, sex, spouse's education, spouse's occupation, typing skills, and number of children were listed as the least important items.

Finally, assistance with resumes, preparation for interviews, and writing cover letters are as close as the Internet. The clearinghouse Riley's Guide (http://www. jobtrak.com/jobguide/) provides information that will be particularly helpful to college students who wish to get tips in these areas. Many of the other websites already listed provide similar information for job seekers. For people who wish to know more about the salaries they should request in their cover letters and in their interviews, Salary Sites (http://www.careerbabe.com/salarysites.html) and Salary Zone (http://www/ioma.com/zone) may provide the information needed. Salary Sites, in particular, contains links to numerous salary surveys for all types of occupations.

Summary

Placement has traditionally been viewed as the culmination of either the career counseling or vocational training process. While this is still true to a degree, many individuals are in need of job placement because they lost their current jobs. In some instances, these individuals will engage in some type of career planning; in other situations, they will be more concerned about getting the first available job. It is apparent that regardless of the reasons for undergoing a job search, modern-day job hunters must be properly equipped with a set of specific skills if they are to be successful. Personnel officers have definite preferences regarding resumes and certain biases against certain types of interview behavior. Unless job hunters have the skills to search out available jobs, write appropriate letters, develop attractive resumes, and interview properly, they will be severely limited in the job search. Fortunately, career development specialists have the tools they need to develop job-hunting skills and have proved to be effective in this area.

It is also clear that several different types of placement operations will be needed in a work force where literally millions of people seek to enter first jobs or find replacements for old ones. Part-time placement offices in high schools and postsecondary institutions can not only provide students with jobs, but also facilitate their career development. Private placement agencies can provide specialized job placement services, and outplacement operations can help relocate the displaced worker. Placement offices in high schools, vocational–technical schools, colleges, and elsewhere can help students find that critical first job. These job placement agencies working independently, but with the same purpose, can alleviate much of the anxiety of being without a job.

References

Atkins, C. P., & Kent, R. L. (1988). What do recruiters consider important during the employment interview? *Journal of Employment Counseling, 25,* 98–103.

Azrin, N. H., & Besadel, V. B. (1979). *Job club counselor's manual: A behavioral approach to vocational counseling.* Baltimore, MD: University Park Press.

Bloch, D. (1989). *The job winning resume.* Lincolnwood, IL: VGM Books.

Bohl, D. L. (Ed.). (1987). *Responsible reduction in force.* New York: American Management Association Publication Division.

Brammer, L. M., & Humberger, F. E. (1984). *Outplacement and inplacement counseling.* Englewood Cliffs, NJ: Prentice-Hall.

Eck, A. (1993, October). Job-related education and training: Their impact on earnings. *Monthly Labor Review*, 21–38.

Eden, D., & Avarim, A. (1993). Self-efficacy training to speed reemployment: Helping people to help themselves. *Journal of Applied Psychology, 78*, 352–360.

Eisenstadt, S. (1995, October 24). Information highway offers new route to jobs. *The News and Observer.* Raleigh, NC.

Farr, J. M. (1989). *Getting the job you really want.* Indianapolis, IN: JIST.

Helwig, A. A. (1987). Information required for job hunting: 1121 counselors respond. *Journal of Employment Counseling, 24*, 184–190.

Helwig, A. D. (1985). Corporate recruits preferences for three résumé styles. *Vocational Guidance Quarterly, 34*, 99–105.

Jones, M. L., Ulicny, G. R., Czyzewski, M. J., & Plante, T. G. (1987). Employment in caregiving jobs for mentally disabled young adults: A feasibility study. *Journal of Employment Counseling, 24*, 122–129.

Kanchier, C. (1990). Career education for adults with mental disabilities. *Journal of Employment Counseling, 27*, 23–36.

Lam, C. S. (1986). Comparison of sheltered and supported work programs: A pilot study. *Rehabilitation Counseling Bulletin, 30*, 66–82.

Lilley, W. (1978). Job hunters, beware. *Canadian Business, 51*, 36–37, 99–100.

Lopez, F. G. (1983). The victims of corporate failures: Some preliminary findings. *Personal and Guidance Journal, 61*, 631–632.

Morin, W. J., & York, L. (1982). *Outplacement techniques: A positive approach to terminating employees.* New York: AMACON.

Murray, N. (1993, Spring). Bridge for the X's: A new career services model. *Journal of Career Planning and Employment*, 28–35.

Platt, J. J., Husband, S. D., Hermalin, J., Cater, J., & Metzger, D. (1993). A cognitive problem solving employment readiness intervention for methadone clients. *Journal of Cognitive Psychotherapy: An International Quarterly, 7*, 21–33.

Ports, M. H. (1993, October). Trends in job search methods. *Monthly Labor Review, 63*–67.

Rife, J. C., & Belcher, J. R. (1993). Social support and job search intensity among older unemployed workers. Implications for employment counselors. *Journal of Employment Counseling, 30*, 98–107.

Riggio, R. E., & Throckmorton, B. (1987). Effects of prior training and verbal errors on students' performance in job interviews. *Journal of Employment Counseling, 29*, 10–16.

Ryland, E. K., & Rosen, B. (1987). Personnel professionals' reactions to chronological and functional resume formats. *Career Development Quarterly, 35*, 228–238.

Silliker, S. A. (1993). The role of social contacts in the successful job search. *Journal of Employment Counseling, 30*, 25–34.

Stephens, D. B., Watt, J. T., & Hobbs, W. S. (1979). Getting through the resume preparation image: Some empirically based guidelines for resume format. *Vocational Guidance Quarterly, 28*, 25–34.

Subich, L. (1994). Annual review: Practice and research in career counseling and development. *Career Development Quarterly, 43*, 114–151.

Wegman, L., Chapman, I., & Johnson, T. (1989). *Work in the new economy.* Indianapolis, IN: JIST.

Yates, C. J. (1987). Job hunters' perspective on their needs during the job search process. *Journal of Employment Counseling, 24,* 155–165.

Zunker, V. G. (1990). *Career counseling: Applied concepts of life planning* (3rd ed.). Monterey, CA: Brooks/Cole.

Important Websites

For Information about Employability Skills Such as Resumes and Interviewing   Go To

Riley's Guide	http://www.jobtrak.com/jobguide/
Proven Resumes	http://www.provenresumes.com/toc.html

Information about Available Jobs (general)

America's Job Bank	http://www.ajb.dni.us/
Career Mosaic	http://www.careermosaic.com/
CareerWeb	http://www.cweb.com/
CareerSite	http://careersite.com/
Internet Career Connection	http://iccweb.com/Default.asp
Monster Board	http://monster.com:80/
Best Jobs in the USA Today	http://www.bestjobsusa.com/
Careers On-Line	http://www.disserv.stu.umn.edu/TC/Grants/COL/

Information about Jobs for Students in Colleges

Riley's Guide	http://www.jobtrak.com/jobguide/

Information about Jobs Listed in Newspapers in 25 Cities

CareerPath	http://www.careerpath.com/

Information about Exotic Places to Work

Cool Works	http://coolworks.com.showme/

Information about Salaries

Salary Zone	http://www/ioma.com/zone
Salary Sites	http://www.careerbabe.com/salarysites.html

17

Career Development in Business and Industry

The term *career development* takes on a more circumscribed meaning in the business context. Thus far, we have discussed career development as a lifelong process that results in the choice, entrance, and adjustment to a series of occupations that together can be characterized as a person's career. Hall (1990) pointed out the fundamental difference between the vocational psychologists, such as Donald Super, and organizational psychologists, such as himself, who are concerned with business and industry. Vocational psychologists are more concerned with the individual processes of development, while industrial psychologists focus more on the situational variables associated with adjustment in the business setting. Job performance, commitment to the organization, job mobility, family–work interactions, and other similar variables are of greatest concern to career development specialists in business and industry (Hall, 1990).

Gutteridge (1986) depicts career development in business and industry as being comprised of two processes: "career planning which is an individual process, and career management, which is an institutional process" (p. 55). Career development, according to Gutteridge, is a joint process, or perhaps more appropriately, *should* be a joint process. Many businesses engage in career management without reference to the employee's career needs. Gutteridge indicates that, in the past, businesses have not typically integrated career planning and career management in a manner that is either responsive to the career needs of the employees or the staffing needs of the corporation. As we see in the next section, the rationale for coordinating these two processes is becoming more compelling.

It is also useful to consider the potential services that may be offered by career counselors in business settings. Osipow (1982) elaborated a list of services that includes the following: (1) help employees assess their work styles and help them change those aspects of their styles that may be ineffective; (2) help managers identify the negative effects of repetitive work, forced relocation, and job loss; (3) identify the strains associated with two-career families and presumably help ameliorate the stresses growing out of those relationships; (4) help managers identify the hazards associated with stress and work; (5) prepare people for retirement; (6) improve the process of performance appraisal; and (7) identify the special concerns of professionals such as scientists.

Osipow (1982) indicated that his "shopping list" is not exhaustive. In fact, several potential functions of the career counselor should be added: building effective work teams, designing and implementing substance and alcohol abuse programs and treatment programs for abusers, and designing and implementing programs to improve employees' health (Wilbur & Vermilyea, 1982).

There is little doubt that improving physical health, mental health, and dealing with substance and alcohol abuse programs are related to improved work performance and these roles usually fall to health educators, directors of occupational health and safety, psychologists, counselors, and others involved with the employee assistance program. This chapter focuses on enhancing individual career planning and organizational career management processes and not on health-related issues.

Finally, just as the meaning of career development changes somewhat in an organizational context, so must the philosophy of the career counselor. Wilbur and Vermilyea (1982) suggested that this shift must occur along four lines: identity, profit motive, emphasis on organizational development, and level of evidence acceptable for decision making. These authors suggested that career counselors must take on the identity of businesspeople first and counselors or psychologists second. In individual counseling, the only concerns are client satisfaction and change. As a career counselor in business and industry engaged in designing and selling services, "operational quality, and efficiency, customer satisfaction, market penetration, resource allocation, and demonstration of impact" (pp. 31–32) become concerns. These are of concern because every business is dedicated first to making a profit. Counselors who are accustomed to putting individual growth first will somehow have to reconcile these two goals, just as they will the idea that organizational development takes precedence over individual development. This is not to suggest that these two areas are incompatible, but if one must be emphasized, individual development will typically be given a lower priority. Also, counselors and psychologists are systematically trained to look for scientific proof that an intervention works. Business decisions are usually not based on hard evidence, and managers are much more likely to rely on their intuition and experience to make decisions (Wilbur & Vermilyea, 1982), something that may be frustrating to the person trained to think more scientifically.

Programming for Career Development

Knowdell (1982, 1984) traced the origins of career development programs in business to the early 1970s, when governmental regulation placed pressure on businesses to provide equal employment opportunity. While Knowdell is undoubtedly correct about the development of comprehensive career development programs for all employees, specialized programs aimed at orienting, socializing, and enhancing the careers of managers probably began much earlier (Hall, 1990). However, the focus of this chapter is on the generalized programming efforts aimed at promoting the careers of employees.

In 1987 Keller and Piotrowski reported that 10 percent of the *Fortune* 500 companies had initiated formal career development programs. Citicorp, General Electric, AT&T, and NASA were among the first corporations to implement comprehensive programs. Ford Motor Company, American Airlines, Glaxo, Pfizer, and numerous other companies have initiated programs in the last few years. The number is increasing steadily, albeit relatively slowly, if one uses as the criterion for inclusion in the list that the program be comprehensive. It is likely that all major corporations in this country have a program aimed at orienting new hires to the business that has employed them and to their specific jobs, and socializing the employees by imparting the corporation's values. Many corporations also provide extensive educational programs aimed at assisting their employees to function more effectively in their current positions and to acquire new job skills that will enhance their opportunity for advancement. It is possible for employees in a few corporations to earn baccalaureate and advanced college degrees with the assistance and support of their businesses. However, what distinguishes these rudimentary career development programs from those that are more highly developed is that comprehensive programs are systematic and focused. A career development system within a business is "an organized, formalized, planned effort to achieve a balance between the individuals' career needs and the organizations' work force requirements" (Leibowitz, Farren, & Kaye, 1986, p. 4). The remainder of this chapter focuses on the rationale for design and implementation of comprehensive career development systems.

Rationale

As Knowdell (1982, 1984) suggested, one of the primary forces behind the development of career development programs in business and industry has been external pressure to provide equality of employment opportunity. Many businesses have been pressured to demonstrate fairness in their recruitment, retention, and promotion procedures. Career development programs that make employees aware not only of their own potential but of job openings with the company have been seen as one means of enhancing equal employment.

London and Stumpf (1986) note that the impetus for career development programs may be primarily internal to the business. They suggest that career development programs are needed to develop career motivation that they believe is based in career resilience, career insight, and career identity. Career resilience is workers' ability to keep a positive perspective even when their careers are not going as well as they would like. Career insight has to do with personal realism about one's own career potential and requires feedback about performance to develop. Career identity is the extent to which workers' personal identities are related to their careers and are reflected in their career directions and goals.

Leibowitz, Farren, and Kaye (1986) also suggest that the current rationale for developing a career development program grows out of meeting internal needs rather than succumbing to external pressure. Career development programs allow businesses to make better use of their employees' skills, increase the loyalty of employees, enhance communication, increase employee retention, contribute to the effectiveness of personnel systems such as performance appraisal and promotion, and help to classify organizational goals. These organizational benefits accrue because managers and employees learn how to manage their own careers; increase their understanding of the organization and its policies; and are better able to give and receive feedback about their performance, to establish realistic goals about their careers, and to increase the sense of personal responsibility for themselves.

Reports from business organizations such as the National Alliance of Business (1986) have made corporate executives aware that it will become increasingly important for corporations to develop and enhance their current employees' work-related capabilities if they are to remain competitive. It is a truism that the labor force of most businesses for the next 10 to 15 years is in place and that well-conceived corporate strategies designed to orient, train, and promote current workers will enhance organizational functioning. In short, corporate executives are concluding that career development programs are good business.

Initiating the Program

Early Steps

There are certain prerequisites to initiating a successful career development program. Among the more important of these are sanctions from top-level executives. Career development programs require various types of organizational changes, and without support from the power structure these changes are unlikely to occur. One CEO sent a memorandum to all managers that "career development will be our number one priority." Not surprisingly, that corporation has one of the finest career development programs in existence.

Establishing a budget to support the program is also an important early step. Choosing a manager who can develop the program is also an important prerequisite to change. The credentials of the manager and the amount budgeted for the development of the program will depend on the type of program to be developed. The manager should be knowledgeable about career development, testing, and career counseling. Moreover, a successful manager needs a basic understanding of organizational functioning, management principles and practices, as well as the general area of human resource planning and development. Specialized knowledge of management information systems, performance appraisal systems, personnel selection and development practices, instructional technology, and a whole host of other skills would of course be useful to the manager of a career development program.

Budgeting for the career development program requires setting forth a developmental budget as well as an operating budget. The initiation of a program in a major corporation can easily cost $300,000 to $400,000, again depending on the nature of the program. A budget for the development of a career development program should include the following lines:

- Manager's salary
- Support personnel salaries
- Consultant's fees/expenses
- Travel expenses to model programs
- Materials acquisition
- Furnishings—desks, bookcases
- Equipment, including computers, printers, and typewriters
- Computer programming assistance
- Printing in-house materials, brochures, and so forth
- Training expenses (orienting managers, training workshop leaders)

The actual cost of operating the program may actually be quite modest depending on the size of the corporation and the type of programs to be delivered. The budget for the program will contain many of the aforementioned budgetary lines, although the amounts for consultant's fees, travel, materials acquisition, equipment procurement, furnishings, printing, and training should be reduced greatly. However, an additional line—evaluation costs—should be added to the operating cost budget.

One additional step should be taken at the outset of the program: determining an organizational niche for the career development program. Typically, these programs are placed under the umbrella of the vice president or director of human resource development (HRD). Leibowitz, Farren, and Kaye (1986) note the importance of the current HRD effort in most corporations, which involves activities such as training new hires and veteran employees, posting job vacancies, evaluating the compensation plan, enhancing employee performance appraisal, and designing a career development program that enhances all of these efforts. For example, one of the jobs assigned to HRD is inventorying the available labor supply (i.e., determining the skills available to focus on the mission of the organization). The career development program can be designed in a manner that will enhance the assessment of employees' skills and thus improve this effort. The career development program can also be instrumental in identifying which employees are engaged in acquiring various types of new skills and thus make the forecasts of needs to recruit employees outside the corporation more accurate.

Needs Assessment

Accurately assessing employee needs is another important early step in the design of a career development program. The needs assessment should be designed in a manner that will answer several key questions such as, "What is the extent of our need for career development programming?" and "What type of program should we have?" However, several questions must be answered prior to embarking on a needs assessment. These questions include: What data collection procedure should be employed? What domains of employee concerns should be sampled? and How will the needs of special groups of employees be identified?

Data Collection Procedures

Some corporations have used employee interviews to determine their need for a career development program. This may be satisfactory as a means of ascertaining top-level management's perceptions of needs but is generally too time-consuming and expensive to use with all employees. A questionnaire should be sent either to a random sample or to all employees, depending on tradition and preference. Obviously, sampling reduces the cost, but if the corporation routinely surveys all employees in its data-gathering efforts, a census should be conducted.

The extent to which follow-up procedures will be employed to increase return rates will be dependent on such factors as the availability of funds and representatives of return rates. Every effort should be made to ensure that returns are both representative of the employees and accurate in their portrayal of employee attitudes. With regard to the latter, every effort should be made to guarantee employee anonymity if the returns are to accurately reflect employee career development needs. Some corporations utilize outside firms for data collection as one means of ensuring confidentiality. If this is not possible, questionnaires and return envelopes should be designed in such a manner that they can be returned without identifying the respondent. Unmarked envelopes that can be placed in central (as opposed to departmental) receptacles can help protect the identity of respondents.

Domains to Be Sampled

The needs assessment questionnaire should be designed to collect information in the following domains: (1) desire for assistance with career planning; (2) preferred source of assistance with career development (e.g., manager, career counselor); (3) preferences for types of career development activities; (4) aversions, if any, to career development activities; and (5) evaluation of current career development activities (if they exist).

Desire for Assistance: Although research has shown that as many as 77 percent of employees may participate in some aspects of the career development program (Wowk, Williams, & Halstead, 1983), it is important for program design purposes to know how many people expect to participate and to be able to estimate when they might participate if various types of career development activities are made available. Thus, direct questions regarding employees' interest in participating in the career development program should be included in the instrument. So should indirect indicators of interest such as degree of satisfaction with current position. People who are dissatisfied with their current jobs may very well be the first to volunteer to participate in the program. Sample items follow:

1. Rate your interest in exploring other career opportunities within the company.
2. Indicate the extent to which you are satisfied in your current position.

Source of Assistance: It is possible to deliver career development services through managers, career counselors employed by the corporation, external consultants, computerized programs, and so forth. Employees should be queried with regard to the people and/or delivery services they would prefer to provide career development services. If an outside firm is being considered, reactions to this option should be explored. All possible options considered feasible by the managers in charge of program development can be presented on the questionnaire for reaction. Some sample items are as follows:

1. Indicate the extent to which you would find each of the following people acceptable as sources of assistance with your own career planning:
   a. Your immediate supervisor
   b. A professional career counselor employed by the corporation
   c. A career counselor outside the corporation who would be brought in to provide assistance to employees
   d. Other—please specify

Types of Career Development Activities Preferred and Aversions, If Any: Recently, at a meeting of representatives from a corporation considering the implementation of a career development program, a debate about the wisdom of utilizing a particular personality inventory as a part of a career development program developed. This debate highlighted that some individuals are uncomfortable with values and personality inventories and perhaps other activities that are often included in career development programs. It is therefore important to ascertain how employees feel about such activities as discussions of interests, values, personality, decision-making style, and career change. If there is widespread aversion to activities such as taking and discussing work values inventories, either among managers or employees, these should either not be included in the program or they should be designed as optional activities. If employees feel uncomfortable with an activity, it is unlikely that their responses to questions or their participation in the activity will reflect their true values or attitudes. Items for sampling attitudes in this domain might include the following:

1. The following is a list of activities that are often included in career development programs. Please rate the extent to which you would feel comfortable participating in each of them:
   a. Completing an interest inventory
   b. Completing a personality inventory
   c. Discussing my work values
   d. Discussing long- and short-term career goals
   e. Discussing my ideal work setting
   f. And so forth

Evaluation of Existing Efforts: Most companies have some aspects of a career development program, usually in the form of job-related feedback during the performance evaluation. All aspects of a program currently in place should be evaluated in the needs assessment process so decisions can be made about their retention and/or modification. It is also useful to ascertain whether or not employees are aware of the opportunities that are now being offered by the corporation, such as paid educational experiences, in-house staff-development sabbatical programs, and so forth. These activities will become more important as the career development program evolves and people take an active role in managing their own careers. The needs assessment may point to an increased need for information about these programs or even to modifications that need to be made in them. Sample items might include the following:

1. To what extent has your performance appraisal been useful to you in your career planning?
2. Rate the degree to which the corporate educational leave policy is useful to you.

Identifying Special Needs

The design of the career development program can be enhanced by sampling the aforementioned five domains. However, the needs assessment will not be complete unless it focuses on the special needs of various subgroups of employees such as women, minorities, and new hires.

The purpose of a career development program is to benefit both the company and the employee by helping to develop employee potential. As noted earlier, corporations that fail to develop talent from within will find themselves hard pressed to compete (e.g., National Alliance of Business, 1986). The career development program must be designed not only to identify talent, but also to help develop that talent.

The needs assessment questionnaire should be designed to determine the extent to which new hires and others understand the corporate occupational structure and the degree to which it offers them opportunity for advancement. These data may be useful in designing employee recruitment and orientation programs as well as in providing information to employees who have considerable tenure with the company.

The career development needs assessment should also be structured so that it identifies barriers to career mobility. Women may have child care problems. Minorities and poor whites may have had poor educational opportunities or have attended substandard schools. Both groups may have observed or experienced discrimination. For example, a recent Gallup survey revealed that 62 percent of the African Americans had observed discrimination in the workplace, either directed toward themselves or others (NCDA, 1988).

Many corporate executives are extremely sensitive about asking questions on the employee survey about emotionally laden issues such as discrimination. While this is understandable, if a decision is reached not to ask these questions on the needs assessment questionnaire, other means of ascertaining this information should be devised, such as hiring external consultants to conduct interviews with various groups of employees.

The special needs of subgroups of employees can be determined if employees are asked to provide certain types of demographic data (e.g., gender, race, employment status, type of job held, years of employment, etc.) and if questions are included in the data collection process that highlight potential problems. Literature reviews of the career development programs encountered by various subgroups can be a useful way of identifying needs that should be addressed.

It would not be unexpected to determine not only that male and female employees have different career development needs, but also that employees working in different departments or units have differing concerns. For example, it is literally impossible for the sales staff of many corporations to attend career development workshops, but they can utilize audiocassettes and workbooks that address career development issues. Some departments may have provided every employee with a personal computer and, thus, would prefer an interactive career development computer program to a workbook or workshop.

It is also likely that the desire for career development activities will vary across departments and units, and the types and levels of activities desired will be markedly different. These and the other factors mentioned affect the design of the career development program and should, therefore, be anticipated in the development of a needs assessment questionnaire.

A Word about Mechanics and Planning

As noted earlier, the needs assessment survey may be embedded in a routine employee opinionnaire or administered separately. Such typical issues as concerns about confidentiality must be attended to if results are to accurately reflect employee opinions. One atypical concern that arises in the assessment of career development needs is that some managers are concerned that the data collection process itself will raise false expectations about career development programming (Leibowitz, Farren, & Kaye, 1986, p. 36). This can be avoided in two ways: through a disclaimer and/or item selection.

If the career development needs assessment survey is conducted as an exploratory step to provide data for the planning of a career development program, this should be stated in the introduction to the questionnaire. If time lines have been established for the initiation of a program, then these should be stated as well. By telling employees that the company is soliciting employee input as one way of informing the decision-making process regarding the implementation of a career development program, raising false expectations can be avoided. Similarly, if the company plans to implement a career development program 2 years hence, indicating this on the questionnaire will lead to realistic expectations about when the program will be implemented. Also, no questions should be placed on the career development needs assessment questionnaire that are not realistic alternatives for inclusion in the program. For example, if no consideration is being given to the development of a computerized career development system, this should not be posed as an option for delivering the program.

Designing the Program

The California Lawrence Livermore National Laboratory program has served as the prototype for many career development programs in other organizations (Knowdell, 1982). This program focuses on career and life planning and has three major components. The first of these is the Career Resource Center (CRC), which contains college catalogs, career information, self-help books, and other information. In the "Livermore Labs" program, CRC personnel also assist employees in developing internal or external resumes. The internal resume is developed for use in pursuing job changes within the organization, whereas the external resume is used in pursuing a new job outside the corporation. Understandably, many corporations have not included an external resume development service as a part of their programs.

The second component of the Livermore Labs program is individual career counseling. However, the counselors who provide this service also provide assistance with financial planning, preparation for retirement, family problems, and a host of other concerns (Knowdell, 1982).

Career assessment workshops constitute the third component of the Livermore Labs program. These consist of 40 hours of intensive career exploration. The content of the workshop sessions at the Livermore Labs program is as follows (Knowdell, 1984):

Week 1—Orientation to career planning (4 hrs)

Week 2—Assessment of work values, personality style, interests; also training in career decision making (16 hrs)

Week 3—Individual interview—a structured interview focusing on past achievements is videotaped (1 hr)

Week 4—Mini seminars made up of small groups of employees work to identify "motivated skills" and effective work style (10 hrs)

Week 5—Individual counseling session focuses on developing an individual career development plan (1 hr)

Week 6—Individuals independently gather information and work on career development plan (varies)

Week 7—Each person presents the what, how, when, and where of a career development plan to other seminar participants (8 hrs)

The actual content of individual seminars may vary to some degree in other corporations. For example, resumes may be developed, interviewing skills may be practiced, and organizational needs may be discussed. But generally speaking, the outcome hoped for in most of these programs is the development of a career development plan for each individual.

One type of information that can be used in developing a career plan is career paths. Career paths represent sequential lines of career progression in an organization (Leibowitz, Ferren, & Kaye, 1986). As can be seen in Figure 17.1, the entry job

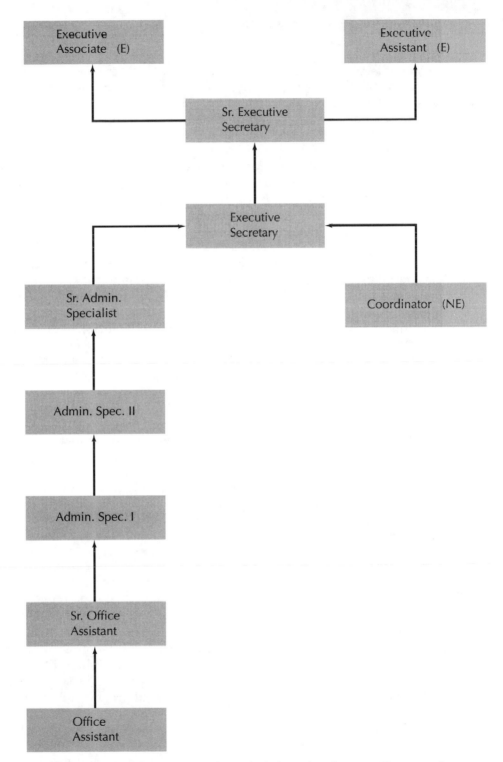

FIGURE 17.1 Career Ladder for Administrative Support Personnel

for administrative support personnel may be as an office assistant, and the corporate accountant (see Figure 17.2) typically enters the system as a financial systems analyst. These and other career paths are developed on the actual experience of employees who have moved to supervisory and managerial experience and thus reflect the promotion practices of the corporation.

Glaxo Wellcome, the second-largest pharmaceutical company in the world (located in Research Triangle Park, NC), has developed a program that is parallel in many ways to the Livermore Labs program. However, Glaxo, as a part of its occupational information, has provided employees with career pathing information for many of the top supervisory and management positions.

American Airlines elected not to offer workshops as a part of its career development program. However, career development specialists have made access to information about jobs and job vacancies readily available to employees. They have also developed policies that enable employees to shadow other employees in jobs of interest. For example, if a reservation agent wished to explore the duties of flight attendants, it would be possible for that agent to take a 2- or 3-day trip with a crew of flight attendants to gain firsthand information about their job responsibilities.

Ford Motor Company, in conjunction with the United Auto Workers (UAW–Ford, 1987), has developed what it terms an employee development and training program. This program uses a series of Life/Education Advisors who conduct one-on-one advising sessions with employees to assist them with educational and personal development planning and goal setting. These advisors also conduct life/education planning workshops; provide information to employees regarding educational, career, and personal growth needs; and collect material about training opportunities.

One of the expected outcomes of the UAW–Ford program is personal growth. A second is career development. However, it is relatively clear that in this program less emphasis is placed on career exploration, interests, and decision making and more emphasis is placed on educational planning than in the other programs discussed.

The Essential Components

Gutteridge (1986) lists five general types of organizational tools: (1) self-assessment tools, (2) individual counseling, (3) internal labor market information/placement exchanges, (4) organizational potential assessment processes, and (5) developmental programs. The Livermore Labs program uses workshops as its essential self-assessment tool. Glaxo Wellcome Corporation offers workshops in which assessment devices are administered, scored, and interpreted. It also provides workbooks that assist in self-assessment. The UAW–Ford program relies on workshop activities for assessment.

Many corporations provide no individual career counseling using trained career counselors. Frequently, supervisors or managers provide "career counseling," coaching, or advice as a part of their performance appraisal meetings. As Gutteridge (1986) noted, this is one of the more controversial aspects of the program,

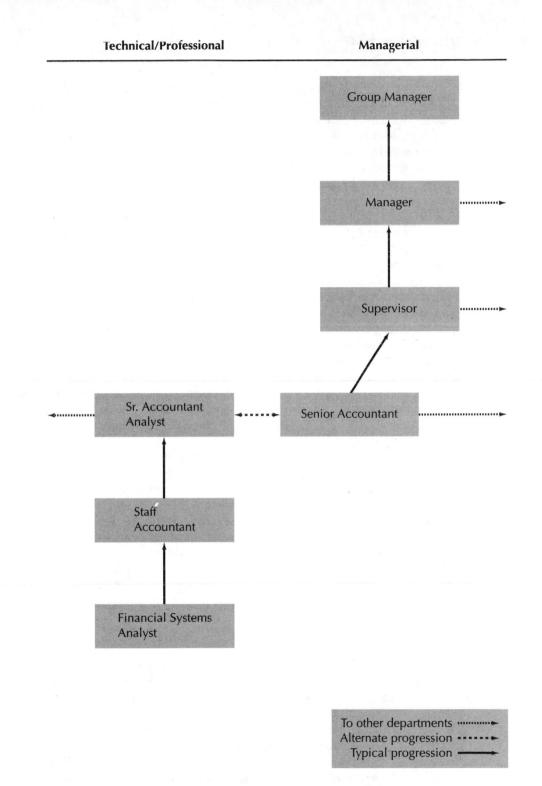

FIGURE 17.2   Career Path: Corporate Accounting

and as Brooks (1984) stated, "Despite claims that managers can or should provide career counseling for employees, managers seldom have either the skill or the inclination to provide these services" (p. 397).

Effective career development programs must have an adequate description of the duties performed by the workers in their organization and the minimum requirements (education and skills) for performing those duties. It is also important that information about career ladders/paths be provided and that all information be readily accessible to employees. For those companies that are prepared to assist workers seek employment outside the corporation, information about careers in the local area, state, and region must be made available. Educational information, like occupational information, may be of two types: internal and external. Most corporations offer ongoing training to employees. Many also offer the opportunities to explore additional education and training outside the corporate structure. Information about these opportunities must also be readily available.

Communicating information about job openings via job posting is one aspect of helping employees identify and pursue career opportunities. Helping employees develop internal resumes and job interviewing skills is another important aspect of this function. Often a CRC is established and staffed to provide these services. However, some companies rely on employee newsletters, bulletins posted in employee lounges and other places, and computerized systems to help employees identify job opportunities and to pursue them.

Every successful organization has an ongoing program to assess the potential of its employees to fill key roles in the organization. In the case of upper-level management, succession planning is engaged in to make sure that there is continuity in organizational leadership. Promotability forecasts are also developed, partially on the basis of performance appraisal information. In some instances, promotability forecasts are developed on the basis of performance in assessment centers, although these centers are primarily used to assess potential for supervisory and managerial positions (Gutteridge, 1986). When assessment centers are used, corporate assessors design a variety of individual and group exercises that are related to functioning as a manager. This assessor then constitutes a panel, usually made up of managers who observe and evaluate employees' performance. As Gutteridge (1986) notes, the panel's recommendation is typically in the form of a "go–no go" recommendation. Skills inventories, which are detailed descriptions of the employee's work history, training, and accomplishments, may also be used in making a final decision.

Developmental programs such as the American Airlines "walk in my shoes" program help employees implement their plans. As already noted, internal and external training programs are also important in this regard as are mentoring systems, training reimbursement, and job rotation programs. Job rotation involves the systematic rotation of an employee through a number of careers, which may be lateral moves designed to introduce variety into the career or develop those skills needed to move vertically in the organization (Gutteridge, 1986).

Of the developmental programs that are offered in various organizations, perhaps none has received more attention than mentoring. Kram (1986) suggested that mentoring, which she defines as "relationships between junior and senior colleagues that contribute to career development" (p. 161), serves two functions: psychosocial and career. Career functions are those that help the junior members of the relationships prepare for advancement in their organizations, while psychosocial functions enhance their feelings of competency and clarify their identities.

To fulfill the career function, mentors "sponsor" junior members by helping them make interpersonal connections, give feedback about relevant job performance, provide support, create opportunities to demonstrate competence, and provide challenging work opportunities. The psychosocial function is fulfilled by role modeling of appropriate organizational behaviors of personal and professional concern, providing ongoing support and reinforcement, and acting as a friend (Kram, 1986).

Although the obvious beneficiary of the mentoring relationship is the junior member, Kram (1985, 1986) also suggested that the senior member benefits as well. Feelings of involvement, making a contribution to the organization, the reciprocal support from the junior member of the dyad, and reliving earlier trials and successes are all benefits of being a mentor.

Mentoring is not without its pitfalls, particularly in cross-gender situations. Martin, Harrison, and DiNitto (1983) reported that cross-gender mentoring can reduce performance as well as feelings of competence and well-being. Kram (1985, 1986) identifies five reasons for these outcomes:

1. Anxiety about the boundaries of the relationships, particularly concerns about intimacy and sexual attraction
2. Reliance on traditional sex roles, which results in a protective attitude by the male and a failure to establish independent roles
3. Ineffective role modeling by males because of different expectations for females in male-dominated organizations.
4. Cross-gender mentoring relations are often viewed suspiciously by managers and employees, with the result that the public image of the relationship becomes of primary concern rather than the well-being of the female.
5. When a woman working in a male-dominated organization is given special attention, peer resentment results because of concern about "unfair" competition. The result is that the woman is forced to choose between her mentor and her peers, with either choice being detrimental to her development.

Bowen (1985) also reiterated many of Kram's (1985, 1986) concerns about cross-gender mentoring. He concluded from his study that gender related problems may not be as great as some might anticipate although envy, jealousy by spouses and others, and snide remarks by colleagues can all result from cross-gender mentoring relationships.

Almost everyone agrees that some form of mentoring occurs within most organizations and that it generally facilitates career development, a point that has been substantiated in a number of research studies which examined the careers of managers (e.g., Reich, 1985). Formal mentoring programs where junior hires are linked to senior mentors are increasingly popular, but it seems that the process of assigning mentors to protégés is tantamount to program failure (Kram, 1986). Instead of involuntary assignment, which often leads to resentment and role confusion, carefully screening potential mentors, enlisting their voluntary participation in the program, preparing them to become mentors through formal training about the role of the mentor, developing mentoring skills, orienting them to the relationship of the mentoring program to the organization and acquainting them with the potential problems associated with cross-gender and cross-cultural mentoring processes, and allowing the mentoring process to occur normally instead of forcing it seems best (Kram, 1985, 1986).

The actual design of each program will be dependent to some degree on employees' needs. It will also be related to the resources available, the culture of the organization, the goals of the organization, and the extent to which the program has been integrated with the other HRD functions.

Integration with HRD

The career development program should be designed in a manner that will enhance the overall function of the human resources development program. The following are examples of how this may be accomplished:

Performance Appraisal: This HRD function can be enhanced by designing activities that prepare employees to ask specific questions of their supervisors at the time of the performance appraisal. For example, employees may want to ask

- How does my current performance affect my promotability?
- What are my deficiencies and how can I remediate them?
- Based on your knowledge of the company, how can I best prepare myself for advancement?
- What are the strategies that I can employ that will most enhance my current job performance?

Many employees report that their managers are uncomfortable in their performance appraisal sessions, with the result that the sessions are brief and the feedback terse. Of course, managers can also be trained to be more specific in their feedback and in discussing the implications of the employee's performance and to provide "advice" regarding the directions the employee should take.

Training: Materials about the company's training policies should be included in the CRC and distributed in career counseling sessions as well as in workshops.

Job Posting: Employees who participate in the program should be made aware of the job posting procedure as well as general hiring practices.

Skills Inventories/Promotability Forecasts: The results of skills profiles developed in workshops can be placed in employees' records and thus help managers gain a more complete picture of the availability of talent and the potential promotability of various employees.

Compensation Systems: Information gained in workshops regarding employees' perceptions of the fairness and adequacy of the compensation system can be communicated to managers.

Program Implementation

Leibowitz, Farren, and Kaye (1986) recommend that a career development program be built on existing programs and practices. As has already been stated, for maximum effectiveness the program should not only be built on existing programs, but also be carefully integrated with them (Gutteridge, 1986; Mirabile, 1986). Mirabile (1986) also pointed out that while methodology and program design are important, unless managerial and employee ownership of the program are gained, the program is likely to struggle. Leibowitz, Farren, and Kaye (1985, 1986) suggested that advisory groups made up of managers and employees may be an effective way of gaining the support that is needed to make the career development program viable. Mirabile (1986) provided even more specific suggestions, such as meeting with the executive vice president of the organization to clarify the organization commitment, to solicit input regarding the program's content, and to clarify the goals of the program as they relate to the organization's goal. He also suggested similar meetings with divisional vice presidents, a cross-section of employees, and other key personnel in the HRD organization.

After the program has been designed, a small pilot program should be implemented and evaluated (Gutteridge, 1986; Leibowitz, Farren, & Kaye, 1985, 1986; Mirabile, 1986). The evaluation of the pilot must necessarily have a focus: employee and organizational needs. Early research (Wowk, Williams, & Halstead, 1983) suggested that when formal career development programs are offered, well over 60 percent of the employees participate in some aspect of the program, with the heaviest participation being in accessing career information. They also report that managers' perceptions of the benefits of the programs include reduced turnover and increased productivity and profitability. However, it has been suggested repeatedly (e.g., Brooks, 1984; Hall, 1986; Hall & Lerner, 1980) that we need better designed evaluation studies that will produce information that relates to both managerial and employee needs.

The needs assessment discussed at the outset should be one of the reference points in designing the evaluation of the pilot programs. If the program has not met the needs of the participants, it cannot be deemed effective. It is also true that records of attendance, turnover, performance, productivity, and profitability are regularly kept by all organizations, and all existing data sources can be monitored as a source of evaluative data.

Finally, with regard to evaluation, these studies need not always be elaborate. Moravec (1982) reported that a career counseling program saved one bank nearly $2 million in 1 year by reducing employee turnover, increasing productivity, and enhancing promotability. It seems likely that both managers and employees would be quite satisfied with a program of this type.

Once evaluative data of the pilot program are collected, the program will need to be fine-tuned and offered to employees throughout the organization. Perhaps the only cautionary word that should be added at this juncture is that widespread participation can be expected and that programming for full implementation should take this into account. To reintegrate and expand on the earlier report of the Wowk and associates (1983) study, 77 percent of the employees in organizations that offered formalized career counseling programs had participated by accessing career information, 74 percent had participated in human resource planning, 70 percent had taken advantage of training and workshops, 61 percent had been involved in career evaluation, 60 percent had engaged in career counseling, and 47 percent had participated in special groups. While Wowk and her associates did not specify the time period in which the participation occurred, 71 percent of the programs surveyed had been implemented in the 5 years prior to their survey, and for most the participation in the programs occurred within a relatively short period of time.

Benefits

Even though career counselors in business and industry may need to concern themselves more with profit, they should still be concerned with the impact on individuals of the programs they design. Knowdell (1982) reported that the results of the follow-up of managers and supervisors in Livermore Labs revealed that 66 percent of both groups believed that employee morale had improved, 88 percent of the supervisors felt that the company would recoup the costs associated with the program, and 73 percent of the employees reported making significant changes in their careers or lives as a result of the program.

Schmidt (1990) summarized the evaluation results from a number of programs in her review of the literature on the effectiveness of career development programs in business and industry. For example, in evaluations of the IBM career development program in San Jose, California, employees reported improvement in their ability to engage in self-assessment and planning. They also reported higher acceptance of responsibility and ownership of their career plan and increased awareness of career opportunities within the company. Schmidt also reports on the successes of programs located in two banks. The managers of the

Third National Corporate program reported that the career development program was worthwhile but time consuming (Goodstein, 1987), whereas employees seemed to have experienced major improvements in their attitudes as a result of the program in the National Bank of Washington. Managers in both banks also reported a dramatic improvement in customer deposits, return on assets, and stock returns, which was one of the reasons for promoting career development (Johnson & Bell, 1987). The Dow Jones & Company employees and managers reported that communication had improved and that job changes were now viewed more positively by employees (Brozeit, 1986) as a result of their program. None of these reports is as dramatic as the 1-year saving of $2 million that resulted from the implementation of a career development program in a bank reported by Moravec (1982). However, they are generally supportive of the idea that both organizational and individual goals are enhanced.

Summary

Career development in business and industry is a relatively new phenomenon, one that is likely to continue and expand. Increasingly, evidence suggests that both employers and employees benefit from these programs. As documentation of the benefits increases, so should the number and scope of these programs.

The exact nature of career development programs in business and industry will vary with the needs of the employees and the resources of the business and, just as is the case in other institutions, some programs will be minimal while others will be exemplary. However, the central elements in all programs will be accurate information about the jobs in the business, mechanisms to communicate this information, and a system that will allow employees to traverse organizational boundaries to pursue, train for, and enter new careers within the organization. Some organizations will undoubtedly rely on technology such as computerized systems to deliver these components, while others will depend more on people-oriented approaches. It is probably the case that both technology and people are needed to deliver high-quality career development programs in business and industry.

References

Bowen, D. D. (1985). Were men meant to mentor women? *Training and Development Journal,* 44, 30–34.

Brooks, L. (1984). Career planning in the work place. In D. Brown, L. Brooks, & associates (Eds.), *Career choice and development: Applying contemporary theories to practice* (pp. 386–405). San Francisco: Jossey-Bass.

Brozeit, R. K. (1986). If I had my druthers. *Personnel Journal, 65,* 84–90.

Goodstein, H. (1987). Career planning. *The Bunker's Magazine, 170,* 58–64.

Gutteridge, T. G. (1986). Organizational career development systems: The state of the practice. In D. T. Hall & associates (Eds.), *Career development in organizations* (pp. 50–94). San Francisco: Jossey-Bass.

Hall, D. T. (1986). Career development in organization: Where do we go from here? In D. T. Hall & associates (Eds.), *Career development in organizations* (pp. 332–351). San Francisco: Jossey-Bass.

Hall, D. T. (1990). Career development theory in organizations. In D. Brown, L. Brooks, & associates (Eds.), *Career choice and development* (2nd ed., pp. 422–454). San Francisco: Jossey-Bass.

Hall, D. T., & Lerner, P. (1980). Career development in work organizations: Research and practice. *Professional Psychology, 11,* 428–435.

Johnson, P., & Bell, D. (1987). Focused vision for focused performance. *Training and Development Journal, 45,* 56–59.

Keller, J., & Piotrowski, C. (1987). Career development programs in Fortune 500 firms. *Psychological Reports, 16,* 920–922.

Knowdell, R. L. (1982). Comprehensive career guidance programs in the workplace. *Vocational Guidance Quarterly, 30,* 323–326.

Knowdell, R. L. (1984). Career planning and development programs in the workplace. In N. C. Gysbers & associates (Eds.), *Designing careers* (pp. 482–507). San Francisco: Jossey-Bass.

Kram, K. E. (1985). *Mentoring at work.* Glenview, IL: Scott, Foresman.

Kram, K. E. (1986). *Mentoring in the workplace.* In D. T. Hall & associates (Eds.), *Career development in organizations* (pp. 160–201). San Francisco: Jossey-Bass.

Leibowitz, Z. B., Farren, C., & Kaye, B. L. (1985). The 12-fold path to CD enlightenment. *Training and Development Journal, 43,* 29–32.

Leibowitz, Z. B., Farren, C., & Kaye, B. L. (1986). *Designing career development systems.* San Francisco: Jossey-Bass.

London, M., & Stumpf, S. A. (1986). Individual and organizational career development in changing times. In D. T. Hall & associates (Eds.), *Career development in organizations* (pp. 21–49). San Francisco: Jossey-Bass.

Martin, P. Y., Harrison, D., & DiNitto, D. (1983). Advancement for women to hierarchical organization: Analysis of problems and prospects. *Journal of Applied Behavioral Science, 19,* 18–33.

Mirabile, R. J. (1986). Designing CD programs the OD way. *Training and Development Journal, 44,* 38–41.

Moravec, M. (1982). A cost effective career planning program requires a strategy. *Personnel Administration, 27,* 28–32.

National Alliance of Business. (1986). *Employment policies: Looking to the year 2000.* Washington, DC: Author.

NCDA. (1988). *Planning for and working in America: Report of a national survey.* Alexandria, VA: Author.

Osipow, S. H. (1982). Counseling psychology: Applications in the world of work. *The Counseling Psychologist, 10,* 19–25.

Reich, M. H. (1985). Executive views from both sides of mentoring. *Personnel, 62,* 42–46.

Schmidt, S. (1990). Career development programs in business and industry. *Journal of Employment Counseling, 27,* 76–83.

UAW–Ford. (1987). *Life education planning program.* A status report in the UAW–Ford program. Dearborn, MI: UAW–Ford National Development and Training Center.

Wilbur, C. S., & Vermilyea, C. J. (1982). Some business advice for counseling psychologist. *The Counseling Psychologist, 10,* 29–30.

Wowk, R., Williams, D., & Halstead, G. (1983). Do formal career development programs really increase employee participation? *Training and Development Journal, 44,* 82–83.

18

Career Counselors in Private Practice

There are literally thousands of counselors, psychologists, social workers, and other mental health professionals in private practice delivering a variety of mental health services. It is likely that a few hundred of these professionals, primarily counselors and counseling psychologists, provide career counseling services to the public. It is also likely that this number will grow because adults in our society seem to be relying increasingly on career counselors for assistance. Over 31 percent of adults surveyed in a recent NCDA Gallup Survey indicated that they had, at some time in their lives, consulted a professional career counselor in a school or college about career choices. However, the answer to one question included in the survey (Hoyt & Lester, 1995) is more enlightening when considering the matter of private practice. Adults surveyed were asked if they had ever visited a "fee charging career counseling agency" to consider their career choices. Almost 9 percent of the respondents responded affirmatively. This means that approximately 11 million adults have paid to receive some type of assistance with their careers. Because of the number of people changing jobs voluntarily and involuntarily, it seems likely that increasing numbers of people will seek assistance from private practitioners in the future.

Qualifications

In Chapter 14, the basic qualifications for practice as a career counselor were outlined. That discussion is not repeated here. However, it is important to note that many states have licensure, certification, and registry laws that regulate the practice of psychologists, counselors, social workers, and others. For example, all fifty states have licensure laws for psychologists, and approximately forty states have licensure laws or some form of regulatory statute for counselors. For the most part, the licensure laws for psychologists require that people who purport to be psychologists must be licensed whether they practice in public institutions or are engaged in private practice. On the other hand, the regulatory statutes for counselors are primarily aimed at regulating practice in the private domain. Unfortunately, these laws often have loopholes that allow some private practitioners to evade regulation (Brown & Srebalus, 1996). For example, an Idaho statute established licensure for counselors that permits professionals interested in becoming licensed to meet the requirements (e.g., meeting the training and supervision requirements and passing a test to demonstrate knowledge) and call themselves licensed Practicing Counselors. However, counselors who wish to enter private practice, including offering career counseling services, do not have to be licensed and may use the titles counselor, career counselor, career consultant, along with any other title as long as they do not call themselves Registered Practicing Counselors. Although the regulatory statutes for counselors are much more stringent in states such as Mississippi, Virginia, and Florida, the extent of regulation varies considerably in other states, with nine states having no regulation.

One state, New Jersey, adopted a statute that requires employment agencies and employment agents to be licensed and career consulting and outplacement firms to be registered with the Chief of Bureau of Employment and Personnel Services. Admittedly, the New Jersey statute establishes a minimum criteria for providing placement and counseling services, but it is a landmark effort to regulate a wide range of services. It seems likely that specialty standards for career counselors will evolve in the near future in many states and that some will adopt statutes similar to New Jersey's. The only reliable means of determining the nature of the regulatory statutes in your state is to contact the licensing boards and get copies of the regulatory statutes as well as the rules established by the board to govern practitioners in your specialty.

Guidelines for Consumers

Caveat emptor, or "let the consumer beware," is probably the best advice for consumers who are seeking assistance with career-related problems. The reason for this, as has already been noted, is that in many states career counselors are unregulated by statute. To assist consumers to make wise choices, the National Career Development Association has issued consumer guidelines for selecting a career counselor (NCDA, 1988). These guidelines are paraphrased as follows:

Credentials

Career counselors should have earned graduate degrees in an appropriate mental health specialty such as counseling, counseling psychology, or social work.

As a part of their training they should have completed supervised field experience which involved career counseling.

They should have appropriate work experience.

They should have developed knowledge bases that will support their activities as career counselors, including knowledge about career development, assessment, occupational information, employability skills, the integration of life roles, and the stresses of working, job loss, and/or career transitions.

Fees

Career counselors should have established fees and allow clients to choose services, terminate whenever they deem appropriate, and pay for only those services that have been provided.

Promises

Professional career counselors should refrain from making claims such as promising careers that have higher salaries or claims that they can provide immediate resolution to career problems.

Ethics

Career counselors follow ethical codes such as those published by the American Psychological Association or the American Counseling Association.

Even if consumers were aware of the guidelines developed by the National Career Development Association, it is likely that they may still be confused by the number of people who call themselves career counselors. For example, there are job placement counselors who offer resume preparation services, outplacement counselors who assist people whose jobs have been terminated find suitable employment, and a variety of other people offering "career counseling." Unfortunately, some of these people have little training in career counseling, while others may have completed a 1- or 2-week training course and received impressive certificates from what appear to be creditable organizations.

As suggested earlier, many states are considering more stringent legislation to regulate career counseling because it is virtually impossible to sort out qualified from unqualified practitioners. Until professional organizations can inform the public and stringent legislation can eliminate the unqualified people, "let the consumer beware" is the best advice that can be offered.

Establishing a Private Practice

Almost everyone who has been involved in setting up a private practice will attest to the difficulty involved in the process, particularly if the practitioner chooses not to join a group practice where referrals are immediately available from other professionals. Many psychologists and counselors who enter private practice enter a group practice, and then choose to offer both personal and career counseling. Often they find that their group practice colleagues refer their "career cases" to them because they lack the skill to provide the service themselves. Other career counselors choose to set up independent practices and offer only career development services. In this section some of the general concerns regarding establishing a private practice are discussed.

Types of Services

Career counselors often offer a wide variety of services, including career counseling with individuals and groups, consultations, job placement, testing, outplacement, resume development and the development of other employability skills, retirement planning, career/life role integration counseling, spousal relocation, training, program evaluation, work adjustment counseling, and vocational appraisal services. Because marketing is a critical part of a successful private practice, practitioners must realistically determine if they have the skills to offer a service and whether there is a market for that service. The following are potential clients for each of the aforementioned services:

Service	*Potential Clients*
Individual and group career counseling	The general public; may target specialized groups such as transitional workers, women, or retirees
Testing	The general public; may target high school students doing career planning or other groups
Outplacement	Business and industry involved in reducing their work force and seeking placement services; often specialize in white-collar workers
Job placement	Members of the general public; specialization often occurs in that some agencies specialize in clerical, technical, or other types of workers (see Chapter 16)
Headhunters	A specialized form of job placement; often involves recruiting and placing corporate executives, school superintendents, scientists

Resume and employability skills development	General public; often targets young workers (e.g., college students), workers in transition, and those who have lost their jobs
Retirement planning	Workers preparing for retirement; may target military or other people from a specific industry
Career/life role integration	General public; may target workers at midlife or new entrants to labor force
Training	Other professionals who want to upgrade their skills in various areas; may target those interested in setting up a private practice
Consultation	Businesses, governmental agencies, schools, colleges and universities, federal programs (e.g., Job Training Partnership Act)
Career development program evaluation	Businesses, governmental agencies, schools, colleges and universities, federal programs with career development programs
Work adjustment counseling	The general public; on a contract basis to businesses
Spousal relocation	Businesses; primarily those businesses interested in transferring executives who have employed spouses who are seeking careers
Vocational appraisal	Social Security Administration; insurance companies; others interested in establishing extent of vocational disability
Career information	Develop customized information packets for clients who do not wish to pursue information independently

In addition to determining whether they have the skills to offer a service and whether there is a client group available in their area, practitioners must assess the degree to which competition is available. For example, outplacement has become highly competitive, and large outplacement firms such as Drake Beam Marin not only have well-developed outplacement programs, but also have a national network of offices that can be called on to assist workers find jobs in a wide variety of job markets. These same firms often offer a spousal relocation service that not only is lucrative, but also helps them establish corporate contacts. Only a few individuals can compete with the large outplacement firms. However, a number of career counselors have developed outplacement services for small companies in areas where relocation does not entail extensive geographic relocation.

Location of the Office

Many private practitioners find it convenient and less expensive to use portions of their residences for their offices. Obviously, this eliminates commuting, rental fees, janitorial services, and so on. Some parking must be provided for clients, and this may become a major issue in some areas, particularly if group counseling is provided for eight to twelve clients at a time. Using one's residence as a business office is impossible in some residential areas because of zoning restrictions.

Many counselors locate offices in settings that cater to professionals because of accessibility, the availability of parking, opportunities to share experiences with other professionals regarding the services of a receptionist or a telephone answering service and perhaps billing services, and opportunities to increase the likelihood of referrals. An office located in a professional office building also helps project the professional image that many career counselors desire, particularly if they are involved with consultation in business and industry. The exact location and nature of the office will depend on the types of services to be offered, costs, desire for professional image, and convenience.

Services to Be Offered

As has already been noted, career counselors may offer a variety of services to the public. The backbone of most private practices is career counseling, but many practitioners are engaged in many other services. Although it is probably true that many private practitioners simply begin their businesses and let them evolve, a careful plan should be developed to offer services and market them to the public.

In deciding what services to offer, the following questions should be posed (Ridgewood Financial Institute, 1995). First: Am I really in business? It is certainly the case that many private practitioners hedge on this question simply because their private practice is a part-time practice. Before deciding what type of services are to be offered, the response to this question must be in the affirmative and must be followed by the obvious question: If I am in business, what business am I in? Will I specialize in career counseling? If yes, which services will I offer? Are there any underserved groups in my community? Are there career development services being offered that could be offered more effectively? At less cost? Once private practitioners decide that they are really in business, that their private practice is really more than a hobby, and the business they are in, it is time to ask a series of other questions.

Chief among the other questions to be answered is: Am I projecting the right image? (Ridgewood Financial Institute, 1995). It is certainly possible to build a successful private practice that specializes in career counseling operating out of an office in the home. It is less likely that a private practitioner can build a highly successful consultation or outplacement out of a home office, primarily because of the need to establish an image that will attract potential clients. For example, it may be difficult for a corporate executive to have confidence that a "shoestring" operation can provide services to twenty executives who need to be relocated because their jobs have been terminated. In real estate, there are three rules for selecting property: location, location, location. In private practice, particularly if there is an expectation of competing with well-established outplacement and corporate counseling firms, the three rules may well be image, image, image. Credentials, office space, stationery, business cards, personal dress and demeanor, and written and verbal presentations are all a part of one's business image and must be attended to in building a practice.

To assess image, compare facilities, equipment, stationery, dress, and so on, to those of the competition and ask: Which would I choose? Some potential private practitioners, after making this comparison, have decided to join group practices so that they can learn to project the "right" image. Others have elected not to compete for business in certain arenas.

In the following section, marketing a private practice is discussed. However, in assessing whether to start or expand a current practice, the question arises: Do I know how to market my current services, or if I elect, to expand a new service? (Ridgewood Financial Institute, 1995). There are literally dozens of ways to market services. Private practitioners must be aware of these and, perhaps more important, be apprised of which ones are actually cost effective. If a knowledge of marketing strategies and their effectiveness has not been developed, marketing consultants may be contacted.

Ultimately a business plan must be developed with specific objectives. Marketing, selection of office space, image, and a host of other decisions and activities grow out of the objectives that are established.

Marketing the Service

Most career counselors working in public institutions are aware of the need to market their programs, but because they are paid regularly by a public or private institution, the immediate need to market is less pressing. Private practitioners are paid by their clients, and thus no clients—no income. This is precisely the reason why many private practitioners start working in institutional settings, initiate part-time private practices, gradually expand their practices, and once a client base is built, sever their relationships with their employers. These successful private practitioners have learned to market their services successfully. There are many strategies that can be employed to market career development services. But before any strategy is employed, the first step is to get comfortable with the idea of advertising. Many counselors who have worked in public institutions have an aversion to advertising (Ridgewood Financial Institute, 1995) because it almost seems unprofessional. Advertising is legal, it is professional, and it is essential to the establishment and maintenance of your private practice. Obviously, advertisements should be tastefully done, but there are no limitations on where they can be placed. Newspapers, newsletters, magazine ads, billboards, television and radio spots, and posters are a few of the potential ways to advertise a service. Another way to advertise your service is a tasteful brochure that outlines your services and solicits business (see Figure 18.1).

One of the best types of advertisements is the nonad. One psychologist in private practice writes regularly for an airlines magazine. Because of the exposure he has received, he is invited to conduct more than a hundred workshops per year. Another prepares a weekly column for a local newspaper. Still others serve in high-visibility volunteer positions where their names will be mentioned frequently in the local news media. Making appearances at several clubs, parent groups, and professional associations to discuss career counseling and development is another nonad marketing strategy employed by many practitioners. To use this strategy effectively, the private practitioner must have good public speaking skills and must be able to project a professional image. Name recognition is an important part of marketing any service, and depending on the nonad activity, the service provided can help build the desired image.

A marketing campaign may begin with nonads, but soon a target group must be developed, a list of the strategies to be employed must be compiled, an advertising budget must be developed, and an advertising calendar must be laid out.

FIGURE 18.1   Portions of Brochure of Career Directions, Hackensack, NJ

Is Career Counseling or Planning for You?
- I would like to examine my career options
- I would like to assess my abilities and interests
- I am not satisfied with my present position
- I cannot decide on a career
- I am uncertain how to change my career after the age of 35
- I am registered with fifteen employment agencies and not one has contacted me for an interview
- I don't know how to set up a complete employment search campaign
- I feel nervous and uncomfortable in an interview
- I want to return to school but cannot decide on a course of study

About New Directions
- Career Planning and Decision Making
- Preretirement
- Midcareer Change
- Job Market Reentry
- Employment Search Skills
- Job Campaign Strategy
- Complete Resume Writing Service
- Interview Skills
- Aptitude, Achievement, and Interest Testing
- Advanced Educational Planning

This campaign will be tied to what services are to be offered. For example, a private practitioner might decide to run weekly advertisements in the local newspaper to publicize a resume development service in January through May, because many high school and college students are beginning the job hunt at this time. These advertisements might be supplemented with posters placed in dormitories and on high school bulletin boards. The following are tips from successful practitioners about marketing a private practice.

> *Private career counseling demands flexibility on the part of the owner/counselor along with creativity since private practice income fluctuates. Career counseling expertise needs to be marketed to several sectors other than private clients. Seminars, consulting, writing newspaper columns, teaching, and outreach counseling for nonprofit groups are necessary in order to advertise the practice, "grow the business," and make an adequate income.*
>
> Joan F. Youngblood,
> Creative Career Counseling

> *In order to make a private career counseling practice thrive, you need to attract clients. Advertising and publicity are two ways of attracting clients. Know the difference between advertising and publicity. Advertising costs you money. Publicity brings you money.*
> *To get your private career counseling practice going, (i.e., making money), you will need to spend up to 50 percent of your time in marketing and sales activities. Marketing and sales are* not *like counseling activities. If marketing and sales are not activities that you enjoy, you should think long and hard about spending so much time in an activity that you don't like. Think about this— Would you advise a client to spend 50 percent of his or her time in an activity that the client dislikes?*
>
> Richard L. Knowdell,
> National Certified Career Counselor

> *Networking and visibility within the communities you are planning to serve is essential. Because counselors are often uncomfortable doing marketing, they often do too little to promote themselves. Referrals come from a broad marketing campaign, encompassing contact development with friends, colleagues, and other professionals who potentially serve your client profile in other capacities. Initially, 50 percent of your time should be spent in marketing activities to generate referrals and a client base. Advertising, workshops, and community service are other techniques that are essential in your marketing plan to increase credibility and visibility as an expert in your field.*
>
> Barbara Tartaglione,
> Career Connection

Networking is a process by which counselors interact with other professionals for the purpose of gaining access to business opportunities and/or referrals. Career counselors often attend local, regional, and statewide professional meetings for counselors to develop and reinforce their own expertise and to enhance the likelihood that clients will be referred to them by other professionals. Career counselors who offer consultation to business and industry should probably extend their networking to organizations like the American Society for Training and Development along with local meetings of counselors and psychologists, because people employed in local businesses belong to this association.

Direct solicitation of services via mail, telephone, or personal contact is also a method of gaining clients, particularly if consultation services are offered. These types of contacts can also be used to extend networks and perhaps gain referrals for other services offered, such as career counseling. Some career counselors believe that the best contacts are made in informal meetings, such as over lunch. While there is no data to support this supposition, the business lunch seems to be widely employed as a marketing strategy.

All forms of advertisement should adhere to the ethical guidelines of the practitioner's profession. Generally speaking, advertisements may contain a listing of the person's highest relevant degree, licenses and certifications, and professional services offered. Advertisements may not include endorsements for past clients and may not make claims of likely success, even if these statements do represent the facts (NBCC, 1996). Sample advertisements are shown in Figure 18.2.

It is also worth noting that networking strategies, advertisements, public appearances, direct solicitations, and other marketing strategies, although they do yield immediate results, do not necessarily result in great numbers of clients or multiple offers to engage in lucrative counseling jobs. The marketing of a private practice can take months and perhaps years. Moreover, marketing *never* stops. Clients terminate and consultation contracts end. To continue to earn, clients must be found and new contracts negotiated. Marketing may become easier, but it always remains an essential task for private practitioners.

Budgeting

A private practice is a for-profit business which requires a great deal of planning, including the development of a careful budget. Figure 18.3 shows a budget planning sheet utilized by Frank Karpati of Career Directions.

It is also imperative that careful logs be kept for income tax purposes; many commercially developed log books are available. Any type of record, including ordinary date books, will suffice so long as the records are backed up by receipts for all expenses. In determining whether a deduction is legitimate the IRS expects the taxpayer to establish a clear relationship between the expense and the business. An emergency room physician successfully argued that a garage door opener allowed him to get to emergencies sooner. A noted speaker who gives 100 to 150 speeches per year also argued that a jacuzzi was essential to help him deal with the stresses of travel. However, both cases are on the "fringes of acceptability" and

Professional RESUMES

CONSULTATION • DESIGN • PRINTING

Career Counseling, Testing
Interviewing Skills Training
Employment Search Strategy
Planning
BY NATIONAL CERTIFIED
Professional Career Counselor

CAREER DIRECTIONS

THE PROFESSIONAL RESUME PEOPLE
NO FEE for initial Consultation
(DAY OR EVENING APPOINTMENTS)
487 - 0808

Professional CAREER COUNSELING & TESTING SERVICES RESUMES

Employment Search,
Interviewing & Salary
Negotiating Skills Training
by NATIONAL CERTIFIED
Professional Career Counselor

CAREER DIRECTIONS

NO FEE for initial Consultation
487 - 0808
(DAY OR EVENING APPTS.)

CAREER DIRECTIONS

PROFESSIONAL RESUMES
CAREER COUNSELING TESTING
INTERVIEWING SKILLS TRAINING &
Employment Search Strategy Planning

by NATIONAL CERTIFIED
PROFESSIONAL CAREER
COUNSELOR

No Fee For Initial Counsultation
DAY OR EVENING APPOINTMENTS

Hackensack Area 487-0808

Professional RESUMES
Career Counseling, Testing
Interviewing Skills Training
Employment Search Strategy
Planning

CONSULTATION•DESIGN•PRINTING
Frank S. Karpall, M.A., N.C.C., N.J.C.C., N.C.C.C., ABVE-Diplomate
NATIONAL CERTIFIED
professional career counselor

CAREER DIRECTIONS

NO FEE for initial Consultation
(DAY OR EVENING APPOINTMENTS)
487 - 0808

FIGURE 18.2 Sample Telephone Directory Advertisements for Career Directions, Hackensack, NJ

FIGURE 18.3 Annual Budget Planning/Expenses Sheet

Advertising
Yellow Pages _____
Other Printed Material _____
Mailing/Postage _____
Total $_____

Automobile
Purchase _____
Depreciation _____
Insurance/Registration _____
Repairs/Maintenance _____
Fuel _____
Total $_____

Professional Membership and Dues
Total $_____

Publications
Library _____
Depreciation _____
Total $_____

Professional Liability Insurance
Total $_____

Computerized Services
Software _____
Supplies _____
Printing _____

Business Travel
Air Transportation _____
Ground Transportation _____
Lodging _____
Meals _____
Miscellaneous _____
Total $_____

Outside Contractors
Administrative Service _____
Consultants & Training _____
Total $_____

Rent
Total $_____

Office Equipment
Service Contracts _____
Computer _____
Depreciation _____
Typewriter _____
Depreciation _____
HP Laser _____
Depreciation _____
Copier
Depreciation _____
Total $_____

Office Furniture
Desks _____
Depreciation _____
Chairs _____
Depreciation _____
Filing Cabinets _____
Depreciation _____
Other _____
Total $_____

Telephone
Office _____
Home _____
Total $_____

Public Relations/Entertainment
Total $_____

might have been disallowed by another auditor. Entertainment, travel, meals, equipment purchases, furniture, malpractice insurance, and continuing education are all legitimate expenses if records are kept properly. However, a consultation with a knowledgeable accountant may be the first step to take in setting up a private practice, and continuing consultation regarding the legitimacy of expenses may be the best means of avoiding problems with the IRS.

Fees

The guideline established for fee setting by the National Board of Certified Counselors (1996) suggests that the career counselor must take into account the financial status of the client. Although this is the guideline most practitioners adhere to, it does not answer the question: Assuming that the client has adequate financial resources, what should I charge? There are several possible answers to this question. One of the most common ways of setting fees in career counseling is to look at the fees of competitors and establish a commensurate fee schedule (Ridgewood Financial Institute, 1995). Another is to set fees in accordance with those being charged for psychotherapy, apparently based on the assumption that the practitioner's time and services are as valuable as those of the psychotherapist. A common fee-setting strategy is to charge less for group counseling than for individual counseling. Unfortunately, there are no data that provide definitive answers to the question: What are career counselors charging for various services?

There are surveys that provide data about the cost of psychotherapy (Ridgewood Financial Institute, 1995), which suggest that fees ranging from $35 to $150 per hour and beyond are charged by various mental health practitioners for psychotherapy. As suggested earlier, some practitioners gear their fee structure to that of psychotherapy. Most clients are probably paying $60 to $80 per hour for career counseling based on this one source. However, many career counselors also charge assessment fees for interest inventories, personality assessments, and aptitude tests, and these can run to $300 and beyond in some instances.

If the data about the fees for career counseling are unclear, those regarding career development consultation are simply unavailable. Whereas some consultants who work with business and industry to set up career development programs, design performance appraisal systems, and improve employee–employer relations charge $1000 to $1200 per day based on private feedback to the authors, it is likely that the range of fees for consultation services is much broader—perhaps ranging from $500 to $5000 per day, depending on the problem and the reputation of the consultant.

In addition, relatively little information about fees is available in the area of outplacement work. Outplacement firms and individual practitioners have demanded and received a fee based on the employee's salary for 3 months (see Chapter 16). Therefore, if the employee is paid $5000 per month, the outplacement fee would be $15,000. However, these fees have been charged for outplacement of middle- and upper-management personnel. When businesses hire outplacement firms to work with blue-collar workers, the fee is typically much smaller, although the number of employees is usually larger.

The fee schedule should be established at the time the service is initiated along with the method of payment. The following statement appears in the contract signed by each client of Career Directions.

Fee Schedule
The fee for a 70–120 minute consultation is $180.00 payable at the time of the conference. This fee also includes counselor research, preparation and testing ser-

vices. Therefore, for the fee the client should expect to receive 2-½ to 3 hours of professional services. Although the exact number of sessions cannot be initially determined, counseling is usually completed within four *to* six *sessions.*

In order for the counseling service to maintain its ability to function and provide the services you need, it is necessary to require of all clients that they be responsible for the time set aside for their consultation. This is particularly essential since a counselor's time is allotted to you alone for the duration of your session, and cannot be used in any other way. In the event that illness or emergency prevents your coming for counseling, you must notify the agency at least 24 hours in advance. The counselor will be happy to discuss this matter with you at length if you deem it appropriate.

One factor that plays a major role in the establishment of fees for psychotherapy that cannot be counted on in providing reimbursement for career counseling is health insurance. Many clients who come for psychotherapy have health insurance that pays some or all of the expense of the treatment. In those instances where insurance pays a portion (80 percent) of an established fee (perhaps $70 per hour) or any established fee ($50 per hour), psychotherapists often charge more for the service since the out-of-pocket cost to the client is not great. However, unless the client also has a mental health problem that can be treated simultaneously with the career problem, health insurance will not pay for the service. This fact alone may dictate that fees for career counseling be lower than those for psychotherapy.

Billing

One inevitable aspect of all forms of private practice is the need to collect fees. Many practitioners request that payment by check or credit card be made at the time the counseling is provided. However, whenever bills are unpaid, regardless of the circumstances, billing agencies and even collection agencies are often utilized to collect overdue accounts. The amount of money spent on collection and lost as a result of unpaid bills will vary with the situation. However, bad debts are a realistic part of all business and reduce expected income.

The Ridgewood Financial Institute (1995) suggests that there are several ways to increase payment for services. For example, collect complete information on every client including name, address, telephone number, and Social Security number so that collection can be expedited. Perhaps more important, when clients fill out information forms about themselves they should also be informed of their financial obligation, how payment is expected (cash, check, or credit card), and what will happen on past-due accounts. Some practitioners charge late fee penalties, sometimes labeled as business costs. Payment at time of service delivery is a means of lowering unpaid bills. This will not prevent receipt of bad checks, but it will probably reduce the number of outstanding bills to be collected.

Many practitioners have a series of "collection letters," with the message ranging from a friendly reminder that payment is past due to a warning that the bill is about to be turned over to a collection agency. The use of a collection agency is a last resort, because their fees often run to 50 percent of the debt and ultimately many of these agencies rely on threats to credit ratings as a basic collection strategy. Finally, some practitioners bring suit in small claims courts, have office assistants telephone people in arrears, and even accept in-kind services (such as repairs to home or office) as payments. Whereas none of these methods is particularly desirable, they all result in increased income and should be considered as alternative methods for increasing the profitability of the practice.

Other Business Details

The establishment of a private practice involves dealing with a host of other details including establishing a recordkeeping system, considering the possibility of using an answering service (versus an answering machine), hiring assistants and/or clerical workers, choosing an appropriate liability insurance policy, and selecting an accountant. Some of these decisions are relatively simple. For example, most practitioners purchase liability insurance from companies that offer group rates through professional associations such as the American Association for Counseling and Development and the American Psychological Association. Other decisions will depend on costs, the image that is being projected, and the personal preference of the practitioner.

Developing a Testing File

One detail that deserves special consideration is the establishment of a testing file. All private practitioners are faced with identifying and securing a set of tests and inventories that can be used to facilitate their clients' career development. The first consideration in this process is to "qualify" to purchase tests. Publishing companies that produce, distribute, and in many instances score the results require that people who order tests provide proof that they are qualified by virtue of training, licensing, and/or certification to administer and interpret the tests that they wish to purchase. Professional ethics also dictate that competence be considered a primary consideration when using tests and inventories. Finally, the potential for malpractice suits against people who carelessly use tests and inventories is considerable.

Establishing a Career Information Center

Earlier, the importance of a career information center was discussed as well as some guidelines for establishing a center. The National Career Development Association publication *Designing and Implementing a Career Information Center* (Brown & Brown, 1990) can also serve as a useful guide. However, an objective for the private practitioner must be to minimize costs while providing an adequate information source to meet client needs. Answering the questions "Who are (or will be) my clients?" and "What will their informational needs be?" is the starting place for establishing the center. The next step is probably to determine what information can be obtained inexpensively through your state Career Information Delivery System (CIDS) and through government publications such as *Occupational Outlook Handbook,* the *Guide to Occupational Information,* and special publications from the Department of Labor's Bureau of Labor Statistics. Once this process has been completed, materials can be purchased from the numerous commercial publishers to complete the library.

Summary

Career counseling in private practice offers a rewarding if challenging career option. However, it also requires a set of skills in addition to those taught in most graduate programs. Career counseling in private practice requires that counselors be able to conceptualize and market a business operation, which involves everything from selecting an office to designing a marketing comparison. Individuals considering this option must carefully consider whether they are equipped personally and professionally to take on such an enterprise. The professional and economic rewards will probably be substantial for those who successfully develop a private practice, although, as is the case with most small businesses, the risk of failure measured in economic terms will be high.

References

Brown, S. T., & Brown, D. (1990). *Designing and implementing a career information center.* Alexandria, VA: National Career Development Association.

Brown, D., & Srebalus, D. J. (1996). *Introduction to the counseling profession.* Englewood Cliffs, NJ: Prentice-Hall.

Gallup Organization. (1989). *A Gallup survey regarding career development.* Princeton, NJ: Author.

Hoyt, K. B., & Lester, J. L. (1995). *Learning to work: The NCDA Gallup survey.* Alexandria, VA: National Career Development Association.

NBCC. (1996). *Certification information and application.* Alexandria, VA: National Board for Certified Counselors.

NCDA. (1988). *The professional practice of career counseling and consultation: A resource document.* Alexandria, VA: National Career Development Association.

Ridgewood Financial Institute. (1995). *Guide to private practice* (2nd ed.). Hawthorne, NJ: Author.

19

Trends and Issues in Career Information, Career Counseling, and Career Development Programming

In this chapter an attempt will be made to identify the trends and issues that will affect career development theory, research, and practice in the year 2000 and beyond. Of course, predicting the future can be risky as well as rewarding. For example, Herr (1974), writing in the National Vocational Guidance Association's decennial volume *Vocational Guidance and Human Development*, made the following predictions for the decade following the publication of the volume: (1) There will be increased specificity in the objectives of vocational guidance programs; (2) the counselor will increasingly act as an agent of change, and "he or she will proffer his (or her) skills indirectly rather than directly in behalf of those he (or she) serves" (p. 564); and (3) the emphasis of vocational guidance in the next decade will be on prevention rather than remediation. History has documented the accuracy of Herr's prediction that career development programs are designed to produce specific results, and they are currently more likely to be evaluated on their ability to produce specific outcomes. However, the predicted shift in counselors' roles from working with individuals to functioning as environmental agents of change has never materialized. We have seen a rise in the number of preventive career development programs in the career education movement of the 1970s, but by 1981 when Ronald Reagan assumed the presidency, the back-to-basics educational movement had all but eliminated these programs in most of our country's schools. There are still preventive career development programs in place, but in

1989 and 1995 only about 40 percent of American adults were in their current positions because of planning (Brown & Minor, 1989, 1992; Hoyt & Lester, 1995), which suggests that large numbers of people are not being affected by any type of program. These same Gallup surveys suggest that 10 to 12 million adults each year need assistance in finding jobs, again suggesting that preventive programs are either not in place or are not working.

Ten years after Herr's (1974) projections, Gysbers (1984) took on a similar task, again writing for the National Vocational Guidance Association. He made the following projections regarding career development theory and practice:

1. The meanings given to career and career development continue to evolve from simply new words for vocation (occupation) and vocational development (occupational development) to words that describe human careers in terms of life roles, life settings, and life events that develop over the life span.
2. Substantial changes have taken place and will continue to occur in the economic, occupational, industrial, and social environments and structure in which the human career develops and interacts and in which career guidance and counseling take place.
3. The number, diversity, and quality of career development programs, tools, and techniques will continue to increase in almost geometric progression.
4. The population served by career development programming and the settings where career development programs and services take place have increased and will continue to do so. (p. 619)

Gysbers's (1984) predictions are somewhat more general than those set forth by Herr (1974) and as such had a higher probability of being accurate when they were cast. However, at this writing it is still unclear whether the meaning of career development is actually going to broaden, as Gysbers (1984) suggested. Some, like McDaniels (1989), certainly seem to be pushing in that direction by defining *career* as something other than the occupations held over the life span. Others, like Holland (1997), seem to be more in favor of the traditional idea of career. However, economic, social, and industrial changes have been accelerated; the number and diversity of career development tools (although *not* the quality) have increased rapidly; and the populations and settings served by career development specialists certainly have increased since 1984.

Both Herr (1974) and Gysbers (1984) made relatively few predictions about the future of career development and, as has already been noted, took somewhat different approaches to doing so (general vs. specific). Zunker (1990), on the other hand, made nearly two dozen projections, focusing primarily on the issues that will confront workers in the future. For example, he projected that the future would provide alternative work patterns such as job sharing and telecommuting (working in the home on a computer), trends that are well documented by McDaniels (1989). However, he also predicted that the job market of the future would make some dramatic shifts, a prediction that is clearly contradicted by the data presented earlier in this volume. Similarly, Zunkers's (1990) projection that workers would place less value on financial rewards seems not to be well founded, probably because the "data" that he used seem to be drawn from armchair philosophy rather than empirical sources.

For the most part, Herr (1974), Gysbers (1984), and Zunker (1990) were on target with their projections. When they became quite specific in their projections or relied on "faulty" databases, predictions appeared to be less accurate. The projections of trends and issues that follow are, like those of others, likely to be subject to error. However, they are made in an attempt to prepare readers to anticipate those forces that will impinge on them and their clients.

The sixth edition of this book contained 15 predictions about the future of career information, career counseling, and career development. With two exceptions, these predictions have been supported by the events that occurred between that edition and this one. The most notable of these exceptions has to do with our prediction that there would be a convergence in thinking and practice about providing counseling services to cultural minorities. The fact is that ideas about and recommendations for practices regarding career counseling for cultural minorities have diverged quite sharply since the last edition (e.g., Leong, 1995). This divergence has been so dramatic that this prediction will be altered in this edition. The second prediction that was not supported by events was that there would be a convergence in recommendations regarding career counseling for men and women. Differences in recommendations between career counseling for men and women have persisted because of the continuing need to address equity, role participation, and initial career choice issues when dealing with women (Melamed, 1995). Because of events since 1997, some of the predictions included in the sixth edition will be retained and others discarded. A few new predictions will be added as well.

Trends: Career Information

1. There will be a continuing effort to improve the delivery of occupational information. Throughout this book, numerous innovations regarding the delivery of occupational information have been illustrated. Recent events, such as placing O*NET and the *Occupational Outlook Handbook* on the Internet, are but two of these innovations. The development of America's Job Bank is another important step in the improvement of occupational information at the national level, and there are many parallel moves in many of the states spearheaded by the SOICCs. Moreover, the development of new classification systems such as those described in Chapter 5 should make the interpretation of occupational information that is collected by various federal agencies easier to interpret and use.

However, efforts to improve the delivery of occupational information are being, and will continue to be, augmented by businesses that have traditionally been involved in publishing various types of occupational information and new businesses interested in profiting from the potential of the Internet to provide occupational information for a fee. The efforts of governmental agencies will also be extended by individuals, businesses, and institutions such as colleges and universities that hope to improve the quality and availability of occupational information.

2. There will be an increased sensitivity to, as well as increased efforts to meet, the occupational information needs of adults. The national survey commissioned by the National Career Development Association in conjunction with NOICC (Hoyt & Lester, 1995) suggested that large numbers of adults have never accessed any type of occupational information. The problem is most acute among those adults who never finished high school (40 percent reported using no source) and Hispanics (35 percent reported using no source), but even one-fifth of college graduates reported using no source of occupational information. When these data are paired with other information (e.g., only 41 percent of the employed respondents reported being in their current jobs because they followed a definite plan, and 27 percent believed they needed assistance finding occupational information), the problem of helping adults access and use career information seems acute.

3. Interactive, computerized informational systems will become more widely utilized. The provisions for designing and implementing a comprehensive career information program at any level are fraught with problems (Brown & Brown, 1990). For example, information must be continuously updated, stored to maximize access, and selected so that the target audience will be motivated to use it. Print materials, needle sorts, microfiche, and other mechanical systems are difficult to keep up to date and store, and often are not highly attractive to the reader. Some of the early computerized systems produced data too slowly because of the capacity of the computers and did not allow for random assess and thus were rigid. With the introduction of laser technology, compact discs are being developed that contain both visual and audio messages. Interactive systems provide users the opportunity to respond to questions posed by the informational system as well as pose questions to the system. The introduction of visual images of college campuses, workers, technical training faculties, work settings, and so forth, will increase motivation to use these systems. Perhaps just as important, subscriber services will update these systems routinely. Currently, career counselors are largely relying on print materials, traditional audiovisual materials, and computerized systems that, while interactive, are still somewhat slow and devoid of a visual dimension. The future will see a decreasing reliance on print material and outdated computerized programs as technology advances and the cost of interactive compact discs decreases.

4. Graduate school courses emphasizing career information will continue to decrease. A survey of counselor education programs (Sampson & Liberty, 1989) suggests that the textbooks used in the preparation of counselors in the area of career development increasingly emphasize career counseling and focus on occupational information. At the time when members of our society need more career information, training programs appear to be placing less emphasis on orienting counselors and psychologists to identifying, evaluating, and using information. This is partially why the NOICC (1986) commissioned the development of *Using Labor Market Information in Career Exploration and Decision Making: A Resource Guide* and developed an extensive in-service training program to help counselor educators and counseling psychologists enhance their ability to train career counselors.

The reduction in time spent on career information is partially due to the recognition of the need to pay more attention to career counseling, which is a healthy sign. However, since most counselors and counseling psychologists are required to take only one course that deals with the various aspects of career development, career counseling coverage is replacing time spent on career information. The result of all this is that career counselors and career development specialists will increasingly have to rely on their own study and in-service training for their knowledge of career information.

5. Our basic understanding of how to select and use occupational information will continue to receive a low priority by researchers. Except for Krumboltz and associates (e.g., Krumboltz & Schroeder, 1965; Krumboltz & Thoreson, 1964), few researchers have made attempts to identify factors that lead to the effective uses of occupational information, and with a few exceptions (e.g., Brown, 1990; Prediger, 1974) the entire area has received little comment. Perhaps researchers assume that career development specialists understand how to select, evaluate, and use career information. Regardless of the reasons for omission, it is expected that career development specialists will continue to ignore the general topic of career information.

6. Career counselors and members of the general public will have increasing access to career information through systems like O*NET and through computer-assisted career guidance systems (CACGS) provided by their State Occupational Information Coordinating Committees (SOICCs). SOICCs in almost all states have either adapted or developed their own CACGS, which have state-level occupational and educational information in them. Some of the databases in these systems are now available on the Worldwide Web and this number will undoubtedly increase. The result of these and other developments will be that occupational information will be available in the homes of millions of people who have computers with modems and the capability of accessing the Worldwide Web, employment security offices destined to become parts of what are termed One-Stop Job Centers, libraries, public schools, community colleges, and colleges and universities.

7. Information about job openings will increasingly be made available on the Worldwide Web. As noted in Chapter 16, numerous job posting services have surfaced in the last few years. While posting job openings on the Internet is fraught with problems, not the least of which is that employers and recruiters may receive thousands of resumes via e-mail, these problems will be solved by screening programs and other devices analagous to the manual screening that now occurs. Employers and potential employees alike will come to see the recruitment of workers via the Worldwide Web as an efficient, effective strategy.

Trends: Career Counseling

1. Career counseling will be increasingly recognized as a counseling specialty that requires expertise in both personal and career counseling as well as related assessment strategies. Crites (1981) was one of the early advocates of this position. More recently numerous books (e.g., Brown & Brooks, 1991; Gysbers & Moore, 1987; Spokane, 1991) and articles (e.g., Brown, 1995; Krumboltz, 1993; Subich, 1993) have taken a similar position by emphasizing the interrelationship of mental health and career concerns and asserted that counselors and psychologists need to be prepared to deal with both. Also, NBCC (1996) has reiterated its stand on the need for generic counseling preparation by reaffirming its requirement that professionals seeking certification as National Certified Career Counselors first obtain certification as NCCs, National Certified Counselors.

2. Certification of career counselors will become an increasing concern among counselors and psychologists. To date, most psychological licensure laws provide licensees with a generic license to practice and, for the most part, psychology has not been concerned about the credentials of career counselors. On the other hand, the very first licensing law passed for counselors (Virginia) contained a provision for recognizing career counseling specialists. Similarly, the national effort to develop certification standards for counselors was initiated primarily for the purpose of recognizing specialists (Brown & Srebalus, 1996). Currently, the National Board of Certified Counselors (NBCC, 1996) certifies career counselors. One of the requirements for obtaining and becoming recognized as a National Certified Career Counselor is that one must first become a NCC (National Certified Counselor), which is a generic certification.

3. There will be a continued divergence of thinking about the career counseling practices for men and women. Most current career counseling books contain sections on the special career counseling needs of women (e.g., Herr & Cramer, 1996). A few (e.g., Zunker, 1990) also contain chapters on the special needs of men, while others consider the topic of gender simultaneously (e.g., Brown & Brooks, 1991). A few books (e.g., Yost & Corbishley, 1987) address this issue only to a slight degree.

The biological fact that women bear children and men do not must be a consideration in career counseling. So must the socialization of gender roles and the impact this makes on career development and career choice. Unfortunately, continuing realities regarding initial career choice, role participation, and discrimination in the workplace must be addressed when counseling women faced with career issues.

4. Increasing attention will be given to the issues involved in counseling cultural minorities. One result of this focus will be the adoption of different strategies at each stage of the process when providing career counseling for minorities. For example, there is well-founded speculation that Native Americans are more likely to be visual than auditory learners (Okun, Fried, & Okun, 1999). This has profound implications for the presentation of occupational information and test interpretation. Leong's (1993) finding that some Asian Americans prefer a dependent decision-making style also has tremendous implications for providing counseling services to this group because much career development literature is predicated on the idea that clients will prefer an independent decision-making style. Other factors that will require changes in career counseling practices for ethnic minorities are differences in time perspective, the display of emotions, and difference in the nonverbal and verbal styles (Okun et al., 1999).

As has been noted throughout this book, career counselors need to be sensitive to cultural and ethnic variables (e.g., Bowman, 1993) sexual orientation (e.g., Gelberg & Chojnacki, 1995), as well as other differentiating factors in the career counseling process. These articles have focused our attention on factors such as communications and decision-making styles, as well as other variables that will undoubtedly influence both the processes and outcomes of career counseling. As Betz (1993) suggests, information from the multicultural counseling literature should be incorporated into the career counseling literature.

5. John Holland's theory (1997) will continue to be dominant in the assessment of interests and research on variables such as occupational satisfaction. However, the sociocognitive theory of Lent, Brown, and Hackett (1996) and Gottfredson's (1996) developmental theory of circumscription and compromise are likely to receive increasing attention. Thus far the interest in Gottfredson's theory has been primarily shown by researchers, and it seems unlikely to have a major impact on practice in the future. As the authors of the sociocognitive theory have shown (Lent et al., 1996), there is an upsurge of interest by researchers in sociocognitive theory, and this interest may translate into an increase in use by practitioners, depending on the products and practices this research yields. Conversely, Super's (1990) developmental theory seems likely to receive less attention from practitioners and researchers alike because its segmental construction makes it hard to generate testable hypotheses and its complexity makes it difficult to translate into practice. Krumboltz's (Mitchell & Krumboltz, 1996) social learning theory may also receive less attention, perhaps because of the similarity between it and the one crafted by Lent and others (1996). Lent and his associates incorporated Bandura's (1986) self-efficacy construct into their theory, whereas Krumboltz has placed less emphasis on it. One fact that is damaging to Krumboltz's theory is that Bandura revised the social learning theory (Bandura, 1977) on which his theory is based and placed more emphasis on the role of self-efficacy and cognitions and less emphasis on learning histories (Bandura, 1986) in the revision. However, Krumboltz (Mitchell & Krumboltz, 1996) has articulated an approach to career counseling based on his theory that may gain acceptance by practitioners. The future influence of the other theories of career development discussed in Chapter 2 is harder to forecast, although it seems likely that all of them will have some impact on both research and practice. The Theory of Work Adjustment has been in the professional literature since the late 1960s, was fully articulated almost two decades ago (Dawis & Lofquist, 1984), and has still not drawn widespread support from practitioners. Perhaps it never will, even though it has much to offer. The other theories set forth in Chapter 2 are too new to make an adequate assessment of their likely influence.

6. As computers are more widely used by the public, it seems likely that much routine "career counseling" will be provided by CACGS. As was reported in Chapter 8, it can be estimated that over 10 million adults have used a computer-assisted career guidance system to explore career options at some time in their lives. If the number of children and adolescents who currently use these systems in states such as Texas and Wisconsin to get occupational information or explore career options is added to this number, it would escalate dramatically. As the children from across the country who are being introduced to CACGS in their schools become adults, the demand for, and usage of, CAGGS will increase.

Trends: Career Development Programming

1. Career counseling and career development programming will continue to operate without a solid empirical basis. Herr and Cramer (1996) identified a number of areas within the career development domain that need empirical investigation. In many ways, it would be easier to identify those areas that do not warrant additional research: none. Many of Holland's (1997) propositions have received widespread support, and we have found that almost any type of interpretation of tests and inventories improves client knowledge (Goodyear, 1990). However, we have not even begun to answer the classic question: What types of intervention are most useful with which types of clients? Neither have we answered basic questions about types of counselors or counseling that are most effective or begun to understand fully the interaction of human and computerized systems (Sampson, 1990). As Herr and Cramer suggest, there is much research that needs to be conducted.

2. Although career development programming will continue to be important, it will be secondary to the school reform movement that grips many of this country's schools. The result is that comprehensive, districtwide, career development programming such as that discussed in Chapters 9 and 10 will be difficult to implement. This is not to suggest that individual schools cannot have outstanding career development programs, or that the comprehensive programs are impossible to develop. It does suggest that career development advocates must find ways to link career development programming to the hoped for outcomes of school reform. Specifically, career development counselors must strive to identify linkages between their programs and academic achievement, school completion, enrollment in postsecondary institutions, and success in those institutions

Summary

A few of what are expected to be the most important trends and issues in career development have been outlined in this final chapter. At the outset, prognostication was portrayed as risky at best, and only time will tell about the accuracy of the predictions made here. It is unlikely that all the trends and issues that will arise in the decade to come have been identified. Career counselors need to learn to be their own futurists and to adapt to changes as they occur.

References

Bandura, A. (1977). *Social learning theory.* Englewood Cliffs, NJ: Prentice-Hall.

Bandura, A. (1986). *Social foundation of thought and action: A social–cognitive theory.* Englewood Cliffs, NJ: Prentice-Hall.

Betz, N. E. (1993). Toward the integration of multicultural and career psychology. *Career Development Quarterly, 42,* 53–55.

Betz, N. E., & Hackett, G. (1981). The relationship of career-related self-efficacy expectations to perceive career operations in college men and women. *Journal of Counseling Psychology, 27,* 44–62.

Bowman, S. L. (1993). Career interventions for ethnic minorities. *Career Development Quarterly, 42,* 14–25.

Brooks, L. (1990). Recent developments in theory building. In D. Brown, L. Brooks, & associates (Eds.), *Career choice and development* (pp. 364–394)). San Francisco: Jossey-Bass.

Brown, D. (1990). Summary, comparison, and critique of the major theories. In D. Brown, L. Brooks, & associates (Eds.), *Career choice and development* (pp. 338–363). San Francisco: Jossey-Bass.

Brown, D., (1995). A values-based approach to facilitating career transitions. *Career Development Quarterly, 44,* 4–11.

Brown, D., & Brooks, L. (1991). *Career counseling techniques.* Boston: Allyn & Bacon.

Brown, D., & Brooks, L. (1996). Introduction to career development. In D. Brown, L. Brooks and associates (Eds.), *Career choice and development* (3rd ed.). San Francisco: Jossey-Bass.

Brown, D., & Minor, C. W. (1989). *Working in America.* Alexandria, VA: National Career Development Association.

Brown, D., & Minor, C. W. (1992). *Career needs in a diverse work force: Implications of NCDA Gallup survey.* Alexandria, VA: National Career Development Association.

Brown, D., & Srebalus, D. J. (1996). *Introduction to the counseling profession* (2nd ed.). Englewood Cliffs, NJ: Prentice-Hall.

Brown, S. T., & Brown, D. (1990). *Designing a career information center.* Garrett Park, MD: Garrett Park Press.

Crites, J. O. (1981). *Career counseling: Models, methods, and materials.* New York: McGraw-Hill.

Dawis, R. V., & Lofquist, L. (1984). *A psychological theory of work adjustment.* Minneapolis: University of Minnesota Press.

Gelberg, S., & Chojnacki, J. T. (1995). Developmental transitions of gay/lesbian/bisexual-affirmative, heterosexual counselors. *Career Development Quarterly, 43,* 267–273.

Goodyear, R. K. (1990). Research on the effects of test interpretation: A review. *The Counseling Psychologist, 18,* 240–257.

Gottfredson, L. (1996). Circumscription and compromise: A revision. In D. Brown, L. Brooks & associates (Eds.), *Career choice and development* (3rd ed.). San Francisco: Jossey-Bass.

Gysbers, N. C. (1984). Major trends in career development theory and practice. In N. C. Gysbers & associates (Eds.), *Designing careers: Counseling to enhance education, work, and leisure* (pp. 618–632). San Francisco: Jossey-Bass.

Herr, E. L. (1974). The decade in prospect: Some implications for vocational guidance. In E. L. Herr (Ed.), *Vocational guidance and human development* (pp. 551–574). Boston: Houghton Mifflin Co.

Herr, E. L., & Cramer, S. H. (1996). *Career guidance and counseling through the life span: Systematic approaches* (5th ed.). Glenview, IL: Scott, Foresman.

Holland, J. L. (1997). *Making vocational choices: A theory of vocational personalities and work environment* (3rd ed.). Englewood Cliffs, NJ: Prentice-Hall.

Hosie, T. W., West, J. D., & Mackey, J. A. (1988). Employment and roles of counselors in substance-abuse centers. *Journal of Mental Health Counseling, 10,* 188–189.

Hoyt, K. B., & Lester, J. N. (1995). *Learning to work: The NCDA Gallup survey.* Alexandria, VA: National Career Development Association.

Krumboltz, J. D., & Schroeder, D. (1965). Promoting career guidance through reinforcement and modeling. *Personnel and Guidance Journal, 44,* 19–26.

Krumboltz, J. D. (1993). Integrating career and personal counseling. *Career Development Quarterly, 42,* 143–148.

Krumboltz, J. D., & Thoreson, C. E. (1964). The effects of behavioral counseling on group and individual settings on information-seeking behavior. *Journal of Counseling Psychology, 11,* 323–333.

Lent, R. W., Brown, S. D., & Hackett, G. (1996). Career development from a social cognitive perspective. In D. Brown, L. Brooks, & associates (Eds.), *Career choice and development* (3rd ed.). San Francisco: Jossey-Bass.

Leong, F. T. L. (1993). The career counseling process for racial ethnic minorities: The case of Asian Americans. *Career Development Quarterly, 42,* 26–40.

Leong, F. T. L. (Ed.). (1995). *Career development and vocational behavior of ethnic minorities.* Mahwah, NJ: Lawrence Erlbaum.

McDaniels, C. (1989). *The changing workplace: Career counseling strategies for the 1990s and beyond.* San Francisco: Jossey-Bass.

Melamed, T. (1995). Career success: The moderating effects of gender. *Journal of Vocational Behavior, 47,* 295–314.

Mitchell, L. K., & Krumboltz, J. D. (1996). Social learning approach to career decision making: Krumboltz's theory. In D. Brown, L. Brooks, & associates (Eds.), *Career choice and development* (3rd ed.). San Francisco: Jossey-Bass.

NBCC. (1996). *NBCC counselor certification, 1996.* Alexandria, VA: Author.

NOICC. (1986). *Using labor market information in career exploration and decision making: A resource guide.* Garrett Park, MD: Garrett Park Press.

Okun, B. F., Fried, J., & Okun, M. L. (1999). *Understanding diversity.* Pacific Grove, CA: Brooks/Cole.

Osipow, S. (1990). Convergence in theories of career choice and development. *Journal of Vocational Behavior, 36,* 122–131.

Prediger, D. J. (1974). The role of assessment in career guidance: A reappraisal. *Impact, 3,* 3–4, 15–21.

Sampson, D. E., & Liberty, L. H. (1989). Textbooks used in counselor education programs. *Counselor Education and Supervision, 29,* 111–121.

Sampson, J. P., Jr. (1990). Computer-assisted testing and the goals of counseling psychology. *The Counseling Psychologist, 18,* 227–239.

Savickas, M. L., & Lent, R. W. (Eds.). (1994). *Convergence in career development theories.* Palo Alto, CA: CPP Books.

Spokane, A. (1991). *Career interventions.* Englewood Cliffs, NJ: Prentice-Hall.

Subich, L. M. (1993). How personal is career counseling? *Career Development Quarterly, 42,* 129–131.

Super, D. E. (1990). A life-span, life-space approach to career development. In D. Brown, L. Brooks, & associates (Eds.), *Career choice and development* (pp. 197–261). San Francisco: Jossey-Bass.

Yost, E. B., & Corbishley, M. A. (1987). *Career counseling: A psychological approach.* San Francisco: Jossey-Bass.

Zunker, V. G. (1990). *Career counseling: Applied concepts of life planning* (3rd ed.). Monterey, CA: Brooks/Cole.

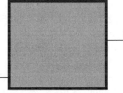

NAME INDEX

SUBJECT INDEX